W9-ADI-108

Our Right to Love

Ginny Vida, Editor

OUR RIGHT TO LOVE
A Lesbian Resource Book

Produced in Cooperation with Women of the National Gay Task Force

Prentice-Hall, Inc., Englewood Cliffs, New Jersey

Our Right to Love: A Lesbian Resource Book
Produced in Cooperation with Women of the National Gay Task
Force
Editor: Ginny Vida, Media Director, National Gay Task Force
Editorial Assistants: Noreen Harnik, Bonnie Gray, Sonia Roth

*Women of the National Gay Task Force Staff and Board of
Directors—1976-77*
Coexecutive Director: Jean O'Leary
Board Cochairperson: Betty J. Powell
Board Members: Sidney Abbott, Pokey Anderson, Charlotte
Bunch, Jean Crosby, Frances Doughty, Meryl Friedman, Barbara
Gittings, Barbara Love, Joan Nixon, Dorothy Riddle, Kay
Whitlock.
Interviewers: Jan Coughlan, Susan James, Catherine Kotter,
Karol Lightner, and Ginny Vida.
Photographers: Chris Almvig, Joan E. Biren, Liza Cowan, Denise
Crippen, Diana Davies, Robin Evans, Donna Gray, Linda Guth-
rie, Cary Herz, Bettye Lane, Bruce Larson, Cynthia MacAdams,
Robert McKeever, Marcelina L. Martin, Chie Nishio, Anita
Schloss, Richard Stanley, Nicole Symons, Kay Tobin, E K
Waller, Sue N. Williams, F. Carol Wood, and Irene Young.
Bibliography: Karol D. Lightner
Consultants: Charlotte Bunch, Jan Crawford, Barbara Gittings,
and Nancy Krody

The National Gay Task Force, 80 Fifth Avenue
New York, New York

NGTF is the largest gay civil rights organization in the country.
It is a clearinghouse for the national gay movement and a political force promoting gay rights legislation and a positive image of
lesbians and gay men in the media.

Art Director: Hal Siegel
Designer: Joan Ann Jacobus

Copyright © 1978 by Virginia Vida

All rights reserved. No part of this book may be reproduced in
any form or by any means, except for the inclusion of brief
quotations in a review, without permission in writing from the
publisher.
Printed in the United States of America
Prentice-Hall International, Inc., London/Prentice-Hall of Australia, Pty. Ltd., Sydney/Prentice-Hall of Canada, Ltd., Toronto/
Prentice-Hall of India Private Ltd., New Delhi/Prentice-Hall of
Japan, Inc., Tokyo/Prentice-Hall of Southeast Asia Pte. Ltd.,
Singapore/Whitehall Books Limited, Wellington, New Zealand
10 9 8 7 6 5 4 3 2 1

Library of Congress Cataloging in Publication Data
Main entry under title:

Our right to love.

  Bibliography: p.
  1. Lesbianism—United States—Addresses, essays, lectures.
2. Lesbians—United States—Addresses, essays, lectures. I. Vida,
Ginny. II. National Gay Task Force.
HQ75.6.U509   301.41'57   77-20184
ISBN 0-13-644401-6

Contributors

Sidney Abbott ○ Bella Abzug ○ Ginny Apuzzo ○ Sarah Lanier Barber ○ Batya Bauman ○ Betty Berzon ○ Ginny Berson ○ Sandra Blair, Esq. ○ Jill Boskey ○ Rita Mae Brown ○ Charlotte Bunch ○ Barbara Cameron ○ Eleanor Cooper ○ Jan Crawford ○ Margaret Cruikshank ○ Betsy Damon ○ Jeri Dilno ○ Frances Doughty ○ Katharine English ○ Ivonne Elias ○ Meryl C. Friedman ○ Vicki Gabriner ○ Sally Miller Gearhart ○ Nancy Gertner, Esq. ○ Barbara Gittings ○ Lois Gould ○ Sasha Gregory-Lewis ○ Harmony Hammond ○ Noreen Harnik ○ Bertha Harris ○ Wilma Scott Heide ○ Shere Hite ○ Elaine Howe ○ Karla Jay ○ The Reverend Dolores Jackson ○ Florynce Kennedy, Esq. ○ Polly Kellogg ○ Linda R. Lachman ○ Joan Larkin ○ J. Lee Lehman ○ Yee Lin ○ Chana Lopez ○ Barbara Love ○ Audre Lorde ○ Doris Lunden ○ Phyllis Lyon ○ Del Martin ○ The Reverend Rhea Y. Miller ○ Kate Millett ○ Esther Morgan ○ Ken Morgan ○ Joan Nixon ○ The Nomadic Sisters ○ Dolores Noll ○ Betty O'Leary ○ Jean O'Leary ○ Betty J. Powell ○ Dorothy Riddle ○ Rhonda Rivera, Esq. ○ Zulma Rivera ○ Susan Rosen ○ Alma Routsong ○ Jackie St. Joan ○ Barbara E. Sang ○ Elizabeth Shanklin ○ Mitzi Simmons ○ Charlotte Spitzer ○ Judi Stein ○ Gloria Steinem ○ Mary L. Stevens, J.D. ○ Roberta Stone ○ Kay Tobin ○ Nancy Toder ○ Lily Tomlin ○ Ginny Vida ○ Joan Waitkevicz, M.D. ○ Susan Wells ○ Kay Whitlock ○ The Womanshare Collective

Notes on Authors of Articles

Sidney Abbott is a member of NGTF's Board of Directors and coauthor, with Barbara Love, of *Sappho Was a Right-On Woman.* She was the first co-coordinator of the National Sexuality and Lesbianism Task Force of the National Organization for Women.

Ginny Berson is a founder and member of the Olivia Records collective. She was a founding member of The Furies, a lesbian feminist newspaper collective. In her spare time she studies Tae Kwon Do Karate, plays with her cat Pooter, and rides a motorcycle.

Betty Berzon is a marriage and family counselor specializing in the problems of gay people. She is a member of the Association of Gay Psychologists, a former board member of the Gay Community Services Center in Los Angeles, and cochairperson of the Greater Los Angeles Chapter of the Western Gay Academic Union.

Sandra Blair is an attorney in private practice at Blair & LeGrand in San Francisco, a law firm specializing in providing legal services to women from a feminist perspective. Her speciality is family and business law (including nonprofit groups). She teaches at the Sex Discrimination Clinic at Hastings College of the Law, and serves on the Police-District Attorney Committee on Battered Women, the Legal Referral Service Committee of the San Francisco Bar Association, and the Board of Bay Area Lawyers for the Arts. She also chairs the Queen's Bench Membership.

Jill Boskey and **Noreen Harnik** have participated in the activities of various socialist feminist gay and antiwar organizations over the past ten years.

Rita Mae Brown is one of the founders of radicalesbians and The Furies Collective. Active in the feminist and gay movements since 1966, she has written five books, including *Rubyfruit Jungle* and *In Her Day,* and is presently working on a sixth. At age thirty-two she is a Mother of the Movement.

Charlotte Bunch is an editor of *Quest: A Feminist Quarterly,* and a board member of the National Gay Task Force. A cofounder of The Furies, she is one of the leading theoreticians of the politics of lesbian feminism, and has taught and written extensively in this field. She is the editor of *Not by Degrees: Essays in Feminist Education.*

Eleanor Cooper is an active member of Lesbian Feminist Liberation and a former spokeswoman of that organization. She is also a staff member of the Women's Center in New York City, a spokesperson for the New York State Coalition of Gay Organizations, and that organization's representative to the New York Women's Lobby.

Jan Crawford is a licensed massage therapist and postural integrator with a private practice in New York City.

Dr. Margaret Cruikshank directed the women's studies program of Mankato State University from 1975 to 1977. Her book on T. B. Macaulay has been published by the Twayne English Author Series. She is presently editing a collection of personal narratives by lesbians.

Betsy Damon is a performer, sculptor, visual artist and mother. She founded a feminist studio in Ithaca, New York, and has recently moved to New York City.

Jeri Dilno is administrative coordinator of the Gay Center for Social Services of San Diego. She is a vice-president of the San Diego Democratic Club, and a member of the Gay Media Task Force and the Feminist Action Committee.

Frances Doughty is a teacher of English and Latin in New York City and a member of the Working Committee of the U. S. National Women's Agenda. She is an NGTF board member and its former cochairperson.

Katharine English is a law student at Lewis and Clark Northwestern School of Law in Portland, Oregon. She is a member of the Community Law Project, a collective law firm of eight women; and a member of Feminist Divorce Collective which published Oregon's feminist self-help divorce handbook, *Parting.* She is gay, and the mother of two sons.

Meryl C. Friedman is a lesbian feminist activist and teacher from Brooklyn, New York. She is a member of the NGTF Board of Directors and cospokesperson of the Gay Teachers Association. As a public speaker she enlightens audiences on the role of lesbians in the educational system. In her spare time she haunts old bookstores and plays in the country with her friend and lover.

Vicki Gabriner has been a part of the Atlanta lesbian feminist community from its early birth pangs. She wrote *Sleeping Beauty, A lesbian fairy tale,* and is now a partner in ATTHIS (Workshops and Consultation in Lesbian Sexuality).

Sally Miller Gearhart is a teacher of Speech Communication and Women's Studies at San Francisco State University, a child of the depression and of white southern Christian upbringing through the water-treading middle class, a double Aries with Virgo rising, committed to play, song, sculpture, fantasy fiction, touch football, and lesbian feminism. She is a closet Ph.D.

Nancy Gertner is an attorney whose practice includes a number of gay people. She focuses heavily on criminal cases, civil rights litigation, and cases involving custody issues for gay women. She is with the law firm of Silverglate, Shapiro and Gertner, 217 Lewis Wharf, Boston, Massachusetts 02110.

Barbara Gittings has been a movement activist since 1958 when she joined Daughters of Bilitis. She edited DOB's first national magazine, *The Ladder,* in 1963-66. She marched in the first gay picket lines in Philadelphia and Washington in 1965 and after. Since 1967 she has been a frequent speaker before college audiences, gay rallies, and groups ranging from psychiatrists to PTAs. She is currently a board member of NGTF and coordinator of the American Library Association's Gay Task Force. Her article "Combatting the Lies in the Libraries" appears in *The Gay Academic.*

Sasha Gregory-Lewis is the associate editor of *The Advocate,* a national gay publication, for which she is responsible for news and political coverage and women's issues. During 1972-74 she served in the U. S. Coast Guard Reserve as a petty officer. She received an honorable discharge, despite the fact that she informed her commanding officer, in writing, that she is a lesbian.

Harmony Hammond is a painter and writer who exhibits frequently in New York City. She is a member of the collective publishing *Heresies: A Feminist Publication on Art and Politics,* and is one of the editors of its "Lesbian Art and Artists" issue. She has published material in *Heresies, Women Artists' Newsletter,* and in a book on feminist education edited by Charlotte Bunch. She teaches at universities and feminist art programs and gives workshops and lectures on lesbian and feminist artists.

Bertha Harris is the author of three novels, *Catching Saradove, Confessions of Cherubino,* and *Lover.* She has lectured and written extensively on the subject of lesbianism, especially in the field of literary criticism. She is presently director of Women's Studies, the College of Staten Island, Richmond Division, City University of New York.

Shere Hite is the author of *The Hite Report,* the result of five years of research on female sexuality. *The Hite Report,* a long-term best-seller, has been translated into nine languages. Shere is now doing research on love and on male sexuality. She has a M.A. from the University of Florida and completed work toward a Ph.D. at Columbia, but withdrew when Columbia refused to accept her research on female sexuality as a thesis topic. She teaches at New York University.

Karla Jay is coeditor with Allen Young of *Out of the Closets, After You're Out,* and "Lavender Culture" (in progress). She and Allen Young are also writing a book on lesbian and gay male sex and life-styles, tentatively titled "What Do You People Want Anyway?" to be published in 1978.

Polly Kellogg is a therapist in private practice in New York City specializing in sex therapy for lesbians. She is a member of the American Association of Sex Educators, Counselors and Therapists, and a faculty member of the Institute for Rational Living.

Linda R. Lachman is a research analyst for the Mayor's Office in Boston and secretary of the Board of Directors of the Gay Rights National Lobby. She formerly served as aide to Massachusetts State Representative Elaine Noble and has also worked as managing editor of Gay Community News, as news director/announcer of "Gay Way Radio," and as coproducer of "Lavender Hour." She also sings, writes poetry, and plays the flute.

J. Lee Lehman is director of the National Gay Student Center, editor in chief of the *Gay Academic Union Journal: Gai Saber,* and editor of the book *Gays on Campus.* In her spare time she studies botany at Rutgers University.

Audre Lorde, a black revolutionary poet, has written six books: *The First Cities, Cables to Rage, From a Land Where Other People Live, New York Head Shop and Museum, Coal,* and *Between Our Selves.* She is an associate professor of English at John Jay College of Criminal Justice, City University of New York. *From a Land Where Other People Live* was nominated for the National Book Award, 1974.

Barbara Love is a member of the NGTF Board of Directors and a coauthor, with Sidney Abbott, of *Sappho Was a Right-On Woman,* and with Elizabeth Shanklin, of "Building Matriarchy" (in progress). A founder of the Matriarchists, she has been involved in the women's movement and gay movement since 1967. She currently serves on the Advisory Board of the New York Chapter of the National Organization for Women.

Phyllis Lyon, D.A., is codirector of the National Sex Forum and on the faculty of the Institute for the Advanced Study of Human Sexuality. She is one of the founders of the Daughters of Bilitis (1955) and coauthor of *Lesbian/Woman.* She also serves as commissioner on the San Francisco Human Rights Commission and is active in the gay and feminist movements.

Del Martin is consultant, writer, and lecturer for Ly Mar Associates; chairperson, San Francisco's Commission on the Status of Women; coordinator, National Organization for Women's Task Force on Battered Women/ Household Violence; coauthor, *Lesbian/Woman* (1972), and author, *Battered Wives* (1976).

The Reverend Rhea Y. Miller is pastor of the Metropolitan Community Church in Boulder, Colorado. She is a "people farmer"—a speaker and workshop leader in areas of human sexuality, feminism, community building and alternate lifestyles. She is a lover of the mountains and of the "Passionate Intensity."

Kate Millett is the author of *Sexual Politics, Flying,* and *Sita.* She is also an artist and sculptor. She lives in a SoHo loft in New York City.

Joan Nixon is a board member of NGTF and a former member of the collective for *Lavender Woman,* a now-suspended lesbian publication in Chicago.

Dolores L. Noll, Ph.D., is an associate professor of English at Kent State University and faculty adviser of the Kent Gay Liberation Front. She has been active in the Gay Caucus for the Modern Languages. A frequent speaker on lesbianism and gay liberation, she described her experiences as a lesbian college professor in the November 1974 issue of *College English.*

Betty O'Leary is the mother of Jean O'Leary. She lives in Cleveland, Ohio.

Jean O'Leary, coexecutive director of the National Gay Task Force, was appointed by President Carter to the President's Commission on the Observance of International Women's Year. She was elected a delegate, as an open lesbian, to the 1976 Democratic National Convention and promoted the gay rights issue there. Jean is a Ph.D. candidate, a former nun, and a former spokeswoman of Lesbian Feminist Liberation.

Betty J. Powell is a black lesbian feminist activist. She is a former cochairperson of the National Gay Task Force Board of Directors; past chairperson of 1974–75 Gay Academic Union Conferences. For many years a teacher of French and department chairperson, Betty is now an instructor at Brooklyn College of the City University of New York, where her present areas of specialization are language theory and methodology, and urban sociology.

Dorothy Riddle, Ph.D., is a clinical psychologist in Tucson, Arizona, who does speaking, workshops, and writing on various aspects of homophobia, as well as advocacy work with lesbians. She is a member of the American Psychological Association Task Force on the Status of Lesbian and Gay Male Psychologists, and supervises community mental health training at the University of Arizona.

Rhonda Rivera, Esq., is a professor of law at Ohio University and former assistant dean at the University of Michigan Law School. She is a distinguished graduate of Wayne State University.

Alma Routsong (Isabel Miller) is the author of *Patience and Sarah.* She has been active in the gay movement since 1970.

Jackie St. Joan has been working as a political organizer for over thirteen years. A strong feminist, she has written for *Quest, Big Mama Rag,* and other feminist journals. She is a recent law school graduate and has been employed as a taxi driver, a secretary, and a teacher. She lives in Denver with her two children and frequent visitors.

Barbara Sang, Ph.D., is a therapist in private practice in New York City. She is on the Steering Committee of the Homosexual Community Counseling Center and is a member of the Association for Women in Psychology, the Association of Gay Psychologists, and the Task Force on the Status of Gay and Lesbian Psychologists. She teaches a course on feminist psychology at New York University.

Elizabeth Shanklin began to explore ideas about matriarchy twenty years ago in a graduate seminar in Ancient Greek at Columbia University. She is currently completing her M.A. in Women's History at Sarah Lawrence College and is writing a book, "Building Matriarchy," with Barbara Love. She was a member of the Feminists and is a founder of the Matriarchists.

Judi Stein is co-director of Women's Community Health Center, Inc., a self-help facility in Cambridge, Massachusetts. She has been actively working in the women's health movement for many years and writing and organizing around lesbian health issues for the past few years.

Gloria Steinem is a writer and the editor of *Ms. Magazine.* She is a member of the President's Commission on the Observance of International Women's Year, a convenor of the National Women's Political Caucus and a member of its Advisory Commission, and chairperson of the Board of Directors of the Women's Action Alliance.

Mary L. Stevens, J.D., is a graduate of Rutgers Law School. She was national coordinator of the Lesbian Law Section of the Eighth National Conference on Women and the Law and an Eagleton Institute of Politics fellow (1976-77). She is now writing a public policy book on women and violence. A former editor of the *Women's Rights Law Reporter,* she currently serves on the board of the Gay Rights National Lobby.

Kay Tobin has worked in the gay cause since 1961 and was one of the first lesbians to picket for gay rights in the mid-1960s. Her photos and news reports have appeared frequently in gay publications. She was one of the founders of New York's Gay Activists Alliance, and she coauthored a 1972 paperback book, *The Gay Crusaders.*

Nancy Toder, Ph.D., is a clinical psychologist in private practice in the Los Angeles area. She specializes in therapy with lesbians and has been active in the radical lesbian and women's movements since 1971. She also consults to mental health centers and universities, to train therapists and counselors to work more effectively (and less destructively) with lesbian clients.

Ginny Vida is media director of the National Gay Task Force and editor of the NGTF newsletter, *It's Time.* She is a former board member of NGTF and a former spokeswoman of Lesbian Feminist Liberation. Before joining the NGTF staff she worked for several years as an editor of children's textbooks and as an English teacher. She has an M.A. in English linguistics from New York University.

H. Joan Waitkevicz, M.D., is a physician working at the St. Mark's Clinic in Manhattan and at the People's Health Center in the Bronx, New York, where she helps teach a people's medicine course. Her specialty is internal medicine.

Susan Wells is a professional writer in Atlanta with a degree in journalism from the University of Georgia. She is active in feminist and lesbian groups such as the Atlanta Lesbian Feminist Alliance and the Atlanta Coalition on Rape.

Kay Whitlock, a feminist activist in the National Organization for Women, has served as co-coordinator of the NOW National Task Force on Sexuality and Lesbianism. A board member of NGTF, she lives in Philadelphia and is active in feminist/lesbian-feminist/gay civil rights efforts at local, state, and national levels.

The Womanshare Collective is made up of the women who live and work at Womanshare Feminist Retreat, in Grants Pass, Oregon. They are the authors and publishers of *Country Lesbians: The Story of the Womanshare Collective.*

Acknowledgments

This book has been made possible through the cooperation of many people who have contributed their assistance and expertise to this project. Although I am grateful to everyone who contributed in any way, I would like to mention the names of a few individuals whose participation has been essential.

I am deeply indebted to the women of the National Gay Task Force staff and Board of Directors for contributing articles, personal testimony, and consultation; to Elaine Howe and Sidney Abbott for initiating the project; to Robert Stewart, my editor at Prentice-Hall, for his invaluable guidance and support; to Charlotte Sheedy and Berenice Hoffman for their advice and assistance in drawing up the proposal and helping with legal arrangements; and to Jan Crawford, for suggesting a phrase that I eventually converted to the title.

The women who have put in the most hours with me on this book are my editorial assistants Noreen Harnik, Bonnie Gray, and Sonia Roth. Noreen, who worked with me for several months, contributed a good deal of organizing and planning and consultation and handled the first stages of assembling the National Resource List. Bonnie Gray transcribed and edited a good many personal testimonies from taped interviews and typed hundreds of manuscript pages, and Sonia Roth spent weeks editing the National Resource List and tracking down people for photo releases. As I was coming down to the wire on my delivery date for this book, Polly Kellogg and Karol Lightner provided crucial editorial assistance and moral support.

This project would not have been possible without approval from the full Board of Directors of NGTF, and the support of NGTF Coexecutive Directors Jean O'Leary and Bruce Voeller, who arranged for me to set time aside from my general duties at NGTF to work on this special project. I am also deeply indebted to NGTF Administrator Robert Herrick who assisted with legal arrangements, and to Ronald Gold, who did a good deal more than his share of the general media work at NGTF while I was devoting so much time and energy to the book.

Though the work of more than a dozen photographers is represented here, I wish to extend a special note of thanks to Bettye Lane, Donna Gray, and Kay Tobin, who made special excursions to obtain particular photographs for the book so that we would have ample representation of loving couples, Third World women, and lesbians and their children. Jeanne Cordova of *The Lesbian Tide* was also helpful in this effort.

For personal testimonies I am particularly grateful to Kitty Cotter, who conducted several tape-recorded interviews and transcribed them. And I would like to thank Karol Lightner, who compiled the Bibliography in record time and also helped with the personal testimonies. I am also grateful to Karen Kinney, for library research, and to Charlotte Bunch and Barbara Gittings, for recommending authors and suggesting revisions in the outline.

I would especially like to thank Charlotte Spitzer and Esther and Ken Morgan of Parents of Gays in Los Angeles for taking the trouble to interview each other and send me the tapes after I had erased their original taped interview by mistake. For permission to reprint entries from *Gaia's Guide* and the *Gayellow Pages* in the National Lesbian Resource List, I wish to thank Sandy Horn and Frances Green respectively; and I am also grateful for permission to reprint excerpts from the following works: *Country Lesbians* by the Womanshare Collective, *Loving Women* by the Nomadic Sisters, *Sita* by Kate Millett, *The Hite Report* by Shere Hite, *I've Been Standing on This Street Corner a Hell of a Long Time* by Audre Lorde, and personal testimony by Batya Bauman, reprinted from *Lilith* magazine.

Finally I am grateful to all the women who contributed in any way—as authors, as persons interviewed for personal testimony, as suppliers of information for the Appendix, and as editors, typists, and assistants. We did it together.

—Ginny Vida

Contents

Foreword

RITA MAE BROWN

Lesbians as a group can be very confusing. There are lesbians whose politics are to the right of Genghis Khan. There are lesbians who make Maoists look moderate. There are lesbians who can only be described as dowdy dykes. There are lesbians who can't be described, they simply knock you out with their beauty. There are lesbians who love cats and would never be seen without one. There are lesbians who like dogs. There are lesbians who like men (no parallel intended) and there are lesbians who barely know that men as a group exist. There are Baptist lesbians, born again; there are Catholic lesbians who certainly never violate papal procedure regarding birth control. There are Jewish lesbians and Zen ones, Shinto and all the other religious possibilities. There are even lesbians who don't believe in any religion at all. There are poor lesbians and rich lesbians. There are dumb lesbians (yes, I hate to admit it but there are) and there are smart lesbians. We come in all colors, too. Lesbians are everywhere, even in the morgue. We die like anyone else.

What lesbians have in common with one another amid all our varieties is that people who aren't lesbians think us odd, perhaps even queer. Certain persons (I won't name them—that would be cruel) tell us lesbianism is unnatural. Wrong. Nothing is unnatural—just untried. Other certain persons tell us that lesbians are sex maniacs. Unfortunately, this is not true. I speak from deep personal experience. People who tell us such things are the same people who tell us crime does not pay. And look at Richard Nixon.

Not only do certain persons muddy the waters about homosexuals today, they even tamper with history. For instance, have you heard the ridiculous rumor sponsored by our public school system that Michelangelo was heterosexual? Applesauce, everyone knows he was gay. If Michelangelo had been straight, the Sistine Chapel would have been painted basic white with a roller. And then that terrible fib about Queen Elizabeth. The Virgin Queen, they call her. Try Divergent Queen. Or the scandal about Sappho flinging herself off a cliff into the sea because of love for some ferryboat man. If she cast herself into the waters, you can bet her lover was in the boat. How about the gossip about J. Edgar Hoover? Do we really want to claim him? But you get the general idea. Any person who loved another person who just happened to be of the same sex gets the historical version of a transsexual operation. Makes you wonder about democracies thumping their chests and declaring they tell the truth to their citizens. If they lie about sex, they'll lie about anything.

Not only do they lie about sex, they make rules about it and by extension love. Do you know that in many states in this nation oral sex, "going down" to you trashy readers, is illegal—whether you are visiting the southern hemisphere with a member of the opposite sex, the same sex, or possibly a watermelon. (The law's always been hard on fruits.) The only time going down should be outlawed is when it refers to the stock market. Ah, but that's the whole thing in a nutshell, where it best belongs. If the powers that be have you and me focusing on our private lives, we might not notice the larger issues like the economy. We won't fight for systemic changes, we'll keep fighting for piecemeal changes.

Maybe this concept is more easily understood if we shift focus from a sexual/cultural issue to a traditional material issue:

You and I are paying higher and higher oil costs. Our discontent rests on the Arabs, who we are told gouge us. However, this nation possesses the technology to use solar energy for heating purposes. That equipment won't be available to us until General Electric figures out a way to buy the sun. Got it?

It's one thing if we are lied to by the power structure. It's another thing if we lie to one another. Lesbians just don't want to lie to you. That's really what this whole gay rights business is all about. How can we make common political cause if we don't know the truth about one another? How can we be friends? Remember, a society that denies you your right to be yourself and to be with others is but a step away from denying you rights that on the surface are more obviously political. If you try to tell me how to act and whom to love and it doesn't sit right by me, there's no way we can make a revolution or even a batch of brownies. Maybe it's time

America grows up and learns to value difference instead of trying to homogenize all of us like so much pasteurized milk. If the whole country can't get it together to let people *be*, at least you can. The articles in this book are people trying to tell you about their lives.

What's astonishing is that these women are ready to write truthfully about themselves. In 1968 when we popped the gay rights movement into second gear (its public phase) by starting Student Homophile League at Columbia University, I was just about the only organizer to use my real name. By 1971 a few other people were willing to be honest about their identity. But most lesbians refused to risk coming out even inside the feminist movement. Beyond the various political arenas (which offered cold comfort) people knew better than to tell the truth. Not only were women in the closet—they seemed to be vying for "Miss Garment Bag 1971."

Six years later why are people taking chances and telling you who they are? Heightened political awareness is one reason. You need to *know* the people you work with. Also, strength of community draws people forward. No one is such a Pollyanna as to think she has nothing to fear by coming out, but at least today there is a community. No one need emerge the way I did, totally alone . . . and that's a small but real victory.

Like all people for all centuries we move in a changing web of time, circumstance, economic controls, and natural upheavals. Any of those factors, individually or in combination with others, could influence us. Who is to say if these things have made our task of telling the truth lighter? For all that, I would still bet the authors in this anthology came forward because it's easier to tell the truth. Lies sap energy, plus when you tell one you soon must tell another. These women are reclaiming their energy for themselves. No lies to oil social/political machinery that does not operate in our self-interest. No lies to placate psychological attitudes that are destructive not just to us but to the concept of human rights and dignity. We tell the truth. You either like us as we are or you don't like us at all. At least we will all know where we stand.

This book demonstrates not just how far lesbians have come, but how far America has moved on the issue of individual liberty. Five years ago this book could not have been published. Five years ago the truth was not welcome about us, about poverty, Watergate, racial prejudice, and a host of seemingly unrelated things which are not unrelated at all. Today I write a foreword to a book containing articles by more than forty women. Just a few years ago I would have had to write the whole book. Think how exhilarated I am. Think of the time this saves me!

If you will take some of your time and read what follows, wherever you fall in the sexual/philosophical spectrum, this book will intrigue you. It might even provoke you to examine your own life: your relationship to others, your relationship to yourself, perhaps even your relationship to the economy. Whatever your conclusions about your own life are, I hope that by reading this book you will respect our right to love.

Introduction

GINNY VIDA

This book reflects a growing awareness of the special concerns of lesbians. All gay women and men have, of course, felt isolated from the mainstream culture, but for lesbians the isolation has been much more acute. With far fewer social outlets as a resource, we have had greater difficulty in establishing a sense of community and in organizing political structures. Moreover, the bulk of movement literature has addressed the needs and experience of gay men, whose life-style, in some important respects, differs from our own.

For the most part, society has ignored our existence; people have only the vaguest notion of who we are, of what it means for a woman to love another woman. The nongay media has tended to spotlight gay males in most articles and programs dealing with homosexuality—to such an extent, in fact, that the general population tends to equate "gay" with "gay men." In a culture where women's activities have been regarded as a footnote to male history, it is no wonder that so little attention has been paid to the lives of gay women.

But, as the slogan says, "we are everywhere," though the public may be unaware of our presence. And we are here in large and ever-increasing numbers. Back in 1953 a Kinsey study on female sexuality indicated that 20 percent of the women interviewed had had sexual experience with other women by age forty-five. This study, published twenty-four years ago, didn't include those women with unfulfilled desires and those who were reluctant to disclose their lesbian experience to the interviewer. The real figures were probably much higher then, and are undoubtedly higher now, following the influences of the sexual revolution and the gay and feminist movements, which have encouraged women to explore and define their own sexual and personal needs, and to think beyond the prescribed sex roles which have previously limited our human choices, including whom we may love.

It has become clear to many feminists, for example, that there are obvious advantages to relating to other women in a society where men are socialized to dominate us. Many women have come to believe that lesbian relationships afford greater opportunities for equality and independence (i.e., less role-playing than in heterosexual relationships) and the pursuit of one's individual goals. Furthermore, the fact that both partners share a personal knowledge of the female experience allows for a deeper level of understanding and the very gratifying sexual love that is possible between two people who are so "tuned in" to each other's bodies. We have also discovered that we are capable of providing each other with the deep levels of affection and emotional support that we as women both require and have to offer. These benefits of the lesbian life-style constitute one of the biggest secrets ever kept under wraps in the patriarchal culture.

As a result of their new perceptions, a great many women have "come out"—that is, have adopted a lesbian life-style—within the last few years, and this trend has brought important changes. A new sense of community has begun to develop among lesbians in many areas of the country; a network of social and political outlets is emerging. Lesbians need to be informed of these developments and how to contribute to them. And it is also very important for the public to begin to understand and appreciate our love.

In the fall of 1975 Elaine Howe, who had been promoting the lesbian issue in the women's movement for some time, proposed the idea for a lesbian resource book to Robert Stewart, special projects editor at Prentice-Hall. Robert, recognizing an idea whose time had come, consulted with Elaine and with Sidney Abbott and found his way to me at the National Gay Task Force, where I was involved in media work.

Would I edit the book and would the women of the NGTF staff and Board of Directors cooperate in its preparation? Certainly the value of the project was obvious to us and very much in line with NGTF's commitment to lesbian visibility. Since the founding of the Task Force in 1973, we had all become more conscious of the need to encourage communication among lesbian groups and individuals, increase public awareness of us as a significant segment of the gay and female populations,

and educate people about the benefits and viability of our life-style.

And so, after unanimous and enthusiastic approval of the project by the full board, we plunged ahead. NGTF offered to free two days of my workweek to devote exclusively to the book for a period of one year. They also agreed to contribute toward the expenses of paper, postage, and phone calls, and to help with publicity.

After the contract was signed, I persuaded my good friend Noreen Harnik to provide editorial assistance, and together we worked up an outline. Then with the assistance of women on the NGTF board and staff— in particular, Jean O'Leary, Charlotte Bunch, and Barbara Gittings—I began a national search for the most representative and articulate authors available who had the most expertise in the areas we had designated.

Finding women to write the articles was easy. Even people whose schedules were already jammed accepted eagerly, made room in their busy lives, and offered to cooperate in any way possible. Del Martin and Phyllis Lyon, coauthors of *Lesbian/Woman,* offered their personal reminiscences of the early homophile days; legendary movement pioneer and author Rita Mae Brown agreed to do the Foreword; Linda Lachman arranged to interview Massachusetts State Representative Elaine Noble on the subject of electoral politics; and the Womanshare Collective from Grants Pass, Oregon, rushed excerpts from their book on country living into the mail. Gloria Steinem, always a friend we could count on, agreed to contribute an article to the final essay section, "Some Help from Our Friends." One by one, the articles were assigned, collected, reworked, and slotted in.

We also began to collect personal testimonies, mostly through taped interviews in New York City, on the subjects of coming out, relationships, counseling, discrimination, and so on. Bettye Lane offered the vast resource of her photographic collection, as did other women. And we began to mail out questionnaires to all seventeen hundred lesbian, feminist, and gay groups on our list at NGTF to compile the national listing of groups and services that appears in the Appendix.

Somehow, with lots of help from the women of NGTF and a long list of others and after much burning of midnight oil, *Our Right to Love* came to its present conclusion.

It is not finished. Every time I look at the outline I think of another article to add. But we had to stop somewhere short of *Encyclopedia Lesbiana.* As it is, my original proposal of twenty articles and twenty-five personal testimonies grew to over forty articles and forty personal testimonies.

The process of putting this book together was a personal revelation for me on several levels. Working at NGTF in close contact with so many public lesbians around the country, I had almost begun to take for granted that so many of us are out of the closet. But when I looked at the finished volume it began to dawn on me that never, in one place, have so many lesbians been willing to go on record by signing their names to articles and allowing their photos to be used. For years, prior to the movement, we had no cultural image except the Well of Loneliness. Now here, at least, we have lesbians and cultural image galore.

As I interviewed women for the personal testimonies and read those that were sent in, I was impressed with the strength and courage, and lack of self-pity, on the part of those who had suffered the terrible cruelties of societal prejudice—who had weathered the nightmares of mental institutions, bar raids, and prison sentences, job discrimination, and rejection by their friends and families. All of this, of course, contrasts with the much more important message of pride in their lesbian identities. Such impressions climaxed for me one morning as I was opening my mail on the Sixth Avenue bus and got misty-eyed reading Barbara Cameron's proud statement from Gay American Indians. I am sure that the women who shared their personal experiences with us will have the honor and respect of all readers.

The story of a woman who had come out in her sixties after three previous heterosexual (and fulfilling) marriages was also a revelation. It goes to show that homosexuality and heterosexuality are not discrete categories and that a coming out can take place any time someone gets in touch with her long-suppressed or unrecognized potential for loving women.

I felt somewhat saddened that a few women who had been "out" lesbians a few years ago carrying gay pride signs in the streets had gone back into the closet in 1977. One woman, for example, who had entered law school could no longer afford to be open. Many undergraduates, visibly lesbian a few years ago, did not then have the stake in the system that they have now—a career that they don't want to risk losing.

But a much more important trend is also very clear, as is obvious from the pages of this book: People who *do* have a stake in the system are going public—in impressive numbers. The vast majority of women represented here are not dropouts from the system but people who hold a variety of jobs: teachers, physicians, attorneys, file clerks, therapists, professors, editors, secretaries, taxi drivers, waitresses, shop owners, typesetters, and business executives. They are in every walk of life. We already have one legislator—Elaine Noble—represented here, and in the next few years other public figures will add themselves to the list.

I was gratified that all authors were willing (and very eager!) to sign their names to articles, and even sometimes to personal testimonies, although here in most cases a first name only or a pseudonym was used. Often, this decision had more to do with the intimate nature of the subject than with reluctance to come out as a lesbian.

After I sent out a press release to the lesbian and gay press announcing this project, I got a terrific response from women who expressed interest in writing articles and personal statements and supplying information for the National Resource List. A number of women sent photographs of themselves, their lovers, and their dogs and cats with a note saying, "We'd be proud to be in a lesbian resource book."

Collecting the photographs was great fun and an excursion into some priceless history. At first we had an overabundance of parade scenes and demonstrations and not enough loving couples, rural scenes, and every-day-at-home shots. We also had very few photos of Third World and older women. So, Bettye Lane, Donna Gray, and Kay Tobin went out on special assignment to fill in the gaps. In this effort the cooperation of Salsa Soul Sisters was also critical. In addition several photographers from outside the New York area, including Joan Biren, of Washington, D.C., sent in marvelous photos. Overall, the photographs convey everything the media doesn't tell you about us: that we feel glad to be who we are, that our lives are filled with affection and creativity and self-respect. It was difficult choosing eighty photos out of the more than three hundred that were submitted. Each is truly worth a thousand words.

This book is intended as an aid to survival. Included are lists of the most up-to-date reference material on topics such as where to meet other lesbians, how to find or start a lesbian organization, where to find a therapist who will help you overcome your problems (not your lesbianism), where to buy a lesbian newspaper, how to cope with job discrimination and child custody problems. A variety of articles and nearly a hundred photographs represent a cross section of lesbian America: lesbian mothers, black lesbians, working-class lesbians, lesbians in their teens and their sixties, prosperous lesbians, lesbian lovers, and lesbians alone.

For readers who still suffer from the various misconceptions about us there is plenty of information that will help dispel the mythology that still clouds the public's perception: that we are sick, sex-obsessed, pathetic, unfulfilled, destructive, and "not real women." Replacing those images are the positive alternatives: our warmth and fulfillment, the health of loving one's equal, lesbianism as an active choice (as distinguished from "arrested development," for example), and so on.

Our Right to Love is divided into several sections of essays, some of which are followed by relevant personal testimony. Following the essay section is an appendix, containing a bibliography and a National Lesbian Resource List of more than 1,300 lesbian-oriented organizations and services. For some lesbians who are just beginning to make contact with the movement, the Appendix may well be the most important part of the book.

In the first essay section, "Lesbian Identity," Lee Lehman introduces the general reader to the lesbian life-style, pointing out those aspects that are part of universal human experience and those that distinguish our love. Then Karla Jay, co-editor of *After You're Out,* explores coming out as the gradual and never-ending process that it is. A good deal of personal testimony follows this article, providing insights, on the one hand, into the old premovement days when gay bars were frequently raided by the police, and role-playing was much more prominent; and contrasting this period with the miraculous liberating influences of the lesbian/feminist/gay movements, which helped bring us alternatives to the bars and—for many of us—our first sense of pride in loving women. The movement also inspired many women to announce their sexual preferences to their friends, family, and employers or co-workers, with a very mixed bag of reactions. In the third article, Betty Powell, cochairperson of the NGTF Board of Directors, reviews the accomplishments and problems of lesbians in the world of work. And a number of accompanying photographs of lesbians working productively in a wide variety of jobs are themselves a testament of the coming-out process that says what words cannot say.

The next section, "Relationships," explores a range of possibilities in styles of relating: romantically, monogamously, polygamously, equally, communally—whatever. As an alternative to loneliness and the bars, Eleanor Cooper offers a rundown of the various types of social outlets now available in many areas. Then Alma Routsong, author of *Patience and Sarah,* writes about "Love and Courtship" in a series of vignettes that many of us will find familiar. Therapist Polly Kellogg offers advice on how to recover from a broken heart in "Breaking Up"; Jeri Dilno, director of the Gay Center for Social Services in San Diego, sizes up the arguments on both sides of the always-contemporary debate on monogamy and alternate life-styles; and Kay Whitlock, of the NOW Sexuality and Lesbianism Task Force, focuses on the desirability of implementing feminist principles of equality in love relationships—and the difficulties of doing so. Finally, excerpts from *Country Lesbians* by the Womanshare Collective, Grants Pass, Oregon, give us an idea of lesbian life on a rural commune and feminist retreat; and Betty Berzon offers advice on "Sharing Your Lesbian Identity with Your Children."

In the section on "Research and Therapy," Barbara Sang reviews the research on lesbians (of which there has been little because most [patriarchal] psychiatric studies have ignored lesbians—a mixed blessing, considering the mostly outrageous conclusions) and suggests directions for future studies; and Dorothy Riddle, Tucson clinical psychologist, stresses the importance of finding the *right kind* of therapy (i.e., avoiding the homophobes) and suggests ways to accomplish this goal.

"Sexuality," the topic of the following section, is, among other things, a partial answer to the question often posed by an unbelieving public, "What can two women possibly do in bed?" The fact that women are very successful sexual partners should not surprise anyone who reads the excerpts from *Loving Women,* a lesbian love manual enumerating the favorite techniques.

Nonetheless, like everyone else, we sometimes experience sexual problems—though there has been some reluctance to discuss these in the lesbian community. Women who are having difficulties in this area are likely to find help, and assurance that they're not alone, by reading Nancy Toder's article.

In the "Health" section a panel of lesbian feminist health workers discusses the special concerns of lesbians regarding health care, and Jan Crawford makes a case for lesbian feminists as the logical healers of women.

The "Lesbian Activism" section is a chronicle of progress in building a movement. We have made inroads into every institution in society—we have put lesbians like Elaine Noble in public office, we have gained much support for the lesbian issue in the feminist movement, we have begun to emerge as visible, healthy role models in the public schools, we have seen a lesbian ordained as an Episcopal priest, we have formed gay caucuses in nearly all of the major religious and professional institutions of society, and we have also created our own institutions—lesbian organizations that have sprung up all over the country.

These subjects, and a history of lesbians and the left (where progress has been minimal), are treated by more than a dozen authors, including Del Martin and Phyllis Lyon, co-authors of *Lesbian/Woman;* Sidney Abbott, co-author of *Sappho Was a Right-On Woman;* Barbara Gittings, a gay movement veteran of eighteen years; Mankato State University Women's Studies Director Peg Cruikshank; Rhea Miller, pastor of the Metropolitan Community Church in Boulder, Colorado; and Dolores Noll, professor of English at Kent State.

The next section, "Visions," presents articles by lesbian theorists. Charlotte Bunch explores the relationship between lesbianism and feminism in her article, cautioning against allowing our own concerns to be swallowed up by either the feminist or gay movements; and Barbara Love and Liz Shanklin envision a society based on matriarchal principles of nurturance. Finally, Sally Gearhart, who teaches women's studies at San Jose State University, proposes a woman-centered spiritual alternative to patriarchal religions.

In "Legal Problems and Remedies," Jean O'Leary, coexecutive director of the National Gay Task Force, outlines the major areas of discrimination faced by gay people and summarizes legislative progress. Two critical areas of discrimination are addressed further in separate articles: Mary Stevens, convenor of the Lesbian Law Section of the 1976 Conference on Women and the Law, offers advice to lesbian mothers with child custody or visitation problems (the court may decide that lesbianism automatically makes a woman an "unfit mother"), and Sasha Gregory-Lewis gives survival information to lesbians in the military, many of whom have been hounded out in gay witch-hunts and discharged dishonorably because of the military's ban on homosexuals. A fourth article by a collective of lesbian attorneys addresses legal problems in relationships, resulting from denial of the right to marry.

In "The Spectrum of Lesbian Experience," we focus almost entirely on personal testimony from women who speak or write from the perspective of race, class, age, and religious background. Lesbians are as diversified as the entire society, and many of us have additional kinds of discrimination to cope with besides those associated with being gay and female. The tendency for us to ignore the barriers that separate us from each other has made it difficult for us to put into practice the lesbian feminist principles we subscribe to. It is important that many women are reflecting on these barriers and working to overcome them.

In "Lesbians and the Media," Jackie St. Joan, of *Big Mama Rag,* a feminist newspaper published in Denver, gives a review of lesbian publications and articles and suggests ways in which we can communicate more effectively with each other through our own media. My own article examines the image of lesbians in the nongay media and offers guidelines for making effective use of the mass communications system to educate the public and reach out to our own people.

The "Lesbian Culture" section includes information on our literary heritage by novelist Bertha Harris, an article on women musicians by NGTF board member Joan Nixon and Olivia Records' Ginny Berson, and personal statements from two lesbian visual artists. This section is also rich in photographs, particularly of lesbian musicians, who have captured our imaginations so well that they are almost a movement in themselves. Wherever they go, the lesbian community turns out in droves.

The "Some Help from Our Friends" section says the kind of thing we'd all like to hear from our families and friends: We love you, we support you, we respect your rights and dignities as loving human beings. I will never forget a program sponsored by Lesbian Feminist Liberation in New York in 1973 at the old Firehouse on Wooster Street at which two hundred lesbians jammed in to hear mothers of lesbians come to speak to us about their love for their lesbian daughters. There was not a dry eye in the house—and it was because each of us wishes our parents could say the same.

It is our hope that this book will contribute toward improving public attitudes; and that some of the terrible pain and repression many lesbians and their families have suffered because of ignorance will be alleviated because of what we and our friends have said here.

If books like this one had existed when I was growing up, I wouldn't have wasted years of my life trying to pretend to myself and the world that I was heterosexual. I don't have to pretend anymore, to myself or anyone, and it feels wonderful. Still, few of us can afford to be so open. And so, to those of you who are still "in the closet," we say that we understand why, and as Barbara Gittings would say, "Courage, folks. Those of us who are out are oiling the closet doors as fast as we can."

The points of view represented here reflect the wide spectrum of thinking in the movement today—not a party line from NGTF. You or I may disagree with some ideas expressed here—about separatism, about working with men, or with heterosexuals, or about the wisdom of serving in the military. But it is important that this broad range of views be included.

As media director of the National Gay Task Force, I can think of no better way to encourage communication than through a book like this. On behalf of the women who contributed to this book, each in her own unique style and from her own experience, we send you our love, and hope that you find this book helpful and informative.

1.
Lesbian Identity

What It Means to Love Another Woman

J. LEE LEHMAN

What is a lesbian? She is a female homosexual. She is a woman who prefers other women on many levels: psychologically, emotionally, psychically, sometimes politically, and sexually. A lesbian may form lasting emotional and sexual bonds with another woman or women or she may form satisfying friendships with other women which are never acted out sexually. There are many different "life-styles" selected by the millions of lesbians in this country. No matter what the choice, however, there is an omnipresent shadow: prejudice.

In different times and cultures, lesbianism has been seen in different ways. It may be totally acceptable (even expected), acceptable (or expected) up until a certain age, or unacceptable. In Western society lesbianism has been flaunted by some (such as Sappho and her disciples), encouraged for pragmatic reasons (such as keeping the illegitimacy rate down), discouraged as sinful (by the Catholic and some other churches), or even presumed to be nonexistent (what can two women do in bed together anyway?). Homosexuality was punishable by burning during the Reformation, death in the Nazi concentration camps, and commitment to mental institutions in the United States. It is only in the seventies that health professionals—psychologists and psychia-

trists—are recognizing that there is nothing inherently bad or "sick" about lesbianism.

Even today, lesbianism remains an enigma. No psychologist, no physician, no scientist, has been adequately able to explain whether there is a "cause," genetic or environmental. The best statistics on its incidence are nearly thirty years old. Of course, "science" hasn't explained the "cause(s)" of heterosexuality either, but this fact has been generally overlooked. Part of the reason, I believe, is that lesbianism has been viewed as sexual activity rather than sexual preference; something a woman does in bed rather than the way she lives her life. Lesbianism is a very complex behavior pattern which is not readily accessible to simplistic analysis. The important distinction is *not* that we have sex with other women, but that we love them, and it is this love that profoundly affects our lives and, in this society, sets us apart.

Love is something that none of us understands fully, but most cherish. Lesbians fall in love: love at first sight, a friendship that develops into something more, an intuitive flash that says, "Get to know this woman!" The effect of falling in love may have different ramifications. If both women have already "come out" (acknowledged their lesbianism), then the process is much easier. It can be disconcerting for a woman who has not acknowledged the strength of her feelings for other women. She may say to herself, "What a wonderful friend!" and then wonder why she gets tongue-tied in that woman's presence, or jealous of anyone the woman sees, or just why she is obsessed with thinking about her. Few of us have been raised to be more than vaguely aware that lesbianism exists, much less that it could be a viable alternative. As a result, it may never occur to her that she is "in love" with the other woman. This realization can take years. In my own case, I had a habit of becoming extremely attached to whoever was my best friend. In high school I suffered through jealousy attacks whenever one of my friends started dating. (Why is she wasting her time on him? What does she see in him?) I freely acknowledged that I preferred women, and I vaguely knew I wasn't going to change. But I didn't recognize any of these feelings as sexual in nature. Finally, in my late teens, it took the prodding of a straight friend who realized I had a crush on her to push me into exploring my sexuality, but not with her!

If, on the other hand, the woman is aware of her preferences, the path of love is more direct, though not necessarily easy. The feelings may not be mutual, may not be of the same intensity, or may not follow the same time sequence. Lesbian love is no harder or easier than any other romantic love. However, there is an additional twist. A lesbian may find herself falling in love with a woman who has no lesbian inclinations. Many of us have experienced this at some point, and it can be very painful to realize that one is "stuck" with unrequited love. We may try to rationalize that the other woman just hasn't come out yet, but this is not always so. The impossibility of love because of circumstance is a theme familiar enough, but as a minority of the population, it can be exasperating to be surrounded by a majority that is unavailable.

The fact that the law of averages is not in our favor introduces one of the major differences in our life-styles. Unlike heterosexual men, we cannot assume that all women around us are potential partners. Like gay men, we have to do something to change the odds to our favor. For this reason we separate from the mainstream of society into our own "subculture" or "community." In this world, we can drop the "straight" disguise that many feel the need to wear "outside." In our own places, we are assured that the other women we meet are lesbians. Whether the need is for light conversation, a friendship, a relationship, or a night of sex, we know we aren't going to be hassled. Of course, our subculture serves two very different functions: providing a place to meet other lesbians and providing an escape from the pressures of a frequently hostile world. Sometimes these may be blurred: many lesbians are so completely separate in the "straight" and "gay" worlds that they are almost two separate women.

The lesbian subculture differs in some essential ways from the gay male one. The two are seldom completely separate. Depending on the location, for example, there may be separate women's and men's bars, or the bar(s) may be mixed. Many lesbians have gay male friends, and their social circles may be separate or mixed. No matter what the choice, lesbian spaces tend to be much less "cruisy" than gay male ones. Cruising, the process of surveying one's surroundings with hope to pick someone up, usually for a one-night stand, is much more common in the gay male community. Some lesbians do cruise, but the process is less acknowledged, that is to say, more subtle. To complicate matters, many lesbians use the word "cruising" to simply denote looking. At any rate, the emphasis on "tricking" (one-night stands) so common in gay male situations is much less evident in lesbian ones. For better or worse, there is a much heavier stress on "relationships" in lesbian circles.

The name of the game, then, is relationships. The meaning of this word is almost as difficult to define as love. Instead of being fool enough to try, I will simply list some of the more common kinds.

1. Monogamous relationships. This is the closest equivalent to the heterosexual marriage concept. The women usually don't go through a wedding ceremony (they can have a religious ceremony in some churches), but they may pool their incomes, buy property together, live together, and share their lives for years.

2. Nonmonogamous relationships. This is probably closest to the heterosexual "open marriage" idea. The women may define their relationship as primary, with each free to develop relationships with others, sexual or otherwise. As with monogamous relationships, the women may live together, own property together, or share the greater part of their lives. Like other nonmonogamous relationships, this type has pitfalls as well as advantages: While it can take the pressure off a

relationship since it frees the women from trying to fill 100 percent of each other's needs, it can also add jealousy.

3. The affair. A relationship between two women can be primarily or exclusively sexual in nature. It is satisfactory when both partners are comfortable with the idea that no one person can (or should) meet all their needs.

4. Friendships. Many lesbians put special emphasis on friendships. Sometimes the friendship may have a sexual element, but this is not the only possibility. For some, the combination of affairs with some and friendships with others is quite satisfactory; for others friendships are an additional bulwark besides more involved relationships. In any case, friendships provide insight, fun, and emotional support regardless of any sexual content. However, the fear of sexual involvement can impair one's ability to have friends when one is involved in a monogamous relationship.

5. Groups. Some lesbians choose to live communally with a group of other lesbians. The main definition of the group is as a household; sexual relationships may or may not be present between members of the household. In either case, this is one very good method of obtaining multiple viewpoints and a strong emotional support structure provided that the women involved are compatible.

WOMAN TO WOMAN: LESBIAN INTIMACY

No matter what the choice of relationship(s), lesbians have had to tread on publicly unexplored territory: the building and maintenance of intimacy between two women. There are certain advantages to two women relating to each other. In a society that has placed such emphasis on separating the sexes, there is considerable empathy possible within each camp. I know another woman intuitively in ways I cannot know a man, because to know another woman is (partially) to know myself. Women have been encouraged to develop their emotional sides, and two women together usually don't have to waste as much time trying to get the other to admit to having feelings. A lesbian does not have to explain to another woman what it means to *be* a woman. Because the woman-woman relationship has been left as comparatively undefined, there is more latitude to develop a unique relationship based on meeting needs rather than fulfilling roles.

Within the lesbian community, there is considerable support for relationships, but far less for intimacy. The "goal" is to find Princess Charming and live happily ever after with her, but no one is telling how to do either. One of the side effects of this emphasis on relationships, I believe, is the very common situation of many lesbians in their late teens and early twenties. Many get involved in (usually) monogamous relationships, begin to live together, and then break up after two years or less. Within six months, both of the former "partners" are in similar relationships with someone else.

Their goal is to be involved, but in the midst of dreams of togetherness, they do not learn how to relate to each other. When they reach a crisis in their relationship, they break up. Fortunately, many lesbians acquire the necessary relationship and intimacy skills as they grow older.

Feminism in general and lesbian feminism in particular encourages women to become stronger individuals. Like most women, we have been raised to put all of our energy into relationships; when the relationship fails, we believe that we have failed. This tendency to practically define oneself in terms of one's relationships puts an undue stress on the relationship. The development of a stronger sense of self—frequently a beneficial side effect of the process of coming out—allows many lesbians to build their relationships between two strong people. For some, consciousness-raising groups, cocounseling situations, or therapy may be ways to further this process. While most lesbians do not choose these alternatives, they are available in most larger cities and many smaller ones where there are feminist and/or lesbian therapists willing to set up or facilitate these groups.

There is some doubt whether a successful relationship necessarily requires large doses of intimacy. More probably it requires a proper ratio of personal space and intimacy. Certainly many women find the right balance, because many spend the greater part of their lives in one relationship. When two women live together for years, the neighbors may choose to accept them as good friends, two "old maids" who get what little comfort they can from each other, relatives, or afraid to live alone. When I came out to my parents several years ago, they told me that they didn't know any other lesbians. I couldn't help thinking of the "roommates" and "friends" I had been introduced to, and the "best friends" with whom my parents used to play bridge! In this respect, it appears to be much easier for two women to live together without raising straight eyebrows than for two men to do the same thing.

The difference in "blind spot" between two women living together and two men doing the same is quite interesting. In the case of two men, everyone seems capable of imagining what they can do together, even if it is the "love that dare not speak its name." With women, all aspects of the relationship are granted as acceptable except any sexual dynamic, which is either unimaginable or unthinkable. Women are almost expected to be intimate emotionally with each other. It is a well-recognized fact that communication is different between two women, a woman and a man, and between two men. A rather amusing illustration was provided by the early attempts to form all-male CR groups using the model of the CR groups that have been so helpful to many women. In one case the men were told that they could talk about anything except business, sports, cars, politics, and religion. There was silence for ten minutes! Women are far more used to discussing feelings with each other than men are. As a result, it is scarcely surprising that society has recognized that two women are very capable of giving each other emotional support. After all, women have been defined almost exclusively as

emotional. To carry the point a bit further, since men are given less credit for being able to give each other such support, it is hardly surprising that straight people's minds wander to other topics when two men live together. The difference is easily demonstrated: In most communities two women can walk down the street holding hands and few people will notice. (Kissing may be another matter!) If two men do it, they may be arrested for inciting a riot!

This does not mean that lesbians suffer less discrimination than gay men. Once the label "lesbian" is applied, one is seen almost exclusively as a sexual being. In fact, studies have shown that lesbians are believed to be far more sexual than other women. There is no scientific evidence to support this belief, but that hasn't stopped many people from thinking that lesbians are sex-crazed. This misinformation has led to a host of other myths, including:

1. "Lesbians are child molesters." Lesbians are no more guilty of this offense than heterosexual women. Women in general are rarely child molesters. More than 90 percent of child molestation is committed by *heterosexual men.*

2. "All a lesbian needs is sex with a man to 'cure' her." In fact, many if not most of us have had sex with men and it obviously hasn't done a thing for us! Isn't this idea an interesting commentary on men's perceptions of their own sexuality? Sex with a man is supposed to be so great that lesbians would willingly give up their assumed greater sexual appetite for it! Needless to say, this idea isn't true, in fact the *opposite* is true if one is strictly looking at sexual performance standards. According to Masters and Johnson, a woman is most likely to have an orgasm while masturbating, with lesbian sex a close second and heterosexual intercourse a poor third. Of course, the most important consideration in sexual pleasure is the psychology of the situation, and a lesbian is going to prefer having sex with a woman and a heterosexual woman is going to prefer having sex with a man.

3. "Lesbians are 'that way' because they are afraid of or hate men." While this may be true of some lesbians, there is no evidence that it is true of a large proportion. It is probably just as true that heterosexual women are "that way" because they fear or hate other women. But since straight scientists think that heterosexuality is the norm, which doesn't have to be explained, there hasn't been any research on the latter subject.

4. "All two lesbians want from each other is sex, sex, sex!" (And to think of all the times I have avoided sex at all cost with another lesbian in order to preserve the friendship.)

Garbage, garbage, garbage! Lesbians are "that way" because they prefer other women for love and emotional support. It's as simple as that.

The need for emotional support from other lesbians is increased considerably by the societal "cost" of being a lesbian. To be a lesbian is to reject the most basic thing one has ever been told about the definition of "woman." We are faced with how to come to grips with this situation during the process of coming out. Coming out can be on several levels, including:

1. Coming out to oneself: the process of discovering and accepting one's lesbianism.

2. Coming out sexually: going to bed with another woman.

3. Coming out to friends and/or family.

4. Coming out publicly; making one's lesbianism a generally known fact.

5. Coming out politically: becoming involved with lesbian feminism, the gay movement, or the women's movement in order to change the status of lesbians in society.

Besides the decisions about whether to open the closet door, keep it closed, or dynamite it, one has to define a self-identity which encompasses the various places. As a lesbian one does not fit the ideal of wife and mother. Lesbians have generally tried three different ways of adapting to this situation. The first two solutions are based on the traditional model of the straight marriage; while these patterns are diminishing in importance, they should still be mentioned.

1. The "femme" role. This is an attempt to keep all the definitions intact except the lover choice. The femme is usually indistinguishable from the average heterosexual woman, at least to the straight world. However, she is likely to be more aware that she is playing a "role" than a straight woman would be. (A friend of mine described it as "being in drag and knowing it.")

2. The "butch" role. This is a rejection of all definitions of "woman" and to varying degrees becoming its antithesis. The classic butch dresses in a motorcycle jacket or a suit and tie, swears a lot, and swaggers. Few lesbians go this far, but their appearance and behavior may approximate that of men to a greater or lesser degree.

3. By attempting to redefine "woman." Few lesbians (and few other women as well) totally fit the stereotypic roles of the ideal woman or its antithesis without a lot of pushing and shoving. The women's and gay movements have encouraged all women (and men as well) to redefine themselves as persons, not as halves to be completed by the opposite half. As a result, an increasing number of lesbians are defining themselves as having both "sides": the rational/aggressive and the nurturing/emotional. A lesbian relationship then becomes the meeting of two equals, not a contest in mutual leaning. Lesbians are increasingly discovering that it is easier—as well as more honest—to be themselves rather than a character in someone else's play.

Lesbians are a very diverse group, and I have barely scratched the surface in this article. I have probably come closer to defining what lesbians are *not* than to defining what we are. Lesbianism defies simple explanations. We are complex human beings in search of many things. In recent years, as we have begun to define ourselves instead of allowing others to do so, we have been struck by our differences. If it weren't for the discrimination against us, we would have much less in common. Yet through all the variables, in our love and caring for women we are united.

"I am always aware, when we are making love, of women's close connection with the earth and all growing, living things."

Falling in love with a woman was the easiest thing in the world. It was like slipping into a velvet suit and finding that it feels wonderful.

I was an immature thirty-one, she was a mature twenty-six. I had discovered Lesbian Feminist Liberation a year previously, and spent that year intoxicated with the warmth of working with my sisters. I had affairs and enjoyed them all tremendously, and after a year I met Teresa. The time and place were right, but at first we didn't take much notice of each other. We were both on the same committee, and we were both blinded by a beautiful and sweet Scandinavian member, who did not respond to either of us.

Then one day, I listened carefully to Teri's opinions as she clarified a point she was making, and realized how intelligent and insightful she was. Here was someone who carefully thought out her opinions before verbalizing them, who made rational judgments based on logical criteria, and presented them in a forthright, simple, undogmatic manner. My admiration for her intelligence grew, and I started to see her in a new light. I began to see her as beautiful, and she became more and more beautiful each day I saw her.

As I got to know her, I responded to her easygoing manner. I loved the way she could take things in her stride as they came along, never worrying too much about the future. She was dependable; I could always rely on her to keep her word. Her personality suited me.

Of course, nobody's perfect; even Teri has a "flaw." She is over seven inches taller than I am. Short people will understand; there is always an imbalance of power when one is taller than the other, plus an aesthetic imbalance: Together we look like Mutt and Jeff. Nothing can be done to remedy this basic inequality. Perhaps my one regret will always be that I have never had a lover shorter than I am.

I fell in love because Teri had many qualities that I saw and liked in myself, like loyalty and dependability, and some qualities that I admired though lacked in myself, like constraint and self-assuredness.

We are alike, both Capricorns, but she is a double Capricorn, conservative in outlook although liberal in politics, always reticent and somewhat reclusive. There is a bit of the devil in her, but it needs someone to bring it out, to make her laugh, and push her to be more sociable. I am her court jester.

In return, her presence always calms me. I am always the pessimist, negative and cynical. She is the eternal optimist, always assuring me things will work out. We perceive events in similar, but subtly different ways. We like the same people, and often the same activities. We are compatible.

I seduced her after knowing her a few months—quite deliberately. She was easy to seduce; from the dance floor up to my bed seemed a short and easy step. Making love with her was beautiful, and we added sexual compatibility to our relationship.

Exploring each other's bodies day after day was the most exciting voyage I have taken. A woman's body is the most exotic continent—soft hills, oceans, valleys, even quicksand, but no deserts or glaciers—nothing hard, craggy, dry or cold. I am always aware, when we are making love, of women's close connection with the earth and all growing, living things. When her body moves, I feel as if the tide is pulling at my ankles as I walk along the shore, the sand slipping through my toes.

I had never felt this intensely before; our growing love had added this new dimension. She would knock on my door and anticipation would rush through me; I felt weak and invigorated at the same time; I was vulnerable; I was invincible.

We were cautious. Neither of us wanted to commit ourselves before we were positive our feelings were reciprocated. Over a period of months, each of us gave more of ourselves to the other, and received more, until we knew the other was ready to commit herself. Neither of us wanted to be the only one in love. When we knew we were ready, we told each other of our love; I spoke first, but it did not matter, for our emotions were equal.

We are both monogamous in nature and ready for a permanent, stable relationship; one that would strive for harmony and equality, working together for common goals without loss of our individual identities. It isn't always easy; we have occasional quarrels. But they have never lasted more than a few hours, in the four years we have lived together. Since we are both women, we will always have the ability to understand each other's emotions and perceptions, share each other's pain and joy, empathize and learn from each other. I may be pessimistic about everything else, but I know this relationship will last.

—Diana

"Our friendship deepened and we were both aware that there was love between us."

I was past sixty when I had my first homosexual experience. My life before then, though varied and full, with all the pluses and minuses that make up most long lives, did not include, as far as I remember, even the thought of anything but "straight" heterosexual relationships. I have been married three times, and they were on the whole good marriages. So it would be untrue to say that discovering that I could love another woman was the result of having had unhappy or unsatisfying experiences with men.

Of course, the teachings and influences of my growing-up years were very definitely in one direction only, and any talent or interest, including friendship with another girl, was secondary to "life's great goal"—marriage and children. Women were competition, a threat—one did not touch another girl, and even within whatever friendships did develop, there was the tacit, and even explicit, understanding that a man could, and even should, come between. Homosexual women, lesbians, were completely outside my ken. I knew only the name, which represented something vaguely unacceptable. As for homosexual men, they were simply offensive. I have no doubt that I infected my own children with the distaste I remember feeling. All in all, it was another world, and had nothing to do with me.

The extent that I have developed or grown in my thinking and general attitudes since those years is due largely to the "rubbing off" on me of the work and ideas of the various women's movements. I say "rubbed off" because I have not taken an active part or even attended a meeting of any group.

When I first got to know Cindy I didn't realize she was gay. Both my husband and I liked her and found her attractive, and when my husband told me she was clearly gay, I remember my curiosity. I had never known a lesbian. Our friendship, however, as it progressed with Cindy, my husband, and me, had nothing to do with Cindy's personal or intimate life, which was not touched on. The three of us simply liked each other. The sudden death of my husband somehow brought Cindy and me closer together. Our friendship grew and there was a mutual exchange and interest in our very different lives and backgrounds—and I, for my part, remember the shock of learning through Cindy about discrimination against gays, and how that discrimination had shaped, even distorted, her life. As our interest in each other grew, our friendship deepened and we were both aware that there was love between us.

Love, however, is different from "in love." Along about that time I remember remarking flippantly to my straight friends how Cindy "brings out all my latent homosexual tendencies." As a matter of fact, I remember saying it to my husband while he was still alive. He undoubtedly thought I was being "cute" and I, for my part, probably thought so too. I do know I didn't take either the words or the thought seriously.

I first began to recognize "in love" feelings one evening after a movie when Cindy, a gay friend of hers, and I got into Cindy's car. Cindy drove and I sat in the middle. I remember the experience of pleasure in finding myself next to Cindy rather than on the window side, and simply feeling *right* that I was next to her. There was a slight touching of thighs, and I felt "at home." I do not believe there is any difference between feeling or being in love at sixteen or sixty.

During the weeks that followed, Cindy began getting different kinds of vibes, as she called them, from me, and eventually it was out in the open. Did I want to do anything about it? Certainly not, and I had no doubts about that. I was simply happy to be with her, to be in love, and of course I had inhibitions. My inhibitions were due, in good part, to my age, and the fact that Cindy was many years younger. But there was also fear of the unknown and I hadn't the remotest idea what would happen. I had never read anything on homosexual love or even discussed it. So I was unsure, fearful of making a fool of myself—I was happy where I was, and I didn't want to spoil it.

However, we both knew there was a strong sexual attraction and Cindy had no inhibitions, other than a wish not to harm me. When we did finally come together in bed, I became aware, almost instantly, that the attraction we both felt was not only unusually powerful but unlike, in intensity, any that I could remember sensing with the men I had known. To me the mystery was, and still is, that I can feel so completely comfortable, natural, and right in loving another woman.

—Ruth

"My feelings toward Sarah frightened me so that my reaction was to flee. . . ."

I'm not sure I know how Sarah and I fell in love. I think everyone would like the answer to what it is that makes two people fall in love. I had just recovered from an unhappy and tragic situation and had just achieved some distance from it, but was still feeling very bruised and hurt. I was really not terribly interested in getting involved with anyone at all, and I came to New York with a friend and a colleague to play and have fun. Through a serendipitous series of experiences I met Sarah at the Duchess, a women's bar. We were introduced there. I don't know how to explain what happened, other than to say that the very moment I met her and laid eyes on her, I just knew that this was going to be a very special relationship and I fell in love with her. I don't think we said two words to each other. I have no recollection of what we talked about that evening. Sarah says I talked with her about doctoral studies in English literature. I can't imagine that I did, because I don't know anything about that subject.

I was in New York for a very brief period of time, and my feelings toward Sarah frightened me so that my reaction was to flee from what was happening. Sarah invited me to her apartment to have a drink and that sent me into a panic. I didn't think that we would really see each other again. After deciding to flee from the situation, when I got back to the apartment I realized that I wanted to see her, but to my horror I couldn't find her in the phone book. I spent a sleepless night wondering how I was going to find her and track her down. At ten the next morning Sarah called me. She had somehow gotten the telephone number of the apartment where I was staying.

Later that spring we spent ten days together in the mountains, where we really got to know one another better, and I think those ten days confirmed our feelings of interest for each other. We found we had lots of values and interests in common: music, the out-of-doors, nature, our commitment to feminism, to a lesbian lifestyle—to as open a life-style as possible. Then began the difficult process of my traveling from Florida to New York, and Sarah's flying south to visit me. I think the fact that we survived those three years with the help of Eastern Airlines is a monumental accomplishment.

Eventually I moved here and we got an apartment together. I think we are less concerned about keeping our relationship going and more concerned about how we can foster the growth of the relationship and the growth of each of us as individuals. I think the relationships that I have seen that have survived are those between two women who have very definite individual personalities.

We have an agreement that we will discuss and open up all areas that are troubling to each of us. We won't go underground with it. We feel that's very important. I don't think the issue of monogamy is an important issue. I think what's much more important is the kind of openness that we are trying to achieve with one another.

We are very conscious about avoiding the role-playing game. We've never sat down to divide the chores by saying, "You do this and I'll do that." But we both appreciate that each of us has different talents and preferences, and we are tuned into each other enough to respect that. I like to cook and I think Sarah enjoys having me cook for her, and Sarah cleans up afterward. On the other hand, when it happens that I'm working late or whatever, Sarah does the cooking. When major decisions are being made having to do with expenditure of time or money, we simply sit down and try to arrive at decisions that are mutual rather than unilateral decisions. For example, if a decision has to be made about how we're going to spend a weekend, I think we're sensitive about consulting with one another.

We both feel comfortable about the way in which we are sharing the apartment. We each pay half the rent.

I think there are definite advantages to a lesbian relationship. I think loving a woman is just about the greatest advantage in the whole world. We don't have the cultural and social supports that straight relationships have, but I think that we are required then to be more sensitive to one another, to be consciously supportive of one another, and our relationships have that nurturing quality.

There may be problems associated with this to watch out for. Often what can happen in a lesbian relationship—because there are so many external pressures—is that the couple sometimes tend to get very tight with one another and turn more to each other for support in a way, I think, that begins to blur the personal identities of the two people involved. I think that's a danger that lesbian couples need be mindful of, and need to find ways to promote the autonomy and individuality of each one in the relationship.

—Gloria

Coming Out as Process[1]

KARLA JAY

When lesbians ask me, "How long have you been out?" I generally respond, "I came out when I was four years old!" The answer may sound glib, but there is the simple truth that I did have an erotic homosexual experience at age four when I unabashedly climbed into the bed of a camp counselor, and a more profound truth that coming out is a lifelong process, which for some of us, at least, starts near the point of birth. A continuing process rather than a quick, sexual (orgasmic or preorgasmic) act that is completed at any given moment.

But first let me tell you about why I give such a glib and somewhat curt answer. Quite simply, I have been asked this question literally thousands of times so that it bores me in the same way I am irritated and bored when women ask me my sun sign (Pisces, if you're now wondering) and then use that slim piece of information to label me, box me, categorize me. It's not that I'm against astrology; in fact, I'm an ardent believer in the subject. That's what makes me rather hostile to the question, for my sun sign is only one twelfth of my astrological makeup, just as my coming out is only one point of reference in my entire emotional life. And like my astrological chart it's too complicated for quick, small talk or verbal stroking questions such as "How are you?"

But like a sun sign to some people, one's coming out can constitute an important point of reference. I think of it as marking a point that is the exact opposite of immigration in that immigration is the moment of one's arrival to a new land whereas one's coming out indicates a point of exit from mainstream heterosexist culture. And just as knowing how long a person has been in this country can sometimes tell you a great deal about what she knows, what her frame of reference is, knowing how long a woman has been "out"—away from the mainstream life of America—can often tell you a great deal about what she knows about lesbian life, what her frame of reference is, what kind of a world she came out into. For example, the date of coming out can indicate whether she came out into the world where bars were virtually the only meeting place, the bars where butch-femme roles were often the only alternative, or whether she arrived in the post-Stonewall era, perhaps out of the feminist or left movements, in a time when there were already alternatives to the bars and when a new consciousness offered role-free life-styles. But of course such a reference system can be misleading because of exceptions. Many Leos aren't kings (or queens), and many

immigrants have lived with American families abroad and therefore have a deep-rooted awareness of our country. By analogy, some longtime lesbians were or are in role-free relationships, and some recent lesbians aren't. Again, it's complex.

In addition, there can be a negative side to the question. The analogy to immigrants is again apt in that immigrants traditionally refer to their length of stay in a country as a sign of status, lord it over more recent arrivals, and try to force the latter into subservient roles in relation to society (usually jobs) on the basis of their seniority. Among lesbians, too, there has been some conflict between "realesbians" who have been "out" since teens, usually through biological urges, and "politicalesbians" who came out through political consciousness. Although these distinctions are somewhat arbitrary and again too simple to contain profound truth and although these particular distinctions will perhaps disappear when the Stonewall generation of lesbians is gone, it is still happening that longtime lesbians occasionally try to put down, shame, or otherwise discredit newer lesbians as having suffered less or having not yet earned enough lavender stripes to lead our dubious army.

At the extreme end of this spectrum are the dyke separatists who exclude straight women completely (for example, Alix Dobkin, a separatist singer and musician, once asked straight women to leave one of her concerts in Woodstock, New York) and who very often force those who are most likely to be sympathetic to our cause to become "enemies" because they are simply not allowed to remain friends. Or at best we force potential lesbians to remain straight.

Again, the fundamental problem here is that to label a woman as "straight" because she hasn't come out as of *now* denies process, and that's what coming out is rather than a sexual performance or an initiation rite, after which the heretofore heterosexual lady wakes up a new woman, with a lavender star or "L" emblazoned in the middle of her forehead! This line of reasoning also contains the illogical presumption that if a woman hasn't come out by a certain age, she is no longer eligible for the benefits of a lesbian life-style. And even if one can presume—and I think one can, even though there are no firm statistics that I trust—that most lesbians come out during teens or in their twenties, there are still lesbians who come out in their forties and fifties. In fact, I tend to especially admire women who have the courage to make a deep-rooted change long after most of us have become thoroughly crystalized in our habits.

And just because I came out at the age of four (although a claim has been made that I made a brief pass at another female child in the sandbox at age two), I make no claim that at that age I was a fully formed dyke (although I must admit that others have made that claim in my behalf), that I am one now, or that I have come out according to the "correct line," whatever that might be.

Like everyone else, my coming-out story is unique,

[1] © 1977 by Karla Jay.

complex, sometimes funny, and sometimes tragic. I was quite open with people until I found out in my late teens that lesbianism, usually referred to as "It" by my parents and their friends and neighbors, was something I was supposed to have outgrown, like a pair of denims. Perhaps I was supposed to have traded it in with my training bra. I didn't (quite obviously), but I did discover that It was not the wonderful thing I had always supposed—at least not in the eyes of the world. So after I had been out for most of my life, I began to hide It.

I even became frightened about It, during my first week at Barnard College, where I discovered that two women had been thrown out the previous year when a boy at Columbia (which is directly across the street) had seen them making love as he peered in dormitory windows with a pair of binoculars. They were expelled, and that creep was probably given an award for his invasion of privacy. Thus I decided to hide It (as even *I* now called lesbianism) from everyone, including my roommates. The only exceptions were my lovers—there was no hiding It from them, although we probably called ourselves "experimental" rather than lesbian if we even dared mention what we were doing at all—even to each other. I even had a nonsexual relationship with a (male) Yalie for the four years of college, and now I'm convinced he was probably a closeted gay person also, although we too were imprisoned in silence, and I used him to cover up my "experimentation." I also cruised in all the right (what I *thought* were the right) places at Barnard (the gym, lurking around the lockers, and the stacks in the library which contained what little homophobic literature there was—and I do mean homophobic), but never met another lesbian there. Had I not met some women elsewhere, I would have come to the unfortunate conclusion that everyone else had indeed outgrown It.

One good experience was that I did remember summer camp, and so I became a counselor. I even became the counselor I had always dreamed about (except that I was interested in other counselors, not children). But this and other good experiences were overshadowed by a fear of being exposed, and consequently expelled from society.

When I finally came out publicly again, shortly after my graduation from Barnard, I found it easiest to tell new people but most difficult to tell those who had presumed I was straight. Maybe it was guilt because my earlier pretense had probably caused their incorrect inference. But there were terrible cases of blindness on the part of heterosexuals. I had one straight roommate twice in New York and in Los Angeles, and she seemed not to notice an incredible number of women who paraded into my bedroom at night and who emerged only the next morning. She also assumed that my marching in gay liberation parades and going to gay liberation meetings were acts of sympathy, and once she came in while I was engaged in a bit of foreplay (to phrase it genteelly) with a lover. Later she told me (after someone finally told her I'm a lesbian—a fact that after all this took her

by surprise) that she thought I had been "comforting her."

This experience is not some peculiar exception, and lesbians should take note that heterosexuals have an amazing capacity for blindness, or perhaps they refuse to notice It in the way any polite person might refuse to see another's dandruff. If I had to give an award to the blindest heterosexual I've known, it would be a tough decision. The prize might go to a friend of mine for twelve years now, who stayed with my lover and me for a week, during which time we were openly affectionate, and upon leaving told me how wonderfully I got on with a roommate. Only in 1976 when she announced her marriage—a year after it had happened—and told me that I was probably the last person to know of it, I told her, "You're probably the last person to know I'm gay." The prize might also go jointly to my parents, who were surprised to discover in 1976 that I'm a lesbian (It)— their discovery occurred when they saw me on Tom Snyder's *Tomorrow Show*. How they didn't know was what surprised me. After all, I had lived with the same lover until 1975 for over five years, we had bought a car jointly, we had moved twice together, and then there was the fact that I had coedited two gay liberation anthologies. But they never had to confront it, and I never told them in explicit enough terms (although when I told them that I loved the woman I was living with— what could be more explicit than *that*—they thought it was fine to have "such good friends"), and they were doing such a wonderful job of ignoring the obvious that I let it pass. And now that they can no longer deny my lesbianism, they still don't accept It, as my lesbianism is still referred to in family circles.

The process didn't end with my parents' discovery, and it will never end, for I live in a heterosexist world where the presumption is that I'm straight, so that every time I meet a new person (and that's quite often), I have to recommence that coming-out process. And still I decide whether it's worth telling someone. After all, I do discuss subjects other than sexuality, and often I have other things in common with straight people so that I try to find a balance between being a lesbian and a humanist.

But every time I blithely assume absolutely everyone must know I'm gay, something comes up to convince me to the contrary. For example, one day at work (where I assume everyone has been told I'm "queer"), a woman told me that she had just discovered that a co-worker is gay. After he had telephoned two women to inform them that he was running a bit late, she made a crack about his having lots of girl friends. "I don't have *any* girl friends, if you know what I mean," was his casual, openly gay remark. She told me the story at dinner confiding in me how she had "found him out." "Well," I answered, "there are more gay people in this department than you would ever think of, if you know what I mean!" She practically hit the floor!

Thus, we spend our lives coming out, and the reality is that none of us is completely "out" or "in." As

Allen Young pointed out in his foreword to *After You're Out,* buying a gay book, such as this one, could be your first act of coming out, the salesclerk the first person to behold you with "suspicious homosexual material."

And because we are all—even me, the four-year-old dyke—somewhere in the middle, it's unkind and rude to exclude women as being straight or "not out enough." I had plenty of time to make my commitment to a lesbian life-style. Others should have the same options.

That also means that we shouldn't pressure women to "come out," and there *is* pressure to be public (not pressure to get into or out of bed; the pressure seems to begin shortly after the honeymoon is over!). It's ironic, I suppose, that at one time gay people most often came out because *heterosexuals* presented us with a dismal alternative: blackmail. Now it's some lesbians who are arm-twisting other lesbians.

Of course, there are a lot of good reasons behind the rhetoric of the slogan, "Come Out!" First of all, if we all came out, there would be so many of us that societal change would happen more quickly. Part of the reason that acceptance of lesbianism has been this slow is that the presumption of heterosexuality again denies our very existence, and most of us are invisible. (How I love the button, How Dare You Presume I'm a Heterosexual!) Moreover, the majority of lesbians in the closet (or teetering somewhere in a revolving door) puts a greater burden on those few of us who stand up and face the wrath of male heterosexist powers. And what wrath! Remember that men want you to hate them or preferably to love them, but to ignore them is absolutely intolerable! So the few of us who openly ignore penises face phallic hatred. Thus some of the "out" lesbians feel angry, oppressed, and thwarted by those lesbians perceived to be "in the closet."

If the latter category were viewed as "on their way out" instead of as "in the closet" (another static phrase denying process), then we might be more understanding, extend others a helping hand, realize that we are in the same position (even if we are a bit further down the road to outdom), and we would not let our good ends justify oppressive means. We might also, instead of expressing anger toward those less "out," feel empathy with the fears of our sisters, for we ourselves have been fearful too, and with good cause, as I was in college. Coming out at the wrong time to employers, to friends, to one's family, could be economically or psychologically suicidal. And the still bitter truth is that many lesbians who have come out *have* lost children, families, jobs, friends, educations. To lie and deny that possibility is to change the truth for ideological purposes, and we lesbians should recognize that old male trip (they, the temporary victors over the matriarchies, have written history to suit their ends). Furthermore, no ideology can assuage the terror a lesbian might feel about losing whatever is at stake at that particular moment. To dismiss that terror as being insignificant or to tell an impoverished lesbian that being free will be better than her paycheck is laying a trip on her and is outright oppressive. After all, we know what it was like when men judged our oppression as less important than racism and classism (read: freeing black males and lower-class males). Judge not—for we have been judged. And how wrongly!

Instead, we must all get in touch with that terror within each of us, for as I have pointed out, we are all coming out, perpetually, together. First, we must feel that terror and then realize at our own rate that terror can be exorcized. That happens when one realizes deeply (not from rhetoric or guilt trips) that no job is ever worth one's self-esteem, that no friend is a true ally who thinks you are someone you aren't, that the love and respect of your family is little if you hate yourself. That consciousness changes your own values first and then it spreads outward in the same way that the mother grows to better embrace the fetus in her womb. We are all pregnant with our liberated selves, and we should be midwives to others and to ourselves in giving birth to that beautiful little lesbian inside each of us.

"When I told her of my feelings, she jumped off the couch [and] almost knocked the lamp over. . . ."

I was married at twenty-five, and my marriage lasted for two years. Breaking up with my husband was somewhat traumatic, but an important experience in terms of my growth, because I became an adult after that break and realized I had to create my own self and make my way in the world. I continued to be very heterosexual for the next three years or so.

I was teaching at a university. At that time I was going through a very personal kind of searching in terms of my sexuality, but I didn't at all think I was homosexual. I wanted to be more authentic, more fulfilled, in heterosexual life, and I began to set up values and criteria for my relating to men. I found that most of my criteria were not met and I began to try to deal with why that was, what did I want in a relationship? Did I want to get married again?

I was not tuned in to the feminist movement in any deep way, but being somewhat aware of what went on in the world, I did unconsciously begin to internalize some of the feminist thinking. I was reading about it and hearing about it but not directly involved in it—I also read some humanistic psychology. I've never traced my psychological Odyssey, but at that time there was a movement toward becoming more and more free to make choices, even if those choices went against the norm.

I came to my lesbianism almost in an intellectual way. I was having a very beautiful friendship with my present lover, Ginny, who was also teaching at the university. We were becoming increasingly close after my first year teaching there. That meant having dinners together and lunches that would go on into the evening. We were very much in tune with each other in terms of our social ideas, politics, aesthetic taste, etc.

As I had been doing all this thinking and reading and opening up myself, I came to the point where I was able to understand that when I was getting ready to see Ginny, I felt more excited about going out with her than about any of the men I was going out with. I was able to let those feelings happen.

I came to this conclusion: "Aha, here we have all the components of love for another person. Everything I feel for her is feelings I would have if I were in love with a man, and the only problem is an artificial barrier. I had always allowed my feelings to grow until they reached that line I did not allow myself to cross, the sexual expression that should go with those feelings." I said to myself, "That's the only problem. There are only two choices—either you stay on this side of the line, and have just a friendship, or you cross that line, and you're into a whole different universe of values and behavior." I didn't name my feeling as homosexual or lesbian. I didn't name it and therefore I wasn't afraid of it.

Then for six months the feelings for her were getting more and more intense. I needed to state this to her, and I had no reason to doubt that she might have the same feelings for me. I wanted to convince her in some way that we could have a beautiful life together, and I did this, not having any real knowledge of whether she was a lesbian or not. It didn't occur to me that maybe she was not a lesbian and would not be receptive.

It turned out that she was, but I didn't know it. When I told her of my feelings, she jumped off the couch, almost knocked the lamp over, came around in front of me, and said, "That's not where I am, not where I've been, not where I'm going. You don't need this problem. You're a woman, you're black, and now you want to be a lesbian? Crazy! We've got to talk about this." She left at six o'clock that morning, and we spent the next week talking about it; we didn't touch each other, and the next day, she called and said, "How are you? Are you coming to your senses?" We went bike riding. We were both teaching at the university, so we'd ride to school together, eat dinner together, and talk. By the end of the week we had resolved that we did love each other, and that was the beginning of our life. We've been together ever since. It'll be our fifth anniversary soon.

—Betty

"This may sound corny, but . . . as I was making love to her, I actually thought about a rose."

When all my girl friends began getting married, I felt left out, but deep down I knew it was women who looked awful good to me. My girl friend, who knew me very

well, asked, "What if you were gay?" But I thought, "I can't be gay." My impression of lesbians was that they were dykes, butches, mean, hard women. I thought, "I'll lead an asexual life rather than be a lesbian."

Finally I married the man I'd been dating for ten years, and in some way the marriage brought all my hidden feelings to the surface. The anxiety was terrible. I felt people were looking at me, thinking I was a lesbian. The marriage lasted only two months. Afterward I spent some time just doing nothing.

Then I saw lesbians on a show on TV. I watched it and I decided to do some reading. One of the first things I read was *Sappho Was a Right-On Woman*. Then something just clicked. I began to develop a feeling of total self-acceptance. I started going out to Greenwich Village. I went to meetings and got to meet people. I went into therapy with a lesbian therapist. I began to notice my sexual feeling for women.

When I decided to come out, I weighed 220 pounds, and I have since lost 62. My family was totally amazed. I was jumping around and I would dance. You know, if you're black, people automatically assume you can dance. Well, I didn't, until after I came out. I kept saying to myself, "If they [my family] only knew why I was this new person." My aunt asked, "What are you doing?" because she wanted to do whatever it was I was doing. I guess she assumed it had to do with hetero-sexuality.

When I first came out, I felt alienated because I did not see other black women, and in my growing awareness I wanted to speak out. I felt a burden of responsibility to speak as a black. It was painful. I thought, "I'm the only black one here. I have to make a good showing . . . maybe set a good example of black women."

Now I'm part of Salsa Soul Sisters, a Third World lesbian group, and I go to other groups, too. I wonder why there aren't more black women in the bars, at the dances, etc. I do think it is important for the black women who are coming out now to have that immediate color identification. That is one reason why Salsa Soul Sisters is important.

Now I feel better about myself. If people say negative things about me, I don't take it personally. I figure it's their problem. I walk better and do better on my job. I wear this question-mark necklace purposely to say to people who are wondering, "Well, go ahead and wonder." I go to work dressed as I want, and I don't try to hide that I'm a lesbian. I won't hide. I just feel terrific.

The prospect of sex with women was initially intimidating and I didn't want to do it right away. I was afraid of women's pubic area. I didn't want to look at women's genitals. Then I fell in love with a woman. We planned a fine intimate "friendship" but my inner soul took control. I always used to fear technique. We made love, and I just didn't think about it. It was fantastic. I think about it to this day. Sometimes it stops me from having casual sex. I thought I would be concerned about oral sex and whether it would smell, but it didn't bother me. I didn't even smell her, it was just a soft wonderful thing. Okay, this may sound corny, but in my head as I was making love to her I actually thought about a rose.

—Zoredea

"He was upset that he was losing his wife to women and he could not fight it in any way."

I knew I was different when I was a little girl, but not exactly how. I wanted the privileges the boys had, and I didn't identify with a lot of the girls in school. I did have close girl friends, though. At thirteen I had a sexual, exploration kind of thing with one of them. It wasn't a full sexual experience, but then at that time I didn't have any sense of genital sex, with men or women.

Anything I ever read about sex was bad. Sex was like a dirty joke to my family, something disgusting. I didn't know anything about lesbians. I don't remember when I first heard about them, but it must have been awful. I thought they were sick, perverts. I never saw them, of course. Sometimes people would say, "He's queer," and it was a joke. But there weren't any women around that anyone would say were lesbians.

In college I put up one of the greatest fronts of all time, giving everyone the impression that I was interested in men. I was a virgin at the time, but from the way I talked, you'd think I wasn't. I was really interested in women, and I couldn't let anyone know. I spent a lot of time thinking about killing myself because I could not be that type of person—a lesbian. I was something that I thought was very wrong.

A counselor at school told me when I was eighteen that if I had not had an experience with a woman yet, that I wasn't a lesbian. I grabbed onto this and continued to repress my sexuality. When I left college I came to New York with my friend Susan and we lived together as roommates. I fell in love with her, and I told her this. She said she couldn't deal with it and immediately left and went back to her parents. She just freaked out.

I felt totally blown away because this was the first time in my life I had ever admitted my lesbian feelings. So I tried to reassure her that I was straight—that I must have developed these feelings for her because I was lonely. I said, "Don't leave me. Don't reject me this way. Just be my friend." But she left. And all I had was my work. I'd go to work and come home and cry.

Susan did decide to come back but she met a young man, and he moved into the apartment with us. It was a small place without much privacy. They slept in a double bed and I slept on a single bed diagonally opposite them. There was no door that shut between— just a big archway. It was just torture for me—I was so jealous.

But through Susan's lover I met Frank, who fell in love with me. I needed a place to go, so I moved in with him. I told him I wasn't in love with him, but I told myself, "He loves me; this is wonderful." I figured it would take me time. I was not afraid of men sexually—I was afraid of sex in general. A year later we got married. Frank helped me learn about sex, my reactions, and my body. I began to get in touch with my sexuality and started reading lesbian literature.

I wanted Frank to be aware of my changes. It was painful, but only fair. He admitted to me that he had had homosexual experiences, but he was not very accepting of the whole idea. He was violent about it, and although he didn't hurt me physically, he'd break furniture and yell. He intimidated me. He was upset that he was losing his wife to women and he could not fight it in any way. There was nothing he could do to prevent me from being a lesbian, and there was nobody to win me back from. So he was in a position of no power, at all. I knew I was hurting him, but it was necessary. I had been hurting myself all my life, and I had to be true to myself.

Then I met Barbara. I was very infatuated with her and we connected sexually. Then I knew that that's who I was all along. I said the word "lesbian" to myself. It began to take on a different meaning to me. It began to mean who I am, and not—wrong.

We made love, and I went home in a taxi, smiling. Though I only slept with Barbara once, I was sure after that evening, and right after that I left my husband. I didn't leave for Barbara—I left for me.

—Karen

"I picked up that my mother considered homosexuality a mental disorder."

I was born in Puerto Rico and we moved to New York when I was six. I feel that I've always been a lesbian, though I only revealed this fact to my sisters and mother very recently.

I've experienced different phases of coming out. My first coming out was telling my best friend of my feelings. That was when I was seventeen. Her reaction was that this was just a stage I was going though. She seemed not to mind, but I felt our friendship suffered. We stopped communicating—and we had been very best friends.

At that time, when I was seventeen, it was very heavy because I didn't understand my own feelings. But other straight friends have reacted more positively. This is more recently, of course.

My second coming out was when I was nineteen, the first time I slept with a woman. My third coming out was only three or four years ago when I accepted my sexuality, when I started going to therapy. My last coming out was to my family, and that was very recently. So I've gone through four phases.

I was scared to tell my family . . . my not accepting myself held me back, of course; my religious background (Catholic), my ethnic background. I felt it was something that had to be kept from everyone ... I thought it would kill my parents if they found out. I remember one time when I was still living at home, I was getting ready to go out one evening. At that time I did not dress in a super-feminine way, and my mother looked at me and said, "I don't know if you're my son Nello or my daughter Nelly." I almost died. That little comment ate at me for weeks.

A similar sort of thing happened later when I was living with Adrienne. We worked in the same company and people could see that we got along together well, and if a bunch of us went out together after work for a drink, Adrienne and I would be together. A rumor started going around the office that Adrienne and I were gay. Her reaction was, "So what?" which was great—but the rumor made me crazy. I immediately changed my dressing habits, tried to look more feminine, grew my hair, bleached it—the works.

Finally, I began to come out to my family—in stages. First, I told my sister. She came to live with me for a while and I felt I'd go crazy if I didn't tell her. We cared about each other and there was so much she didn't know about me. Her reaction was that she already knew and it made no difference to her. I felt great about it.

My mother's reaction was different. I was breaking up with my lover at the time and going through an enormously difficult time. I remember I called up my mother and asked her to come over to my place. I had to be with someone. I really wanted to tell her right then. My world was falling apart, the person I loved had left me—all that stuff—and mothers are supposed to be there to comfort you.

Well, she came over, of course, and the moment she got in the door—she could see how I looked—she said, "If you're going to tell me something that will upset me, don't say it." So I didn't, and she went about doing things to make me comfortable, like getting me some food, without ever acknowledging what was going on. She was well aware that I was going through something emotional and on the one hand, she wanted to know why, and on the other hand she really didn't want to know. To me, of course, it was quite a normal breakup. I wanted her to understand that my emotional state had to do with a loss, not with my sexuality.

Later on, when I did tell her, her reaction was very complicated. First she said she'd suspected it. She said that a few years ago when she heard I was going into therapy she had thought it was to straighten out my sexuality. I picked up that my mother considered homosexuality a mental disorder. Then she began to feel guilty. She thought that it might have been caused by my upbringing, my not being with her for so many years, or my stepfather. I assured her I felt my sexuality had no cause. It always seemed to me to be predetermined.

I feel glad that I told her—totally, totally relieved. I had to tell her because she knew nothing about me, really. Of course, she still has problems. My stepfather detests homosexuals; he views them as sick people. But the last thing my mother said to me the night I told her was, "I hope you're not going to stop coming to the house."

—Nelly

"Emotionally it's very easy for women to try to become each other in a way that men and women don't."

When I first entered the women's movement in 1971, I got caught up in the excitement of it and was very high for months, and that high has lasted to some degree ever since. From the beginning I began to respond to women in a way that I never had before, and became very close to one particular woman. I became her political protégé. She guided me as my consciousness opened up to new ideas and feelings. Within the excitement and affection of that relationship, I began to realize that the previous limits on my relationships with women were falsely imposed. I began to realize I could sexually love women, but I was living a heterosexual life at the time. Then, as I began to see women, I considered myself bisexual. However, within a period of a few months, I made the choice to have physical and emotional relationships with women only. There were all kinds of political reasons that I could give, but the real personal reasons are that my relationships with women are so much more emotionally satisfying than with men, and also that I enjoy more of my sexuality with women.

I feel very grateful that I was there when the women's movement was so exciting and new; we were all so brave and full of ideas. That was a tremendous stimulation to feeling loving toward women. I remember the first time I slept with a woman it was like crossing through a concrete wall, and within moments of becoming intimate, we both laughed a lot about how unnecessarily frightened we'd been. Once I got two inches over the barriers to sexuality between women it was very clear to me the barriers are bullshit. It's sad that not everyone is able to see that, or experience it, because of the constraints, the horror actually, that this society builds around women loving women.

The advantages of being a lesbian were that now I could really share the excitement of what was happening in the women's movement. I had been seeing a man when I first entered the movement, in England, and he appeared pleased in his letters about my enthusiastic feminism. But the moment he arrived in the States, we started talking and he had no interest in my new feminist perceptions, yet I never met a woman who wasn't interested in exploring these things with me—visions, concepts, and feelings. All the women I've known have stimulated me to grow in different kinds of ways. It's not a Pollyanna story. There was pain involved also.

Because women experience similar things, although not exactly the same things, sexually, it can be easy to get into comparison or competition. It's an advantage because you know how to make love to each other—it's a disadvantage because sometimes it comes down to who has the biggest orgasm. With a man it's such a different experience for him that he can't compare it.

Emotionally it's very easy for women to *become each other* in a way that men and women don't. If the relationship doesn't work, you literally have to reshape yourself in a way that you don't with a man, because you have kept different boundaries with a woman than with a man. It is easier on some levels to lose your identity with a woman. That's been my experience, anyway. Also, in the women's movement it's been painful sometimes because the world has set it up so that there are few rewards, so there's often jealousy and competition among movement leaders over the few rewards that exist.

Everybody is growing in different directions at the same time. Some women are very excited right now about the idea of polygamy, while others are interested in having a monogamous relationship. They often meet each other at different parts of the cycle. That's a universal problem.

I must say how wonderful lesbian lovemaking is. But we are delicate sexually, too. Therefore those people who aren't experiencing glorious, consistent sexuality, for whatever reasons, feel inferior or unacceptable, when in fact in all parts of society, there are long periods of time when many people have no sex at all.

Because I made the decision to love women through feminism, I have felt apart from the gay community. In the gay community, people don't always consider their lesbianism a choice, for reasons that I think have to do with hiding their sexuality for so many years. It causes problems for me in terms of identifying not as a "gay person" but as a "lesbian feminist" despite the fact that we both suffer the same oppression. Our feelings about lesbianism or homosexuality are very different, and to me that's a frustrating experience.

Whereas many gay women have kind, generous, loving feelings toward gay men, and feel like they share a lot of the experiences of gay men, I in general don't see gay men any differently than I see straight men. If they are mimicking women in ways that women don't want to behave, then I find them insulting. I don't have an identification with gay men, and that is a big problem between me and women I respect who have different feelings about them.

—Jan

"Nineteen seventy-seven is not perfect, but it beats the hell out of thirty years ago."

In 1945 the Village gay bars in New York City were of the nightclub style, strictly for tourists. Straight couples got the best tables; then by the usual order of who could tip best, gay men were seated, with lesbians often assigned rear tables. Those waiting on tables (all gay) were in heavy drag and the men most often doubled as entertainers (remember "Honeysuckle Rose"?) with lesbians occasionally allowed to sing.

The atmosphere was oppressive and somewhat awesome to young and not-so-young women without much money and a simple need to socialize. Many of the lesbians working in the bars eventually were conned or coerced into seedy and dubious activities by the mob front-money people in order to keep their fairly lucrative jobs.

It was thoroughly debasing and exploitive. Nineteen seventy-seven is not perfect, but it beats the hell out of thirty years ago. As a middle-aged woman with thirty-eight years as a lesbian, I feel a very personal good fortune to be around.

Our vulnerability in those early days was not merely an "endless series of small humiliations," but a constant erosion of self-esteem. A fearful and schizophrenic existence, one in which being "out" was tantamount to social suicide. For those who say this was also true for gay men—we know it must be multiplied many times for women.

There were problems for us as individuals with all of the social institutions, and virtually *no one* was there with empathetic support or help. We had not even the ethnic or racial ghetto to go home to for shared compassion, and most certainly (with few exceptions) *we were denied even the comfort of an understanding family.* I cannot begin to imagine the lesbian experience for a black, a first-generation American, or a sister from a strict fundamentalist family. Even though we socialized, it was almost never "at home," and racial alienation kept us even more estranged from our black sisters. *Our excessive isolation was shattering.*

The toll was heavy, particularly for younger women who had not yet built in defensive savvy or who were outraged at having a need to do so. Sometimes they were institutionalized for their life-style, sometimes for their social dysfunction or for a nebulous combination of the two. Far too many tragically lost the fight, ending in mental hospitals or prisons, along with those gone from suicide, drugs, alcohol, and street or domestic violence. All clearly compounded by the social denial of our lesbian life-style.

Although the struggle for our choice of life-style remains a painfully slow process, for me it seems phenomenal to have come this far in the last decade. I, for one, am most grateful for the progression of civil rights movements and especially proud of the women who have brought us this far. So right on, sisters.

—Lest we forget, Elaine Howe

"The headline said . . . '64 Women and One Man Arrested in Bar.'"

I was "kicked out of the closet" in a bar raid in 1953. I was about sixteen. I had known for some time that I was a lesbian, but I was in the closet, and I heard about a lesbian bar called the Goldenrod, on the outskirts of New Orleans. I went there and I was very happy. I discovered a lot of lesbians, more than I dreamed ever existed. But about the third time I was there, the bar was raided by the police. They came in both doors with flashlights and turned all the lights on, shut off the jukebox, and they took us all to jail and charged us with disturbing the peace by playing the jukebox too loud. I spent the night in jail and the owner got us out early in the morning. All the women were released on bond.

I was absolutely stunned when the police came in. I didn't know that something like that might happen. I was with a girl who was sixteen. We had both been in reform school, and I was really afraid once the police came that I would have to go back to reform school, and so I lied about my age. She didn't lie about her age, and that was the last time I saw her. I'm sure she did go back to reform school.

There were only a few cells in the jail and a lot of women. Everybody was freaking out. Most of these women had families there in the city, and jobs, and they were talking about a reporter being around and about their fear that it would be in the paper. I didn't even think about that. I worried that my father would be angry because I didn't know when I was going to get out of there. So it was a great relief when we were released early in the morning, and I actually met my father on his way to work as I was coming in. He was irritated, to say the least, at the hour I was coming in.

Then later that day when I got up I went to the drugstore and bought a newspaper. They had a section in the paper called "Police Reports" and I thought that's where this would be, and I was worried because my father always read the Police Reports. I looked and it wasn't there. Then I turned back to the first page to see what the big news of the day was, and it turned out to be me. I couldn't believe it. The headline said something like "64 Women and One Man Arrested in Bar" and they hinted very broadly about what kind of a bar it was. There it was on the front page, and all our names and addresses were listed. So I was kicked out of the closet. A lot of people had reached the point of suspecting that I was a lesbian—and this proved it. My father was very upset, and I had a fight with my brother and was knocked down a flight of stairs, hurting my leg very badly, and went to a friend's house to stay. She took me to the hospital. I had torn all the tissues in my knee, and I was bleeding internally and I had a cast put on. I stayed with her because I didn't feel I could protect myself if I went back home.

Then I had to go to court. I was really scared about what was going to happen. I thought I might be sent to jail, and I had no money for fines. But the courtroom scene was really astounding because they had raided *all* the gay bars in New Orleans the very same night, and the courtroom was absolutely packed with gay people. The judge dismissed the case. I guess there wasn't any legal way to hold all the people in the bar responsible for the volume of the jukebox.

I was arrested many times after that. The charges would range from "vagrancy" to "no honest visible means of support," "wearing the clothes of the opposite sex," or "disorderly conduct"—anything that they could write down. Mostly these charges were dismissed—it was just harassment. If the charges weren't dismissed I had to pay a fine, usually twenty-five dollars plus another five dollars to get a bondsman.

I think the Goldenrod went out of business after that. Most of those women were middle-class working women who were very much in the closet, and I think a lot of lives were wrecked that night. Raids were a common occurrence in the bars in the French Quarter, and the people that were being arrested there were mostly people that were not "out." Many were not from New Orleans but from other parts of the country.

Some few months later I went back to visit my father, and I was in love with a woman, living with her happily, and I wanted to share that with him. But he couldn't deal with it. First he said, "I'd rather see you dead." Then he began to talk about how the cause was perhaps some sexual practices between himself and my mother, and then he offered to have me return and live with him. He said he would do for me what my lover did for me. And that's the last time I ever talked to my father. I just felt sick. After that he said he had no daughter, as far as he was concerned. He died about eight or nine years ago, I guess, and I never had any further communication with him.

—Doris Lunden

"They transported me to the Women's House of Detention. That was terrible, really terrible."

Twenty years ago my mother had me arrested. I ended up spending two weeks in a Catholic home and three and a half weeks in the Women's House of Detention. It was in 1956, and I was nineteen.

I thought I was secure, being over eighteen. I thought I was an adult according to the law, and I was working. I was living in the city with my lover, and my mother learned we were gay. She came to visit me and said, "If you don't come home, I'm going to have you arrested." It seemed impossible. She couldn't have me arrested, I thought. I was working for a living, and I had a security clearance. I was working for a company that made atomic boilers for nuclear submarines, and it was a good job.

I said, "Well, I don't think you can do that. Call the police if you like." She did. These two policemen came and one of them said, "Listen, you don't really know the law. Yes, we can arrest you, and if you let us take you, you're going to be in a lot of trouble. It's not that easy to walk away once we take you." I said, "I don't agree with you. I know my rights. I want to straighten this out because she can't lean on me this way."

We went to the precinct. It took six hours for a policewoman to come because they were scarce then. From there, sure enough, I was sent to a Catholic home for two weeks. Ironically it was on the same block I lived, East Seventeenth Street. One night I left the group on the fifth floor and tried to escape, but I couldn't find my way out. I found a nun sitting at the bottom of the door, so they caught me. After that, they kept very good watch. From there they transported me to the Women's House of Detention. That was terrible, really terrible.

The charge, as I understand it, was that I was a "wayward minor." Nobody ever discussed charges or anything else with me. It was simple and clear-cut. Your parents think you're living in some lewd manner, or somebody's contributing to your delinquency, and until this is straightened out, you're out of your parents' custody.

My mother, who hadn't realized how involved this was, was surprised, too. She just wanted to throw up her hands and say, "I don't want this to happen, I don't want her to go to that place." She had no right to say that, anymore.

I was so worried about my lover; I think that's what upset me more than anything. I lost my memory; I had a cat, and I couldn't remember the cat's name. It was traumatic.

When I was taken to prison, these gates opened and I came through this dark area and was told to strip and take a shower. All it did was trickle cold water. There were women running around and yelling. I was examined by a doctor who made a crack about, "Nobody's a virgin anymore." From there, we were sent to the sixth floor. Because I was a lesbian, they didn't put me with the under-twenty-one-year-olds. I was put into another wing with the addicts, pushers, and murderers. It was incredible, a terrible experience. I'm a cleanliness nut. In the dining area there would be a woman sitting at the doorway and the shift coming out would give their utensils to her. She would drop them in a pail of soapy water and wipe them off with a dirty cloth and hand them to the new people coming in.

There was only one other lesbian there. She was a swell person. There were people who never should have been there, a girl in her eighth month of pregnancy, for example. Somebody on the subway accused her of pickpocketing.

After over three weeks in the Women's House of Detention, I saw an uncle of mine who was an attorney. I had been examined I don't know how many times. I was told there would be a court situation. I was frightened to death because a lot of prisoners were being sent to "villages," prisons away from the city, until they were twenty-one. I was very frightened about that. I thought perhaps they had arrested my lover, because she was twenty-five and I was nineteen.

Then I went to court. My mother was there. The judge sent my mother out of the room and I was released. I said, "I can support myself. I realize maybe I wasn't doing the right thing. I will stay with my mother." They thought I had "reformed." They gave me a card with a list of lesbian bars where I was not allowed to go. I had to get a job. I was supposed to report every two weeks. I did get a job. I reported only once, and

then I left my mother's home and didn't see my family until I was over twenty-one.

When I was inside the women's prison, I didn't think that my lover knew where I was. I realized she did know when I arrived for my court appearance. A friend of ours who lived next door had played detective and met me in the court hallway pretending he was an attorney. He gave me a note from her; it was the most wonderful thing that ever happened to me. I stayed home for a couple of weeks. I couldn't live there because I missed my lover. We talked daily, although I was supposed to have no contact with her. I left and started my life again. I changed my name and got another job, and that was the beginning of a very happy life since then.

—Melissa

"She had promised God that if He would let her be an opera singer, she would never have a full sexual experience with a woman."

For a long time I'd realized that I wasn't like the other girls in high school, because I really couldn't understand why they were always going around talking about boys and getting upset if they didn't get asked out on dates. They seemed to feel about boys the way I felt about girls. When I was fifteen I ran across *The Well of Loneliness,* and I can still remember my relief at realizing I wasn't the only one in the world who felt like that. I was sure that as soon as I got away to college, I'd find a lot of women like me, and everything would be different.

I went to a music conservatory in New England when I was sixteen, and I did fall in love with another woman student who loved me, too. But that never got acted out because she'd had a relationship in high school and had been wiped out by her guilt over it. She had promised God that if he would let her be an opera singer, she would never have a full sexual experience with a woman. So we'd go just so far before she'd call quits. That nearly drove us both up the wall. I found out years later that she had gotten over that, but it didn't happen with me.

I didn't have a full sexual experience until I was eighteen. When I was home on vacation, I came into New York on the train and took a taxi down to the Village. I didn't have any idea where to go, so I asked the driver if he knew of a bar that was just for women. He was very shocked and fatherly and disapproving, but in the end he let me off just a little ways from the Bagatelle. I stood around for a while, and then saw two women who looked gay go into a drugstore. I sat down next to them at the counter and finally got up the courage to ask them if they knew any place. They said, "Well, you look kind of young." I said, "I'm old enough." They said, "Well, just two doors up there's the Bagatelle."

The bars were pretty awful, although I made some

good platonic friends who kept me out of trouble. Everyone was into role-playing in the early fifties; you were either a butch or a femme. Naturally I took the butch role, since I didn't want to be trapped as a "helpless female." Somewhere along the line I went to bed with someone, and while I didn't get all that much pleasure from it, it was exciting to my mind and heart, I guess, to finally find out what everyone made such a big fuss about. I had a series of affairs over the next few months. I didn't let myself get physically involved with anyone I wasn't "in love" with, but I was adept at convincing myself that I was "in love" with a number of unlikely women.

After I transferred into Smith College, I dropped the bar scene completely, and was pretty well in despair because there didn't seem to be anything possible between women except the kind of tragic situation and suffering that Radclyffe Hall had written about, or the awful bar scene with people just going from partner to partner. I finally talked to a college church worker about this, and she arranged for me to meet with a woman—a department head—who had been in a relationship with another woman for something like twenty-five years. When I went to her office, I guess we were both pretty paralyzed.

I remember we sat and looked at each other for what seemed ages, and finally I thanked her for seeing me. Then another long, embarrassed time. Then I said, "I understand that you and Miss So-and-so have lived together for a long time." The professor nodded, and said they had. I hesitated, then said, "Then it is possible?" And she said, "Yes, it is possible." We sat and looked at each other a bit longer, and then I thanked her and left.

It seems such a small thing, and it couldn't have been more than five minutes, but I don't know of anything I'm more grateful for. She had shown me that there was a possibility of a growing, honorable and lasting relationship, that the propaganda was a lie. It still takes my breath away, looking back on it, to think of that woman's guts. She didn't know anything at all about me, and if I'd blown the whistle on her in 1954, you know, at Smith College, you can guess what would have happened. And she knew that, and was taking that chance to help out a much younger sister. Now that I'm getting on too, I've tried to do the same for some of the younger women I've met who are confused or troubled. I know it's easier in 1977 than it was for her then, but it still takes courage, and I know that my courage comes from hers way back then. It gets passed on.

—Chris

Betty Powell, language instructor

Lesbians at Work

BETTY J. POWELL

All women are oppressed notwithstanding their socio-economic status. Central to this feminist analysis is the idea that although a woman factory worker and a woman professor have to contend with different environments, they both find themselves at the mercy of men's power, privilege, and varying degrees of hostility. Women who are lesbians may escape the personal oppression of individual male/female relationships, but to society they are still women. And, like all women engaged in the commerce of the world, they rarely escape the manifold attempts to keep them in their place.

However, with the explosion of the women's movement as an expression of the specificity of female talents, interests, and capabilities that have been historically aborted, the social activity we know as work has assumed new meaning and potential in the lives of many women. While the vast majority of lesbians, as with heterosexual women, continue to engage in the limited spheres of work-related activity which the female personality has been shaped to submit to, many others are moving into uncharted fields or seek to function in traditional ones in ways that upset the basic assumptions on which society has so comfortably rested.

In the search for a representative spectrum of lesbians for this article we have chosen to focus on six women whose work or visions of their work in some way challenge these assumptions.

Lesbians threaten the ideology of male supremacy by destroying the lie about female inferiority, weakness, and passivity. This rejection of their proper "role" in society is in itself sufficient cause for harassment and oppression by male society. Compound this with an independent presentation of self in the labor market, and the lesbian is confronted by those who are only too eager to attack, subvert, minimize, and even destroy her—psychically and economically. For this reason some of the women who agreed to share their thoughts, feelings, and experiences with us asked not to have their names revealed. The day has not yet come when even the most daring of lesbians among us is totally free. In these instances, however, it is only the name, but none of the experiences, that has been changed.

Since it is a basic socially accepted value that a man is measured by what he does, the more he confirms his grasp on the world in action and work, the greater his value. It would follow, then, that in order to maintain his superior human worth there must be some things that women will not and must not be allowed to do. Therefore the social organization of work is so construed that women's access to certain occupations, disciplines, and areas of expertise is impossible, or at least severely limited. As a student at Berkeley in California, set on entering the School of Architecture there, Susan Fieldston found herself knocking at the door of one of those "No Females Allowed" clubs. Intimidated by such male-identified requirements as advanced math and physical science, and the very obvious unwelcoming attitudes, she decided to continue her training in design at Berkeley and New York's Parsons School of Design. Today Susan is president of her own firm, which has been operating successfully for the past ten years.

Although Susan's company is technically known as a contract designer firm, her work inevitably spills over into the field of architecture—both areas being renowned as among the most cutthroat, macho-type professions. Fortunate in having landed her first job with a female-run firm, Susan was given a great deal of support, encouragement, and license to extend her expertise into the areas of lighting, carpentry, plumbing, hardware, and actual construction. Increased experiences over the years, and simply daring to go, led her to discover the talents and creativity that extend far beyond her training. In challenging and trampling the "mystique" of the architectural design profession Susan found that she was able to effect design and construction in a much more integrated way than so many of the less qualified architects she encountered.

When asked about the relationship of her lesbianism to her work, Susan chose first to focus on the effect of femaleness on what she creates and how she functions in her field. She began by stating, "We're stuck with these damn boxes that the boys build us. . . . Women would never design that way. Left to our own devices things would be very low and very rounded. So we have to do it within the boxes. . . . Whenever you start to see lots of curved surfaces where all the elements, including lighting, take place in a space in such a way as to break the monotony, it's highly probable that a woman has designed it." Also, she added, "I love what I do, because we [her firm] very seldom repeat what we do." Susan's company specializes in restaurants, hotels, stores, embassies, "very few offices," and is one of the few companies in the country that do the designing for cruise ships. In each instance, creativity and imagination are the guiding lights. It is Susan's observation that one of the biggest reasons businesses make money in America is because of repetition. By sacrificing some of the profits gained through mass production (i.e., repetition) and through the male-identified system of kickbacks, Susan maintains her standards of variety, vitality, originality, and above all, quality in her work.

As for her lesbianism, Susan informed us that up until six years ago she had related only to men. With her first intimate involvement with a woman came the first time that she really felt comfortable in a relationship. Once having totally embraced her lesbianism, she no longer felt the pressure to be this mythical, perfect someone as she had in her heterosexual relations. Unhampered by this tension-making kind of expectation, she found herself relaxing in such a way that it flowed into every part of her life. "It certainly became a part of the design aspect," she noted, ". . . in that design becomes softer now, becomes a more fluid line. Also it becomes a more sensual experience to develop fabrics and materials. I think it's all because of a kind of emotional security that is reflected in how I develop and defend what I create as being okay because I'm okay. . . . Not that everything is easy," she continued, ". . . but the experience of working on a relationship that you know is basically good and sticking with it even when the going is rough, is one that definitely enhances the way I work at my craft, and the actual running of my business." Then she added, "You know it's also the way I feel about being gay in general now. I mean when you really think that religiously, politically, in all segments of the society they're really talking about it now. It indicates the real concern we've been able to generate. And because we know that it's basically good we've got to stick with it until the fight is won!"

Speaking of some of the battles that she must continually wage in her work, Susan told the age-old axiom in the architectural world, and its more contemporary twist. It seems it used to be that if a woman was successful it meant she was either a bitch (i.e., strong, independent woman) or sleeping with the clients. Now the successful woman is either a bitch or a dyke. Ironic, how even the language of oppression adapts to social change.

Refusing to compromise her assertiveness or drive for excellence leaves a woman like Susan no cushion

Carol Solomon, silversmith

against the oftentimes brutal assaults of the male mentality in her profession. However, because her work is so well received by the profession, Susan takes advantage of her indisputable talent to counter every attack against women or gays as she goes about her daily activities. Susan likens being a woman and somewhat of an activist in this apolitical field to a kind of isolation that parallels itself to gayness. Precisely because of this connection she feels that she is strengthened and can continue, even if she makes only a bit of a dent in consciousnesses where women and gays are concerned. Susan is active on three professional boards in her field, the most personally interesting one for her being the Illuminating Engineers Society Board. It's in the chambers of these formerly all-male clubs that Susan and some of the few other women like her wonder if even their most active attempts to in some way reshape the minds of men will have any lasting effect. "So many give up," Susan remarked sadly. But she immediately countered, ". . . but we can't get tired, we just can't. What we do right now will help those coming after us—lesbians, women, gay men, blacks, Asian-Americans, all those whose only strike against them is that they're different from these fair-haired boys who run this whole damn country."

While tenacity is one of the qualities that shapes Eileen McPhearson's life also, it has helped her survive in circumstances quite different from those of Susan Fieldston. At twenty-two years old, one of five children of working-class parents, Eileen is a secretary for a small import-exporting firm by day and a part-time waitress by night. She has spent almost two years working at these two jobs in order to be able to go to law school next year. When asked why she had set her sights on a career in law, Eileen responded, ". . . to protect people from the System, and in the process educate them about the nature of its abuses, break down the mystique, make them question the whole mess . . . and, well I could go on and on, but that's basically it."

Compared to what motivates most people to enter the legal profession, Eileen's personal objectives are somewhat unique indeed. For training geared toward these humanistic and, in essence, very political goals, Eileen couldn't have chosen a more appropriate institution at which to pursue her studies. Next fall she will be entering the Antioch School of Law in Washington, D.C. This alternative type law school's philosophy is based on the concept of advocacy law, which undergirds and permeates all of its courses and pedagogical approaches. The school focuses much of its students' training on legal knowledge and experiences that will best serve the poor, minorities, the dissident, and the disenfranchised.

At a school such as Antioch, Eileen suspects that the whole enlightened tone already established there will preclude some of the negative responses and experiences she might have in most other law schools as a woman and outfront lesbian feminist. However, the situation she finds herself in at the jobs she presently holds is quite

another story. Both are viewed by the culture as the typical kind of women's work which demand the typical kind of subservient behavior befitting the "role" of woman on this earth. Eileen's reaction to that expectation is, "No way!" In both situations she went about learning the ropes in an aggressive, assertive, astute manner, which she felt was very natural to her. She feigned none of the feminine wiles and limitations that conditioning and survival dictate to all women in this culture. As a waitress this behavior caused her the greatest difficulty, mostly she concluded, because the scatterbrained quality was lacking. It was as if the manager didn't know at all how to deal with a waitress, that is, "one of his girls" who engaged him directly and fearlessly as if she were "one of the boys." After several weeks on the job there occurred a major confrontation which Eileen perceived was set up by the manager as a kind of power play. During the course of the heated exchange, in what he thought to be his ultimate male coup, he loudly proclaimed, "If you're one of those lessies who think you can do anything a man can do, then there's no room for you here—except my bedroom upstairs where I could teach you a thing or two about real life, sweetie." Eileen's response was quick and equally biting, "Yes, I am a lesbian and proud of it. And the thing that's really eating your guts out, sweetie, is that in and outside of the bedroom I *can* do anything a man can do—only in most cases better. Furthermore, one of those things is that I can and will bring suit against you if you continue to hassle me or even attempt to fire me because of my sexual preference." Case closed! Well, Eileen smilingly confessed to me that she knew that the gay civil rights bill which would assure her protection against just such discrimination had actually failed to pass in the City Council for the third time. But she also knew that chances were the manager didn't know that, or even the meaning of sexual preference.

I connected this experience with something that Susan Fieldston had discussed with me about breaking that mystique of the architectural design field. What it came down to was nothing more than male ego. In very practical or abstract problem-solving situations she came to find that they didn't always know the answers. "But," she explained, "because they have been posturing ever since they were babies, they're very, very good at it, and can get away with looking and sounding like they know a thing when they really don't know zip."

Well, Eileen McPhearson turned the tables, assumed the posture of knowing, and used it positively in behalf of her economic and psychic survival. It's a rare instance that a lesbian can pull off such an encounter without suffering physical and/or economic reprisal. Therefore, the consequences of Eileen's experience were surprising to her. After that, she told me, the championer of male superiority backed off but remains very hostile and aloof. And for whatever their reasons, the other workers in the restaurant have come to sort of adopt her as their "kid who is going to law school."

At the import-exporting firm where she works,

Eileen described how her sexual orientation was much more subtly handled. It was only after several months on the job that the subject was broached through Eileen's direct response concerning her weekend "dates." The process was one that quite a few lesbians are said to experience. It is based primarily on the fact that it is virtually impossible for the human mind to sustain two contradictory pieces of information at the same time. Therefore, the eight people in Eileen's office having all come to really admire her as a person, respect her performance on the job, and applaud her intention of entering law school had a very hard choice to make when she informed two of them that her "dates" were with women. As she had been very open about her feminist attitudes, and even led some consciousness-raising discussions during lunch hours, her co-workers at first tried to interpret her remarks as referring to her sociopolitical involvement with other feminists. Eileen patiently clarified, then waited for the deafening silence to be filled with the clatter of back-to-work sounds. Well, the word got around rather quickly. Whereupon the two younger women in the office began and continue to have an approach-avoidance relationship with her. All the men, except one, seemed stunned and somehow personally wounded—a kind of "How could a nice [i.e., normal] girl like you. . . ?" response. They have not yet, however, directed any overt hostility toward her. It makes Eileen anxious though to be almost always on guard for whatever and whenever it does come. The one other male took the occasion to confide that he was bisexual, but in more of a kinky than serious way, Eileen decided. Her immediate supervisor, a male, seems still not to know what to do with this revelation. So he continues to interact with her as if nothing has changed. However, he unknowingly gives verbal and nonverbal indications that surely this is just a phase that will pass. The most directly positive response has come from the two slightly past middle age women, one married and one not, who now question and talk to her more openly about feminism. They even ask her for material and suggested books to read, but have never raised the issue of lesbianism. Eileen sums up the situation on this job as familiarity breeding some level of tolerance, and to a small degree, even openness.

Janine Braithwaite is a black lesbian feminist who has found the overall response to her lesbian life-style to be somewhat analogous to Eileen McPhearson's experience at the import-exporting company. Janine has been working for a social and political service organization for two years. The organization is a national one that gears its work predominantly toward blacks, but also some groups of Hispanic women. As the national coordinator of field services, Janine is responsible for delivering the programs, projects, and issue areas in which her organization is involved out to the field. These issues range from housing to hunger, education, politics, and many others. In an area such as political education Janine serves as catalyst for grass-roots organizing, training women in the nitty-gritty aspects of how to get govern-

ment to work for them in their communities. The use of volunteerism and other traditional roles to go about getting the social change needed is a particularly effective approach used by the organization. A project with which she is immediately involved in planning is a two-day conference on black women in higher education, and all the follow-up work that will flow from this program.

When asked how her job in any way relates to her lesbianism, Janine replied that her responsibilities include keeping coverage of all women's issues. In the course of attending meetings and coordinating efforts around these issues it is her feminism that most overtly affects her work. But in the process of discussing, refining, and directing movement in these areas she feels that it has helped sharpen her definition of herself as a political lesbian feminist.

Although she is not completely out in her office some of the staff and supervisors have been directly told, or have indirectly concluded, that she is a lesbian, based on her honest responses about her private life. It is very interesting, Janine points out, that for almost all of the secretarial staff she is probably the first and only lesbian, or gay person, they have ever known personally. Whatever myths or fears they have had to overcome, it doesn't show. What does come through, Janine states, is that "they really like me because they dig the way I am professionally. It makes my work much easier," she continued, "and in a way is a gain for them." She explained this by quoting one of the secretaries as saying that unlike the other professional women in the office, she was "not seditty."* Consequently they feel valued and take pride in doing whatever is required to facilitate her work. Janine analyzed this by saying that being a lesbian, or perhaps more accurately, a feminist who is a lesbian, she can be a more genuine human person; and that because she felt closer to women than her heterosexual peers, she had a whole different feeling and regard for women. Perhaps it is the clear evidence of this in her attitudes and mode of interaction that helps the secretarial staff respond only to the humanity that they can see and experience.

Finally, in reflecting on any possible connection between her lesbianism and a creative approach to her work, Janine speculated that because she is not constrained by the need to effect socially mandated (i.e., feminine) behavior or postures alien to her real personhood, there is space to generate energies that flow into her work, resulting in the imaginative or the creative. "I guess it has to do with the fact that whatever I'm doing it's really me."

Janine confided, however, that interesting and exciting as her work has been in the past years, she is very much feeling the need to move on to something else now. Having majored in journalism in college, worked in public relations during the Lindsay administration in New York, and also in reform politics, Janine has a strong desire now to blend all these skills and experi-

---

*A black term meaning condescending, uppity.

Barbara Levy, attorney

Zulma Rivera, employment interviewer

ences with her lesbian feminism in an integrated way. "My dream," she tells us, "is to pour my skills, training, talents, and personal/political interests into the making of a magazine for black feminist lesbians." There seems little doubt that this independent, very capable woman will someday do just that. Move over *Essence*—a lesbian with a vision is on her way!

The last three women interviewed for this article are illustrative of the socially productive character of the work that women freely choose to do and design for themselves. The narration of their struggles, while not as lengthy as the preceding ones, is no less significant. To the contrary, the nature of some of their experiences speaks more pointedly to the diverse grievances and the oppression that most lesbians still suffer in their widely varied arenas of work.

Concetta Peron, Isabella Rossi, and Leslie Kramarsky have banded together to run a small printing business whose primary product is a community service newsletter. This newsletter functions as a medium for the political education of many inhabitants of East Harlem in New York. The three women, who have struggled to keep this business alive for the past three years, have very different histories, are headed in very different directions, but for the moment are committed to a single project which they deem socially productive. Besides their social consciousness, their single most common link is their lesbianism.

Concetta Peron, a Hispanic woman of fifty-six years, is a former New York City social worker who started the printing operation, and intends to continue it with the help of primarily younger lesbians who, she knows, will come and go as the exigencies of their lives dictate. In her community she is known and accepted as a lesbian, which is quite a phenomenal reality. But because of her many years of working with and for this poverty-stricken yet very vital community, her otherwise "reprehensible" life-style is almost completely overlooked. She is seen instead as part of their survival—physically and psychically. How incredible and unpredictable the ways of human beings. Among an ethnic group notorious for its unrelenting machismo, this blindness to an ordinarily intolerable deviance from the female role gives one a kind of perverse hope in human potential.

The New York City Department of Social Welfare, however, was very predictable in its response, and in no way humane, when they abruptly terminated Concetta's service upon receiving information that she was a lesbian. Concetta had worked fifteen years for the city of New York, yet was denied any letters of reference in seeking other employment and all benefits accrued over the years. She has been fighting to bring this act of injustice before the courts for the past five years, but without success. She vows to continue her struggle.

Isabella Rossi is a twenty-four-year-old woman from Brattleboro, Vermont—"a hick from the sticks," she jokingly adds. After college and before coming to New York, Isabella spent a year living communally on a collective farm in northern Massachusetts. At that time she was considering enrolling in a forestry school and was thoroughly enjoying the rugged experience of farm life. The only discomfort was in discovering her lesbianism in a supposedly heterosexual (males and females) commune. When members of the commune learned of this, she was literally banished from what she had come to consider her "family." The pain of that kind of human betrayal still weighs heavy in Isabella's heart.

Life after that led her to the School of Social Work at Fordham University, where she met Concetta during one of the professional conferences there. Isabella has her master's in social work now, but couldn't face the thought of working in a field where she would have to suppress her identity, or suffer the fate of Concetta at some unknown point in her career. And so, Isabella now finds herself training to be a feminist therapist, and grows very excited when talking about the real possibility of being able to do intern work at Identity House, a highly respected counseling agency for lesbians, gay men, bisexuals, and heterosexuals too.

Leslie Kramarsky plans to own her own solar energy company in about five years. A chemistry major in college, she dropped out during her third year to dedicate all of her energies to the anti-Vietnam War movement. From the movement she went on to travel across country enrolling in Free University classes as she stopped for months in various places. Of the six jobs that she held during this odyssey, she was fired from five of them because she refused to dissemble her lesbian identity in any way. "Those were hard lessons and hungry times," Leslie recalls, "but I wouldn't have done it any other way. I just hope the movement can really begin to make a difference in the individual lives of people like me." Meanwhile, Leslie is headed back to Boston this summer to formally finish her last year at Boston University. She has applied to Stanford and MIT for January 1978, "because," she says, "they have the top people in environmental studies, and the best facilities for working with solar energy."

All the lesbians whose lives we've looked at very briefly here are symbolic of our finding our way of being, our new identity in relation to how and what we do as work. This can only be interpreted as the beginning of a new degree of personal and social power over the way we live our lives.

"I would drop names so they would get the idea I was straight."

I used to worry that I might lose my job if my employer found out I was a lesbian, but it was the social stigma that bothered me more than anything. I was afraid that the women I liked at work would shun me.

I always kept it a secret, especially during my twenties. I felt a strong need to be thought of as an attractive, sexual person. People in my office were always talking about their boy friends or their husbands, so I would mention some of my gay male friends' names. I didn't go all out—I didn't say I was seeing so-and-so—but I would drop names so they would get the idea I was straight.

I guess when I went into my thirties I didn't care as much about what they thought. Also my consciousness was being raised. Like why should *I* try to impress *you* when I don't even like the way you live? I think I had been ashamed of it, and really very frightened.

I don't care so much now what people think. I guess my being a lesbian is much more legitimate to me now than years ago when I first came out sexually. There was no literature then; there was nothing. People said "queer" and "pervert" and it was just awful. There was no positive identification with anybody, no role models, there was no one to look to.

I think the people in my office might be aware that I'm a lesbian, but I'm not sure. I don't get any phone calls from men and I don't mention the names of any men there, now. I don't dress like the rest of the women there and I don't wear makeup. They just might think I'm a spinster, though. I'm very withdrawn at work, and it's bad, because I don't feel I can relate to them freely, and that's what bothers me most. It would be good to tell everyone, and let them work it out—make them deal with it.

I guess I had been afraid I would be ridiculed. That's happened occasionally—people have called me names on the street, and I've been stared at. But I think my fear was really excessive, because I didn't recognize that society can be wrong. In every discussion my gay friends and I would get into we would say, "Such-and-such a movie star is gay, etc." We said this, I suppose, in order to make ourselves feel better, but we never questioned society. All the anger we felt for being outcasts we directed toward each other.

Makeup now looks very strange to me on women. It indicates how much they depend on an image. They're covering up their faces. If it's subtle makeup and enhances the way women look, and makes them feel good, then fine. But I used to go through hours of anxiety about wearing makeup. I'd have to get up very early and put on the eyebrows, and they wouldn't match, and I would get hysterical trying to get one just like the other one. I always felt like I was posing. You couldn't touch your face, you couldn't scratch your eye, you left lipstick prints all over the place—it was just disgusting.

I never wear dresses anymore—who benefits from them, anyway? Your legs are simply on display. I never liked dresses, unless it's for a practical reason, since they can be cooler in the summertime. I dislike unwelcome male attention, and when I stopped wearing dresses and skirts and makeup, I hardly got any comments. There was none of that, "Hey, baby" stuff. And slacks are much more comfortable. I used to sit on the subway in a dress, and especially if it was short, my stomach muscles

Nancy Johnson and Dinah Utah, graphic artists

would be sore, because I was sitting there all tense with my knees together so some creepy man wouldn't look up my dress. It's like being on display. Presenting a feminine image has nothing to do with the person you are—what you're doing, or what you're thinking.

—Jo Ann

". . . a black woman is always supposed to be on her knees, either praying, scrubbing a floor, or giving a blowjob."

I have a self-awareness of what it is to be black, and a self-awareness of what it is to be gay and be a woman. These things are referred to by black lesbians as the "triple oppression."

I tried to get a job in personnel psychology years ago. It was ridiculous. I couldn't get a job to save my life. I had a degree, and I knew white people who could get a job in the field. I was forced to work as an attendant in hospitals. This kind of racism made me feel bad about myself. Sexism operated, but the racism was foremost, and being a lesbian, with all of its bad connotations, made job interviews a hell. They asked me about myself, and I would become very paranoid, very sensitive, very crazy. There was no mechanism to deal with it.

Now I teach at a college, and the health profession I'm involved with is pretty small. People know each other pretty well. Nationally your reputation is made pretty quickly. Being black, it's very easy for me to be identified. There are not many black women in that profession, and that bothers me, because it inhibits my coming out. People get hired by word of mouth and reputation. I've never come out as being gay, but nobody has ever asked me. It's inhibiting and frustrating, because I would like to come out, but I don't feel like juggling it all.

I'm not so worried about losing the job I have presently, but I'd like to change jobs and I would worry about that if I were out. It's a licensed profession, and a lot of licenses are written in terms of good moral character. They use very broad terminology, which leaves room to be fucked over. Being black and being a woman and being a lesbian, you really can get fucked over.

I find that I struggle with another -ism, ageism. It's very real. If I was younger I think I would come out, but I have to deal with ageism, as well as being black, gay, and a woman.

I have a very unique situation right now. I have a gay male roommate. On my job I refer to my roommate by name. That kind of keeps everybody confused. They don't know gay people can live together. But I felt all of my life that I was obviously gay, and that everybody knew I was gay, and that I didn't have to pretend anything.

I feel I have at times had job discrimination problems because I'm gay. I lost a job at a mental health

agency once. I never knew whether it was sexism, racism, which -ism was operating. I was suddenly accused of being incompetent, after working there seven or eight years and being promoted with fantastic evaluations. What might have happened was I had an involvement with a woman who I think might have been a patient of somebody on the staff. Somebody might have been horrified that I had a lesbian relationship, especially since the woman was nineteen. I think that might have been it. I've never been able to prove it. All of a sudden eighty-five people started calling me incompetent.

I went to the city agencies with documentation that their accusations were ridiculous, but that's how it is with black people. When they get ready to screw you, I don't care what the mechanisms are, you get screwed. If you've incorporated a lot of the negative images that have been laid on you anyway, even though you can be strong, you're still very vulnerable. It's painful and hard to fight. At the time it happened, I could not really fight it, because I had a personal tragedy, and I could not devote much time to it. As it worked out, it was one of the best things that ever happened, because I went on unemployment for a number of months and did some research I wanted to do, and ended up changing my whole career completely. It worked out nicely.

I feel being an aggressive black woman has never been too cool. Being a lesbian, there's a tendency for me to be aggressive. A black woman is not supposed to be aggressive, not supposed to question. We're supposed to clean up and take care of people. I used to tell people that a black woman is always supposed to be on her knees, either praying, scrubbing a floor, or giving a blowjob. If you're not doing any of those things, it's hard for people to deal with you, and that was very much so in the fifties. You could get a job scrubbing a floor—you'd better be on your knees. Being a lesbian, I wasn't about to give no blowjobs, or scrub no floors, and I had no time to be in church.

In one sense the scene has changed a lot, in terms of different support groups coming together. The thing that is disappointing is that lesbians still reflect the rest of American society in terms of not coming to grips with racism. History has been tied up intimately with sexism and racism. Lesbians have got to deal with the history of sexism and racism together.

—Lynn

2. Relationships

Social Outlets

ELEANOR COOPER

It used to be, prior to the movement, that it took many years for a lesbian to build up the small circle of friends to which her social life was limited. We met a few lesbians in bars, but few friends. Our friends were mostly ex-lovers and their ex-lovers. There were many barriers to our recognition of other lesbians and it was even necessary to be securely involved in a relationship to assure that we would be welcome in the company of other lesbian couples. Each woman held on to her lover in the realistic fear that she would be hard to replace; a lesbian without a lover was seen as a threat to other relationships and was therefore cut off from her friends.

The bars came closest to being a community and a social institution, but not very close. They were violent, confusing, expensive, and exploiting. They gave lesbianism a bad name. They manufactured the worst lesbian stereotypes, and drove nonstereotypical lesbians back to isolation thinking, "I'm not one of those."

Times have changed and we now have some alternative social outlets. Even the bars are not as oppressive as they used to be and not all of them are run by organized crime. The local lesbian switchboards or women's centers or the publications that serve as bar/organization guides can fill you in on the current situation and the problems of bar raids and other police harassment, which is less of a problem than it has been in the past.

What are the functions of our social outlets? Spending time enjoyably, meeting friends and lovers, sharing consciousness and experiences, being with women to take us and our relationships and emotions seriously. We can hardly know ourselves without the company of other lesbians. For lesbian social outlets have been deeply involved in our identity as lesbians. Our politics and political movement have been intertwined with our socializing from the beginning, even when we have denied or failed to recognize it. We have always been in the double bind of fearing, on the one hand, to reveal our lesbianism in order to keep our jobs and homes and other forms of economic security and often even the loving support of our families, and on the other hand needing to identify ourselves to other lesbians who might offer us the community of lovers and friendship we need.

The variety of social experiences that lesbians may need or want can be seen as changing with life changes. It is hard to separate the social functions from the emotional support functions of rap groups, consciousness-raising groups, and coming-out groups, for example, which perform both functions. We form social bonds with the women who have shared our lives in such an intimate way. At the same time, we may lack the confidence to have close relationships while coming out and prefer nonthreatening contacts.

What has determined the possibilities, however, is the proximity of other lesbians. Most of us have the memory of feeling like the only one, then one of a very small minority. We sought out lesbians just because they were lesbians, even though we might have shared no other interests.

When we want to find each other as friends and/or potential lovers, lesbians are not free to assume that any woman they meet is a potential lesbian unless the woman appears in a lesbian-identified situation, as well as appearing to have emotional reactions which we perceive as lesbian in nature. We need an atmosphere which offers support and security. Lesbians are not as easy to identify as the old stereotypes would suggest and lesbians are not into the casual sexual encounter or "street cruising" that are a familiar part of the gay men's scene.

We need patience and determination to make contact with other lesbians. There are few ways to get to know a broad cross section of lesbians. Lesbian organizations offer the best opportunity that I know, especially in big cities. Whatever political differences there are among the groups, they all offer a supportive atmosphere for lesbians.

It takes time to relate to an organization. Try to speak first to other women, who may be even shyer than you, despite the fact that they seem to know what's happening and you seem to be the outsider. Many lesbians prefer to remain anonymous until they are at ease in a group. Keep going back until you feel comfortable.

What organizations have to offer is the opportunity to get to know other lesbians in a less pressured social situation while sharing projects. It is a way to get to know much more about each other than the "small talk" that most social situations are limited to.

Other locations for lesbians in cities include coffeehouses, bookstores, church groups, lesbian centers, women's centers, and a great variety of private parties and events. There are neighborhoods in some cities with a large percentage of lesbian and/or gay male residents.

Gay groups that include both men and women have their problems in that there are usually fewer women than men. There is often a problem of sexist attitudes of some gay men. In many isolated parts of the country, however, lesbians are glad to share consciousness with other gay people.

In middle-sized cities we find lesbians who are active participants in feminist groups such as the National Organization for Women. There are lesbian task forces in NOW. Many of the lesbians will be closeted women who don't like bars and don't want to be identified as lesbians. One must be discreet about revealing other lesbians to nonlesbians and be aware that there may be homophobic attitudes in some women's organizations.

It is fair to assume that most of the women in movement organizations are in their twenties and thirties, with fewer women under eighteen or over forty. There are specialized groups for older women such as Gay Older Women's Liberation or Gay Women's Alternative in New York City. Women under eighteen will find that the gay youth groups are predominantly male. College campuses are likely to have groups. For specialized groups and services for your age group, check the local equivalent of a lesbian switchboard (a telephone service/hotline for information on events, activities, groups, referrals, etc., in the lesbian community).

Newspapers, magazines, newsletters, and other publications are useful for finding likely places to socialize with other lesbians. The publications that are directed at the lesbian, feminist, and gay communities such as L.A.'s *Lesbian Tide* and Boston's *Gay Community News* are the most likely to have what we're looking for. So are community newspapers like *The Village Voice,* which is aimed at the Greenwich Village gay ghetto of New York, and will have notices for gay residents.

You can also use a nationally distributed publication such as *Lesbian Connection* to locate lesbians all over the country. In these publications there are individuals who are listed as Contact Dykes as well as listings of events and organizations. This may be very useful, as nationally distributed bar/organization guides are usually out of date fairly quickly.

There are also publications in which women might advertise to meet other lesbians by means of "personal" ads. It is important to add a word of caution here: It is impossible to know from the ad what sort of person may have placed it.

The underground papers with sex ads are the worst place to try. Even services such as the *Wishing Well,* which only provides pen pals under the most cautious circumstances, can't guarantee whom you're corresponding with.

Women in isolated situations are always having to weigh the risks involved in revealing themselves as lesbians. You may have to decide whether or not to "come out" to a friend by suggesting that she become a lover. Small towns and close communities can be the harshest places to be a public lesbian. Women who are lesbians often have been married and now have the added problem of their children. Women may become lesbians while they are still married. Despite all hazards women do manage to find each other and share love:

Terry came out in a small midwestern town in the 1970s with a determined young woman who pursued her insisting that Terry must be a lesbian because she "looked like one." After they had lived together for a while they began to track down the rumors that other lesbians could be found in one local bar on a particular night of the week. After they finally established contact with these women (it took nearly a year) they began to run into some of them at the hospital where they worked. They also eventually found that there were small groups of lesbians at the concerts of a particular country music star. They occasionally traveled with their friends to St. Louis to see real lesbian bars and finally located an annual lesbian homecoming party on a nearby college campus.

When Terry was ready to leave the Midwest, a friend loaned her a copy of Gayellow Pages. She wrote to Lesbian Feminist Liberation in New York City. The answer she received helped her to decide to move there and work out a better life for herself where there were lots of lesbians.

She found LFL listed in the New York phone book and went to the address at the Women's Center on West Twentieth Street on her second day in town. She also found *Majority Report,* a feminist newspaper with a calendar of events and ads for most of the lesbian events in the city. She found that at one of her favorite places, the Women's Coffee House, there are weekly concerts by lesbian musicians.

From any social event you can organize, you can begin a mailing list. Women in the West and Southwest semirural areas that I know of have organized monthly (or even weekly) open houses where it becomes known by word of mouth that an event will take place. They also have regular softball games which are social events for local lesbians. They have discreet mailing lists for anyone who wants to be notified of special parties, and scheduled games or playing times in many places. They may be found by checking a newspaper that lists events for lesbians or with organizations, churches, and bars that serve lesbians. Word of mouth is still more common, so anyone who is looking for lesbian sports activities should check with other women who are likely to have heard about them.

Lesbian groups have grown out of all kinds of organizations that include women and gay people. There are gay and lesbian caucuses and meetings of political organizations, for example, Gay Democrats, the Lesbian Task Force of the National Organization for Women, Integrity (in the Episcopal Church), Dignity (in the Catholic Church), and churches that are entirely gay such as the Metropolitan Community Church (found in major cities). Gay professional organizations, such as Gay Nurses Association, Gay Teachers Association, the Lesbian Writers Collective, Lesbian Artists, the Gay Academic Union, can be found by telephoning the National Gay Task Force or any women's, gay, or lesbian organization listed in the telephone book.

Beth and her lover, now both in their late thirties, are both active members of a lesbian chapter of Alcoholics Anonymous. They spend most of their social life with other lesbians who are active in the AA program. They feel most comfortable with small groups of women friends who share their values and who take their struggle to change their own lives as seriously as they themselves do.

There are also other services for other needs we have. Coming out and breaking up with your lover and isolation from other lesbians are tremendous pressures that we all have to deal with. We need institutionalized peer counseling to remind us that the world is crazy and that it's not our own distorted way of looking at things. Basically we need to know that each of us is not the "only one" who has these feelings. Call the Lesbian Switchboard or any other lesbian service organization and ask for a rap group, peer counseling, feminist therapy, or a consciousness-raising group as well as the local bars and organizations.

Marge's first semester in a small California college was also when she had her first lesbian experience. She was living in a women's dorm and had no idea of what a lesbian was. Fortunately, she attended the annual symposium of Glide Foundation in San Francisco. She had an opportunity to visit the homes of gay people and to see gays being open and comfortable. For the first time she saw lesbianism as a viable life-style.

The pressure of being known as a lesbian in her college proved to be too much and she left school for six months. She retreated to an isolated part of the Mojave desert where she lived with friends. She sought out a local junior college women's consciousness-raising group. Though she was the only out lesbian at the beginning, within six months all the women had come out and one of them became her lover. They found time to travel to the Los Angeles Gay Community Center and the Feminist Women's Health Center, where she learned about self-help techniques and setting up self-help groups. These brought her in touch with other lesbians. Marge moved to Los Angeles with her lover, who wanted to go back to school. Marge couldn't stand living in a city and moved to Santa Cruz with another woman friend and two gay men—old friends from high school—who were very involved in the gay movement. She characterizes her social life from coming out at eighteen through

about twenty-one as reflecting her fluid self-definition and life-style. Friends and lovers were interchangeable. She in no way wanted to be considered part of a couple. Her circle of friends agreed on the viability of bisexuality and also agreed with her that they didn't want to be "defined."

As she helped organize a campus/town gay group, she found that she preferred being with the nonstudents, who seemed more down-to-earth. But she enjoyed being able to share the on-campus concerts, lectures, and plays with her college friends.

Marge found her living arrangements no longer workable as she felt less like living with men, even gay men. It was a slow change, but a complete break came because of the men's jealousy of her happy relationships with women.

For the first time, Marge lived on her own instead of in a low-cost group-living situation. It was a good way to make the transition that solidified her first long-term relationship and her lesbian identity.

Lesbians now have more opportunities to share social experiences with each other. But we have to seek them out.

You can begin with the obvious check of the phone book for listings under Gay, Lesbian, and Women's. (These listings may be preceded by the name of the city or county.) You can locate bookstores that might have newspapers and magazines and gay guides such as *Gaia's Guide* for lesbians and the Gayellow Pages. There are special gay and women's bookstores, and literature tables at gay centers, women's centers, and gay women's conferences. There are national gay groups and national headquarters of similar organizations and churches, in large cities such as New York, Chicago, and Los Angeles, which can refer you to your local chapters and groups if you can't find them in your local area.

If all else fails, you can start your own.

Love and Courtship

ALMA ROUTSONG

Love. My assignment was Romance and Courtship, but I don't like the connotations of unrealism in the word "romance"; only what is real is truly interesting. Love is real.

I do not have a definition of love. I have tried for years and have not been able to come up with one that covers all the cases I know to be love. Not even "love is caring" covers all cases.

I cannot understand the lesbian liberation movement except as an assertion that ardent love, fervent love, is essential to healthy functioning; we have a right to love because we have a right to be healthy. Liberation will save the original purity and joy of this love and let our inner child go on generating it as birds go on singing. Unliberation brings fear as fast as joy, and sometimes faster. Unliberation can really make a mess out of love.

I am bewildered by lesbians who will shout in the streets for liberation and then reject ardor in favor of something more bland that won't interfere with the other parts of their lives. Why be an outcast except for something essential? Why not marry a man and have a house in Westchester if you don't know that ardent love is essential?

Without love, we are cynical, pessimistic, preoccupied with petty things, unfond of the human race, dyspeptic, materialistic, tense; many have died of lack of love alone, some without knowing why.

With love, we are kind, calm, generous, courageous, and beautiful. The embrace of true lovers is where body and soul meet. It is an authentic experience of the divine.

Love is not reliable. It is given to us by a will not our own, and taken back again in the same way. We can't control its mysterious, moonlike waxings and wanings, or make it stop when it begins to hurt.

Marriage is an attempt to make love reliable, to keep it available but untroublesome. The form persists, like a painted picture of the moon or a moon-shaped lampshade, but love has slipped out from under and gone to where it is welcome. Only the free can love.

Power (which includes money) is the main rival of love and love's antithesis. Power and love cannot coexist. In the pursuit of power, men have gutted and befouled the earth. In the exercise of power, they have covered little girls with napalm and then these men have died of bitterness and confusion because nobody is grateful, nobody loves them. Lyndon Johnson's heart broke, literally. How could so much power so fearlessly wielded fail to attract love? People who care for power come in all sizes. Some people's only power is to have a headache or a temper tantrum or keep you waiting for a table in a restaurant, so that's what they do. Like Lyndon Johnson, they're really trying to make friends. Power is ugly. We should think about it no more than is necessary for learning to protect ourselves from it.

Work, on the other hand, can and should coexist with love. They glorify each other. Since this is not generally known, love is often sacrificed for work. But work achieved at the expense of love is not done well, and is better left undone. Who can be healed by a physician who is not a lover, or trust the decision of a judge who is not a lover, or be nourished by food provided by a farmer or a cook who is not a lover? Preservatives and additives are not what's killing us, it is the lack of one additional additive. Would you buy a used car from a woman who is not a lover? Read a book by, whistle a song by, learn French from, tell your troubles to, have your boots reheeled by, a woman who is not a lover?

Courtship. All right. You agree. You're in love with your friend. Both you and she have been injured by the coldness and incomprehension of other people. You long to lie down with her and do your share of ridding the world of war and pestilence and grief. How do you go about bringing that about?

Here are some stories about how women have courted each other, with moral appended where appropriate and outcome, if known.

A and B play together on the same amateur softball team. They are attracted to each other. A has just come out of a long lesbian relationship which appeared to be monogamous but was in fact asexual. B has just come out of a series of short, disappointing affairs. B falls in love with A and immediately proposes marriage. A says, "No, I've done that. I'm not going to be confined that way again. I'm going to be a free person and live emotionally and sleep with the women I love. I won't marry you, but I'll sleep with you." B says, "I'm tired of not being committed. I'm tired of playing around. I want something serious and lasting. I won't sleep with you unless you marry me." A says, "Forget it." B takes to getting drunk and calling A in the middle of the night, urging marriage. A keeps repeating, "I'll sleep with you but I won't marry you." Comes a softball game at which B again urges marriage and A says no and gets into her car. B, who is drunk, stands in front of the car with her arms over the hood to prevent A from driving away and vomits all over the hood of A's car. A says, "Okay, I'll marry you." And she did. This relationship is still going on. I want to warn against B's methods unless you are beautiful and brilliant and a partner in your firm—an all-round good catch. An ordinary klutz couldn't get away with it.

C and D are middle-aged lesbians who have been through many painful or boring relationships and are feeling discouraged. They are introduced by a mutual friend. They have dinner a few times and talk about their work. They like each other, but agree they can never be lovers because they are both femmes, old style. C has read in *Patience and Sarah* about gazing into a woman's eyes as a means of bringing about an embrace. In a spirit of experiment, she gazes into D's eyes—an eyelock. D begins to tremble. C later in the night calls the friend who introduced them and asks her to feed C's cat. Five days later the friend is still feeding the cat because C has not gone home. D wants to live with C, but C says, "I can't stand your dogs." D, with great difficulty because the dogs are elderly, finds good homes for all of them. C and D together rent a pleasant apartment in Brooklyn, where C has sworn she will never live. D does not retaliate about the dogs by asking C to give up her cat. They have been together ten years.

E and F are in a consciousness-raising group together. E is much older than F and although she finds F attractive she doesn't expect the attraction to be mutual. Warm feelings develop because of the intimacy and continuity of CR. One cold night when they are leaving a group meeting together, F asks if she may go home with E. E is pleased and surprised. As soon as they enter E's house, F seizes E's guitar and plays and sings for many hours. E considers this unusual but since she knows that no two women are alike she listens and waits. They finally go to bed at about three in the morning, F in all her clothes. E reaches over and takes F's hand. F immediately leaps out of bed, saying that her abdomen has begun to cramp and that she has to go right home. This courtship ends in friendship.

G and H are writers who admire each other's work. G is a lesbian. H is heterosexual but inactive. H invites G to her house. They have a long talk about writing and reading and sexuality. Each advocates her own orientation. H believes that youth is the time for love and middle age is the time to write about one's memories of love. G is determined to wander off into the snow like an old Eskimo when the time of love ends for her, which she hopes will not happen soon. It is time for G to leave. She says, "See me to the door and kiss me." H turns at the door and leans into G's arms. They kiss. H is transformed by the kiss and begins to look very Jewish. When she resumes her customary Gentile mask, G knows the kiss is over and goes home and writes a beautiful poem about H's transformed face. H is moved by the poem, but becoming a lesbian would invalidate her work. Why must G *call* it lesbianism? Emily Dickinson didn't. Jane Austen didn't. G, who believes what she saw in H's face, begins a courtship that turns mostly on love letters (since writing is what she does best) and an occasional meeting. H responds with hostility. This courtship ends in estrangement. The moral is, poems and letters have been known not to work, even with women who like to read.

J and K are members of Daughters of Bilitis during its final struggle. J is a young graduate student who lives with a young woman she met at college. K is middle-aged and in a passionate love affair that is ending against her will. J and K have many long conversations. K tells J things she is not accustomed to hearing, such as that lesbians should not cut class and lesbians should be excellent. One day J phones K and asks if she may come over. K is very tired of talking about Daughters of Bilitis, but she says yes. J arrives with carnations, sits on K's couch, and says, "I've been saying your name in my sleep and my lover said, 'Don't just stand there, do something.' So here I am." K sees this as an opportunity to take some of the pressure off her departing lover, and accepts J's embrace. But Eros is not obedient, and K is unable to love J erotically. In all other ways, K loves J and gives her many hours-long hugs which send her off beautiful to talk about gay rights on radio and television. J wants to keep trying for Eros. K says, "I warn you, if you wake up you'll become someone who cries on the street." J says, "Too late. I want to wake up." K is never able to have erotic feeling for J and J goes away and loves other women better than she did before. This is not an unhappy ending.

L belongs to a lesbian organization that meets in a building heated by a very old, crotchety, and ravenous coal furnace, which L tends. M begins to take a great interest in the furnace and in its boiler. Whenever L goes to the basement to shovel coal or ashes, M comes along and studies the boiler. M begins dropping by the organization office during the hours when L is womaning the switchboard. They sit many days telling each other about their lives and their former lovers but never mentioning the possibility that they themselves might become lovers. One night they leave a meeting together with feeling so heavy between them they can hardly walk and head toward L's house. L is thinking, "She's going to ask if she can stay, and I'm going to say yes." They reach L's house. When L turns from unlocking the downstairs door, she sees M running down the street. The next morning L telephones M and says, "What happened last night? I thought you were going to stay." M says, "I wanted to, but I got scared. May I come over now?" This relationship does them both a lot of good and then evolves into a good friendship.

N is an actively heterosexual woman who comes to lesbian meetings because her daughter is a lesbian and she wants to understand lesbianism better. N is very attractive and easily makes friends among the lesbians. She lets it be known that she considers bisexuality an ideal and that she wishes to become capable of it. O is one of N's lesbian friends. O feels that she is perfect for N because, unlike most lesbians, she will not be repelled by the idea that N is also seeing men. O waits until all the other lesbians have failed in their courtships of N and then O asks N out for a drink. O tells N that she has concluded that if none of those great women could move N, O herself probably can't either. N says one should not make decisions for other people or decide in advance what their reaction will be. One should let the people in whom one is interested know that one is interested. O says, "I'm interested." N says, "Well, if I did have an affair with a woman, it would have to be very discreet." O says, "I can't do it, then. It took me too long to get out of the closet. I'm not going back." N never does achieve bisexuality. N and O are friends.

Dancing as a way of changing friends into lovers cannot be overestimated. It is not at all necessary to dance well. Neither P nor Q can dance at all. But one night at a lesbian dance they hold each other and sway. It's not certain they move their feet at all. The song to which they dance may be fast or slow. It is a very hot night and they are sweating. They pour sweat all over each other, as well as some other awesome and sacred emanation which neither of them can understand, now or in the future. They fall together and apart for many years. The end is not yet known.

R is a scientist who has just completed a project for a United States government agency and is working eighteen hours a day to write up the results. Her psychiatrist assures her she is not really a lesbian and that her one lesbian relationship was an accident brought about by her lover's happening to look like R's mother. S is a respectable gray-haired matron, a pillar of her church and community, who frequently telephones R and suggests dinner or a concert. R accepts these invitations but always finds someone else to bring along. One evening R and S are alone together briefly at R's house. S pounds her fists on the table, shouting, "Dammit, I am not a mad rapist! You don't need a chaperone with me." The chaperone arrives and they all go to a concert, but afterward R and S go back to R's house and kiss. R says, "This is terrible. I'll fall in love with you, and all I'll want to do is make love, and I won't get my study done on time." Next day, emergency session, R's psychiatrist tells R that if she continues with S, R will become an outcast, barred from her profession. He says that if she makes such a choice, she will be showing such disregard for him professionally as to make further psychotherapy impossible. R, he says, must choose between being "fairly happy" with S and becoming "perfect" under his guidance. R, a good scientist with a gift for statistics, realizes at once that "fairly happy" is the best offer she's ever had. She chooses S. R and S make love many times a day, reducing R's work time. Nevertheless, she finishes her study two months ahead of schedule, and the bureaucrat who gave her the grant tells her it is the only useful study the government got in return for its grant money during the whole year. R functions very comfortably without her psychiatrist and without the tranquilizers he has been doping her with. Her blood pressure goes down to normal. Within a year, R and S move to a distant city where they make a home together. They both succeed in their professions. Moral: Not living your lesbianism can make you sick.

"People are often surprised that our relationship has lasted twenty-six years."

I "married" Muriel at age thirty; I consider it very much a marriage. I had lots of relationships before, lasting anywhere from five minutes to one year. I couldn't always deal with rejecting a woman, so I waited until conditions were ready for them to leave me. While I didn't do anything terrible, it was pretty obvious that the relationships weren't right.

I met Muriel when I was thirty and she was thirty-seven. She had never had a homosexual relationship before. I thought she was very attractive.

I met her in Schrafft's. Those days are over—you don't meet them in Schrafft's like that anymore. Schrafft's doesn't even exist anymore. (I guess maybe they thought that if this is what it can lead to, this chain is going downhill.) I liked her, and it became obvious to me in talking to her that she was not gay. That didn't stop my pursuit, but it had to be a different type of courtship.

She had been having an affair with her business partner for a number of years. He was ill. Part of my courtship was being just swell and marvelous and best friends. I used to drive her to the hospital to visit him. She was the art director; he was the business end, so I helped her with some of the business things in his

absence: keeping the books and payrolls. I never declared myself a lesbian, so she didn't know; I don't think she even suspected, because she doesn't think in terms of sex. She didn't then, and still doesn't. She's a people person; if she likes people, it doesn't matter what they are. Her sexual experience had been all heterosexual—minimal, I might add, for a thirty-six-year-old woman. I think there might have been two men in her life.

I was being so marvelous and irresistible, but nothing was happening, except we were turning out to be swell friends. I tried to make myself indispensable. Then one night I got very drunk and called her about twelve o'clock and said, "I have to talk to you." She said, "I'm in bed." I said, "That's wonderful, don't make a move." So I went up there, blind out of my skull. In those days ladies wore "divine housecoats," for entertaining, and she looked smashing. She made me a drink, got back into bed, and I sat alongside her, and said, "Muriel, I have to tell you, I'm a lesbian." She said, "I'm not, you know," so I said, "Don't worry about it, I'll think of something." That was a big fiasco; even if I wanted to do something I wasn't able to. Even as I said it, I wanted to kill myself. But she didn't fall down when I told her, and I wound myself up and went home.

The next morning, I couldn't face her. I was embarrassed, uncomfortable, riddled with guilt. I didn't go for a couple of days, I sent flowers with a tasteful note, "I'm very sorry; we can still be friends."

I don't know how it evolved, maybe another six months of seeing each other went by, and I don't even know how we got into bed, or how we even kissed. I don't remember, but it happened, and it was so spontaneous and very easy, and there wasn't any guilt or discomfort. She responded to me and was very dear.

I had said to her that after this other woman I was living with, I would never fall in love with another woman. "I'm thirty and I've had it with that stuff," I said, "but I must get out of that mess." My "roommate" was making it with men, women, field mice, whatever—I had the perfect excuse when I found out it was a field mouse that she'd been fooling with! I told Muriel that my situation with Edith was just untenable and I had to find an apartment. I couldn't afford a big place, and she said, "I have an extra closet, since we're already sharing a bed." So for all intents and purposes I moved into her "closet" for a while. We were lovers by then. We slept on a studio couch for several years in a marvelous, beautiful, and very loving relationship. One day, Muriel said, "I think there'll be an apartment available in the floor above our office," and I said, "Wonderful."

The romance was taking very well. Her partner's illness was beyond repair and he would never be able to come back into the business. She asked me if I would come in and be her partner. Our working and living relationships were absolutely marvelous from the beginning. She was the art director of the agency; I was the business manager. We worked and lived together, but we weren't constantly with each other. I just loved being with her. She was my best friend. She still is. I love her, and I like her tremendously. She's a very attractive person.

I don't understand why people are often surprised that our relationship has lasted twenty-six years. The young ones are the most surprised—twenty-, thirty-, even forty-year-olds. I'm fifty-six; that's the big difference. Today, women meet and share a beer and hop into bed, and if that's not good enough, right away it's got to be draperies and Van Gogh reprints and maple furniture, and they haven't gotten to know each other.

When I met Muriel, I knew subconsciously she was the person that I would spend the rest of my life with. I've looked at a lot of other women, but nobody has even remotely threatened our relationship. I've cheated five times in twenty-six years, but there's always been five thousand miles between us at the time. I might be in Puerto Rico, she might be in New York. I knew Muriel would never find out. Some people don't have these needs; I did.

I once said to Muriel, "Never ask a question unless you're prepared to deal with the answer," so we've never talked about it. When I'm ready to fool around I always hope I'll meet somebody who looks like Muriel, acts like Muriel, and is not Muriel, but there's only one Muriel. That's why it's been very minimal. I never felt guilty, because I was not denying anything to her. An open-end marriage is not for me—I don't think it helps for a long-range relationship. I guess I am basically monogamous—I know Muriel is.

Look at gay men. They're always saying they've been together twelve thousand years. They've been together ten minutes, and right away they're cruising the bars. Among lesbians it's much more an emotional kind of thing, and while sex isn't parenthetic, it's part of the total.

Those five times were wonderful little episodes. I would have wanted to tell Muriel because I had such a good time, but of course I wouldn't. I was not denying Muriel anything of myself. She comes first.

If she has had similar experiences, I wouldn't know about it. If I found out about it, I wouldn't dare be upset, because maybe she had had the same needs I have had. I would rather not discuss it, though. You can intellectualize a thing to death, and make much more of it than is really important.

You have to respect each other, be kind to each other, and communicate. So often women have an argument over something dumb and somebody's hurt. Then they bleed and brood, but don't say anything. A month goes by, another situation occurs, and now the brooding gets a little longer. I usually set a time limit, maybe fifteen minutes, for my brooding. I want to clear the air.

No relationship is perfect—mine certainly isn't. We've had our ups and downs, but fortunately we talk about it. I always know when I have hurt Muriel. She'll never say anything, because she's a bleeder, but I won't allow that. I say to her, "Honey, we've got to talk. I've done something wrong, I'm sure, tell me. Unless you're having such a good time suffering, then call me when you're ready, don't make it too long."

I won't allow anything to get heavy. I may be right, and I may be wrong, and one must allow the other person to be right and be wrong. I used to be very aggressive and want to make all the decisions. I'm still aggressive, but Muriel makes decisions too—why should only I be right or wrong? She's a person, too.

I know six sets of lesbians that are breaking up their relationship. None of them should have gotten involved with each other because they didn't know each other well enough. I believe in long engagements. They weren't communicating, either. I asked, "When did you try last to communicate with her? Maybe you need a third person who can be objective, it needn't be a professional. Say in front of each other what's bothering you."

If you care, you say, "Talk to me about it—if I'm wrong, next time I'll try not to do it again. I'm glad you told me, I wasn't aware." What's wrong about admitting to being wrong? If you care about each other, you will.

—Paula

"I had just unearthed my lovable lesbian heart, and here it was broken."

I wasn't prepared for the pain I felt when my first full-blown relationship ended. I had never been "in love" before. For thirty years my big, loving, lesbian heart had been under wraps in the closet, and it had grown huge with the yearning to love. These yearnings surfaced with all the intensity of (overdue) adolescence. Every cell and nerve ending in my body and psyche wanted to love a woman and to hold and be held by her. Given these enormous needs, plus the romantic Hollywood tapes in my head, I was a setup for love.

So when I met Sue, practically as soon as we kissed, we set up housekeeping—home-cooked meals, curtains, stereo. The need for domestic warmth, a "home," was strong in me. I had felt like a loner all my life. Now I was no longer "on the run" from my lesbianism. I was coming "home" to my lesbianism and wanted nothing more than to rest in our monogamous domestic nest. So happily, with much help from Sue, I turned myself over to "us." We gave full reign to our dependency needs. We did *everything together*. The togetherness, which was at first a refuge from a hostile society, turned sour as we overdosed on each other.

Three years later the breakup began with her saying she needed to be nonmonogamous. I confidently agreed; but the first night she spent away from me, I cried hysterically all night. I felt crazy and alone. For years I'd leaned exclusively on her, and here I was devastated and she wasn't there to talk to. For two months I denied that we were breaking up and tried to work at nonmonogamy. I was shocked to find myself snooping for letters and straining to overhear phone conversations in a crazed state of mind. But jealousy was easier to deal with than breaking up; I needed the time to prepare my system, to believe that it was really over.

We had shared immense struggles: breaking from our families, coming out, curing her alcoholism, grad school, and setting up a business together. I had centered myself totally on the relationship. Who was I without it? Would I go to a hotel? A panicky emptiness gripped me. My whole system froze in disbelief: I had just unearthed my lovable lesbian heart, and here it was broken. How could the love I'd yearned for and given so much to suddenly end? I doubted my sanity; hadn't we been planning a life together last month? My emotions were very physical: I felt raw, wounded, open the way skin is when a scab's been torn off. I was tired, restless, empty, and my heart would literally ache. I felt in shock and I couldn't shake the feeling. I took long walks, started a journal, couldn't concentrate, and was very forgetful. I kept telling myself I was in recovery from a trauma and needed time to digest what had happened and to heal. I wanted to go to a rest home for a month and recuperate.

My first night in my own apartment in Berkeley wasn't as bad as I'd expected. It had taken me months to make the move, but once I was out, I didn't want to go back even to get the rest of my things. At first I had no one to talk to since we had isolated ourselves from the lesbian community in our coupledom. One day I just walked into the woman's center and cried with strangers —a hard thing for a strong woman to do! Luckily I made friends fast. For the first time in my life I was able to cry about lesbian problems and get held by women other than a lover. This was a precious feeling, like having support, a gang, a real lesbian family at last.

Crying with people was helpful: I needed to hear myself telling people how hard the alcoholism, especially, had been on me and to hear the anger I'd been denying all along to be "in love." One day I poured out to a friend all the things about Sue I didn't like. This day was a breakthrough; the illusions finally dissolved and I realized I was glad we'd broken up. Healing was steady after this. I contacted old friends and picked up my old activities again. Slowly my sense of self and my sanity returned, but it took an astonishing amount of time—a full eight months.

Since I learned that my common sense can desert me when a good woman kisses me, I made rules to protect myself: Don't get involved instantly. Keep a circle of friends. Don't move in together. Keep a journal on problems in the relationship and daily annoyances. And devote as much energy to my work and the lesbian community as to a lover. In my next relationship, I kept about half these rules, and the breakup after two years was much easier and more friendly. So to paraphrase Alix Dobkin, "We don't learn easy, but we learn." Or so I hope.

—Nancy

Breaking Up

POLLY KELLOGG

Very strong women—women who've survived all sorts of hell in their lives—can often be thrown by a breakup with a lover. There are many reasons why breakups are so hard. First of all, we relate very deeply and intimately, and the loss of this is sad. Women are good at communication and caring, and when women love each other, the mutual exchange of this energy is incredibly intense and beautiful.

Of course, we will regret the end of real love, but the devastation that often comes with breakups has its roots in the pressures of a homophobic society, and may get cured someday as we cure society. For example, living in a hostile society causes us to overload our relationships; we get no support from our family, TV, religion, or jobs, so we're thrown back on each other for all our needs: Our lover becomes our family, our protection from a toxic environment, and perhaps our only "best friend" or confidante. How terrifying when we have a fight if there's no friend or mother to turn to! Breaking up can make us feel that all our supports are being pulled from under us at once.

Our lover often serves another subtle function: She is the reflection or validation of my lesbianism. Traveling "out there," I'm invisible, I'm assumed out of existence. So in order to exist, I need a daily dose of lesbianism from somewhere: hence the tendency to go everywhere with a lover, to get jobs together, or to talk to each other several times a day from work. It's damn lonely "out there" and I need a hand to hold onto. It's not surprising that during a breakup many women experience a flash of the disturbing question, "Am I really a lesbian?"

Most of us don't come out at puberty, and may go through years of denying our love for women. We come out in a state of unmitigated starvation: bursting with hugs that have been held in or directed only toward our cat (s, dogs, horses, plants). When we finally find a piece of love, we hang onto it like a dog with its first pork chop. These immense needs artificially exaggerate our dependency and can make breakups devastating.

Another cause of dependency is that it's very hard for a woman to find work that builds self-esteem, identity, and confidence. It's hard for women to find work, period, much less ego-building careers. For lesbians there's the additional problem of finding work where the closet isn't too oppressive. Being stuck in a "shit job," it's easy to get overfocused on the importance of love.

Hollywood romanticism, like religion, is ingested mostly by women. The cultural view of love involves a tragic, overdependent bonding till death. A sicker notion can hardly be imagined. "I'm nobody till somebody loves me" . . . I found myself when I found you. We're told over and over again that unrequited love is worse than death ... so the lesbian who's had plenty of crushes on straight women has her pain fed royally. And of course, you can't love two people at once, and if your lover tries, you might as well head for the nearest ten-story window. To survive a breakup, *don't* play the radio. And remind yourself that you may have lost a companion, but you have *not* lost your *self.*

It's quixotic that as strong and independent as most of us are, we can get so dependent in relationships. During breakups, it helps to remind yourself that you have probably handled many difficult situations alone, and can do so again. The weakness is phony: We fall into the habit of dependency, for the reasons discussed above, and then we *think* we can't do things without our lover, and this just isn't true.

It's very important to make friends and connections to the lesbian community. You need other lesbians to talk to, share problems with, play with, and feel like a lesbian with. Otherwise your lesbian identity isn't nurtured; you're like a plant without sunshine and water, or a petunia in an onion patch. And individually and as a couple you fail to grow. And during a breakup you feel terribly alone if you don't have gay friends. We all know the high we get from a lesbian conference, concert, Lesbian Pride Week, or a weekend at a woman's retreat. It takes planning to get that affirmation as often as possible by finding out about every event, throwing parties, joining or forming groups, and making friends. If you're getting hugs from the community, you don't choke a lover with all your friendship needs.

Living in a homophobic society is rough and creates built-in pressures on our relationships. A relationship can go bad because of these pressures, not because of any fault of either individual. And breakups are harder now than they need be. As a movement we are beginning to talk about creating community, "over-coupling," losing identity in relationships, becoming overly dependent, and nonmonogamy. But we are just at the beginning of all this. It's new for all of us. The movement started in 1969, so in a sense, the oldest of us is only eight years old, and no one has the answers. As the Woman's Place brochure says, "We are here as innocent children on their first journey out to play." We might as well be gentle on ourselves and each other as we make mistakes while learning to love in an onion patch.

Monogamy and Alternate Life-Styles

JERI DILNO

To gain some perspective on the variety of lesbian life-styles, I spoke to several women, each in a unique relationship. Two of the women are in an open relationship, one is a single lesbian, one is having multiple relationships, and one has a monogamous commitment. I also participated in a rap group with nine other women, discussing the topic of changing life-styles. This article is based on these dialogues, filtered through my own experience as a forty-year-old lesbian who came out in 1954 at the age of eighteen.

EFFECTS OF SOCIALIZATION

For a number of political and sociological reasons, women and men have been conditioned to play particular roles essential to the preservation of our patriarchal society. A strict definition of roles has been necessary to provide and maintain certain functions in this society. The services rendered by these roles were most efficiently carried out and controlled by institutionalizing specific role relationships in a tradition that has come to be known as marriage.

The ideal of marriage as "the life-style" has been refined over the years. Today it permeates every facet of our culture. It has become essential for the preservation of the "order of things." Two of the societal functions of marriage are child-rearing and identification of heirs. An important by-product of these functions is the containment and control of sexual activity—thus monogamy.

To assure the perpetuation of this system, young people are carefully trained to fill roles that are defined for them by gender. For women, this biological destiny provides us access to a single, narrow part of our personhood. We are societally defined as the nurturer; the caretaker of the emotional; dependent on "the other" for most of our external needs. In playing this role, we have denied our independent self.

The traditional heterosexual marriage is a proving ground for the concepts of roles. The male is "the other," expected to provide security, guidance, and material support to the female. Her contribution is emotional support, primarily functioning as wife and mother. Together they form the basis for the family unit which is effectively held in check by current laws and customs. One of the most significant rules imposed on this relationship is that of monogamy, an extremely well entrenched code, completely supported by law, religion, and custom. Upon this framework, taught by parents, schools, churches, synagogues, the law, medicine, and reenforced by the media, women and men are expected to build their lives.

Many lesbians are questioning the basic marriage model of relationships. At the same time they are confronted by the fact it is the only established pattern available to use in constructing their relationships. The resulting dichotomy can be seen in the rejection of the arbitrary assignments within the union while maintaining many of the external indicators of "marriage." Monogamy seems to be the most well established sign of coupledom.

The issue of monogamy versus nonmonogamy is being debated in women's communities everywhere. It would seem a logical step for lesbians to extend their rejection of the standards of heterosexual marriage to include monogamy. It isn't that easy. The society that brought us up, that we live in most of the time, and that provides us with the cultural reenforcement that helps to shade our identities, is strongly couple-oriented. We tend to place each other in groups of twos rather than ones or threes or infinities. With the exception of large cities, where political and cultural experiments are the norm, there is little support for women who are exploring new ways of relating to each other, living together, and sharing life.

OBSTACLES TO EXPERIMENTATION

Women who are beginning to examine new ways of relating, who are trying innovative structures in their relationships, are encountering difficulties. The cultural message is strong. It surfaces in the opinions of peers and in the self-doubts of the experimenters.

Ann T. and Sheila R., both in their middle twenties, define their relationship as open. They have encountered a lack of understanding and acceptance for their life-style.

Ann explains, "I've had problems with other women I'm involved with hassling me because they think I'm 'married.' They feel pressure that we're [she and Sheila] 'married.' I think a lot of that is sociological stereotypes. If you have a primary relationship—a two-car garage—you're married."

"The feeling from the people we were relating to was, well, if their relationship was really that good they wouldn't be looking around," adds Sheila.

Ann sums up the attitudes they have found: "Even if we don't want to be a couple, people relate to us as such."

Another roadblock for women in creating new ways of relating is our indoctrination, which prepares us to be dependent beings. We are programmed with the rules of a system that denies us access to essential truths about ourselves. We are taught to find our validation outside ourselves. We are trained to fit into marriage as the partner primarily concerned with fostering the

growth and development of the union. This assignment cannot be carried out by meeting our own needs outside the marriage.

Being a lesbian is a political statement whether the individual woman is aware of that or not. We are evidence that the cultural lessons can be rejected. Our existence challenges the system. We bring our experience as women in this society, tempered by our lesbian divergence from it, to our relationships.

VARIETIES OF LESBIAN LIFE-STYLES

Monogamy

Monogamy is the life-style of most lesbian couples, a reflection, perhaps, of the overwhelming cultural example to all couples. There are benefits, aside from societal and peer approval, to choosing a monogamous relationship.

A sense of security, as you build upon a history with one person, is one advantage. An emotional sense of security is developed by knowing your partner well, a certain predictability occurs that is valued by many. A practical sense of security is provided by the knowledge you stand a good chance of not growing old alone.

The energy level required for a monogamous relationship is less than needed in more experimental life-styles. This is a practical and realistic advantage for people who choose to devote high levels of energy to a job, politics, school, or special projects.

In several ways each lesbian relationship challenges the status quo by its very existence. Who is the nurturer between two women? Who is "the other" between two partners whose jobs give them parity and equal access to the outside world? How are roles determined? Is there a "masculine" and "feminine" breakdown of chores and responsibilities? If there is, it is certainly not based on gender. However, in some lesbian relationships, roles are still prominent and definite. The partners are influenced by the cultural definition of masculine/feminine. They seek to emulate the majority by creating the best "marriage" they can. An extreme case is the relationship of Terry P. and Betty F. Terry stays at home playing "wife" while Betty works as the "provider." They both come from middle-class backgrounds, bringing with them explicit concepts of what is allowed in their roles.

Some lesbians have adopted the heterosexual model as the basis for a pair-bond, which resembles a traditional marriage. Not all women who pursue this life-style carry it to the extreme that Terry P. and Betty F. do in their rigid adherence to well-defined roles. Many couples, who would not consciously define any roles or restrictions within their relationships, still maintain strict rules regarding the partnership per se. Often this takes the form of economic control. The person who handles the money is able to wield power over the other and thus manipulate the relationship structure. Clearly, though subtly, this is a role behavior culturally assigned to males.

Lesbian expression of the heterosexual traditional marriage is a continuum ranging from the replication of masculine/feminine roles to the total absence of any arbitrary assignments within the relationship. It is entirely possible for a monogamous union to be free from roles. Women who have chosen this style have been able to recognize their socialization and bring a new perspective to monogamy.

Mickey D., who defines her present situation as one to one and monogamous, explains, "To me monogamy is a relationship that's chosen because it's good for those two people at that particular time. It involves intense growth together." She and others like her have elected to be in a monogamous situation that is not necessarily static. They feel this is different from the traditional, heterosexual model. According to Mickey, "The only understanding of monogamy when I was married [heterosexually] was that piece of paper, it wasn't anything I'd thought out—it was expected. You signed the paper, you were monogamous. In this [her present lesbian relationship] monogamy has come about on terms that are important to me. Things I've thought about as a way to relate now."

Celibacy

Many celibate women recognize their lesbian feelings and choose not to act on them at a given time in their lives (i.e., between relationships). The choice may be imposed by lack of opportunity, as in the case of a woman living in a small town who is unable to make contact with other lesbians. For many women, the opportunity to exercise their option of lesbianism has never been possible. This phenomenon was more common in a time when women were not allowed any expression of sexuality. In most communities you can find an "old maid/aunt/schoolteacher" living alone. A friend recently told me this story, which provides an insight to the feelings of "spinsters" in our midst:

"My lover and I and two other couples were on a trip to Mexico. My mother, who knew the score, was with us. She brought a friend with her, a seventy-seven-year-old woman. We, my friends and I, weren't sure if she was aware of the situation. At one time we were all riding together in the back of a pickup truck, talking openly about our lives. My mother's friend listened, then told us about herself. She had always experienced feelings toward women, but had never acted upon them. Until meeting us she had never suspected such a life-style was possible!"

Not all celibate lesbians are asexual. Many have chosen not to relate sexually for reasons of religion, career, or other personal considerations. The period of celibacy may be temporary or a permanent choice.

Multiple Relationships/Open Marriage

Other single lesbians are relating in what might be called multiple relationships. These may include sexual activity or they may be intensely emotional. Often, both components are present. This pattern of living requires a woman to place herself as the top priority for her attention and energy. Being selfish in this way is a radical stance for a well-trained nurturer to take.

Women are also experimenting with the concept of "open marriage." Lesbians in this life-style spend the majority of their energy developing and maintaining high levels of intimacy with people in addition to their partner. One woman I spoke to described her ultimate goal as being "able to relate to two or three women in a primary sense at the same time." She elaborated that this would take a lot of time and energy as well as require partners whose goals were similar.

Women in these nontraditional relationships spoke of prior experiences in monogamous unions, both heterosexual and lesbian. They discussed disadvantages that had led them to try other ways of relating.

A tendency to become "lost" in the other person was a common complaint. An overwhelming sense of dependency (either on their partner or being directed toward themselves) was a strong reason for the choice to experiment. Many women felt limited by jealousy, fear, and/or uncertainty in extending themselves beyond the traditional relationship. A feeling of lost opportunity for personal growth led these women to make the decision to try something other than a monogamous relationship.

PERSONAL IMPLICATIONS

Lesbians, as illustrated by the conversations I had with women preparing for this article, share a common experience in the difficulty of living a life contradictory to the expectations of families, friends, and society. The inconsistency between training and practice produces conflict for the majority of lesbians. We do not all react the same to the ensuing mental struggle. I have noted our different behaviors fall into two major categories. One is our rejection of societal training. This is expressed on a scale ranging from radical-lesbian/feminist politics as a relationship basis to practicing lesbians who deny any of the political implications of lesbianism. The other is the degree of openness in our expression of rebellion against expectations. The gamut runs from demonstrator to closet lesbian who maintains an extra bedroom for "appearance's sake." These variances are not opposite poles but a continuum of behavior. We have all experienced movement in either direction on the scale, influenced by the prevailing circumstance of our life.

My observation is that the further the variation is from the acceptable role, an open relationship with several participants, for example, the more up-front the women are apt to be. This candidness, or lack of same, extends to individual interpersonal relationships. Very traditional and role-bound situations are usually maintained by women who are deeply hidden in their closets.

Personal testimony from the women I talked with, all of whom are experimenting with new concepts in relating, stands as proof of the conflict produced by rejection of the female role model. These women have spent hours examining their philosophy and reconciling the emotional and intellectual split caused by their determination to be self-defined. Their words are descriptive and need no further comment:

A participant of the rap group said, "I'm most comfortable with monogamy but my head says different. When I realize I'm sexually attracted to someone and I can't do anything about it—then I feel hemmed in."

Shelia R., in describing her initial reactions to her open relationship, stated, "I spent hours crying about stuff that kept me from feeling important. As soon as I could see my importance it became easy to even encourage other relationships."

Her partner, Ann T., expresses her feelings: "It's hard for me to think of Shelia relating to other people, but that's a distress born of my insecurities that I can counsel on to get rid of and do. The only time I've felt bad about her relating to other people is when I'm not feeling secure about my self-worth."

Sarah D., a lesbian who formerly practiced serial monogamy within a couple framework and is now single, speaks about her single experience: "I'm intellectually comfortable with nonmonogamy but I also know emotionally I could not deal with it in a couple situation. I'm even having trouble dating more than one person at a time. It's a conflict for me."

Joanne S., who is beginning to deal with her need to relate to other women in addition to Jackie, her lover of six years, describes the reactions of others to her current life-style: "Most of the couples Jackie and I know see what's happening as a threat to them. They are waiting to see what happens between Kay and me. If we appear to be relating well, people expect me to leave Jackie and move right in with Kay. If we are not getting along, they say, 'I knew it couldn't work.' "

CONCLUSION

Lesbians have come to their space, individually and collectively, with little or no affirmation from society at large. Once we turned our energies away from doing what was expected, we were on our own. At this point we create a lesbian perspective which grows to become part of our lives. A point of view that also affects the ways we choose to relate to other women.

Speaking from my own experience, in 1954 the only option I was aware of as an acceptable relationship was a monogamous pair-bond that closely resembled the model marriage of mother and father. The difference between the lesbian union and that of Mr. and Mrs. Average was the lesbian perspective.

A lesbian community does exist regardless of the levels of individual awareness or the political consciousness of its members. The personal experience of being different from other little girls, rejecting at some level our role assignment, and questioning, however subtly, the "natural order of things," is extended as the universal lesbian experience.

What, then, is the lesbian relationship? It is a reflection of our move from the passive to the assertive. It is an indicator of our process of change in ourselves and the effect that has on the institutions that surround

us. It is not easily definable. The women I spoke to are not representative of *the* lesbian relationship. They are experiencing *a* lesbian relationship. Each one of us is living the experience. Our unique, individual way of relating is both personal and an integral part of the lesbian community.

Younger lesbians are sometimes critical of older lesbians, seeing them as static, without growth in their relationships. The lesbians of small towns do not always understand the political radicalism that churns in large metropolitan areas like New York City, San Francisco, Boston, etc. The one issue that seems to divide and threaten more than any other is the definition of the lesbian relationship. Is monogamy a cop-out to the system? Is the relationship of women with each other a political statement?

Yes and no to both of these questions. I have met women whose addiction to monogamy has become an excuse for the stagnation of personal growth. I also know women whose devotion to "the political" has denied them access to their humanity and kept them from personal growth. How we are different is not as important as how we are alike.

The special quality of being a lesbian is part of our total personhood. Lesbianism is the source of knowledge we have discovered about ourselves, our lives, and our relationships. It gives direction to our challenge of the status quo. Society has failed to standardize us! No matter how hard some of us try to imitate the majority, those relationships will always be a copy of someone else's way. Given our cultural framework, it is impossible for two women to relate with the same dynamic present between a man and woman or two men. I rejoice in that!

Monogamy is our life-style. Open marriage is our life-style. Multiple relationships is our life-style. Singleness is our life-style. The essence of being in a lesbian relationship is only fully understood by being in one. As women with a unique outlook on our environment, whose lives are living criticism of our culture, we are creating options in ways of relating for the future.

"I feel that monogamy, like role-playing, is aping some of the worst aspects of the heterosexual life-style."

I am basically a nonmonogamist—one of the few around who will even admit to it. I enjoy being my own person, living by myself, and relating sexually and sensually to many women. I do not feel a need to limit myself to one woman, or even one at a time. I figure, why love one person when I can love lots? And, believe me, there are certainly a lot of wonderful women out there to love— that I have found!

In becoming a nonmonogamist (in truth, I cannot say it is the easiest thing in the world to do), I have discovered that I have been able to rid myself of a lot of mythologies—archaic, even sexist concepts about lovers and loving. I've learned to question and work through feelings of possession and jealousy, the fear of abandonment and loss, the feelings of being half a person, and useless, without a lover. I am still learning to be a whole person, self-contained, and I can now bring that to my loving relationships. I've learned that I can discover "sisterhood" even with lovers! I know, too, that any lovers I relate to will have the same choices and freedoms that I have—it's understood. (And I *say* that because I have met many so-called "nonmonogamists" who, it turns out, feel it's okay for them to relate to others, but don't want their partners to do it! This, to say the least, is pretty much "male-identified," not to mention sexist.)

I've observed that a lot of things that go down in a one-to-one relationship are quite negative: they interfere, in many cases, with true loving. In a lesbian community, I think monogamy can be isolating, not only to members of that community but to the couple themselves, who *do* need to devote a lot of time and energy to making their relationship work. There are exceptions to this, but I have noticed a pattern: Most relationships, in the end, do not work. They might last for a few months, a few years—but in the end, the women split, and many times cannot even be friends afterward! What good has it been if they cannot be friends? What did it all mean? What good, ultimately, is a system like that?

I am amazed at the undying optimism with which most monogamists, who have been through a whole series of relationships, approach each new affair with the self-assurance that "this one will last forever." It must be due to some romantic myth, rooted in childhood omnipotence and encouraged by the pop culture surrounding us. I am also amazed that these same women treat those who are searching for alternatives as if we were pariahs.

I feel that monogamy, like role-playing, is aping some of the worst aspects of the heterosexual life-style. We are socialized to be heterosexual, and monogamous (especially the women), from the time we are babies . . . it's pounded into our brains. Monogamy *is* a socialization, one that needs to be examined.

Some people tell me they feel that humans are basically monogamous, as if it were a built-in biological need. I am not convinced of that at all; humans, to me, seem to encompass almost every kind of social-sexual behavior that can be invented. I don't want to rap on theories and concepts of the development or evolvement of monogamy. Let me say only that I don't think it works very well; not for us, not for heterosexuals. One thing we may have going for us: We can often extricate ourselves from monogamous messes with less pain than our heterosexual counterparts; they're trapped—by children, mortgages, possessions, debts—and many times they just deaden themselves and stay together.

I've been in a few fairly monogamous relationships; two of them were live-in relationships, lasting well over a year. I am happy to say that most of my ex-lovers are now my dearest and best friends—whether I parted from them, they from me, or it was mutual. When my most recent ex-lover complained to another ex-lover of mine that I was moving out on her, the second woman retorted, "She's moving out? Now you're *really* stuck with her!"

And, believe me, I am *truly* monogamous with my friends!

It's just that I don't want to pour a lot of time and energy into one, single human being: I want that energy for myself, for the movement, for my sisters and friends, as well as lovers (who are also sisters and friends). It's really as simple as that—and as complicated. . . .

—Karol

"I thought nonmonogamy was fantastic—eating your cake and having it, too."

I am presently in a monogamous relationship with a woman. She's twenty-five and I'm thirty-two; we live together in an apartment with eight cats and a dog. We have had a very changing relationship over the years. Our first year together was the typical sort of "husband/wife" kind of relationship, where I worked and she worked and I came home and watched *Star Trek* and she cooked dinner. Then we went to sleep.

It wasn't notably successful; we broke up a year after we started living together. I really hadn't paid enough attention to Caroline. I didn't have an idea of what I wanted and we had gotten into the relationship almost accidentally; it was almost a "marriage of convenience." I had very little idea of what Caroline's needs were. She had somewhat more of an idea of what my needs were.

I would leave her for weekends and go home to my parents. During this time she was unfaithful a couple of times—if you could call it that. Mainly she wanted to attract my attention; she wanted to get some reaction and some more attention out of me. But the scheme backfired and, instead of making me more attentive, it just made me resentful and angry, and I withdrew even more.

We spent seven months apart—in different parts of the country with no communication at all—and we both got heavily involved with other people at this time. At the end of that seven months, my lover returned to New York and after a sort of dating period we resumed the relationship. We decided to start it off on quite a different footing; we both picked out an apartment together, moved to a different part of town, and we more or less started all over again. At this point, though, we hadn't joined the movement and, as far as we knew, there was no viable alternative to monogamy—or "monotany" as a friend of mine calls it.

By the time she left, we more or less talked ourselves into believing it would be better that way. It wasn't until we'd been apart and been in other relationships that we realized the value of the relationship that we had had together. After we had been living together for about a year, I fell in love with another woman and had an affair with her, and assumed that, since I was in love with her, I would leave Caroline and move in with the other woman.

After this broke up, we worked through a lot of resentment and a lot of negative feelings, but decided that just because one of us fell in love with another person, it didn't mean that we had to break up. It meant perhaps that our relationship changed, but that we could try to explore different ways of having relationships. We were also in Lesbian Feminist Liberation at that point, and nonmonogamy was all the rage. So, we thought we'd try it out.

We experimented. Caroline had a couple of affairs; I had somewhat more than a couple of affairs and that continued. We both toyed with the idea of leaving each other all through these affairs, but after we'd had a relationship with another person for maybe two or three months we found that we missed each other so much that we dropped the other relationship and went back together.

Our relationship changed tremendously during this time. Nonmonogamy introduced all sorts of reasons for friction, negative feelings, and jealousy—which I was less able to deal with than Caroline was.

The only time it really worked was when we were both going out with people we were not too attached to—and then we would come back and discuss these other relationships with each other. That was only a short period of time—maybe three or four months—and that was the only time I would think that we were totally what you would consider nonmonogamous."

In all cases except one, our other lovers were fairly sanguine about the situation. Only one lover was really so upset that it influenced a lot of what was going on. I think almost all my lovers really realized that they were on a different plane, and they never expected that much from me. The one woman who was upset by my relationship with Caroline was a woman who wanted me to live with her.

Most of Caroline's lovers were very antagonistic toward me, and with good reason: I wasn't particularly happy when she was going out with anyone else. It was perfectly all right for me to play around, but I was upset when she did it.

The main problem with nonmonogamy is jealousy. I suppose it's possible to work out a relationship in which neither partner is that jealous, but that assumes either an awful lot of stability or perhaps a partnership relationship instead of a "lover" relationship.

In my case, being nonmonogamous proved even more strongly in my mind that Caroline is the one person I want to spend the rest of my life with. While all these relationships were exciting, and many of them fulfilling, and they certainly taught me a lot about myself and other people, in the end, it was Caroline that I wanted to get back to. She seemed to fit me the best and accept me the way I am, and seemed to be the

"proper complement." While I can't say we will never have more affairs, I think my days of searching for the ideal affair are over.

What one thinks of monogamy and nonmonogamy has an awful lot to do with what one is experiencing at the time. When I was at the high point of another relationship, ignoring the pain I was causing, I thought nonmonogamy was fantastic—eating your cake and having it, too. But now, as I look back on it, there was an awful lot of pain on both sides. In fact, I ended my last relationship because there was too much pain involved—I couldn't continue to hurt Caroline, and the other woman.

That's how I feel about it now. Certainly had I been interviewed six months earlier, I might have said something different. I might feel differently in another six months. But right now monogamy is where I want to be.

—Susan

"She will go to a lover to stay overnight, and when I wake up in the morning, I feel, 'Oh, no.'"

My ideal is to have a mate for life. That's my goal. I would like a lifetime partner, someone I can depend on. I don't know if relationships for most people were meant to go on that long, anyway, but I prefer relating to one person, basically.

My lover and I have seen each other for two years, and been strictly monogamous, but recently she said she wanted to sleep with a woman she had met at work. I got terribly frightened, and reacted with hostility, and was depressed and cried. I think it's all right now, because she reassured me that ours was the relationship she was interested in keeping, and she loved me. She said, "It's just unrealistic to think you're going to be turned on to only one person the rest of your life. If you end up resenting that person because you can't sleep with anyone else, the relationship is bound to end." I thought she could say that because she wasn't the one being left alone. Otherwise I tend to agree with her, but it's difficult to make it work. I haven't heard of too many people who have had successful nonmonogamous relationships.

My first and second relationships were monogamous. My long-term one was basically monogamous, but there were moments when I sneaked off, and I felt guilty and lousy. I suppose if my lover had been less inflexible, perhaps we would have stayed together.

With my present relationship I could see someone else if I wanted to. She is now seeing other people, which causes a lot of anxiety. The jealousy is incredible—I can't shut my mind off. She will go to a lover to stay overnight, and when I wake up in the morning, I feel, "Oh, no." There's some relief because I know I can do the same thing. So, we'll try it this way. I don't know what the answer is. I think if people make a commitment to be monogamous, then they have to deal with frustrations if they want to sleep with someone else. That's one way of keeping emotional turmoil at its lowest but I don't know if it's the best thing. I think if you feel that you're loved and your relationship isn't threatened, it's okay to go off and fool around, but every time someone else comes into the picture there's going to be a lot of anxiety, because this may be your lover's "big love." But that could happen anyway.

—Jo Ann

"Nervous people don't like messes. Better for me to cope with myself and one other person . . ."

One of the aspects I found most appealing about slipping into the homosexual subculture was its freedom from social convention. Since my lesbian lover and I had moved beyond the legal and religious pale, our "marriage" could be whatever style we chose it to be. So what did we choose? Monogamy, that's what.

First, I am by nature very nervous. I break into a sweat at the mere *idea* of trying to satisfy, appease, and perhaps even entertain a duo or trio of lesbians. Our relationships, as intricately woven as a Persian rug, would inevitably become a tangled mess. Nervous people don't like messes. Better for me to cope with myself and one other person—that is, my lover—in all our multitude of desires, demands, and periods. There are days when we barely get to work on time, clean, clothed, and somewhat fed. Things are complicated enough with just two, thank you.

Second, monogamy is an easy, sometimes lazy framework from which your lesbian friends can be approached. It's true there's no longer that zingy sexual tension at MCC gatherings and bar nights, but I get enough of that at home. I have gratefully ceased being the hunter, and other women are no longer the prey. They are Sue and Doris and Vickie as *people*.

Third, and finally, my lover strongly believes in monogamy. She lived that way (in a straight marriage) for eighteen years previous to our seven. One thing's for sure: If your lover abhors bigamy and all that playing around, you're sure as blazes going to be monogamous, period. And she'll watch you like a hawk to be sure you stay that way!

—Jane

"We were only lesbians in bed. During the day we were husband and wife . . ."

My first lesbian experience was with a younger woman. I thought that since she was younger, I would have to be the butch partner. But she was very dominant and very physically strong, and I think at her age she interpreted this as being important and meaning she was a butch. She was more heavily built than I was, and bigger and stronger, butchier-looking. One day she put her foot down and said that she wanted to be the butch. I said, "Fine—it doesn't matter to me," I was just playing a game. I kept on with the same way of dressing, same way of acting, basically.

In my second relationship, role-playing became a little more important. I thought that if I identified myself heavily as a typical, perfect wife, the perfect "woman," I would make the relationship succeed. And I really did it all the way. I was the perfect wife—from eight o'clock in the morning until I was asleep.

That meant doing all the house chores, all the things a woman is supposed to do in a house, plus dressing up, the stylish way of feminine dressing—rushing home to take care of my daughter and lover, and sacrificing myself by always being a baby-sitter and wife. I couldn't go out; *she* could go out and I would stay with my child because I was acting the wife and the mother. I did everything that up to now has been considered the female role, the typical heterosexual female. We were only lesbians in bed. During the day we were husband and wife, even to the point of her calling me her wife and me calling her my husband.

I felt very uncomfortable in this role-playing, and I felt mine was the heavier emotional burden. I was the real breadwinner in the relationship. She really cared and helped, but I was the one that paid the bills, fixed things in the house, took care of tickets and the hotel reservations on the trips we took—I did everything. I did everything physical I wasn't supposed to do as a butch and I did all the worrying about the welfare of the family, and the housework, and that tired me out. My earning power was greater than hers, too. She was butchy physically, even though emotionally I was the strong one, but we heavily identified as butch and femme, respectively.

Around three years ago, I began to realize I was getting tired of carrying the whole load. I started meeting other women that were not into roles, where before I had met only women who identified that way.

I started seeing the freedom of non-role-playing. These women functioned as *women*. They did not have to function only in a certain way. My old relationship was wearing out, and I think it was due to both of us being tired of the same attitudes. That's when I met the person who became my third lover. This woman was not into roles at all. With her I saw a chance of being me. I was appreciated for myself. I could dress the way I wanted to, go where I wanted, and act any way I preferred. For the first time I was in a free relationship, where I felt I could be open. It has worked like that, ever since. I also started getting involved in the gay liberation movement, and reading about lesbian issues. I started being aware of a lot of things, whereas I had no interest in the gay scene before. I realized these roles had been oppressing me for a long time and they would oppress anybody who would fall into them. Thus I started living my full life as a lesbian without oppressive roles.

—Ivonne Elias

Striving Toward Equality in Loving Relationships

KAY WHITLOCK

Let's get one issue clarified at the outset. When we enter into relationships, love *won't* keep us together. It's doubtful that it ever did. In spite of the efforts of social propagandists to assure us that all we really need is love, lesbian feminists are aware that a better basis for loving relationships is equality.

It has taken us a long time to realize that without equality, a relationship, for however long it may last, is bound to exact a price many of us are no longer willing to pay. Moreover, we know that without egalitarian relationships, "love" becomes just one more rationalization for excusing or accepting imbalances of power or exploitation in our personal lives. It is difficult, if not impossible, to imagine real loving (which is, in its most comprehensive sense, a dynamic, active process that continually values personal growth and that implies respect for the autonomy of each individual within the relationship) between or among lovers in the absence of equality.

In the days before the emergence of lesbian feminism, we tried to establish relationships that accepted, without criticism, heterosexual norms. Legions of lesbians lived imitation heterosexual lives. It comes as no surprise to realize that many women are still uncritically accepting heterosexual models and norms because they do not yet perceive of other ways of living.

Illustrative of this is the answer given to me by a lesbian, an urban planner in her late thirties, when I asked if she had been consciously aware of seeking equality in a relationship prior to her identification of herself as a feminist:

"No, I never thought of it. I very clearly accepted without thought two premises which a lot of us who are "older" lesbians accepted. One was that we were not quite acceptable as people. And the corollary of that was that in order to be more acceptable to ourselves and to society, our relationships had to emulate as closely as possible the ideal heterosexual relationship: monogamy,

butch-femme—the whole role system, 'till death do us part.' People would talk about getting married! I never did that. I could not bring myself to do it! But people did. And not until the feminist movement, not until a long time after I knew about the beginnings, did I realize that not only didn't it have to be that way, but wasn't healthy that way. But it was a long time coming. I lived a long time with the stereotypes and the preconceptions about homosexuality that had been given to me by society."

This sort of pressure is reinforced by those, both gay and straight, who refuse to see or who are afraid to see lesbianism as something more than sex between women. The viewing of lesbianism in purely sexual terms is part and parcel of the popular patriarchal mythology because it refuses to acknowledge the very real political implications of lesbian-feminist ideology.

To be a lesbian attempting to live life as an imitation heterosexual implies its own obvious contradictions. Those contradictions have been spelled out in detail by other writers (Martin and Lyon, Abbot and Love, etc.). What is particularly fascinating to me is the manner in which society chooses to deal with lesbians. On one hand, we are encouraged to emulate heterosexual models and norms as closely as possible, but when we do, we are labeled "butch-femme," and we are attacked from all sides—by straight male society, by straight feminist society, and even by other lesbians who came out after the emergence of the second wave of feminism and the development of lesbian feminism. I am especially intrigued by a common feminist response to the phenomenon of lesbians in butch-femme relationships. "Isn't it *revolting*," some "enlightened" feminist may proclaim, "to see butch-femme couples?"

What an interesting response. Such remarks are more likely to come from straight feminists than from lesbians since most lesbians do understand one thing quite clearly, whether we identify ourselves as feminists or not: We understand the pressures on gays to conform, the pressures to adopt the models and norms of the dominant class. We understand that in the popular mind, "butch-femme" boils down to "heterosexual"—in form at least, if not in sexual practice. We know that the straight feminist who is so revolted by butch-femme dynamics is not equally revolted by the heterosexuals—her own class—who provide the models for us to imitate. We know that the straight feminist so often does not see the connection. Nor does she usually understand the meaning of her remarks. Writer Charlotte Bunch makes the point in precise terms:

. . . lesbian role-playing doesn't compare to that of heterosexuals where most women are *the "femme" and considered "natural," not anti-feminist, even by many feminists. As such, criticism of "butch" lesbians is a criticism of any woman who steps* out *of her role.*[1]

---

[1] Charlotte Bunch, "Introduction," Nancy Myron and Charlotte Bunch, eds., *Lesbianism and the Women's Movement* (Baltimore: Diana Press, 1975), p. 12.

Lesbians understand one other thing, and that is the grotesque peculiarity of being part of an oppressed group which so frequently attempts to minimize the pain of that oppression by being as "acceptable" as possible, within certain obvious constraints. Unlike groups oppressed on the basis of sex alone, or on the basis of race, we have the option of remaining invisible, and often lesbians opt for that invisibility because we believe we can still be more acceptable if no one knows that we're gay. The exercising of that option rather than confronting the real source of oppression has its own terrible cost, but many do exercise it. In a society that worships conformity, it is not difficult to understand personal fear at being seen as the "other." In our desire to be as "normal" as possible, lesbians were not immune to incorporating many elements of heterosexism into our personal lives. After all, inequality is acceptable *and desired* in sexist society. Traditional (and senseless) gender-based roles are acceptable *and desired* in sexist society. We did not escape our conditioning entirely.

As women in society, we were devalued. As lesbians, we knew we were despised. Our personal relationships provided us with some shelter from a patriarchal, heterosexist world, if only because we went home to other women who did not despise us. We tried to forget our oppression in the arms of our lovers. Until recent years, we rarely even thought about the concept of equality in our personal relationships. We were too busy trying to survive.

And so, we'd often inadvertently hang what Rita Mae Brown has referred to as "the albatross of love oppression"[2] around our necks and try to feel like complete human beings by finding validation through our lovers. Somehow, we thought, we'd make it through all of the hassles as long as we had Love. That was, again in Rita Mae's words, "the lie of the Individual Solution."[3] It was Love, of course, that was supposed to make the I.S. operable:

Love was the answer. It solved all problems and if allowed to flow free it could solve the problems of the world. All a woman had to do was find that four-letter word, love, and that other four-letter word, life, just opened up and bloomed with eternal joy.[4]

With the development of feminist thought and lesbian-feminist ideology, we began to realize that feminism requires the *destruction* of male supremacy. While many cautious feminists dealt with this realization by gently trying to rearrange sex roles or labor divisions predicated upon traditional sex roles, lesbian feminists focused more directly on sex *power*. In the words of Charlotte Bunch, ". . . it is not the roles themselves that women and men play, but the power behind those roles that is oppressive."[5] The truth of this is apparent when we

analyze attempts to reform only role assignments within a relationship without confronting the underlying power imbalance *demanded by the institution of heterosexuality.* Bunch has pointed out that "the social necessity for strictly defined roles has decreased in recent years."[6] Feminism has certainly impacted in this area, and the contribution is a valuable one. Yet the process has, too, been co-opted by the accompanying deluge of open marriage self-help books with their facile Amy Vanderbilt-like social codes and guidelines for the smugly "liberated." The great failure of such surface reform efforts is their refusal to examine heterosexuality as "an ideology and an institution that oppresses us all."[7] It is their refusal to acknowledge heterosexuality as far more than sex between a man and a woman. Without analysis and understanding that the *normative status* of heterosexuality is a basic underpinning of male supremacy, the glib how-to's of the open marriage treatises are next to worthless. They treat symptoms, not causes, by offering such inscrutable advice as "the partners must grant equality to one another." Are we to actually believe that equality can be achieved without analysis of power? Shall we be content with shallow attempts at defining equality as equal numbers of household chores on lists divided up between lovers? Shall we forget the numerous subtle ways in which power over others is exercised, through emotional manipulation, economic bondage, ad infinitum?

I do not pretend that lesbian relationships are automatically more egalitarian than heterosexual relationships. I do not believe the issue is one of convincing all women to become lesbians. I do believe that it is necessary for *all* women to challenge heterosexist ideology (not individual sexual preference). For lesbians, this is crucial if we are ever to achieve equality in our personal lives and relationships, and if we are ever to effectively confront the sources of our oppression. Writing in *Ms.,* Charlotte Bunch pointed out in unmistakable terms why this challenge is so important:

In our society, heterosexuality goes hand in hand with the sexist assumption that each woman exists for a man—her body, her children, and her services are his property. . . . Heterosexism depends on the idea that heterosexuality is both the only natural and the superior form of human sexuality, thus providing ideological support to male supremacy. Heterosexism is basic to women's oppression in the family and to discrimination against single or other women who live outside the nuclear family.[8]

In order that we not participate further in our own oppression, it is necessary that lesbians integrate this lesbian-feminist analysis into our own lives and into our relationships. Merely to be a lesbian does not mean we

---

[2]Rita May Brown, "Living with Other Women," ibid., p. 64.
[3]Ibid.
[4]Ibid.
[5]Bunch, loc. cit.

[6]Ibid.
[7]Ibid.
[8]Charlotte Bunch, "Forum: Learning From Lesbian Separatism," *Ms.,* Vol. V, No. 5 (November 1976), p. 99.

have necessarily divested ourselves of vestiges of heterosexism.

Conditioning, as I said, runs deep. How has heterosexism worked within lesbian relationships to maintain inequality? Let me count the ways!

Traditional heterosexual relationship norms encourage loving partners to "find fulfillment" through one another. They do not teach us to develop a strong sense of personal autonomy, and then to value autonomy in those we love. Traditional heterosexual relationship norms encourage us to adhere to real notions of possessiveness and ownership with regard to one's lover(s). The concept of "my woman" is real and prevalent: How many times do we hear of "Joan and *her* woman"? We are taught to submerge our own identities in relationships by finding our own primary self-importance vicariously through attachment to various "others" (whether children, husband, lesbian lover, etc.). We are taught to define ourselves according to the sum total of functions we perform for the benefit of those others. We are taught that it is desirable (for women, at any rate) to sacrifice one's own needs, ambitions, interests, and emotions for the perceived "greater good" of the relationship. We are taught to manipulate and to be manipulated emotionally; to question our own perceptions. We are taught that virtually every need we have must be fulfilled within our primary relationship, and that something must be wrong if there are any needs that are not fulfilled within that relationship. If a relationship is having problems, we are taught that it is probably all our fault, or that it's all someone else's fault. We are seldom taught that relationships are complex, and when there are difficulties, the solutions may be just as complex, or that everyone involved might bear a little responsibility. We are taught to blame ourselves continually for having a single thought, need, emotion, interest, that does not perfectly coincide with that of our lover(s). In short, again and again, we are bludgeoned with a club equally comprised of chunks of guilt, self-doubt, submissiveness, self-denial, and fear. These aspects of traditional heterosexual relationship norms act to maintain the relative powerlessness of females. Increasingly, lesbians have seen the need to deal wtih such power games and to avoid imitating them in their own lives.

In the course of talking with many lesbians about equality in loving relationships, I found this concept of power mentioned again and again. They invariably said, in one form or another, that the question of equality is tied to that of personal autonomy for each woman within the relationship. In the absence of a strong sense of personal autonomy for each, power games are inevitably played. Power is then used to control or modify the behavior, actions, freedom, of the woman who has compromised her own autonomy. Those who enjoy wielding power over others inevitably exploit other people; those who continue to allow others to wield power over them will inevitably be exploited. Fortunately, many lesbians are rejecting such games, recognizing them to be destructive to individuals within relationships and to the relationship itself. One woman I spoke with addressed the problem in direct terms as she talked about a former relationship: "The power was virtually all mine, and I was not comfortable with that. When the power is all yours, the relationship is, too. And the responsibility for making sure the relationship continues and the power to change it don't go together. You can only change yourself. You can't change somebody else."

I discovered this basic truth myself—the hard way! In a former relationship, I lived with a woman who felt it harmed our relationship for me ever to get angry. Not just at her. At anything, including my job or other external aggravations. It made her feel uptight, she said, and any display of anger on my part was detrimental to our relationship since it showed I was insensitive to her. Her solution was to make me feel terribly guilty about my insensitivity so that I would change. For the longest time, I stopped showing anger. I felt it was my problem, totally, and since I allowed her to exercise power over me, I tried to be what she wanted me to be. This, of course, made me angry, but not at her. At myself, for not being precisely what she wanted me to be. This example is a minor one, but it is illustrative. The truth is that in many ways, I tried to be what she felt I should be. I denied my own emotions, perceptions, feelings, because I apparently thought her opinions had more validity than mine. Besides, I didn't want to jeopardize the relationship. In the end, of course, the relationship was shot to hell since no matter how hard I tried (and toward the end, I quit trying), I couldn't change who I was. Later, with the support of numerous women friends, I decided my basic need was to change not my whole being, but that aspect of me that totally acquiesced to another person. I decided to be myself rather than an appendage of someone else.

Retaining a strong personal sense of autonomy within a relationship does not mean acting without regard to one's lover(s). It does mean respecting oneself, one's needs, one's emotions. It does mean considering one's own feelings and needs at least as important as those of the other person. Women together in relationships owe it to ourselves, at least, to decide what we are willing to put up with and what we aren't. We owe it to ourselves to understand that there may be times when differences in personal needs, ambitions, goals, can no longer be accommodated within a relationship. We owe it to ourselves to divest ourselves of the need to exercise power over others in our relationships. We owe it to ourselves to realize that our personal meaning must not be defined in terms of whom we are with, but in terms of who we, ourselves, are. We must accord our lovers the same respect in terms of autonomy.

The reader will note that I have avoided speaking of structural changes that must be made in order for an egalitarian relationship to be actualized. That is because I do not believe that structural changes in and of themselves guarantee equality. Nor do I believe that there are any basic structural forms that guarantee equality. Women must decide for themselves in this regard. Monogamy, neither a total good nor an absolute evil in and of itself, may be desired by some lesbians, rejected by others. The important thing is that a commitment to monogamy or nonmonogamy be a freely chosen one, not an enforced decision. Living in collectives may work for some; others may want space that is totally their own. Divisions of labor should be mutually decided upon, mutually agreed to. Women must decide for themselves to what degree and in what areas their relationship will reflect individual independence and mutual interdependence. It would be insufferably dogmatic of me to begin to suggest that there is a single "best" way of structuring relationships.

Nor, alas, is there any single pat formula; any single set of guidelines for developing a sense of personal autonomy within each woman or within each relationship. There is no easy answer for developing ways of living that do not depend on exercising power over others. The most I can offer is a rather modest discussion of some issues that are important, and the observation that women are beginning to build relationships based not only on love, but on equality as well. These same women who are willing to deal with the concept of power and who are willing to challenge traditional heterosexist norms believe that the personal really is political. We can learn a great deal from them, and we can learn a great deal from our own efforts to create egalitarian relationships.

Communal Living

WOMANSHARE COLLECTIVE, GRANTS PASS, OREGON

The following excerpts from the book *Country Lesbians: The Story of the Womanshare Collective* (Womanshare, 1977) describe life on a feminist rural retreat.

Commenting on their financial survival, the collective wrote in a letter:

"Our Womanshare sessions over the year pay about one year's land payments which are $150 a month. We charge $10 to $15 per day, which includes a room and all meals. In the past we have supplemented our income by doing odd jobs, teaching at the local college (sewing), waitressing, farm labor, tree planting, dividends, and collecting unemployment. Lately we have formed a carpentry collective with two women next door. We wrote our book, *Country Lesbians,* and distribute it ourselves to bring in some income.

"We bought 100,000 worms from a firm in California for $500 to start a worm bin. Our worms never multiplied as they were supposed to. We were given more. This spring they look better, but what one counts on in the worm business is for them to double themselves every two months. We had planned to have thirty-two bins by last September. It is now April and we have five. Whether it is a viable business we don't know."

We do not see the way we live as *the answer* for all women, nor even as the answer for all of us forever, since we are changing all the time.

We are lesbian separatists, giving our primary emotional, sexual, economic, political, and work energy to women.

We believe in structure. We find it necessary for dealing with the problems of daily life and with our feelings. We accomplish more if we organize our days, our work, our living environment, and sometimes even our relationships. Sometimes other women laugh at us for planning things so carefully. We are also involved in nonrational thinking . . . with spiritual experiences . . . alternative health care, making pottery, the study of Tarot, etc. For all of us it means seeing beyond our old limits of what life means and being open to new ways of creating a new women's culture.

We are in our late twenties or early thirties, of different class backgrounds and life experiences. We own 23 acres of land in a fairly well populated part of the country, two miles from a very small village. At the present time we all share the monthly land payments, as well as taxes and improvements. The land is owned by the five of us. If any of us die, the land goes to the remaining others. We have agreed to put in our personal wills the stipulation that if all of us die, the land will go to the Oregon Women's Land Trust, so that our male relatives can never inherit the land.

Inevitable questions arise from group ownership of land:

1. What we will do if a woman wants to leave the land, either (a) temporarily or (b) permanently:
   (a) If a woman must be away temporarily and cannot participate in collective decisions about the land, then she must delegate her decision-making powers to the other women.
   (b) If a woman wants to leave the collective and the land permanently, she can have her name removed from the deed. But she also agrees that the land cannot be sold unless *all* of us agree to sell. She cannot sell her share. As a collective and a family we all agree we will try to help her out financially, but this will not be considered "buying out" her share of the land.
2. What we will do if a woman wants to join us: We will have an agreed upon time period in which all of us will decide if we want to live together and share ownership of the land. A woman does not have to "buy in" in order to join us. . . . If a woman joins with us she will be

expected to contribute to the land payments, utility bills, etc.

3. What we will do if we have a conflict that we can't solve by ourselves:

We all agree to mediation with an outside woman or women.

If our collective decides to split up we agree to mediation as a way of deciding what to do with the land. We each agree that we would not individually hire lawyers to represent our personal interests.

4. What are some of our choices for dealing with the land if the collective splits up?

(a) Have a waiting period of six months to one year before selling the land; and all women who own the land must agree to sell.

(b) Give the land to the Oregon Women's Land Trust.

(c) Sell the land and divide the money equally.

5. If we decide to sell the land who would we sell it to?

(a) Lesbian feminist separatists are our first preference. We would sell to them for the cost of the land plus improvements plus cost of living increase. We do not want to make a profit selling this land to women.

(b) If there were no women interested in buying the land we would sell it to men for a profit above the original cost of the land with improvements and cost of living increase. . . .

Money. A constant worry. Where to get it? Who has the most? What to spend it on? Can we share it? Living collectively brings the question of money into sharp focus in our daily lives. . . . One of the things that helps a lot is knowing each other's class backgrounds. But understanding where we come from and where our attitudes were formed is only a part of the process, we must *deal* with it. . . . Money is tied to and entwined with our feelings of independence, security, power, and self-worth. This makes it emotionally hard when we must decide what to do with the money we have, or when we want to do something and don't have the money to do it. . . . We are trying several different ways of dealing with money. We share some, and also have individual money. We each invested $200 in Womanshare when it began and we all share the money that is made by Womanshare . . . that money goes toward land payments, some car repairs, and for electrical work. We each spend about $50 a month on food, though some of us get food stamps. We each also spend about $50-$100 a month for utility bills, house and car maintenance, tools, amusements and personal expenses. . . .

We came to our land with several advantages . . . we all had enough money to support ourselves, which brought us time to put our energy into building alternate life-support systems. We all had skills that we hoped would be useful for creating a collective business. Teaching, feminist therapy, and food business experience. . . .

Nelly had already lived in the country for several years and had acquired survival skills such as carpentry and chainsawing. But being women and city people, most of us did not have the country survival skills like splitting wood, building fires, plumbing, auto mechanics, carpentry, and gardening, so we had to put out lots of extra energy to learn these skills as fast and as well as we could. . . . We are women who are trying to fix things we've never dreamed of fixing before, like freezing pipes. What's more, because we live in the country, we are very dependent on our cars and often have to struggle to keep them in good running condition. It's truly a never-ending struggle dealing with the physical plane while living in the country—but those are the dues you pay to live here.

Most of us have, at one time or another, worked at traditional jobs in the area such as tree-planting, teaching at the local college, waitressing, farm labor. In these jobs men boss us, men have power over us. For the most part, these jobs have not paid well . . . we get very little money for hard, often demeaning work. We are always looking for alternate ways. We want to continue to live in the country and we must find ways to support ourselves in a nonoppressive fashion. . . .

The cooking, dishes and housecleaning lists are posted in the kitchen. The cooking list is made up randomly, and is faithfully followed unless someone is away . . . when we make a new list until the absent woman returns.

The cleaning system hasn't always been so effective. We discovered that each of us has different standards of cleanliness. Some of us feel that the houses are kept in fairly good order most of the time—others often see the place as a total mess. Most of the time we live peacefully with these differences. But there are occasional flareups. Sometimes anger about a messy kitchen is really displaced anger stemming from another cause and sometimes it is simple irritation at not being able to find a clean place to make breakfast. After many struggles about keeping the place clean, we have recently experimented with a new idea that has revolutionized our housekeeping headaches. Each woman is responsible for doing a half-hour of housework daily for five days a week or a total of two and one-half hours per week. This new system takes the pressure off the ones who feel that they must keep the place clean for the rest of us and it gives us all the choice of what we want to clean and we aren't stuck with the same disgusting job for months on end.

We also have schedules for wood runs to cut firewood and work on the worm business; getting manure, watering the bins, building bins, and harvesting.

Everyone here feels she needs her own space . . . which means her own room. Having our own rooms helps us to keep a sense of ourselves . . . it is a way of centering, a private space away from the everyday chaos.

When we began living together we had a problem about this . . . there was not enough space to meet our needs. Nelly was finding her space, the crooked house, unlivable—it wouldn't heat up and it leaked! Then Dian remembered that whoever lived in the chicken coop was to be renegotiated on January 1st. (It was a preferred space and Carol had been living there.) Carol said she wouldn't mind being in the main house (where there is one bedroom) as she still saw it important to be separate from Billie—not to have her room in the same house. Billie said she could make a new room in the other house where the unused kitchen was. Dian felt reluctant to leave the room she'd painted yellow and had built the bed to suit her, but she needed more quiet than her present room gave her. She would move to Billie's old room. Nelly got the coop. In the end everyone changed rooms except Sue. Later when the Hexagon was built, Nelly moved there and Carol went back to the coop . . . and we now even have a spare room!

Within our family we have feelings and thoughts about what collectivity means to us. . . .

As individuals in a friend-to-friend way, we lack something. We are five and then we are two plus two plus one. And when I feel like one, I feel very alone here. There's not much room for just hanging out. Mostly we make space for being "conscious" which means to us knowing what our thoughts and feelings are about things; and for working together on projects. . . . I think we each feel very strongly about our ideas and beliefs about "Lesbian Nation" and, at the moment, our ideas are like stone walls between us. Disagreement is taken as nonsupport. Our political differences seem harder to deal with when other things in our individual and collective lives become difficult. For me it comes down to beliefs about "political correctness" and as lesbians and women much of this depends upon how we conduct ourselves in our personal relationships. After all, the personal is political. But I see us calling couples bad and singles good. And, at the moment, it's driving me up a wall. This is what always bothered me about politics before the women's movement . . . for me there is not one proper way of behaving or relating. I feel I've been many different kinds of people in my life and I've had many different types of relationships. And I think it's going to continue that way.

Living collectively also means we don't each need one of everything; it's economical and less wasteful. I know that learning to share what I have and learning to cooperate encourages the best in me. Living collectively has increased my understanding of emotions and relationships. I have learned to speak some awful angry words instead of hiding my feelings . . . real communication can then occur. And from that, true understanding does grow.

The night before some of us had been in a heavy discussion and I had been thinking about all of our struggles; about class, about opening our collective up to other women, about how we all needed to assert our individuality once again. I kept seeing this scene in my mind . . . all of us fighting each other . . . in physical combat! I was really scared that our struggles might divide us. I decided to write out my fantasies to trans-

form the scary, negative energy into creative, if not quite positive. But writing did not solve all of my problems! Once I knew that I was afraid of being alone, I had to work it out with the rest of my family. We all talked, yelled, worried, cried, and fought our way through once again. My fears of aloneness were not just mine; every woman in my family was feeling similar fear—and we got through our fright in the way we knew best—as a group.

Collectivity means not having to always struggle alone. Collectivity provides a support system through which I can deal with the heaviest issues in my life—money, sex, and the work on the physical plane that needs to be done. It provides an outside barometer through which I can analyze my growth . . . the women I live with inspire me when I am stagnating. The larger culture has not provided us with many models for the way we want to live, to be, to create the new world we want to create. On the other hand, collectivity means not only struggling with my own problems and blocks, but also sharing the struggles of the women I live with. Sometimes it feels as if I do the emotional work of five; it seems like whenever I achieve some peace in my personal life, there are always problems in the other women's lives I must cope with. Collectivity is ecologically sound. By sharing, we use up less of the earth's limited natural resources. Collectivity allows me to live less expensively.

Collectivity is my chosen way to change and grow . . . I need other women . . . I have found that I become stronger when I band together with other women. . . . Collectivity means learning to build and fix things, to make a garden, to make money without oppressing myself or other women. If I am to do all the physical things I want to do, including making myself healthier and stronger, I must have other women to help, teach, and encourage me. . . . Collectivity means sharing what I know. I want to study and make things and draw and write and sing and have the kind of fun women do who go through really heavy times together. One of my secret wishes is to be a visionary, to dream of the future and to see my dreams come true. I have to live collectively to create a new world . . . I can't do it alone.

I live here with these four women because I need a "home." I need a connection with group beyond myself, and a connection with the earth that endures. I see our land go through the changes of the seasons. Similarly, I see my friends change too, and yet we are still together. We are still on the land. We may not always be the same five women. We may not always live on this land. But I know I must be with women and that we must be connected to the earth. This way of life gives me the support I need to be a lesbian-feminist—to be who I really am in this sick world we live in. Now I am no longer alone. I am part of the collective *we*, and we endure.

RESOURCES

Following is a list of feminist retreats or planned rural communes listed in *Lesbian Connection.* For the complete annotated list, write to: Lesbian Connection, Ambitious Amazons, Box 811, East Lansing, Mich. 48823. Ask for the Directory of Country Living.

Land Trusts for Women, c/o Oregon Women's Land Trust, Box 1713, Eugene, Ore. 97401.

Women on Land, P.O. Box 521, Fayetteville, Ark. 72701.

Sappha Survival School, Box 4D, Aeneaes Valley Road, Tonasket, Wash. 98855.

Another Demention, Sisters of Diana, Inc., RR1, Box 42A, Tishomingo, Okla. 73460.

Four Women, Contact Joanie, 3100 Ridgewood Rd., Willits, Calif. 95490 (707 459-5776).

Nourishing Space for Women, Cave Canyon Ranch, P.O. Box D-11, Vail, Ariz. 85641. Include a stamped, self-addressed envelope.

Ashfield Farm Women, Samson Road Farm, Samson Rd., Ashfield, Mass. 01330.

Womanshare, 1531 Gray's Creek Rd., Grants Pass, Ore. 97526.

A Woman's Place, Athol, N.Y. 12810 (518 623-9541).

Dearest Womyn, c/o KD & Barb Aehle, Rt. 3, Box 1708, Port Angles, Wash. 98362 (206 452-2435).

Janus South: Growth Center for Women, 39 Circuit St., Halifax, Mass. 02338.

Sharing Your Lesbian Identity with Your Children: A Case for Openness

BETTY BERZON, M.S.

The handsome, bright, professional woman sat in my office shaking her head, saying over and over again, "I just can't. I just can't see any reason that makes sense for telling the children that I'm a lesbian."

Her children were in early adolescence. We talked about the possibilities of their learning about lesbianism from sources considerably less considerate of their sensibilities than she was, their ill-informed peers, pornographic literature, comedians' jokes, a variety of homophobic adults. Yes, she could see that it would be better

if they heard positive, accurate personalized information from her. But, still, she wasn't sure.... How might it affect their own sexual identity? How would they feel about her? Whom might they tell? What kind of an experience would that be for them? Important questions. We dealt with them one by one. Still, she didn't know....

She had recently ended her marriage and became involved with a lover who was about to move into the house with her and her children. I asked if something happened to her, an accident or a sudden illness, would the children call her lover. "No, they wouldn't. They'd call their father, some of my relatives. They'd have no reason to call ———." I asked how she felt about that. "I don't like it. That would be terrible."

I pointed out that she could hardly blame her children for not calling her lover, whom they'd been led to believe was just a friend. She pondered that a long time. We probed more deeply into her fears about disclosing her gayness to her children, and her own ambivalent feelings about her identity began to emerge. Telling her children was like looking into a mirror for her, in which there would be reflected the final undeniable image of herself as a lesbian. It was that image she was not ready to face. As she began to sort out the various elements of her dilemma she was soon able to work them through sufficiently to reach a decision to disclose herself to her daughter and son. She did, effectively, and that created a new potential for depth in her relationship with her children.

This woman's concern about the sexual identity of her children being affected by her own sexual orientation is shared by many lesbian mothers. This concern is reinforced by popular notions of appropriate gender behavior and what affects it, same-sex role models being considered critical to the development of properly feminine/masculine identity. Sex researchers agree, however, that the essentials of gender identity are established very early in childhood and by a process that is complex and so far unyielding to explanation. There is even speculation now that prenatal programming plays an important part in the determination of gender identity.

A more productive concern, I believe, would be for the young person's orientation to sexuality itself. That is strongly affected by parental attitudes and behavior.

If there is secrecy and tension around the topic of sexuality in the home, the children may grow up believing that sex is something to be frightened of and to keep hidden. Homosexuality is not contagious. Fear and shame are. Children are especially sensitive to the feelings underlying communication by adults.

Of course the children's age should make a difference in how they are approached. Preschool children are likely to be concerned with changes in mother's behavior or in the household routine primarily as it might directly affect the attention they are getting.

After a child starts school there is likely to be a new interest in comparing the family situation with those of classmates. The interest, however, is not likely

Judy Burns and daughter Jenny

to be in the sexual arrangement but in how similar or different the situation is to that of other children. This might be a good time to talk to the children about the many differences there are among people and how they live. The important thing is not to be defensive or apologetic about a life-style that is different, but to present it matter-of-factly as a reasonable expression of the needs and preferences of given persons.

The time for particular alertness to the effect of disclosure should be during early adolescence when a youngster is forming her/his own personal orientation to sexuality and to life. Emphasis here should be on establishing a clear separation of the youngster's sexual development from that of the mother. A matter-of-fact attitude toward all variants of sexual preference is recommended. One should not be judged more desirable than another. What should be valued is the individual's right to follow the path that is most personally suitable.

The mother should keep in mind that adolescence is a time when peer approval is of great importance to youngsters. This might mean being prepared to deal with some initial rejection of anything that might threaten disapproval from peers, in this instance, her own sexual orientation and life-style.

Another concern lesbian mothers often have is whether or not they should give some special attention to their male children. I do think there is a basis for making sure it is communicated that Mother's noninvolvement with a male partner does not reflect a rejection of her son as a male person. The origin of the concern is probably of more importance. It is usually other adults in the mother's environment who fear the son won't have sufficient male influence in his life to counterbalance the influence of the women around him.

I believe the lesbian mother should not make this her special burden to bear. People have the same concerns about sons of divorced, nongay mothers. But homosexuality bothers people more than divorce, so the expressions of concern might be louder and stronger and taken more seriously by the woman who is a lesbian in addition to being divorced. The action I recommend is to put this matter in proper perspective. Strong expressions of concern here usually reflect an overinvestment in sex-role stereotypes and an underinformed protest against homosexuality. They should be dealt with as such.

Needless to say, the woman who has been openly gay around her children since they were infants will have worked through most of these dilemmas. It is to the woman who is just evolving into a gay life-style or just connecting with the possibilities for more openness with her children that these remarks are mainly addressed.

I am a strong advocate of *planning* for disclosure events about important subject matter. All too often the decision for disclosure of a mother's lesbianism is made by default.

There is a sudden and unexpected confrontation by the children, or by a relative or friend or ex-spouse in the children's presence. The disclosure is made, without preparation, without the important working through to a conviction that this is the right thing to do and the right time to do it. There has not been an opportunity to choose the time, the place, the conditions, or the supporting cast. Mother is in the high-speed lane of the freeway during rush hour, the car is full of her children and their friends. Her son asks if sleeping every night with the same woman the way she does makes you a lesbian, and is she one?

On the other hand, a decision to disclose, followed by careful preparation with the help of a friend or professional person, thinking through what, how, when, and where can make the difference between a constructive experience and a calamity.

I am most hopeful for positive outcome of disclosure when I hear reasons for the decision like the following:

I value my emotional life enough to want to share it with my children. I want them to learn to trust and value their emotional life and I want to help them do that, by example. I want there to be as much honesty and truth as possible in my relationship with my children. I want them to understand that a relationship with a woman lover is a special close and serious one for me. I want them to understand why I choose to spend so much time with such a person, especially when it might mean excluding them in the process.

For most people making the decision is just the beginning. How, when, where, what, and "what can I expect," come next. Let's take these questions one at a time.

SHALL I WAIT UNTIL I'M ASKED OR SHALL I TAKE THE INITIATIVE?

I believe it is important, whenever possible, to take the initiative in order to be able to exercise some control over the conditions of disclosure. It is best if the children can be prepared ahead of time. "I have something I want to talk to you about that is important to you and to me." And, incidentally, a long face foreshadowing doom is not the best introduction to a discussion of your gay identity. Assuming that you will have worked through much of your own ambivalence about your sexuality your attitude should be upbeat and positive. Hopefully, you are sharing something with your children that you prize and they should be given the best possible chance to do that also.

A related matter is that of avoiding the act of disclosure by forcing the children to tell *you* what you are trying to tell *them*. The nervous mother, unable to get the words out, might ask, "You know what I'm trying to tell you, don't you?" Unfair. The disclosure of your lesbianism is an act of faith in your children. Give them and yourself the best chance for a successful outcome by participating as *fully* as possible in this personal affirmation of your relationship with them.

SHALL I TELL THEM ONE AT A TIME OR ALL TOGETHER?

If there is a large difference in your children's ages, you might want to tell them in different ways. In addition, telling your children separately might give them a special feeling that will enhance the experience you have with them. If you tell them separately, you should not let too long a period elapse between the times you tell each of them. If your children are close in age and it is a usual event in your family to talk things over as a group, it is probably best to tell them together. However you choose to do this, your own judgment is your best guide. You know how each of your children reacts to you and to the others. You are the final expert on this matter.

IS THERE ANYTHING IMPORTANT ABOUT WHEN AND WHERE THEY SHOULD BE TOLD?

Yes, I think it's important to arrange for a place that is quiet and private and a time in which you won't be interrupted or distracted. It is particularly important to have plenty of time planned in for explanations and expression of feelings.

WHAT DO I SAY?

In working with lesbian mothers struggling with the coming-out process I have been surprised, at times, to see extremely bright, articulate, sometimes eloquent women at such a total loss for the words to use with their children. There are, of course, no universally applicable guidelines. And there are no magic words. However, planning gives you time to think through some possibilities and decide what feels best for you. I present below a device to help with such preparation. It is a questionnaire including some of the basic questions children ask, allowing for age differences and levels of sophistication, of course. Following each question I have listed some possibilities for answers, again to be adjusted for age and sophistication level. I suggest you try to answer each question for yourself, modifying or adding to what I have offered. It has been my experience that women who are particularly troubled by what to say are able to approach disclosure much more easily once they have gone through this kind of exercise.

Question 1. What does being gay mean? What is a lesbian?
Being gay means being attracted to a person who is the same sex you are. It means being attracted in such a way that you might fall in love with the person. You might want to be very close to the person, as people are when they're married, or when they love each other and live together as though they were married. A lesbian is a woman who feels this way about another woman.

Many children of school age will have heard the words "gay" and "lesbian" already. They may think they know what they mean and tell you there's no need to explain them. It is, however, very important that you do supply your own explanations. The odds are that what your children have heard already is derogatory, ridiculing, or frightening. They have probably learned that lesbians and gay men are people to be wary of, to feel sorry for, or to laugh about. How fortunate that you have an opportunity to correct those impressions.

Question 2. What makes a person gay?
No one knows exactly what makes a person choose one kind of a partner to love and be close to rather than another kind. It's probably for a lot of different reasons. I wonder if your question might really be, "Will I be gay?"

Question 3. Will I be gay?
You won't be gay just because I am. You have a different makeup and different life experiences from mine. You are a separate person. You'll be whatever you are going to be because of your own makeup and your own experiences. What I hope is that you'll be a person who has interesting and loving relationships with people, and who is open to whatever life has to offer. Whatever you are I hope you'll be a happy and self-fulfilled person.

Question 4. How can you tell if someone's gay?
You can't just by looking at them. All kinds of people are gay. Gay people are women and men, young and old, skinny and fat, poor and rich, mothers and fathers, daughters and sons, athletes and bankers and teachers and doctors and lawyers and farmers and business people. So many different kinds of people are gay they couldn't possibly all look alike.

Question 5. Are there a lot of gay people? Yes, millions in the United States and millions more all over the world.

Question 6. Where are all the gay people?
A lot of lesbians and gay men *hide* the fact that they are gay. They hide it because there are still many people who don't really understand what being gay means. Because they don't understand it they think there's something bad about it and they make life difficult for those people who are gay. But that's changing now. In the last few years gay people have started talking about themselves a lot more so there is beginning to be better understanding. As more and more people understand what being gay is about there is not so much need for gay people to hide.

Question 7. What do you think I should tell my friends about this?
First of all, remember that a lot of people don't understand what it means to be gay and they put it down. Some of your friends may find it interesting. Some may want to make jokes or say critical things about it. That's

the way it is with their parents and that's probably the way it will be with them. If there are friends you'd really like to tell, who you think would understand, try it out. If you have a bad experience, let's talk about it. We can learn together about the best ways of talking to people about it.

There are additional questions that children frequently ask that are best answered, I believe, from an entirely personal point of view. For instance, *"How can you tell if you're gay?"* You would do well to inquire into the personal meaning of the question for your child because the question is more likely, *"How will I know if I'm gay?"* I think that is best answered by the mother discussing her own experience, perhaps then leading into the abstractions offered above in answer to the question "Will I be gay?"

Other questions often asked are:

"Why did you marry and have children if you are a lesbian?"

"Do you hate men?" ("Do you hate me?" your son might be asking.)

"Is this why you got divorced?"

If you are introducing a lover into your household for the first time, you should be careful about not causing it to appear as if this development (your gayness) is purely a function of your relationship with *this* woman. In this event your children might come to regard her as the "villain" who turned their mother into a lesbian. It is sometimes easy for women to disclose their lesbianism to their children strictly in terms of their relationship with a particular lover. It might be very important to their acceptance of this person to understand that your gayness is a function of *your* needs and preferences, not something that's being done to you by an outsider.

WHAT CAN I EXPECT?

The answer to this question, of course, depends entirely on the kind of relationship you have with your children to begin with, how old and how sophisticated the children are, and how comfortable you are with your lesbian identity. If all of those systems are "go," your disclosure will probably be relatively trouble-free and a good experience. If, however, there are reasons for a child to react negatively, that reaction might come in the form of name-calling, expression of angry feelings, or total silence. You should be prepared for any of the three.

Name-calling and Angry Feelings
"You're a *queer*!"

"Dyke!"

"You *lesbian*." (angrily)

Terrible to hear? Stirs up your own anger? Want to retaliate? Or is your inclination to deal with the *words*? "I don't want to hear that kind of language from you!!"

What is the real issue to be dealt with? This young person has been given a hot potato to handle and is

saying, "Ouch!!" You wouldn't object to your child's emotional response if it was a *physical* discomfort being experienced. It would seem a "natural" reaction. So is this one. If you can hold onto that idea and not cut off the reaction through retaliatory anger of refocusing on the words being used, you will be opening an important channel for expression of feelings around this touchy subject. It is infinitely better for your daughter or son to express these feelings with you than to turn them inward or act them out destructively. You can help further by recognizing that these words are a way of giving voice to the strong feelings that have been touched off. And you can say so. "This is making you pretty angry right now."

Total Silence
If your child meets your disclosure in total silence, it is best to recognize, again, that s(he) is having a difficult time with this information. You might try to gently draw feelings out, or if that seems unworkable to invite further discussion as soon as possible. At least make it clear that you are available any time and want very much to hear whatever feelings or questions there are.

OTHERS IN THE FAMILY

What about others in the family? Your ex-husband. Does he know you are gay? If not, that is something you should take care of, if at all possible, before you make your disclosure to the children. If your ex-husband knows you are gay but you're not sure how he is feeling about it, talk with him again, if possible. Try to assure yourself, insofar as you can, that there will be support and understanding from this source if your children choose to use it. If that is an impossible dream, as is sometimes the case, unfortunately, at least you will know where you stand and what you are getting into, and you can then prepare the children.

What about other family members, grandparents, the children's aunts and uncles, and so on? If your children are close to any of these family members, you should, again if possible, be sure that (1) they know you are gay, (2) they understand what that means to you, and (3) they are supportive of you. It is particularly helpful if these relatives can accept and reinforce the positive attitudes your children develop toward your gayness.

FINALLY . . .

Finally, there are two things to remember.

First, keep the channels of communication open with your children. Continue to talk about the topic of your lesbian identity as often as seems appropriate. Hopefully you will be able to do this comfortably and it will become a natural subject for conversation in your household.

Second, trust yourself. You are the world's leading

expert on *your* mother-child relationship. The real clues for the decision on disclosure to your children, how, when, where, what to say, etc., are in your intimate knowledge of that relationship. Use it to put the suggestions of this writer, and everyone else offering help in this important personal matter, in perspective.

"I walked out of the class and realized that I had just come out to Kate's teacher."

I came out to my daughter Kate about three years ago, when she was six, not long after I came out. From the beginning, when I was involved with women I never hid anything from her. If there was a woman who slept over, if we hugged or kissed, or whatever, I never made any attempt to hide it. She was having dinner out with me and a friend of mine, and she asked, "What does *lesbian* mean?" because she heard us using the word in our conversation. I replied that a lesbian was a woman who loved other women. Later on, when I was working with a friend, we used the word "lesbian" frequently in our conversation and talked about lesbian mothers, and the kids started teasing and joking with us: "Lesbian, lesbian, that's all you ever talk about," and she said to her friend, "We're lesbian kids, aren't we?" and Ellie and I looked at each other wondering which one of them was going to be the first to bring it up at Show and Tell.

We talked about it again on our way to her school and she said, "How come I've seen women kissing other women and I've seen women kissing men but I've never seen men kissing men?" I said, "You may not have seen it, but there are men who like to kiss other men, and they're called homosexuals," so we got into definitions, and we arrived at the school and she said, "I think we better stop talking about this now." I asked why, and she said, "Because we haven't gotten to sex yet in my class." Without my ever having explained taboos to her, she had a very clear sense of them. I saw she would not bring it up in a context where it was going to result in something painful to her; she had a delicate, subtle sense. I think kids do know what's going on; they know how other people feel about things, and it doesn't have to come from the parents. That was reassuring to me, because I knew that she would know how to protect herself. This came after the time in the restaurant when I had to define the word for her. I had said, "You know that *I* am a lesbian, don't you?" and she said yes. She didn't have the name for it earlier, I think, but she understood I was relating to women. She accepted it as something natural. I think she's always understood that I wasn't the stereotypic mother in the TV commercial, and there's a lot of difference in life-styles in the neighborhood where I live. I think she spoke about it the first time she wanted an explanation and a definition.

About a year and a half ago, my daughter and I did a TV interview. I was apprehensive beforehand, because we hadn't had any heavy conversation, and I wanted to prepare her. I wanted to make sure she was ready for whatever might come from kids in her class who might happen to see the program. I asked her how she felt about being on it, and she was excited about being on a television program, and a little nervous about having attention focused on her. I made sure she understood that there are people who are negative about homosexuality and asked her if she felt all right about being on the program under those circumstances. She said, "I know, but they're really stupid, aren't they?" She's a very strong feminist, and very sure that what we do and the way we live is okay, and it's different from what other people do.

On the program the interviewer set her up for a negative answer by asking her what a lesbian is. Her answer was, "It's a woman who loves another woman," and he said, "When your mother told you that she was a lesbian, were you shocked or upset?" "No." "How did you feel?" "I felt regular." That was great. I was very proud of her, and it was true.

There are lots of things that don't get talked about explicitly with children, between children and adults, that are communicated very strongly anyway. One of the things that she carried an impression away with that day was that while the interviewer was exploitative and frightened by the subject, the women and children interviewed on the program were very strong and forceful and centered and sure of who they were.

A few of her friends told her they saw her on TV. I asked her if they said anything about it and she said no. I've never really known for sure how this may have affected the attitudes of other kids in her class or the parents of those children. There is one parent that hasn't called me for a couple of years, and I have no way of knowing whether it was related to that event or not. There's a friend of Kate's whom she's just as close to as she ever was before. If she were being ostracized or suffering over it, I have some sense from other situations that she would be talking about it.

More recently we were both interviewed for another television program. I went to her school and told her fourth-grade teacher that I would have to pick her up early that day because TV people were coming to our house, and he asked me what the program was about. I said, "Lesbian mothers and their children," and he said "Wonderful" and I walked out of the class and realized that I had just come out to Kate's teacher. When I went to the school again for a conference, he was very negative: "The last time you were here you threw this word 'lesbian' at me and I don't think that was a very wise decision; there were children standing around." I looked at him with utter disbelief. He's a white man who is married to a black woman and I assume that he's experienced prejudice. I said, "I don't know if any children heard what I said, but if they had and raised questions, it would be very important to explain that that's a normal part of human sexuality. I think the children should be exposed to those words. You can't hide the difference if you're black, but I don't think hiding differences is very good for people, and I don't see anything wrong with who I am and I don't think those children need protection from that piece of information." Of course the real problem was not the children; he wanted me to protect him from the information because he couldn't deal with it. He had made his accommodations, and he was typical of many liberals, very threatened. I had a real consciousness-raising session with him and gave him a lot of analogies between my situation and his. It's very amusing, because since then he has bent over backwards to prove himself as a wonderful teacher to me.

Even though I said all the right things that you say in that situation, I walked out of that school and burst into tears. It takes a daily struggle to be ready if you're going to be out, and it's important to me, but sometimes you're in a very alien environment. That's part of being a lesbian mother, dealing with teachers and schools. I have friends who are lesbian mothers who recently went to open school night together. They had a nice experience with their kid's teacher, who is very open and a strong feminist and very supportive, but certainly not everybody is going to experience that.

It would be much harder to deal with coming out to an adolescent, I think, a kid who's going through questions about his or her own identity. I would be paying a very big price in terms of my relationship if I were hiding the primary intensity of my relationships with women from my daughter, or if I were sealing off my sexual self. The bedroom door is closed, certainly, but sexuality isn't just what happens in the bedroom. There are all kinds of affection and love and warmth, and being able to experience that is communicating to her something of the whole range of human sexuality. This is also a way of saying to her, "I like who I am; you can feel good about who you are." Why save that and make it some terribly painful revelation?

I think a lot of women don't come out to their children because they're afraid it may come up as a custody issue if they're divorced. I worried about that. In my case it wasn't a realistic fear, because my ex-husband was a passive person, not very emotionally involved with Kate or committed to parenting, and he didn't spend very much time with her. There may be a very real threat of loss of custody for some women, though, and I certainly wouldn't cavalierly say that anybody should just feel free about coming out, but I think it is important to really assess the situation and think it through and see whether it is a reality. It would be bad for the kid to spill the beans, and then a custody case results and the child has to carry the burden of guilt for having told the secret.

I told my daughter, "If you want to tell your father about it, it's okay," and she said, "I already told him about it." My guess is that he had picked up a long time ago that I was a lesbian. There was always at least one other woman in the apartment when he came to pick up Kate. He was aware that I was relating to women

Joan Larkin and daughter Kate

and not to men. Fear on the part of lesbian mothers, and other lesbians, is often some piece of guilt and inability to accept lesbianism oneself.

Lesbianism for me involves a radically different way of seeing myself and my whole life. Kate has been exposed not just to me, but to lots of strong women who define themselves not by their relationship with somebody else. I think that centeredness and self-acceptance and strength is a very positive adult model for her to have. People always approach this subject in terms of what are the problems, but there are some wonderful advantages—especially when two lesbians are living together and doing the parenting. I wasn't living with another woman until recently, but my life and Kate's have both changed enormously as a result, and now there's another warm, loving adult in the household who emotionally is much more available to her than most men would be, given the way they've been socialized and given the way they've been taught to relate to children. It's wonderful for her. We've been fortunate in that she and my lover have a very good relationship with each other on their own, where before with Kate there was a kind of sibling rivalry with women who were my lovers; she doesn't have any siblings to have that competition with. That hasn't been the case with her and the woman I live with, and it's been very warm and loving. *I* also feel better, because there's somebody to share experiences with—both joys and problems relating to taking care of Kate. She isn't totally my own responsibility anymore.

I don't know what Kate's sexuality is going to be,

and I don't know more than anyone else does where sexual preference comes from. Whatever her choice is, it's hers, but it strikes me that after experiencing the strength of the women that come to our house, I can't imagine why she would want anything less than that. I have the natural parental wish for her not to have to go through awful suffering and loss of her own direction in the course of trying out relationships. You can't protect your children from everything, and I suppose I have some kind of idealized picture that with women there would be more support of her own direction. I have never said this before because I have always been eager to stop at saying, "I have no ax to grind," because one thing that comes up in custody cases is the fear the child is going to be depraved and corrupted and forced into homosexuality.

I used to feel apologetic about all the ways that we were different from Mom's apple pie. Now I understand that the more exposure to different kinds of people that a child has, the better equipped she's going to be to deal with the world as it really is. Individual difference is the essence of civilization, and it's got to be accepted and nourished. I think she's a stronger person because of this, whether she becomes a lesbian or not. There's a whole range of experience that she knows about that a lot of kids are not aware of. Far from hurting her, it makes her a much richer person, and I think it is a preparation for accepting other kinds of difference too. She's just a fantastic kid. It's a joy to watch her grow.

—Joan Larkin
(edited from a taped interview)

"I feel like he's just as much my child, although none of this is legitimized by the society."

(Sue and Roberta have been together since 1973. Sue has a seven-year-old son, Jody. Mark, Sue's ex-husband, does not use his knowledge of their lesbianism to influence Jody against his mother. Jody sees his father every other weekend. Both Sue and Roberta's testimony is presented below.)

Sue: Being a mother is a very respected role in the lesbian feminist community. Most people are impressed. But perhaps we're not that much involved with the community. We've hesitated to bring Jody into contact with it because some of the lesbian feminists we've met give off very negative vibrations towards males. I don't want him to feel there is something wrong with him because he's a boy.

We want him to know mature men who like kids; they could be either straight or gay. But we do want men around him, and not just for role models, but because he needs to be confident in his ability to relate to other males as well as women.

Roberta: We talked with a group of lesbian feminists who were starting a lesbian-feminist commune. We asked what would be the place of a male child in such a commune. It was a shock to them because I don't think they had even thought about it, and the idea of an all-female environment is not an alternative for us.

Sue: Jody, my son, has some idea what gay is, and he knows the jewelry we wear means *gay*. At first he used to wonder if our belonging to the Gay Teachers Association meant that we were just happy, but last Christmas we had a party, and we hung a lesbian symbol on the tree, and our gay male friends hung a gay symbol on the tree, and he asked what those things meant. I said one was a sign about women loving women, and the other a sign about men who love men, and ultimately he understood that's what gay meant. We don't describe to him what we do in bed. He knows we sleep together because we love each other, and that's part of our relationship. The issue hasn't come up yet; I wish it would come from him, before I mention it.

As he gets older more and more things come up. At first he was jealous, but he didn't relate it to sex. He was only four then. He knows how babies are born, but as far as describing sexual acts I am waiting for him to ask a question I can respond to directly. At some point he asked if we were married. He understands that our relationship is permanent, and that Roberta is going to be here, and sometimes he calls her his roommate, and sometimes his friend.

Roberta: At times when we are traveling together, either the three of us, or just myself and Jody, and I'm acting as the other responsible parent, he'll refer to me as "Mother" in order not to have to explain, "This is my mother's roommate who lives with us." And I'll refer to him as my son.

Sue: He doesn't protest; he is happy about it. He sees us three as a family. His school had him drew a picture of his family, and he drew Mark, me and Roberta, and himself.

Roberta: I feel like I am Jody's other parent because we're a family unit, more a parent than Mark because Sue and I make the day-to-day decisions together. I think we have an equal share. When I first moved in, I felt it wasn't my territory, because I moved into an apartment that wasn't mine, with a child that wasn't mine, and I felt like an outsider. Maybe I didn't want the responsibility, but we did a lot of talking, and I got to know Jody better, and took more responsibility, and now I feel at home in talking about what should be done for Jody. I feel like he's just as much my child, although none of this is legitimized by the society.

We try to be open and aggressive about people recognizing our relationship. When Jody was in day care, I got involved in his school. The director knew we were gay, and that made it easier for us to say, "We're both responsible. If Sue is not home and I answer the phone, then talk to me."

The school he is in now is different, but we've signed all his cards together, and I am the other responsible person in the household. We both take an active role. I meet Jody's teachers together with Sue. We make it apparent that we're both equally responsible and concerned about Jody.

Sue: I went to a single parents' night at Jody's old day-care center, and when my turn came I explained that I wasn't really a single parent, and most of the teachers there ended up knowing about us. I want Roberta, who has all the hardships of being a parent, to also have the name and respect that goes with it. I really feel like I have to insist on that.

The front-office people in his new school are very snooty, very conventional-minded. They insisted upon sending my ex-husband the same invitations to parents' night I received. He went with his wife, and Roberta wasn't invited—I thought it was very presumptuous of them—Roberta and I pay the school bill with our joint checking account.

Another time Roberta went to talk to one of the administrators about observing a class, and they had the attitude, "You're not a parent; why do you want to do this?" and they really frosted her out. I blew up, and it was instantly corrected, and Roberta went and observed and after that we never got hassled again. Simply by insisting on her right to be the other parent, we've made our place in the school. We still didn't go to the parents' square dance, though.

One creepy woman—the mother of one of Jody's friends—insisted upon calling Roberta "the baby-sitter" and Jody explained that Roberta was his roommate. But another mother said, "I always treat Roberta as if she were the other parent; that's her role."

Roberta: When I had to go into the hospital, I wanted Sue to be the other person consulted. They didn't ask me once they knew I wasn't "married." We made things clear by having a lesbian friend as my nurse. There are situations that come up all the time where you want to be recognized as a legal couple—and we have to pull it off with our brazenness.

We would like to have the same health plan straight married couples have, and file joint taxes, but it's the social pressure that we have to battle against. What *does* bother me is that if anything ever happened to Sue I know I would have *no* control over what happened to Jody. I would like to think his father would consult me, but it probably wouldn't happen.

Sue: We're angry when we think how the advantages of living in an urban environment ties us down to the city—where maybe one day Jody'll get killed by someone who wants his bicycle or something. We have the same reasons for wanting to leave the city as most other middle-class parents.

Roberta: We often think about moving, but the possibility of taking Jody from a private school where we can pretty much dictate what we want done with him is scary for us. I've worked in the public school system and seen children referred to the guidance counselor because the mother was a lesbian. Picking a place with a good school means more than just reading; it means where are we going to go where our child isn't going to be told, "Your parents are sick" or "You're sick because you have lesbians in your family."

—Susan Rosen and Roberta Stone

3.
Reseach and Therapy

Lesbian Research: A Critical Evaluation

BARBARA E. SANG, Ph.D.

What relevance does a paper on "lesbian research" have for the lesbian community? In this paper I will attempt to show how research, often done in the name of "science," has continued to perpetuate negative myths and misconceptions about lesbians and women in general.[1] Such research can be damaging to lesbians in all areas of their lives: feelings of self-worth, relationships to family, lovers, and friends, openness about self in school and job situations, child custody, etc. It is important that we develop research that relates to our own life experience.

As lesbians we need to become aware of the biases in research that "put us down." In this way we can be in a better position to (1) refuse to participate in studies that are offensive, (2) educate the public as to the inadequacies in existing research, (3) formulate alternative research questions and designs that have meaning to us as persons. It is also about time we got away from research that asks, "Who is healthier, gays or straights?" Once again, gays are put in the position of having to

---

[1] I would like to extend my thanks to Ann Wallingford, who contributed many helpful ideas and suggestions to this article.

explain their preference. In recent years, a number of better designed studies, using larger samples of lesbians, have found that lesbians are as well adjusted as straight women. In fact, on certain measures, lesbians were found to be more competent, autonomous, and self-fulfilled in terms of using their adult potential.

First, I will briefly show how the psychoanalytic model takes the position that lesbianism is some form of arrest in development. This was done despite absence of experimental evidence to substantiate their thinking. In the next section, entitled, "The Transitional Phase," I will critically examine some of the research that has been done on lesbianism, pointing out areas of faulty logic and research biases. In a paper of this scope it is not possible to do justice to the vast body of literature that has been accumulating on lesbianism over the last ten years. Thus, I will attempt to describe some trends and issues as I see them. References to other studies, or to more detailed reviews of the literature, will be provided for those who wish to explore this area in greater depth. Finally, I would like to conclude this survey with my own suggestions for future directions and processes in research.

PART I: HISTORICAL ANALYSIS

A number of major books and position papers on the subject of lesbianism, written by psychiatrists and psychologists, began to appear in the 1950s. Women who were trying to decide if they were lesbians or women seeking to validate their own experience were faced with the following description of themselves: Homosexuality was considered a form of "immaturity" or "pathology" which many felt could and should be "cured." In the psychoanalytic literature, lesbianism was described as "an outgrowth of failings in human relationships," "an ego defect," "an arrest in normal sexual development," and "denial of female genitality." Loving a member of one's own sex was thought of as an extension of love for oneself, which was then labeled "narcissistic" or "self-centered." (Deutsh, 1944; Bergler, 1951; Fried, 1960). It is simplistic to think that if you love someone with the same genitals as yourself, that person is an extension of you. Two people of the opposite sex can be similar in more respects than persons of the same sex.

Even the psychoanalyst Clara Thompson (1964), whose views on women were considered "radical for her time," felt that "homosexuality" is but a symptom of more general personality difficulties. She believed that homosexuality was acceptable if nothing else existed; however, it would (should) disappear when more satisfactory gratifications were available. Thompson speculated that if the culture made no sex restrictions, people would get the most satisfactory type of sexual gratification from the union of male and female genitals. Thompson died in 1958; therefore, she did not have the benefit of later research and reports from masses of women exposing the "myth of the vaginal orgasm." This research has shown that for sexual climax most women need clitoral stimulation rather than vaginal penetration. (Koedt, 1970; Seaman, 1972; Hite, 1976.)

In one of the most widely available books on lesbianism today, written by the psychiatrist Frank Caprio, in 1954, the lesbian is further described as "jealous," "insecure," "possessive," "sadomasochistic," and basically "unhappy." He claims, "Psychoanalysts are in agreement that all women who prefer a homosexual way of life suffer from a distorted sense of values and betray their emotional immaturity in their attitudes toward men, sex and marriage." As Abbott and Love (1972) point out, "A woman can only achieve the label of maturity when she serves the needs of the system and submits to a male." Caprio himself is well known for his view that lesbianism is a reenactment of the mother-child relationship. His reasoning is as follows: "Love is feminine in origin. Hence, it is logical to conclude that female homosexuality is a regression to mother love, a need for maternal protection and security." The logic of this statement is clearly questionable. Unfortunately, Caprio's view, as well as pathologically oriented models in general, have served to be emotionally detrimental to lesbians themselves. (Sang, 1974, 1977.) In most relationships individuals differ in their style of relating to the world. It is easy to fall into the trap of labeling these differences "child" or "adult," "immature" or "mature." Were we to observe any relationship between two people, we could easily polarize each of these individuals into one or the other position. (Lowenherz and Sang, 1975.) More current research suggests that lesbian relationships may create a better emotional environment for realized adult potential. Cotton (1957), Furgeri (1976), and Oberstone and Sukoneck (1976) report that lesbians may be more reciprocal and egalitarian than traditional males and females in their relationships.

For further methodological weaknesses and faulty assumptions in the work of Caprio and others, the reader is referred to Dolores Klaich's analysis of "Post-Freud American Confusion" in *Woman + Woman* (1974). Klaich also provides an excellent critique of the work of the sexologist Krafft-Ebbing, a nineteenth-century moralist who helped implant the association of "degenerate" with lesbianism.

Psychoanalytic literature on lesbianism is likely to seem as though the observations and conclusions made are based on actual research. However, this is not at all the case: It was found that within the *Psychological Abstracts*, between the years 1939 and 1960, there was a total of only twenty-two articles that mention lesbianism. Pathetically, most of the "studies," which often used only one or two subjects, focused on the physical "causes" of lesbianism or the effects of hormones or electric shock on removing this sexual orientation. The largest study reported during this period was done on fourteen "delinquent" girls. (Shifrin, 1977.)

Thus, general theories about lesbians were based on little more than newspaper clippings, a few select

"patients" in psychotherapy, and prejudices of the period.

Caprio's own personal belief is that "love, sex and survival are all interrelated." If sex does not also serve a procreative function, it is "aberrant" and "sick." If research were to be performed by someone holding this view of adjustment, lesbians by such a naïve criterion would have to be considered "maladjusted." One can only question how Caprio would interpret the phenomenon of mothers who are also lesbians.

Looking back on the position that lesbianism is a form of "abnormality," it is now easier to see how many assumptions, taken to be truth about lesbianism, were merely reflections of the social beliefs and prejudices of the time. Nussdorf (1977) states: "As long as society devalues homosexuals as compared to heterosexuals, or devalues women as compared to men, then all research findings must be thought of as being undeterminately biased." Sadly, many of the books which project antiquated viewpoints are very accessible today, due to the surge of interest in the psychology of women; however, books with opposing points of view are not always so available. For lesbians exploring "coming out" or for those wishing to know more about lesbianism, these older books can be highly misleading. Presently, there is a strong trend to include one chapter on lesbianism in each new anthology on female psychology. It is disappointing that some of these current anthologies offer, as their only lesbian chapter, articles by authors whose views are almost identical to the pathological models previously discussed. (Eisenbud, 1969; McDougall, 1970.)

The notion that homosexuality was a form of mental problem or aberration was perpetuated by the *Diagnostic and Statistical Manual* put out by the American Psychiatric Association. A large number of mental health practitioners use this manual; thus, it has a wide impact on mental health thinking and services in general. In the 1952 edition of this manual, homosexuals were classified with people who committed crimes of a destructive or anti-social nature. The revised 1968 edition listed homosexuality as a "sexual deviation" along with individuals who are child molesters, voyeurs, and exhibitionists. In 1973 the American Psychiatric Association went on record as saying that in their diagnostic manual homosexuality would be listed as a "Sexual Orientation Disturbance," and removed from the mental disorder list. This label, they said, would only apply if the person herself/himself felt internal conflict or wished to change his/her sexual orientation. It has been pointed out, however, that this statement is ambiguous and could lead to psychotherapy that is harmful to gays. Many lesbians have gone into psychotherapy to feel good about their lesbianism, only to find themselves once again trying to be "heterosexual." Persons seeking therapy need a genuine option that it's all right to be gay. There are many therapists today who are not sure how they feel about a gay life-style as an option. Their uncertainty at this time can be limiting and oppressive. Numerous women have consulted with me who have spent time and money with psychotherapists who encouraged them to go straight. (Sang, 1974, 1977.) Some women struggling with the issue of "coming out" might benefit from self-exploration in a supportive peer or consciousness-raising group; others might better benefit from seeking out therapists who view lesbianism as a viable life-style.

In 1975 the American Psychological Association (APA) adopted a resolution stating that homosexuality per se implies no impairment in judgment, stability, reliability, or general social or vocational capabilities. The APA further urged all mental health professionals to take the lead in removing the stigma long associated with homosexuality. With this aim in mind, a Task Force on the Status of Lesbian and Gay Psychologists was formed within the American Psychological Association. The task force has been responsible for passing an APA resolution stating that persons not be discriminated against on the basis of affectional or sexual preference, either regarding the care or custody of their own children, or as foster or adoptive parents. At the present time, the task force is preparing an information and resource packet for educating psychologists to gay life-styles. Also, the task force has designed and is conducting a study of the professional and personal experiences of lesbian and male psychologists. To date, eighty-two female respondents have identified themselves as lesbian, eighteen bisexual. Although the data has not been completely analyzed, it does appear that many of these women hold "high status" professional positions. About 27 percent in the sample are openly lesbian. None reported that "coming out" was a mistake. However, women in the "closet" feared losing their current job status. Almost all the women stated that being gay has given them insight into social-psychological issues. These results suggest that many well-qualified lesbian researchers who are familiar with lesbian and feminist life-styles may be unable to do research for fear of being known as homosexual. Many lesbian and gay male support groups for people in the helping professions meet regularly throughout the country.

PART II: THE "TRANSITIONAL PHASE"

The 1960s marked the beginning of a more active gay movement and a surge in vitality within the feminist movement. The subject of homosexuality was more out in the open. With the increased awareness that psychology was male-oriented, and the realization that virtually all studies on homosexuality used males as subjects, it finally occurred to researchers to study lesbianism. Between 1960 and 1969 Shifrin (1977) found a total of twenty-three articles on lesbianism listed in the *Psychological Abstracts*. Only half of these "studies" were based on twenty-five or more subjects. Some trends noted were a general decrease in psychoanalytic thought and the study of lesbianism from a "social perspective."

An attempt to "study" the lesbian community increased in focus.

During this period, more lesbians were attending homophile organizations and were, therefore, for the first time, accessible to researchers. It was now possible to obtain samples as large as one hundred or more.[2] Incidentally, I was a subject in several studies during this time and found many of the questions difficult to answer. For example, I was often asked to describe myself or family as "passive" or "active"; but passive or active in respect to what? Many questions that were asked did not seem to tap the wealth of experience that I knew to exist in the lesbian community. At the same time that lesbians were being studied, lesbians were coming together for the first time in groups to compare and contrast their own experiences. To me, this marked the beginnings of a new lesbian awareness. Such a sharing and contrasting of ideas by lesbians in different groups continues to be an alternative form of study and knowledge. I will elaborate on this new process in research in the last section of this paper.

Between 1970 and 1975 we see the first beginnings of a feminist and gay impact on the psychological literature. As a result, lesbianism is studied as a separate area of concern as opposed to being a subcategory of male homosexuality. A total of fifty-four studies on lesbianism were reported during this period. (Shifrin, 1977.) We continue to see research on who is better adjusted—lesbian or heterosexual women.

Kristiann Mannion (1975) has done a thorough review of the theory and research on female homosexuality. She provides a good methodological critique of a large number of studies. Mannion sees a relationship between theory, methods used, and the results obtained. In other words, studies that attempt to validate psychoanalytic theory with more "ambiguous measures," such as projective tests, are more likely to pick up "disturbance" because they lend themselves to it. She goes on to point out, however, that when psychologists were asked to distinguish between the test responses of gay and straight persons, they could not do so.

As stated previously, a number of studies have shown lesbians in general to be more assertive, autonomous, self-actualizing, and inner-directed than heterosexual women. These finds are not surprising in view of the fact that most lesbians assume that they will have to provide for themselves and to not be taken care of by

---

[2]Since most lesbian studies used subjects recruited from homophile organizations, many gays felt that any picture obtained from such a "select" population could not be extended to fit "all" lesbians. It was argued that we had no idea of who the population was. Many lesbians were too afraid to "come out." At this time many progay researchers are no longer interested in obtaining *the* representative samples of lesbians. Morin (1977) has emphasized that lesbians are not a unified group and lesbianism does not represent a personality style. Also, most people are neither "all heterosexual" or "all homosexual" although we may choose to label ourselves as such.

others. In a paper entitled, "A Case for Lesbians as Role Models for Healthy Adult Women," Barbara Love (1975) states: "Lesbians . . . must be recognized as pioneers in breaking role barriers for women, not only by loving women, which is not nearly as important as being independent, self-defined and equal to men." I think we will soon see—we should soon see the same realization in the field of psychology as we have seen in the women's movement—that the qualities associated with the lesbian life-style can be viewed as positive and not negative, and not just acceptable either.

Many investigators are aware that studies on lesbians must be interpreted within the context of changing attitudes toward sex-role stereotypes. As a result, a number of doctoral dissertations of interest have come out on lesbianism over the last few years.[3] Freedman (1975) reports that his research on lesbians found them to score higher than a heterosexual control group on autonomy, spontaneity, orientation toward the present, as opposed to preoccupation with the past and future, and sensitivity to one's own needs and feelings. Freedman administered behavioral tests "measuring neuroticism and emotional stability" to eighty-two members of the DOB, a homophile organization in California, and sixty-seven "heterosexual controls" from a women's service organization. Oberstone (1976) explored female homosexuality within the total framework of preferred styles of life. She found no major differences in psychological adjustment between the women with a preferred homosexual orientation or heterosexual orientation. Brown (1977) compared eighty-six lesbians and eighty-two heterosexual women on several personality scales which, according to the bulk of the literature on lesbian personality, differentiate lesbians from heterosexual women. Lesbians were not found to be more "pathological" than heterosexual women. The results also did not support contentions of poorer self-concept, or of lesser satisfactions with interpersonal relations. No support was offered for contentions of more "masculine" personality or greater levels of aggression and/or dominance. Support was also not found for the viewpoint that lesbians had more negative feelings toward their sexuality.

Now that homosexuality is considered to be more "acceptable" and to be a "legitimate" area of investigation, a recent trend has appeared in lesbian research. Well-intentioned investigators (often male) who have little familiarity or understanding of lesbianism and feminism are attempting to dispel the notion that lesbians are less adjusted than heterosexual women. In essence, some of the questions being asked, the methods being used, and the interpretations of the findings reflect "heterosexist" and/or sexist bias.[4]

A few select examples of such biased studies are as follows:

(1) the naïve assumption that a group of single heterosexual women have the same relationship status as a group of "single" lesbian women (lesbians may be in a committed couple relationship although they are legally considered "single");

(2) the use of clinical jargon that comes from an "illness model," for example, "homosexual *condition*" or "cross gender *symptoms*." In one study, significantly more homosexual women were found to identify themselves as "masculine" (whatever this means), as compared to heterosexual women. The same authors consider "tomboyishness" as an "avoidance of appropriate sex-type behavior" (Saghir and Robins, 1973);

(3) the reporting of differences between lesbian and heterosexual women devoid of a social context: Although Saghir and Robins found lesbians to be no more "neurotic" than heterosexual women, in reporting their findings, they state that more lesbians, as compared to heterosexual women, frequent bars and drop out of college more often. This could give the impression that lesbians are less "stable" than heterosexual women. It needs to be made clear that lesbians have few opportunities to meet other than in bars. College can also be a painful experience for the lesbian; not only does she feel pressured to "hide" who she is, but she also has few opportunities to meet and relate to women with feelings like herself. It takes considerable strength to make it through college considering these conditions.

A study that has been given considerable attention in the women's literature was conducted by the psychoanalyst Charlotte Wolf (*Love Between Women*, England, 1971). I have noted that everyone who reports on this study has come away with a different interpretation of the findings. One recent textbook used in Psychology of Women classes called, *Half the Human Experience—The Psychology of Women* (1976), states that "some would argue that this search for 'causes' implies a classification of lesbianism as abnormal. However, as psychologists, we find this logic unsatisfying, since we must always concern ourselves with the development of behavior, be it criminal behavior or genius." Others, like myself, would argue that studies can't simply be done on "behavior." Depending on your value system you will focus on certain issues and not others. You will attribute different meanings to what you see. It is important to note that the editors of the above text present a three-page presentation of lesbianism entitled, "Research on the Genesis of Lesbianism" based on Wolff's findings. Within this report we read that "mothers of lesbians were significantly higher on destructive maternal attitudes; they tended to be either indifferent or neglectful"; "The typical mother of lesbians was thus frequently narcissistic and immature."

The following report excerpted from a book review is my interpretation of the Wolff study. If my own analysis has any validity, the reader will share my

---

[3] Because these researchers were expected to comply with a model that was acceptable to their university, the methods used were not always ones of personal choice.

[4] Lesbian Book Review section of the *Homosexual Counseling Journal*, Vol. I, Nos. 1 and 3 (1974).

concern with the noncritical manner in which results on lesbianism are reported:

In the last section of her book, Wolff reports on a study she made in which she compared 108 lesbians from a homophile organization in London to "normal" women. While it is not reported where the heterosexual women were recruited, they are said to have been matched with the "deviates" on the basis of occupation, family background, and age. All participants were given questionnaires, only the lesbians were interviewed and asked to write "emotional autobiographies." A few select findings showed that significantly more lesbians, as compared to the controls, were (1) only children; (2) wanted to be boys as children; (3) had a higher incidence of alcoholism; (4) had a higher incidence of violence. Sexually, lesbians were found to show a lower incidence of frigidity than their controls. In several instances, findings that were reported as "significant" in the text were not "significant" in the corresponding tables. In discussing her findings, Wolff often strays too far from the data she has obtained. Much is made of the finding that lesbians reported themselves to be their mothers' favorites and to have mothers who were less loving than those of heterosexual women. Wolff treats this difference as fact, yet one can only wonder if we are not dealing with different conceptions of the role of mother. Love Between Women *can be recommended only for the controversy and issues it raises. On the whole, this book lacks integration, and its tone is one of condescension."*[5]

PART III: WHO ARE WE AND WHERE DO WE WANT TO GO IN THE FUTURE? NEW DIRECTIONS IN LESBIAN-FEMINIST RESEARCH

I have always felt that nothing is going to change in our society unless there can be a new approach to the doing of social change.

— from Ruth Falk, *Women Loving*

An Emerging System of Feminist and Lesbian Research Values:

Lesbians and feminists began to realize that traditional models of psychology were not conducive to their emotional development. Many, therefore, began to experiment with alternative forms of learning about themselves. (Kent, 1969; Boston Women's Health Book Collective, 1971.) One of the top priorities that grew out of women's own experience was the commitment to facilitate the growth and self-actualization of all individuals; judgments about what constitutes "health" were being challenged. (Posin, 1973, 1977; Douvan, 1974; Keiffer, 1975-1977; Miller, 1976; Javors and Schwab, 1976; Vaughter, 1976.)

In most research as it exists today, one's own personal experience is not considered valid data for

"scientific inquiry." Yet, we have seen that the so-called objective measures of science can also be biased. In the lesbian community research of a different, but equally valid nature has been going on for many years. We make statements about our individual experience through personal testimony, correspondence, fiction, and unpublished position papers. Lesbians also compare and contrast their experiences in small intimate groups or in larger conferences or workshops.[6] This ongoing dialogue that lesbians are having with one another has resulted in a growing body of knowledge and new theory. Some of this new thinking is just beginning to find its way into the "professional literature." Vaughter (1976) notes that there is a growing trend among lesbians and feminists to work cooperatively rather than competitively. An individual person's work or contribution is also seen as a part of an ongoing process rather than *the* final product. (Miller, 1976.)

We are in the process of trying to clarify and sort out what is relevant to our own experience as women and lesbians, always conscious of the fact that who we are stems from oppression as women and lesbians, as well as our social class, backgrounds, and personal experience. At times it feels that despite many similarities as a group, there are also numerous differences.

A few weeks ago, in conjunction with another project. I was browsing through some old copies of *The Ladder,* the publication of the Daughters of Bilitis (DOB), a lesbian organization. There was an issue entitled, "DOB Questionnaire Reveals Some Facts About Lesbians." This study was conducted in 1958. It seemed amazing that that which lesbians knew about themselves almost twenty years ago still has relevance for everyone today. What astounded me most was that during this time lesbians did not have the benefit of feminist language and concepts, but they were challenging conventional sex role stereotyped relationships in a radical way:

A number of persons indicated specifically that they recognized both "masculine and feminine" elements in themselves. It is probable that a large majority of persons, lesbian and otherwise, have a mixture of elements, but that awareness of this mixture, as well as the mixture itself, varies from person to person. It also seems likely that awareness of either the "masculine" or the "feminine" qualities may be heightened by contrast with a partner who has a different combination of them.

Although this DOB study was done in 1958, it has been included in this section because it is an example of the new process and direction discussed previously: (1) the study was done as a collaborative effort; (2) the way in

---

[6]The concept of the *Lesbian Herstory Archives* was evolved by a group of women who met at the Gay Academic Union Conference in 1973. The Archives seeks to preserve for the future all expressions of lesbian identity: written, spoken, drawn, filmed, photographed, and recorded. Intended as a center for all women, the Archives represents a "commitment to rediscovery of our past, controlling our present and speaking to our future."

which the findings of this survey are reported are in striking contrast to the rigid and dogmatic way ideas about lesbianism were presented during this period. Some highlights of the DOB questionnaire are as follows: Over 500 questionnaires were sent out to readers of *The Ladder* to gether some general data on lesbians who probably would otherwise not come to the attention of researchers (157 returned). The median age was thirty-two years. Most responders did better than average in their college work or had above-average income. The professional group was more numerous than any other group. A high percentage of persons (27 percent) had been married. Almost all reported knowing they were homosexual when they married but did so to avoid social and family pressures.

What Kinds of Research Do Lesbians Wish to See in Order to Improve the Quality of Their Lives?

The following section of this paper will consist of several suggestions as to the direction and nature of lesbian research. Each individual is, of course, free to determine if these priorities are consistent with her/his own values. It will be noted that there is considerable overlap between areas that have been categorized separately.

1. Documentation of lesbian oppression. We will need: (1) to make necessary changes in social values and attitudes, (2) to provide support and validation for individuals struggling with the effects of gay oppression, (3) to develop skills and techniques necessary to ensure that lesbians lead more satisfactory and productive lives.

Dianne Greene (1976) intensively interviewed eighteen self-identified lesbians ranging in age from twenty-three to thirty-three. She found that the younger women "came out" at a later age but acted on their feelings sooner. These women felt better about themselves as persons. However, in contrast, women who were older recognized lesbian feelings at an earlier age but waited until much later in life to act on them. These women had internalized negative stereotypes about lesbians and did not feel as good about themselves. We need to know more about the strengths and assets of lesbians who did not have the validating information and the lesbian peer-group support that is more available to lesbians today.

2. Issues relevant to the lives of lesbians. Lesbians are experimenting with new forms of relating and living. We have much to learn from our own experiences. Some possible areas to explore might be: (1) relating to one another as "equals," (2) dealing with differences in age, educational level, income, and class background, (3) handling relationships to other women friends and to former lovers, (4) relating to women who are uncertain about their sexual orientation, (5) maintaining lesbian relationships and heterosexual marriage simultaneously, (6) experiencing alternative "life-style," for example, nonmonogomy, all-women's communes or communities, bisexuality, (7) helping children with a lesbian parent(s) to cope with being "different" in a society that values conformity.

A recent study that is especially relevant to the lesbian community was conducted by Lena Furgeri (1976). She compared lesbians over forty and under thirty years of age. It was assumed that the older couples experienced lesbian relationships at a time when the social taboos against lesbianism were the strongest. Furgeri conducted in-depth interviews and administered a questionnaire to ninety-four self-acknowledged lesbians from New York. Her sample included women from different class backgrounds. Most of the younger couples met in the movement, whereas the older women met socially. Both members of each couple worked. Ease and openness of communication existed among the younger couples. Most of the couples structured their chores according to interest and time availability. Couples were monogamous although "open-closed" relationships were an issue. There was more tension among the older couples who longed for the freedom and openness of younger lesbian couples. Role relationships seemed related to social class, education, and age. One surprising finding was that older couples shared their life-styles more openly with their families while the younger couples seemed more open about themselves at work. Older women acknowledged the benefits of the gay movement, but had negative attitudes toward "younger" women and their wish to be separate from gay men. The younger women were more involved in social reform.

3. New directions. We need a view of human development and personality that is neither sexist nor heterosexist in order that each individual realizes her or his unique potential. No longer do we want to make comparisons between individuals based on preconceived value judgments of health. At some point we may be in a position to make comparisons between groups which could then improve the lives of all people. Schwartz (1977) plans to study the interpersonal relationships of male homosexuals, lesbians, and heterosexual couples on the decision-making process. Different groups may have different knowledge or skills to offer one another. Comparisons between lesbian and male homosexuals could prove similarly useful. Cotton[7] (1975) suggests that some of the differences he found between lesbians and gay men are due to the difference in the nature of discrimination between the sexes. For instance, it is more dangerous for a woman to live alone than it is for a man, and more men than women can afford to live alone.

Another form of comparative study was done by Sara Beck Fein and Elaine Nuehring (1975). They studied the youthful male-female integrated gay community. This community was found to be more socially oriented as opposed to sexually oriented. The differences observed between males and females within the integrated community were minimal as compared to female and male homosexuals studied in gender-

---

[7]Excerpted from a media review by Barbara Trilling in the *Homosexual Counseling Journal*, October 1975.

segregated communities. Women were found to be as politically active as males.

In summary, it appears that lesbian research, as reflected in the professional literature, has begun to move away from studies of "causes" and "adjustment." These priorities in research do continue, however, and often reflect an underlying assumption that lesbian and male homosexuality is unnatural and undesirable. (Falk, 1975, Morin, 1977.) Now there are a number of studies that show gays to be as well adjusted as straights. In the future our energies, our time and money can be better spent on research that helps to maximize the growth potential of the individuals being studied. Several alternative directions and processes for new research have been suggested. Eventually, we may not only be asking different questions but also making significant changes in the nature of research itself.

RESOURCES

Lesbian Research and Mental Health
I. Organizations for Mental Health Workers. Offer support, information, exchange of ideas and action for social change. Most of these organizations publish regular newsletters and hold conferences on research.

Association of Gay Psychologists (AGP). P.O. Box 29527, Atlanta, Ga. 30359.

Association for Women in Psychology (AWP). Newsletter editor (1977) Kathy Gardy, 721 Carroll St., Brooklyn, N.Y. 11215.

The Task Force on the Status of Lesbian and Gay Psychologists (The American Psychological Association Board of Social and Ethical Responsibility). The Task Force invites interested persons to express their concerns and priorities regarding the status of lesbian and gay male psychologists by writing to the Task Force in care of BSERP, American Psychological Association, 1200 17th St., N.W., Washington, D.C. 20036.

Gay Public Health Workers. A caucus of the American Public Health Association. 206 N. 35th St., Philadelphia, Pa. 19104.

Gay Academic Union, Inc. Box 480, Lenox Hill Station, New York, N.Y. 10021. One of the priorities of this organization is to promote new approaches to the study of gay experience.

II. Selected Bibliographies or Reviews of Lesbian Research.

Morin, Steve. "An Annotated Bibliography on Lesbian and Male Homosexuals (1967-1974)." *JSAS* Catalogue of Selected Documents in Psychology, 1976. MS. 1247.

Mannion, Kristiann. "Female Homosexuality: A Comprehensive Review of Theory and Research." *JSAS* Catalogue of Selected Documents in Psychology, 1976. MS. 1247.

Reisman, Betty. "Research on Female Homosexuality: A Review." *The Homosexual Counseling Journal,* in press.

Other
KNOW, Inc. A feminist press with an excellent selection of research papers and theory on the psychology of women. P.O. Box 86031, Pittsburgh, Pa. 15221.

The Lesbian Herstory Archives. Collects information on the lives, writings, and experiences of lesbians. P.O. Box 1258, New York, N.Y. 10001.

The Homosexual Counseling Journal. Papers on a variety of subjects relating to the lesbian and gay male experience. For information on subscribing to the journal or obtaining out-of-print issues, write to HCCC, Inc., 30 E. 60th St., New York, N.Y. 10022.

BIBLIOGRAPHY

Abbott, Sidney, and Love, Barbara. *Sappho Was a Right-On Woman.* New York: Stein & Day, 1972.

Beck Fein, Sara, and Nuehring, Elaine. "Perspectives on the Gender-integrated Gay Community: Its Formal Structure and Social Functions." *Homosexual Counseling Journal,* 1975, No. 2, pp. 150-63.

Bergler, Edmund. *Homosexuality, Disease or Way of Life?* New York: Collier Books, 1956.

Boston Women's Health Book Collective. *Our Bodies Ourselves.* New York: Simon & Schuster, 1971.

Brown, Laura. "A Comparison of Some Personality Variables in Lesbian and Heterosexual Women." *Journal of Abnormal Psychology.* In press.

Caprio, Frank. *Female Homosexuality: A Modern Study of Lesbianism.* New York: Grove Press, 1954.

Cotton W. L. "Social and Sexual Relationships of Lesbians." *The Journal of Sex Research,* 1975, No. 11, pp. 139-48.

Daughters of Bilitis. "DOB Questionnaire Reveals Some Facts About Lesbians." 1958. *The Ladder.* 9 vol. New York: Arno Press, 1976. Also in *Homosexual Counseling Journal.* In press.

Douvan, Elizabeth. "Directions and Needs of Research on Women." In Dorothy McGuigan, ed., *New Research on Women and Sex Roles.* Michigan: The Center for Continuing Education of Women, 1976.

Eisenbud, Ruth-Jean. "Female Homosexuality: A Sweet Enfranchisement." In George Goldmen and Donald Milman, eds., *Modern Woman: Her Psychology and Sexuality.* Illinois: Charles C. Thomas, 1969.

Falk, Ruth. *Women Loving.* New York: Random House, 1975.

Freedman, Mark. "Homosexuals May Be Healthier than Straights." *Psychology Today,* March 1975, pp. 28-32.

———. "Homosexuality Among Women and Psychological Adjustment." Unpublished doctoral dissertation, 1967.

Fried, Edrita. *The Ego in Love and Sexuality.* New York: Grune and Stratton, 1960.

Furgeri, Lena Blanco. "The Lesbian/Feminist Movement and Social Change: Female Homosociality, a New Consciousness." Unpublished doctoral dissertation, 1976.

Greene, Diane. "Women Loving Women: An Exploration into Feelings and Life Experiences." Unpublished doctoral dissertation, City University of New York, 1976.

Hite, Shere. *The Hite Report.* New York, Macmillan Publishing Co., 1976.

Hyde, Janet Shibley, and Rosenberg, B. G., eds. *Half of the Human Experience: The Psychology of Women.* Lexington, Mass.: Heath & Co., 1976.

Javors, Irene, and Schwab, Charlotte. "In Feminist Therapy, It's Also 'Buyer Beware.'" *Majority Report,* June 12-25, 1976.

Keiffer, Miriam. Personal communication (1975-77) on the subject of conflict resolution in human sexuality.

Klaich, Dolores. *Woman + Woman: Attitudes Toward Lesbianism.* New York: Simon & Schuster, 1974.

Koedt, Anne. *The Myth of the Vaginal Orgasm,* 1970. Reprinted by KNOW, Inc., Box 86031, Pittsburgh, Pa. 15221.

Love, Barbara. "A Case for Lesbians as Role Models for Healthy Adult Women." Paper presented at the meetings of the American Psychological Association, Chicago, 1975.

Lowenhertz, Lila, and Sang, Barbara. "Personism: Towards the Elimination of Interpersonal Oppression." Paper presented at the meetings of the American Psychological Association, Chicago, 1975.

McDougall, Joyce. "Homosexuality in Women." In Signe Hammer, ed., *Women Body and Culture* (essays on the sexuality of women in a changing society). New York: Harper & Row, 1975.

Mannion, Kristiann. "Female Homosexuality: A Comprehensive Review of Theory and Research." *JSAS—Catalogue of Selected Documents in Psychology,* 1976, No. 6, MS 1247.

Miller, Jean Baker. *Toward a New Psychology of Women.* Boston: Beacon Press, 1976.

Morin, Stephen. "An Annotated Bibliography of Research on Lesbianism and Male Homosexuality (1967-1974)." *JSAS—Catalogue of Selected Documents in Psychology,* 1976, No. 15, MS 1191.

——. "Heterosexual Bias in Psychological Research on Lesbianism and Male Homosexuality." *American Psychologist,* 1977.

Nussdorf, Gerrie. "The Emerging Homosexual. Consciousness as the Basis for a Reappraisal of Homosexuality as a Diagnostic Category." Unpublished paper, 1971. Personal communication, 1977.

Oberstone, Andrea, and Sukoneck, Harriet. "Psychological Adjustment and Life Style of Single Lesbians and Single Heterosexual Women." *Psychology of Women Quarterly,* 1976. No. 2, pp. 172-88.

Posin, Robyn. "Transition: A Woman's Document." *Quadrille.* Bennington: 1975, Vol. 9, p. 13.

——. Selected poems (unpublished), 1975.

——. Correspondence, 1973-1977.

Rosen, David. *Lesbianism.* Illinois: Charles C. Thomas, 1974.

Rush, Anne Kent. *Getting Clear.* New York: Random House, 1973.

Saghir, Marcel, and Robins, Eli. *Male and Female Homosexuality.* Baltimore: Williams & Wilkins, 1973.

Sang, Barbara. "Psychotherapy with Lesbians—Some Observations and Tentative Generalizations." Paper presented at the meetings of the American Psychological Association, New Orleans, 1974. Also in Edna Rawlings and Dianne Carter, eds., *Psychotherapy for Women: Treatment Towards Equality.* Illinois: Charles C. Thomas, 1977.

Schwartz, Pepper. Department of Sociology, University of Washington. Personal communication, 1977.

Seaman, Barbara. *Free and Female.* New York: Coward, McCann & Geoghegan, 1972.

Shrifin, Francine. "Citations on the Subject of Lesbianism in the *Psychological Abstracts* (1950-1976)." Unpublished paper, 1977.

Thompson, Clara. "On Women." In Maurice Green, ed., *Interpersonal Psychoanalysis.* New York: Basic Books, 1964.

Trilling, Barbara. "Lesbianism and Its Relation to the Changing Social and Psychological Role of Women." Paper presented at the meetings of the American Psychological Association, 1975.

Vaughter, Reesa. "Review Essay—Psychology." *SIGNS* (Journal of Women in Culture and Society), 1976, No. 2, pp. 120-46.

Wolff, Charlotte. *Love Between Women.* New York: Harper & Row, 1971.

Finding Supportive Therapy

DOROTHY I. RIDDLE, Ph.D.

Like other persons, lesbians get depressed, confused, nervous, or unsure of themselves. Sometimes these are passing moods, and sometimes the moods persist. Sometimes the person needs no outside help, and sometimes she does.

Lesbians have particular difficulty getting appropriate professional help for personal problems. There are still relatively few lesbian therapists available, and heterosexual therapists have been socialized to be just as heterosexist[1] as other heterosexuals. The purpose of this article is to help lesbians become aware of the biases of professional therapists, the stresses in gay life that therapists often overlook or minimize, and what therapeutic alternatives are available.

THERAPIST BIASES

A therapist is a person with certain specific professional skills. Going to a therapist is like buying a friend. You are paying someone to be impartial, to be supportive, to help you identify options of which you may not be aware, and/or to help you learn particular skills for living. If you want a therapist to be helpful to you, you must be sure that you want help with something about which the therapist is an expert.

Differences Among Therapists

Professional therapists come in several different varieties: psychiatrists, psychoanalysts, clinical psychologists, psychiatric social workers, etc. The differences among these have to do both with training and with legal authority. Psychiatrists have a medical degree, plus a three-year residency in psychiatry. Psychoanalysts usually are psychiatrists who have then done training through a psychoanalytic institute. Clinical psychologists have a doctorate in psychology with special training in both therapy and psychological assessment (testing), plus a year's clinical internship. Psychiatric social workers have a degree in social work, with special training in therapeutic work.

Differences in legal authority have to do with medications, hospitalization, and confidentiality. Only therapists with a medical degree may prescribe medication or admit persons to psychiatric wards or institutions. Every therapist is bound by professional ethics to honor your confidence unless you give permission for information to be shared. However, whether or not your sessions are "privileged" communication—that is, your therapist may not be required, if subpoenaed, to testify without your permission—depends upon state statutes. In most states, therapists with medical degrees and clinical psychologists are covered by confidentiality statutes, while other kinds of therapists usually are not covered unless their discipline has lobbied successfully for coverage.

Therapeutic Orientation

The issue of "what causes lesbianism" is a crucial one in forming the orientation of the therapist. For example,

anyone trained in the medical model tends to be pathology-oriented and to view lesbians as sick persons to be cured. Or they may see homosexuality as genetically or endocrinologically determined, and therefore pity lesbians for not really having free choice. Anyone trained psychoanalytically tends to assume that problems are rooted in childhood and family pathology, and to view same-sex relationships as regressive or immature. Social-learning theorists assume that we learn same-sex or opposite-sex preference through role models or social reinforcement, and that anything that has been learned (i.e., lesbianism) can be unlearned. Thus, homosexuality can be seen as "just a phase" that we grow into and mature out of.

Most therapists assume the superiority of the monogamous heterosexual nuclear family life-style. Even therapists who want to be supportive of lesbians often take the position that "being gay is fine, but don't close out the option of heterosexuality." These therapists overlook the fact that heterosexuals are the ones who generally act without choices, since most lesbians are functionally bisexual. In addition, research shows that women who view themselves as "bisexual" are not nearly as well adjusted as those who feel comfortable being lesbians.

Many lesbians have pushed for homosexuality to be viewed as predetermined or unchangeable because that lowers the likelihood that therapists will push to change lesbians. However, seeing lesbianism as predetermined increases the likelihood that the therapist will be patronizing ("You poor dear, you've adjusted awfully well given the circumstances").

Research has found that homophobia[2] is most strongly correlated with a commitment to traditional sex roles, rather than to particular sexual attitudes or behavior. In other words, the "phobia" is a fear of the breakdown of traditional roles and the blurring of what it means to be a woman or a man, rather than a fear of same-sex sexuality. Thus, therapists' sexist assumptions— for example, that females are naturally more passive, less sexual, more nurturing, or less achievement-oriented than males—are as important a bias as their heterosexist assumptions. Liberal equal-rights therapists may still want women to be "real women" and men to be "real men," with all that that attitude implies.

Therapeutic Expertise

In general, therapists have expertise in discovering motives for actions, becoming aware of and dealing with complex emotions, developing self-esteem, and determining goals and values. Some therapists have specific areas of expertise—like sexual dysfunction, conflict resolution, depression, etc.

Very few therapists have any expertise in what life as a lesbian is like or what the particular issues and stresses are. They are often oblivious to, or naïve about,

---

[1] Heterosexism is a set of beliefs or attitudes holding that opposite-sex relationships are better than, more mature than, or to be preferred to same-sex relationships.

[2] Homophobia, an outgrowth of heterosexism, is the fear of same-sex intimacy.

the pressure on lesbians to either "pass for straight" or "come out" and risk the reactions of others. This constant stress is so much a part of everyday life that many lesbians forget about it. But stress is cumulative and may result in falling apart one day over what might seem like a trivial episode or issue.

THE STRESSES OF BEING A LESBIAN

"Coming out" is not a linear process. We come out to ourselves and others in bits and pieces all our lives. Coming out involves a highly personal series of choices, some of which are binding (e.g., coming out to your family) and some of which can be reversed (e.g., being affectionate on the street) and thus must be faced again and again. Every moment of the day one has to make new decisions about whether or not to risk being out in a particular situation:

- Are you smiling too intimately at your lover in the supermarket?
- Can you go repeatedly to a small lecture or concert series with your lover?
- Should you make sure to be seen in public with an eligible male?
- Can you hold hands at the movies?
- Can you afford to have people to your home and risk questions about your living arrangements?
- How affectionately can you kiss hello and good-bye at the airport?
- When others start talking about "those homos," should you intervene?

The fear of repercussions is constant and realistic. Because of the potentially high cost involved in coming out—for example, loss of job, housing, friends, family, children—the safest course is not to take risks. But that can result in a very tight, constrained feeling. If you feel that there is something about yourself that you cannot afford to reveal, you will constantly have to monitor your emotional responses and so will feel tense and on guard. It is hard to be enthused about yourself while feeling that, at the core, you have some basic flaw.

Coming Out to Yourself
The process of coming out to yourself is crucial to any real sense of self-worth. Because of the prejudice with which we all grow up, women may excuse each same-sex relationship as exceptional, or slide over the same issue with "so I've known I was queer since I was sixteen, so what?" or try to "go straight" because that's "what's natural." Sometimes coming out involves coming to terms with the life-style you have been living but have been ashamed of. Or it may involve facing and integrating your potential for relating intimately with women after years of heterosexual identity. Wherever you are coming from, you have to deal with all the stereotypes of lesbians: "Does this mean that I'm a man-hater/ unfeminine/immature/sinful/neurotic?"

Coming out to yourself means a total redefinition

of self. It means getting rid of socialized prejudices that women are less talented or interesting than men, and feeling good about being a woman. It means stepping outside the system of gaining respect and prestige by virtue of the man with whom you are identified, and being willing to be related to on your own merits. Affirming your lesbian identity also involves giving up social support for your relationships—giving up fantasies about being taken care of by a male, or planning your life around caring for a male.

Coming out means questioning societal norms and values and coming to terms with yourself separate from those expectations. For lesbians, in particular, this society is an alien place. We are bombarded with the heterosexual life-style in books, newspapers, television shows, movies, plays, etc. All of us need places where we can be accepted and affirmed as ourselves, totally ourselves, rather than being tolerated or feared or treated as invisible.

Being Closeted
If you are determined to remain very closeted, then a tremendous amount of energy gets tied up in the game of "who knows." Each interaction must be scrutinized for slipups, inadvertent indications that you are gay. You may find yourself settling for a secure, but unchallenging and eventually boring, position in order to avoid questions about your life-style. Each time there is a gay function, you must decide if you can risk being seen there. And, if you have any gay friends, you place yourself in double jeopardy because your identity becomes suspect if the friend becomes known as gay.

As a closeted lesbian, you must also endure being assumed to be a single, eligible female. Depending upon your age, this view may or may not be coupled with pity that you have not yet married or remarried. You will have to deal with friendly offers to "fix you up." You will have to find some solution to administrative entertainment obligations or business socializing—always going alone, inviting a willing male friend as an escort, or declining and seeming unsociable.

Being Openly Gay
On the other hand, if you decide to be open about your life-style, you will have other stresses to handle. You may feel more whole within yourself, but you will have to put up with others' homophobic responses to your life-style. You run a high risk of being related to stereotypically—"I'd rather you didn't stay alone with my children," "Why do you hate men?" "It's too bad you never had a good sexual relationship with a man," etc. Or you may be treated as a one-dimensional person, interested only in gay issues. And you will be constantly vulnerable to the hurt of finding out that previous friends or family members reject you for your life-style choice.

Probably the most difficult part about being openly gay is the fact that you then function as a kind of "Typhoid Mary." Any woman with whom you are seen, who is not obviously relating to a man, becomes automatically suspect. Any woman with whom you are lovers may be inadvertently "brought out at any time." Once you are out of the closet, it is very difficult to go back in and close the door after yourself!

Relationship Issues

A relationship between two persons who have been socialized to be nurturing, supportive, and (to some degree) emotionally intimate will be different from a relationship between a person who has been socialized to be nurturing and a person who has been socialized to be aggressive and dominant. Thus, heterosexual models are not appropriate for lesbian relationships because of the power patterns assumed. For lesbians, everything is up for grabs—which may be exciting, or may be very scary and demoralizing.

Each lesbian comes to the task of evolving nontraditional, interdependent patterns of relating from a slightly different place. If you have "made it" by being very aggressive and independent, you will have to struggle with how to share responsibility and be supportive of another's lead-taking. If you have accepted the conditioning to be more passive, you will need to learn to take initiative and assume appropriate responsibility for yourself.

Much of the jealousy attributed to lesbian couples comes from the fact that in so many settings the relationship cannot be acknowledged or validated. There is always the real threat that one partner may opt for a more socially acceptable relationship with a male simply in order to escape the stress of a closeted relationship. And so mutual trust becomes a critical issue. Developing a shared problem-solving, decision-making process is a challenging task. It is even more challenging if it must be done in the closet, squeezed in between work demands and family pressures.

Living with Children

When there are children involved, the stress becomes much more intense. You are constantly on guard so that custody will not be challenged, and continually worrying about what the children will say about the relationship. You also have the fear that the children may be embarrassed or avoided because of living in a nontraditional family situation. Many lesbians stay in heterosexual relationships and/or give up lover relationships simply so that they will not hurt or lose their children.

In addition, there is the issue of balancing a lover relationship and raising children. All parents face this, but gay parents are under particular strains. Because same-sex relationships are not condoned, the natural physical affection between lovers has to be artificially circumscribed.

Then, too, there are the tensions of working out child-care and discipline issues with the nonparental partner. There are no role models for gay families. Somehow adults and children must develop some description of the family constellation, and some viable relationship between the nonparental partner and the father of the children. Finding ways in which the family unit can enjoy itself publicly becomes a real challenge.

THERAPEUTIC ALTERNATIVES

When you are feeling vulnerable, depressed, or generally unable to cope, the last thing you want to do is to begin a tedious evaluation of the existing mental health resources in your community. Usually you are too upset to be thinking particularly clearly, and you want help immediately.

Kinds of Problems In deciding where to go for help, you need to have some idea of what the problem is and how it relates to your life-style. There are a number of general problems in living that may or may not be related to your life-style—for example, not feeling good about yourself; persistent uncomfortable emotions (e.g., depression, anxiety, phobias, etc.); situations that are particularly puzzling or stressful; or personal pattern changes that you wish to make.

Generally speaking, we begin to "break down" psychologically when we are not getting all of our personal needs met. One important self-help skill is to review the way in which you are spending your time: What kinds of activities are important to you? Are you getting each of these needs met each week? In what ways are you able to be "out" and be your whole self.

In a number of communities, lesbians have formed (with or without professional help) rap or support groups modeled on the feminist consciousness-raising groups. Support groups can be helpful in several different ways: as a place to ask questions and explore options regarding your life-style; as an environment where you can be your own self; as a place to examine your own fears and stereotypes about being gay; as a place to provide a sense of community and support.

If you feel you need more individual help, you may have the option of gay peer counseling through a gay service group or going to a gay therapist who has skills compatible with your problem. Remember that a traditional heterosexual therapist does not really have the expertise to be helpful with problems that stem from, or are related to, your life-style. However, a gay therapist who does not feel comfortable with her own life-style may not be of any more help. If you do go to a heterosexual therapist, you need to try to build in gay advocacy for yourself within that traditional therapeutic setting—that is, have another lesbian go with you or review with you what is being focused on in the sessions.

Resource Services

Several kinds of services have evolved to help you find support. One kind of service is the crisis line or switchboard (either general or gay in orientation). If you feel you must talk with someone immediately, a crisis service is usually your best bet since other services generally have an appointment delay. You can always make an appointment with a therapist to go into a problem in more detail once you have gotten some initial help or support from a crisis service.

There are also feminist and/or gay referral services which help clients find appropriate therapists. These referral services may or may not include providing paraprofessional help or advocacy. The information given by these referral services may be based on an individual's experience, or on having surveyed or interviewed all available therapists in the area. In making use of these services, you need to keep in mind that a therapist who is good with one individual may not be good with another. In addition, there are national organizations, like the Association of Gay Psychologists, that maintain a listing of gay therapists known to them.

Selecting a Therapist

Your task in selecting a therapist is to find someone who is good for *you*. In addition to making use of available referral services, you can ask friends, peers, and other professionals for suggestions. Then call up the person's office, read over any literature available about fees and services provided, and talk with the therapist about her/his approach. If you feel really uncomfortable anywhere along the line, then seriously reconsider.

Unfortunately, therapists usually are not trained to explain to lay persons what they do or to acknowledge that they have limits on what issues and with whom they work effectively. Rather, traditional therapeutic approaches depend upon the client perceiving the therapist as all-powerful and all-knowing. In addition, therapists usually are trained to believe that they, rather than the client, know best what the therapeutic issues are. Thus, any questioning on your part may be interpreted as resistance, running away from the "real" problem, acting out, etc.

Despite the professional pressure to be uncritical of the therapist you select, there are several factors to keep in mind. One of these is the sex of the therapist. If you go to a heterosexual male therapist, then you may run the risk of that man being very chauvinistic or not being able to resist the idea that you are gay because you haven't found "the man." Gay male therapists may also be chauvinistic, though they are likely to be more supportive than heterosexual males. Women therapists, especially those with some feminist awareness, are more likely to be helpful because they know what it is like to be a woman and are not as likely to denigrate women's issues. However, heterosexual women therapists may be very threatened by your life-style because of the implications for themselves.

When lesbian therapists are not available, heterosexual feminist therapists may be an excellent alternative, provided they have taken a look at their own homophobia and built in some kind of accountability. For example, do they have a group of lesbians with whom they consult about potential heterosexual bias? Are they in study groups about lesbianism and feminism? Are they open to, or do they encourage, an advocacy model—i.e., having a gay paraprofessional participate as your support? Will they pay you to spend a session educating them about your life-style?

If you want to do group work (bioenergetics, gestalt, etc.), be very wary of being the isolated gay person in a heterosexual group. Never underestimate the power of homophobia and never be naïve enough to think that it won't surface. You are very likely to find, at the very least, that you spend your energy helping others deal with their homophobia so that they are able to be supportive of you—a nice high, but it won't get you very far on your own issues, unless the issue is being accepted by heterosexuals.

SUMMARY

Given the present bias of our society, problems lesbians have are always somehow related to being gay because of the pressures around being "out." Most heterosexual therapists either are still oblivious to the realistic stresses of gay life or see gay life as pathological. Thus, as a lesbian you must decide whether the help you can potentially get from a heterosexual therapist is worth the price you are likely to pay in patronage or objectification (missed focus).

If you feel good about your life-style and have lots of support as a lesbian, then you may want to select the therapist who has the skills that will be most useful to you, regardless of sex or life-style. If you have questions or concerns relating to your life-style or your lover relationship, you may want to pick a gay paraprofessional over a heterosexual professional therapist if there are no gay professionals available. In any case, if you feel at all shaky because of your lesbianism, then you need to be very careful to build in gay support of some kind.

RESOURCES

"Off the Couch: A Woman's Guide to Therapy," by the Women and Therapy Collective, 1975. Goddard-Cambridge Graduate Program in Social Change, 5 Upland Road, Cambridge, Mass. 02140. 617 492-0700. $2.00

"Her attitude was that . . . I should 'put my sexuality in the refrigerator.' "

When I was about twenty I had a confrontation with my parents about my homosexuality. My parents' first reaction was how to protect the neighbors' daughter from me, and I found myself in a psychiatrist's office on Park Avenue. He said he would see me, under the condition that I give up my homosexual relationship. I knew that was an impossible thing for me to do. I guess my parents didn't know where else to turn. If I was twenty-one I must have signed my own commitment papers; if I wasn't, they probably did. That is kind of a blur. So I ended up in a mental hospital. There I found the atmosphere with my therapist supportive, and there were no conditions, and I could call my lover or see her.

As soon as my parents realized that the hospital would not be punitive, they moved me from that hospital to another. I remained there about six months. My psychiatrist was a Catholic woman. I feel very strongly that her Catholicism colored the way she looked at me as a patient. She felt homosexuality was a sin, that it was evil. That was her religious conviction. She told me she had driven to a beach and had seen two women there, obviously very fond of each other, touching each other. She had thought to herself, "What a sad thing it is to see these two women together." This was a very painful story for me because I fantasized all the time about all these billions of people who had the freedom to get on a subway, go to the beach, or even make a phone call, because I didn't have that freedom.

The first month or so at the second institution the issue of my homosexuality was not discussed. My lover hadn't the remotest idea of where I was, so that was a grave concern to me. I spent a great deal of my initial therapy trying to beat the system to sneak a letter out to her through another patient. I finally found a patient who would take the letter out, but she got nervous and on visiting day told my father she had a letter he should know about. The letter ended up back in the psychiatrist's hands. Her attitude was that I had had two lesbian experiences and "three strikes and you're out." Until I could get myself together I should "put my sexuality in the refrigerator"—that's the actual image she used.

There was nothing from her to help me see that being gay might be a way that I could live my life with dignity or any kind of pleasure. It never entered my mind that I might never go back to my lesbian relationship—I knew that's where I belonged and that's who I was. But I knew that was not my passport to getting out of the hospital. I got out by repressing not only my sexuality but rage for any feelings I felt might keep me there longer, so if I was feeling agitated or angry or depressed I did my best not to verbalize it with her. That's a very bad therapeutic situation, when you really are looking at the therapist as someone to get around, and cannot be honest with her.

I was told by my psychiatrist that most patients' records were public for the nurses to see, but that mine were private. I assumed that the reason why they had to be kept private was this really dangerous part of me—my homosexuality, which shouldn't be discussed. I felt I had no control over my release, other than to play the games that I thought I had to play with the therapist. It never entered my mind to stand up and say, "Wait a minute—I don't think I really belong here, and I'd like to get out."

There was one young woman my age in there for drinking problems, and she and I were wildly attracted to each other, and would sneak into the ladies' room—which of course had no doors—and kiss frantically for one second. We couldn't even go into our bedrooms and close the doors—we weren't allowed to have our doors closed. And we expended a great deal of energy on when we could see each other and have just fleeting moments of contact. When patients were well behaved, they could invite another patient over to tea. This was a big privilege and meant you were getting healthy. I wanted Sandy to have tea with me, and my psychiatrist said, "We're not going to honor your invitation because we don't feel the two of you should really see each other. This is not healthy." I think Sandy was also pretending to be straight so she could get out.

I think it would be very helpful to me if I could talk to another lesbian who had this same experience.

—Sarah

"Frankly, I was getting more out of tennis than the therapy."

Until I came out in my early thirties I thought lesbianism was a mental illness. When I was thirteen I developed a crush on the principal's daughter, and from then on I fell in love with a succession of girls, and then women, but never acted on my feelings. I felt starved—I had no interest in men, but since society expected it of me, I felt like a failure.

In college I finally hinted at my feelings to a psychologist I was seeing, but she said, "I don't think you're a homosexual. Homosexuals have a tendency to destroy each other." I felt relieved; there was "hope" for me.

When I was twenty-six, after fleeing from a relationship with a man who loved me and wanted to marry me, I decided to go into therapy to work through my "problems" with men. A psychoanalyst at the graduate school I was attending told me that my problem was deep-seated and would require several years of psychoanalysis involving four to five appointments a week. All of this made me feel terribly important, but I did not have the financial resources necessary to see a psychoanalyst four or five times a week for several years. I applied to the Psychoanalytic Institute for free therapy but was turned down, for what reason I could never learn. I then, in desperation, turned to my family for financial help, which they supplied reluctantly.

After two years of lying on the couch four nights a week, after all that investment of time and money, I had to admit to myself that I didn't feel any better about men than I felt when I had started. Meanwhile, I had started taking tennis lessons and had begun to experience a new freedom of movement with my body. I wanted to play tennis all year around—but couldn't afford to play indoors if I continued the therapy. So one day I screwed up my courage and walked into my analyst's office in my tennis shorts and proceeded to lie down on the couch and explain why I had decided to discontinue therapy. (Frankly, I was getting more out of tennis than the therapy.) He was really startled, and he even made the supreme gesture of saying, "Look, you can sit up; we can look at each other." But it was too late. I left for the tennis courts, crying all the way.

About a year later I entered therapy again, however, after fleeing from another relationship with a man who loved me. I felt I would just go on this way hurting people I didn't want to hurt. And I finally began to consider the possibility that I might accept my homosexual feelings and make the best of my "sickness."

So, I went to see a resident psychiatrist twice a week. And right from the beginning I told him I couldn't promise that I'd make a choice for men. He completely surprised me by saying, "I'm only here to help *you* find out what you want for yourself."

His comment really floored me, and I never forgot it. It was one of the best things anyone ever said to me. Looking back, I was so vulnerable and full of self-hatred then that I think if he had told me I had to walk the straight and narrow, I would have continued that useless pursuit.

I did continue to see men, but when the opportunity came up in my life to get close to another woman, I was more open to it on some level—even though I felt it was 90 percent unthinkable! When I finally did begin to get involved with a woman, my psychiatrist reacted warmly—not with analytic distance. He smiled, and he said, "You seem very happy." And I could see that he was actually *happy for me.* I cried and cried. I opened up in my therapy and I began to feel love instead of resentment for him. He was not going to deprive me of the first real relationship with a woman that I'd had in my life, after starving all these years.

Through the lesbian and gay movements I began to question the "mental illness" theory about homosexuality and to realize that a majority of the people *can* be wrong. I saw that what was being passed off as "mental health" was a hoax, and that gay love was perfectly healthy and normal. What had been abnormal, for me and for millions of others, was the stifling of our feelings of love for other women, in the name of mental health.

—Ginny

4. Sexuality

Making Love*

I. HASTE MAKES WASTE (OR TIME WELL SPENT)

The degree of arousal in many women is enhanced by ample foreplay. For most women, foreplay is as important or more important than that ecstatic moment which usually culminates the sexual experience. Holding, hugging, talking, stroking and kissing have always been pointed out as very important from the female point of view, possibly because it relates so directly to the intensity of the sexual climax.

Women usually find that foreplay is a wonderful sensual experience since orgasm can occur at any time and having more than one orgasm is not uncommon. The timing of each person's climax is strictly up to the women making love, so the possibilities for activities prior to and after climax are limitless. In fact, climax can be viewed as a very pleasant addition to the many nice vibrations generated during lovemaking.

Obsession with orgasm can reduce the enjoyment of the sensuousness of sharing another woman's body. There's no need to hurry; relax, enjoy and share all delightful sensations with each other. Linger on what feels good and move on if something is not a turn-on.

*Exerpted from *Loving Women*, by the Nomadic Sisters. Copyright © by the Nomadic Sisters, 1976.

Women have a distinct advantage when making love with other women since they already are aware of their own erogenous areas. Don't assume, however, that what is exciting for you will also be exciting for your partner. Watch for her reactions carefully. Ask her to tell you what feels good; tell her what feels good to you.

Usually, foreplay is thought of as actual touching, but there are other possibilities that should be mentioned before touching. Since sexual excitement is so closely associated with a person's state of mind, any of the following activities could enhance the sharing and enjoying that women feel during sexual play.

Dancing can be part of foreplay or might be the activity which starts the two of you toward the bedroom in the first place. Close dancing, clothed or nude, can be very stimulating. Rubbing breasts together or fondling them, pressing and rubbing pubic areas or cupping her buttocks and pushing her pubis against yours are all tried and true ways of sexually exciting a partner and yourself. If you are nude, you could just go from a standing to a prone position and carry on into other lovemaking techniques. We wouldn't suggest this on a crowded dance floor, however, unless your social group is extremely liberated.

Undressing each other or for each other can be a nice way to begin an evening. There is something much more erotic about another person unbuttoning your clothes, releasing your breasts or slowly pulling down your pants than going through this daily routine yourself. Having your friend watch, however, while you undress with the intent of exciting her can be very sensual and you both can fantasize about what is going to happen once you are nude.

Since women are usually concerned about cleanliness during sexual play, the bath and bathroom activities can be incorporated into foreplay. Even a kiss or a hug becomes something special when water is added. Shower or bathe together, taking turns slowly soaping one another or washing each other's hair. Be particularly attentive when soaping breasts, buttocks and the insides of thighs. But be careful about strong soaps against the sensitive vulva tissue or around the anus since they can burn and irritate.

If you have a hand-held shower head, you may want to bring your partner to her first climax by holding her while playing the water around her clitoris.... But *never shoot water up the vagina.* In the bathtub you can sit facing one another, pressing your vulvas together and playing water on both of you at once....

Spend some time drying each other, powdering, applying lotion and playing with one another's hair. Combing and brushing her hair can be extremely pleasant for her. Massaging her scalp or playing your hair over her body can both be very sensual.

Reading pornography together or to each other, listening to erotic or romantic music, reading poetry, looking at erotic pictures or photographing one another (a Polaroid is really helpful here) can all be sexually stimulating for you both. If you are particularly courageous, you might want to attend an erotic movie prior to lovemaking. We have found that all of the above can be very exciting foreplay for women.

Touching is one of the nicest things two people can do together. Massaging and/or stroking are pleasant ways to relax each other. We would differentiate between full body massage and stroking, however, since the intent of a complete massage is total relaxation and peace. Therefore, "real massage" using one of the many fine manuals available as a guide is probably an end in itself rather than a foreplay method. A full massage after lovemaking may be a good way to end an evening. Or if orgasm is not in the cards that night, massage might be just the ticket for her well-being and happiness.

We will define touching as anything which feels good. You can rub, knead, pinch, stroke, drag, slap, press, push or tickle any part of your friend's body and she yours. The neck, back, buttocks, inner thighs and breasts are all good places to start; but move quickly to another area if your partner indicates by her reaction that she is not enjoying what you are doing, or might enjoy something else more. Leave her wanting just a little more of what you're doing rather than keeping one thing going so long that it gets boring. Try giving her three sensual wishes in which she can send you to any area of her body with whatever touching techniques she chooses. Don't be surprised if you end up rubbing her buttocks, sucking her toe or biting an earlobe. Then again, she may be so aroused that she sends you directly to her clitoris and vagina and you will know that foreplay has come to a successful conclusion.

Stimulating your lover's breasts may be wonderful foreplay since some women seem to have a wire between their breasts and clitoris. Kiss and nuzzle all parts of her breasts. Suck them gently, then harder if she enjoys hard sucking and pulling. Take as much as you can get in your mouth then slowly pull it out, holding onto the nipple as long as possible. Lick and flick one nipple with your tongue while gently fingering the other. If her breasts are large, press them together while sucking and licking both nipples or go quickly from one to the other.

We have gone into some detail about breast play not because we necessarily favor this area, but because we wish to provide an example of extensive foreplay involving one body part. You might find that your friend feels especially erotic about her ears or having her back bitten or being tickled with feathers. The key is to find each other's special buttons and push them in as many different ways as the two of you can dream up.

II. GOING DOWN, DOWN, DOWN . . .

Oral sex is a common method of lovemaking between women. The use of the mouth and tongue on the genitals is not only soft and warm but very intimate. Participating in oral sex is an affirmation that the genital area is beautiful and sensitive, responsive and healthy.

The "missionary position" of oral sex is one in which one partner is on her back; the other is on her stomach between her partner's spread legs. Choose the most comfortable moment for both of you during foreplay to move into this position. Approach the genital area gradually with kisses to her breasts, stomach, navel, and then the vulva. Move your body down hers as you kiss.

The following description is from your point of view as the woman who is "going down." In no way does this imply that the role of your partner is one of passivity. She should feel free to move about, make noise, tell you what feels best, move your head or indicate if she would prefer another position.

So there you are in the missionary position—what next?

You're now in a perfect place to put into play all those techniques that you've been enjoying everywhere else during foreplay. Kiss, nibble and tongue the entire area from the navel to mid-thigh. Spend some time on this.

Add an element of surprise—don't let her know where you'll touch her next. At this point, if your lover wishes she could reach down and part her pubic hair for you. Or you may do this yourself with your fingers or tongue. The experience is subtly different with each of these variations.

Touch the lips of her vulva with your lips. Very gently slide your moistened tongue up from the bottom of the entrance to the vagina to the clitoris. Try exhaling slowly throughout this journey; the warm air is a delicious sensation. Now create: Move your moistened tongue all over this inner area, trace the outline of the lips, circle the clitoris, tease the vagina by gently inserting your tongue, then withdrawing to circle its entrance. (There may be plenty of moisture at this point. If not, make it your responsibility to keep the area wet with your tongue.) Run the flat of your tongue up each side of the lips of the vulva. Always keep the pressure light; depend on your partner to indicate if she wants it increased. She should feel free to take hold of your head at any time to express a need for any difference in pressure or more attention to a specific area.

Responding to your own inclinations and her reactions, you might begin concentrating on the clitoris. Lightly suck the clitoris, run your tongue around the edge of it, suck the sides, lick it all over. Rotate your moistened lips around and over the whole area. Hold her labia together while you insert your tongue against her clitoris. Dart down to the vagina, slip your tongue in, then quickly move back to the clitoris. Spend time with all of these. Move from one to the other and back again.

Your partner may need constant stimulation of the clitoris using one of these methods (or any other you devise) for quite a period of time before she reaches orgasm. So narrow your attention on the clitoris to one (or two) movement pattern(s) which seem to be most pleasurable for her. Be careful not to overstimulate the clitoris (too much pressure can be painful). Watch for clues—she may move her body more with one stimula-

tion, she may moan or take hold of your head, she may become perfectly still in concentration or she just may tell you what she enjoys the most.

These same clues can be a signal that she is approaching orgasm. What happens then is unique for each woman. You may recognize that she is experiencing it or you may be completely unaware until afterwards. She may not want any more stimulation and move away. She may push you away or pull you closer, enclosing you between her legs. She may thrash around so violently that you need to hold on to maintain your contact. Any response should not be considered unusual. A woman may scream, cry, laugh, moan, sigh—or remain silent with only her facial expression to let you know. And don't be surprised at anything she might say.

The missionary position is but one way to enjoy oral sex. The "69" position with both partners performing oral stimulation while on their sides or with one on top of the other is quite common. Mutual orgasm in this position is certainly possible and for some may be a very high experience. It has, though, all the pitfalls of other attempts at mutual orgasm; namely, it is awfully hard to concentrate on stimulating her while you are feeling the overwhelming pleasure of her mouth on you. We heartily recommend this position for those couples who can keep their minds on two things at once.

Lying on your back while your lover straddles your face is very effective since it allows an excellent angle for watching each other. It also offers more involvement for the woman on top because she can slide up and down on your tongue and easily move her clitoris into positions that excite her. In addition to the positions previously mentioned, you might extend your legs over the edge of the bed while your partner kneels on the floor; lean against or sit upon a stool or countertop while she kneels or leans to get into position.

Don't be hesitant to introduce other devices or techniques in combination with all of the described positions. If your friend enjoys vaginal stimulation, she may transcend higher and higher with the combined stimulations.

Other things need to be mentioned about oral lovemaking. The clitoris must be stimulated for most women to experience orgasm, but contact directly on the clitoris such as biting or banging it with your teeth could quickly reduce her passion.

Some women have an aversion to the smell, taste, wetness and, in some cases, the idea of such intimate contact. If you experience these feelings, you should let your partner know since few things can cause as much conflict in bed as one person wanting another to do something she is not eager to do. Try to deal with whatever is upsetting to either of you or choose to use another method.

If one partner really wants oral stimulation and the other is willing to work through her hesitations, they can try several suggestions.

Since the female genital area includes the urethra and anus, we would recommend a careful cleansing of the area before she goes down on you. There are also creams and other items that can be rubbed on the vaginal area which will change the smell and taste of the sexual juices. (Commercial "love potions" are sold in pornography stores and head shops, and "feminine sprays" sold in drug stores; but until we know what chemicals they actually contain, we are reluctant to recommend their use.) Some foods such as yogurt, whipped cream, honey and liqueurs can be placed on the vulva and licked or eaten off, but towels might be in order. Honey, in particular, may taste good, but it turns into a very sticky situation for the person on whom it is used.

The amount of sexual wetness women experience varies from dryness to a constant flow and both types may distract from the pleasure. A lubricating jelly or saliva can be used if she is dry; in the case of a very wet lover, you may wish to insert a thumb or other item into the vagina during oral stimulation. The wetness is, however, very stimulating for some and rubbing it over your friend's body may be a real turn-on for both of you. The pH (acid-alkaline) balance of her juices may be irritating to your skin and we would recommend washing your face after oral contact if dry skin or the lingering sexual smell is a problem for you.

However, there are many women who view their odor as natural and basic. We applaud this fact and support a continuing protest against the trip that the multi-million dollar feminine spray industry is trying to lay on us.

Since oral sex is probably the most intimate method you will use, it is essential that you listen carefully to each other's feelings concerning oral contact (or any other sexual techniques). Open communication and mutual caring are paramount in a good sexual relationship. A sense of fun and humor is also essential in all your lovemaking, because sex *is* fun! Taking lovemaking too seriously can lead to anxious or unhappy bed partners, a situation not quite compatible with the joyous, free attitude we hope surrounds your sexual activities.

III. GIVE THE LADY A HAND . . .

Making love with your hands is as easy and enjoyable as masturbating and many of the techniques described above will work beautifully with a partner. A common position is lying side by side while one or both use any or all of the following methods.

A slow stroking and fingering of your lover's entire vulva combined with short visits to her clitoris should put the wheels in motion. At this point, gentle circling, lifting or easy pinching of the clitoris is probably most effective while increasing the pressure and speed of your movement as she moves toward orgasm.

Pinching the lips of the vulva together and rubbing the clitoris between them can be quite pleasant. Shaking her pubis with the heel of your hand while fingering her clitoris or vagina or a gentle shaking of the clitoris and the skin around it can result in full orgasm.

Too much attention or a heavy touch may over-stimulate the clitoris. If this should happen, go back to stroking and gentle fingering, perhaps concentrating on the vagina until she wants you to return to her clitoris.

You can kneel beside her and stimulate the clitoris with one hand and the vagina with the other. This position is effective because you can coordinate a simultaneous pushing and pulling motion against the vagina and the clitoris.

Vary the two-handed technique by lying on top of her while you move your fingers in and out of her vagina. Total body contact can also be increased by positioning her on her front or on her hands and knees with you entering from the rear using both hands or by holding her close with one while stimulating her vulva with the other. This position offers a good angle for pushing your thumb in and out of her vagina while fingering her clitoris, and perhaps gently massaging her anus.

She can also straddle you while you lie on your back and work her clitoris and vagina against your fingers and pubic bone. Sitting in chairs, standing and kneeling are all positions that you and your partner can incorporate in your lovemaking.

Some women lie on top of their lover and rub the vulva area against the pubic bone until orgasm occurs. Lying between each other's legs with full contact of both genital areas (X position) can be stimulating because the position permits rubbing and pulling against each other with the possibility of simultaneous orgasm. Probably the best advice on the positions you choose is to try these, try your own and if they feel good, use them!! They all lend themselves to foreplay and could all lead to orgasm.

Introducing implements such as vibrators or dildos into your lovemaking could be a marvelous addition to all the other things you are doing. For some it can pose the threat of needing an "outsider" for sexual satisfaction, but the stand we take is that *anything that is safe and adds to a woman's enjoyment should be explored as a viable possibility.*

Dildos can be hand-held, strapped on to free the hands or used in combination with oral sex, the hands, or vibrators for vaginal stimulation. These and other implements must feel comfortable and one woman's pleasure could be another woman's pain. Check on the size of your partner's vagina with your fingers first and be sure to use a lubricant if there is any chance that the dildo won't slide in easily. We would also suggest watching what you are doing since in this case you can't let your fingers do the walking. (Besides, watching can be a real turn-on.)

The angle of penetration should be performed with the same care you would take when inserting your fingers or a tampon. Since the first third of a woman's vagina is the most sensitive to pleasure *and* pain, asking her to help the first time may be the best solution.

The last point we wish to mention is to exercise loving care when using implements. Keep in mind how easily vaginal infections can be transmitted and take greater care if there is any chance of sharing one of these common but irritating bugs.

We wish to reiterate our recommendation for enjoying all those things which feel good to you and your partner. Uptightness or moral judgment regarding any technique that is enjoyed by women can only add to the already long years of sexual oppression of women.

RESOURCES

Loving Women, by the Nomadic Sisters, 1976. Copies are available from The Nomadic Sisters, P.O. Box 793, Sonora, Calif. 95370, for $3.75 plus 50¢ postage and handling. California residents add 6% sales tax.

"Dyketactics," a film on lesbian love-making by Barbara Hammer. 4 min., color, sound. Rental $20 ($10 for women's groups); sale $100. Order from Multi-Media Resource Center, 1525 Franklin St., San Francisco, Calif. 94209. 415 673-5100.

"We Are Ourselves," a National Sex Forum Film on lesbian love-making by Ann Hershey. 15 min., color, sound. Rental $35, sale $200. Order from Multi-Media Resource Center (see above).

The Joy of Lesbian Sex, by Emily L. Sisley, Ph.D., and Bertha Harris, Crown Publishers, 1977. $12.95.

What Lesbians Do, by Godiva, 1975. Order from Amazon Reality, P.O. Box 95, Eugene, Oregon 97401. $4.50.

Liberating Masturbation: A Meditation on Self-Love, by Betty Dodson, 1974. Order from Betty Dodson, Box 1933, New York, N.Y. 10001. $3.50.

Lesbian Love and Liberation: The Book of Sex, by Del Martin and Phyllis Lyon, 1973. Multi-Media Resource Center, 1525 Franklin St., San Francisco, Calif. 94109. 415 673-5100. $1.95 (first class add 40¢)

The Hite Report, by Shere Hite, Macmillan, 1976. Note especially the chapter on "Lesbianism."

"The sensation was so new and wild that I had a very sudden climax."

I felt I was the only lesbian in Des Moines, and I finally moved to Iowa City with the express purpose of either coming out or trying to compromise something. I went into therapy, and took my mother's advice and tried men first. It was "so-so"! I ran across a woman who seemed to be coming on to me and I found myself coming on to her. We began to have feelings for each other, but she was not very far out—she'd had a couple of minor experiences, and I had no experience with women.

We got to the point where we would get more

affectionate—we would hug, and the hugs got longer. One night we started kissing each other on the cheek and our mouths brushed together for half an instant. I was afraid. I'd never kissed a woman like that before. We finally slept together. Neither of us had any idea what we would do. It's strange to come out with someone who is also coming out, but it's also very sweet and spontaneous.

Neither of us had any expectations, except that we both knew we wanted to please each other. After a very jittery dinner together we began to hug and kiss and I confessed I had been so nervous that day that I had taken *two* baths; she told me she was so scared, she had taken *three*! That broke the ice. We began to undress each other slowly. I was shaking like a leaf. I wasn't sure what to do and so began to do just what I wanted to do. There she was, naked and she wanted me—I began to touch and stroke her all over—especially her breasts and parts I had never been able to touch before—Jesus, after twenty-six years! We kissed and touched for some time and then I got on top of her. We moved our bodies together (the clinical term is "tribadize") and she was quite receptive to that.

I fell to her side and began to explore her with my hands. She told me earlier she had never had an orgasm; I manipulated her clitoris very gently, put my fingers inside of her, following the same rhythmic patterns she was doing with her body. She moved around quite a bit, reminding me of ocean waves. She would slow down and then start up again. At one point her breathing changed and her face tensed up but then it stopped. She said, "I think that was *it*," but I noticed she still wanted to move around and her clitoris was not that sensitive to my touch. It is, you know, immediately after a woman has had an orgasm. We let it go at that, temporarily. She made love to me, next, in the same way. Her hands explored, it was really nice! We did this all night long and on the second time around, when I again made love to her, all of a sudden her breathing got very heavy, almost panting, and she began to moan. I knew, I just *knew* she was coming—she gasped, "Oh, my God—what is *that*!" and I said, "That's *it*, honey!" She went off like a rocket. . . .

We were very pleased that not only had we brought each other out, but she had experienced her first orgasm. It was very rewarding for both of us. Oddly enough, I did not have an orgasm that night. I had experienced them before, both in masturbation and with men. They came to me easily, from the beginning. Ironically, before this affair, I had been trying to repress my sexuality, with the help of the University of Iowa's Hospital Outpatient Clinic. The shrinks had kindly given me a prescription for Stelazine. One week before we first slept together, I had thrown out my pills, but the pills were still in my system, so I was not able to experience orgasm for about a week into the affair.

The Midwest is not the best place, I have found, to learn about oral sex. Most of the midwestern dykes I've run across are into digital sex. I experimented with oral sex, but I didn't know what I was doing and there was no one to teach me. The first time I had an orgasm with oral sex, my lover and I were in a motel and she was exploring down there. She accidentally managed to cover my clitoris with her mouth and slightly stroked it with her tongue. It was a *weird* feeling, like some sort of "liquid force" was enveloping me, and the sensation was so new and wild that I had a very sudden climax.

I never really got into oral sex until I came East. Lucky for me, the first woman I ran into here had a Ph.D. in the Oral Arts. She knew *all* the strokes—and I learned them from her. I learned that not only could I do all sorts of innovative things when I went down on a woman, but I could stay down there almost indefinitely. I could use any number of different tongue-strokes, patterns, etc., and penetrate inside with my tongue. I love oral sex—I like doing it to other women and I enjoy being gone down on, too, especially by someone who knows what she is doing; that will send me into space faster than anything else!

I think the fourth lover I had in the Midwest was probably unique in sexual history. She was a woman who, when she reached the point of orgasm, fainted. (Fortunately she told me about it ahead of time: I would have had a nervous breakdown otherwise.) She liked to be penetrated, even to the point where I could get my whole hand inside her, and she would get so worked up, just go crazy, almost. She would reach the point of orgasm and right in the middle of coming, she would just go limp! She would pass out completely. I knew what was happening so I would just hold her, caress her, and wait for her to come to, in about thirty seconds.

This woman was married and supposedly "straight." She had to out-and-out proposition me before I was going to touch this straight, married woman. We got into bed and I was all ready to show her the ropes, you know, the "big butch" act. I was on top of her when she suddenly pitched me off, rolled me over on my back, and began to make love to me. I said, "Wait a minute. I'm supposed to be bringing *you* out—let me go first and show you." She stuck her lower lip out and said, "*I* want to go first!" I said, "Oh . . . okay." She was quite good for someone who'd never slept with a woman before. She likes to initiate things; she always "goes first."

On my thirty-first birthday, I had a brief affair with a woman who was quite a good lover and she and I discovered that I was able to have multiple orgasms. She was good with her hands; also with oral sex and she knew how to combine them. I had been curious about anal sex before I met her and had discovered, through masturbation, that I could experience orgasm by inserting a tiny vibrator into my anus. I found that the sensations caused me to feel excited. I had thought only men could have anal orgasms, and then *I* had one; I liked it and told my new lover about it. She did something to me that I really dug; first, she went down on me and, at the same time, put three or four fingers inside of me, then she took her other hand and inserted one finger into my anus. So there were three things going on at

once and there I was, all plugged up. Talk about an orgasm!

After that, she withdrew her fingers, but did not take her mouth from my clitoris: She stayed stock-still for a minute, and then very slowly, gently, began to manipulate my clitoris with her tongue, again. I thought, "Oh, I won't be able to *bear* this." I was always very sensitive in that area after climaxing. I wondered if I was going to be able to ride out the feeling of irritation in the clitoral area and, sure enough, within a minute the irritation passed and I went right back up, again. And again, and again!

Anal sex seems a freaky thing at first. One lover went even a step further. One time she was constipated and I teased her about giving her an enema. She became serious and I realized that she wanted me to, and the idea turned her on! I was a bit freaked, but I bought a baby-enema syringe and, following the instructions, gave her an enema. She really got off on it, sensually. There's a word for that: It's called "klismaphilia," which is a sexual love of having enemas. I let her give me one one time, but I don't have these feelings back. It feels slightly uncomfortable to me, although not totally unpleasurable.

There have been a couple of women in my life who were into dancing. That can be very sexual and I had one unique experience with a woman on the dance floor. She was a sexy dancer and knew how to manipulate her body against mine. Suddenly I found myself experiencing a light orgasm.

I don't feel that someone should do anything she doesn't feel comfortable doing. I don't like to "trick"—I enjoy getting to know a woman first. I like a bit of courtship. I have never gone home with a woman I have met the same night, and rarely anyone I've seen only once or twice. The one time I came closest to a "trick" was such a bad experience that I was glad to go in the morning.

I enjoy being with a woman who knows how to use her hands and fingers, all silky-smooth and gentle—I don't like people to be rough with their hands. I enjoy lots of affection and cuddling, tons of foreplay. I appreciate, most of all, a woman who knows how to go down on me. No matter what my state of mind, even if I were dead, I think I could have an orgasm if she goes down on me and knows what to do.

Once in a while, I might get into a 69 position, but it's not a comfortable position for me, top or bottom, or sides, even. I find it hard to concentrate on what I am doing when I am being done at the same time. Just once, though, I was able to break through that and come at the same time my partner came.

I have also initiated a situation where the other woman knelt and I slipped my head underneath her—I don't "go down" on her, she "comes down" on me. I can't do that back, though. I have trouble sitting up, or kneeling, or standing when someone is making love to me—I just get spacy and fall over. One lover went down on me while we were in the shower together, and I fell over in the tub. I can't have an orgasm if I am not lying down. Once or twice I tried to see if I could get through sex trying to lie perfectly still. It is virtually impossible for me.

I know that I had no problems with sex or orgasms at all, once I came out. I didn't even know people *had* trouble with orgasms until I met a woman who did. I have just not had any hang-ups about it, except when I finally make love with a woman that I have wanted for a long time (months, or even years) I may find myself so worked up that I can't come.

I will use a vibrator now and then, if someone wants me to. I don't prefer them. I much prefer to make love with my own parts. I have a vibrator I utilize for masturbatory purposes, both externally and internally. I have found, though, that I cannot use it every day as it tends to "numb me out." If I used a vibrator, say, and found myself later that day in a sexual situation, I would not be as intensely aroused as I might be, and I might not even experience an orgasm. I use it sparingly. Once every few days is enough.

One thing I employ in my lovemaking is massage, sensual and sexual. I give back rubs before and/or after sex. If I am rubbing her back I may begin to not only rub, but kiss and stroke it, too. I like to take my tongue and, starting at the base of the spine, very lightly brush the tongue over the fine, small hairs along the backbone and run up the entire length to the neck. One of my ex-lovers said, "I like this better than sex!" Unfortunately for me, she did! Massage and back rubs are good ways to start foreplay and make nice afterplay, too. It's a fine way to help someone come down and go to sleep.

Most anything a woman wants me to do, with the exception of S&M, all she has to do is say what she wants and I will say, "Your command is my wish!" and do it. I love the way women look when I am making love to them: the way their faces look, the way they tense up before orgasm, the way they move their bodies, the noises they make; God, they're beautiful. . . .

—Karol

Excerpt from *Sita**

KATE MILLETT

I had brought her daffodils, poking about the little wooden cart in front of the flower shop on Solano, wondering what I could get for the cash I had with me,

*This passage is excerpted from *Sita*, by Kate Millett, with the permission of Farrar, Straus and Giroux, Inc. Copyright © 1976, 1977 by Kate Millett. The book is about the end of a love affair. Ed.

realizing only gradually that it was Valentine's Day. Sentimental crap of course. Feeling a bit silly as I carried them up to the front door, then completely disarmed by the delight in her face. "How yellow they are, Kate, how much like spring!" The spirit of the day takes over, asserts itself against all better judgment, all hanging back. "I have something for you too, dear lady," she sings at me, brandishing a champagne bottle. Silver paper, great pink ribbon, she has been to Barber and Stewart, had it gift-wrapped. All for me. She has remembered. What if I hadn't absentmindedly bought those daffodils? She would have beaten me at what I had thought was my game.

But it is hers tonight as well. She has become the benevolent dictator, the fairy godmother. We'll have dinner at the Marina, she says, celebrate. The lift of her at times like this, the call in her eyes, in the movement of her head. First we'll have a drink, wait till the sunset is just ripe before we watch it across the water. "The champagne now?" "No, let's save it for later; when we come back we'll build a fire, drink it before we go to bed." Something's up. Suddenly she is all romance, witchery, good fortune. Mellow the talk, the mood, the fine evening; like the past come back. She is restored to me in states, in a glance, in a smile, in the full warm brown of her eyes. I do not want to believe but I feel myself sliding, persuaded. At dinner she is flirtatious, saying again that she does not want to lose me, her eyes full on me, the power of them open and compelling. I am being called, beckoned, even pleaded with. She is courting me from across the table, with a look or a smile or a joke, with teasing and reminiscing, with the flattering recall of a detail, an occasion, a friend.

The lilt of her at times like this, the call in her eyes, in the movement of her head. The pleading nearly in those fine brown eyes, the pathos of this aging and beautiful woman asking me not to leave her. "It's that I never felt or, rather, never felt before that you had any respect for me." "Sita, don't be absurd." "It's true. You never gave me the feeling that I was worth anything in your eyes." Maneuvers, I think, of course she must know how I admire her in everything, I have told her so a thousand times. And she has even used it against me. "I had to make you respect me." "You have only made me miserable." "Until this time, until you came out here this time, I've never been anything more than a shadow in your life, tagging along, someone in the background." "That's ridiculous." "It's how I feel. It's how I've always felt." I look at the great beauty in her eyes, the utter sincerity, the unimpeachable conviction. All completely of the moment, all true, all false. She has persuaded herself of this during the past five minutes and believes it completely. Five minutes ago or hence, she will be imperious again, mouthing speeches about her freedom, or full of sentiment, persuading me that what we suffer now is merely a moment in our long relationship, a mere segment in the band of time that unites us, will unite us always, each passage like a pattern in a bolt of cloth,

now one color, now another, now a leaf, now an arabesque, now a flower or a hill. "We have come to a very wonderful place in our relationship," she goes on. "We have come to a point of struggle where all the initial conflicts had to explode, be resolved. We will be more equal now, we've reached a point of separateness, independence. We've grown up in a sense." "I have no more expectations," I tell her, afraid even to say this, controlling the bitterness and the soreness of what I say. But she does not hear me, telling me again how deeply she loves me, the one great passionate love of her life.

There is no resisting her eyes, the softness of her voice, its little thrill of an accent speaking a word, softening it, making it intimate, nearly as intimate as the Italian words she used to say making love to me—*"tesoro bello," "ti voglio bene,"* the most intimate sounds I had ever heard. I even forgot that she no longer says them. Listening to her now, the gesture of her throat courting me, the liquid of her eyes pleading or snapping into the flirtation of wit, the coaxing of her humor, her mischievousness. Even her infidelities are proofs of her love; ploys, sleights, gestures to strengthen the fiber of this wonderful creation that lies between us.

We are at our old place on the Marina, Solomon Grundy's, with the sea and the city spread out beyond the glass walls, the gulls sweeping, the last sailboats hurrying home, their great wings brushing by our windows. Beauty of sky, sea, the lights of the bridges, and the city. This is our place, we are at home, each great moment of our affair played out somehow, echoed against this scene which is as much Sita as it is itself. She who is always California for me. If I should lose it . . . a tear stinging the thought. But before me now her whole self dedicated to the idea of retrieving me. Yes, I have expectations. "There's a Persian proverb I'll tell you when we're comfortably installed in front of the fire," she says.

Just as I light the fire, New York interrupts us with a quarrel and a petition, long, convoluted prose recited over three thousand miles of telephone wire and demanding immediate attention: prisoners and denunciations, informers and accusations, arrests, positions of principle. I want very much to say, "Look, I just happen to be busy making love now and cannot quite enter your mood." But I don't say it; no one ever does.

After this, the peace of the fire and the room and our quietude. We have hours to make love. Leisure. I will wait and let her seduce me, sitting back from the flames on a low stool next to the red Chinese table, watching the fire, sipping champagne as, gradually, by the slowest and most insidious of motions, her hand winds its way up the full sleeve of my gown. It is so deliberate, so agreed upon, so assured. The entire evening is prelude only to this moment, pledged to it, all preparation and diplomacy toward this consummation. Our talk is only a summons to this actualization.

Remembering how she took me sitting down, sitting on a low stool, her hand reaching under my long skirt, entering me as I sit. Legs apart, perched forward but still sitting. The little straw stool, drumlike, made of string and bamboo, curiously and elaborately fashioned over a straw frame. Pakistani, fruit of one of our enchanted shopping sprees at the import houses of San Francisco, on fine mornings two years ago when I first furnished my apartment in Sacramento, the great luxurious weekend visits of our first love, rapt hours of lovemaking at the Sausalito Hotel. Now the fire and her figure crouched on the floor next to me, her hand searching, reaming, digging within me. Somehow it is particularly exciting that I sit, that I am sitting just above her as she reclines on the rug, her arm extending up inside me. Sitting. The frisson of perversity in it. Forcing myself almost to go on sitting, which is difficult. So excited I am, so much I long to sprawl on the floor under her so she may hover above me, nearly mount me, and my legs flung wide and open. But sitting still, or if not still, yet maintaining myself on the little stool through the pure ecstasy of her explorations, her little touches, her experiments, her caresses, her attacks. Those long, strong fingers plunging into me, then withdrawn to hang about the lips of love, the small bud of clitoris erect, swollen, full almost to crying out. And still upon this little stool, this curious sedate little chair, gasping into her mouth, take me, take me, our tongues crowding into each other, divine intercourse each its penis and protrusion, or turn about, womb and cave-like the mouth arches and waits the other's tongue, pleading and prodding to fill, overwhelm.

Still perched upon the little stool. And finally can bear no more confinement but must have the floor, the great red Persian under me and the fire before me as I groan under her full thrusts, having quietly slid the stool away, slowly surrendering the strange gratification it gave, its limits and discipline. Now for the full open force of her, the full stretch of my legs, buttocks tense and taut as they raise me against her terrible entry, its power and fire. Hot you have made me, so hot, I whisper. Her tongue in my ear for answer, coquetry. Knowing so well her mastery, her authority. I would give her everything, blood, self, life. Open for her, whispering into her ear as she takes the higher inner ridge of flesh in me, wrings it and makes it come like rain, juices weep upon her hand, telling her as she brings one cloudburst after another from this strange hidden height, telling her I am hers, her creature her thing her woman her cunt her own to have, do unto, surrendering with each gush of that pink and hidden place she has only to press and it flows, surrendering self as well as body.

Sexual Problems of Lesbians

NANCY TODER, Ph.D.

When I told a friend that I had been asked to write an article on sexual problems of lesbians and that I had a three-week deadline, my friend replied, "Oh, that's plenty of time; lesbians don't have many sexual problems." I find this attitude, that all lesbians have great sex all the time, to be one of the most popular and destructive myths in the lesbian community. The result of this myth is, on the one hand, an implicit lack of permission for women to acknowledge, let alone talk about, the real sexual problems they may be experiencing, while on the other hand, women whose sex lives are quite satisfying may be convinced that they have a sexual problem, just because sex isn't dynamite every single time. These illusions survive because although there is much bantering about sexuality, it has been my experience, both professionally and personally, that outside of the joking, teasing, and flirting, there are few opportunities for lesbians to talk freely and seriously with each other about sexuality. (The main exceptions seem to be the CR group, where women tend to be more honest and disclosing about their sexuality.)

In this article, I want first to place women's sexual problems in a societal perspective and to deal with the basic issues of defining a sexual problem. Then I will describe specific sexual problems of lesbians and will discuss the causes and treatments of these problems.

As most women are filled with insecurities about their sexual adequacy, a state of mind created and perpetuated by the mass media and other institutions in our society, they are always looking outside themselves to see whether they have sexual problems. Given the lack of honest communication among women about sexuality, women have no reference points to judge their own sexuality. In the absence of real norms, women's insecurities create unrealistic norms based on misinformation spread by male authorities (the professions, media, religions, etc.). It is my opinion that women's sharing their experiences and generating reality-based norms of female sexual response can be very helpful, by giving us knowledge about the diversity and range of female response, as well as by providing support from the recognition that other women have experiences similar to our own. This support from sisters has been helpful in all aspects of our exploration of our identities and our growing solidarity as women.

Some feminists object to talking about sexual

norms, because they are fearful of the ways that norms can be (mis)used, primarily to label someone as abnormal. As lesbians, we know that this fear is reality-based; our culture is very judgmental, and most of us have experienced great conformity pressures in all aspects of our lives. However, I feel that knowledge of the true norms and range of female response (based on our own observations and data, not the interpretations and conclusions of men) is likely to be comforting to most women.

This discussion raises more fundamental questions: Who defines what a sexual problem is? Are there clear-cut objective standards for determining which behaviors, feelings, and inhibitions are problems? Are these standards determined by certain values or assumptions, or are they simply based on a statistical concept of normality?

In my opinion, a woman has a sexual problem if she herself feels frustrated with her sexuality. What one woman may define as a problem, another woman will be totally comfortable with. For example, one woman may feel she has a problem if she doesn't like oral sex, whereas a different woman may feel that this inhibition is perfectly fine, that there are plenty of other sexual behaviors that she can and does enjoy, and that her pleasure is not significantly affected by this one inhibition. However, a problem can still arise if this woman is in a relationship that is important to her, and her lover is frustrated by the limitations imposed on their love-making.

At one time, women were expected not to enjoy sex; sex was supposed to be something a woman submitted to for functional reasons. Now, women are pressured to be turned on all the time, to have orgasms every time they make love, to have and enjoy sex with any partner, and to be able to engage in any sexual practice, anywhere, anytime. No one lives that way, of course, but all of us are affected by these myths and pressures. This means that many women who previously might not have labeled themselves as having a sexual problem, now would.

The information that most women are capable of multiple orgasms or that most women have orgasms at all can be very intimidating for a woman who has never had an orgasm but enjoys sexual contact. This woman would be more likely today to define herself as having a sexual problem than she would have been twenty years ago. But on the other hand, twenty years ago many straight women didn't think they were capable of or had the right to demand an orgasm for themselves, and so many women settled for less sexual pleasure than they could have had. In fact, orgasms are a very pleasant part of sexual satisfaction.

We need to be able to express our desires and to feel we have the right to fulfillment, yet it seems that our desires and expectations have been shaped and elevated by the latest Madison Avenue type. Madison Avenue and Hollywood keep us insecure all the time—we're not sexy enough or turned on enough—and set standards for our sexual response that are outside of ourselves and don't take our particular uniquenesses into account.

How can a woman know when a particular need or expectation is truly her own, rather than an internalization of a societal pressure? This is a very difficult question. All I can say is that there is a difference between knowing that your body isn't getting what it wants and is frustrated, and the feeling of inferiority and inadequacy that results from knowing you're not living up to some mythological norm. It is likely that a woman's sense of self must be fairly developed and stable before she can easily feel that difference.

SEXUAL PROBLEMS

What are some of the common problems that lesbians experience? One category of sexual problems is sexual dysfunctions; these are inhibitions of sexual response that block the natural flow of sexual arousal and release.

Sexual dysfunctions in women are commonly divided into three syndromes: orgasmic dysfunction, general sexual dysfunction, and vaginismus. Lesbians experience many of the same sexual dysfunctions as heterosexual women; however, there are also some noticeable differences. For example, it is very rare (I have never heard of a case) for a lesbian to complain of vaginismus—the tightening of the muscles surrounding the vaginal entrance and preventing vaginal penetration—whereas this is a more common, yet still relatively infrequent, complaint of heterosexual women who are unable to have intercourse. Obviously (although it wasn't obvious to me until I had done some thinking about it), the differences between the ways lesbians commonly make love and the ways heterosexual women commonly make love place a different emphasis on what is likely to be seen or experienced as a problem, as well as possibly causing differences in the incidence of different dysfunctions. At this time, there is no research to indicate whether lesbians simply do not have vaginismus (a definite possibility, as the insertion of a finger is unlikely to arouse the same degree of fear and muscular tension as the insertion of a penis), or whether some lesbians do suffer from vaginismus but do not define this as a problem, simply refraining from vaginal penetration while making love. There may be differences in the likelihood of vaginismus between lesbians who have had recent sexual experiences with men (especially unpleasant experiences) and those women who have been lesbians for a long time. Again, this is speculation on my part. The sample of women I've worked with is too small to draw any conclusions, and no research has been done in this area.

Perhaps the most common sexual complaint among women is orgasmic difficulties. The term orgasmic dysfunction refers to the specific inhibition of the orgasmic component of the sexual response. Masters and Johnson have suggested that female sexual response is divided into four phases: *excitement,* when a woman first becomes sexually aroused and begins to lubricate, the vagina expands and lengthens, and blood accumulates in the pelvic area; *plateau,* when a woman reaches a high level of stimulation, the vaginal opening narrows from the engorging of the outer third of the vagina with blood (this process is known as the orgasmic platform), the inner two thirds of the vagina continues to expand, the uterus elevates fully, and the clitoris retracts under its hood; *orgasm,* when the sexual tension is released by a body reflex characterized by involuntary vaginal, uterine, and anal contractions; and *resolution,* when muscle tension and blood congestion disappear from the pelvic area and the entire body returns to its nonaroused state.

The woman with orgasmic dysfunction does not go beyond the plateau phase. Masters and Johnson have refining the concept of orgasmic dysfunction by subdividing it into two diagnostic categories—primary and secondary—and then further subdividing these categories into absolute and situational. A woman has primary orgasmic dysfunction if she has never experienced an orgasm, whereas a secondary orgasmic dysfunction develops after a period of time in which the woman was orgasmic. In absolute orgasmic dysfunction, a woman is unable to have an orgasm under any circumstances of stimulation, whereas a woman has situational orgasmic dysfunction if she can have an orgasm, but only under specific circumstances. In the most common situational dysfunction, a woman is able to masturbate to orgasm, but is unable to have an orgasm with a partner.

Masters and Johnson report that primary orgasmic dysfunction is frequently related to a corresponding dysfunction in the woman's partner (assumed by Masters and Johnson to be male). In other words, a woman may never have experienced an orgasm because she has never been stimulated adequately during lovemaking. In my clinical experience, this is rarely true for lesbians—which may suggest a lower incidence of orgasmic dysfunction among lesbians than among heterosexual women. The role of the clitoris in lovemaking may have surprised the heterosexual world in the last ten years, but it is not news to lesbians.

The third sexual dysfunction commonly ascribed to women is labeled general sexual dysfunction. A woman who is generally dysfunctional experiences little if any erotic arousal from sexual stimulation. Physiologically, she is suffering from an inhibition of the vasocongestive (engorging of blood) component of the sexual response: She does not lubricate, her vagina does not expand, and no orgasmic platform is formed. She may also be inorgasmic, but not necessarily. My hunch (again there is no research) is that general dysfunction is less common among lesbians than among heterosexual women. Certainly it is more rare for lesbians to present general dysfunction as a problem.

A problem that seems more common in the lesbian community is the fear of some women of being touched in a sexual way. These women are comfortable about making love to a woman, but refuse to allow a woman to make love to them. It is possible that some of these women are generally sexually dysfunctional and are better able to protect themselves from unpleasurable sexual stimulation in the context of a lesbian relationship. (It is not unheard-of for a problem of this sort to be accepted in a lesbian relationship for long periods of time, whereas I imagine that few men would accept this behavior for any length of time, as it would preclude intercourse.) For other women, the refusal to allow women to make love to them may reflect "old gay" notions of appropriate roles. A woman who is playing butch to the hilt, who identifies herself as the man or husband in the relationship, is likely to be very uncomfortable with her surprisingly very female genitals. This woman might also be uncomfortable about being fully naked with her lover, thus dispelling the illusion of her maleness, as well as horrified by the notion of her lover playing an "aggressive" role in bed. It is likely that for many of the women in this predicament, the alienation that they feel from their genitals is expressed in general sexual dysfunction, but again, not necessarily. My impression is that as the feminist and lesbian movements have grown, the number of women who adhere to rigid role-playing has diminished, and that role-playing is becoming a somewhat archaic form in the American lesbian world.

Another problem unique to the lesbian community is the reverse of the above: the refusal of some women to make love to their partners. This passivity may be a function of intrapsychic conflict and/or societal conditioning (factors to be discussed later in more detail), but is more likely to be a reflection of the woman's ambivalence toward the lesbian relationship. Some women who are involved in sexual relationships with women continue to identify themselves as primarily or exclusively heterosexual. This is justified in their minds by the fact that *they* are not making love to a woman, and therefore they think they are not engaging in homosexual behaviors. Negative consequences for the committed lesbian involved in such a relationship may be many. The continual rejection of her sexuality and her body by her "lover" may result in an internalization of intense negative feelings about her own desirability, and these feelings may in turn precipitate sexual dysfunction in future relationships. The imbalance of such a relationship is also likely to produce lowered self-esteem. Thus, a woman who enters into such a one-way sexual relationship feeling relatively good about her body and herself may not leave the relationship in as good a state of mind.

A different type of sexual problem is sexual inhibitions; these include sexual phobias and rigid or restrictive lovemaking patterns. With lesbian couples, the most common presenting problem of this sort is that one woman in the couple dislikes or fears oral sex. If both partners dislike or are indifferent to oral sex, and they enjoy other sexual behaviors, there is no problem. However, if oral sex is very pleasurable and important to one woman and aversive to the other, then there is a relationship problem.

It is interesting that lesbian couples are more likely to define a woman's dislike of oral sex as a problem than are heterosexual couples. Colleagues who work with

heterosexual couples tell me that these couples very rarely seek sex therapy because of one or both partners' discomfort with oral sex. In contrast, many lesbians clearly feel that oral sex is an important part of sexual fulfillment, as lesbians are frequently motivated to seek therapy to overcome an oral sex inhibition, even when the rest of the sexual relationship is in many respects highly satisfying. In other less positive instances, a woman may feel pressured into working on her "problems with oral sex" because her lover is defining this problem for her. The lover may feel deprived of a very pleasurable type of lovemaking, and/or she may have internalized some distinctly lesbian myths that can be very destructive when used against a lover. A prime example is, "A woman is not a *real* lesbian if she doesn't like oral sex." Variations on the same theme are, "Any lesbian who is not into oral sex is clearly not capable of deep passion for another woman," and the more catastrophic assertion, "If you don't want to go down on me, it's obvious you don't really love me." The above statements are examples of ways in which we intimidate each other sexually and set narrow definitions of acceptable erotic behavior.

Some lesbians have developed phobic reactions to different parts of their bodies. The most common areas of the body affected seem to be the breasts, anus, and vagina. Women who have such phobic reactions may prohibit touching of these areas or may only allow them to be touched under very special conditions and in very special ways. Additionally, some women complain that they are able to enjoy sex and/or be orgasmic only if they engage in a particular sequence or type of lovemaking or fantasy. These women often feel frustrated by the rigidity and limitations imposed on their sexual response.

A difference in desire for frequency of sex is a very common problem for which lesbian couples seek help. The woman with greater needs often feels frustrated, rejected, and resentful, while the woman with less frequent desire often feels pressured, inadequate, and resentful. The longer the discrepancy in demand for sex, the greater the likelihood of hostility and dysfunctional behavior patterns.

In a large proportion of lesbian couples complaining of different needs for frequency of sex, both partners report that when they do have sex, the sex is good to fantastic. My clinical impression is that a higher proportion of lesbians than of heterosexuals have both high-quality sex and frequency problems; heterosexual couples with quantity problems are more likely to have quality problems, too. In fact, among heterosexual couples, poor quality of sex for one of the partners (usually the woman) often results in that partner's avoiding sexual contact. In contrast, my work with lesbians indicates that discrepancies in demand for sex are likely to be a function of a real difference in needs or a reflection of other relationship problems. Similarly, many heterosexual women complain that their partner is unwilling to be affectionate and that sex is too goal-

oriented. This complaint is rarely heard from lesbians. Many lesbians in long-term relationships report plenty of hugs and kisses, but not enough nitty-gritty sex.

CAUSES OF PROBLEMS

Before moving on to issues in the treatment of sexual problems, it will be helpful to look at some of the causes of sexual dysfunction in individuals and in relationships, as treatment decisions are often based on the causes of the dysfunction, as well as on its specific nature.

Sexual dysfunctions in women are rarely a product of pathology in the sex organs. In a clear-cut situational pattern of dysfunction, the physical soundness of a woman's sex organs is established, indicating that the cause of the dysfunction is most likely psychological. However, if a woman is experiencing discomfort or a dampening of sexual excitement during sexual contact, then the first step should be a complete medical examination to rule out the possibility of organic complications, such as vaginal infections or clitoral adhesions. (Many gynecologists not only are insensitive to women who experience sexual problems but also are not up to date on the various organic factors that can affect sexual satisfaction. Thus, a woman who wants a sexological examination should either get a referral from a sex clinic or go to a gynecologist she knows and trusts.)

General loss of interest in or responsiveness to sex may be the product of fatigue, depression, illness, or drug use. However, orgasmic functioning is not likely to be affected by such factors.

The great majority of sexual problems are psychologically determined. Helen Kaplan, in her excellent book *The New Sex Therapy,* suggests that these psychological factors may be a function of both immediate and remote causes. Common immediate causes are the failure of lovers to communicate honestly their genuine feelings and desires; misinformation about the normal range of female sexuality; and sexual anxieties stemming from fear of failure, pressure to perform, an excessive need to please the partner (which prevents a woman from focusing on her own satisfaction), or fear of rejection. The fear of losing control, of fainting, screaming, or urinating while having an orgasm, is common among preorgasmic women. These various conflicts and fears may create defenses that interfere with a woman's ability to abandon herself to the sexual experience. Another common reaction, labeled by Masters and Johnson as "spectatoring," refers to the experience of observing one's own lovemaking, usually as a response to performance fears.

On the other hand, sexual anxieties, guilts, and fears may derive from deeply ingrained intrapsychic conflicts. These conflicts may have arisen from early family experiences, such as religious orthodoxy or constrictive upbringing, or they may have come from a more general exposure to our antisexual and antifemale culture. From religious doctrine and general attitudes that permeate our entire society, we learn that our genitals are dirty;

that our primary task in life is to make some man happy, including "servicing" him sexually; and that our own sexuality somehow is both a trifle not worth bothering about and an overwhelming, insatiable force that must be suppressed, lest it make us unfit for our holy roles as wife, mother, and guardian of society's "morality."

It is not surprising, then, that many women experience intense conflicts, often unconscious, between enjoyment of sex, and fear of punishment (learned from childhood experiences) or feelings of guilt (associated with "sinful" or "unnatural" behavior). For the lesbian, the fear and guilt are compounded by the fact that she is stepping totally out of the realm of acceptable sexual feelings and behaviors. Her experience is likely to be condemned as anti-God, anti-Man, anti-Nature, and anti-Life. And on some level, even the youngest and most sheltered of women experiencing lesbian feelings knows the degree to which the expression of her feelings will violate the most basic of society's rules. Not exactly a healthy or supportive atmosphere for getting it on!

Sexual dysfunctions are also acquired through behavioral conditioning and reinforcement. In contrast with dysfunctions caused by learned attitudes toward sexuality, behaviorally conditioned dysfunctions do not involve the same degree of intrapsychic conflict; instead, they are a response to certain specific experiences. The most common of these experiences are childhood sexual traumas, such as rape or incestuous seductions, or negative sexual experiences as a young woman, which may range from mild (setting certain patterns of sexual response) to severe (rape). One uniquely lesbian set of experiences involves young women in all-women environments, such as all-girl schools, convents, and the military. The consequences of getting caught making love in such situations are severe, and the likelihood great, so that the lovemaking is often rushed and accompanied by fear and guilt. With time, these experiences may result in orgasmic dysfunction, avoidance of foreplay, and an inhibition of movement and sounds during lovemaking.

Finally, sexual difficulties may be not an expression of one person's intrapsychic conflict, but rather may reflect sexual or more general problems in a relationship. Sexual problems in a relationship may be due to a destructive sexual system between the two lovers that encourages and perpetuates anxieties about sexual performance and failure. Communication difficulties may exacerbate the problem; these may arise from culturally induced shame and guilt about talking openly about sexual matters, or they may reflect a more deeply rooted communication problem of the couple. Often in couples that seem sexually incompatible, underlying ambivalences, hostilities, and anxieties are being acted out in the sexual relationship; women are often unaware of the subtle forces that have turned them off to each other sexually. Sometimes, a woman who is generally unassertive and who feels intimidated by her lover will choose sex as a way to express resentments, because she is afraid to express her anger in more direct ways. Kaplan suggests some dynamic explanations for rage at a lover and fear of abandonment (two feelings that can affect the couple's sexual relationship adversely), including failure to establish trust and intimacy, unresolved conflicts with parents that are acted out on the lover (transferences), power struggles, unrealistic expectations of the lover or the relationship, and excessive dependency and demands. The anger or fear may directly inhibit the sexual response (for example, secondary orgasmic dysfunction), or it may be acted out in different maneuvers aimed at sabotage of the sexual interaction (for example, choosing to make love when both partners are too tired).

TREATMENT

If you feel that you do have a sexual problem, and maybe have some idea of why you're having the problem, your first decision is whether you can deal with the problem alone (or with a lover) or whether you should seek help. Sometimes just recognizing the problem and talking about it with your lover or a friend can help. If your difficulty seems to be the result of misinformation, lack of information, or lack of support, you may want to join a lesbian CR group. For most sexual dysfunctions, therapy is your best bet. (Some additional options are available if you are preorgasmic; I will discuss these later.) Therapy is also in order if your problem is in the context of a relationship, and if you and your lover have exhausted your own resources for trying to solve the problem.

In some of the larger cities, you may be able to locate lesbian therapists who have expertise in working with sexual problems. In a greater number of areas, you may have access to straight feminist therapists, who are unlikely to have antilesbian attitudes and who should have more liberated and less stereotypic notions of female sexuality than their more traditional colleagues.

In my opinion, the therapist's knowledge of and experience in working with sexual problems are as important as her feminist "credentials." A therapist who knows nothing about behavioral sex therapy techniques may focus attention on the remote causes of sexual problems and ignore the immediate causes. This exclusive focus on remote causes can result in many years of therapy, huge costs, and little progress in solving the sexual problem. In general, the rapid-treatment behavioral approach has been much more successful in treating sexual problems. The ideal sex therapist is flexible enough to use behavioral techniques for treating the immediate causes, and more insight-oriented strategies for dealing with the deeper elements of the problem when necessary.

How to find a therapist? Your friends may be your best resource. If a therapist comes highly recommended by a lesbian friend, that's a good start. Other resources are local women's organizations, many of which keep lists of feminist therapists with notes on their particular expertise. If you live near a university or medical school, you can call the psychology or psychiatry department and ask whether the school has a sex clinic. If you go to a sex clinic, ask for a female therapist, preferably one with some experience in working with lesbians. (A competent and imaginative sex therapist, however, can generally work successfully with a lesbian or a lesbian couple even without prior experience.)

You may want to make one appointment each with several prospective therapists, and then choose the one you like best. In these initial appointments, ask each therapist about her therapeutic orientation and her training and qualifications in both general and sexual therapy, tell her what you want out of therapy, and ask her what you can expect in therapy with her. Don't be afraid to ask specific questions, and trust your judgment: If you don't feel good about the prospect of working with a certain therapist, probably your instincts are telling you something important.

Once you go into sex therapy, you can expect the course of treatment to be something like this: First, you and the therapist will define your problem. Next, the therapist will ask you for a detailed sex history (including your experiences, feelings, and expectations), and will probably take copious notes. Do not be surprised if the sex history takes several sessions; this time investment will pay off by enabling the therapist to develop a specific and suitable treatment plan for you. After the sex history is complete, the therapist will summarize for you the aspects of the history that clarify the nature and origin of your sexual problem, and she and you will set goals for the treatment. The treatment will probably include both sex education (to counter myths, misinformation, and unrealistic expectations) and structured homework assignments. These assignments will be sexual and erotic experiences designed to reduce performance anxieties, to provide a relaxed and supportive atmosphere for you to explore your sexuality, and to relieve your specific problems.

Whatever the nature of your sexual problem, if you are involved in a primary relationship, then it is most helpful for both women to participate in the therapy together. This permits the couple to deal with the inevitable frustrations and misunderstandings that have resulted from the problem, and ensures the cooperative and active participation of both women in the problem-solving process. Conjoint sex therapy examines the myths and misconceptions about each other's behaviors and feelings, delineates the problem situations, and finds more adaptive ways to deal with these situations.

Sex therapists make a distinction between sexual problems that seem to be a function of anxiety and those that seem to arise from anger. If anxiety is the primary cause of the problem, then sex therapy from a behavioral perspective, with some attention to changing destructive sexual attitudes, is appropriate. However, if the sexual problem is arising from underlying hostilities and resentments in the relationship, then a more traditional therapy, which will help identify dynamic problems in the relationship and provide a safe outlet for expressing feelings and solving the problems, is needed.

One way to help determine whether the sexual problem is stemming from anxiety or anger is to see when the problem began. If you have always had the problem, then it is likely to be caused by anxiety. If the problem is specific to your present relationship, then it may be either anxiety or anger. If, however, you and your lover had good sex for a while, and then a problem arose—say, after one of you had an affair, or after you began to fight frequently—then the sex problem is more likely to be caused by anger.

Often a couple will identify one of the two women as having the problem: She doesn't have orgasms, or she rarely wants to make love. Again, let me stress that even if only one woman is dysfunctional or inhibited, the problem is still a relationship problem, and it is important for both women to be involved in the process of therapy. When both women are involved, not only will their sex life together be enhanced, but their communication and intimacy in all areas of their relationship are likely to improve.

If you are preorgasmic and live in a large city, you may be able to find a therapist who offers groups for preorgasmic women. The advantages of such a group over individual or couple therapy are that the group provides additional support and more varied viewpoints, and costs less. On the other hand, you get more of the therapist's time and attention in individual therapy, and your lover cannot participate in the therapy if it takes place in a group. If you can't imagine talking about the intimate details of your sexuality in a group, then you may be more comfortable in individual therapy.

Two books are now available to help women expand their sexual awareness and become orgasmic: Lonnie Barbach's *For Yourself: The Fulfillment of Female Sexuality,* and Julie Heiman, Leslie LoPiccolo, and Joseph LoPiccolo's *Becoming Orgasmic: A Sexual Growth Program for Women.* I prefer Barbach's book, as it is firmly entrenched in a woman's perspective, has a little more awareness of lesbian realities, and effectively stresses individual differences by including the reactions and responses of many women to the different stages of the treatment program. If you feel optimistic about your ability to solve the problem on your own with some guidance, or if therapy is a financial impossibility, get one or both of the books and give it a try.

MEN

In conclusion, I want to mention a topic that is taboo in the lesbian community—a topic about which women are filled with shame, anxiety, and fear—namely, the experience of sexual feelings, fantasies, or dreams about men, or the actual experience of having sex with a man. As lesbians almost never talk about these experiences, many lesbians assume that other lesbians never have them, and literally panic when they have a sexual fantasy or dream that includes men. Many women immediately begin to

question their identity: Am I really a lesbian? Does this mean that I should pick up a man and go to bed with him?

In my work with lesbians, I have found that many women have sexual feelings or dreams about men, or engage in sexual contact with men, for many different reasons. Women who are still insecure about their lesbian identity (and how many of us aren't at one time or another, given the societal pressures we face daily?) will sometimes go to bed with a man to prove to themselves that they still can do it, or that their lesbianism is a choice and not (as society says) a rejection by men. This often happens to women when they visit their parents; isolated from lesbian supports and realities, women sometimes succumb to pressure to be heterosexual.

Some lesbians engage in sexual fantasies about or behaviors with men out of curiosity. For those women who have never had sex with men, it is a new experience; for women who once were actively heterosexual and who have been lesbians for some time, sex with men is an old forgotten experience. Sometimes women who live relatively separatist lives find themselves missing men; a dream may communicate this message to a woman, or quick sex may be an easy way to make limited contact. Other times, a woman may decide to sleep with a man because of anger: One woman with whom I was working was angry with the women's community because she was having a hard time finding a lover, and a big part of her desire to sleep with a man was really a desire to say "fuck you" to her lesbian friends.

I bring up this taboo subject in order to reassure women that many lesbians share these feelings and experiences, and to make a plea for recognition and acceptance of *all* parts of ourselves. Until we recognize those parts of ourselves that are disquieting and inconsistent, until we respect our individual differences, the unity we build is false. More fundamentally, when we limit ourselves by imposing rigid and punitive rules for acceptable sexual feelings and behaviors, we are in fact capitulating to the same forces that we struggle against in asserting our lesbianism.

RECOMMENDATIONS FOR FURTHER READING

The following books provide accurate factual information on female sexual response and sexual dysfunction. Unfortunately, all of these books are heterosexual in orientation.

Barbach, Lonnie Garfield. *For Yourself.* New York: Doubleday & Co., 1975. Excellent description of a group therapy program for preorgasmic women. Also includes a chapter on the anatomy and physiology of female sexuality.

Belliveau, Fred, and Richter, Lin. *Understanding Human Sexual Inadequacy.* New York: Bantam Book/ Little Brown & Co., 1970. A readable discussion of the therapy principles and techniques used by Masters and Johnson in their treatment of sexual dysfunctions.

Boston Women's Health Collective. *Our Bodies, Our Selves.* 2nd ed. New York: Simon & Schuster, 1976. Written from a feminist perspective. Includes a well-written chapter on the anatomy and physiology of sexuality, with excellent photographs and drawings of female pelvic organs.

Heiman, Julia; LoPiccolo, Leslie; and LoPiccolo, Joseph. *Becoming Orgasmic: A Sexual Growth Program for Women.* Englewood Cliffs, N.J.: Prentice-Hall, 1976. An individual program for preorgasmic women. Very heterosexual in assumptions, but contains some useful information and techniques.

Kaplan, Helen Singer. *The New Sex Therapy.* New York: Quadrangle Books, 1974. Highly informative and useful. Technical but accessible. Focuses on sexual dysfunction, but includes excellent chapters on the anatomy and physiology of sexual response and on the effects of illness, drugs, and age on sexuality.

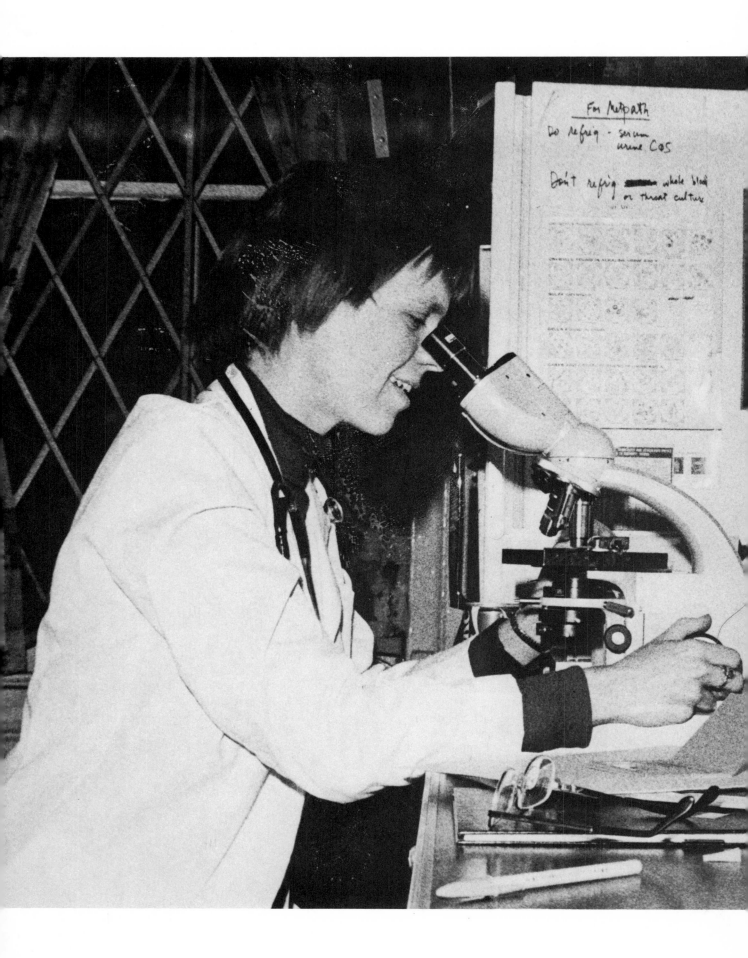

5. Health

Lesbian Health Issues

Health care has been of particular concern for many lesbians who have found it difficult to deal with the homophobic attitudes of heterosexuals and the sexism of male physicians. The first two parts of the following article were edited from a transcript of a panel sponsored by the Gay Public Health Workers' Caucus held at the 1976 convention of the American Public Health Association in Miami Beach.

First, Dr. Joan Waitkevicz, a physician at the St. Mark's Clinic in New York City, explains the rationale for setting aside a special Gay Women's Night to deal with the special problems of lesbians; then Judi Stein, codirector of Women's Community Health, a self-help health center in Cambridge, elaborates further on lesbian health issues; and, finally, a recovered alcoholic addresses the problem of alcoholism and discusses the value of lesbian AA groups.—Ed.

ST. MARK'S CLINIC, NEW YORK CITY

First, I would like to give some background information on the Women's Night at St. Mark's Clinic. St. Mark's is located in the East Village area of New York City, traditionally an area where a large number of gay people live. In 1973 a lesbian woman from the community had to have major surgery for cervical cancer; she had not had a Pap test in many years. Some of her friends, also lesbians, were working as paramedical staff at the clinic.

They realized that St. Mark's, though known as an "alternative clinic," was providing no more outreach or services for lesbians than any other health facility, because policy was made, as always, by heterosexual male professionals. These women sought out other women with various medical training, professional and nonprofessional, and a few months later set up a Gay Women's Night once a week.

Four years later, the Women's Night still emphasizes health screening tests, such as the Pap test, blood pressure, testing for anemia and tuberculosis; in addition, care is given for a wide range of medical problems. "Primary Care"—interviews and testing—is done by six "primary health workers," while diagnosis and treatment are done by one physician and one physician's assistant. Though no woman is excluded, lesbians and older single women (with whom we have a lot in common) are encouraged to attend.

Why do people come to a lesbian clinic and what do they expect? First of all, they expect a comfortable space where they can talk freely with other women. A lot of valuable information is exchanged in the waiting room, and rap groups have been formed around special health problems like alcoholism.

Second, they expect a woman's lover, or any woman she brings with her, to be given the respect usually accorded to a spouse or relative. We invite the other women into the examining room to add to the medical history, participate in the examination, and ask questions. Often we learn a lot about the person from her friend; whether she eats enough, sleeps enough, overworks; where she spends her time (especially important in tracing winter strep and flu epidemics). She may also bring home more information from the visit if she can check out what was said with her friend when they get home.

Third, women coming to our clinic expect to get information on how their illness affects their sex life, from a health worker who is herself a lesbian, without embarrassment.

Like other lesbian clinics, we find that very few women who relate only to women have syphilis or gonorrhea—much less so than heterosexuals or gay men. However, we routinely ask if a woman wishes VD screening tests, and many do.

Infections transmitted through the bowel, such as hepatitis, all parasites including amoeba, and bacterial and viral diarrheas are a problem for all people who have oral sex. A person who is ill with one of these infections in the contagious stage should not be the recipient in oral sex. We take the initiative in telling people this. Unfortunately, most straight health care workers still don't—probably resulting in epidemics among gays and straights alike.

The three main vaginal infections (monilia, trichomonas, and "nonspecific") usually cannot be transmitted to the mouth or throat. (One possible exception is that people on cortisonelike hormones or anticancer drugs can get oral monilia.)

These vaginal infections can be spread to the vaginal area of another woman by fingers, vibrators, tub bath water, etc., and we advise lovers to be careful if one woman has an infection and the other does not. The lover of a woman with one of these infections usually does not have to be checked, unless she wants to be. There are three exceptions: if the woman has trichomonas (which is more catching), if she has repeated infections of the same type, and of course if the lover has a discharge.

We also warn women with "cold sores" or fever blisters on their mouth or face to avoid making love orally until the infection is gone. The "cold sore" virus is very similar to the virus causing genital herpes, a painful infection of the labia (vaginal lips), which carries a slightly higher risk of future cancer. Although no connection has yet been made between the cold sore herpes virus and the genital herpes virus, we feel it is better to be careful.

Finally, many women attend Women's Night because they expect some give-and-take with the staff with regard to medical treatment. Most women who have been through several vaginal infections, or several bouts of asthma or uncontrolled high blood pressure, have strong preferences in terms of the medications and the nonmedicinal treatment prescribed, and doctors rarely ask. We encourage women to discuss which among the available medicines they prefer, to work out a treatment plan they can live with, and in general to be more self-sufficient around their health care.

—H. Joan Waitkevicz, M.D.

WOMEN'S COMMUNITY HEALTH

I'm codirector of Women's Community Health, a woman owned and controlled self-help center in Cambridge, Massachusetts.

Some issues all women face when we seek health care are (1) high cost, (2) bad or poor availability, (3) disrespect and rudeness, (4) lack of adequate information, (5) misinformation or lies, (6) condescension, (7) mystification of our bodies, (8) mystification of the role of practitioner, (9) humiliation and sexual abuse, (10) lack of input into decision making, (11) ignorance by the practitioner of well-woman functions and healthy life functions such as menstruation, childbirth, pregnancy, and menopause, (12) institutional ageism, racism, classism, and sexism; in other words, total lack of control.

The issues that lesbians face when we seek health care are all of the above, and then two more: heterosexism (defined as the assumption that everyone is or wants to be a practicing heterosexual) and homophobia (defined as "the extreme rage and fear reaction to homosexuals . . . a severe disturbance which has a powerful effect on the person who has it, as well as on the people with whom he or she comes into contact.") Lesbians are often put in the position of having their overt or sus-

pected lesbianism used as an interfering factor in their health care.

Lesbianism is often seen by medical practitioners as the *cause* of other health conditions, such as colitis and alcoholism; lesbians find they must fight to choose *not* to obtain a birth control method; lesbians find that answers are unavailable to them for common questions about transmission of vaginal conditions or sexually transmitted disease; lesbians are often denied the right to visit with or accompany lovers in the hospital, in the doctor's office, in the emergency rooms, in the intensive-care unit; lesbians are often subject to inquisitions—sometimes malicious, sometimes merely curious, as to their lesbianism and many details of their personal lives. Or, lesbians are subjected to monologues, lectures, and anecdotes designed to convince them that the practitioner is not sexist, heterosexist, or homophobic—and besides which, some women who live in his or her neighborhood are "that way."

Lesbians, by and large, are not in control of health care experience any more than most of us are in control of most of our lives. One answer is the self-help movement.

Women's Community Health is a self-help health center collectively owned and controlled by the women who work at the center. Self-help means sharing information and skills so that we have the ability to make responsible decisions about our health care. Self-help involves demystifying the roles of medical professionals and the current notions of health and illness so that we, as women, are in control of those aspects of our lives, such as menstruation, pregnancy, or childbirth, that can be aspects of a woman's normal life-span. By sharing information and skills, women can begin to take control of our health care; by taking control of our lives in one aspect, we learn to regain control over our total lives.

Self-help centers have worked hard for a long time at developing a high consciousness and visibility about lesbian health issues. I am working on a lesbian health pamphlet, and that is considered part of my workweek. In 1975 we held our annual women's health weekend. At the lesbian health workshop that weekend, some lesbians asked, "Why don't you have lesbian health workers?" We wrote the following statement in reply.

At Women's Community Health, we do not make any assumptions about women's sexual preferences or lifestyle. We support every woman in her own choice, and hope we create an environment in which women feel free to express their sexuality-related health needs. We have considered making lesbian health workers available, and after much discussion we decided not to supply this option because: (1) it may help perpetuate divisions between heterosexual and lesbian women, (2) we should also have to create categories on the basis of race and age, which is not functionally feasible right now, and (3) each of us would have to label her own sexuality, which many of us are not willing or able to do.

We feel that a more productive goal is for each of

us to confront her sexual biases and eliminate them, and openly support all forms of sexuality.

This statement on sexuality becomes part of a woman's medical record, so she can see it. Efforts *have* been made in self-help centers to acknowledge the presence of lesbians and lesbian issues and to make sure that some of those issues that women face seeking health care are not compounded for lesbians.

—Judi Stein

"Isolation is the groundwork for alcoholism and any lesbian in this society is going to feel isolated."

Lesbians may be more vulnerable to alcoholism than other women. I think the percentage of lesbians, gays in general, who are alcoholic is very high. There hasn't been too much research, but the guesses are as high as one in three. I was asked, "Do you think that being a lesbian had something to do with your becoming an alcoholic?" and in two senses it has. Isolation is the groundwork for alcoholism and any lesbian in this society is going to feel isolated. The other thing is that up until recently, all lesbian social activity has been in the bars, or other drinking situations. I know that I was able to hide from myself for many years the fact that I had a drinking problem. I thought I was in the bars for social contact. Of course, when you're there, you drink. If all of my social contact hadn't been in bars, I would have had to look at how frequently I drank and how much I drank.

It was through Alcoholics Anonymous meetings that I got sober. I had to go to a hospital and be detoxed, but it was at the meetings where I learned about alcoholism and how not to cure it but control it. I was uncomfortable in heterosexual AA groups. I had difficulty coming out in fear of how they would react to me. I couldn't have stood the rejection, if that had been the case. Eventually some other women and I in AA decided we would have a lesbian AA meeting. There was already a gay AA meeting, but it was mostly gay men. Women were not attracted to that group. So we started this lesbian AA group, and at the time there were only about seven or eight sober lesbians that we knew of in AA.

The way the AA meeting works, you have a speaker and then discussion afterward. You hear the speaker's story, and we thought with eight women, we'd have eight weeks of meetings, and we'd hear those eight stories and then what would happen? Where would we get more speakers? But we never had that problem. The first meeting was eight, the second meeting was fifteen, the third was twenty-five, and I think there have been times when we had as many as fifty women at the meeting. A lot of women got into AA sooner as a result of lesbian AA being in existence—women who wouldn't

go to straight AA because they felt it wouldn't be for *them*. It's interesting that after they come to the lesbian AA meetings for a while and stop drinking, they go on to other lesbian organizations and meetings, too.

A woman came from Philadelphia and wanted to know how to start a group there. I believe there's a group in Washington, one on the West Coast, and a lot of other lesbian AA groups starting.

There was an article in the *Advocate* on alcoholism. They had some statistics and a resource list for the gay alcoholic and information on alcoholism. Here in New York I've been giving out information to the lesbian community on alcoholism. I've been on panels on alcoholism done at Lesbian Feminist Liberation, and I've done workshops on alcoholism at A Woman's Place (Athol, in upstate New York) and at the Health and Healing Conference. More recently I've started talking to the staffs of alcoholism programs about treatment of the gay alcoholic. I did a seminar at St. Luke's Alcoholism Program and a couple of drug programs. I think the problems are similar.

I give people at these programs the same information that I give to any group about homosexuality. The problem is that they're ignorant about it. They work in a psychiatric framework and tend to view the gay alcoholic as sick *because she's gay*. They view the behavior of gay people in alcoholism programs differently than they view the same behavior from heterosexuals.

I would like to add that my name is appearing below as Doris L. because there's a tradition in AA that members remain anonymous at the level of press on radio and television. That's to protect the organization which we all depend upon for our lives. It bothers me to be anonymous because as a lesbian I want to be as out as I possibly can be. But this takes precedence here.

—Doris L.

RESOURCES

Alcoholics Anonymous, AA World Services, P.O. Box 459, Grand Central Station, New York, N.Y. 10017.

The Alcoholism Center for Women, 1147 S. Alvarado St., Los Angeles, Calif. 90006. 213 381-7805. The Center's rehabilitative and self-development services are available to all women, but the program has a special emphasis and concern for the lesbian alchoholic.

"Alcoholism and the Lesbian Community," by Brenda Weathers, 1976. An excellent survey of the problem, with suggestions for treatment programs. Order from The Alcoholism Center for Women (see above).

Feeling Our Way

JAN CRAWFORD

In the summer of 1975 I spent a month at A Woman's Place, a rural retreat at Athol, New York. I was then moving from a career in advertising and establishment feminist activities toward a life more consistent with my growing radical feminism. At A Woman's Place I received my first full massage. During the massage I felt at home in my body for the first time since childhood. Not only was my body comforted, but that massage became the first conscious step toward the serious acknowledgment of the connection between my physical and inner selves. After that experience I felt a new strength and new sufficiency. I felt more generous and loving toward other women because I was reacting from a source deeper within my self. In a revelatory way my politics and deepest feelings had come together and enriched each other as I experienced the expansion of my own feminism into new physical and spiritual realms.

When I arrived back in Manhattan I began intensive study of many forms of massage and alternative medicine. Today I do body therapy, feminist counseling, and teach courses in healing using primarily Oriental massage and postural realignment techniques. I work only with women.

One of the rewards of my practice is the pleasure I share with women who walk in exhausted by their efforts to survive and walk out feeling strong, filled up with themselves again. I have been able to help women with disease and physical pain which are in my view a response to the patriarchal force of life-negativity surrounding us. When they are released from physical pain and armoring through body work, women artists and writers have often allowed new creative energy up from deep inside themselves. Some severely depressed women have resensed their physical selves within the bodyless state of depression and responded more strongly to their own desire to live. But it is just as rewarding to see women simply begin to feel more sensitive and loving toward their bodies. I have the pleasure of watching women learn how to receive guiltlessly.

A sometimes maddening frustration of this work, however, is encountering the resistance many of us still have to experiencing healing and pleasure. In touch-oriented therapies like massage therapy, resistance seems to be related to the degree of wounding each of us has sustained and the degree to which we are still—often unconsciously—subject to men's health imperatives for women. These are my observations of what some of those imperatives, many of which are remnants of patriarchal religious teachings, dictate:

1. Women comfort. Men heal.
2. Only the highly credentialed can heal. And only expensive health care is quality health care.
3. Touch is sexual. As little touch as possible should occur in the healing process.
4. Modesty and shyness in women are virtues. Comfort with one's body is narcissistic at best.
5. Pleasure in women is self-indulgent. Women should be self-sacrificing civilizers of men.
6. Women's bodies are mysterious beyond their understanding. And self-knowledge, were it possible, is too heavy a responsibility for women.
7. Women exaggerate pain.
8. We do not have to participate in our own healing. Doctors and/or God controls our health.
9. A certain amount of pain is to be tolerated in this earthly life.

All women need healing from the paralyzing effect of these rigid parameters of existence. As women who commit ourselves to other women, we lesbians face even greater challenges to wholeness. One of those challenges is the fact that we are not affirmed by our culture. By choosing to love women we have often had to sacrifice family, religion, acceptance in schools and work. If we have chosen inner integrity, we have had to live without full membership in these traditonal support systems. And only when we do completely face the fact that we are Virginia Woolf's "Outsider's Society" can we begin to build woman-natured forms of communion and support with free hearts. This acknowledgment, however, is almost always accompanied by some pain of loss and separation, and it is a process for which we require healing.

Women who choose to build new worlds of being are often deeply disappointed, confused between old and new values, exhausted from risk-taking. We need healing from the process of revolution itself, and we need good physical and spiritual contact to remind us of our material presence within this abstract chaos of change.

Very few of us are totally "out" as lesbians. Even among the bravest or most privileged there are still areas of our lives in which we must be dishonest. The stress and anxiety that forced hypocrisy creates is hurtful to us emotionally and physically.

I believe one of the other characteristics lesbian feminists share is that we are idealists by our very decision to be lesbians. We are dissatisfied with constricted female roles and with the limitations of sexual/emotional relations with men. But as perfectionists, we are often tormented by the comparison between the lives we are forced to live and the lives we know are possible.

As lesbians we have been taught that we are not only social but physical monstrosities, that we are defective men or women physiologically. And because we do sustain so many challenges to our value as human beings, many of us have assumed "armored" and physically rigid

postures. For example, our high, tight shoulders essentially say, "This is my world too, and I won't be abused." We are forced into defensiveness, and the cost is often blocked energy use and physical pain. We need experiences like massage as consistent ways of remembering the beauty and truthfulness of our bodies.

Despite all this, we can give ourselves and other women a quality of healing attention never before experienced between women. Dorothy Krieger, a nationally recognized scientific researcher into the effects of the laying on of hands, has pointed out that the strong intent to help or to heal another person is one of the critical factors in helping a sick person become better. As a group I believe lesbian feminists are developing the most conscious intent to help women. We are in the best position to know that men's health imperatives for women are myths from which only the men who created them benefit. We have less fear of or distortion of physical contact between women. And, as importantly, we recognize that women deserve healing first. For these reasons we are in fact the most logical healers of women.

There will be important differences in the healing we have experienced and the healing we women can provide for ourselves. We are beginning to develop women's health imperatives for women. The following ideals reflect my experience of a growing feminist philosophy shared to one degree or another by thousands of women inside and outside the establishment health care system:

1. Women can heal—ourselves and others.

2. There are many routes to health, and establishment credentials do not in themselves indicate the quality of care being delivered. The cost of health care can sometimes indicate corruption rather than quality of care.

3. Touch is essential. Almost all of us suffer from touch deficiency.

4. Women who feel comfortable with and loving toward their bodies are healthy.

5. We have been self-sacrificing too long.

6. We can know our bodies. And women doing healing work should be careful not to mystify our work with the body. We should also make it clear that we have not solved all the problems confronting women seeking help from us.

7. We should respect each woman's experience of pain.

8. We must participate in our own health. Women in the health field must try to involve women in making choices in our own healing processes.

9. Pleasure, comfort, and health are each woman's natural right. In my own life I have found that I can now rid myself of many headaches, back problems, and allergy problems using self-massage, color healing, herbs, and nutritional changes and meditations. I may suddenly find after months of frustrating work that a subtle adjustment to the position of my shoulder allows my breath to deepen. Or I may notice that I am standing

more fully grounded or supported by the earth than ever before. The beginning rewards of the physical and emotional disarmoring that results during the healing process have also allowed me the first clear memories of my early childhood and the most insightful dreams of my life. I am beginning to live more and more from the inside out.

It is clear that my involvement in healing and self-healing is simply not a personal phenomenon. Recent signs in the lesbian feminist movement on the East Coast show that large numbers of women are beginning to share these feelings. The Boston Spirituality Conference in April of 1976 was the first major gathering on the East Coast to express the existence of women's physical and spiritual selves in feminist terms. It had a significant focus on the healing arts. There were workshops on topics like "Natural Healing and Massage" and "Psychic Skills and Healing."

Because of the great interest in healing at the Boston Conference, a conference called "Womancraft" was held at Woodstock, New York, in September of 1976. Two months later a similar conference was held in New York City, "A Celebration of the Beguines." It was the first women's conference in this city to concentrate on sharing healing skills. Lesbian feminists were prominent in the planning of all these gatherings.

Individual women and small groups of women had been doing important work in this area for years. And those of us who are involved in feminist healing arts are grateful to the women in the gynecological self-help movement who showed us that we could begin to control and improve our own health. We are also grateful to magazines like *Womanspirit* and *Country Women* that have given and continue to give us much information and encouragement.

There are now a multitude of forms in which we are expressing our desire to comfort, heal, and please each other. Consciousness-raising groups, for example, are often healing experiences. Women are teaching each other about the use of fasting, meditation, yoga, herbs and healthful foods, different massage forms, color and sound healing, writing, masturbation, chanting, iris diagnosis, breathing exercises, Eastern and Western medicine, ritual, feminist psychotherapies, astrology, music, wicca (witchcraft), physical movement, art, self-expressive theater, all of which can be used for healing and prevention of illness. And tomorrow we will create or adapt other forms.

My personal hope for lesbian feminists in particular, and all women in general, is that:

We will desire health.

We will learn to care for ourselves.

We will begin to honor and satisfy our inner lives as well as respect the necessities and pleasures of living in the external world.

Our lives will be safer, more comfortable, and lustier.

We will no longer think in dichotomized terms like those I have had to use in this article—i.e., mind/body/spirit, inner life/external world—but we will find new words to describe new organic realities.

We will be able to make health care and loving attention equally available to all women.

From this fuller integration of ourselves, from simply feeling good, I believe a new generosity will increasingly characterize our relations with each other. Through this new self-sufficiency and more substantive interdependency we will develop ways of living together that are a true reflection of our most ecstatic dreams, knowing now that we can all be the healers and the healed.

RESOURCES

Country Women, Box 51, Albion, Calif. 95410

Womanspirit, Box 263, Wolf Creek, Ore. 97497

Women and Health, 223 Stonehill Road, Old Westbury, N.Y. 11568

Health Rite, 175 Fifth Avenue, New York, N.Y. 10010

6. Lesbian Activism

Reminis- cences of Two Female Homophiles

PHYLLIS LYON and DEL MARTIN

When we first got together as a lesbian couple in San Francisco in 1953, we knew little about the gay subculture. There were gay bars, but we always felt like tourists when we went to them. We were too shy to speak to the women we saw there. Our failure to make friends with other women like ourselves made us feel isolated and alone.

We did have some close heterosexual friends who knew and understood about "us," and eventually we met some gay men. But still that wasn't enough. We wanted so desperately to know other lesbian women.

A fateful telephone call on a sunny Saturday afternoon in September 1955 changed our lives drastically. A lesbian acquaintance, whom we had met through some gay men, called to ask if we wanted to be involved in the formation of a new social club for gay women. That was the beginning of the Daughters of Bilitis.

In the twenty-two years since, we have seen incredible changes—changes in society that we never dreamed would take place in our lifetime. DOB, like the Mattachine Society and ONE, was born in the shadow of the Joe McCarthy witch-hunts and the sweeping purges of homosexuals from the U.S. State Department. Constantly harassed by the police, many gays were beaten up and ordered to leave town or face imprisonment. Gay bars, our only social meeting place, were subject to periodic raids. We never knew when the paddy wagon would pull up in front and all of the patrons would be loaded in and taken to the station. They were usually charged with "visiting a house of ill repute" or "disturbing the peace." Police notified employers when they made such arrests. Most homosexuals pleaded guilty to get off with a suspended sentence and a small fine. But they had a police record, which counted against them when seeking employment. Additionally, both female and male undercover agents frequented gay bars to entice patrons into making a pass so that they could make arrests for "lewd and lascivious" behavior or solicitation.

We were lucky we never got arrested. We escaped that experience—once by a night and another time by a week. But we didn't escape the effects of what we read about homosexuality. What little literature was available on the subject was to be found in the library under the heading of "abnormal psychology" or "sexual deviance." The inference was that whatever applied to male homosexuals also applied to females. The few so-called scientific books dealing with lesbians were written by men and were totally biased. The subjects came from captive populations—women in prison or in therapy. We couldn't identify with what was being said about women who loved women. Novels painted a somewhat truer picture, but according to the plot formula demanded by publishers the heroine always came to a tragic end. She lost her lover to a man or committed suicide. (As a consequence Dr. Frank Caprio—following the true scientific method—concluded that lesbians were prone to suicide.) Newspapers and magazines refused to carry articles on homosexuality other than news reports on police raids or murder victims. *The New York Times* wouldn't even run an advertisement for a book with the dread word in its title.

DOB began under this repressive climate. With its potential members branded by society as illegal, immoral, and sick, the going was slow and laborious. Hardly anyone was out of the closet. The fear of discovery and its consequences were very real. Although many lesbians hungered for contact with their gay sisters, they didn't want to risk having their names on a membership or mailing list. This fear of being involved and the difficulty we had letting anybody know that DOB existed hampered the organization's growth.

Oddly enough, the only woman we are aware of who ever got into any trouble because of her involvement in DOB was a heterosexual woman, Dr. Vera Plunkett, who was investigated by the San Francisco Chiropractic Society. Her interrogators asked her if she was a lesbian. She replied, "It's none of your business! I don't ask you who you go to bed with, and I'm certainly not going to tell you who I go to bed with." The investigation was eventually dropped. The Daughters of Bilitis was open to women—both gay and "straight." And certainly we didn't take a bed check of our members.

The name of the organization was taken from "Songs of Bilitis," a narrative lesbian love poem by Pierre Louÿs published in 1894. Bilitis was characterized as a contemporary of Sappho. Daughters of Bilitis sounded like just another women's lodge, such as the Daughters of the Nile or the Daughters of the American Revolution. The DOB could be explained away as a women's group studying early Greek poetry. Only those "in the know" would be aware of the real nature of the club. At the time we chose the name we had no idea of going public, nor how many times in the future we would be required to explain its origin.

Although started as a more or less "secret" social club, DOB changed its character considerably just a year later. To overcome problems of lesbian fear and self-image, the organization decided to publish *The Ladder* as an outreach to the public and to other lesbians across the country. The first issue was sent to every lesbian any of our members knew or had heard of. The second issue, which contained an article "Your Name Is Safe," citing a 1953 U. S. Supreme Court decision upholding the right of a publisher to refuse to reveal the names of purchasers of reading material to a congressional investigating committee, was mailed to all the women attorneys listed in the San Francisco telephone directory. The response from the lesbians, for the most part, was positive. But receiving a lesbian publication panicked the women attorneys, most of whom threatened to report us to the postal authorities unless we removed their names from our mailing list immediately. (This guilt by association also plagued DOB in its effort to find professional women as speakers for its first national lesbian convention held in San Francisco in 1960.)

The Ladder also announced the first of a series of monthly public discussion meetings to be held in a downtown hall. There being no other means of publicizing these meetings, the "public" attending was primarily gay, with a smattering of straight friends and relatives. But calling them public meetings allowed gays to come and hear about "those" people, presumably without being identified themselves. The earlier sessions were geared toward dispelling myths and alleviating anxieties, apprising homosexuals of their legal rights, and introducing them to professionals (attorneys, psychologists, psychiatrists, employment and marriage counselors) who "understood" and offered their help.

The membership grew, and by 1958 DOB had formed two more chapters in Los Angeles and New York City. Later chapters were to emerge, flourish, lie dormant, or go defunct in most major cities of the United States and in Melbourne, Australia. Most of the members and authors published in *The Ladder* used pseudonyms for personal protection. Phyllis, who edited *The Ladder* from its inception until 1960, took the name of Ann Ferguson. This posed a problem at public discussion meetings when people asked to meet the editor. Members found that Phyllis was completely oblivious to the name Ann. Only when they shouted "Phyllis!" did she respond. The fourth issue of *The Ladder* carried an

obituary, complete with heavy border. We killed Ann Ferguson—it was the only thing to do. And Phyllis Lyon came out.

Del had an equally dramatic coming out. At the 1960 DOB convention just as we were sitting down to lunch the "Homosexual Detail" of San Francisco's Vice Squad arrived. As national president Del had to deal with the police officers who wanted to know what this DOB organization was all about. "Do you advocate dressing in the clothes of the opposite sex?" she was asked. "Look around," she replied. "Does it look like it?" There we all were dressed in our finest from high heels to earrings. To get rid of the cops Del gave them her given name, Dorothy, and her phone numbers at work, home, and the DOB office. She offered to meet with them at a later date to explain the organization in more detail. Interestingly enough, she never heard from them again, although the police had checked out DOB with the manager of the office building when the fact that San Francisco harbored the national headquarters of two homophile organizations—DOB and Mattachine—became an issue in the 1959 mayoralty campaign. (In the seventies Del experienced another name problem. She was asked to endorse a political candidate, but had to decline because she was registered to vote under her legal name. Who the hell knew Dorothy Martin? She has since reregistered as Del.)

DOB's four-part statement of purpose, printed inside the front cover of *The Ladder* for so many years, has caused a certain amount of consternation and questions from more recent lesbians—especially the part about "advocating a mode of dress and behavior acceptable to society." To today's more militant and secure lesbians it must seem like a complete sellout. But, for the most part, lesbians of the fifties were not secure in either fact or self-image.

Phyllis still remembers vividly the first time she went out in the neighborhood after she and Del had moved in together. She "knew" everyone on the street could see she was a lesbian. Intellectually she was aware this was crazy. She had walked the same streets in the same jeans and shirt before—before she became a practicing lesbian. She didn't look any different (only maybe happier) but the feeling of being "different" in the eyes of others was there at a gut level. It took a while to meld feelings and intellect into one good and positive self-image.

The climate of the fifties was not the climate of the seventies. DOB members feared disclosure of their sexual orientation more than anything else. They felt that lesbians who flaunted themselves, who wore men's clothes (which usually meant only men's pants and shirts and perhaps "mannish" shoes), were a threat. If you were seen with one who was "obvious," you were apt to be tarred with the same brush. (Once when Del wore a tailored *women's* pantsuit to a DOB brunch, we were shocked to learn later that members were disturbed that a DOB officer would wear a man's suit.)

There were other reasons for DOB's "dress code."

Members felt that gay women should not be restricted as to where they could go because of the clothes they wore. As Helen Sanders once said, "We should be able to go anywhere and be as comfortable in an evening gown as in slacks." And certainly in the fifties there were few restaurants where you could go in pants; such attire was even frowned upon for shopping downtown. In the second issue of *The Ladder* a reader put it this way: "I find that because now I am wearing women's slacks and letting my hair grow long I am getting a wider variety of friends and I have neighbors instead of people next door. I no longer have the feeling that everyone is watching."

Of course, we all wore slacks at DOB meetings and parties held in our homes. But in public we generally wore skirts—even had an annual fund-raising, dress-up cocktail party to which men were invited. Gay men expected their lesbian sisters to wear skirts in public, and some gay bars would not allow women in if they wore pants.

As the years passed and DOB and its members became more secure the dress code became an empty statement more honored in the breach than in the enforcement. But it did serve its purpose. DOB members, by and large, were a pretty self-confident bunch and certainly did a lot to change the public's image of the lesbian as a pseudomale. By the time of the first demonstrations by homosexual women and men at Independence Hall in Philadelphia and the White House in Washington, D.C., many DOB members expressed their displeasure that the organizers insisted that the women wear skirts.

Another turnabout happened in 1960 when we sent out press releases announcing that DOB was holding the first national lesbian convention. Hal Call, national president of the Mattachine Society, wrote us a letter of protest, saying he was appalled at our audacity. He pointed out that homophile organizations had always billed themselves as organizations dealing with the problem of homosexuality, certainly not as homosexual societies. He added that he seriously doubted if members of Mattachine would be able to attend the DOB convention under the circumstances. Mattachine, like ONE, was open to women, but its membership was 99 percent male. So Jaye Bell, president of the hosting chapter, responded, "If the members of Mattachine dress with decorum and behave properly, we are sure that no one will mistake them for lesbians." In all fairness, however, Del must admit that just two years earlier when she rented our first office she told the building manager that DOB was "an organization dealing with the sociological problems of single women." But the 1959 mayoralty election blew our cover, and DOB decided there was no more point in camouflaging our identity.

At the convention luncheon that the police had interrupted, the Reverend Fordyce Eastburn, Episcopal chaplain at St. Luke's Hospital, was the featured speaker. The reason this is significant was that, although clergy had previously participated in Mattachine and ONE conventions, they had attended out of personal concern and did not reveal nor speak for their denominations. Originally we had asked the late Bishop James Pike and Rabbi Alvin Fine, both of whom had politely declined. Then we tackled the Council of Churches for a speaker. After a couple of months DOB received a reply apologizing for the delay and admitting they had "never received a request of this nature before and quite frankly we didn't know how to deal with it." We had visions of delight over the turmoil our request had provoked in San Francisco's church circles.

Mr. Eastburn came to us as an official spokesperson of the California Episcopal Diocese. His speech was anything but comforting to gays. He said that we would be accepted in the church, as all sinners are. But once there, we would be expected to change—either that or remain celibate. The wife of a psychiatrist was appalled by his note of doom and asked Del afterward, "Don't you feel that this will destroy all the good you have managed to build? Won't it set your members back?" But Del didn't think so. "We've already been called every name there is to call us. We look at it this way: We've opened the door to communication with the church." Indeed, Mr. Eastburn has kept in touch with us over the years and has a far more enlightened attitude than he did in 1960. And his superior, Bishop Pike, was to appoint a Joint Committee on Homosexuality to continue the dialogue between the church and the gay community.

People have asked us, too, to clarify some of the language used in the early days of the gay movement. In DOB's statement of purpose we referred to the "variant" which in those days was really very avant-garde. Deviant (against the norm) had more popular usage, but variant placed homosexuality properly as a variation on the Kinsey scale of human sexuality. The word "homophile" comes from the Greek and means love of same. The term was adopted by West Coast organizations to deemphasize the three letters in homo*sex*uality, which tends to be a hang-up in our society. Homophile, we felt, better expressed a sense of the whole person. In *The Ladder* we always upper-cased "lesbian," just as "gay" is often capitalized today.

In the latter part of the sixties the East Coast Homophile Organizations made moves to get homophile into the dictionary. In the process they declared that homophile could only be used as an adjective and only in reference to an organization or movement. We disagreed. Having used the word in our vocabulary both as a noun and as an adjective for more than a decade, we were not about to be told that we couldn't do so anymore. Then along came gay liberation and we were told we couldn't use the word at all, that we needed to put *sex* back into homosexuality. And in the seventies when gay became the accepted term we had come full circle, since gay had been used as an "in" password in the old days when we were *all* in the closet.

The fact that we enlisted professional speakers, who volunteered their services and many times opened themselves up to suspicion and criticism from their colleagues, did not stem from our inability to recognize that we were indeed the "experts" and could speak for ourselves. Rather, it was an acknowledgment, first, that few of us were in a position to speak out publicly, and second, that professionals are the public opinion makers. In February 1966 at the first meeting of the North American Conference of Homophile Organizations in Kansas City a declaration that "we are not sick" became a major controversy. Opposition came from those of us who felt such a statement could easily be rejected by the retort, "You are, too!" and would accomplish nothing. On the other hand, we worked actively to change professional opinion, always pointing out that conclusions had been based upon theory and not fact.

In 1958 DOB conducted its own survey on the background and behavior of lesbians in an effort to stimulate research on gay women. In 1960 a second survey was conducted to call attention to the differences between homosexual women and men. Previously the professional literature dealt almost solely with male homosexuals and gave only casual mention to lesbians, who were assumed to be their female counterparts. The DOB surveys were successful in bringing about research that dispelled some of the myths about lesbians. Members were the guinea pigs for Armon (1960), Prosin (1962), Gundlach and Riess (1968), Freedman (1968), Kaye (1971), Saghir and Robins (1971), and Rosen (1974). The dates are publishing dates, not the time when the research was conducted. Armon, unable to find many clear-cut differences between the lesbians and the heterosexual control group in her study, concluded that homosexuality is not a clinical entity. Aside from Kaye, who concluded that, because most lesbians had had some heterosexual experience, they were bisexual and therefore treatable, the researchers generally found that gay women were no more neurotic than heterosexual women.

By 1968 DOB's research director, Florence Conrad, decided it was high time we found out if there had been any change in attitude among mental health professionals. Aware that they would not be apt to respond readily to a questionnaire from a lesbian organization, she took her idea to Dr. Joel Fort, who was director of the San Francisco Health Department's Center for Special Problems. Together with Dr. Claude Steiner they conducted an opinion survey among Bay Area psychiatrists, psychologists, and social workers who were picked at random. The results were far more encouraging than expected. More than 90 percent felt that public misunderstanding had arisen from the terms "illness" or "disease" as applied to homosexuality, and 96 percent did not see any reason why the average homosexual should be required to undergo therapy. Also, 97 percent admitted that in dealing with a homosexual "patient" they would work with a goal other than change to a heterosexual orientation—the other goals being self-acceptance, self-assertiveness, and improved interpersonal relationships.

Editors of professional journals were not eager to publish data that was contrary to traditional concepts of homosexuality as a "personality disorder." The survey remained unpublished until October 1971 when it was finally accepted by *Psychological Reports.* That same year Dr. Kent Robinson, a Baltimore psychiatrist, sponsored the first gay panel at the American Psychiatric Association's annual meeting in Washington, D.C. He also arranged a meeting with members of the Nomenclature Committee to begin negotiations to remove homosexuality from the organization's Standard Diagnostic Manual. By 1974 it was an accomplished fact.

A great deal of misunderstanding also exists today around the fact that early DOB goals included education of the lesbian "to enable her to understand herself and make her adjustment to society." What was meant is perhaps best explained in Del's editorial in the second issue of *The Ladder*:

To the uninformed this difference [being a Lesbian] may constitute "a sin against nature," with all its moral and legal implications. To the informed this difference merely means another form of individual adjustment to self and society.

The salvation of the Lesbian lies in her acceptance of herself without guilt or anxiety, in her awareness of her capabilities and her limitations, and in pursuit of a constructive way of life without misgivings or apology.

That was our intent and the extent of our philosophy, ideology, or politics at the time. We knew that if the lesbian was to find her niche in society she could not allow herself to be bogged down by what "they" said. Far more important was her self-concept. Years later the women's movement was to undergo the same struggle. Change from a negative to a positive self-image is necessary in any oppressed group before its members can even conceive of undertaking an activist liberation movement.

Gay Pride grew out of resistance to the bullying tactics of police. On the West Coast it happened at the costume ball in San Francisco on New Year's Day 1965 at a benefit held for the newly formed Council on Religion and the Homosexual. A cadre of police intent upon making wholesale arrests parked a paddy wagon in front of California Hall, flooded the entrance with lights, and took photos—still and movie—of everyone going in or out of the building. More than five hundred gay women and men, bolstered by the support of clergy and their wives, crossed that picket line of cops. Six arrests were made, among them three attorneys and a housewife. The next day seven angry ministers held a press conference denouncing the Gestapo-like police behavior. The American Civil Liberties Union took the case, and charges were dismissed by the judge without the defense presenting even one word of testimony.

On the East Coast in 1969 homosexuals rioted against police harassment at Stonewall, a gay bar in New York City. That marked a change in grass-roots consciousness and the change from the homophile to the gay liberation movement. Since then, from coast to coast, Gay Pride celebrations are held annually. But the resistance, the militance, and the joy of "coming out" could only have happened because of the groundwork laid by the homophile organizations of the fifties and sixties.

As we said at the beginning of this article, we have seen changes in our society that we never dreamed would happen in our lifetime. We have seen police officers appointed to act as a liaison to the gay community to iron out difficulties as they arise. We have seen gay studies included in the curriculum of colleges and universities. We have seen repressive sex laws repealed in almost twenty states and civil rights ordinances for gays enacted in many cities and counties. We have seen an up-front lesbian elected to the Massachusetts legislature. And we have even seen an incumbent President and his challenger forced to take a stand on issues that affect gay citizens.

As for ourselves, we were recently appointed by the mayor of San Francisco to city commissions: Phyllis to the Human Rights Commission and Del to the Commission on the Status of Women. And one fond memory we shall always hold dear is that we danced together at the mayor's Inaugural Ball.

Del Martin and Phyllis Lyon, authors of Lesbian / Woman

Electoral Politics: An Interview with Elaine Noble

LINDA LACHMAN

Note: Elaine Noble was the first open lesbian to be elected to public office. In 1974 she ran on the Democratic ticket in the Fenway district of Boston and was elected state representative. Since that time she has received wide attention by the media and has campaigned for a variety of issues, including the rights of women and gays, in the Massachusetts State Legislature.

The following interview was conducted by Linda Lachman, a former member of Elaine's staff. –Ed.

L: Why should lesbians run for office?

E: We have to understand why women haven't, in general, become involved in politics, from a historical basis. Educational institutions, city and state government, the church, have always been, in the history of the Western world, controlled by, designed by, and open primarily to men. It has only been in the last one hundred years that women have realized that in order to get control over their own lives, they have one of two alternatives: either to completely withdraw from the systems that govern and try to build alternative ones, or to take a look at the systems to which they've been denied access and to try to get into those processes. There are good arguments for both of them, but living in a conservative Western world, we're born political, because we cannot have grown up in America without having some amount of contact with some institutions at some point in our lives.

The luxury of withdrawing from institutions only comes after you've been through some of the better ones. It is primarily the white upper- and middle-class lesbians who can sometimes have the luxury of saying they want to build an alternative. The poor, Third World lesbians, who live in ghettos or live in projects, whether it be in New York, Georgia, or elsewhere, realize that their key to freedom is through institutions, learning how to read and write and work through that institution. As women, we get our working papers through institutions.

L: A great many workingwomen involve themselves in health collectives and other alternative structures because it takes a lot of money to be able to run for office.

E: That's true, but you're still building an institution, and my premise is that you can't get away from institutions as it stands now. You can build alternative ones, but they still become institutions, and therefore if you're going to have one institution, why not take over one? I'm not saying that one is more valid than the other, but that the last male bastion of power to really be infiltrated by women and minorities is politics, and it is the most major institution that governs every other aspect of institutions in our lives. We don't have a legacy, or a heritage, at building alternative political structures, because the ones that stand are so formidable.

L: Many women say that participating in the government, in the system, will take too much time for the changes to happen and that the alternative systems will make things happen faster.

E: I don't agree with that. I think if you want to work in an alternative system, fine, but when you stay out of politics, what happens is that you create a vacuum of power which the very people we don't want governing our lives absorb, and that's a very difficult angle that people have got to understand. It's certainly something the blacks understood in the sixties. There was never a question when they had to register to vote, when they started putting it together and integrating public facilities and institutions. They realized that they didn't have an option of building alternative structures, but that they had to get into the structures that existed in order to get some power over their own lives. They couldn't build an alternative bus system, so they had to take over the bus system so they could sit wherever they wanted. I think for women, we have to realize that the longer we stay out of the system, the longer decisions will be made by others about our lives on health care, on sexual preference, sexuality, shelters for battered women, rape. Legislation either will not exist or will come out so badly mutilated that it won't even bear any resemblance to what a woman's original piece of legislation looked like.

The main argument for this is that if it doesn't touch your life in the political process, it doesn't become your priority. Most legislators in Massachusetts deal with eight thousand or more pieces of legislation in a year, so if it is not one of their legislative priorities, it doesn't happen. It's no accident that in male legislative bodies, women's bills and gay bills have never been a priority, because you have to get people into that process who value them and begin to make allegiances.

Connecticut Senator Betty Hudson's tremendous coup was heading the Human Services Committee handling the gay bill, and at the same time building up a great allegiance with unions who are now in back of the gay bill and her women's bills. The unions consider her one of their own, so they want to go along with her legislation. It's a priority for Betty Hudson, and without Betty in that form of government, it just wouldn't happen.

If I weren't in the Massachusetts State House, you wouldn't have a new consenting adults bill in this state; you'd have the same old bill that was written years ago

and submitted every year. I don't care how liberal the man is, if it's not a priority in his life, he isn't going to rework that bill, or if she's a straight woman, she's not going to spend as much time tediously going over the bills, seeking out help from the attorney general's office, because it isn't one of their priorities in terms of their own small life. I believe that who you are and what you're about comes out in your political structures. I think that for that reason alone I'm convinced that the structures are built to keep people out. Anyplace that I go that people say, "Stay out," I want to get into, just to say, "You're not going to keep me out!"

L: Is there any other more specific reason that lesbians should be more involved?

E: I think that we can't trust the men, and I don't mean that in a paranoid way. Gay men to a certain extent have similar priorities, and we can work comfortably together on some levels, but we have the responsibility to carry our issues.

In child custody cases, for examples, lesbians have a different row to hoe, especially financially. Traditionally, women don't have as much money as men in court cases and it's up to those lesbians who are political to build up defense funds. I also think that often gay men can be as piggy as straight men and don't necessarily view us any differently.

Priorities are just a hard-core political reality. Take the reverse now—the representative from Brookline deals with election laws. If he asks me, I'll help him, but it's not a priority of mine. It's his responsibility to submit the best bills he can put together and so on. There are so many bills you just can't function without having some specific areas that are priorities and they are always the ones that touch your life. If lesbians don't decide that they're going to carry their own issues, they won't get done.

I just think women have to get involved. I've paid my dues in the feminist movement in terms of straight women's issues—abortion, birth control, day care—and I think because of that I'm able to get the respect and support of a whole lot of women and it's time for that, but if we think they're going to do it for us, we're kidding ourselves.

L: By choosing to work in the system, many women say that you are forced to compromise yourself.

E: I think that whatever work you do, you make compromises, and people confuse compromise with being co-opted. There is a distinction. I work in the last bastion of male power, and if I walk into that House chamber and I am not together personally, if I do not know what my agenda is, then they can smell it a mile away. If I'm confused, then they can feed me a line of bull on a bill, but it is my confusion that leads me into the mistake, and that's how co-optation begins. I don't have to compromise with anyone if I don't want to do so, or on things that I feel I don't want to compromise on. Under pressure you just weigh the situation, what's involved for all sides, what it's worth to the people you're representing, and you make a deal. That's how life is. I push as hard as I can for the best deal for my constituency and my agenda.

There's another reason for running for office—it's rewarding and exciting! One of the most exciting times for me was being in that chamber during the joint convention of both houses of the legislature and participating in that bitter battle to get the ERA on the ballot. If there hadn't been three key women linking up with more experienced women, that would have never happened. Within thirty seconds history would have been rewritten. But the fact that we were there, fighting on the floor, changed the course of Massachusetts history, and the course of history of this country, perhaps, because we are considered one of the pivotal states. Some of the younger women were pushing some of the older women, persuading them to lead, which they were really delighted to do. They knew the maneuvers and taught us a lot—bam! Thirty seconds in this state and we might not have had the ERA on the ballot and no ERA in this state.

And being in the decision-making body, and to understand acutely that thirty seconds can change the course of history for women, is pretty exciting and meaningful for me. I don't feel powerless. I can take the self-hate that has been taught to me all my life and that is so prevalent in the lesbian community, and push it outward onto those responsible. I have more control over my life.

I see a wave of conservatism coming down the pike, and if we don't use our talents—it should be a mandate that we use our talents for the betterment of people—it's our own fault. We also have an unusual burden to bear right now, because lesbians have had to carry the straight women's issues too—and our issues have been tied in with gay men's issues, and we have really not come into our own. Because there aren't enough lesbian feminists around to take control, the gay guys take charge. We just have to have more of us who will take the responsibility.

With our feminist awareness, we realize that the hatred that denies us access or tells us what terrible people we are, is the same hatred that denies political access to blacks and other oppressed people. The people who would repeal a racial imbalance law are the same people who would vote against a gay rights bill or a women's bill. I think women understand that and that it's our duty to raise those issues as well as our own. Women just seem to be more sensitive; they know oppression and that it's transferable at any moment.

Somewhere along the line, all of us have to begin to put ourselves on the line to open up that system. I don't always like what I do or where I work, because it's very hard work, but it has to be done, and for the next people who come along, it will be a lot easier. That notion is a comfort for me, and I have to keep that vision in front of me, as do other women. But I just don't see how we can afford not to be involved, because every time a lesbian mother is denied custody, or a lesbian is denied a bank loan for a mortgage, that's political, because there's no law that protects you. There are some people who don't want to put themselves on the line to change that. There are different kinds of people to do different kinds of tasks, but there should be more strategists who are committed to changing and infiltrating political structure on all levels. I think women have to realize that we're at a time in our history where everything is going to be difficult the first time around.

L: What about campaigning?

E: Prejudice is high and people aren't going to elect a black candidate because they're black, any more than they're going to elect a lesbian feminist because she's a lesbian feminist! In terms of the way you get elected, nobody runs on a one-issue or two-issue campaign. You run on ten or twenty issues. It's just an extension of that philosophy I mentioned, seeing where the oppression and injustices occur and talking about housing and minorities, for example, and I think that that's necessary and appropriate.

L: For your first campaign, to get your foot in the door,

Elaine Noble, Massachusetts State Representative

you already had a great deal of previous community activity. That was important to you, wasn't it?

E: Yes, I had thirteen years of community experience such as working in settlement houses while I was a college student—it was one of the ways I subsidized going through school. I think at that time if anyone had said I would be running for office, I would have told them they were crazy, because the political process was something foreign to me. I didn't know the difference between City Hall and the State House. Even after I started lobbying with parents and with NOW women for day care or school reform, I was pretty intimidated by the place. I realize now that environment is really important. Structures intimidate people, and the marble mazes control us to a certain extent—it's incredible. It was hard for me.

I didn't know I was involved. I thought I was on the side of the true and the just, and I didn't know that it was political action.

L: Eventually you began to infiltrate, shall we say, into other women's organizations. How did that affect your career?

E: It taught me a great deal about the political process and persistence—about being there all the time; running lesbians for any office available, and letting all women get to know us and why they shouldn't be afraid of us. It was a long process and I did it not by setting up little lectures, "now we will talk about lesbianism," but by functioning around that issue and a series of other issues. They were nervous for a while, but it worked out okay, and, as a result, those women came out and worked in my election.

Then, while I was involved with the National Women's Political Caucus and teaching, the House was redistricted and one of the new districts was where I had lived. Several friends said to me, "You know it like the back of your hand; you've lived there, worked there; why don't you run?" They did not drag me kicking and screaming into it; I think it was suggested twice!

I said, "I don't have any qualifications," but they said, "You're already a politician, look at what you've done." We tend not to value our own work sometimes. So I started looking and realized, sure I was qualified, and in many ways better than some of the political people who were running.

To me, life is paying your dues and putting yourself on the line, and I figured that since I had struggled through who I was and what I was about, in many ways I had already won. I wasn't going to be a candidate who was running just to raise issues, but I was running to win. You burn a lot of bridges and you take a lot of risks, and that's what I think being alive and being political means.

I have to add another aspect, however. I don't think anyone should be in politics all of their adult lives. I don't care if you're running a paper, or a health collective, or whatever, you should expand; use your tools, and teach somebody else, and then get out for a while to rejuvenate yourself. It's unhealthy for one person to be doing the same stuff all the time. It's unhealthy for the community; it's unhealthy for the person. I guess that's why I have a vested interest in bringing other people along, because the burden is then lifted. I hope soon! I don't want to spend my life as the only one—I think that's fair, fairer for everyone.

Here I am thirty-three years old with an invitation from one of the most formidable male institutions in the country for me to come back and finish my doctorate. Then I find out that the job market, especially because I was political, is very small for me. So now I'm looking at law school so at least I can have control over my own life, and have a tangible tool or trade. I have to change directions, make a major career change, alter my trade, and it's because of the lack of political lesbians in those institutions that I'm being denied access; I'm still considered a risk. I have to do a forty-five-degree turn and go into law rather than into the philosophy of education, my own discipline which I dearly love. I feel very acutely how important it is to be political, but I've narrowed my choices because I have been political. In many ways, though, I think that by doing that I've opened up choices to other women. I think I've blown the system wide open. When a lesbian feminist, in a conservative town and state, can get elected, there's absolutely no reason why anybody can't get elected anywhere in this country. There's no excuse now. There are districts like mine in every city, and you go to a district where you can win. You go to a district where you feel comfortable living, where you pay your dues in community activities, and you start from the roots up. I wouldn't move to a very conservative town; that would be crazy. I don't want to fail. At the same time my own personal options have narrowed because there haven't been women there for me. Hopefully, women who are even ten years younger than I am won't have to face that. For at least the next hundred years we'll all face some kind of discrimination, but we can legislate against it and make people realize that they're going to have to pay for their bigotry. If they don't obey the law, they go to jail or they get fined. And you work on making judges at the appellate court or the supreme court level uphold the laws, and that's an exciting concept, to realize that on a federal or state level you can now say, "No, you can't discriminate against women anymore." To me that's a trip, that's just incredibly exciting, and it can be extended if more lesbians get into the process.

L: Can you be more specific as to how you put your first campaign together?

E: I started off with about seven people in a room.

L: What were their various political experiences?

E: None, absolutely none. The most experienced person in my campaign was the office manager, the sixteen-year-old daughter of a friend who had grown up in a very political family. None of us had any electoral process experience. We just decided we'd learn the rules and we went out and we studied. We read and we talked to people. I went down to City Hall and sat down with the elections officials to find out, "How do you get on the ballot?" "You need signatures." "How many signatures?" "What does it mean that signatures can be invalidated?" I learned all that and had the biggest drive for signatures ever and turned in more than anyone had ever seen for a state office. It was my way of serving notice that I'm here, and I'm not going away. It also scared some of the opposition away. Then I learned what you do with those lists. If they signed my petition, I should thank them for signing it. So I worked from the list, and many of them simply couldn't believe that they got a letter saying "thank you," not "vote for me." Of course, they got that later!

My campaign was interesting because it was a new district—though I think it would work in other districts too. Most good politicians represent people, but educate them, too. Most people didn't know about the district, so I informed them that this was a new district and that this rep or that rep was no longer their rep and that they had to go and register, and thus and such were the lines of the district, and, "Oh, by the way, I'm a candidate." People were so freaked out that I was giving them information, and low-keying my candidacy, that I think they were really shocked. I just said, "This is what I've done, in terms of the community, and this is what I want to do." I made, through my campaigning on the issues, a contract with the people, so that this time around I could go back and say, "Look, I've worked hard, and here's what I've done that I said I would do." The day after I was sworn in I began living up to my part of the contract, so that two years later when they stood in line to vote on a street that had never been lit before, I could point to the streetlights, and other things, the tangible things as well as issues.

L: Would you say your first campaign was door-to-door?

E: What I tried to do was one-on-one, trying to meet everybody in my district who was a potential voter and following it up with a piece of literature in the mail.

People really want to see how well you run. People would see Elaine Noble at the bus stop at 6:30 A.M. I had people spit at me and yell nasty things at me—and it did freak me, I must admit—I don't think I'll ever get used to that—but I kept myself together, and what it did to the other decent people getting on the bus is that it radicalized them. They would watch the way in which I handled that and people want to see how you handle situations. I would be at the supermarket and rather than trying to stop people with their grocery bags, I would say, "Can I give you a hand with this?" and then, "Oh, by the way, is it okay if I put some of my literature in?" "Okay." "Thanks." I got muscles like a Green Bay Packer, but I also got votes! You know, it's those funny little touches that come with the political process, and maybe it's weird, and maybe not, but I did that as well as maintaining involvement in community meetings and always being up-front with people.

I really had an advantage over the other candidates in some ways because people knew me over a series of years, and you have to remember that people usually vote for people most like themselves. I don't mean you'll find everyone agreeing with you all the time, nor do I want to try to be all things to all people, but people vote for someone who they think thinks like them or feels like them on certain issues. If the majority of my district changed radically, and the majority of the people didn't think the way I do, they'd get themselves another rep. And I think that's appropriate, rather than my shifting my public views on things to adjust to a new constituency. That's why a great many legislators begin to lose their integrity, because they try to change their views to meet a new constituency and people know it isn't them. People sense that.

People may not always agree with me, but they give me a vote for being direct and honest with them. That's how I won the first election, by constantly going back to them over and over again, talking to them, letting them know who I was, and making them aware that I didn't have horns and a tail, just maybe a few different ideas or opinions. I let them know that I would give them a good deal, that I would represent them like a good lawyer represents a client, trying to get the best deal I could for them. I just have ultimate faith and wisdom in how intelligent people are. There are a great many politicians who think that people are really stupid, but they're not. They're very sensitive and they pick up more than those pols give them credit for. If you give people a good reason for voting for you, they will. I've been told I'm too idealistic, that I think people are smarter than they really are, by some seasoned politicians. But I think they are smart—I think that the process has been designed to make it difficult for them to show it, but I think the voters are a hell of a lot better than most of the political structure reflects. I try to deal with everyone on a level of respect, assuming that their problems are valid until I find out otherwise. So, in order to get elected you just have to show people why they should vote for you.

L: Without the groundwork, though, the community work, would that work out?

E: Of course, you have to pay your dues, to have something to show. However, even if you put in two years of community work, that's extremely valid. There are so many candidates who just pop up, move into the district, and they haven't done a damn thing; they posture themselves as America's guests. The majority of politicians are just that—we pay for their lunch—and it's terrible. So many women could win an election. It's just learning the process and everyone makes it seem so difficult, purposely. You just begin by learning what governs the process where you are and how it works, and you find out what step A is and you start. The community action involvement helps you to understand your local political process. That I can't stress enough. You can't run just on women's issues. Oftentimes, I think, we can tend to get overinvolved in our women's things and forget there are other oppressed people with whom we can share our fight.

One important thing I learned, as well, is that once you're committed as a candidate, you have to have very committed people with you. In other words, you don't want people who are going to always be questioning your judgment, in the sense of your issues. As a candidate, you don't have time to sit up until 3:00 A.M. rapping, convincing your workers. If they aren't convinced, then they simply shouldn't be with you—throw them out and get somebody else. They're sapping your energy in a way that they have no right to sap. If you believe in me as a candidate, you offer me your services and you want to help, fine. If I have to sell my volunteers on me, that's just screwy. I think that that's been the demise of some women candidates, where they just felt responsible for everyone; and believe me, "sickies" do hang on and around campaigns, and they sap your energy. I've seen that happen in the movement—the show-me-that-you're-holier-than-thou. Once you get your volunteers and that campaign process going, just remember that, in an election, people who work for you in any sense are an extension of you and you have the right to ask them to do that in a way that suits you, and how you see yourself or want yourself reflected.

Another decision you have to make if you want to run is whether to run as a Republican, Democrat, or independent. In Massachusetts the Democrats run the show, and I wanted to be in that club, because if I ran as an independent they wouldn't have to take me seriously, and also, they wouldn't have to give me any money for my final fight. On the other hand, as the Democratic nominee, they had to give me that money, and welcome me into that club and help seat me. I didn't run as a Republican because there were only about seventy-six Republicans registered to vote in my district! It costs more money, because you have to mount a primary campaign, and it's a longer run, but I felt it was well worth it. You have to get in where the pie is being sliced, and the Democrats own it in this state, and that's just part of the process.

Finding a person who is good at handling volunteers for a campaign manager, and a good bookkeeper—a good finance person—and so on, the people you get to work for you are so important. I just went around to my friends and to friends of friends. They all had the skills even though they hadn't used them in a political campaign before, and it was exciting because it was our own, and we all learned and were in it together. I had a couple of seasoned political people help me out and advise me, and I can't stress enough how vital that is. I think it's virtually impossible to do by yourself without a political mentor to help map out what a campaign should look like. Once you have that blueprint, though, you can pretty much move it along. It's frightening to think of mapping your life for a year. You make your life public, probably more public than at any other time, and it's an incredible intrusion, but it has to be done and you learn

what to respond to and what not to respond to. The key is having very loyal and caring people with you. For me it was pretty much the same people the second time except that I expanded my base, broadened my coalition; it was a little more sophisticated.

L: You were in office this time, too, and that makes a difference.

E: Yes, I couldn't spend all my time campaigning; I had my job to do and I wanted to continue doing it well. The first time around I really nickled and dimed it. I had to do that, I wasn't known, had established few contacts, and had all my time to campaign. This time around I had earned union endorsement, for example, and had a broader coalition.

L: Then to get your foot in the door, the first campaign, is really different.

E: By all means, everything the first time is always different from the second time around. In some ways it gets easier, but in some ways it just changes; the complexities of it are different. The first step, though, is one that really doesn't change. It's just understanding your constituency and reflecting that. It means going to community hearings and community meetings, and testifying and making input and being there for people when they need you. It's showing you have the kind of mettle it takes to be someone who will take their wishes and philosophies to the state level. It's time, lots of it. It's day and night and it's hard, hardest the first time out. It cuts into your personal life, into a lot of things, but so does running a women's newspaper, or a health center. It's pretty rewarding work, and if I start getting bitter about it, I'll get out. I can see how people can get bitter about it. People only come to a politician when they're in need, in trouble, and it's a crisis. I do crisis intervention work all the time, and people just don't understand on Thanksgiving or Christmas Day, or on Sundays, whenever, why I'm not helping fix a leak, or bringing a city official to help out with something. It's part of that thing that you pledged, to take care of them, and they just don't understand, sometimes, that you're human, too. Most politicians have worked through that and can deal with it, but it's those kinds of things that eat away at you so you have to stop every once in a while and refuel, and then go back. It's finding time to refuel that can be a problem, but you have to remember to do it. If you don't stop to refuel, you're of no use to anybody, but if you remember to take care of yourself, as well as your constituents, you'll have a long and healthy relationship. The feeling of accomplishment that comes with knowing you're helping people and doing your part to the best of your abilities is important for all of us.

RESOURCES

"A Woman's Place Is in the House: A Portrait of Elaine Noble," color videotape by Nancy Porter, 1975, 29 mins. WGBH Educational Foundation, 125 Western Ave., Boston, Mass. 02134.

Nurturing a Lesbian Organization

VICKI GABRINER and SUSAN WELLS

In the last six years, lesbian organizations have multiplied rapidly in the United States. These groups are part of the growing lesbian feminist culture. Our needs are met neither by the larger society nor by the feminist or gay movements. In the feminist movement we are outnumbered by straight women and find our energies diverted toward issues of limited personal concern for lesbians. In the gay movement we are outnumbered by men due to the greater freedom men have in this society to be politically and socially open, and therefore our energies are diverted toward issues such as harassment on streets, also of limited personal concern to lesbians. We are now developing a political power base for ourselves.

In surveying a national cross section of lesbian groups, we found a common theme of support for lesbians in their fight against oppression. Each group had a different way of responding to the needs of the women in its area, but forming a lesbian group, whether it was social, political, or project-oriented, filled a vital need of lesbians in their areas. Several women in small towns or rural areas have written desperate letters to existing lesbian organizations saying there are no outlets for them in their areas. Clearly, there is a need for lesbian groups in all parts of the country.

To help lesbians deal with the practical considerations of forming new groups, we have extracted information gathered from eleven lesbian organizations[1] which replied in depth to a questionnaire sent to more than one hundred lesbian groups across the country. These include health centers, newspapers and presses, student groups, gay churches and religious groups, political action groups, lesbian therapy groups, social groups and lesbian mothers and other special interest groups, information centers and a national organization with

[1] Lesbian Feminist Liberation, New York; Yalesbians, New Haven; NOW Sexuality Task Force, Washington, D.C.; Sapphic Sisters, Denville, N.J.; Lesbian Resource Center, Seattle; Lesbian Union, Amherst, Mass.; Daughters of Bilitis, San Francisco; Central Ohio Lesbians, Columbus; Women's Center, Tampa; United Sisters, Garwood, New Jersey; Atlanta Lesbian Feminist Alliance, Atlanta.

chapters in several states. We will talk about the experience of these groups in terms of membership, outreach, structure, fund raising, and politics; we will then provide case studies of Yalesbians of New Haven and the Atlanta Lesbian Feminist Alliance (ALFA) of which we are members.

The problem with a lesbian organization is not starting it, but sustaining it. The major problems are external. We are lesbians and society is not fond of us, so it is difficult to find safe, comfortable, inexpensive meeting places and funding.

The student groups (Yalesbians and Lesbian Union of Amherst) did have hassles with their college administrations, but both groups were finally granted official recognition as student organizations and given meeting space and money, although, according to Lesbian Union, not nearly enough. Yalesbians shares an office with the gay men's group on campus and finds it adequate.

Lesbian organizations looking for members and a place to meet might consider the facilities of a college in their area, at least as a beginning. Resources helpful to other groups were the YWCA and the National Organization for Women, both of which were able to provide money and meeting places. Many NOW chapters either have a Lesbianism and Sexuality Task Force or might be interested in forming one.

A woman in Washington, D.C., has been holding an open house in her home each week for lesbians for several years. The event is purely social, and has served to bring women together in a nonthreatening situation. This type of meeting can be either advertised or publicized by word of mouth among friends.

Another suggestion is to look into churches in your area. Some lesbian groups have found space to meet in church buildings and some have been able to hold dances and other functions there. Unitarian and Episcopal churches have often responded favorably. In many areas gay churches, such as the Metropolitan Community Church, may offer meeting space, as might existing gay men's organizations.

Membership solicitation has been accomplished by advertising social events and meetings in feminist publications, local newspapers, and leafleting lesbian bars. Once a membership is established, most groups run into two major problems: forming a structure and choosing a political stance.

Many lesbian groups, eager to avoid male hierarchical structures, have organized collectively without designated leaders. However, as Yalesbians points out, "We're finding, like so many other movement groups, that not having a designated leadership structure has a tendency to be extremely frustrating, since there are obviously leaders anyway." A structure usually functions best if it establishes some clear lines of accountability within the group by making certain people responsible for certain activities.

Forming committees allows women to participate in those activities of an organization which they find most appealing. Committee chairwomen are usually selected by vote or volunteer if only one person is interested. Flexibility in structure is a must for most groups. After five years, ALFA is now reorganizing, as is the Lesbian Resource Center in Seattle after six years, which reports that "we are still trying on structure and functions."

One rule usually holds true: The larger the group, the more need there is for a tight structure. Large groups trying to arrive collectively at decisions may find their meetings chaotic or dragging on for hours unless some kind of guidelines for decision making are followed, and someone is given the power to "chair" the meeting. Following a simplified version of Robert's Rules of Order may be better than a four-hour meeting where sixty people talk at once, drift from the topic, reach no conclusions, and leave feeling unsisterly.

Once the group's activities are defined, a structure to accomplish its goals may suggest itself. Keep in mind that as the organization grows, it will evolve in many different stages. The structure of the group will have to change as needs change. An ad-hoc committee to protest a particular TV show could evolve into a standing media committee, for example.

To be political or not, and to what extent, is a difficult choice for individual lesbians and lesbian groups. The very existence of a lesbian organization is a political statement, but beyond that, the degree and variation is endless. The needs of the women involved determine the thrust of the group. Several of the groups that answered our survey reported conflicts between women who wanted the group to be primarily political and those who wanted it to be social. Political groups usually find it expedient to continue their social activities, which bring nonpolitical lesbians into the community, and can usually mix political and social activities. An example is Lesbian Feminist Liberation's Sunday panels, which may have an overtly "political" topic, such as "Legislative and Judicial Reform," or a topic concerning life-styles, such as "Lesbians and Alcoholism," and serve both as an educational and a social outlet.

One answer is a committee structure adopted by both ALFA and Lesbian Feminist Liberation that allows political women to express themselves within the group, in legislative or media committees, for example, but does not require all members to be politically committed, as they can be active in health committees, fund-raising committees, self-defense, etc. If there are several lesbian groups in a city, it may be possible to specialize in particular areas: an example would be Dykes and Tykes, a New York organization of lesbians relating to children.

Being project-oriented (e.g., sponsoring a series of regular programs) can serve to give the membership a sense of accomplishment that increases momentum for the next event. Fund-raising and outreach programs often go hand in hand. In many areas, social activities for lesbians are so rare that it isn't difficult to attract women to a dance, picnic, etc. These activities can be excellent fund raisers, especially if you can get volunteer

The Atlanta Lesbian Feminist Alliance softball team

labor, and charge a small admission fee, offering refreshments and other incentives. You can get women interested in participating further in your activities this way.

ALFA and several other groups reported phenomenal success with sports programs. When ALFA sponsored a softball team in 1973, its membership doubled. The team played as an outfront lesbian team in a city league which provided constant free publicity for the organization. Since then, ALFA has had teams every year which have generated a tremendous amount of interest and activity. During the six-month softball season, however, much of the organizational energy is drained into sports.

Fund raising is a major problem in most groups. Few reported having enough money to provide the services they wanted to offer their members and the community. Dues and donations were the most common avenues for funding, but as one group pointed out, "Most lesbians are in low-paying jobs or unemployed and cannot contribute much." Those lesbians who have high-paying jobs are often hesitant to write out a check to a lesbian organization. Some groups raise money by selling literature, bumper stickers, having garage sales. One organization even holds Sarah Coventry jewelry parties. One or two groups have incorporated to facilitate some fund-raising activities. Your group may wish to consult an attorney about the advantages of incorporating.

ALFA has raised money by having a women's bar sponsor various events and through theater performances given by a group of mostly ALFA members. ALFA also sponsored the Great Southeast Lesbian Conference in 1975 and raised several hundred dollars. Regular rent parties also supplement the group's income.

A few gay groups have been able to secure large amounts of money through grants. Usually, these funds are given to organizations that offer definite services to the community or to their members. The Lesbian Resource Center in Los Angeles operates through the Gay Community Services Center, which obtains most of its $400,000 annual budget through grants. The Gay Community Services Center in Los Angeles is an excellent source of information about grants for gay groups. Organizations providing services for the community can sometimes find city grant money. The Women's Alcohol Program of Los Angeles operates under a city grant. Women in organizations such as NOW who have fundraising expertise may be helpful in suggesting ways to generate revenue.

One hassle with raising money is handling it properly. It is often difficult to keep track of where money is spent and how much is coming in. Sometimes a finance committee can perform all money-handling functions; other times a single treasurer is enough. Be aware, however, that problems arising out of money hassles are some of the most difficult to handle and can cause the most severe unsisterly feelings in a group. Very careful managing of the group's money is essential to keep that pressure off the organization's sometimes fragile balance.

Space is of primary importance and is usually the group's major expense. It must be as secure as possible against theft, and it should have the minimum number of fire exits required by law for whatever size gatherings you're going to have.

The space must be an adequate size, with adequate bathroom facilities and lighting outlets. Although it ideally ought to be in a safe and convenient neighborhood, it is necessary to locate in an area and building where music and dancing will not disturb the neighbors in nearby homes or the floor below. If a group opts for a deserted factory street, they sacrifice some safety, but gain freedom of activity. It is usually necessary to seek a compromise.

The importance of staffing the phone during regular, publicized hours cannot be overemphasized. Much of your outreach will be wasted if it can't be followed up when interested women call or visit. If you have a telephone, but can't staff it regularly, the group might consider investing in an answering machine to take messages.

A newsletter is vital to most organizations. Every group that answered our questionnaire reported providing at least some kind of regular communication to its members. A monthly calendar and news of the group's activities can be one of the organization's best means of reaching new members and keeping old ones active and aware. Both a regular publication and a space for the group require money and committed women to maintain them, but they are also excellent ways to give the group a sense of identity.

Working with the media, both gay and straight, counterculture and "legitimate," can be one of the most important ways of reaching potential members and informing the community of your activities. It is surprisingly easy to get coverage from some media sources and exceedingly difficult from others. We have found that radio stations and small newspapers are the most receptive to announcing events and covering off-beat stories (which is what lesbian activities are considered). Some TV stations and larger newspapers can also be interested if you are persistent. Naming one contact person in your group who can deal with the press on a regular basis is a good idea. (Additional suggestions on media outreach are offered in the section "Lesbians and the Media.")

Following is a more specific view of how two groups, very different in nature, saw the needs of the women they represent and are meeting these needs.

ATLANTA LESBIAN FEMINIST ALLIANCE

ALFA formed in the summer of 1972 under a set of circumstances that birthed many of the lesbian feminist organizations in the United States: Atlanta Women's Liberation was too straight and the Gay Liberation Front was too male.

Atlanta's homosexual community has always been very large. It is the gay capital of the South with lesbians and homosexual men coming there from all over the Deep South for survival reasons. Before 1970, lesbians drew their collective strength from their social circles; there was no outfront lesbian feminist community. Over the years, many lesbians have moved into the neighborhood in which the ALFA house is located, personal relationships have developed, and groups with overlapping memberships (e.g., theater and political groups) have formed. ALFA has 115 members, basically white, middle class, in the eighteen to forty age group.

ALFA has chosen not to take a defined political stance, but to provide different outlets to women in the community; this has both positive and negative sides. The criticism has been made that she tries to be all things to all lesbians and can satisfy none. In general, ALFA has moved from a more consciously political to a more socially and athletically oriented organization.

ALFA's most important political activities have been to mobilize in opposition to the homophobic policies of Atlanta's newspapers; to participate in coalition work for the Equal Rights Amendment and Gay Pride Week; and to organize the Great Southeast Lesbian Conference in 1975 which gathered about six hundred women from around the South.

Other important outreach activities to the non-lesbian community have been public presentations at local schools and on radio and TV.

The activity that has drawn the largest participation of ALFA women and increased its membership has been its sponsorship of lesbian softball teams which play in the city league.[2]

About fifteen women for whom ALFA did not fulfill political needs formed Dykes for the Second American Revolution (DARII). It is committed to developing lesbian-feminist-socialist politics and functions separately from, but cooperatively with, ALFA.

ALFA has always been run as a nonhierarchical collective, with newsletter, library, media, finance, house, and political committees. From time to time, a small steering committee will oversee the general functioning. Its structure is nonauthoritarian, but it also lacks clearly defined expectations and ground rules.

Fund raising and finances have been major headaches. ALFA needs about $260 a month to operate. Money comes from yearly $6 dues, monthly pledges (slim pickings), selling literature, donations in time of crisis, cosponsoring events with the Tower (the women's bar in Atlanta with which ALFA has established a continuing supportive relationship), rent parties, and special events.

Throughout ALFA's life she has had a house, which has been an important focus for her activities and one of her major expenses. It is used for monthly business meetings, open houses, play and poetry readings,

committee meetings, workshops, bimonthly Socialist Feminist Women's Union meetings (paying ALFA a small rental sum), as well as nightly staffing by ALFA members. It has a library, pool table, telephone, and a small room available for transient dykes.

One of the energy patterns which has plagued ALFA, as it has other groups, is the unequal distribution of womanpower: Only a few of the 115 membership do the actual work. So an informal hierarchy of power exists around those who do the work. The few women who do the bulk of the work burn out and drop out. A frequent complaint is that the friendship circles, while very important to the continuing life of ALFA, tend to make it hard for new women to become involved. Another problem is that very few women are really willing and able to be completely open about their lesbianism, so certain kinds of political activity are limited to them. ALFA has had its ups and downs, but its importance to the community is proven by its continued existence and large membership.

YALESBIANS

Yalesbians was founded in September 1975 as a subgroup of the basically male Gay Alliance (GA). When it became obvious that their interests were different, Yalesbians became a separate group. Their broad goal is to work for the eradication of sexism and heterosexism at Yale, in New Haven, and in society in general.

They consider the support aspect of their work most important. ("Yale is enough to drive any well-balanced dyke crazy!") Next in importance is their consciousness raising. ("Students from Yale and similar schools are . . . going to be running this country someday. . . . We think it's important to get to them now while we have access to them. Hopefully their policies won't be as homophobic as they might have been without our influence.")

Yalesbians membership is one-third non-Yale affiliated. There are about fifty women, ages eighteen to forty, racially mixed, mostly middle class. The women's community in which they function has drawn closer together in the last year and a half as a result of the grand jury/FBI harassment around Susan Saxe and Kathy Power.

As a student organization, they pay no rent for their office, which is on campus and shared with GA. The office is used for the meetings of several groups as well as a coffeehouse on Friday nights (mostly for men).

Activities of Yalesbians include a speaker's bureau, work on the New Haven gay rights bill, sponsorship of feminist and lesbian feminist speakers on campus, monthly potlucks and dances at the New Haven Women's Liberation Center, and a weekly radio show shared with GA.

Yalesbians has no formal leadership structure, which they are finding frustrating, and they expressed a need to form a good working structure.

---

[2]For more detailed discussion of ALFA's participation in ERA and softball, see two articles by Vicki Gabriner in *Quest: A Feminist Quarterly*, "ERA: The Year of the Rabble," Vol. I, No. 2, and "Come Out Slugging," Vol. II, No. 3.

RESOURCES

"Getting Your Share: An Introduction to Fundraising," Women's Action Alliance, 370 Lexington Ave., New York, N.Y. 10017. Includes information on how to apply for grants, and a resource list of groups and materials. $2.00

Lesbian Resource Center, 1213 N. Highland Ave., Los Angeles, Calif. 90038. 213 464-7485.

Lesbians and the Women's Movement

SIDNEY ABBOTT

The women's movement and the gay movement have a great deal to offer each other, and, since 1970, lesbians have been developing linkages in theory and organization that enable the two movements to relate to one another.

The women's rights movement was a seed sown by Betty Friedan and the founding group of the National Organization for Women on the fertile liberal ground that had supported and financed the black struggle for equal voting and economic rights in the late fifties and early sixties.

The gay liberation movement began as a coming together of the homophile rights movement and gay members of the New Left who saw during the 1969 Stonewall riots in New York's Greenwich Village that gays also were an oppressed group with revolutionary potential.

Gay women have had to struggle within both movements for their place. By and large we have won, but it feels a little like trying to scale glass mountains; that is, if you stop to rest for a single minute, you begin sliding backward. Even today the apparently "natural" tendency of both movements is to conceive some new efforts without visible participation of lesbians, leading some activist lesbians to dream of a national lesbian feminist movement separate from the two existing movements.

Lesbians have been the ones who listened to what both the women's movement and the gay movement were saying and wove the themes into one coherent theory of sexist oppression. This effort, expanding the scope of concern of both movements, has the continual potential to strengthen both movements.

To the gay movement, they said, "Homophobia is not the cause of our oppression as homosexuals. Sexism

is the cause. Homophobia, the hatred of homosexuals, is a part of sexism, a part of sexual stereotyping." The benchmark of lesbian success in the gay movement came when the National Gay Task Force founding Board of Directors in 1973 voted to include a phrase in the new organization's statement of purpose indicating that sexism is the cause of homosexual oppression.

To the women's movement, lesbians said, "Expand your idea of sex role stereotyping to include us, because we are a key proof of female oppression. If any one of you is successful outside the home, what is the first thing you are called—a ballbreaker, a lesbian, that is, a sort of man, no longer a woman or womanly. Expand your concept of woman to include us and our life-styles and you free yourselves; you could free all women. Don't just say that women are suffering and in pain; also say women are strong and capable and while some can express these things within the heterosexist structure, others choose to step out of that structure altogether to express who they are as people. It is normal for women to live independently and as equals of men. Look at us; we do it every day."

Early on, in the 1960s, the women's movement was a women's rights movement. The thrust was toward changing laws and regulations of governmental and other major institutions, to give equal opportunity to women. The women worried about respectability and credibility. The fear was that men would regard the movement as just another kind of women's club, a kind of auxiliary to the human rights movement, a footnote to human progress.

So the idea was to do a great deal of research, to marshal legions of facts, and to appear sober-headed, serious, and professional, lest men laugh. The obvious—to us today—discrimination against women needed to be documented and presented to the society. The women knew that the burden was on them to be more intelligent and to work harder than men, because to succeed in changing laws and rules and regulations, the votes and approval of overwhelmingly male legislatures and other centers of male power were needed. The National Organization for Women developed this style to a great degree of effectiveness.

But soon they felt besieged from within. First, along came the radical feminists, earliest represented by Ti-Grace Atkinson, who resigned as president of New York NOW in a display of fireworks that had members ripping up their membership cards and leaving to join her new group, the feminists, or to set up other groups. Next, the lesbians appeared.

There had always been lesbians working within the women's movement, but in hiding. Now the lesbians began coming out.

Soon the media was filled with, on the one hand, stories of the activities of the "bra burners," that is, the radicals, as in the Atlantic City Miss America pageant action; and vague references, on the other hand, to lesbianism. The media began to portray "women's libbers" as being, somehow, not real women.

Those who sat for hours going through children's textbooks, or struggling to draft pro-abortion laws, or surveying how many hours women *would* work if given a chance, those women who labored long and hard far from the television cameras on the nitty-gritty that precedes legislative packages, grew resentful.

The radicals had split off to form their own organizations. Some lesbians did too, and some went off to try to relate to the emerging gay liberation groups. But many lesbians stayed in the women's movement and many stayed in NOW because they felt identified with the other women across the vast range of women's issues.

NOW has gone through a number of stages in dealing with lesbians. At first, few lesbians came out in NOW and fewer came out in public. A large number of lesbians remained closeted. They felt this ensured them the freedom to work on any issue they chose, and not just on lesbian issues.

Just as there was a sound enough base, in reality, for the feelings women in the early women's movement expressed that gaining credibility would be a battle in itself, there was a reality base to a decision to remain more or less closeted.

For the very feminism of lesbians who did come out was questioned, in the sense of saying, "If you are with us, how can you risk rocking or swamping the boat? Why don't you just keep quiet and work with us? Is your fight really a part of our fight?" The bottom-line question was rarely clearly stated, but it underlay certain attitudes: "Is a lesbian a woman?" Woman is culturally, not biologically, defined. That is, every female human past puberty is not necessarily a woman. Woman has been defined by loving a man, having children, giving freely of herself, and taking little, or only covertly, for herself. But can she live for herself and love another female and struggle day in and out to support herself and still be a woman? Isn't she then a sort of a man?

Worst of all was the accusation, "If you really cared for the women's movement and for women, you would keep quiet and help us. If you come out, *you,* not the men, will defeat us."

The National Organization for Women Supporting Gay Issues in the 1976 Christopher St. March

Many lesbian and heterosexual women felt that it was vital to present the male authority structure with real women, in order to win reform.

The fears of the heterosexual women multiplied as their own activities began to endanger their marriages. Hours and energies spent away from home led to fights within the home. Increasing independence and competence made them unruly and not apt to return to dependence. Marriages faltered and crumbled.

Suddenly large numbers of women were separating from their husbands and divorcing. They underwent economic shock. They sought to find men who were supportive and, at that time, the selection was sparse indeed. Men were hostile and cynical.

Angry at having their feminism questioned, the lesbians' rhetoric, meanwhile, had escalated. Lesbians argued back. Lesbians now saw themselves as the symbolic vanguard of the women's movement, the women who were independent of men, who proved it could be done. The theme of sisterhood in the early women's movement had been expanded by lesbians to include caring and love for women, and it included sexual love.

Previously heterosexual women began to approach each other and known lesbians for warmth, affection, and love. A number of women became lesbians. Others became bisexual.

However, some of those women now felt rootless and frightened. They had stepped from beyond the male system of economic and personal support into what? They went to lesbian bars and events and felt alienated. They saw some lesbians imitating male dress and behavior. They discovered male attitudes in their lesbian friends and in themselves and were horrified. Some suffered severe anxiety in all-lesbian groups. They sometimes did not understand that the attitudes they heard, the jokes they listened to, and the anger they saw were part of lesbian oppression and consequently low self-esteem, and their identity crisis continued.

Articles were written by feminists defining the new woman who loved women as different from lesbians, and some accusations were hurled at lesbians for supposedly male behavior and attitudes toward other women.

What was happening here? Are lesbians really so strange and different? Every outgroup, whether oppressed for reasons of race, ethnicity, economic class, sex, or sexual preference, is psychologically hurt and angered by its oppression; at the same time some of the oppression is internalized. Lesbians, like gay men, are no exception. Further, a group that is just raising its head after centuries of bowing it under the weight of prejudice, cruelty, and exclusion wants to celebrate, not conduct self-criticism. Lesbians were no different. They wanted at last to feel free to dress and act as they wished, exactly as everyone else was doing in the middle and late 1960s. Also they knew within their own subculture what was to be taken seriously and what was minority humor—a kind of feedback loop of what society had said about lesbians. They knew that some of the humor and expressed attitudes were somewhat self-disparaging. But lesbians also had stored up rage because of the status and privileges of heterosexual women.

Those trying out lesbian relationships bewildered heterosexual feminists. If lesbians were sick, disturbed people from birth, how is it that Mrs. John Smith, my best friend, who joined the women's movement with me, is now sleeping with women? How is it she has left her husband and taken her children to live with a woman? Who is she, and who, then, am I? Female sexuality did not seem to be fixed but very changeable.

Gradually, things sorted themselves out. Those heterosexual feminists who remained primarily heterosexual regained their sense of orientation. Lesbians expanded their social and sexual lives out of the bars into the women's movement and into a variety of new social, cultural, and political activities. New lesbians gained confidence, began to enjoy their new freedoms, and to experiment with who it was, after all, they wanted to be as lesbians. Did they want monogamy? Did they want blue jeans and shorter hair? Did they want to remain essentially as they were before, except that they loved women or a woman?

As the women's movement succeeded in some of its goals, some men became less overtly hostile, and some feminists were able to form improved relationships with men. Some men call themselves feminists; others pragmatically learned to make concessions to keep their homes. Some proclaimed that their marriages were better now that their wives had new interests.

Part of the historical importance of the women's movement from a lesbian perspective is that it has been a doorway out of the closet of mental and physical ghettoization. Gay women have had the unique experience, not shared by gay men, of dealing with large numbers of straight people of their own sex day after day, meeting after meeting, year after year, as themselves—that is, as lesbians—and gaining confidence and learning from the interaction about their own strengths. Gay women have had a tremendous historic opportunity to grow as people and to feel that their oppression is part of women's oppression. They suddenly saw themselves as part of a surging majority, one half of the human race.

But the struggle in the women's movement has never been easy, not for a moment. In its first part, this article tells why it was difficult on an interpersonal basis. In addition, there were strictly political considerations such as what was the goal of the women's movement? Reform or revolution? Especially since the American withdrawal from Vietnam and the end of the antiwar movement, revolutionary forces have concentrated their organizing on the women's movement and the gay movement. "We're the only action in town," as one woman commented.

A contravening force, slowing revolutionary fervor, has been the economic recession bringing a scarcity of jobs for women and increasing fears about losing their jobs that gay people have. Some have found their own revolutionary energies and those of others curtailed by personal needs and needs for immediate reform. In general, the women's movement has moved slightly left and the gay movement has moved toward the center.

This important fact must not be lost sight of: that lesbians in the women's movement span the entire political spectrum. Lesbians as a group are not left, right, or moderate. Lesbians are everywhere. There probably has never been a unified lesbian vote in any women's or mixed gay (male and female) organization. Some lesbians want reform, some want revolution, some see one as leading to the other. Some lesbians who are active feminists believe that lesbian issues should wait until other feminists' goals are reached, such as passage of the ERA (Equal Rights Amendment).

While NOW is only one feminist organization, it is the oldest, the largest, and the one where virtually every major issue, from equal pay for equal work, abortion, and lesbian rights, to the troubles of battered women, has surfaced first. NOW is ten years old this year. But for its first eight years, or until that Philadelphia Conference in 1975, it was seen as an organization of middle-class professional women and suburban housewives. In Philadelphia, for the first time the younger denim crowd was numerous. But, in fact, a lot of the key issues were brought to the forefront by the stereotyped white-gloved women of NOW. NOW was always more diverse than it appeared. NOW always contained a mixture of women who had left or radical backgrounds, of conservative women and liberal women. There was always a left, right, and center to NOW, although in the early years the prevailing views were moderate or centrist.

Since the "Lesbian Issue," so called, first surfaced in late 1969 in NOW, and during 1970 when the key struggles to bring the issue to light were fought, all three political orientations have had reasons why lesbians and lesbian rights should not be dealt with. The left-oriented women came from a political background that was traditionally antihomosexual, and in the early days wanted feminism, not to speak of lesbianism, subordinated to the economic and class struggle. Currently, there are still reservations about the priority of feminist and lesbian issues in relation to issues of class and race. The conservative women feared that any discussion of lesbianism would queer the movement's bid for the respectability of its issues and mean that the political system and the establishment would not act legally and legislatively on women's rights. The liberals and moderates sympathized with the emotions of the lesbian women, their needs and anger, but counseled waiting until the time was right—that is, after key pieces of legislation, especially the ERA, were passed.

On the other hand, individual women identified with all three orientations—conservative, liberal, and radical—have intervened at crisis moments to help lesbian feminists active in the women's movement on their road to visibility and open support.

In NOW, at least, the lesbian issue was often treated as a political football—that is, used to endanger individual women's personal or political reputations. A prolesbian stance was said to mean something about reliability on other feminist issues where no such linkage existed—as in "If you're for the lesbian resolution [or issue] you're against or don't care about the ERA," or "You don't believe in the class struggle or support the issue of race."

It was obvious from studying the political environment that radicals, liberals, and conservatives were all reluctant to assign a top priority to the lesbian issue when placed against the spectrum of their more traditional concerns. Hence the only possible strategy of the NOW National Task Force on Sexuality and Lesbianism was to remain open to all three camps and to pick up support where possible depending on the prevailing winds. Sometimes it was possible to maximize on the very tactic of the issue being linked with other issues. Essentially, however, the furor surrounding lesbian activities and goals meant that those most concerned about the lesbian issue at root could not get caught up in the fortunes of other issues and power struggles unless some benefit for lesbians was foreseen. "Keep truckin' and pick up support when and where you can—and don't be surprised if you have no support or different support tomorrow"—that was the outlook that worked.

With this pragmatic and incrementalist approach, solid gains were made for lesbians from 1970 on. In December 1971 top officers in National NOW, feminist authors, and leaders from a broad spectrum of political stances supported Kate Millett at a press conference in New York. The press conference was a reply to *Time* magazine's effort to discredit her because of her bisexuality. On Labor Day weekend of 1971, the National NOW conference, meeting in Los Angeles, adopted a resolution that recognized the right of a woman to define and express her own sexuality; recognized lesbians as doubly oppressed as women and homosexuals; and acknowledged their oppression as a legitimate concern of NOW. In February 1973 the first Lesbian Caucus (and the first large-scale organized caucus in the organization's history) was formed at the National Conference, chaired by Elaine Noble and myself. Some 10 percent of the two thousand women at the conference participated in the caucus. At the same conference an implementing resolution urging NOW to take certain specific actions was passed to strengthen the more philosophic 1971 national resolution. In Washington the first open lesbian, Del Martin of San Francisco, was elected to the Board of Directors. In July 1973 the National Task Force on Sexuality and Lesbianism was officially launched by the approval of the appointments of Sidney Abbott and H. Jayne Vogan at a Board of Directors meeting in San Francisco. Obtaining the task force alone had taken nearly three years.

Following each forward movement there was a degree of backlash and resistance. It was difficult for the new task force to obtain sufficient funding or even to get a mailing sent out by the national office in Chicago. Yet chapters around the country began, slowly, to establish local task forces. At the next national conference in Houston in 1974 the entire conference became a battle-ground. Specific actions on lesbian issues were gobbled up in the atmosphere of political struggle that ended, however, in the emergence of a new president, Karen DeCrow, an open supporter of lesbian rights. She was elected by a narrow enough margin so that her victory could be credited, in part, to support by a number of lesbians. However, on this vote as on all others, lesbians did not vote in a block. Numbers of lesbians voted for other candidates. Numbers of active lesbian feminists in NOW remained in the more moderate political camps. However, they began to see that they had better speak up, or else the issue would be owned by the winning camp. It was made even clearer in Houston than in Washington in 1973 that the issue could produce votes for candidates.

Thus, at the 1975 National Conference in Philadelphia everyone, all three major candidates for president, and in fact virtually all candidates, whether major or minor, were for the lesbian issue and for a conference resolution on lesbianism. The only question was which resolution. A proposal drafted by a board member labeled "moderate" by some and "conservative" by others addressed the real world of legal and legislative needs on local, state, and federal levels and addressed the issue of sufficient budgeting. As national coordinator, I backed that resolution, while stating that I would not campaign for any candidate or align myself with any group but would hold the caucus open as a place for the serious presentation of all views where all candidates could be heard.

Since the election would be close, to align myself and/or the caucus with any one candidate would be to risk the defeat of the resolution. However, this stand meant offering myself as the target for unceasing political pressure from all camps. Best friends accused me of being a traitor to one group or another. Strangers accosted me angrily. One woman circulated the unfounded rumor that I was a CIA agent.

But enough of us held to our position, so that the caucus was open to all candidates and all views. We picked up the needed critical mass of support. The resolution was amended at several open caucus meetings. By the last and largest of those meetings some 150 women from all political camps—some of whom would not speak to each other anywhere except in that room—cooperatively amended the resolution so that it had the support of all factions. We got the lesbian resolution moved sufficiently high up on the agenda to be able to use parliamentary procedure to get it to the floor.

The lesbian resolution got to the floor and passed unanimously. More than twenty other issue-oriented resolutions never made it to the floor. The reason was that voting for officers was so close that voting procedures were being questioned. The American Arbitration Society called for revotes for major offices. Conference time was rapidly consumed by matters pertaining to the legalities of votes and voters.

After the conference, I thought of all the women

and task force leaders whose issues had never made it to the floor in the chaos of the conference. The bottleneck caused by the election of officers meant that no new policy was made at the conference in most of the twenty issue areas important to NOW.

The conference had not been used to educate the more than two thousand women present from all across the country on the pressing policy needs of the organization. The election of officers had consumed almost the entire conference. The issue-oriented task force coordinators, generally not political by nature, were despondent. Chapter representatives were furious and confused by the intensity and bitterness of the political struggle they had witnessed. They had been buffeted and battered for days and had had to watch legalistic procedural questions prevail over substantive issues. They had had to stand in line to 10:00 or 11:00 P.M. to get to vote since reballoting was necessary. As a winner in this frustrating environment, the National Task Force on Sexuality and Lesbianism foresaw tough times ahead.

This has proved to be the case. Although under fresh and energetic leadership, the task force has had to fight to realize even a percentage of the gains promised in the resolution.

From the vantage point of NOW, where the issue has meant an incredible emotional and political struggle for many women from the beginning in 1969, the progress of the issue in other national organizations appears calm.

A week before the February 1973 NOW National Conference in Washington, D.C., the National Women's Political Caucus met in national conference in Houston, Texas. There a Special Caucus was formed according to NWPC procedure with many heterosexual women joining gay women in signing the required petition. The New York delegation, made up mostly of heterosexual women, signed en masse to support the petition. The delegation included such NWPC founders as Gloria Steinem, Brenda Feigen-Fasteau, and Bella Abzug.

In 1976 the NWPC issued a position paper supporting equal rights for lesbians in employment, housing, education, credit, and in state or federally funded programs. The position paper states that this stand is the policy of NWPC.

Membership in the National Women's Political Caucus is less broadly based than that of NOW. Members are usually interested in running for local, state, or national office and often have a background in clubhouse politics. With little publicity and with considerable political skill they quietly moved to support lesbian rights.

The National Women's Agenda, begun in 1975, a project of the Women's Action Alliance, included the issue of sexual preference in its preamble. The needs of lesbians are being addressed in the Task Force on Respect for the Individual. (Other concerns listed by the task force are age, work roles, physical appearance, and marital status.) Coconvenors of the area are Frances Doughty, past Board cochair of the National Gay Task Force, and Ronni Smith, of the New York State Division of Human Rights. Frances Doughty and Charlotte Bunch, a member of the Board of Directors of the National Gay Task Force, have been the only open lesbians on the central working committee that coordinates the various issues areas of the agenda. Frances and Charlotte see as an important part of their role educating the representatives to the agenda from the many participating women's organizations on the needs of lesbians.

Groups participating in the agenda include a number of traditional women's groups, such as the Girl Scouts and the YWCA. (The YWCA issued a policy statement supporting equal rights for homosexuals in the early 1970s.) While there has been no open opposition on the agenda, there was a quiet flurry when Frances was seated on the stage while presidential candidate Jimmy Carter was addressing the Agenda National Conference in October 1976, and some consternation was evident when lesbian feminist singer Maxine Feldman performed lesbian feminist songs that evening.

But the bad ole days are not entirely gone. Recently the staff of the commission in the State Department that is planning the events for International Women's Year circulated a paper reportedly entitled, "Is Lesbianism a Feminist Issue?" Back to square one. And the commission, at first, decided *not* to suggest a workshop on lesbian issues in the materials it circulated to its appointed state planning committees. And workshops held would have to be initiated by groups of gay women in each state petitioning the committees. It took active intervention on the part of Jean O'Leary, coexecutive director of the National Gay Task Force and a member of the National Commission, to reverse this position several months later.

This has occurred, as stated above, after every major national women's group has at least accepted lesbian equal rights as a viable issue.

What does all of this mean for lesbians around the country who are thinking of becoming active in feminism?

It means that you can work in feminism openly as a lesbian, if you wish, and work on lesbian issues or other issues. Chances are, your degree of comfort will depend on your geographic location (East and West Coasts and parts of the Southwest are more relaxed than parts of the midwest, for example), your age, and your experience being out with others. Being out is a very personal decision, as well as a political one, of course, and it should be given the careful consideration of any important personal decision. A miserable hero does nobody much good.

If you wish to remain closeted or to be open only with a few close friends, you may be making the right assessment. There are many reasons for discretion— disgruntled ex-husbands, sensitive jobs, towns or cities with histories of repression of homosexuals. Lesbian feminists have received important help in the past from closeted sisters. What lesbians must guard against is feeling paranoia about the open lesbians. On the other hand, being out and being yourself is a matchless feeling, fulfilling almost of itself.

Looking back now on eight years of visible lesbian feminists in national feminist organizations, we can ask again the most loaded questions and begin to answer them.

Has the lesbian issue hurt the ERA? The ERA has had a difficult time in the ratification process. Yes, lesbianism in the women's movement and homosexuality in general have been raised as issues in many states. But this came about only in part because there are admitted lesbians in the women's movement.

The other cause is the amendment itself. Many people interpret it as blurring male and female gender identity and thereby blurring sexual roles. It is hard to explain to people how the ERA will and will not affect their everyday lives. Many women see it as removing traditional areas of protection (while advocates see it as extending protection to men).

People experienced a loss of orientation when male hippies grew long hair and carried handbags and gave out flowers.

Any change in the relationship between the sexes, whether in the area of legal rights, or in dress or behavior, can cause anxiety. The interesting part is that charges of lesbianism were leveled at feminists in Europe in the early 1900s and here before any lesbians became public or any of the national organizations took up the issue.

All of this seems to add up to the probability that the name-calling would have happened anyway, outfront lesbians or no. Lesbians going public and visible at least gives everyone a chance to find out what we are like and decide on their position. Admitted lesbianism in the women's movement didn't help the ERA, but perhaps in the end it helped diffuse the issue, so that the professional bigots found it harder to sway fairer-minded people.

Has lesbianism driven heterosexual women away from the women's movement? No doubt the presence of more or less open lesbians has caused individual women to withdraw from organizations. However, the usual pattern seems to be to move to another area within the same organization. Thus, a given committee will, one year, be "lesbian-dominated," and the next "straight-dominated." Gay women also like to work with their friends, so they tend to drift together in terms of activities and work areas. It could be said that while the women's movement as a whole is "integrated" in terms of sexual preference, subgroups may well contain a preponderance of straight or gay women.

But the best answer to the question is the simple fact that tens of thousands of women are actively involved in the women's movement nationally, and the highest percentage of lesbians would not exceed 30 percent and maybe, nationwide, much closer to 20 percent. This means that 70 to 80 percent of the women probably are heterosexual. So who's scared?

Above all there is the sense of the historic moment, that instinct about the timing of social change that any group needs to improve its lot. Clearly, the decade of the 1960s was such a moment. She who did not seize the moment might have been lost forever in the abominable pit society reserves for lesbians.

Lesbians and International Women's Year: A Report on Three Conferences

FRANCES DOUGHTY

Three major international conferences marked International Women's Year, 1975: the double conferences in Mexico City in June/July, consisting of the official United Nations conference and the Tribune, organized by the nongovernmental organizations of the United Nations; the World Congress for International Women's Year, which took place in East Berlin in October 1975; and the International Tribunal on Crimes against Women, held in Brussels in March 1976.

The International Tribunal on Crimes against Women was the only conference that officially included lesbians as members of the community of women. It was also the only conference that was conceived and executed by feminists. This connection between support of lesbians and feminism was also made clear, though in a negative sense, at the World Congress in East Berlin, where feminism was discredited by every means possible, including oppression of lesbians. The seriousness with which the Communists (capitalized to indicate the Russian model) viewed feminism as a threat convinced me that we ourselves need to develop our view of feminism as a worldwide ideology and a force equal to capitalism and Communism.

For lesbians to flourish, changes must be made in concepts of power, especially concerning sex-role stereotypes, so that power is seen as self-determination, rather than domination/submission. In the course of International Women's Year, I came to see bringing about these changes as the task of feminism, and each conference then became not only a forum concerning the status of lesbians but also a model for methods of social change. I began to feel that I was living through a process of thesis (Mexico City and capitalism), antithesis (East Berlin and Communism), and, I hoped, synthesis (Brussels and feminism).

Even in Protestant countries of the Western bloc, where lesbians fare best, recognition of lesbians' existence is at the whim of the males who control these countries. The official invisibility of lesbians in the United Nations conferences in Mexico City reflected this fact, but was somewhat mitigated by our being allowed to speak and hold workshops at the Tribune. In East Berlin another woman and I were both cut off when we attempted to speak publicly about lesbianism. In no totalitarian regime are deviants permitted: Homosexuals were/are persecuted both in fascist Germany and in Communist Cuba. Lesbian invisibility should not be taken to mean that lesbians do not exist in countries where there is no lesbian or feminist movement. At these conferences, I myself met, or heard of from others, lesbians on every continent in countries of all political persuasions.

Lesbians were totally absent from materials publicizing both the official United Nations conference and the unofficial Tribune, held in Mexico City from June 19 to July 2, 1975.

There was no answer from the official U.N. conference to a letter pointing out the omission of lesbians from International Women's Year, nor, as far as I know, was lesbianism ever discussed at its meetings in Mexico City. The women leading the Tribune replied jointly, with thanks for the "thoughtful letter" and the information that groups wanting "to raise issues for special consideration" would have facilities to do so.

Because both conferences were so poorly publicized, it was almost impossible to mobilize lesbians in advance, so I simply went to the open mike at the first plenary session of the Tribune. After speaking of the use of the word "developed" to describe the United States, whose only development is technological, I said that I was not only a member of the United States, but also of a group whose name had not been mentioned in connection with International Women's Year, even though our whole lives were involved with women. As the word "lesbian" came through the headphones in simultaneous translation, there was first silence, then a buzz (someone told me later that some women thought I had made the announcement to get dates!).

By the end of that first weekend, three days later, we had met with a group of lesbians and homosexuals who wanted to start a gay liberation movement in Mexico; we had met with the more radical segment of the Mexican women's movement; we had discovered that in certain Indian villages in Mexico, there are women-sorcerers who pass their information from mother to daughter, and who are lesbians; and we had appeared on the front pages of the Mexican press.

"We" evolved into the International Lesbian-Feminist Caucus, consisting of Linda Fowler, Carol Lease, Ingrid Stone, and myself from the United States; Laurie Bebbington, of Melbourne, Australia; and others who cannot be named here because of the dangers of being publicly known as lesbians. Our activities continued in the following week: a speech by Laurie in another plenary session of the Tribune on sex-role stereotyping and the family, translated verbatim by the Mexican press; two workshops, addressing a total of four hundred women, mainly Spanish-speaking; two press releases: one from the caucus, one from a group of Mexican lesbians who had to remain anonymous; interviews with the Mexican press and television, Canadian and Australian radio, *Time* magazine; an article on lesbianism by Linda Fowler and Carol Lease in *Xilonen,* the daily newspaper of the Tribune; development of a close liaison with Nancy Cardenas, a prominent theater director and proponent of gay rights who had recently produced a highly controversial Mexican version of *Boys in the Band*; and a request from the Mexican government's sex education program for more information on homosexuality.

The American Embassy held an open house for women at the Tribune to meet the official American delegation to the United Nations conference, at which I made a statement on the use of women by developing countries as a surplus labor pool and on the intimate connection between lesbianism and feminism. Reactions were mixed: The woman who spoke after me called for unity among all women, then added that she was proud to be a mother, a grandmother, and as God made her. Jill Ruckelshaus, one of our three official delegates to the United Nations conference, and at that time presiding officer of the National Commission on the Observance of International Women's Year, made a point of coming over and asking for information on the position of lesbians in the United States. Gloria Steinem, Bella Abzug, and Flo Kennedy all emphasized the necessity of supporting lesbians as part of the feminist position in various speeches given during the Tribune.

On the human level, we found enormous support and gratitude from women at the Tribune, especially those from Mexico and other Spanish-speaking countries. A frequent comment was that this subject had never been discussed openly in Mexico before; another Spanish-speaking woman said that our workshops were the only place in either conference where women's sexuality had been discussed at all; the Tribune staff went out of their way to deal with our space problems (the overflow crowd at the first workshop was backed up all the way around the hall outside); many women at the second workshop applauded a speech on Spanish machismo, as well as another statement, also in Spanish, that "sex with a man is no sex at all."

Participating in the Tribune, despite the joy of its immediate human impact, made me aware of many ironies: Mexico was supposedly the site of the conferences because its outgoing President was campaigning to be elected Secretary-General of the United Nations; on account of diplomatic protocol, the official United Nations conference's presiding officer was head of the host country's delegation, the Mexican Attorney General, not only a man, but the man in charge of internal security in the country in which the Partido Revolucionario Institucional (the Institutional Revolutionary Party—the very name is a paradox) has been in power since the revolution's end in 1920; the United Nations conference met where students were shot in demonstrations during the 1968 Olympics; after women at the Tribune, which was open to all who could afford to come but had no power, from many different countries worked together for a week making amendments to the World Plan of Action, they were told that their amendments would not be presented to the official United Nations conference.

Although Mexico has the reputation of being one of the most liberal Latin-American countries, a sense of threat underlay the sophistication of Mexico City. Homosexuality, for example, is legal as long as it is "discreet" and between consenting adults. *But,* it is a criminal offense to publish anything pertaining to a "vice." *But,* there had been a raid shortly before the beginning of the conference at which over a hundred male homosexuals had been charged with possession of (planted) drugs and weapons. *But,* when a group of us were walking on the Paseo de la Reforma late after a lesbian dance, a man purposely speeded up his car at a light with sufficient force to knock one woman down.

The incongruities between the world of the United Nations conferences and the actual lives of women, in particular of the women who lived in the country we were visiting, made the whole show seem a bone tossed us by the powers that be. In spite of the tremendous sense of energy and excitement generated by the coming together of well over five thousand women at the Tribune, and in spite of the very moving feeling that our presence there as open lesbians had touched a great many women, I came home feeling that I had participated in the capitalist male version of International Women's Year, and wondered what was next.

The answer was waiting when I returned from Mexico City: an invitation to be on the United States Preparatory Committee of the World Congress for International Women's Year, to take place in the German Democratic Republic (East Berlin, East Germany), October 20-24, 1975. The conference was sponsored by

the Women's International League for Peace and freedom and the Women's International Democratic Federation, the Soviet-bloc women's organization, composed of 117 member organizations in 101 countries. Its president, Freda Brown, of Australia, also presided over the two thousand women attending the World Congress in East Berlin.

I did not expect the conference itself to be more than a propaganda showpiece, but I thought somehow that the United States delegation would be different, operating in the same individualistic manner I had enjoyed in Mexico City. I was also encouraged to go by the concern expressed by Judy Joseph of WILPF that lesbians be represented in the delegation. The one hundred delegates allotted to the United States by the International Preparatory Committee were chosen by race, ethnic group, class, occupation, geographic distribution, and religion. The diversity of women in the United States delegation, the apparent openness to lesbians, and my curiosity about life in East Berlin were the decisive factors in my decision to attend the conference.

I was naïvely unprepared for almost every aspect of what actually happened. I had not realized that it would be such a highly structured, formal conference, in which everything, even housing, seating, and individual speakers, would reflect national politics and party lines. Speeches in the plenary sessions were rhetorical formalities, given in front of the conference symbol, an outline of a woman's head with eyes, a nose, and no mouth at all; the nine smaller commissions, on topics such as women and the law, the family, education, and the media, also consisted in large part of set speeches containing much rhetoric. I also did not know that every effort would be made to discredit feminism, especially within the United States delegation, by associating it with lesbianism, the middle class, and, most strongly and painfully, with racism. It turned out to be one of the most embattled, exhausting, and educational experiences of my life.

On our arrival in East Berlin, when we left the airport building to board our bus to the hotel, we were met by a row of schoolchildren, each with a red rose, which they handed to each of us—a touch that reminded me of all the accounts I had read of visits to socialist countries. I was feeling rather supercilious about being too sophisticated to be taken in by such tricks, when the woman behind me, black, said in a voice full of emotion that she had never had a cut flower before. I stopped feeling supercilious and started thinking about other women's lives.

On arriving at our hotel, we found we were the only guests, and the twenty-four-hour presence of two men on each floor was a constant reminder that we were in the power of the state. All food, housing, and local transportation for the two thousand women at the conference were free. We were told that most of the money, which must have been an enormous sum, came from the women of East Germany.

Since the U.S. delegation was so isolated, and since

there was no free interchange between individuals at the meetings of the conference, I began what I came to call "cruising the plenary," wandering around the halls and snack bars looking for women who looked talkable to. I met some other feminists, but few lesbians from other countries until the last day of the conference. I was told, however, that the German Democratic Republic had no laws against homosexuality but regarded lesbians as sick, though I don't know what "treatment" they are given. It seemed impossible to make contact with other women in East Berlin than those at the conference, but I did meet some lesbians from West Berlin there, who invited us to come to the women's pub the last night of the conference.

As far as I know, lesbianism was discussed publicly only twice, once by a Danish woman and once by myself, in speeches at commission meetings. We were both cut off, even though the Danish woman was a member of the prestigious International Preparatory Committee. The hostility to me as a lesbian was even stronger, however, from other members of the U.S. delegation, one of whom told me I was wrong if I thought that my "gaiety" made me a liberated woman; somewhat more sympathetically, someone else informed me that it just wasn't time for us.

In the first few days together, the internal politics of our delegation became clearer: women who were either members of or closely affiliated with the Communist party, U.S.A.; women who were non-Communist socialists, some feminist, some not; women from the more recent women's movement, from organizations such as the National Women's Political Caucus, the National Organization for Women, and the National Gay Task Force; a few radical feminists (Laura Zelmachild and Diana Russell, organizing the International Tribunal on Crimes Against Women, from Berkeley, and Jan Peterson, of the Congress of Neighborhood Women); some women who were not overtly political; and many women subsequent events prevented me from knowing.

The major issue within the U.S. delegation was one I did not understand until the conference was over, even though Jan Peterson pointed it out to me at the time: the discrediting of feminism. What I saw and responded to were attacks on individual women: on Laura Zelmachild for being disruptive, on myself as a lesbian, but most vehemently on Diana Russell of the International Tribunal on Crimes Against Women, for being a racist. Her book *The Politics of Rape* had been criticized as racist by Angela Davis prior to the conference. Using this charge of racism as a focus, those anxious to discredit the most actively feminist women polarized the delegation. By the midpoint of the conference, women weren't speaking to each other even in the dining room. By Thursday, well after midnight, Diana Russell was seated in front of the delegation in a room so highly charged that nothing rational she might have said would have altered the situation. The responses were not to what she had said or written (only one woman in the delegation had read the book), but to the speakers' experiences with the racism of our culture. The threat of physical violence hung in the air. The meeting was dissolved amid threats and actions that could have set off real fighting. Communication had been effectively broken for over half the time we were at the conference and was never restored.

When the closing ceremonies were finally over the next day, I felt exhaustion, relief, a great desire to be held. The isolation, the attacks on individual women, the experience of living in a totally unfamiliar and threatening situation, added up to a sense of having been in hand-to-hand combat for a week. The emotional intensity of the conference was matched by the number of things it gave me to think about.

The sense of being individually embattled and exhausted by the struggles within our delegation, besides keeping me from understanding clearly that the issue to be dealt with was feminism, not individual problems or racism, also made me want to be with women who understood and supported me, rather than to make the effort needed to find and to talk to women who were unfamiliar with or frightened by lesbianism and feminism. The experience showed me how a culture can limit the spread of whatever it considers deviant by isolating it and creating an environment so hostile that those considered deviant remain grouped together for mutual support rather than circulating freely through the culture at large. If this analysis is correct, lesbian separatism should then be regarded as a means of resourcement only, not as a long-term strategy.

The conference also showed me the hunger of women from the United States who are not white, middle class, college-"educated," for recognition, for an escape, from racism, for care to be given to the pain that our "classless" society has inflicted. I think that the most universal ideological attractions of feminism are its holistic view of the dominant male culture's pecking-order mentality as inherently oppressive, as the single source of racism *and* sexism *and* classism; and its vision of the possibility of a world in which "power over" would not be the dominant mode of relating. But this message gets lost when the most vocal and visible feminists are from those same categories that most other women have learned to distrust.

As I tried to see how this message could be conveyed, I was quite surprised to find that I kept having an image of missionaries. I understood that the roses, the free food, lodging, and transportation offered at the conference were in some ways similar to the "services" given by missionaries as a way of saying; Look, we offer not just words, but material improvement in your daily life. What could we offer, whose resources are so limited? Would it have to be intangibles: respect, a sense of being valued, support for each woman in fighting the oppression that she felt most severely? Another missionary image came to mind: that of bearing witness. Could we make our lives such that those who came in contact with us would feel that they too could find in feminism both an organizing intellectual principle and an emotionally sustaining force?

How *do* you change values without using coercion? What are feminism's major strengths and how can they most effectively be presented? What would a feminist society be like, how would we run the hospitals and the subways and collect the garbage? Do we *want* to see ourselves as a major "ism"?

These are some of the questions I hoped to find answers to, or at least discuss, at the International Tribunal on Crimes Against Women, which took place in Brussels, March 4-8, 1976. (It seemed appropriate that our own conference should be the year *after* the fanfare of the official conferences in which women served as a pretext to further the ends of the men in charge.) Organized by an international committee out of conversations and workshops at the women's camp on the Danish island of Femo and the International Feminist Conference in Frankfurt in November 1974, the Tribunal was created on the model of Bertrand Russell's tribunal on the war in Vietnam, to make public the full range of crimes, both violently brutal and subtly discriminatory, committed against women of all cultures. Most of the over two thousand women attending were Europeans, but many came from such countries as Japan, Australia, South Africa, Chile, Brazil, India, the United States, and Taiwan. A number of testimonies were heard from women who could not attend, in the form of letters or tapes.

Topics covered included medical crimes, economic crimes, minority women, rape, political prisoners, lesbians, wife-beating, prostitution, pornography, and femicide. The testimonies given formally had simultaneous translations; the workshops had to be conducted in a patient Babel of translations by whatever women happened to be fluent in two or more languages. I was very painfully aware here, as at the other conferences, that, like too many citizens of the United States, I could not speak one major European language fluently.

The lesbian caucus met at least once a day for three days. Most of the time was spent in planning a demonstration to show that lesbians are everywhere and that lesbianism is a political, not just a sexual, choice. The demonstration was full of good feeling, singing, and the European lesbian sign, not a fist but hands extended to form a much more woman-shaped opening. The oppression and fear of lesbians were graphically demonstrated by women who covered their heads with paper bags decorated with faces and women's symbols.

A Belgian woman who spoke both Spanish and English told me that lesbianism is so taboo in Spain that some Spanish women at the Tribunal were afraid to come out, even to their Spanish sisters from the newly active women's movement who had come to the Tribunal with them. One woman had had letters to her from abroad opened by the government. But by the last day of the lesbian caucus, the Spanish lesbians were there, shyly trying to follow the discussion as it was translated by the Belgian women.

As well as organizing a demonstration, some of the lesbians also put on a dance, at which a German rock group with an English name (the Flying Lesbians) played and sang their own songs. Not only was the band very American, but the whole lesbian and feminist movement in Germany seemed amazingly similar to that of the United States. German lesbians were demonstrating self-help; four women from the (separatist) Lesbian Action Center in Berlin gave an excellent prepared testimony on oppression of lesbians in Germany; a feminist publishing house, Frauenoffensive, was operating in Munich; there was even a counterpart, though more seriously ideological, to the Liberated Women's Engagement Calendar. The Germans were by far the largest group at the Tribunal.

The French lesbians, on the other hand, seemed far less influenced by currents from the United States. They appeared to be more theoretical and cerebral, often coming from a background of activity in the Left, and less involved in demonstrations, in publicly coming out, or in consciousness-raising. The French category of things "not done" includes public declarations of one's private life, and a number of French lesbians apparently consider their lesbianism in that light. An American living in Paris did tell me, though, that a lesbian-feminist group had recently formed there; and a rape case involving two lesbians camping in the South of France was widely publicized in the women's community.

In Scandinavia the center of lesbian activity seems to be Copenhagen, where there are a number of women's organizations, including a Women's House. In Sweden, where there is a strong sense of social conformity, I was told that there is little organized activity either among women in general or among lesbians. A Norwegian woman who gave testimony talked about the geographical isolation of lesbians in Norway, whose chief center of both feminist and lesbian activity is Oslo, where there is a Women's House, a lesbian newspaper, a visual arts workshop, and a bookstore in the Women's House. The Norwegian witness described having been forced to have intercourse with (i.e., to be raped by) her husband regularly for six months while in a mental institution because she no longer wanted marital relations with him (she thanked the United States—bitterly—for having originated this kind of "therapy"). There is a Scandinavian lesbian communications network, as well as regular seminars for lesbians from Norway, Sweden, Finland, and Denmark.

A lesbian from Holland presented spontaneous testimony that sounded depressingly similar to stories from the United States: after coming out, she lost both her job and her children.

One of the testimonies I remember most vividly was one not given in person or on tape (because the voice could be too easily traced), but in an anonymous letter from a woman in Mozambique, saying that she was "hesitant ... to support these struggles for liberation when they deny my right to existence and reject my collaboration once they gain power." She is forced to choose between a life of exile and the risk of rehabilitation camps where lesbians "learn through self-criticism the correct line about themselves."

The European lesbians seemed very mobile: A

network of acquaintances and romances criss-crossed all of Europe.

A Danish woman who was studying social medicine in Germany told me of having done her dissertation on prostitution and finding that a number of prostitutes were women from Africa who had had clitoridectomies. The cutting out of the clitoris, usually in primitive conditions, using a piece of glass or a piece of a broken pot, by older females, is a rite of passage practiced widely (up to 85%) from Iran, throughout the Middle East, all the way across Africa to Guinea on the Atlantic Ocean. In addition, a woman's labia are sometimes stiched together if her husband must be away from home.

Divorce does not exist in Ireland, but a woman's husband may sue her lover for damage to his property. In Spain, even giving information leading to an abortion may make one an accomplice, punishable by up to six years in jail for a first offense and as many as eighteen years for repeated offenses. The Catholic Church has universally aligned itself with forces opposing women's rights.

The list could go on and on. Though the Tribunal did not answer the questions I had posed after the Berlin conference, nor did it fully articulate the possibility of feminism as a possible synthesis of the present opposition of capitalism and communism, it did confirm that the oppression of women in general and of lesbians in particular is truly worldwide. It also showed that the status of lesbians reflects the status of women from culture to culture. The means of expressing hatred and objectification of women vary, but the message is the same.

The experience of meeting women from all over the world at these three conferences brought home the enormous differences in the material conditions in which women live; but it also made me think that, rather than argue over who is oppressed; it sometimes makes more sense to compare the degrees to which women are oppressed within their own cultures. And, finally, I returned with the conviction that lesbians have more freedom and more support among feminists than anywhere else. As feminists, we must take ourselves seriously; as lesbians, we must make ourselves visible, must bear witness over and over again, to break the conspiracy of invisibility and ignorance that keeps people thinking that all lesbians are someplace else; as women, we must think of ourselves as a global force seeking new and more humane social forms.

International Women's Year—our Year—and our conferences were used by too many men for their own purposes. The issue of women's self-determination has a myriad of forms specific to each woman's own life, but it is the same issue, regardless of its economic or political context.

Lesbians and the Gay Movement

BARBARA GITTINGS AND KAY TOBIN

The straight lawyer made a deprecating remark about a popular gay bar.

"Can you think of a better place for us to go?" replied the lesbian.

The lawyer had gone to the bar to hunt a witness to help a lesbian client. The lesbian who spoke was trying to explain why lesbians frequented the bar. The exchange could have taken place in real life; in fact it was played before millions of people watching an NBC television movie aired in February 1977.

Is there a better place for lesbians to go than the gay bars? If so, it's not common knowledge as reflected in the film script. The organized gay movement in America has been around since 1951 and has finally achieved wide public notice as a movement for social change, but its other major role as the better place for gay people to meet is still obscure.

How well has the gay movement done at providing lesbians with a better place to go? We believe it's been a mixed success and that certain features of the movement have tended to deter gay women from joining or to limit their participation. Sexism in gay men is often cited as a main problem, but we think there are other deterrents too. We want to take a critical look at these and the issue of sexism.

While some lesbians joined in common cause with gay men in the earliest gay groups (Mattachine and ONE) and many more have done so in today's hundreds of gay groups, there's also a long tradition for separate lesbian organizations. Some gay women's groups have often cooperated with all-male or mixed organizations while retaining their separate identity. Generally, gay women and men have found it most useful to work together, pooling brains and resources, when battling the bigotries and barriers in our antigay society. Generally, gay women and men have found it most congenial to hold separate social functions, even while enjoying some mixed functions as well.

Daughters of Bilitis, the pioneer lesbian organization and for fourteen years the only all-women's gay group in the movement, was launched in 1955 to provide a place other than the bars where lesbians could meet other lesbians. Its calendar had business meetings, socials, discussion groups, and public forums and panels. At the outset DOB drew up a statement of purpose that included research, law reform, education of the lesbian, and education of the public. An ambitious program!

Still, most lesbians who came to DOB came more

Barbara Gittings at gay rally

to meet other lesbians than to work for social change. In our view this is the real draw of exclusively lesbian organizations, whether it's a stated purpose or not. Given the difficulties gay women encounter when they first set out to find a congenial gay milieu with promise of friendships and love, lesbian organizations are a natural for them to turn to.

Since DOB met such a basic need among lesbians, it should have been a runaway success from the start, attracting scores and then hundreds and thousands of gay women. But that didn't happen. DOB did grow, but very slowly. Membership at its peak was only a couple of hundred, and subscriptions to DOB's magazine eventually reached one thousand.

There were problems, especially in the fifties and sixties, that DOB could not surmount. With the subject of homosexuality still shrouded in silence, it was difficult for gay groups to break into mass media and to get distribution for gay publications. And even when they managed to hear of DOB's existence, many gay women felt too threatened to attend DOB gatherings, fearful of being seen there, fearful that somehow their cover would be blown and they would be publicly exposed as being lesbian. They felt safer either in a very private social circle, if they had managed to find one, or, oddly enough, in the impersonal atmosphere of lesbian bars, where they took their chances on sizing up strangers. Even today many lesbians avoid organized gay groups for the same reasons and make the same social choices.

But we believe that DOB itself was a turnoff to many gay women because of an unrealistic attitude about the lesbian that suffused its work. A basic DOB theme was that lesbians generally needed to shape up in order to be fit for "integration into society," DOB's

overall goal. For instance, the group's statement of purpose advocated "a mode of behavior and dress acceptable to society." (Efforts by some DOB members to remove this clause did not succeed until 1967.) A message from the president in an early issue of DOB's magazine, *The Ladder,* noted that "our organization has already converted a few to remembering that they are women first and a butch or fem secondly, so their attitude should be that which society accepts. Contrary to belief, we have shown them that there is a place for them in society, but only if they wish to make it so. They now do."

DOB's teacher-pupil atmosphere, with self-appointed teachers exhorting and educating a mythical laggard lesbian, was doomed to have limited appeal. In reality, most lesbians then as now were already integrated into the mainstream of society—at the price of concealing their gayness. They didn't need upgrading to fit in, they needed relief from such problems as fear of losing their jobs or the love of their families, and of prejudice from psychiatry and the churches.

Not that DOB neglected these issues. Far from it. Along with the handful of other gay groups in those early years, DOB laid essential groundwork for all the diverse activities of the movement today. Besides providing social events, it made referrals and did other informal social services; it established ties with people in the fields of law and religion and the behavioral sciences —people the general public of the time looked to as experts on homosexuality; it put into print a subject still deeply taboo; it confronted public officials and supported resistance to police and postal crackdowns.

Yet there was always the message that the lesbian should earn her acceptance by society. DOB sold the lesbian short as a class, and even in its best days DOB failed to attract large numbers of gay women.

Today's movement is much larger and more diverse and has the advantage of being known about everywhere. But in our opinion much of today's movement is also failing to appeal to the vast majority of gay women, because of unrealistic views about the lesbian and what she needs.

Example. Some lesbians in the movement believe that lesbians are so weakened by their double oppression as women and as gays that they must band together not simply to find one another, but to find strength. The lesbian is thought to be in fundamental need, not merely of a social group, but of a "support group" and maybe consciousness-raising as well. While the old teacher-pupil ambience is gone (or is it?) the unexamined notion persists in these quarters that the lesbian as a class needs special strengthening in order to cope with the world.

Of course, some lesbians do want special help in coping—though we think much of that would recede if good social alternatives existed for them—and those who do ought to be able to get it from supportive peers or professionals. But groups that operate on the assumption that all lesbians *qua* lesbians need help make themselves irrelevant to most lesbians who feel intrinsically all right as they are and who are competent actors in the real world, busy carving out for themselves satisfactory lives against whatever odds. Few lesbians are so crippled by being both female and gay that they need a group dedicated to psychic hand-holding to make them feel and function better. More likely, the majority of lesbians need a social group and perhaps a chance to find someone special for personal hand-holding.

Lesbians know perfectly well what are the injustices gay people face, and they may wish for a group geared to dealing with these. But unfortunately groups that dwell on analyzing oppression are often short on practical plans for alleviating it here and now. Contrarily, they may promote "a false aristocracy of suffering instead of excellence and achievement," as Elaine Sinclair put it in an open letter to her New York group. Lesbians obviously are not flocking to the movement to be schooled in oppression or to join such an aristocracy. They sense the insult implicit in a you-poor-thing perspective.

Example. Some lesbians in the movement have a supercharged response to sexism and male chauvinism, to the point that they spend much time and energy attacking the sexism of the handiest men around, the gay men in the movement. In extreme cases, every *faux pas* by gay men may be pounced on and made a battle issue—as if these lesbians were threatened in their very core. Such hostilities often lead to the formation of totally separatist groups on the rationale that the differences between men and women are too great for them to work together in the gay cause. A case in point: In the fall of 1976, a number of women walked out of the Gay Academic Union in New York City after four years of charging the men with sexism.

Yet nowhere outside the gay movement, nowhere in the gay population at large, do we find gay women so arraigned against gay men. If there's any substantial interest among the masses of lesbians in such acrimonious carryings-on, they aren't coming around to say so and join the fray.

Example. Some lesbians in the movement theorize that the lesbian needs more to look forward to than huddling with her downtrodden sisters for strength or rising up angry at her sexist brothers. They propose she move beyond reacting to negatives, into a positive world of independence from men and solidarity with all women. Many of their ideas have been codified in an essay called "Woman-Identified Woman."

In this much-touted essay, which appeared in 1970, the lesbian is defined as "the rage of all women condensed to the point of explosion." She is pictured as an unhappy by-product of a sexist cultural setup. She is supposed to be continually at war with sexism and male supremacy, yet guilty for not meeting society's expectations. The authors then labor mightily to get her out of the fix they've put her in. They plot how she can transcend all that male-identified evil and find her authentic selfhood and maximum autonomy. The catch is, she can gain "maximum autonomy" only after identifying with other people—the batch of human beings who happen to be female—and joining in a collective search

for an authentic selfhood. "Only women can give each other a new sense of self," says the essay. In sum, the lesbian needs a different sense of self and can't be trusted to come up with it on her own without benefit of group-think.

This must seem a pointless prescription to most lesbians who substantially exempt themselves from the traditional female role. Rage, reaction, rebellion? These aren't the central stuff of the lesbian experience. Knowing the traditional female role isn't right for her—that's different from raging and rebelling against it—the lesbian is automatically freed up to invent her own way and be her own person. She doesn't need to join a pack and trade in her satisfying sense of self for a nebulous group-consciousness.

The contorted theory of woman-identified woman is about as realistic and helpful as the old psychoanalytic theories that also claimed that the lesbian was a faulty outcome of a faulty setup and needed reconstructing. The lesbian deserves better than to hear this all over again in different rhetoric from her own movement.

Social scientists are beginning to confirm what most lesbians have known all along: that lesbians, along with gay men, generally feel quite good about themselves and enjoy a heightened sense of personal strength and autonomy and freedom. A partial rundown on these positive findings was done by gay psychologist Mark Freedman in his article "Homosexuals May Be Healthier than Straights."[1]

We believe that the majority of lesbians who come around to any gay group are not looking for analysis or warfare or reconstruction. They come for the same plain reason that motivated the early movement women: They want to meet and mix with other gay women in the legitimate pursuit of friendships and love. The pity is that because of the rhetoric and ideology pushed by some elements of the gay movement, many gay women never come around at all.

Are there good alternatives for gay women? Yes. A few lesbian groups do meet the social needs of lesbians in a direct and uncluttered fashion.

We have a couple of favorites we like to cite. One is Gay Women's Alternative in New York City, which offers a weekly program held in a church hall. The meetings feature speakers on all sorts of current topics (including but not limited to gay and feminist topics) along with wine, cheese, and soft drinks, and time for free-flowing discussion and socializing. The other is the Open House launched by a lesbian sponsor in the Washington, D.C., area. She is an extraordinary woman—cheerful, gracious, generous, warmhearted, and dedicated to her plan. Every Wednesday evening her home is open to gay women (and those who think they may be gay) for conversation and mixing. Simple refreshments for the crowds that turn up are made possible by the presence of a donation can. A carton of gay movement literature is on hand for anyone to help herself.

Both Gay Women's Alternative and Open House

---

[1]*Psychology Today,* March 1975.

have been advertised in their areas. Both are vehicles for bringing gay women together and boosting their awareness of the gay cause—but both are free of ideological slant and prescriptions. GWA has been going for four years and Open House for six, both on a weekly basis. They thrive thanks to meeting the most basic need of the lesbian and paying her the compliment of welcoming her as she is.

What about the gay woman who wants more than socializing, who wants to help make concrete changes in the antigay world? She must go where the action is. Generally, the action-oriented groups are mixed, and often men are in the majority. Some groups, such as the National Gay Task Force and Seattle's the Dorian Group, are so arranged that policy decisions are made equally by women and men, even though the general membership may be predominantly male. But equality by design isn't always necessary; for example, the Task Force on Gay Liberation of the American Library Association, a small and unstructured group, has throughout its seven years had equal or greater participation by women. Mixed action-oriented groups offer the lesbian the opportunity for both friendships and accomplishment, usually without ideological overkill.

Is sexism a real barrier to gay women and men working together? Since this has become an issue within the movement, we asked several gay women who do work in mixed groups to comment, and here are some of the responses:

Sarajane Garten, an Ed.D. candidate in human sexuality, is active in Gay Public Health Workers (gay caucus of the American Public Health Association) and the National Gay Student Center. She writes, "Presently I think there are two main reasons why I choose to continue working in mixed groups. The first reason is that I see them as externally oriented. My sense is that all-women groups . . . are internally focused. That is to say, community work is directed toward the lesbian community. Mixed groups that I have worked with lean toward effecting change in the *total community.* Perhaps the word is 'reformist.' All of my experience has been attempting to create change, reduce homophobia, lessen the social stigma attached to being gay. The organizations which appear to have this as their goal are mixed ones.

"The second reason I continue to choose to work in mixed groups is that I have had a chance to create some good friendships and working relationships with men. . . . It is my experience that better relationships between men and women are more possible when the sexual politics are removed. . . . I have some good male friends and I think this is possible only because we're not interested in fucking each other or fucking over each other. . . .

"In truth, the major disadvantage to my choosing to work in mixed groups is that many lesbians have questioned my feminism, and this translates into 'I am a better feminist because I work in all-lesbian organizations.' "

Sandra Penn writes, "I do not view gay people as separate groups of 'men' and 'women.' I find no difference in working with men or women or both. The problems may differ slightly in detail but are essentially the same." Penn is a former high school teacher; she has been for eleven years part of the administration of the West Side Discussion Group in New York City and she helps run its counseling and professional therapy programs.

Pamela Clerico tells us, "I like men in general, I suppose, and feel our gayness gives us a commonality in working for equal rights for all human beings. . . . There may be some gay men whom I would not want to work with simply because I don't care for the way they act, or what they believe in. . . . I am interested in human beings whom I can like, admire, respect, and work with." Clerico, who manages an office for several lawyers, is vice-president of the Dorian Group in Seattle, a civil rights, educational, and social organization for gay professionals.

Meryl Friedman is cofounder and cospokesperson of the Gay Teachers Association in New York City, and on the Board of Directors of the National Gay Task Force. She says, "Gay teachers are both men and women. As a civil rights organization that is interested in protecting the rights of gay teachers and providing gay teachers the opportunity to meet each other and gain support for each other, it would be utterly foolish not to have the GTA a mixed group. Any other way would be self-defeating."

Marjorie Morgan, a librarian who works with the Task Force on Gay Liberation of the American Library Association and who was in the Gay Media Project of Philadelphia, has this to say: "The women who work with men are more filled with love toward human beings than are the separatists, and also seem more mature and less fanatic. . . . Why alienate oneself from one-half the population, when friendship with men, particularly gay men, can be enriching and rewarding and can bear the fruits of joint labor in the gay movement? As a gay woman, I do not find all gay women likable or easy to work with simply because they are gay women. It is necessary to pick and choose those whom one likes, whether they be male or female. . . . My gay male companions provide me with friendships that are free of the emotional complications that are sometimes present with female friendships. I have had trouble with only one gay male friend since coming out; I since discovered that he is oppressive to both men and women without discrimination. I have had very little problem in the gay movement . . . in encountering hatred of women or extreme sexism."

Joan DeForeest has a somewhat different view. "There is, of course, a lot of sexism among gay men—a fact readily admitted by many of the men themselves. I think it would be less than honest to deny this and dangerously counterproductive to negate it as an important issue that needs to be dealt with by gay men. It is also important to state, I think, that many gay men—at least many involved in the gay movement and thus perhaps more aware of feminist issues—are concerned with their own sexism (as well as that of other men) and are working to become more conscious of this and to eliminate it in their relationships with women, with other men, and with their own self-concept. . . .

"While I would not argue with anyone choosing not to work with men (there are, after all, enough jobs to be done and many ways to do them successfully), there is certainly a great need for women willing to work with men on gay issues that affect both lesbians and gay men. I would therefore encourage any lesbian so inclined to work with gay men in effecting legal and social change, in public education, gay media, and gay social services." DeForeest works with gay men as a public speaker and in her job as director of Community Services at Philadelphia's Eromin Center, a counseling center for erotic minorities.

Freda Smith writes, "I choose to work with gay men because I choose to work within the human family to bring about its unity and an end to the way it divides and oppresses itself. . . . To whatever extent it is within my power, no other gay child (*girl* or *boy*) will grow up to experience the world I knew." Smith is a minister, on the Board of Elders of Metropolitan Community Church; she was a leader in the successful law-reform drive in California and an organizer of gay studies at Sacramento State University.

Betty Berzon tells us she likes to work with gay men because "they are accomplishment-oriented, are conditioned to using resources at hand, and used to accomplishing things. I'm very tuned in to that, very product-oriented." She adds that she likes men a lot and gets along better with them than with women because she feels fewer personal tensions in friendships with men. She notes that some gay issues are specific to gay women and some to gay men, and that by women and men working together both kinds of issues can be represented to the public at large. "When you go to the straight world, more attention is paid to a mixed group, especially a harmonious one, when the gay message is coming from both men and women." She also says, "The only reason I see for separate activity is to bring gay women into the movement." Berzon is a psychologist in private practice; for three years she served on the board of the Gay Community Services Center in Los Angeles, and currently she is in the Gay Juvenile Task Force and the Association of Gay Psychologists.

Lee Lehman points out that "separatism may be an urban luxury" since gay groups tend to be concentrated in big cities while small towns may have only one group or none at all. "Growing up in Stevens Point, Wisconsin, in the sixties, I could fight for my rights as a woman, but I had no recourse as a homosexual. Like many other lesbians, much of my emotional support for coming out came from gay men." Lehman, a Ph.D. candidate in botany, is director of the National Gay Student Center and is editor in chief of the forthcoming *Gay Academic Union Journal.* She is also active in

lesbian-feminist organizations. "Mixed gay groups are usually more direct in getting things done, but are ulcer-inducing to dedicated feminists. At this point in time, I would be lost without being in both sorts of groups. I don't prefer one type because each one meets different needs."

Frances Hanckel says, "It comes down to this for me: Do you really believe people can be individuals, or are you tied to a reverse sexism? I try to relate as much as possible to persons rather than genders, races, or classes; and I do believe there are decent men out there from whom it would be a waste to cut myself off. I have had many personally rewarding friendships with gay men with whom I've worked, and I feel that we have accomplished more productive work together than we could have alone—not really because we were of different sexes but because we were different individuals who did not allow our genders to prevent communication. Funny how defensive this comment makes me feel, as though I were justifying some sort of collaboration." Hanckel is a medical administrator who is active in the American Public Health Association's gay caucus, Gay Public Health Workers, and the Task Force on Gay Liberation of the American Library Association.

Louise Crawford says she works with gay men because "I'm comfortable with them. Why not?" She believes in choosing a group for what it does and who is in it, and not by gender criteria, since "different groups have different orientations regardless of sex." Crawford is head cashier at a university and is majoring in Asian studies; she is vice-president of Gay Academic Union, Inc., and one of the editors of its forthcoming journal.

Terry DeCrescenzo, a social worker, is on the board of the Gay Community Services Center in Los Angeles, is a member of the Gay Juvenile Task Force, and formerly wrote the "Womansbeat" column in the national gay paper *Newswest* (now defunct). She notes that at least 75 percent of her gay movement work has been with men. "I choose to work with gay men for a number of reasons. First of all, I genuinely like men! My decision to work on a project, or join an organization, or serve on a steering committee is based on the merit I see in the particular group, project, etc., and what the payoff for me is likely to be. Sure, sometimes gay men do not have the level of sensitivity to my needs that I wish they did (I imagine I'm less than totally aware of their needs and priorities too). I don't ignore a low level of consciousness when it exists. I challenge it, nonhostilely when possible. . . .

"It is also true, in my opinion, that gay men have a good deal more experience in some areas that lesbians can learn from. And I do not mean that men are in a paternalistic/teaching role which demeans or diminishes me. I simply mean that gay men, who have in general been more visible than gay women, have access to information and people as a result of their earlier activism. I have rarely felt 'put down or tolerated' by gay men in the movement. . . .

"I am interested in achieving real power in the real

world, not just in feeling good with a group of like-minded, supportive sisters who don't have a real power base.... We are in this world together, women and men, and I would not look forward to a separatist community made up of women only. I have been a lesbian for as far back in my life as I can remember, but I have never excluded men from my life, and do not want to, either in my personal life or in movement work.

"It's difficult to advise women to work with men, because the advice is often interpreted as a put-down. I tell women that I believe in the basic sincerity of gay men, even if they do blunder and flounder a bit. They, too, have a lifetime of acculturation which tells them we're little girls to be amused and tolerated, and even when they consciously give up that stance, a lot of what they've integrated 'bleeds through' anyway in their language. As long as I believe in their basic honesty, I will hang in with them, and I advise other women to do the same. I think the hope for the future of the gay movement is a united front."

We too believe in a united front. With so much work to be done—on job discrimination, psychiatric views, the law, the media, religious attitudes, the literature, and much more—the movement needs diversity but can ill afford divisiveness. We believe that the controversy over whether gay women and men can/should work together is largely on the wane. Gay women and men have a long social history as friends and allies that far antedates today's organized gay movement, and we doubt that the general amity between them will ever be shaken.

The gay movement should be a better place for lesbians to go, for friendship and love as well as for constructive work to end the bigotries and barriers against gay people. And in the main it is. Lesbian reader, join us!

Lesbians and the Left

NOREEN HARNIK and JILL BOSKEY

"Commie, pinko, queer!"—the epithet often hurled at demonstrators in the early 1960s embodied a truth that it took the demonstrators close to ten years to come to terms with: gays and leftists have common interests. Both gays and leftists risk loss of jobs, rejection by family and friends, even arrest for being too blatant. The attacks of our enemies often link us together. During the anti-Communist, antihomosexual hysteria of the fifties, Guy George Gabrielson, Republican National Chairman, said, "Perhaps as dangerous as the actual Communists are the sexual perverts who have infiltrated our Govern-

ment in recent years."[1] Joseph McCarthy himself got carried away in his antihomosexual campaign in the midst of the Senate hearings. Senator Tydings felt moved to quip, "Won't you stop this continued heckling about homosexuals and let us get on with the main work of finding Communists!?"[2] But the links exist not only in the minds of the "defenders of the American way."

Historically, many of those who defended homosexual rights also championed the rights of other oppressed peoples. Emma Goldman, one of the first Americans to speak out for the rights of homosexuals, was an anarchist and a feminist. Henry Hay, a founder of the Mattachine Society, was a member of the Communist party.[3] In our own day, the gay movement of the sixties and seventies was born of the same rage against injustice that engendered the struggle for civil rights, the feminist movement, the antiwar movement, and all the various factions of the new Left whose roots were nurtured in the ferment of the 1960s. Our basic cause was human liberation. We felt that all people, black or white, Vietnamese or American, men or women, gay or straight, had the right to the basic freedoms and necessities of life. We had been taught that "all men are created equal" with a right to "life, liberty, and the pursuit of happiness." But we felt that women were created with these same, equal rights. That blacks had the same right to sit at a lunch counter as whites. That Vietnamese people had the same right to choose their own form of government as anyone else. That gays had as much right to congregate in bars as straights. We wanted to try to create a world in which everyone had the right to a job, a decent income, decent housing, decent education, decent medical care, as well as the democratic freedoms of speech, press, and choice of lovers.

The years 1969 and 1970 were in many ways the high point for organized leftists, feminists, and gays in recent United States history. Hundreds of thousands turned out for antiwar demonstrations. Thousands turned out for Christopher Street Liberation Day parades and lesbian dances and events in major cities. Feminist demonstrations also attracted thousands, and the women's movement finally began to acknowledge its own complicity in the continuing oppression of lesbians within the movement. In New York City radical organizations such as Alternate U (which opened its doors for some of the first gay dances ever held) managed to unite the Left, feminist and gay movements under one lively roof.

While the Left was giving its support to the newly organized feminists and gays, these groups were also joining in the general struggle for human rights, including the effort to end the war in Vietnam. Unity reached

[1] Jonathan Katz, *Gay American History: Lesbians and Gay Men in the U.S.A.* (New York: Thomas Y. Crowell Co., 1976), p. 92.
[2] Ibid., p. 93
[3] Ibid., p. 406.

its peak. Most demonstrations against the war had contingents of various groups united around their own interests, for example, blacks, Latins, native Americans, feminists, Jewish leftists. There were political differences, even deep distrust, but all were willing to get together to try to end the war and to support each other's human liberation.

With the advent of the Nixon years, however, a pall fell over the unity enjoyed by these movements—a pall that, for most activists, led to a scattering of energy and a narrowing of vision. The seeds of the coming divisions had been there all along. In fact, it was often our common experiences as women and lesbians working within straight-male-dominated leftist groups that led us to feel the need to explore our own lives more thoroughly. Through this process, many of us began to discover the exhilaration and satisfaction that could come from devoting time and energy and love to other women. Lesbians began to join CR groups and study groups which dealt specifically with our own oppression as lesbian women. Some went on to form lesbian-feminist political organizations which often put out newspapers and tried to formulate a specifically lesbian-feminist political perspective. We tried to develop new cultural forms to express our growing understanding of the beauty and power of women working together. And as time went on, many of us began to doubt our original optimism about the Left.

Though it was true that the Stonewall Rebellion, an event marking the birth of the gay movement of the current generation, would probably never have happened if the Left and feminist movements hadn't been in motion, lesbians began to realize that the Left of the seventies was ignoring the obligations of unity. Men in the Left were mouthing the feminist line but still living their sexism. Many straight women still wanted lesbians to remain in the closet to protect the respectability of the increasingly reformist feminist movement. Sections of the black movement were elevating the heterosexual man-woman-child family to the status of "ideological correctness." Most gay men had no more understanding of the unique position of lesbians as both women and gays than their straight counterparts.

As lesbians and other disparate groups had withdrawn to examine their unique positions in the political scheme, the remnants of the new Left, in disarray and disillusionment, had begun to reformulate their positions. SDS, in particular, had split into several factions with various levels of consciousness and a myriad of viewpoints as to what constituted proper revolutionary behavior and what did not. Of course, these formulations were made almost exclusively by straight white men and reflected the expected bias thereof.

Instead of examining the specific conditions of United States society and history and of the history of the old and the new Left in America, the male Left grasped for a ready-made answer. Many decided that since the revolutionary forces had won in China, Mao must have all the answers. They grafted Mao's political

thinking about China onto the United States. For others, it was Trotsky or Stalin but the result was the same; they rejected the positive lessons they had begun to learn from the feminist and gay movements. Many of these groups began to adopt the social views of the most backward "worker" as their ideology. Groups such as the Revolutionary Union, later the Revolutionary Communist party, and the October League, offshoots of the original SDS, thus began to promote the nuclear family as a basic unit of the revolutionary struggle, defying not only feminist analysis but Marxist analysis as well. Moreover many groups have a stated position that homosexuality is a disease—a "response to the intensification of the contradictions brought about by decaying capitalism."[4] They hold that homosexuality, like the state, will wither away under communism (if not on its own, then with a little help).

Trotskyist parties such as the Socialist Workers party and the Sparticist League voice support for gay liberation and fight for feminist causes like day care and free abortion on demand. But many independent lesbians feel that these groups are really only being opportunistic. They recognized the strength of the women's and gay movements and wanted to recruit women and gays into their organizations. They accept lesbians who devote the required portion of their political efforts to a more economic definition of the revolution while often rejecting the gay and feminist movements themselves as "raising personal predilections to the level of political principles."[5] One's first commitment, according to these groups, must always be support for the party—a commitment that might well include the obligation to defend uncritically with arms as well as words any so-called "deformed workers' state" (e.g., Cuba, the Soviet Union, China) despite its "deformations,"[6] such as imprisoning, murdering, or otherwise persecuting its homosexual populations. Is it any wonder that some of us feel these groups might fail to remember their "gay is okay" line if they ever took power?

The international picture seems even bleaker than that of the United States Left, though the international socialist movement started out with great promise. In December 1917, just a few short weeks after taking power, the Bolshevik government in the Soviet Union was the first government in recorded history to do away with all laws against homosexual acts. This was part of a general program of reform of antiquated sexual morality which the Soviet government undertook and which included the legalization of abortion on demand and an aggressive attack on sexism in all its many ugly forms. With the death of Lenin and the rise of Stalin, however, these first bold steps were brutally stunted and ultimately reversed. In January 1934 the Soviet authorities

---

[4] Unpublished Revolutionary Union position paper on the gay question.
[5] "On 'Gay Liberation': A Marxist Analysis," in *Women and Revolution*, No. 13, Winter 1976-1977.
[6] Ibid.

under the now firmly established leadership of Stalin conducted a series of mass arrests of gay men in Moscow, Leningrad, Kharkov, and Odessa. Lesbians as usual were invisible to the male authorities and thus ignored. In March 1934 a federal statute was introduced in the Soviet Union that forbade homosexual activities between males with penalties of up to five years' imprisonment for consensual acts.[7]

The Cuban revolution, which in so many vital ways has improved the life of the Cuban people, nevertheless has, as a deliberate governmental policy, jailed gay Cubans just for being gay. In 1971 an official document from Cuba stated, "The social pathological character of homosexual deviation is recognized" by the First National Congress on Education and Culture, and it was resolved that "all manifestations of homosexual deviations are to be firmly rejected and prevented from spreading."[8]

In China gays have fared no better. Many American women, having read "Goldflower's Story" and *Fanshen,* had learned to respect the Chinese revolution because it had greatly improved the status of Chinese women. Mao himself had said, "Women held up half the sky" and had made the equality of women one of the cornerstones of his revolutionary thinking. But it began to become clear that lesbians officially "don't exist" in China. *The Great Speckled Bird,* an Atlanta underground newspaper, did an interview with William Hinton, an American who lived in China from 1947 to 1953 and visited there again in 1971. Hinton said, "I didn't ask anybody about homosexuality, but using my eyes and ears I would say that they are under rather serious repression.... It is not something that people in China usually talk about, but they would deny it.... there are gay people and ... they have serious problems because it is generally considered rather a serious abnormal behavior."[9]

Still many lesbians maintain hope for the American revolution. Some few of us have joined groups like the Socialist Workers party or the New American Movement, willing to submerge our lesbian identity. A few leftist lesbians have been able to form socialist organizations in which they believe their political formulations about the nature of sexism are really basic to the groups' purpose. Some women who live in smaller cities and towns have found it easier than lesbians in big cities like New York to work with the male Left where they live. Incidents of activity hostile to both leftists and gays have facilitated cooperation between these groups. Alliances have indeed been formed around grand jury harassment of lesbians, gay men, and straight leftists. And, of course, as recent disclosures have revealed, we have all been subject to FBI surveillance. This, however, is a negative bond and our greatest hope for unity in the future may lie in the hope that revolution in the United States can be different—can usher in much more than "state capitalism" under the pseudonym of socialism. We reason that women's liberation and gay liberation are much stronger in the United States and that each revolution learns from those that precede it. No leftist revolution has yet succeeded in a heavily industrialized nation; that is important and could be a crucial difference.

We want the world to change but we want a change that, while ensuring individual liberties and freedom from sexual oppression, also challenges all the fundamental issues of hierarchy, privilege, and economic injustice. We believe this is possible. But it is not likely to occur through a gay movement or a women's movement that settles for reform—reform that is never capable of challenging the essence of our oppression as lesbians or women. If the Left has failed us as lesbians, so reformism fails us as human beings. A federal gay rights bill or an equal rights amendment for women in our present capitalist society merely lulls us into the belief that things are changing at the heart while in reality we are helping to construct a cosmetic facade. And in the end since the basic balance of power remains unchanged, such reforms may even be used against us as state equal rights amendments have frequently been used to get men into positions that have previously been dominated by women while women remain "unqualified" for higher status, higher paying male-dominated jobs.

Reformism, however, is not a sin of the gay and women's movements alone. It also characterizes an American Left that fails to challenge the nuclear family or any of the other basic trappings of the patriarchy. The exclusion of women, the invisibility of lesbians, the incarceration of gay people, and the dominance of men remain primary facts of life in every so-called socialist nation on this earth. No truly basic move forward in human evolution can occur until this imbalance is obliterated once and for all. We believe that recognition of the need for a multifaceted attack on all the causes of human oppression can bring about a principled unity among the groups that grew out of the sixties. Only together can we create a truly democratic society where all people's needs are met.

[7]For more information, see John Lauritsen and David Thorstad, *The Early Homosexual Rights Movement, 1864-1935* (New York: Times Change Press, 1974).

[8]Quoted in Alan Young and Karla Jay, eds., *Out of the Closets: Voices of Gay Liberation* (New York: Douglas/Links, 1972), p. 246.

[9]From *The Lavender & Red Book,* a gay liberation/socialist anthology (Lavender & Red Union, 6844 Sunset Blvd., Los Angeles, Calif. 90028), pp. 39-40. Reprinted from *Great Speckled Bird.*

Lesbian as Teacher, Teacher as Lesbian

MERYL C. FRIEDMAN

My first years as a lesbian teacher would have proved far less complicated if Brooklyn College had offered me a course entitled "The Lesbian in the Public School System." However, such a course never made it into the curriculum. (I wonder if they feared overcrowded conditions?) After the usual liberal arts and "methods" courses, there I stood facing a class of eighth-graders, unable to take refuge behind the academic and research frameworks that I'd always depended on for new and unnerving situations. Do these kids know I'm a lesbian? Should they know? Should I tell them, or lie, or pretend I'm not gay, be invisible? For many lesbian teachers the lack of any support structure often leads to very real feelings of confusion, fear, and isolation. What is a lesbian teacher to do?

Our experiences with the New York City Council[1] and their tragicomic performance staged for our benefit during the course of the hearings on the gay civil rights bill clearly taught us that to be an open lesbian and a teacher meant to be singled out as an object to be feared and loathed. Let's face it, sisters, we are perceived by the homophobic public to be a tremendous threat to the continuance of heterosexual society; heads of family preservation groups shudder at the mere thought of our existence. Our presence in the classroom is enough to ignite terror in the hearts of these self-righteous folks, who seem to be convinced that lesbian visibility in the classroom will, as a matter of course, undermine the foundations of heterosexuality that have so sacredly been laid. Nongays seem to forget (or ignore) the fact that, although we are lesbians, we were brought up, for the most part, in nongay households and with overwhelmingly antigay attitudes. Yet, here we are, gay women despite all the conditioning not to be.

Up until recently school systems have generally ignored the existence of lesbians on both sides of the school desk. This refusal to acknowledge the presence of a portion of the school population (which can be calculated at a substantial 10 percent) has to affect education in general and lesbian students in particular.

As a lesbian teacher, one question that I am natur-

ally concerned with is how changes can be effected so as to make the school environment more meaningful to lesbian students and also make the school administration aware of and interested in their unique presence and needs.

I was recently contacted by a former student, a young woman of sixteen, who was in the process of recognizing and realizing her lesbianism. Reaching out to me was her first real open acknowledgment of her feelings for women. Her need to talk about and explore these feelings and the confusion she felt is entirely understandable. Her needs reflect the needs of thousands of other young lesbians in our school systems. It becomes more difficult for these young women to get in touch with their feelings, learn about lesbianism as an alternative life-style, find people to talk to and share their thoughts and emotions with other young lesbians, since the school system provides absolutely no means of assistance or information pertaining to lesbianism. In a society where one of the basic goals of education has traditionally been meeting the individual needs of its students, this lack of services and personnel is indeed a sad commentary.

At this time school libraries are seriously lacking in intelligent and positive materials about lesbianism. A school library could easily serve as a reservoir of information about lesbianism, providing students with the opportunity to gain perspective; to learn about themselves in a nonthreatening way.

Counseling for students who are getting in touch with lesbian feelings is virtually nonexistent. Teachers and guidance personnel are at best unaware and untrained in this area, and at worst homophobic. A valuable first step toward enabling counselors and teachers to deal with youngsters' questions about their lesbianism and their sexuality would be for these school personnel to engage in consciousness-raising sessions in an effort to broaden their awareness.

Socially, lesbian students need group or club activities to provide them with the opportunity to discover and meet each other. Such encounters would help to eliminate the depression that results from living the isolated existence that many young lesbians face.

Curricula must also be altered so that the contributions of lesbians and gay men are presented, in both historical and a present-day sense. Our lesbian "daughters" must not be denied the knowledge of their culture and heritage.

And then there is the issue of teachers as role models. Teachers are indeed role models. The inherent assumption about lesbian teachers is that they will be *negative* role models, foisting their "incompleteness" and "perversity" upon the children they teach.

On one level I am so piqued by the obvious stupidity of the "negative role model" theory that I am tempted to ignore the issue completely. However, this issue is very real to the heterosexual community. Lesbian and gay male teachers from the Gay Teachers Association have set out to enlighten the unaware parent

---

[1] The gay civil rights bill was defeated by the New York City Council in 1974 by a vote of 22-19, with two abstentions.

Elementary teacher Kerry Woodward with student

public. We point out that nongay students need help in focusing in on the legitimacy of alternative life-styles, so that they may develop into mature human beings who don't define themselves from strict stereotypical definitions of what is and what is not acceptable. We discuss the needs of gay students—how important it is to help young gays to get in touch with their own feelings, without fear of loss of love, and to learn about their own identity with pride and self-respect.

Lesbian students have a right to know lesbians who are fine, dedicated, warm, loving, and sensitive women. Yes, they especially have a right to *positive* role models to identify with. Young lesbians should not have to be frightened of their sexuality and the legitimacy of their feelings. Neither should they be left to learn about themselves from outdated and offensive books where human feelings are overlooked and negative myths and stereotypes are projected and perpetrated.

Lesbian visibility in the classroom is one way to express the validity of life-styles other than heterosexual. Exposure to various life choices and styles is one way to avoid the bigotry that results from putting people into preconceived molds.

Until recently, acceptable role models for lesbians did not exist. Why? We've been defined by a society that is male-dominated and predominantly heterosexual. We are experienced as threatening, described as "queer" and "unstable." Now, however, times are changing. Lesbians are beginning to define themselves and must continue to do so. The public needs to know that lesbians are not merely "sexual"; we are whole persons who have emotional, intellectual, spiritual, and physical needs. Lesbian teachers, as role models, can help make this clear to the public.

Nonlesbians should no longer be allowed the luxury of ignorance. The lesbian teacher must turn around the homophobe's concept of her as a negative role model. An up-front lesbian teacher, who respects herself and her life-style, can only be a positive role model to lesbians and nonlesbians alike. Lesbian students would then have a woman to identify with and nonlesbian students could come to grips with whatever prejudices about lesbianism that they may have incorporated, and deal with the concept of alternative life-styles in a realistic fashion. In these ways both lesbians and nonlesbians will have the opportunity to grow up as freer human beings.

Prior to the gay movement most lesbian teachers feared that they would be discriminated against, even lose their jobs, if their lesbianism was revealed. Unfortunately this feeling is still prevalent and is often justified. Such fear is detrimental to us not only as teachers but also in its effect on our self-concept as lesbian/women. For many, fear of discovery has motivated an almost fanatical quest for isolated anonymity. The split into two distinct spheres, "my work" and "my life," creates a constant division which can only yield frustration and confusion. With these problems in mind the Gay Teachers Association has attempted to bring about changes on three levels: (1) how gay teachers view themselves and each other, (2) how we are treated and regarded by our employers and society at large, and (3) how we can help meet the needs of gay students.

As cofounder of GTA, I vividly recall our first public meeting in October 1974. The association had been set up to articulate the needs and problems of gay teachers in New York City; to build a support structure; and to integrate gay teachers, as a powerful voice, into the gay rights struggle. The women who came to that initial meeting needed to meet with other lesbian teachers, share their problems and ideas, and find mutual support. The thought of actually coming face to face with other women in similar positions was exhilarating and terrifying. A large vacuum in their lives was beginning to fill. Many of the women somewhat sheepishly confessed later that they were wary that photographers and fingerprint experts from the Board of Education were going to spring out from behind closed doors! Although we didn't dare ask for last names, some women were reluctant to use even first names. The most obvious conversational question, "Where do you teach?" was verboten.

Presently, some of our most active members (those who are now involved with the GTA Speakers' Bureau and Political Action Committee) blush profusely when they reminisce about these first meetings they attended. These women, despite initial fears and misgivings, have become a vital part of GTA. What started off as a felt need metamorphosed into a demand for their rights as people. It is the fulfilling of this need that often compensates for and overcomes the fear. Progress is being made. . . .

Unfortunately many lesbian teachers are still governed by fear of exposure despite the concrete achievements of GTA.[2] Gaining a feeling of security is often a long and tedious process. As a lesbian activist in 1974 I thought of myself as an up-front, movement-oriented woman, openly fighting for gay civil rights since 1971. I'd had the unusual experience of coming out in what I think of as an evolutionary way. I became aware of my lesbianism at twenty-six, at a time when the gay movement was flowering. For me, realizing that I was a lesbian was like coming home—it was literally a whole, new glorious life, one that I embraced securely and happily. These new feelings are incorporated into every aspect of my life. I found my professional life strongly affected by my lesbianism through my involvement in GTA. I learned that "coming out" is not a single step, but a continuing process. Just when I'd think, "That's it, all the closet doors are opened wide," I'd become aware of another obstacle to freeing myself

up to be me. I think of these obstacles as "storage closets." In coming out further and further, the closet has been aired out many times.

For example, recently GTA members actively negotiated with the New York State Teachers' Union (NYSUT) for acknowledgment of our existence and passage of a gay rights support resolution. Since NYSUT is a very large, depersonalized organization, I thought of our lobbying as a very nonthreatening exercise in gay and personal liberation. We could achieve valuable protections without much danger of disclosing the identity of our members. At a NYSUT meeting, however, I found myself unexpectedly face to face with my local union representative. To say I was shocked is an understatement; to describe his response is impossible. Needless to say I quickly explained the importance of the resolution in question, with my adrenaline pumping away!

Thus I have found myself forced to be honest about my identity on every personal and professional level. For me the process has been strengthening.

GTA succeeded not only with NYSUT but also with the New York City teachers' union (UFT). The statewide union newspaper did a feature article with picture about GTA. Although almost all of my colleagues knew I was a lesbian, most preferred not to deal with the issue and ignored it whenever possible. However, after reading the newspaper story, many people loosened up, as if reading about lesbian schoolteachers in a union paper legitimized our existence. The other teachers were now anxious to talk not only about GTA in general, but also more specifically about the role of the lesbian teacher. For the most part, the response was very supportive from both administration and staff.

Most recently I've entered a new level on the continuum of coming out—dealing with the Parents Teachers Association. The president of the PTA happened to be viewing a television talk show on the same day that I appeared along with two other representatives of GTA to discuss "Gay Teachers in the New York City Public School System." The PTA president was outraged that a teacher at his school was a lesbian. "It's bad enough that she's a lesbian, but that she has to discuss being a lesbian teacher on television. . . !" He demanded that the principal dismiss me immediately. Now, I knew that my job was safe and my rights would be protected. Time and again the New York City Board of Education has declared that gay teachers have the same rights as any other teachers, and that appearing on a television show that discussed my involvement with an organization outside the classroom was well within the realm of acceptable activities for any teacher.[3] However, I was heartened that my principal, without hesitation, supported my right to speak out as a lesbian teacher.

GTA has grown as an organization and I have

---

[2] On January 24, 1975, Mr. Frank Arricale, executive director of personnel for the New York City Board of Education, issued a policy statement affirming the rights of gay teachers. In June 1976 the United Federation of Teachers Executive Board adopted a supportive gay rights resolution. In August 1976 the New York State United Teachers passed a supportive gay rights resolution.

[3] GTA was instrumental in getting the executive director of Personnel for the New York City Board of Education to issue a statement guaranteeing the civil rights of gay teachers.

THE BOARD OF EDUCATION
OF THE CITY SCHOOL DISTRICT OF NEW YORK
DIVISION OF PERSONNEL
65 COURT STREET
BROOKLYN, N.Y. 11201

FRANK C. ARRICALE, II
EXECUTIVE DIRECTOR

596-6121/22/23

January 24, 1975

Ms. Meryl Friedman
Gay Teachers Caucus

Dear Ms. Friedman:

As we have discussed both at joint meetings with the Board of
Examiners, ourselves, and the National Gay Task Force, as well as
in private meetings with you and Mark in my office, you can be
assured that homosexuality is not a bar to entrance into teaching
in New York City nor to the continuation of teaching in the City.
This point I made very clear to the members of the City Council
last year when I was questioned on the matter through letters.
I believe you have a copy of the letter I sent to Councilman
Burden on this matter.

Homosexual teachers have exactly the same rights and protection
as any other teacher in the system. Not only are we not involved
in any process of ferreting out homosexual teachers, frankly,
we are not particularly interested in whether or not teachers are
homosexual or not. You will recall that Dr. Rockowitz, Chairperson
of the Board of Examiners, last year made the same point in the
meeting we had with the National Gay Task Force which you attended.

If there are any further questions or concerns, please do not hesitate
to call.

Again, I apologize for the mixup in our appointment dates this past
week, but as you can read from the newspapers, you can understand
how some of us at the Board involved in the battle of the budget so
intensely can begin to get absent-minded.

With every best wish,

Sincerely,

FRANK C. ARRICALE, II
Executive Director

FCA:h

NEW YORK STATE UNITED TEACHERS
80 Wolf Road • Albany, New York 12205 • (518) 459-5400

September 7, 1976

Mr. Marc Rubin
204 Lincoln Place
Brooklyn, New York   11217

Dear Mr. Rubin:

At its August 29-30 meeting, the NYSUT Board of Directors adopted the
following resolution:

> WHEREAS, NYSUT has traditionally supported the civil and human
> rights of its members, and
>
> WHEREAS, NYSUT recognizes the oppression of, and discrimination
> against homosexuals in general and homosexual teachers
> in particular, and
>
> WHEREAS, it is the responsibility of trade unions to provide jobs
> protection for its entire membership from all forms of
> discrimination
>
> THEREFORE BE IT RESOLVED that NYSUT continue to support the civil
> rights of all members, including homosexuals and will continue to
> represent equally all of its members in all NYSUT activities,
> associations and organizations without regard to sexual orientation.

The Board also voted to continue its policy with regard to advertising in the
NEW YORK TEACHER, i.e. not to accept paid advertising from any other membership
organization.

I appreciate the presentation which you and other representatives of the Gay
Teachers Association made before the NYSUT Board of Directors. If you have
further questions concerning the actions of the Board feel free to contact
my office.

Fraternally,

Thomas Y. Hobart, Jr.
President

TYH:ss

Affiliated with the American Federation of Teachers, AFL-CIO

United Federation of Teachers

Local 2, American Federation of Teachers, AFL-CIO

260 Park Avenue South
New York, N.Y. 10010
(212) 777-7500

October 6, 1976

Ms. Meryl Friedman
831 Carroll Street
Brooklyn, New York   11215

Dear Ms. Friedman:

In June, the UFT Executive Board adopted the following resolution:

Resolution on Rights of Homosexual Teachers

WHEREAS, UFT has traditionally supported the civil and human rights of its members; and

WHEREAS, UFT recognizes the oppression of, and discrimination against homosexuals in general and homosexual teachers in particular; and

WHEREAS, it is the responsibility of trade unions to provide their members with protection from all forms of discrimination on the job,

Therefore, be it

RESOLVED, that UFT continue to support the civil rights of all members, including homosexuals, and will continue to represent equally all of its members in all UFT activities, associations, and organizations, without regard to sexual orientation.

As you can see, our organization is ready and willing to stand by any of our members whose civil rights are denied.

Fraternally,

ALBERT SHANKER
President

AS:rdg
OPEIU 153

Affiliated with the New York State AFL-CIO, New York City Central Labor Council and the New York Congress of Teachers

grown as a person through my involvement in the struggles that lesbian teachers face. The awareness of my responsibilities as a lesbian teacher to myself, to students, and to other lesbian teachers is a growing one that has evolved during the course of the last several years. The more involved I become in working for lesbian rights, the freer and prouder I feel. Working openly as a lesbian teacher has made me feel not only better about myself and my abilities, but also more confident and more secure as a professional.

RESOURCES

"Homosexuality Goes to School," an award-winning documentary radio program about gay teachers and students, is available in the form of a transcript and cassette from Options in Education, National Public Radio, 2025 M St., N.W., Washington, D.C. 20036. The transcript is free; the cassette is $5.00.

"The days of guilt and shame are gone."

I am a high school lesbian, a proud lesbian, and I would like to share some of my growing experiences with you.

My first (and only) homosexual experience began two years ago, when I was sixteen. I had never been in love before, and was confused and frightened when the deep love I felt for a close friend grew beyond the boundaries of a friendship. Not knowing what homosexuality was, or that it existed at all, I found it impossible to define my intense longing to be close to the beautiful young woman I so deeply loved. I knew that I couldn't be in love with Jackie, because two women simply cannot feel that way about each other. At least that's what everyone said. When I found out how wrong they were, I was really mixed up. My relationship with her was, in my eyes, the most beautiful experience I had ever had in my life. Yet, why did other students call me "queer" and "lezzie" in the halls at school? Why did people yell rude comments from their cars when we walked down the street together? Why did the only book concerning homosexuality in the school library refer to gay people as being sick and perverted? Why did the Holy Bible, which I had been taught to believe in, condemn me? Why couldn't anyone else understand? Why didn't they try? I had so many questions, so many fears, so much guilt, and too few answers. With the help of some beautiful straight friends, however, I eventually found the answers. The days of guilt and shame are long gone.

Once Jackie and I overcame our uncertainties and guilt, we initiated an effort to raise the consciousnesses of our fellow students, an effort which has had surprising success in a small-town high school. On the first day

of school this year (my senior year) I wore a Gay Pride T-shirt to school and didn't get expelled. As a matter of fact, the faculty has been tolerant of the consciousness-raising activities performed by Jackie and myself, and several teachers have given us warm encouragement. The reactions of students, on the other hand, have been diversified. When I walked into English class wearing my Gay Pride T-shirt and sat down at a table with Jackie, everyone else at that table got up and moved elsewhere. While I would have been upset by this action a year before, I was now able to recognize it as a sign of weakness on the part of the students, rather than myself.

Jackie and I have engaged in a variety of other activities designed to encourage other students to think about and express attitudes toward homosexuality. One was an opinion poll which Jackie gave to the sociology class (she was denied permission to poll the entire school).

At our suggestion, the book *Sappho Was a Right-On Woman* was purchased by the public library, and we plan to make the same suggestion to the library at school. We have also initiated numerous discussions concerning homosexuality and the law in government class. Although many students have been reluctant to participate, I feel that the discussions are beneficial in that they catalyze thought on the subject. Last week a very interesting occurrence took place in our government class. After being given an assignment to write a bill or amendment to be debated and voted on in a mock Senate, Jackie and I wrote an amendment that would establish equality under the law for homosexuals, and would forbid the government to regulate private sexual acts between consenting human beings. As could be expected, this proposal ignited a great deal of heated discussion. Using the Bible as one of its weapons, the opposition defeated the amendment in a vote of 13 to 11, with abstentions. A similar bill did pass in another government class.

Jackie and I, however, were not about to give up. The following day we proposed a bill to legalize the institution of slavery, on the grounds that slavery is permitted and even condoned by the Bible. Our purpose was to illustrate the inconsistency of the logic employed by the class in defeating our bill on homosexuality, and I feel the point was well made.

Since my involvement in trying to raise the consciousness of my fellow students, the gay movement has become the most important aspect of my life. Although I at times feel isolated because I know no other gay students besides Jackie, I feel very proud of what we are doing, and I am looking forward to college. The attitudes of students are changing. Jackie and I no longer hear derogatory names when walking down the halls. Many friends respect us for what we are doing. Other students are forced to think about and acknowledge the existence of homosexuality. We were interviewed by the school newspaper, although the teacher in charge chose not to print the interview.

I realize these are small victories, but it's a start. If

we can raise the consciousness at the high school level, then a foundation is established to build on in the future. The day of equality for all human beings is coming—I dream of it; I feel it; I believe in it. Although I may not live to see that day, I'm going to fight to help it get here.

Mitzi Simmons
(reprinted from *Lesbian Connection*)

Lesbians in the Academic World

MARGARET CRUIKSHANK

I want to discuss the invisibility of lesbians in the academic world and a few recent developments that make me hope we will not always be invisible. But, like others who write on social change, I have more to say about the problem than about the solutions. I believe that the invisibility of lesbian professors and administrators not only affects lesbians themselves but creates obstacles to the full emotional and intellectual development of all women in higher education. Lesbian invisibility can thus be seen as a general feminist concern as well as a gay rights issue.

If our students were told which subjects would be ignored in their classes, they would at least know what they didn't know. But our courses *assume* that everyone is heterosexual, and the assumption is so deeply buried in our consciousness that we fail to see that it is in fact an assumption. Academics like to mock the Victorians for being afraid of sex, but since the only sexual relationships we acknowledge are heterosexual ones, our progress in sexual emancipation is nothing to boast of.

It is true that homosexuality is considered in "deviant behavior" courses and is no doubt mentioned in other courses (at one school it is mentioned right after necrophilia). So rarely, however, is the subject discussed by open homosexuals, either students or teachers, that what is currently said probably disseminates misinformation more often than it dispels ignorance. The university has traditionally been a place where prevailing public opinion could be challenged, but in the case of homosexuality, the university simply mirrors the prejudices and homophobia of American society.

Because women professors on college campuses are greatly outnumbered by their male colleagues, the lesbian undergraduate in need of a role model is far less likely to find one than is the male homosexual student. Thus the self-esteem of the young lesbian is especially threatened by popular beliefs: that lesbians hate men,

that they want to be men, that they dress like men, and that sleeping with men will "cure" them. The crucial error in all of these statements is that men are made the issue. Men are seen as so much more important than women in this society that even lesbianism is viewed as a condition having essentially to do with men. Of course it does not. It is an affirmation of women and is, in the words of Rita Mae Brown, "a life that draws its strength, support, and direction from women." But the invisibility of lesbian professors makes this truth inaccessible to many undergraduate lesbians, who may indeed worry that they are rejecting men and are not therefore whole human beings, or who may assume that all of the women who teach them and have taught them are heterosexual women.

There are other misconceptions about lesbians resulting from lesbian invisibility which all feminists, not only lesbian feminists, must attack: (1) that lesbians are an extremely small group, (2) that they are all the same, and (3) that lesbians are a sinister force.

Because nearly all lesbian professors and administrators are invisible, it is possible to believe that lesbians are a much less significant minority on college campuses than they really are. Impressions are more important here than statistics. If the undergraduate woman thinks of lesbians as a tiny group (perhaps she thinks she has never met one), she is likely to give no thought at all to her own sexuality, assuming heterosexual feelings and behaviors are the only normal ones. Unable to imagine healthy, happy lesbians because she sees none, she naturally assumes she is heterosexual, especially when reading "research" based on lesbians in mental hospitals and prisons. It doesn't occur to her that, for example, studies of German-Americans that focused exclusively on people in prisons and mental hospitals would reach some bizarre conclusions about German-Americans.

Any carelessly assumed notion about oneself is dangerous, and surely one reason we see women in their thirties and forties coming out is that in their college years they did not know that lesbians, although a minority among women, are very well represented on campuses. The invisibility of lesbian professors makes it possible for a young undergraduate to tell herself, "No, that can't be it," when she feels attracted to women but repulsed by the popular image of lesbians. Even when she falls in love with a friend and has a sexual relationship, she may assure herself and her lover that they really *aren't* lesbians, they just happen to love each other.

Thousands of us have had that experience, as college students, as graduate students, and even as professors. Looking back, it seems an incredible game we played: We conspired against ourselves. If a few of our admired professors whom we now know are lesbians had told us then, the label might have lost its frightening connotations. Perhaps those of us who are drawn to academic work have a special need to be respectable. The high grades that allowed us to become scholars gave us a status denied to most women. No wonder we chose not to become the most depised of women—the dyke—even when we were living with the women we loved.

Books like Jane Rule's *Lesbian Images,* while showing that lesbians are more numerous than we previously knew, will also help to eradicate the notion that all lesbians are the same—tough, swaggering women with Gertrude Stein haircuts. When the beautifully dressed, genteel, and soft-spoken specialist in American literature leans over her lectern and tells her class that she is particularly interested in the lesbian interpretation of Emily Dickinson's poetry because she herself is a lesbian, the butch stereotype will begin to crumble. When the dean of women comes out, the diversity of lesbians will be more apparent than it is now. I do not want to argue defensively that we are respectable after all. Some of us most emphatically are not respectable. But lesbian invisibility means that for the great majority of undergraduate women, the term "lesbian" will suggest some exotic and far away woman, Jill Johnston, perhaps, or Kate Millett, and will not suggest, as it should, teacher, dean, neighbor, scout leader, dorm counselor, church worker. In addition, when the differences among lesbians are better understood, the phrase "lesbian feminist" will no longer be synonymous with the phrase "radical feminist." Some of my colleagues see all lesbians as radicals. Of course the term "radical" often simply means someone I fear or cannot identify with, and for many women on campuses today, unfortunately, that is exactly the significance of the term "lesbian."

The third misconception noted above, lesbians as a sinister force, was neatly illustrated for me the first week I was women's studies director, when a middle-aged supporter of the program said to me earnestly that she hoped I would not let "those lesbians" take over the women's center. I soon learned that the women's center staff had never seen a lesbian and wished some would come to their rap sessions. So much for take-over. No doubt some residual fear from the fifties of Communist take-over shapes the view that a function of lesbians is taking over groups, the way playing golf is a function of suburban matrons. When individual lesbians become better known as lesbians, perhaps the myth of lesbians as a sinister force will be exploded.

In one way, of course, we *are* a sinister force: Many of us have taken control of our own lives, and the exuberant happiness that often flows from taking responsibility for one's life is obvious to our straight friends, who are bound to ask themselves what they are getting from marriage or marriage equivalents. Many wives are happy too, no doubt, and some lesbians endure destructive relationships and suffering; but women who have learned to devote their energies to themselves threaten the patriarchal system merely by existing.

Editors of new anthologies based on an images-of-women theme (which means, so far, images of straight women) have shown what very limited roles women have been given—goddess, bitch, whore, wife, symbol of evil—and how difficult it has been to see women in themselves rather than in relation to men. The very narrow butch

role assigned by popular mythology to lesbians is therefore related to a larger problem, the narrow roles imagined for women generally. Just as heterosexual women have been portrayed by male writers as the Other and Alien, lesbians are very readily seen as Other and Alien by women college professors, even by those feminists who vigorously attack sexist views in their classes.

Besides the prevailing belief that heterosexuality is the norm and lesbianism a departure from the norm and therefore alien, there are other compelling reasons why a lesbian professor today who values her privacy and has an instinct for self-preservation will choose not to reveal her sexual identity: first, a fear of local harassment—bricks through her window, damage to her car, obscene phone calls—and second, a greater deterrent, fear of government assaults on her constitutional rights. FBI and grand jury harassments of lesbians, known among ourselves, has now been thoroughly documented in a three-part *New Yorker* series on the Fifth Amendment (April 1976). The lesbian who calls attention to herself instantly loses her anonymity. Although she might like to be a role model for the young lesbians she meets in her classes, she feels that the personal sacrifice would be too great. It may be objected that a closeted lesbian is one who has not fully accepted her emotional-sexual identity, and of some women this is no doubt true; but as long as grave penalties attach to announcing one's lesbianism, only those who are temperamentally suited to long-term strife and fighting will be able to throw away the cloak of invisibility.

There are a few signs, however, that this oppressive situation is slowly changing. Julia Stanley reported in a recent issue of *The Lesbian Tide* (January-February 1977) that the National Council of English Teachers passed a resolution urging that discrimination against homosexuals be ended, whether it occur in hiring and firing, in textbooks or in classroom practices. The NCTE resolution noted, very appropriately, that homosexuals have always been well represented among teachers and students of English. Such public statements cannot ensure that lesbians will become more visible on their campuses but will create a climate in which individuals may feel that coming out is at least one possible choice.

More directly relevant to lesbians are (1) the movement to organize within professions such as nursing and medicine and to sponsor conferences such as the APA's conference on lesbian feminist therapy which was held in October 1977 in San Francisco; and (2) the increasing number of books by lesbians which the feminist presses and lesbian feminist presses are publishing. Works that most of us had never heard of three years ago, as well as good new material by lesbians, are now becoming available. Signs of this burgeoning are the lesbian issue of *Margins* that Beth Hodges edited (August 1975) and more recently the special issue of *Sinister Wisdom* devoted to lesbian writing and publishing (Fall 1976, also edited by Hodges.) Again, the creative outpouring of books by and about lesbians does not guarantee that academic lesbians will become more visible, but greater circulation of our own writings will surely mean that the secrecy surrounding lesbianism can never again be as great as it has been in the past.

Perhaps the greatest hope for ending lesbian invisibility comes from the new and rapidly growing field of women's studies, which has attracted a disproportionate number of lesbians, both as administrators and as students. This is no surprise: Lesbians have a special stake in a thorough investigation of women's past and the encouragement of less stereotyped attitudes toward women. More than eighty of the five hundred women who went to San Francisco for the founding convention of the National Women's Studies Association (January 1977) attended the lesbian resources workshop. And it was clear that they came from strong personal concern for lesbian issues and not as detached observers.

A more dramatic attack on lesbian invisibility occurred during one of the general sessions of this conference, when, to support a statement on ending discrimination against themselves, lesbians in large numbers stood up to show who they were and how many of them were in the room. That was unquestionably a historic moment for women-identified academics in this country.

Even before the first national meeting of the association, women's studies programs had inadvertently served to demonstrate that lesbians are far more numerous than any of us would have supposed ten years ago or even five years ago. If a goal of women's studies is to make the diversity of women better known, a related goal must be to make the diversity of lesbians better known. But this will be hard to do while nearly all lesbian professors and administrators remain invisible.

My own women's studies program would no doubt be attacked if I were an "avowed" lesbian. My solution therefore to the problem of lesbian invisibility has been a series of awkward compromises. I have come out to a few of the students who work for me, to students who tell me that they are lesbians, and to a few other professors who I know are lesbians. Picture a closet with many holes in it. Or, more whimsically, the Cheshire cat's grin without the cat. That is often the way I feel when dealing with colleagues.

But an attitude I notice among a few heterosexual women I work with gives me a slightly hopeful view of the future: They see that the oppression of lesbians is their problem too. They see that as long as lesbian relationships are reviled, their own freedom to form close friendships with other women and to express affection openly is threatened. This sense of community with lesbians is the first step toward breaking down the stereotypes that I have noted above, and women's studies will encourage it.

In the long struggle between fear and ignorance on the one hand and knowledge on the other, some prejudice about human groups has been assailed, but contempt for lesbians has survived. Only now have we begun to demand that we be considered with the same detachment that is (supposedly) brought to the study of other

groups. As the lesbians' caucus at the San Francisco women's studies convention noted, materials on lesbians have been entirely omitted from the college curriculum or badly distorted. But if women academics, at least, can be persuaded that lesbianism is no problem but that fear of lesbians and ignorance of lesbians are the real problems, then lesbian invisibility may someday be far less characteristic of American campuses than it is in the 1970s.

"Our strongest resource is the open lesbian, particularly in an academic community."

I wanted very much to be open about my lesbianism at the college where I teach. It was very important to me. At the time I came out, I wasn't sure why it was important. My coming out was precipitated by a course listed in our college catalog, which grouped homosexuals, drug addicts, alcoholics, and sex-offenders together in a course called "Deviant Subcultures." The stress was on prevention and rehabilitation. That course had been bothering me for a while. Suddenly one night I thought, "I'm going to do something about this." The next morning I called my secretary on the phone and dictated a memo to her. I said that as a colleague in the college community and as a member of the homosexual community I found the course offensive and inaccurate. I asked her to type this and send it to my chairperson and the chairperson of the social science division where the course was offered, plus the dean of the college and the president. The secretary had said, "Do you know what you're saying? Do you really want me to send this?" I said, "Yes." It caused a great deal of agitation in the social science division.

They sent memos to me that they would, of course, look into this right away, and would have a subcommittee to discuss this course. Then silence. The deadline for changing the wording in the catalog or deleting courses was coming, but I had heard nothing from them. I got in touch with the chair of the social science division and demanded, "What's happened to this?" and was told that she had been trying to get me. That's not accurate, because I have a secretary, for one, and I am home every night. She said they had fixed the course up, and she would send me the rewording, and she knew I would be delighted. Well, the rewording was exactly the same except *homosexual* became *homophile*. Still the stress was on rehabilitation, halfway houses, that kind of thing, and we were still lumped with the same category of social deviants. The same impulse that made me dictate the memo precipitated my walking into the president's office all by myself. I just walked in. I didn't make an appointment ahead of time. He was there, and I told him, "Joe, this is what's happened . . . I'm very concerned." At that time the catalog deadline was within twenty-four hours. "I don't think this rewording is at all appropriate; I don't think it's removed the difficulties of the course content. It's still offensive and I feel upset about it." He contacted the dean of faculty, who called an emergency curriculum committee meeting. Within twenty-four hours the course was dropped, and it's never been in the catalog again.

That was three years ago. I still have my job. I haven't gotten any feeling that the declaration to the president was detrimental to me professionally. I had said to the president, "I don't speak just for myself—I speak for other gay colleagues in our community. They are not comfortable about speaking out because they are afraid it will hurt them when they come up for rehiring." He assured me that if the subject of anyone's sex life ever came up during a college-wide meeting he would rule it out of order and call the meeting closed, and would see to it that that was never used against a faculty member.

I still remain the only open gay person at the college. There are maybe a dozen gay men at the college, but no women I know about, and the men are still in the closet although one is becoming more open about his life-style. I have found it extraordinarily liberating to be open. It removed my feeling of alienation at my job. I've become much more forceful in my feelings about feminism. It has reinforced my feelings about being a woman.

There has been very little reaction from my students. They felt it was no big deal at all. I'm open about my lesbianism each time I teach a women's course. Our strongest resource is the open lesbian, particularly in an academic community. Because I've been open I've been able to feel more comfortable about using lesbian materials, whenever I teach a women's course. I could never teach a women's course again without having a lesbian writer, or a book about lesbian experience. My students respond to that. I've never had any difficulty as far as their responses to lesbian novels, or their response to me. The only time I had difficulty was when I had two Vietnam veterans in my class. They baited me and the other women about every issue—abortion, open marriage, sexuality, anything. Lesbianism was just another issue to make snide remarks about.

Three years ago there was a very strong women's group at the college and we got together and decided to have a women's week, with workshops exploring issues relating to women. "Women on the Job" was one of our big areas, and "Women and the Law" was another. I had a student who had been a prostitute who had been in jail, and she did a prostitution workshop. There were some police officials who came and talked about rape. I participated in a "Women Loving Women" workshop, and we had a tremendous turnout. I also did a presentation on lesbianism in the social science class.

One lesbian student and two male students have come out to me since my coming out at the college.

By and large, my colleagues are extremely supportive. My lover, Gloria, and I attended a Christmas party given by the chairperson of the English department. We were the only gay people there. Before the party I wondered, "What are we going to do if people start to dance?" I was very concerned about whether Gloria and I would have to dance, but there was no dancing. We behaved better than some of my colleagues, who got very drunk. I was a little nervous, but it went beautifully. I felt that my openness about homosexuality has earned, maybe not complete understanding from my colleagues, but certainly respect. They showed this respect to Gloria. They knew that Gloria and I had just moved in together and were completely aware of our life-style. The invitation for the party was sent to both of us. It wasn't sent to me with a "P.S. Bring anyone you like."

—Sarah Lanier Barber

Two Stones and One Bird: Religion and the Lesbian

THE REVEREND RHEA Y. MILLER

We come so many full circles in our lifetime. I am again the child who sat in the big green overstuffed chair in the corner reading biographies. For some unknown reason I had decided to read the story of Jesus in one of the Gospels. I was not a reader of the Bible in the normal course of events as a child, but I had picked up the Bible this particular day and was reading about the Crucifixion. Big tears began to roll down my face just when Dad walked through the living room where I was sitting. He saw me crying and asked what was wrong. "How could they do this to Jesus? Leave Him all alone? He loved those people." And Dad replied, "You're well on your way to understanding." I may have been, but it was another fifteen years before I could recapture that spiritual awareness.

I was raised in the Church, my father being a rural midwestern pastor. I took religion and the Church all very seriously but I never considered myself very religious or spiritual because I couldn't pray right (God never spoke or responded to my prayers) and I felt no emotional attachment to God in my heart, or so I thought. I was intrigued by religious people and loved questions about religion. I became a religion major in college because those classes were the only ones that dared ask the questions I had to ask. Who was this Jesus anyway? What makes right and wrong? Isn't God only a

The Rev. Ellen Barrett, first open lesbian ordained an Episcopal priest

rationalization after all? I studied theology voraciously but it all dead-ended with more unanswered questions and seemingly endless rationalizations. I became a master of theological issues and discussions but it all seemed so worthless, so lifeless. And the Church—the Church seemed the epitome of hypocrisy and irrelevancy. The Church in no way seemed to relate to the real world as I saw it. The pain, suffering, and laughter that was life to me was refused mere recognition in churches. Therefore, I left religious discussions and I left the Church.

I entered the secular world unfettered by religious obligations for five years. I finished school, drove a dump truck, sang the lead in a rock combo, and was the baker for a large resort kitchen. About three years into this pilgrimage I discovered and actualized my lesbianism. Religious considerations played no role in this discovery as I'd never been a biblical literalist (a phenomenon of the Enlightenment and not the early Church) nor could I conceive of "loving," regardless of whom, as ever being sinful. In fact, even being the agnostic that I was, I saw my love of a woman as a gift of God. My pilgrimage into the world continued until I hit rock bottom in my personal life. I had successfully isolated myself from my family, professional aspirations, a lover, and any personal expectations. In this state of humility I learned that I had unintentionally hurt a dear friend very badly. There was no way I could forgive myself. And walking swiftly out into the night air heaving sobs of regret, I cried out, "I'm sorry," and without thunder and lightning or visions in the sky, I became aware of "Okay. It's about time. You're forgiven. Just keep walking. You have promises to keep and miles to go before you sleep." It was not just a feeling or a cognitive understanding. It was a whole awareness that filled and joined my entire body. I was in touch again after so many years with my spirituality. Religion became a matter of discovery and not learning or modeling. Everything was new. I was a child again.

In my new discovery I learned how people kept letting words get in the way. I became aware of a Reality in my life that I saw in other people's lives, but unless I spoke about this Reality with the right words, my Reality was denied or considered immature, distorted, or inconsistent. People said that the Bible said homosexuals were sick and yet I knew I wasn't sick and I knew the Reality within me not only accepted but embraced my life as God-given. I learned to show that the Bible did not in truth condemn homosexuality but it seemed only a game to justify what I already knew. People said that God was the Father only and I knew God was also Mother and there is neither male nor female in the risen Christ, and yet all the words seemed so useless. I saw people excluded from realizing their spirituality, especially homosexuals, and more especially lesbians. Yet, somehow, lesbians have survived, relying totally on *their* awareness of the Reality, despite other people's words, and carry on in faith. There can be a no more hopeful sign for the survival of spiritual Reality in our lives than a Christian lesbian.

The established Church continues to get caught up in its words and structures, credentials, and roles, yet homosexuals continue to strive to bring the Reality of Jesus Christ and the Church to people, gay and straight. The Universalist Unitarian Association (UUA) seems to come the nearest to supporting homosexuality as a lifestyle. It has established an Office of Gay Concerns, constructed an excellent human sexuality unit within its educational materials which includes a very up-front discussion of homosexuality. Overall, UUA churches seem to be more receptive to gay persons using their facilities for worship and gatherings, and certainly respond least homophobically of any of the established churches.

The United Church of Christ (UCC), the Presbyterians, Lutherans, and the United Methodist Church (UMC) all have gay caucuses struggling for the recognition, embracing, and acceptance of homosexuals in their respective congregations. The gay Baptists keep trying to form a gay group or caucus, but are currently without funds or staff. Baptist denominations remain totally nonreceptive. The UCC has a woman coordinator of their gay caucus and she estimates a 20 percent lesbian membership. The UCC is concentrating on educating its people and seeking civil rights for homosexuals. They are the first church to have ordained a self-proclaimed homosexual. The Presbyterians are focusing on the study of homosexuality. Their gay caucus is struggling for mere recognition and it is still a highly homophobic church. Lutherans Concerned for Gays is very low key in profile, deliberately not taking a political stance. Their preference is to work toward dialogue and better understanding. There are a growing number of local chapters, some of which do meet regularly for worship. They have an estimated 17 percent female membership.

The United Methodists have taken the stance "we love you but . . ." The UMC supports civil rights but sees the homosexual life-style as incompatible with Christianity. The UMC Gay Caucus has taken a more activist stance than some, partly because of the opportunities afforded by the structure of the UMC. The movement for lesbians in the UMC is happening within the women's caucus, most particularly in the local Task Forces on the Role and Status of Women. Many lesbians are found working within these groups, but not openly. Therefore, the UMC Gay Caucus is primarily male, and the much needed insight and talent of the lesbians are closeted within the feminist movement in the UMC. At least the women are making some headway, in that more and more women are in leadership positions, not to mention their increased numbers in seminaries. The UMC is still basically a very homophobic church.

The Episcopal Church is suffering considerable turmoil over women and the church, not to mention homosexuals and the church. A group known as Integrity has arisen to work with Episcopal gay persons. It was one of the first gay groups to obtain support from a noted theologian, Norman Pittinger. Integrity emphasizes the provision of a support group for religious gay persons and seeks further education and dialogue within the church at large. Although Integrity has gained considerable recognition, the Episcopal Church's stance at present is that homosexuals should be loved as Children of God and given equal rights, but ordination involves issues that need further study. As the Episcopal Church is very sexist, it is no surprise that the percentage of women in Integrity at best is only 10 percent. In January 1977 Bishop Paul Moore of the New York Diocese ordained the first open lesbian to the priesthood, but this represents the exception and not the rule. There are approximately twenty-five local chapters of Integrity, primarily in the more major cities, most of which meet regularly for the Eucharist.

Perhaps the largest gay religious group outside of the Universal Fellowship of Metropolitan Community Churches (UFMCC) is the gay Catholic organization known as Dignity. Dignity has been in existence approximately eight years with currently nearly fifty chapters all over the nation, not including affiliated organizations worldwide. This group stresses education, spiritual development, social involvement, and social events. Its membership comprises up to 25 percent lesbians, decidedly below the norm, but considering the sexist nature of the Roman Catholic Church, not a bad percentage. Dignity too has been supported by the writing of a priest/theologian, Father John McNeill. His most recent work, *The Church and the Homosexual*, is used by gay religious persons across faith and denomination lines.

Gay Jewish groups have also been forming, mostly on either coast in more than a half-dozen cities, not to mention several abroad. This religious group more than any other suffers from centuries of entrenched patriarchic male roles. It is an immense step simply for a group of gay Jewish males to gather. Obviously, however, lesbians are not often found, nor are they actively sought.

All these gay religious groups must fight for mere recognition, much less acceptance. They are so involved with obtaining recognition that many needs of the consituency are not even heard, much less met. One church, however, exists specifically to minister to the needs of gay persons. In 1968 the Universal Fellowship of Metropolitan Community Churches (UFMCC)—a gay Christian church—was founded by Troy Perry. Today there are over ninety UFMCC churches all over the world, including the United States, Canada, Britain, Australia, Union of South Africa, and Nigeria, with a total membership over the twenty-thousand mark. UFMCC began by simply wanting to put itself out of business; that is, when other churches opened their doors to the homosexual life-style, there would be no need for the UFMCC. Obviously, the foreseeable future offers little hope. Meanwhile, UFMCC has begun to grow and mature and to realize that it is not simply about gay Christians. Because from the beginning it sought to reach across denominational boundaries, UFMCC has become a concrete step in ecumenism. It is moving and amazing to see Pentecostals, Catholics, and Baptists working together.

Moreover, UFMCC has consciously decided to confront sexism in its ranks. UFMCC learned that women in the leadership means women in the congregation. Of the seven presiding elders of the UFMCC, one of whom is the founder, Troy Perry himself, three are women. The leading evangelist preacher of UFMCC is a woman with feminist consciousness. Moreover, at their General Conference in Washington, D.C., in 1976, UFMCC resolved to gradually but actively change the sexist language to inclusive language in liturgy, song, and scripture. It went a step further and stated that it "recognizes the spiritual growth among all women at this time and affirms its eagerness to learn and grow from feminist theology." There are exceptions on the local level, of course, but they are decreasing. Thus, UFMCC has become much more than just a "gay church."

Most of these gay religious groups are found in large metropolitan areas, or in "newsletter" form only. The larger metropolitan areas provide the still necessary anonymity which allows homosexuals to gather without fear of exposure and harassment. The UFMCC, Dignity, and Integrity are found in most metropolitan areas. The other groups, excluding the UUA, and a few chapters of the Presbyterian Gay Caucus and Lutherans Concerned for Gays, are not yet developed into local chapter groups. The UFMCC is finally beginning to break into more rural areas, such as Wichita, Kansas; Joplin, Missouri; and Quincy, Illinois.

The concern for lesbians and sexism in gay religious groups goes beyond sexist language and the need for women in leadership positions. Within the gay subculture itself there is very little gay male/female interaction. Thus, the ignorance of the unique problems of lesbians by male homosexuals, not to mention society at large, is almost overwhelming. For example, a large percentage of lesbians, approximately one third, are mothers. Extreme child discord is a common result of a lesbian couple bringing two sets of children into one family. Children often have no concept that they are now part of a new family. Lesbian couples may thus be forced to separate. Many lesbian mothers live in constant fear of exposure by irate husbands and the loss of their children. The whole process of lesbian mothers entering the job market for the first time is also foreign to most males. The problems and concerns of lesbians who are not mothers only adds to this list. This is where churches must minister.

Many lesbians have left the Church altogether, regardless of their stance on homosexuality, primarily because of the apparent lack of concern for their needs. Other lesbians have begun to turn to alternative modes of spirituality and are forming covens, entering witchcraft, etc. There are still lesbians such as myself, however, who are struggling to awaken the Church to new insights and perspectives. These are women who have discovered a core of truth and faith, a Reality, within the patriarchal religion that supersedes and disavows the sexism. Their intuitive, wholistic, relationship-oriented perspective calls attention to people's *needs* and not their shoulds, to the process and not the goals, to the community and not the individual. These are women of vision who dare to call the established and the radical, the male and the female, the gay and the straight, into one community of believers.

There is no place for the lesbian to lay her head, but there are plenty of places to dig in. I see that her digging and her Awareness may yet free the world from its "words." For myself, I must keep in touch with the Reality of loving and being loved, of wholeness, of "not knowing" but trusting, as I experienced as a child. It is all I have. It is all we need.

Prison Ministry

THE REVEREND DOLORES JACKSON

Note: The following statement was edited from a taped interview with the Reverend Dolores (Dee) Jackson, minister of Alpha and Omega Metropolitan Community Church in Brooklyn, New York. (MCC is a gay Christian church.) Dee is a prison chaplain serving women's detention facilities in Manhattan, Brooklyn, and upstate New York. She is also a counselor for drug addicts and alcoholics.—Ed.

I've been involved in the prison ministry about a year. The gay male ministry didn't have any problems getting into the men's facility—they were able to perform services in the "Queen's Tank," the area where the gay men are segregated from the straight male prisoners. But when I tried to get into the women's facility, the administration refused to admit me because they feared I would promote homosexuality.

Then I went through the Board of Corrections and told them the women were being discriminated against. They said that in the women's facility the gay women were not segregated, so I would have access not only to the gay women but to all the women. The superintendent said, "I don't want anyone coming in here converting these women to homosexuality." I looked her in the eye and said, "If I am going to do any converting I would hope it would be to Jesus Christ." At that point she said, "What corridor would you like to work on?" I had the same credentials that any other minister had, and there was really not a good reason for me to be banned from the institution, so they gave me a pass.

I was assigned to a floor with about thirty women on it. Just as many straight women were interested in the counseling as gay women. Many of them came out of curiosity—to see a lesbian minister. I started talking to about three women, and by the third week there were twenty-four. One thing I discovered is that the chaplain's department refused to counsel gay women unless they confessed to being gay and promised never to do it again.

Then I was called down by the administration and told that the counseling requests were getting to be "too much." I requested a time slot like every other church there, to do a worship service, and I said, "From what I understand services are badly attended. Maybe this will inspire members to come to church." They didn't want that, because the whole institution would probably have come. So they limited me to that one corridor.

I tried to get into the New York State facility, Bedford Hills. Years ago I had been employed there as a corrections officer, so I knew the officers and administration. I felt that coming in with "another cap on" might cause a bit of a problem, but because I had specific women I had to see, they couldn't refuse me. Lesbians there are theoretically not discriminated against, but certain things like job programs are not open to them easily. They'll say, "If you don't put on a dress, and earrings, and stockings, we can't send you out" and of course that's going to discourage lesbians right away. When it's time to go before the parole board, they have to dress to prove they have been "rehabilitated." So the women go to the Board of Parole looking very dainty-like, in order to be given the programs. Then there are other agencies like some halfway houses that are not too keen about having openly gay women there.

There are a lot of feminine-looking lesbians in the facility, and if they come out and say, "I'm gay," the administration ignores it. Gay, to them, means looking like a man, so if you don't look like a man you're not gay. At the state facility you may have family members or close friends on your visiting list, but if they think for a minute that it's a gay relationship, they will say that person can't come to see you. In the facility at Riker's Island it's not like that. Anybody can come as long as they come on visiting hours.

A relationship could be strained, though, at the time of your arrest. When they say you have one phone call and it's to your family or lawyer, they might not allow you to call your lover. But things are getting better, because I can remember times when you just wouldn't dare stand before the judge as a lesbian; at least now there are organizations like ours who will fight for you.

The judge will usually give you a longer sentence if you're gay. I had a call from the police department about a woman they were looking for, for robbery. They were interrogating me: "Just answer one question—is she a bulldyke? Is she one of those *he-she's*?" This was the police! Now, I know that when they catch this woman, she's going to have hell, even before she gets to court. And if there's a possibility she didn't commit a crime, they are going to assume she did it anyway, because she's "trying to be a man."

Most of the correction officers are gay themselves. They might come down hard on the lesbian prisoners if they feel the administration is watching them. They can't appear to approve of what the gay prisoners are doing, even if they are gay themselves. The gay administrators have the same problems.

When you take the test for correction officer they

don't ask if you're gay. You can look at some of the correction officers and wonder how they got the job. Their lesbianism is so obvious, and yet one of them might say, "I have three kids," which many lesbians do, and this throws suspicion completely out of the minds of a lot of administrators. On the other hand, they often *want* gay correction officers because they feel they have more stamina and can handle the prisoners better.

One of the stereotypes about gay women is that they are more prone to violence than straight women and that they are going to rape the other prisoners. I have worked in all-girls' facilities and at women's facilities and I've never seen any type of lesbian rape. I understand that rape is common in the male facility (in which case gay men are the *victims,* not the perpetrators), but I've never seen it in the women's facility, or even heard of it.

Basically, I find the relationships very loving. It's hard, of course, to express yourself physically as a lesbian in prison. There's a lot of hand-holding and sitting very close. There's no open display. Sexual encounters are almost impossible, unless an officer turns her back, for someone's convenience. I've asked prisoners, "Where do you get together?" One said, "I'm assigned to work in the kitchen, in the back. There's a potato bin back there and it's a big machine, so you can't see behind it. Sometimes the officer is in the front, and I'm friends with her, and she won't come in the back." If you're on line with other women in front of you and the officer's in front opening the door, you can grab a kiss before she can see the rest of the group. No one's going to rat, because it's no big thing.

At night the women are locked one to a room, but accidentally-on-purpose two women could be locked in the same room. I can remember opening up some mornings and seeing two people coming out of one room.

You can be put in segregation because of open display of homosexuality, which has to be so open the officer has to write it up. If that happens both of you could go to segregation for days or weeks. You lose a certain number of "points," which means if you are to go before the parole board in February, now you might not go until April. Lesbianism has already added to your time, so the inmates are pretty careful. They know just how far to go. If someone says, "May I go in such-and-such's room, she wants to show me something," anything could be going on. A woman might stand outside the cell as a lookout, and if she sees an officer coming, she'll say, "Chickie, Chickie," and that means get yourself together.

Some lesbians come out of jail and start to fall back into drugs, and they have a tendency to come to me, because at least I'm not going to put the gay trip on them, or the religious trip, either. I'm more interested in their problem. Once I feel I have them, then I tell them the religious aspects. I have quite a few people still coming to see me after they have been out of jail six months.

I was interested in making sure the congregation in my church would be ready to accept them. Now I'm getting the congregation and the people ready for the junkie and the prostitute. It's hard to take, let's face it. If you've been sitting down with middle-class, clean people all the time who've never been in trouble, you may not be so receptive; so I've gotten the whole congregation involved in prison ministry. About a quarter of our congregation are ex-offenders. Of that number, just about all of them are ex-drug addicts.

One thing many women would like you to do is talk to their families about being gay, because they can't. There are quite a number of families I'm working with now. I'm also busy with the children of lesbian mothers, because a lot of their children are in day care, or foster care, or with relatives, and when a mother is released from prison, she needs a court order to have that child returned to her. There is no way she is going to get that child back or even be given visiting rights until she has a job and an apartment.

There is still a lot of work that hasn't been done for lesbians in prison. There has to be some organization dealing with just the ex-offender. We have gay groups, but the prison issue is just one of many things they are concerned with. We need a complete program for helping lesbian women get back into society, because I can't find jobs for these women. And we need halfway houses for them. I'm glad we have a women's medical facility now in the Village. I had this woman in Utah sitting in a hospital for detoxification, in a therapy group, and they started hitting her on her clothes and her appearance. She said, "I am not here for my homosexuality; I am here for my drug problem." If we could have programs in the gay community so people wouldn't have to deal with this prejudice, that would be great.

The average lesbian interested in prisons is more interested in the political prisoners than the main-line prisoners. If we had the same kind of strength that we use to raise money for political prisoners, we could have a drug addiction program just for lesbians.

Lesbian organizations should try to make direct contact with women in prisons. They would be allowed in like any other group. If the gay community were saying, "We have such-and-such a program, and one of the things we are trying to do is make the gay woman feel good about herself," and show them a whole social program, they would allow us in, but they are not going to allow you in if you are going to start a problem. They admit they can't deal with some of the problems that gay women have. Let them think you are helping them. We should be saying, "You cannot deal with this. We can; we want to help you."

RESOURCES

"Like a Rose," a 16 mm, black and white, sound, 23-minute documentary film about two gay women serving twenty-five year sentences in the Missouri state penitentiary. Rental $35, sale $250.

Add $3 handling/postage. Order from Tomato Productions, Box 1952, Evergreen, Colorado 80439.

"Daddy Tank: No Touching, No Human Contact—In Cell Block 4200," in *The Lesbian Tide*, Nov./Dec. 1976. Tide Publications, 8855 Cattaraugus Ave., Los Angeles, Calif. 90034. 213 839-7254.

Cordova, Jeanne, "Prison Reform: New Freedoms for Daddy-Tanked Lesbians," in *The Lesbian Tide*, March/April 1977, page 6.

The Prison, Probation and Parole Program at the Gay Community Services Center, 1213 N. Highland Ave., Hollywood, Calif. 90038. 213 464-7485. A positive, supportive program dealing with the needs of gay offenders.

Professional and Union Caucuses

DOLORES L. NOLL, Ph.D.

In the last few years, more and more lesbians and gay men have taken our struggle for liberation into the area of our lives where homophobic oppression often wields its greatest power—into our jobs or professions. The threat of losing a job—or of not getting one in the first place—is very real for most gay people; and the decision to come out at work is not one to be made lightly. Yet if the risks are great, so are the rewards—not only the sense of elation and freedom that so often accompanies the refusal to accept the chains of silence any longer, but also the gratification that comes from joining with other gay people in one's profession to bring about changes that are both concrete and far-reaching. Lesbians have been involved in virtually all of the organizations discussed in this article, often in ways fundamental to the success of the group.

The "first openly gay caucus in a professional organization"[1] was the Task Force on Gay Liberation,[2] a subgroup of the Social Responsibilities Round Table of the American Library Association (ALA). Organized in 1970 by Janet Cooper and Israel Fishman, and coor-

dinated since 1971 by Barbara Gittings, it has pursued with considerable success its goals: "to promote the creation, publication, and dissemination of more and better materials on gay people and the gay movement, and to raise within the library profession issues of discrimination against gay people both as librarians and as library users."

The TFGL's most distinguished contribution has been the publication and widespread distribution of a constantly expanding bibliography of materials that "present or support positive views on the gay experience, that help in understanding a gay-related issue, or that have special historical value." Growing from a list of thirty-seven titles in 1971, the current edition (fifth, 1975; supplement, 1976) contains 252 entries.[3] Over 30,000 copies of the fourth edition alone were distributed. In addition, the TFGL has prepared a "Gay Materials Core Collection List," consisting of seventeen items, "as a recommended inexpensive core collection of gay materials for small and medium-sized libraries"; and it has issued as well "Gay Books in Format for the Blind and Physically Handicapped."

The TFGL has also taken steps to inspire authors and prod publishers to write and issue more progay books. The establishment in 1971 of an annual Gay Book Award was one result of this effort. Four women have won the award so far: Isabel Miller (Alma Routsong), Del Martin and Phyllis Lyon (jointly), and Jeannette Foster. Task Force members Frances Hanckel and John Cunningham have published an article in the *Wilson Library Bulletin*[4] analyzing four novels about adolescent male homosexuals. These writers point out that these books, in addition to neglecting the lesbian experience altogether, perpetuate the view that "being gay has no lasting significance and/or costs someone a terrible price."[5] Published in conjunction with this article are the guidelines drawn up by the TFGL "to help librarians evaluate the treatment of gay themes in children's and YA literature."[6] A current project of a Task Force committee (made up of four women and two men) is to work "as consultants with the Media Selection and Usage Committee of ALA's Young Adult Services Division to produce a mediagraphic essay of gay materials for teenagers."

If the TFGL has conformed to the highest professional standards in its published efforts, it has been less conventional in its projects at the annual ALA conventions. In Dallas in 1971, recognizing the need for publicity, the Task Force members set up a kissing booth, entitled "Hug-a-Homosexual," in the convention exhibit hall. Needless to say, the booth attracted considerable

---

[1] Unless otherwise indicated, all quotations have been taken from the completed *Lesbian Sourcebook* questionnaire or from other materials issued by the group under discussion.

[2] Barbara Gittings, Coordinator; P.O. Box 2383, Philadelphia, Pa. 19103. A comprehensive survey of the TFGL's activities (which I have drawn on for this article) may be found in Barbara Gittings, "Combatting the Lies in the Libraries," in Louie Crew, ed., *The Gay Academic* (ETC Publications, 1977), pp. 107-18.

[3] The cost of the fifth edition of the bibliography, obtainable from Barbara Gittings at P.O. Box 2383, Philadelphia, Pa. 19103, is 25¢ a copy, five copies for $1.00.

[4] "Can Young Gays Find Happiness in YA [Young Adult] Books?" *Wilson Library Bulletin*, No. 50 (March 1976), pp. 528-34.

[5] Ibid., p. 532.

[6] Ibid., p. 532.

attention from hundreds of onlookers as well as two local TV stations and a *Life* photographer. More recent programs have been somewhat more conservative, though no less creative. In 1975, for instance, in a forum entitled "The Children's Hour: Must Gay Be Grim for Jane and Jim?" led by Frances Hanckel, members of the TFGL held up large signs reading "Death" or "Car Crash" each time one of these unfortunate events occurred in the plot narration: "Guffaws broke from the audience by the time the signs were hoisted during the final plot summary."[7] Future programs of the TFGL promise to be equally provocative.

As a gay organization that spans all the academic disciplines, the Gay Academic Union[8] has acted as a catalyst in the formation of gay caucuses in these disciplines. Created in 1973 by a group of sixty-one women and men, the GAU has brought together gay people from academia, facilitating and reinforcing the contacts that lead to the growth of more specialized groups. The GAU's principal contribution in this respect has been its annual conferences, held at a New York City college or university each Thanksgiving weekend since 1973. (No conference was held in 1977.)

From the beginning, sexism and separatism have been major issues at the GAU conferences. In 1973 the Women's Caucus spent many hours debating the question of whether or not to form a separate lesbian group or, if not, what specific recommendations for combating sexism they should present to the organization as a whole. Although the women did decide to remain in the GAU at that time, the two issues continued to create tensions in the following years, coming to a head in the 1975 conference. As a result of these tensions (as well as, presumably, of other factors, such as scanty publicity and the growth of other gay organizations), attendance dropped considerably at the 1976 conference. Despite this, however, women continued to play key roles in the 1976 conference. M. Louise Crawford was the conference chairwoman, and Paula Bennett was the conference cosponsor. These and other women spoke or read papers on such diverse topics as Emily Dickinson's poetry, lesbian/gay patients and therapists, peer-group counseling, a model gay civil rights act, a lesbian dissertation support group, lesbian mothers, and so on. Elly Bulkin, Jan Clausen, Joan Larkin, Susan Sherman, and Fran Winant gave a lesbian-feminist poetry reading; and lesbian writers Kate Millett and Rita Mae Brown also read or spoke.

The national GAU has spawned chapters in Boston, Philadelphia, Chicago, Ann Arbor, and elsewhere. Conferences sponsored by these regional groups include one held at Ann Arbor in 1975 and another in Boston in 1976.

Perhaps one of the most far-reaching of the professional gay caucuses is the Gay Caucus for the Modern Languages,[9] an allied organization of the Modern Language Association, the most prestigious and largest of the scholarly organizations for college and university teachers of English and foreign languages. An average of ten thousand people attend the annual MLA conventions. The creation of the GCML at the 1973 convention was the result of a fortunate coincidence. Dolores Noll read a paper on her life-style as a lesbian college professor at a panel sponsored by the Women's Caucus; and Louis Crompton conducted a seminar entitled "Research in Gay Literature." The lesbians and gay men who met at these meetings decided, at Crompton's seminar, to apply to the MLA for recognition of the Gay Caucus as an allied organization, a status that would give the caucus meeting times and rooms at the annual conventions. The group also decided to work for a forum on "Homosexuality and Literature" for the 1974 convention. (Forums are large public meetings on topics of general interest.) During the following months, both of these efforts were successful. The Gay Caucus became an allied organization; and at the next MLA convention over five hundred people heard Bertha Harris, Christopher Isherwood, and Louis Crompton at the forum. In addition, there were six other gay-related meetings or workshops, as well as a GCML literature table and cash bar. Also, the leadership structure of the caucus was expanded to include fourteen officers; seven women and seven men were elected to these positions.

As a result of a petition circulated by GCML members, the Modern Language Association agreed in 1975 to create a Discussion Group on Gay Studies in Language and Literature, an official subgroup within the MLA membership structure. Thus, there are now two formally distinct but closely related gay groups associated with the MLA. The Discussion Group is concerned primarily with helping to plan and coordinate programs on gay literature and research; the Gay Caucus sponsors workshops on topics of a political or pedagogical nature and pursues political goals within the MLA.

The number of gay-related programs at MLA conventions continues to expand. In 1975 in San Francisco, there were fifteen such meetings, and the following year in New York City the number had grown to over twenty—all listed in the official MLA convention program. Among those of special interest to lesbians have been lesbian-feminist poetry readings and panels on such topics, among others, as "Lesbians and Literature,"[10] "Lesbian Feminist Writing and Publishing," and "Female Self-definition in Literature and in Life."

Lesbians continue to fill leadership positions in both the GCML and the Gay Discussion Group. In 1976 Judith McDaniel replaced me as the coordinator of the caucus, and Paula French became the Discussion Group chair. Half of the other offices in the two groups are held by women; at least half of the approximately seventy-five members of the GCML are women.

Several members of the GCML have been active in the formation of the Gay Caucus for the National Coun-

---

[7] Gittings, *The Gay Academic*, ed. Crew, p. 113.

[8] The address of the GAU is Box 1479, Hunter College, CUNY, New York, N.Y. 10021.

[9] Paula Bennett, Treasurer/Membership Coordinator, Beaver Pond Road, Lincoln, Mass. 01773.

[10] A transcription of the taped 1975 "Lesbians and Literature" panel, moderated by Judith McDaniel, appears in *Sinister Wisdom* (Beth Hodges, ed.,) *Special Issue: Lesbian Writing and Publishing*, Vol. I (Fall 1976), pp. 20-33.

cil of Teachers of English.[11] The NCTE is an 87,000-member professional organization of English teachers from kindergarten through the university level. Initiated by Louie Crew and coconvened by him and Julia Stanley, the caucus made its presence known at the NCTE convention in Chicago in November 1976. Moving immediately into the political arena, the caucus proposed a progay resolution at the NCTE business meeting, a measure that passed by a narrow margin. Also, three lesbians participated in a panel entitled "Towards a Healthy Gay Presence in Textbooks and Classrooms in Secondary Schools and Colleges": Deborah Core, Julia P. Stanley, and Janet Cooper. The caucus, with a membership of thirty people (ten of whom are women), is planning further activities for the 1977 NCTE convention.

The Committee of Gay Historians[12] has been active in the last two years in the 18,000-member American Historical Association. In 1975 the AHA passed a "strongly-worded resolution affirming the rights of gay historians to employment..."; another resolution, "which encourages the teaching of the history of gay people and other sexual minorities," was passed at the 1976 annual business meeting of the association and has been sent to the membership for approval. Before this business meeting, "fifty gay and single historians met to discuss current research and teaching dealing with gay history.... For the first time this meeting was listed in the official correspondence and publications of the Association."

As a result of efforts by individuals or gay groups, all the national teachers' unions have now adopted resolutions opposing discrimination against gay teachers: the National Education Association, the American Federation of Teachers (an AFL-CIO affiliate), and the American Association of University Professors.[13] In New York City the 150-member Gay Teachers Association[14] (half of whom are women) has been instrumental in the passage of antidiscrimination rulings from the United Federation of Teachers and the New York State United Teachers. As all these resolutions are implemented, more and more contracts negotiated by teachers' unions will contain stipulations against gay discrimination.[15]

Lesbians and gay men have also been active politically and professionally in the fields of health and social services. In 1975 the Gay Public Health Workers Caucus[16] was organized at the annual meeting of the American Public Health Association. The caucus succeeded at that time "in obtaining overwhelming approval of the Association's Governing Council of a comprehensive resolution on the rights and health problems of gay people." At the 1976 APHA convention, held in Miami Beach, the GPHW sponsored several workshops, a cash bar, an exhibit, and a hospitality suite. The exhibit concerned "the causes and the way to eradicate homophobia, an unnecessary health hazard." One of the panels cosponsored by the GPHW and the Women's Caucus was on "Lesbian Health Issues." Moderated by Sarajane Garten, the panel consisted of Judi Stein, E. Carolyn Innes, and Joan Waitkevicz. Two women also participated in the workshop on "Gay Issues in Mental Health," Susan Vasbinder and Joan DeForeest. At the conference the GPHW chose as its major project for 1977 the formulation of guidelines "for helping non-gay health services to be responsive to the health needs of gay people." Coordinating the project is Sandy Reder of the Gay Health Collective of Boston.[17] In May 1976 two members of the GPHW Coordinating Committee, Sarajane Garten and William M. Somers, conducted an "in-service training session on homosexuality and the health concerns of the gay community" at a staff meeting of the APHA in Washington, D.C. Presented at the request of the APHA's executive director, the training session was successful in that "the staff asked many questions and the prevailing attitude was a receptive one."[18]

Another gay caucus that met at the APHA convention in 1976 was the Gay Nurses Alliance,[19] an autonomous group in existence since 1973. This group, cofounded by E. Carolyn Innes and G. David Waldron, has mounted exhibits at the 1975 and 1976 conventions of the American Nurses Association. The GNA hopes to become a caucus of the ANA and to sponsor a program, as well as an exhibit, at the ANA convention in Honolulu in 1978. In November 1974 the cochairperson of the Massachusetts chapter of the GNA, Laura Rood, spoke at a meeting of the Human Rights Committee of the Massachusetts Nurses Association, which "expressed interest in the GNA and offered professional support...."[20] Also, in 1975 several members of the GNA (including two women) presented a panel to 150 people at the statewide convention of the MNA.

The Gay Social Services Alliance,[21] organized in January 1976, attempts to bring "a gay/lesbian presence to all social work professional conferences." With a

[11] Julia P. Stanley and Louie Crew, Coordinators; Department of English, University of Nebraska, Lincoln, Neb. 68588 (Stanley); Box 1203, Ft. Valley State College, Ft. Valley, Ga. 31030 (Crew).

[12] Dennis Rubini, Cochair, Department of History, Temple University, Philadelphia, Pa. All information on the Committee on Gay Historians has been obtained from "AHA Votes on Gay Rights," *Chicago Gay Life,* October 1976.

[13] Copies of these resolutions may be obtained from the National Gay Task Force.

[14] Meryl Friedman and Marc Rubin, Cospokespersons, 204 Lincoln Place, Brooklyn, N.Y. 11217.

[15] For instance, the Kent State University faculty union, an affiliate of both the NEA and the AAUP, includes "sexual preference" in the antidiscrimination clause of its contract, currently under negotiation.

[16] Walter J. Lear, 206 N. 35th St., Philadelphia, Pa. 19104.

[17] The address of the Gay Health Collective is 16 Haviland St., Boston, Mass. 02115; phone 617 267-7573.

[18] "Teaching Health," *Gay Community News,* July 3, 1976.

[19] Gay Nurses Alliance—West, E. Carolyn Innes, Co-coordinator, P.O. Box 17593, San Diego, Calif. 92117; Gay Nurses Alliance—East, John C. Lawrence, Co-Coordinator, 130 Pembroke St., A-4, Boston, Mass. 02118.

[20] "Gay Nurses Meet with Mass. Nurses Assoc.," *Gay Community News,* November 30, 1974, p. 3.

[21] Ron Ginsberg, Coordinator, 345 W. 21, #1A, New York, N.Y., 10011.

Alma Routsong (Isabel Miller) and Barbara Gittings at gay kissing booth, American Library Association Convention, 1971

mailing list of about fifty (of whom approximately a quarter are women), the GSSA helped to form a gay caucus at the annual program of the Council on Social Work Education in Philadelphia in March 1976. In addition, the alliance sponsors a Speakers Bureau and a gay foster child program.

A number of gay groups concerned with health care and social services have joined to form the National Gay Health Coalition.[22] As of November 1976, two national meetings had been held, and a third was planned under the auspices of the Gay Academic Union conference. At that time the following groups were members of the coalition: Gay Public Health Workers; Association of Gay Psychologists; Gay Nurses Alliance; Gay Social Services Alliance; Boston Gay Health Collective; Washington, D.C., Gay Men's V.D. Clinic; American Psychological Association Task Force on the Status of Lesbian and Gay Psychologists; New York St. Mark's Clinic; Hunter College Gay Social Workers; Identity House, New York City; Homosexual Community Counseling Center, New York City; Washington, D.C. Free Clinic; New York City Gay Deaf Program; and New York City Gay Men's Health Project.

The Lambda Legal Defense and Education Fund, Inc.,[23] was conceived in early 1972. Although incorporation was originally denied to the group by the New York Appellate Division, "on the grounds that there wasn't a need for such an organization to defend the rights of gay people," the New York Court of Appeals reversed this decision in October 1973. In 1974 the Internal Revenue Service granted tax-exempt status to Lambda, the first-gay-oriented group to receive such status. Lambda's membership, which is coextensive with its Board of Directors, consists of nine lawyers, of whom four are women. Although the group has not attempted "to create a large general membership" because of the specialized nature of its activities, it is now "planning to inaugurate a broad membership drive during the coming year."[24]

Lambda's purpose is "to participate as attorneys in those matters likely to be of significance to gay people as a group," either through providing counsel or acting as cocounsel for a party in a case, or by filing *amicus curiae* briefs. So far, it has participated in thirteen cases. Lambda has also been working within the American Bar Association on gay rights issues. Several years ago, after considerable argument, the ABA did adopt a resolution supporting the repeal of laws against consensual, private sexual conduct; but so far the ABA has refused to take a stand in support of antigay discrimination measures.

At the Eighth National Conference on Women and the Law held in Madison, Wisconsin, in 1977, a one-day, non-separatist Lesbian Law Section[25] took place, which in effect became the first national conference on gay law. At the Section, six hundred law women focused on legal representation of lesbian clients. The legal issues were integrated into the one hundred forty-four panels of the parent conference (two thousand law women).

The sisterhood of gay and nongay law women sharing resources and skills on this scale proved costly in an unexpected way when the Wisconsin Bar Association withdrew its promised grant to the parent conference. But the parent conference never withdrew support for the Lesbian Law Section. Typical of the awakened consciousness and solidarity of participants was a note from a nongay Midwestern attorney who commented that the Section convinced her that lesbian rights was the "frontier and leading edge" of the women's movement. Collective projects and a referral list were two of the byproducts of the Section.

What have been the effects of these professional and union gay caucuses? Resolutions passed, court cases won, or workshops presented can be counted. More subtle results, though more difficult to measure, are no less real. An incident that must have been—and will be—duplicated in one form or another many times was reported by Karen Keener following the National Council of Teachers of English convention:

A post-Caucus-meeting comment spoken to four of us on an elevator by a man who had walked into the meeting late and sat in the back: "In fifty years, this is the first time I've even had the courage to step into a room!" And as he got off the elevator, he turned, smiled, held up his fist, and said, "Dignity. Dignity!"

What even a relatively few gay professionals can accomplish when they turn their skills and talents not only to combating homophobia but also to carving out whole new areas of study is demonstrated by this brief survey. As more and more lesbians and gay men, acting from a new or stronger sense of dignity, join in these efforts, the results surely will challenge the imagination.

RESOURCES

A list entitled "Professional Gay Caucuses" is available from the National Gay Task Force, 80 Fifth Ave., New York, N.Y. 10011. This list, updated regularly, includes names and addresses of persons to contact for each group. Please enclose a stamped, self-addressed envelope.

[22] No address is given.

[23] William J. Thom, Coordinator, P.O. Box 5448, Grand Central Station, New York, N.Y. 10022. For an article on Lambda, see James M. Saslow, "Lambda's General Counsel: E. Carrington Boggan, Esq.," *The Advocate,* February 23, 1977, pp. 16-17, 40.

[24] Ibid., p. 17.

[25] Mary L. Stevens, Coordinator, Box 244M, Morristown, N.J. 07960.

7. Visions

Lesbian-Feminist Theory

CHARLOTTE BUNCH

Lesbianism and feminism are both about women loving and supporting women and women revolting against the so-called supremacy of men and the patriarchal institutions that control us. Politically, understanding the connection between lesbianism and feminism is essential to ending the oppression of all women and of all homosexuals, both female and male. The political theory that embodies and defines that connection is called lesbian feminism. It is a theory that has grown out of the experiences of lesbians in both the feminist and the gay movements; out of both our participation in those movements and our separation from them at various times and places. It is the theory that holds the key to the relationship between homosexual oppression and female oppression—a connection linked in the lives of lesbians. And it is a theory that is unknown or misunderstood by many feminists, lesbians, and gay men.

In this article, I hope to erase that last sentence by clarifying the principles of lesbian feminism: to illustrate to the homosexual that *no queers* will ever be free as long as sexism persists because male supremacy is at the root of both gay oppression and homophobia. To demonstrate to the woman that *no females* will ever be free to choose to be anything until we are also free to choose

to be lesbians, because the domination of heterosexuality is a mainstay of male supremacy. And above all, to show the lesbian (the homosexual and woman) that these two parts of our oppression are linked and not only need not but also should not be separated in our struggles for liberation.

The development of lesbian-feminist theory began for most of us with the recognition on some level that in a male supremacist culture, heterosexuality is a political institution as well as a sexual preference, and, therefore, lesbianism is political as well as personal. "The Woman-Identified Woman" statement,[1] one of the earlier lesbian-feminist documents issued by Radicalesbians in 1970, pointed to the political implications of lesbianism when it stated: "On some level, she [the lesbian] has not been able to accept the limitations and oppressions laid on her by the most basic role of her society—the female role." That paper and subsequent discussion and writings went on to analyze the nascent political power and consciousness in the personal act of being a lesbian in a male supremacist society; it is the act, whether consciously or not, of putting women first in defiance of a culture that has structured the female life around the male. Based on this recognition, the concept of woman-identification came to describe the life stance of self-affirmation and love for women; of primary identification with women that gives energy through a positive sense of self, developed with reference to ourselves, and not in relation to men.

In this context, lesbian feminism takes on its political significance. It is not just a personal choice about life-style, although it involves one in a highly personal and intimate way. It is not limited to civil rights for queers, although equal rights and job protection are absolutely essential. It is more than the dynamic female culture and community that has emerged recently, although that is crucial to our survival and power as a people. Lesbian feminism as it has developed over the past decade involves all of these, but as a political theory, it is primarily a critique of heterosexism—the institutional and ideological domination of heterosexuality, as a fundamental part of male supremacy. This theory extends the feminist analysis of sexual politics to an analysis of sexuality itself, as it is structured into our society today. Its practical application involves an orientation of one's life around women (woman-identification) and a commitment to women as a political force capable of changing society as well as our life-style.

Before discussing lesbian-feminist analysis further, let me clarify my use of terms that have often caused confusion. *Lesbian-feminist theory,* as a critique of male supremacy and heterosexism, is a perspective, analysis,

---

[1] "The Woman-Identified Woman," by Radicalesbians, is included in *Radical Feminism,* edited by Anne Koedt, Ellen Levine and Anita Rapone, Quadrangle, 1973. The article may also be ordered from KNOW, Inc., for 30¢, P.O. Box 86031, Pittsburg, Pa. 15221.

and commitment that can be embraced by anyone, gay or straight, female or male—just as socialism or Pan-Africanism are theories that can be adopted by anyone regardless of race, sex, or class. A *lesbian* is a woman whose sexual/affectional preference is for women, and who has thereby rejected the female role on some level, but she may or may not embrace a lesbian-feminist political analysis. A *Woman-Identified-Woman* is a feminist who adopts a lesbian-feminist ideology and enacts that understanding in her life, whether she is a lesbian sexually or not. All lesbians are not woman-identified; all feminists are not woman-identified; but a clearer understanding of lesbian feminism should enable more of both to unite around this common identification.

As more lesbians recognized the political significance of lesbianism, we began to see that heterosexism functions in every institution that feminists have shown to be oppressive to women: the work place, schools, the family, the media, organized religion, etc. All of society's institutions are based on the assumption that every woman either is or wants to be bonded to a man both economically and emotionally and they depend on the idea that heterosexuality is both the only natural and the superior form of human sexuality. These assumptions—the ideology of heterosexism—help to maintain the institutional oppression of all women and of those men who openly deviate from the heterosexist masculine norm.

The family and women's oppression within it are obviously based on heterosexism, as are forms of discrimination against single women or any who live outside the nuclear family. Less obvious, but equally important, discrimination against women in the work place is also supported by the ideology of heterosexism. Women are defined and exploited as secondary or marginal workers on the assumption that work is not our primary vocation: even if we work outside of the home all of our lives, we are assumed to be primarily committed to family and to have another (major) breadwinner (male) supporting us. This assumption has been proved false repeatedly, not only for lesbians but also for many others, especially Third World and lower-class women. Nevertheless, the myth prevails—the ideology of heterosexism linked with the institution of the nuclear family continues to justify job discrimination and the refusal to regard work as a serious goal for women.

One could similarly describe how heterosexist attitudes permeate all the other institutions of our society. Perhaps most important is how heterosexism has been used to deny women's strength, to tie her self-concept and survival to men. According to society, if you are not with a man, you are not fully a woman; whether celibate or lesbian, you are seen as "queer." If you are independent and aggressive about your life, you are called a "dyke," regardless of sexual preference. Such labels have been used to terrify women—to keep straight women in their place and to keep lesbians in the closet.

Labels are not just name-calling. Behind each label is the implicit threat of social, economic, or physical reprisal—the denial of life-supporting systems or even life itself if you step too far out of line. Thus, the most pervasive and insidious thing that keeps heterosexual domination going is the control over granting or denying women heterosexual privileges: social and family acceptance, economic security, male legitimacy, legal and physical protection. The degree to which you receive these benefits depends on race, sex, and class, and on how much you play by the patriarchy's rules. Through heterosexual privilege, a woman is given a stake in behaving properly (or, in the case of a lesbian, of pretending to behave properly) and thus in maintaining the system that perpetuates her own oppression. Women, no matter what their sexual orientation or personal ties to men, must realize that our ultimate survival is more connected to that of all women than to one man. Heterosexual privileges are not lasting benefits or power but small, short-term bribes in return for giving up lasting self-discovery and collective power.

If we examine the labels and the language that have been used against us from another angle, they reveal the potential power of lesbianism and woman-identification. Why does society equate female assertiveness, independence, and wholeness (ability to live without a man) with the terms "lesbian," "man-hating dyke," "butch" (male imitator or potent one), "ball-breaker," etc.? The language used against us is the language of power and battle. Men sense in the presence of lesbians the power to revolt, to threaten their "supremacy." They perceived this potential power before we ourselves understood it, and they sought to repress our sexuality as one aspect of our potential for independence of them and for changing society.

Lesbian-feminist theory did not spring up in a vacuum; it developed out of our experiences in coming out, from the reaction against us, and particularly from our efforts to understand and analyze that reaction. Most of us who enthusiastically came out and asserted our right to be "lesbian, woman, and proud" in the late sixties and early seventies did not understand fully the threat to patriarchal society of our statements and actions. We had been warned by "older" lesbians about the dangers, but we only learned what a threat lesbianism is by the reactions we experienced both in society and in the movements that we knew—civil rights, feminist, leftist, and even gay male. Then we learned that we are outlaws. We realized that it was not okay to be lesbian in America. And we learned that it is not okay for a reason that goes far beyond individual attitudes and bigotry. It is not okay because self-loving and independent women are a challenge to the idea that men are superior, an idea that patriarchy's institutions strengthen and depend upon.

The lesbian is most clearly the antithesis of patriarchy—an offense to its basic tenets: It is woman-hating; we are woman-loving. It demands female obedience and docility; we seek strength, assertiveness and dignity for women. It bases power and defined roles on one's gender and other physical attributes; we operate outside gender-defined roles and seek a new basis for defining power and relationships. Our very existence is an attack on what men have defined as "their" territory. The lesbian's future lies not in surrendering our position as outlaws for token acceptance but in seizing and using it to bring change in patriarchal society. It is our very situation as outlaws that gives us much of the strength and imagination to challenge male definitions of us and of the social order. Some of the early lesbian slogans and titles caught the essense of that power: The Lavendar Menace; The Furies; Spectre; We Are the Women Your Mother Warned You About.

While working for our civil rights and the space to develop our own life-styles and institutions, we must not think that we can be absorbed into patriarchy as it is. We must be cautious about using the "we are just like you" strategy. We are different. And society needs our differences: our ability to love women in a woman-hating world; our strength and self-sufficiency in a society that says you must have a man; our powers of imagining and discovering new possibilities that come from having to create our lives without models or the support of existing institutions. While all lesbians are obviously not the same, we are also not the same as straights. To deny our differences is to deny both our particular oppression and our particular strength. Rather we must bring our experiences and differences to all who are seeking to develop a new reality for women and thus for men as well. Some of these differences will be shared by others who do not fit society's norms of color, age, physical appearance, marital status, class, etc. In fact, the more any woman is already or steps outside of society's assumptions of who she should be, the more "queer" she is and the more she can usually see how sexist and heterosexist assumptions confine her individually and women as a group.

Since lesbian-feminist theory is also based on our experiences of female oppression, we have come to see that homophobia and gay oppression, even for men, are based in sexism and the institutional power of male supremacy. Gay men have some male privileges in society, particularly if they remain closeted or out-woman-hate heterosexual men. But they will remain scorned as less than men and more like women, as long as women are scorned and as long as real men must fuck and fuck over real women in patriarchy. Their long-term interests therefore lie not in identifying with and attempting to gain more male privilege but in challenging male supremacy along with heterosexual domination. Gay men face a choice similar to that of straight women: They can accept society's offers of short-term benefits (male privilege for one and heterosexual privilege for the other) or they can challenge the patriarchal basis of those very privileges and work for a long-term elimination of the entire system of sexual oppression.

Lesbians as both homosexuals and women have no real stake in maintaining either aspect of sex-based oppression and should be the quickest to see the impor-

tance of lesbian-feminism and to enact it politically and personally. It is, then, the lesbian's ignorance about or indifference toward lesbian-feminism that I find most perplexing and disturbing. To embrace and transform our status as outlaws and challenge the dual problems of sexism and heterosexism may not always be the most comfortable option; it is, however, the most powerful and fulfilling one. No matter what one's particular sphere of activity, it is a perspective that provides the basis for both individual and group strength in the struggle to gain control over our lives and to bring fundamental change in society. It sometimes appears easier to seek acceptance on patriarchy's turf and terms, but ultimately, our freedom depends less on society's acceptance than on changing its basic tenets.

In discussing lesbian-feminist theory and the lesbian as outlaw to patriarchy, I am not speaking about what specific tactics to use when (e.g., legislation versus demonstrations). Rather I am referring to the underlying analysis and approach that we bring to any political action and the view that we have of how heterosexism and male supremacy reinforce one another in maintaining our oppression. Tactics will vary widely according to circumstances, but lesbians must ground ourselves in lesbian-feminist theory. From this point, we can decide which issues to pursue in what manner and we can make alliances with other individuals and groups who also understand that patriarchy does not serve their individual interests or the interests of a more just and humane world order.

The Answer Is Matriarchy

BARBARA LOVE and ELIZABETH SHANKLIN

Just as we have been conditioned to feel negatively toward ourselves as women, as lesbians, and as mothers, we have been very effectively conditioned to feel negatively about matriarchy. When we hear the word "matriarchy," we are conditioned to a number of responses: that matriarchy refers to the past and that matriarchies have never existed; that matriarchy is a hopeless fantasy of female domination, of mothers dominating children, of women being cruel to men; or that matriarchists are reactionaries escaping from capitalist society into a romantic dream of goddesses and tribal life.

Conditioning us so negatively to matriarchy is, of course, in the interests of patriarchs. We are made to feel that patriarchy is natural; we are less likely to question it, and less likely to direct our energies to ending it.

The struggle toward matriarchy has nevertheless been waged in the past century.[1] There is now a vital and conscious movement toward matriarchy.[2] We intend this article to be a theoretical contribution to that movement, and we are going to limit our discussion here to defining the word. What do we mean by "matriarchy"?

TOWARD A DEFINITION OF MATRIARCHY

By "matriarchy" we mean a nonalienated society: a society in which women, those who produce the next generation, define motherhood, determine the conditions of motherhood, and determine the environment in which the next generation is reared.[3]

We now live in a patriarchy. We mean by "patriarchy" a society ruled by fathers. Rule by father implies the expropriation of the child and the exploitation of women as mothers. Mothers bear children for nine months within their bodies, and labor—even risking their lives—to give birth to their children. In patriarchy the child at birth becomes the property of the father. This expropriation of the child is carried out in historic patriarchies through a set of institutions.

Patriarchy then does not refer merely to male domination, but to a specific set of institutions that ensures the alienation of the child from the mother. While some aspects of these institutions change, the basic relationship between the father, the mother, and her child is fundamental to patriarchy.

The expropriation of the child from the mother was more easily recognized in the past. In the United States in the nineteenth century, for example, the law made the father the sole guardian of the mother's child. The father might apprentice the child, determine how and whether it was educated, and make all decisions relative to its well-being and health—in opposition to the mother and to the child. The father could will that at his death a total stranger to the mother become the guardian of her child.

Today, the alienation of the child from the mother persists. But now the alienation occurs less through the power of individual fathers and more through impersonal institutions. Now the mother is permitted to be the legal guardian of her child, but that function no longer carries the decision-making power it used to have. The patriarchal state now decides when, where, and how

---

[1] We need herstories of the matriarchal movement. To date there has been none published. Some indication of the movement in the nineteenth century can be found in Elizabeth Shanklin's paper, "Elizabeth Cady Stanton, Our Revolutionary Mother," presented at CUNY Women's Conference, 1976. Stanton proposed matriarchy as the ultimate goal of women's liberation. Drawing upon Bachofen and Morgan, who did not advocate matriarchy, but who lifted the curtain on the past, Stanton drew her own conclusions. Engels has been a major contributor to the movement. Such a herstory would surely include the contributions of Helen Diner and Robert Briffault. The reception given Briffault's *The Mothers,* a three-volume work explicitly delineating the need for matriarchy, and the way in which his work is ignored today or discredited by "scholars" would be stimulating material for herstorical analysis.

[2] Indications include: the publication of "scholarly" articles by anthropologists and historians stridently "proving that there never was a matriarchy because they don't admit or have the evidence that there was; the publication of *The Inevitability of Patriarchy;* communities across the country that identify themselves as matriarchal; conferences across the country devoted to matriarchy or containing workshops on matriarchy; courses in the politics of motherhood; the day-care movement demanding that mothers control their own centers; movement literature; the interest in matriarchal ritual and matriarchies of the past; the publication of Adrienne Rich's *Of Woman Born;* the publication of this article.

[3] Our set of assumptions includes the following:
1. That whether or not there has ever been a matriarchy like the one we need will not determine whether there will or will not be one in the future.
2. That human nature is maleable in the following way: If people are surrounded by nurturant institutions, i.e., institutions that are nurturant to people and that reward people for being nurturant, then people will tend to become nurturant; if people are surrounded by institutions that are exploitative, i.e., if people are exploited and rewarded for exploiting others, then people will tend to become exploitative.
3. That a woman who chooses to bear a child is interested in its growing to its full potential into a self-regulating, whole person, and that any distortion of that nurturant bond between a mother and her child will have been caused by the environment in which that mother and child have lived and/or continue to live.
4. As long as the design of a society is based on exploitative structures, the genuine liberation of lesbians—or any other group—cannot be achieved.

her child will be employed. Institutions now dictate how her child will be socialized: Each child is conditioned daily through the public schools, the economic structures, the media, and religion so that her/his behavior and attitudes are regulated to serve the interests of the dominant patriarchs.

The mother must, for example, yield up her child at age five to "educational" institutions designed by fathers. She must by law send her child to be socialized in a competitive system that will stratify her child according to the interests of those in power. She must prepare her child to function in a warrior economy.[4] She must resort to the ideas of the father as the sole creator if she wishes her child to belong to any established religion; she must permit her child to be conditioned by corporate interests through television if she wishes her child to share a frame of reference with other children; to have a child "legitimately," she must marry the father. She is then bound to give sexual and domestic service. She must also give the child the father's name as token of his proprietary interest. Typically, if her daughter decides to repeat this pattern, it will be the father who is acknowledged as owner and gives her away to the next possessor.

Therefore, through the institutions of patriarchy, the child is alienated from the mother. The child becomes the property of the father and institutions designed by him. These institutions have usurped the maternal function, and then defined for women what a mother's role is to be. Patriarchal institutions make the mother the servant of patriarchy. Like any servant, the mother is directed in the tasks that she is to perform vis-à-vis the property of the owner. She is made the custodian of his child, and told that her job is to help her child function in institutions designed by men. If she should permit any activity threatening to patriarchs, she can at any time be declared an unfit mother—for example, if she should allow her child to have a lesbian relationship or if she should allow her child to withdraw from public school.

Understanding our society as a patriarchy explains the special oppression of lesbian mothers. The lesbian commitment to women rather than to men is an act of independence improper for the mother's role as servant to patriarchy. While a single mother's child is considered "illegitimate," the single heterosexual mother does not threaten the continuation of patriarchy to the degree that a lesbian mother does. For the lesbian relationship implies commitment to denial of male authority over the

mother's own and her child's life. Therefore, the lesbian mother constitutes a threat to the continuation of patriarchal society.

It's a myth that lesbians aren't mothers. It's a myth that lesbians don't want to be mothers. What is frequently true is that lesbians don't want to pay the price to be mothers in patriarchy: to be reduced to the custodian of one's own child; to be a wife; to be isolated, financially dependent, and stigmatized. What is true is that lesbians don't want to be mothers as men have institutionalized motherhood, usurping the mother's power and rights. Sometimes, lesbians simply don't like being around children, but under different conditions, who knows?

It is in the interests of patriarchy to direct lesbians—a critical revolutionary force—away from bearing and rearing children. It's patriarchal manipulation to say lesbians should not influence children—even their own children—and thus leave them vulnerable to be indoctrinated by fathers and their institutions into patriarchal ways.

Are we implying that every lesbian should be a mother to be a revolutionary? No. What we are saying is that our liberation as women and as lesbians will never be accomplished until we are liberated to be mothers. Until we have the power to define the conditions under which we exercise our biological potential, until we define for ourselves the role of motherhood to include the power to determine the conditions of motherhood and to determine the environment in which our children are reared, we have no real choice. And until we have choices, we are not free.

To say that we must end the expropriation of children by fathers implies the first real revolution known to history. For male "revolutions" have actually meant only a change in the class of men in power, leaving intact the fundamental exploitation of patriarchy—the alienation of the mother from her child. For regardless of which class has been in power in patriarchy—the aristocracy, the middle or working class—the alienation between the mother and the child has persisted. The child has been expropriated by feudal lords, capitalist institutions, and the socialist state.

By "matriarchy" we mean a society in which the mode of child-rearing is nurturant—that is, strengthens the unique will of each individual to form open, trusting, creative bonds with others.

The mode of child-rearing in patriarchy is to control and dominate the child's will. In capitalism the child's will is directed toward serving the interests of corporations; in socialism it is directed toward serving the state. In patriarchy to nurture oneself is actually a revolutionary act.

Therefore, although women are told that they are the nurturers of the world, women in patriarchy do not have the power to nurture—if by nurturance we mean supporting the unique will of the child to grow into its full potential as a self-regulating individual. Capitalism

---

[4]We use the term "warrior economy" to refer to the economies of patriarchy. We use the term as Veblen used it in *The Theory of the Leisure Class*. Marx is replete with descriptions of the warrior character of presocialist economies. The warrior aspect of socialist society, we assert, resides not in its economic base, but persists in its mode of reproduction, i.e., the taking of the child from the person who produced it. A simple definition of a warrior might be a person who survives by taking what others have, or have produced.

and socialism, the institutions of patriarchy—which control the mother and child—both conflict with nurturance.

Under capitalism, mothers are faced with a dilemma. They can force their children to conform to a competitive economy, to a competitive educational system, to competitive games, to bourgeois codes of behavior, dress, and lovemaking. But, if they do all this, they crush their children's desire to live openly, creatively, trustfully, and safely with others. On the other hand, mothers can choose to nurture their children's wills to form open, trusting bonds with others. But if they do this, they are permitting their children to risk exploitation, poverty, stigma, and isolation. Most of us are some amalgam of these two, always in conflict, struggling to find ourselves, to be able to maintain deep and steady contact with others of our choice.

Under socialism, a mother who attempted to nurture the unique will of her child would most likely be denounced or arrested. However, she has the compensation that the socialist patriarchs (at least under Mao) socialized her child to relate to others (and others to her child) in a supportive, noncompetitive way. But this support does not stem from strengthening of the unique being of each individual. Children are not socialized to think for themselves, and are therefore doomed to be prey to political manipulation. Since children have been dominated and indoctrinated instead of nurtured into positive relations with others, they will be dependent on the benevolence of dictators.

The matriarchal mode of child-rearing in which each individual is nurtured rather than dominated from birth provides the rational basis for a genuinely healthy society, a society of self-regulating, positive individuals.[5] Matriarchy, as we define it, then implies the elimination of every institution of patriarchy—its economic, its political, its sexual, its social, and its educational institutions. Each of these institutions defines how the next generation is to be reared.

Each of these institutions structures the mother's role, reducing motherhood to being the custodian of what one has biologically produced. Just as the power of mothers to determine the socialization of their children is increased, in matriarchy the identification of who is a mother would also expand. With the breakdown of the nuclear patriarchal family, collective living arrangements have been emerging in which both women and men without children share the children of other members of the collective. The lesbian community has been developing an expanded sense of motherhood; for example, lovers frequently share children, and movement conferences show a consciousness of the need for sharing responsibility for all children. One need not be a biological mother in order to mother.

---

[5] The ability to nurture oneself and to nurture others is developed through the experience of having been nurtured. The discipline of psychology clearly indicates that our early childhood years are the most influential in establishing character.

By "matriarchy" we mean a society in which all relationships are modeled on the nurturant relationship between a mother and her child.

As a consequence of our alienation from our mothers institutionalized in our patriarchal society, each of has has been denied to some degree the fundamental source of security. We have been denied that interaction between a nurturant person and ourselves throughout our early years. We have been denied that interaction that could have strengthened our capacity to be secure, to be open, to trust, to be ourselves, to realize our sensory, emotional, intellectual, energetic potential.

We become estranged from our real feelings. We learn to suppress, to deny; we project, we fragment. We squander our life's energies in anxieties and angers. We are alienated from ourselves. Being alienated and fragmented, we lead defensive or programmed lives. We lose the capacity to live deeply in contact with ourselves, others, and nature. We lose the capacity to govern ourselves, to be self-regulated. Our alienation from our mothers has left us to some degree crippled for life.

We must go to psychiatrists—to learn what it is to nurture ourselves. We spend years learning how to form a nurturant relationship with another person. For, being to some degree alienated from ourselves, and confronting other alienated people, we form alienated relationships.

We have been taught to base our personal relationships on the warrior mode of competing—beating and conquering our friends and associates in games, in business, and in politics. Our relationships throughout society—our work relationships, movement relationships, love relationships—can only really be understood in terms of how in those situations we deal with our alienation. Genuine contact that persists, genuine openness and trust that is steady, is very rare, and constantly threatened by patriarchal habits of competition.

In matriarchy this basic alienation (as well as the alienation of labor) is eliminated. Institutions do not usurp the mother's right to determine that the environment—both social and natural—be nurturant to her child. The conditions of motherhood, having been defined by women, support the mother and her interest in the child's growth into a self-regulating, trusting individual. The conditions of socialization—the economic, educational, and governmental institutions—reinforce and support the bonds of nurturance.

In matriarchy no institutions conflict with the nurturance of each individual to form open, trusting bonds with others; in addition, each individual is nurtured deeply in a secure relationship with her/his mother. The consequences of deep nurturance and nurturant social structures are that individuals would be capable of relating to others in open, trusting, and supportive ways. More, the energies generated and released under these conditions promise creativity and productivity unimaginable within patriarchy. This is what we mean when we say that in matriarchy all relationships would be modeled on the nurturant relation of the mother and the child: Each of us would learn how to be nurturant to ourselves and to others.

Matriarchy, then, provides the only reasonable basis for a genuinely harmonious society, a society of self-regulating, positive individuals.

By indicating that women, as the bearers of the next generation, should have the power to nurture, we are obviously expanding popular concepts of the scope of nurturance. Nurturing includes not only feeding and clothing and cleaning a child, but strengthening the unique will of the child. Inasmuch as the child is not reared in a vacuum, the bearers of the next generation in order to be nurturant must have the power to determine that the economic, political, educational, and social environment in which the next generation is socialized is nurturant. We are therefore saying that in order to be nurturant, women must determine the social structures of society.

By "matriarchy" we mean a society in which the maternal principle, the nurturance of life, informs all social structures; this implies the elimination of all patriarchal institutions: economic, political, sexual, and educational.

Each institution of patriarchy has an exploitative function. The elimination of every exploitative structure would be necessary in order to create social structures that support the nurturance of the unique will of each individual to trusting, open relationships with others.

Matriarchy, in fact, provides through the liberation of the maternal function from subservience to warrior institutions the basis for the elimination of the patriarchal state. For only through the nurturance of each individual to self-regulation can one expect to eliminate the need for a dominating government or state.

We mean by "matriarchy" a society in which production serves the interests of reproduction; that is, the production of goods is regulated to support the nurturance of life.

In both capitalist and socialist states, the production of things that produce wealth and military power dominates and determines the quality of life in the society. The way in which the next generation is conceived, born, and reared—that is, the mode of reproduction—is dictated by the interests of production.

We mean by matriarchy a society in which the production of things is not to accumulate wealth, to defend or wage war, but to strengthen each individual's capacity to live openly in trust with others. It is not rational to expect a person to live in trust with another so long as one can survive only through the destruction of the other, or the exploitation of the other. Therefore, matriarchy implies a worldwide socialist economic base, but a liberation of reproduction from subordination to the socialist state.

Matriarchy, as we have defined it, is the solution to a number of problems that concern many of us deeply. Men have questioned how to eliminate exploitation, war, racism, classism, sexism, and they have de-vised innumerable answers to these problems. These answers have proven inadequate. They have been inadequate because men have refused to eliminate patriarchy. The question is how to create a nurturant society. The answer is matriarchy.

If the creation of matriarchy seems an impossible dream, it's because we are among the first to overcome the myth of the inevitability of patriarchy and realize the possibility of matriarchy. If the vision of uniting nurturance with economic transactions and political organizations appears a hopeless fantasy to some, it is because it requires our gaining power that men tell us we have never had. If we are torn in facing up to the need for matriarchy, it is because we are paid by patriarchs to support them. If linking motherhood to economic and political power seems to be vain imaginings, it's because patriarchs have conditioned us to link motherhood with powerlessness—and to think of mothering as trivial. If matriarchy seems irrelevant to lesbian liberation, it's because every institution in this society so controls us that we are directed away from examining the total system.

The task of ending patriarchy and creating matriarchy is not so awesome as it might first appear. We will be summoning up energies that are suppressed now; we will be releasing our creative energies, our own buried needs and desires. And we will be aligned with the struggle for life which strongly asserts itself in each new generation as it battles with patriarchal institutions that seek to dominate and subjugate it. We will be aligned with the struggle for life in each oppressed person, and the oppressed are many.

There are innumerable men, women, and children who have not yet become political, but who are dissatisfied with the current system. Many of these people have not become political because they have realized that the patriarchal political movements that promised a classless society, for example, provided no hope of producing people who were capable of a classless society. Matriarchy will.

We believe that the matriarchal movement will find support among people of both sexes, and of all classes, races, and ages. The cry for a more nurturant society has manifested itself in the black movement, the labor movement, the Native American movement, the Third World movement, the environmental movement, the consumer movement, the radical education movement, the radical medicine and psychology movements, and the children's liberation movement, as well as the mother's movement, the gay movement, the lesbian movement, and the women's movement.

Every movement for liberation is, we think, an unconscious movement toward matriarchy. Therefore, we have potential allies who are now struggling, unawakened to the fact that patriarchy is the problem—that under patriarchy we can never create a nurturant society. These various movements have often felt some common denominator with other movements. That common denominator is the need for matriarchy.

Whereas women's liberation and lesbian liberation

have been largely founded around the concepts of freeing ourselves from domination, matriarchal theory provides the rational basis for women to restructure and guide the institutions in society. As the bearers of life, it is our right and responsibility to determine that life is nurtured.

The Spiritual Dimension: Death and Resurrection of a Hallelujah Dyke

SALLY MILLER GEARHART

In trying to get this article together I've taken a long look at the vacated closet where I lived for twenty years. I can't find in that closet or in the fresher air of feminism in 1977 any definition of spirituality that satisfies me. Usually the term is associated with experiences that are fundamentally meaningful, creative, moving, real, and life-ward in their texture. For the present I'd like to call it *any faith in or attention to knowledge and values whose source cannot be proved—that is, cannot be empirically demonstrated—even though that knowledge and those values influence our action.*

From my lesbian feminist perspective I'd like (a) to explore my understanding of lesbianism and (b) to review our participation in traditional religious faiths. Then I'd like (c) to identify a "spirituality" subculture within the women's movement, show how that subculture is attractive to lesbians, and briefly suggest potential dangers within the subculture.

I. I believe that as lesbians we've been defined too long in an *inter*personal way, that is, in terms of our relationships to others. The societal (male) notion of the lesbian is "the woman who has sex with other women." Even the most useful of definitions that comes from among our own ranks is an *inter*personal one: "a woman whose primary erotic, psychological, emotional and social interest is in a member of her own sex, even

though that interest may not be overtly expressed" (12).[1] It's time we defined our selfs less in *inter*personal terms and began thinking of our selfs in ways that say who *we* are, not who our friends/lovers are.

I suggest that *a lesbian is a woman who seeks her own self-nurturance.* That's a very *intra*personal description, one that centers in the lesbian herself and one that for many of us comes closer to the truth. I'm reminded of the woman, now legendary through the speechmaking of Charlotte Bunch, whose first thought on realizing she was a lesbian (after her first sexual experience with another woman) was, "My God. Now I'll have to support myself for the rest of my life." I suspect that as lesbians we've always known that at the very ground level we are the virgin, the original meaning of which is "one unto her self"; we've always known that each of us is a woman who does not want to depend upon a man, who does not even want to depend upon another woman—upon other *women,* yes, in a collective sense, for that's a part of our dream too, but not upon any other single person; either consciously or unconsciously we've known that we have in us a strong tendency toward anarchism in its best sense, that is, a tendency toward self-governance and a desire to give up the habit of governing other people; we've always known that we want our own self-reliance and that of every woman. For sure, very few if any of us have gotten "there" yet; that's no surprise in a society where we've been brought up to hate our selfs. Even to begin to love our self, a woman, in a woman-hating society that has tens of thousands of years of history behind its misogyny is quite an accomplishment (8).

On the surface a description of the lesbian as one who seeks her own self-nurturance seems contradicted by the fact that usually we move to our self-nurturance through other women. It's been our relationships that most often have given us personal strength—whether we are lesbian feminists who came to our identity through the women's movement or lesbian feminists who have always loved other women but who needed the supportive atmosphere of feminism to articulate that reality. What is described by a number of us in our journey to self-nurturance is not so much a contradiction as a process that evolves in the following way.

In interacting with another woman several unconventional benefits enter my life. First, I receive the kind of gratification I've been seeking: I'm not only nurturing another; as well, I am being cared for in return because it's a woman I am loving. I would not have that caring relationship with a man because in all likelihood he has been convinced by society's conditioning that *he cannot* nurture me.

Second, I am validated by standards that, though they are still outside myself, nevertheless come from one who is like me. I don't strive in vain to meet the standards set by the male culture in heterosexual rela-

---

[1]Numbers in parentheses refer to the source list at the end of this article.

tionships; I am no longer a woman-in-that-I-am-not-a-man; I am a woman in that I am a woman.

Finally, I am out of that heavy atmosphere deliberately calculated to make me feel my "half-ness," my inadequacy, my inferiority; I am into one that suggests my potential wholeness. The most deeply engrained of all power dynamics, that of male over female, is now absent from my relational field, and my partner and I are able to play out with each other a wide range of old and new power roles, see them for what they are, and move to change them. We learn how subtle the mechanism of projection is, in what minute ways we expect each other to be something we can only be to our own self. With the male-female dynamic removed and a territory of sameness established, we can each see the more complex and multileveled differences between the two of us as people; we can identify our own unique self in intricate detail.

Wholeness at last seems possible. I begin to see how it would feel to be free of romantic dependencies, to relate to another out of some stronger self (1). I might no longer be afraid, for instance, that I'll "lose" her if I show some weakness; perhaps I'd learn how to handle her preference for being with someone else without crumbling up; maybe she would make room in conversations for me without seeming to "give up" her power "to me"; I could take that room because I want it and not because she expects/wants me to take it.

But the wholeness I reach for requires a *transference* of caring from the other woman to my self, a *transference* from the relationship in which we cling to each other to a relationship in which I depend on my self. I'm prepared for that transfer: (1) I know *how to nurture* because I do nurture her and (2) through her attention to me I *experience nurturance* of myself and come to trust that I can be nurtured. The transfer itself comes in hundreds of changes in behavior and attitude, sometimes consciously, sometimes unconsciously. It happens within the context of one long relationship, or in two, three, or a dozen. The point, I finally realize, is not so much the *achievement* of my self-reliance; I'll probably never manage that. The point is my *commitment* to nurture my self, my commitment to struggle with my self and through the romance of relationships in the cultivation of my self-nurturance.

In addition to the pain and growth involved in my letting go of neurotic dependencies, there is the pain and joy of allowing one I love to become her own self-nurturer. If she wants to be with another woman instead of with me, I may be jealous but at least I understand my reaction—the romantic mode has schooled me well in that (1). But if she wants to be by her self, to be alone instead of being with me, what can I say to that? How can I contend with that rival? Further, my self-hatred flares up because she *can* be by herself; she has found some source of self-reliance that I am only still moving toward. I'm caught on the contradiction of wanting to affirm her self-love and at the same time wanting to be

the most important thing to her, more important even than her self is. There's a way out of my romantic dependencies, but it is never a painless one.

The process continues. I may feel "whole" for long periods of time, perhaps in need of no relationship or unwilling to enter a relationship because it would threaten that wholeness, "cost" me too much. If/when I do relate to another woman (or to the same woman), an entirely new dynamic emerges: the relationship seems healthier because my wholeness (and hopefully hers too) seems in super shape. But I dare not be too confident about this because I'm usually disillusioned: The relationship is not so healthy after all, I'm not as together as I thought I was, a thread of jealousy has sneaked in or I've backslid in some other way that lets me know my self-nurturance is far from assured. I need to do some more work and it is that very work that this new relationship seems chosen to accomplish.

So it goes: back and forth in the tension between self and another, in a dialectic of self-reliance and dependence, in a mutual growth of expanding trust and self-assessment, always—with each turn of the same relationship, with each different relationship, or with each period of being alone—a little closer to our self for each woman concerned. The closer we move to our selfs, the less dependence there is in our coming together and the more like two whole persons each of us will behave.

I'm convinced now that the transference to the self of the nurturing function is not only vital to a woman-to-woman relationship. It is for me *the "final cause"* of such a relationship; that is, it is *the reason for having that relationship at all.* Further, for me this commitment to self-nurturance—in relationship, in aloneness—is only a first step in a greater growth that we'll explore later.

II. As women who love women we have both resisted and been molded by world religions—institutions hardly famous for their hospitality to lesbians. We've spent some miserable centuries in the temples-cathedrals-churches-mosques of the world (when we've been allowed inside them) always cramping and maiming our spirituality in order to fit it into the dictates of some "higher power." I'll concentrate here on the Christian church's treatment of lesbians and women because (1) my own background is Christian, (2) the Judeo-Christian tradition constitutes the fundamental morality and belief system of Western culture, influencing even the lives of "atheists" or "agnostics," and (3) in essential respects, for present purposes, Christianity typifies all world religions. By "the Church" I mean both the institution *and* the body of believers who stake their faith on patriarchal theology's most complex and successful mystification: the unique divinity and redemptive power of Jesus of Nazareth.

I poured decades of creative energy into the church before I found my rage at its intolerance of my lesbianism. It took me another decade to realize that our oppression as lesbians is at its base an oppression of women. Of the twelve references in the Bible to homosexual acts, for instance, only one (Romans 1:26) mentions women. Hebraic law simply classed women with other property—houses, servants, asses, and oxen—and New Testament writers were little better. In spite of my efforts to make the Church meaningful in my life, I finally concluded that (1) the Christian tradition is fundamentally woman-hating, (2) feminism is incompatible with Christianity, and (3) though some lesbians/women may remain in the Church, others daily forsake it.

1. That the Church is misogynist is borne out in its direct expressions—in, for instance, humiliating biblical passages or in a church history which equates woman with Evil, in our exclusion from the power positions in contemporary ecclesiastical systems, in the attitude and intent of church literature where we may play only one of three roles: helpmeet ("Praise."), whore ("For shame!"), or old maid ("What a pity."). Further, its woman-hating is evidenced in the Church's deliberate obliteration of all but its kind of woman from history. Some scholars even show how Hebraic tradition transformed the Great Mother into an androgynous creator of an androgynous humankind; that version was then doctored to permit a male God to create man, from whom woman was born. Finally, the proof of the Church's misogyny rests in its fanatic investment in and perpetuation of the institutions most oppressive to women and particularly to lesbians: *sex-role socialization* (the Big Lie of the patriarchy: that "femininity" and "masculinity" exist) and *the exclusively heterosexually based family structure* (of which there is a recent nuclear model—Daddy-Mommy-baby—and an earlier extended family model—Dad still at the helm of a larger boy-meets-girl ship). Feminist scholars and theologians have documented these evidences and a host more in their analysis of the misogyny characteristic of all world religions (1, 2, 3, 4, 5, 6, 7, 8, 10, 13, 15, 16, 18, 23).

2. Feminism has been for me an atmosphere in which I have begun to find and understand what spirituality means to me as a woman. In comparing traveling pains with other ex-Christian women I've learned that feminism has been experienced similarly by them as a miraculous transformation of their lives (a conversion?), a near inexplicable alteration not only of their relationships and their commitments but of their value system and of their ways of perceiving the material world itself.

Feminism simply won't live in comfort within the Church. Where Christianity preached to me from above, for instances, in that remarkable competitive and self-hating hierarchy of God-over-man-over-woman-over-child-over-animal-over-nature, women were speaking with me eyeball to eyeball about equality and worth. Where the Church told me what I was to be and by what standards (God's and man's) I was to be judged, feminism suggested that I might not be judged at all and that

I define my self by my own (woman's) standards. While God and the boys would have me be the half-person (strictly intuitive, weak, gentle, emotional) who in the magic of heterosexual marriage would find my "other half" (strictly logical, strong, aggressive, intellectual) and with him become "whole," feminism declared that I was potentially whole within my self. And while the Church described to me over and over the joy of the pure-and-holy-love-of-Jesus, Jesus, even when I convinced my self he was around, could never compare to the holdings and healings that I found with strong, loving women.

The hierarchical, authoritarian, competitive structure of the Church and its exclusively male and misogynist theology (see the works of the same feminist scholars as above) are utterly devoid of woman-ness except insofar as exploited womanenergy is the power on which all of Christendom thrives. Any ideology, then, that affirms philogyny (womanlove), equality, and wholeness is a threat to the very nature of the Church.

3. Though it's a mistake to equate the single woman with the lesbian (or the married woman with the heterosexual) it is as an unmarried woman that the lesbian suffers the bulk of the Church's humiliation of her. Until recently, working within the church has been one of the few socially acceptable careers or avocations for the single woman. The Church has happily encouraged its "old maids" who put in so many selfless hours polishing its altars, directing its pageants, pounding its pianos, regimenting its Sunday schools, organizing its bake sales, and singing in its choirs. (How many "alto" voices, through gritted teeth, resented the fact that the tenor line was for men only?)

But feminism has affected the church: It has challenged that institution and its believers to exhibit (its apparently closeted) characteristics of flexibility, tolerance, and humanism; it has dared the institution to state forthrightly its genuine concern for woman. In token ways the Church has responded, in some denominations to the point of ordaining women, even open lesbians.

When a lesbian feminist within the Church understands the misogyny of the Church, she faces the decision to remain within it or leave it. My own choice with lots of reluctance and struggle was to join thousands of other women who were turning away from Christianity; very simply, loving myself and other women was impossible for me there and nothing but sheer masochism could have kept me functioning in that atmosphere (7,8).

There are, however, lesbian feminists and other strong women who elect for good reasons (8) to work within the Church. They remain there fully aware that Christianity has been a magnificent mystification for the sake of male supremacy, a splendid lie built upon woman-hatred; they remain there knowing full well that for the Church to cease its destructive, antilife behavior it would have to demonstrate far more than an equalization of its women with its men; they remain there understanding that if the Church succeeded in making the transformation required of it by feminism—in its structure, in its theology, in its practice as well as in its personnel—it would no longer be an institution, no longer the body of a dehumanized Jesus; it would no longer be the Church.

They remain. And under very special conditions, not the least of which is the love and solidarity they have found there with each other. Out of their struggles to survive and even to make incremental changes within the Church, there is emerging a formidable brand of feminism, one that understands the spiritual nature of woman to be at the heart of our political movement. Lesbian feminists connected still to traditional church structures challenge the institution with a "theology" rising not from the brow of body-hating church fathers but from the self-loving experiences of women; to the embarrassment of the Church itself they put into action highly unorthodox (i.e., feminist) notions of Christian practice. They constitute for the rest of us outside the Church not only a continuing source of creative thinking about spirituality but as well a company of workers fighting on one of the most terrifying battlefronts of the movement's political action: the patriarchal Church, headquarters for all of Western culture's misogynist attitudes.

III. Lesbian feminists who escaped the confines of the Church have nevertheless experienced a need for spiritual fulfillment ("hopelessly religious types" we're sometimes called). Some of us who have turned with hope to the growing Metropolitan Community Church (a church for all people whose membership is largely gay) have been able to work there with the overwhelmingly male membership. For most of us, however, our spiritual inclinations have not found adequate expression in the MCC and we have been drawn in greater numbers, I believe, to a special form of activity which is referred to by many as the "womanspirit" or "spirituality" part of the women's movement (9,14,17,19,20,21,22).

For the most part women working in womanspirit (1) *affirm unorthodox ways of knowing reality*—that is, the "occult," the "unconscious," the "intuitive." They redeem from masculist assumptions and assertions such tools as the Tarot, astrology, the *I Ching,* numerology; they pay attention to dreams, visions, memories, creative modes, rituals, games, celebrations; they discover and reinterpret a buried history of Amazons and matriarchies.

Further, they (2) *seek in the name of women to heal both the human body and the raped planet;* they practice ancient skills of laying on of hands, nutrition, herbalism, midwifery, martial arts; they tend the earth; they ask questions about death, about violence, about a female ethic. It's significant to me that this spirituality is so concerned for *material* things. Such concern suggests that women's kind of spirituality might bring hope for the healing of our age-old rift from nature: the rift resulting, I believe, from that first act of dominance—man over woman—and later institutionalized by the patriarchy into the mind/body split.

Women into this part of the movement often envision a female culture in which men cannot participate (though some suggest that men might be allowed if they embraced female values, e.g., nonviolence, nonhierarchy, noncompetition). Their spiritual expression is in terms of the ancient goddess or the forces of nature. The most unifying concept among them is that of *energy.* They understand that the physical form that energy usually takes is violent and destructive, particularly to anything female. They understand the psychic form of energy, in contrast, to rise from an internal source within individual women and ultimately to be cosmic in its dimensions. Elsewhere I've called the destructive type "improperly sourced *inter*personal energy," typical of the patriarchy, and the psychic type "re-sourced *intra*personal energy" for which I believe women have a unique capacity (9). Women who are into womanspirit work to re-source their energy in themselves, to enhance it, and to share it with each other. Essential to all this is an *absence* of destructive energy; thus many of them move as far as possible from it, into rural areas of the country; others do the work of finding their *intra*personal energy in urban ghettos psychically shielded from heavy patriarchal forces (20).

There's a strong sense in which lesbians who were pillars of the Church are drawn into the activities of womanspirit—for some of the same reasons that they were drawn to patriarchal faiths. A mystic is a mystic is a mystic, as one of our own might say. By the same token, lesbians who never had a deep investment in religion might not seek out the dream circles or the healing rituals of womanspirit. I understand, however, two reasons why womanspirit is attractive to lesbians: (1) it emphasizes the *self as the source* of psychic energy and (2) it sees *bonding between women* as the effective channel of use for that re-sourced energy.

1. If the lesbian is fairly described as a woman who seeks her own self-nurturance, then it follows without much discussion that she might be drawn to women who look inside their selfs for a source of energy; she might be familiar with the *intra*personal dimension of her strength, with that center where she feels least vulnerable to the violent energy raging about her.

2. In the womanbonding of womanspirit I find both an obvious attraction for lesbians and a deeper, more far-reaching one. The obvious attraction is womanspirit's *validation of the lives lesbians have always led.* In quiet subterranean ways we have been bonding for centuries. Even when we were in dark closets or deep into the power games with each other we knew in a part of our selfs that our lives were reminiscent of some ancient woman-culture, of some time in history or in the future when women were/will be strong, self-reliant, independent, and yet together with one another. As groups of women gather for such occasions as solstice celebrations or group healings, the embodiment is taking the place of our unarticulated memories and dreams. To ex-Christians of us such rituals are the closest thing we can imagine to a lesbian "church." What used to be only a fantasy—whispered if spoken at all—is now becoming a

reality: Women without the draining interference of men, women in work, in love, in celebration together, embracing both the self-reliance of each woman and her concern for others. For a hard-core-card-carrying-lesbian-spiritual-buff, even Easter Sunday morning or the hottest revival in town couldn't compare to a scene like that.

On the less obvious level, I discover lesbians, particularly lesbian feminists, being drawn to the woman-bonding of womanspirit because (1) their commitment to self-nurturance—and to the pattern of coupling from which self-nurturance is usually derived—does not fill their spiritual needs and (2) they see in the woman-bonding not only the *spiritual* reality they seek but as well a *political* potential.

1. I believe the commitment to self-nurturance is only a beginning, an absolutely essential beginning, but only a first step in a greater growth. If we spend our lesbian-feminist lives *only* struggling for our own self-reliance, then we are isolated—either in our selves or in a couple—and thus never approach the "spiritual" as I am beginning to understand that term.

It's taken me a long time to articulate my uneasiness with the Christian version of spirituality: the ecstatic face of a saint, the rhapsodic words about bodiless union with "God." I'm convinced now that that kind of spirituality is inevitably an act of solipsism, not only divorced from anything material but as well, totally isolated from other persons.

My growing understanding of a female spirituality involves a *collective* quality. A spiritual experience in female terms not only never separates body and spirit but requires *that the experience be shared.* I don't want to insist that by myself I can't have an experience of female spirituality. I think I can, but when I "have it" I also have the distinct feeling that what I'm in touch with—the self, the earth, the cosmic energy—is connected to other women, perhaps in what more and more feminist thinkers are describing as a kind of "horizontal transcendence." When patriarchal faiths speak of transcendence they refer to something bigger-than-self, to something higher-than-self—to God, to Buddha, Nature, Brahmin, Allah, Tao, the Good, or Universal Mind—destroying even the happier concept of the "community of believers" by resting that concept on the existence of a God-on-high. Feminist spirituality calls for a less vertical, a less comparative, form of transcendence. When women join together in the energy flow that can move among us, there is a discernible sense of a power "beyond" each of us but not one "above" or "bigger." It is simply *there.* It would not be *there* in that unique way if each self participating were not *there* in her unique way, operating out of her commitment to her self-nurturance. This "presencing" (Nelle Morton's word) of women with each other, that joining together of our self-loving selfs, of our re-sourced channels of energy, is then at the same time both *internal* to each woman and *transcendent*—a transcendence created by energy from among equal participants. When, by myself, I re-source and touch that place of spiritual reality, I

experience it as a re-creation of that presencing, as if there were whole reservoirs of womanenergy that my re-sourcing taps. I have myself helped to create those reservoirs both for myself and others by my active presencing with them on other occasions.

I don't believe I can experience "horizontal transcendence" simply by sharing with one other woman in the confines of a relationship. What we touch together in our mutual growth toward self-reliance may be intimate; in "I-thou" flashes it may seem to be grounded in some universal womanness or to participate with all of womanness in some fundamental caring textures; yet I can't call even that deep intimacy "spiritual" if I act on those feelings *only* within the limitations of that relationship. I may grow there, but if I grow *only* there, if my commitment is *only* there, then that relationship becomes an encapsulation only a little "bigger" than the patriarch's isolated and jealously guarded version of spirituality.

I remind myself, incidentally, that patriarchal faiths rely for their survival upon just such isolated couples. In a front-page feature on marriage encounter, a desperate attempt to resurrect both church and synagogue, a Reverend Paddy Colleran says it flat out: "The couple is the central unit of the church. If we renew the couple, we renew the church" (San Francisco *Chronicle,* February 26, 1977). Whether heterosexual as the Church would have it or woman-to-woman as we would have it, pairing has its dangers, its potential for oppression. We may escape some of those dangers and some of that oppression by understanding our coupling as growth toward self-nurturance, but if our concerns go no further than our pairing we buy into precisely the mind set that Patriarchal Headquarters would have us embrace.

Paradoxically, then, the more I move toward self-reliance, the more vividly I understand that I am *not* sufficient unto my self (or that as a couple we are not sufficient unto our selfs). My growth toward self-nurturance is an essential bridge but *only* a bridge between (on the one hand) the romantic dependencies I was conditioned into and (on the other) the phenomenon of collective female spirituality. Among lesbians the more open we become about our life-styles, the more we lean toward a community, the more we seek relations on a variety of levels that go beyond the small circle of our closeted society. We seem to require a being-together of more women like our selfs; we want a matrix, an environment of *multi* dependence where more than one person will fill our needs and where we can fill the needs of more than one person. (I do not necessarily speak here of sexual needs.) I experience this bare beginning of *multi* dependence as a web of support, a network of channels with other women *no one* channel of which is essential but *all* of which literally hold me up and sustain my relational life, my growth toward self-nurturance; further, it is in this support that I begin to experience a female version of spirituality. Just as I am at the center of my web, each other woman is at the center of hers, and her relationship to me is one of many. In this *multi* dependent network, though I could be "sexually monagomous," *no one* relationship bears the burden of *all* my needs.

2. Lesbians may be drawn to the womanbonding of womanspirit because it represents to them a form of political action. They understand, in fact, that there is a deep sense in which, if we have a new concept of spirituality, *the spiritual is political*. Women working in womanspirit have firsthand experience of the power of horizontal transcendence; further they know the healing and life-giving potential of collectivized psychic energy; finally, they understand the planet earth to have been stripped and gouged by violent patriarchal energy. When such women *intend* to use such collectivized healing energy in the service of a violated world, that purpose, that energy, and those agents have to be called political. It's more and more solidly my own conviction that in the spirituality arena of the women's movement there is the world's most radical political potential, for in its redemption of female values and female epistemology, womanspirit returns to and begins again with the fundamental female nature of the race.

Lesbian feminists who are working in the spirituality subculture of the women's movement often are the greatest critics of that subculture, particularly if their own history is one of political activity. I name here without much elaboration the dangers they most frequently see in womanspirit. Each danger is in itself a rich territory for argument, dialogue, and growth.

Danger Number One: that we will be content to struggle *only* for our own personal growth, only for our own self-nurturance or our womanloving pairings. If we are not something new on the face of the earth, if we're not serious about transforming the quality of all human life—of all life—on this planet, then we're doing no more than pursuing a privileged private salvation. Peggy Kornegger has accurately pinned down the threat to women that is posed by Transcendental Meditation, Erhard Seminars Training, and the host of other personal solutions so easily incorporated into the status quo—spiritual alternatives which, while lining the pockets of their male leaders, keep their followers docile, solipsistic, and "blissed out" (11). We can't afford to bliss out, either in meditation or in rural isolation. We need regularly to remind ourselves of the political nature of our task; we need regularly to touch our lives with the heavy destructive energy so that we see clearly how high the stakes are in the accomplishment of that task (20).

Danger Number Two: that we will affirm the woman qualities (intuition, emotionality, gentleness, nonviolence, synchronicity, and the like) and forget that we also have valuable analytic and logical functions, that strength and leadership don't have to mean power-mongering, that the occult is not the only passageway to knowledge.

Danger Number Three: that we will expect our spiritual/political growth to come without effort. There's lots to be said for the influence on material

reality of believing and of fantasizing. Further, it's important for us to celebrate. But faith, celebration, and all the easy laid-back flow in the world will not substitute for the hard disciplined work that the development of our skills requires. Serious and extensive practice is essential to any craft. Women's spiritual expression is no exception.

Danger Number Four: that we will lose our horizontal transcendence, that in our attempt to share energy we will institutionalize our rituals or approach some "party line" of women's spirituality. If any one of us ever feels uneasy or "spiritually incorrect" (and the tiny ways that that can happen are infinite), then it's time to look hard at what we're doing, at the assumptions we're making, at the expectations we're putting on each other; it's time to examine our selfs for differences among us—most obviously the differences of class—that will divide us and make our spirituality seem mighty like an old-fashioned power trip.

I'm convinced all over again that lesbianism has always tended toward self-reliance, toward the *intra*personal dimension of human reality. For centuries we have been an underground culture of women leaning toward one another and toward our own self-love. Those centuries-old spiritual leanings are now clearly linked to womanspirit activities, to the use, among *multi*dependent women, of internally sourced and horizontally transcendent power. We are on the brink of realizing the potential of our female spirituality and we are beginning to understand the political commitment that that spirituality involves.

We are a far cry from the "sinners" many of us once were, crouching below the pulpit seeking personal forgiveness. Maybe it's the memory of that patriarchal history that makes our free-standing selfs more joyous and the joining of our lives more committed. If so, then that's cause enough in itself for a "Hallelujah!" or a "Blessed be."

SOURCES

1. Cleveland, Peggy, and Gearhart, Sally. "On the Prevalence of Stilips." *Quest: A Feminist Quarterly* (P. O. Box 8843, Washington, D.C. 20003). Vol. I, No. 4 (Spring 1975)
2. Collins, Sheila. *A Different Heaven and Earth*. Philadelphia: Judson Press, 1974.
3. Daly, Mary. *The Church and the Second Sex*. New York: Harper & Row, 1968.
4. Daly, Mary. *Beyond God the Father*. Boston: Beacon Press, 1973.
5. Doely, Sarah Bentley, ed. *Women's Liberation and the Church*. New York: Association Press, 1970.
6. Fischer, C. B.; Brennenman, Betsy; and Bennett, Ann, eds. *Women in a Strange Land*. Philadelphia: Fortress Press, 1975.

7. Gearhart, Sally. "The Lesbian and God-the-Father or All the Church Needs is a Good Lay—On Its Side." *Radical Religion,* Vol. I, No. 2 (Spring 1974). (The Radical Religion Collective, 2323 Hearst Street, Berkeley, Calif. 94709.) Also excerpted in *Womanspirit,* Vol. I, No. 1 (Autumn Equinox 1974). (Nox 263, Wolf Creek, Ore. 97497.)

8. Gearhart, Sally. "The Miracle of Lesbianism." *Loving Women/Loving Men: Gay Liberation and the Church,* by Sally Gearhart and William Johnson. San Francisco: Glide Publications, 1974. (330 Ellis, San Francisco, Calif. 94102.)

9. Gearhart, Sally. "Womanpower: Energy Resourcement." *Companions for the Journey: An Anthology of Women and Spirituality.* Edited by Juanita Weaver, 1710 19th St. N.W., Washington, D.C. 20009. 1977. Also excerpted in *Womanspirit,* Vol. III, No. 7 (Spring Equinox, 1976). (Box 263, Wolf Creek, Ore. 97497.)

10. Hageman, Alice, ed. *Sexist Religion and Women in the Church: No More Silence.* New York: Associated Press, 1974.

11. Kornegger, Peggy. "The Spirituality Ripoff." *The Second Wave,* Spring 1976.

12. Martin, Del, and Lyon, Phyllis. *Lesbian/Woman.* San Francisco: Glide Publications, 1972. (330 Ellis, San Francisco, Calif. 94102.) Also in paper from Bantam.

13. Morton, Nelle. "How Images Function." *Quest: A Feminist Quarterly,* Vol. III, No. 2(Fall 1976). (P.O. Box 8843, Washington, D.C. 20003.)

14. *Quest: A Feminist Quarterly.* P. O. Box 8843, Washington, D.C. 20003. See particularly issues on Spirituality (Vol. I, No. 4, Spring 1975) and on Selfhood (Vol. I, No. 3, Winter 1975).

15. Ruether, Rosemary Radford. *New Woman/New Earth.* New York: Seabury Press, 1975.

16. Ruether, Rosemary Radford, ed. *Religion and Sexism: Images of Women in Jewish and Christian Traditions.* New York: Simon & Schuster, 1974.

17. Rush, Ann Kent. *Moon, Moon.* San Francisco: Moon Books/Random House, 1976.

18. Scanzoni, L. and Hardesty, N. *All We Are Meant to Be: A Biblical Liberation.* Waco, Tex.: Word Press, 1974.

19. Stone, Merlin. *When God Was a Woman.* New York: Dial Press, 1976.

20. "View-of-the-Moon Dialogue." *Womanspirit,* Vol. III, No. 9 (Fall Equinox 1976). (Box 263, Wolf Creek, Ore. 97497). A response to "Womanpower: Energy Resourcement" entitled "A View of the Moon from the City Streets," by Sherrie Cohen, Ann Yarabinee, Linda S. Norwood, T. Cardea Tinder, and Judy Mendelsohn. A response to their article by Sally Gearhart entitled "And Her View of the Same Moon from Another City's Streets" and a response entitled "Response" by Batya Podos in Vol. III, No. 10 (Winter Solstice 1976).

21. Wittig, Monique. *Les Guerilleres.* Translated by David LeVay. New York: Avon Books, 1969.

22. *Womanspirit.* Box 263, Wolf Creek, Ore. 97497.

23. *Women and the Word: Toward a Whole Theology.* Berkeley, Calif.: Office of Women's Affairs, 1972. (2465 LeConte, Berkeley, Calif. 94709.)

8.
Lesbians and the Law

Jean O'Leary

Legal Problems and Remedies

JEAN O'LEARY

In addition to the discrimination we face as women, lesbians encounter many legal problems in this country because the laws of our land discriminate unjustly on the basis of sexual or affectional preference. We are routinely denied government employment in many areas, turned down for security clearances, cashiered out of the armed forces, rejected as immigrants, denied custody of our own children, taxed at higher rates, and excluded from the benefits of many social programs. A legal injustice requires a legal remedy: Such laws and policies must be changed legislatively, or struck down in the courts.

Besides the various forms of legal discrimination, there is also an abundant variety of *extra*-legal discrimination, on the part of private individuals, that is both socially condemned and legally barred when it comes to other minorities, yet is widely sanctioned in both law and social attitudes when it comes to us. Private discrimination against gays is not even considered a fit topic for investigation by the U. S. Civil Rights Commission, the "nation's conscience" on matters of minority

rights,[1] and in the meantime in most parts of the country employers are free to fire or refuse to hire otherwise qualified persons merely because they are gay; property owners may refuse to rent, lease, or sell to gays; and operators of public accommodations may declare their establishments off limits to "overtly" gay would-be customers. To these injustices there is at least a partial remedy: Gays must be legally recognized as having the same civil rights as any other citizens, and these rights must be upheld at least as vigorously as is done for any other minority. In the end, of course, only massive shifts in social attitudes can assure us full rights, but gay civil rights legislation is an essential step toward first-class citizenship.

Ironically, oppression of gay people is both mitigated and facilitated by our "invisibility." Contrary to popular stereotypes the vast majority of lesbians and gay men can very easily "pass" as "straight." But while this ability protects many of us from overt discrimination on our jobs and in other areas, *having* to live one's life "under cover" in this way is psychologically unhealthy. Moreover, this "invisibility" hides the true extent of our oppression even from ourselves, and encourages society to dismiss our problems as of concern only to some minute fringe of "kooks and queers."

Nonetheless, we are really everywhere, in numbers most reliably estimated as amounting to nearly one-tenth the population—in the United States that's more than 20 million people! Homosexuality cuts across all lines of class, race, religion, education, political ideology, or economic status—and across the line between the sexes. Most people when they hear the word "gay" still think in terms of gay males, but there are millions of lesbians, and we, of course, also have a stake in ending antihomosexual discrimination. We also have perhaps even better means and opportunities to accomplish this, since working through both the gay and the feminist movements gives us a double political strength; and since sexism and sex-role stereotyping oppress both women and gays, the two movements are natural allies.

For lesbians, the most obvious sort of discrimination occurs in the area of child custody, since many lesbians who have been married and had children are unfairly denied custody of them—and sometimes even adequate visitation rights—following a divorce. For gay men, the most obvious discrimination is in the unequal (selective) enforcement of the "sodomy" laws still on the books in many states, which prohibit specific sexual acts (such as oral and anal sex) even between consenting adults in private—and even when the laws putatively apply to heterosexuals.

But virtually every other form of discrimination

---

1. The U.S. Civil Rights Commission has, however, acknowledged its authority to investigate antigay bias in the area of "Administration of Justice," which includes police harassment, the courts, federal prisons, etc.

against gays affects both lesbians and gay males similarly. And, though lesbians are not prosecuted for violation of the "sodomy" laws, their existence makes every sexually active lesbian in states with such laws a presumed felon who can then be discriminated against in other ways—or at least denied equal protection of the law. It means, even though one is not put in jail, that one is presumed to be untrustworthy, contemptuous of legal authority, socially deviant, of bad moral character—in a word, *criminal.* However thankless and seemingly superfluous the task, repeal of consensual sex laws is a necessary precondition for any widespread and *lasting* civil rights reform.

DECRIMINALIZATION OF CONSENSUAL SEX LAWS

Under the Constitution, it is not possible for any state (or Congress) to make it illegal to *be* homosexual, that is, to have a homosexual orientation or preference. However, in March 1976 the U. S. Supreme Court, in a widely criticized decision, affirmed the right of states to prohibit certain sexual *acts* between persons of the same sex (usually oral or anal intercourse, but sometimes even acts not involving "penetration," such as mutual masturbation).

Of course, the High Court in no way said that state legislatures *must* pass, or retain, such laws, and even after that decision several more states joined the ranks of those having repealed their antigay "sodomy" statutes. At this writing slightly more than one third of the states have thus "decriminalized" sexual activities between consenting adults in private. It would have been wonderful if the Supreme Court had chosen to invalidate all remaining such laws in "one fell swoop," and it could still do so at a future date. But its failure to do so is no disaster; it only means that the work of repealing these laws must continue to be carried on piecemeal, legislature by legislature, until gays in every state are free from the threat of criminal prosecution for expressing natural feelings. Moreover, as in other areas where a temporary setback may actually help ensure final victory, the tremendous publicity given to the Court's action brought the issue into the public's consciousness. Many of the country's major newspapers and virtually every civil rights organization came down strongly on the side of decriminalization, usually providing well-argued editorials or statements and public opinion polls (in our support!) that can be used by gay lobbyists working in the state legislatures.

In most cases, except, for example, California, "sodomy" law reform has been achieved as part of a general state criminal law reform. Ever since 1962, when the American Law Institute proposed its U. S. Model Penal Code, it has been accepted in enlightened legal circles that government really has no business trying to regulate the sexual activities in which adult citizens engage in private. The Kinsey reports revealed that "the abominable and detestable crime against nature," far from being a rare "perversion" engaged in by a tiny fraction of the population, was in fact enjoyed so widely that fair enforcement of the laws against it would put most of the country (heterosexuals, included) behind bars. This realization has probably been the major factor making "sodomy" law repeal palatable even to relatively conservative legislatures; it has even in some cases been presented as a way of "preserving the sanctity of the marriage bed" from the prying eyes of government!

Unfortunately, here as elsewhere a double standard often prevails. Legislators willing to sanction any consensual sexual practices between heterosexual married couples may not be tolerant of unmarried ones, and still less of gays. When a general consensual sex law is repealed, efforts are sometimes made—and sometimes succeed (as in Idaho and quite recently in Arkansas)—to reinstate a more narrow prohibition limited to acts performed by members of the same sex or by unmarried persons.

Similarly, when "sodomy" law repeal is brought up as a separate issue, instead of in a broader legislative "package" including other issues such as complete penal code revision or all laws concerning sexual conduct, there is less chance of the legislation passing.

In view of this, perhaps the best general strategy is *not* to press for decriminalization of gays as a separate issue. If the state in question has not had a recent complete recodification of its criminal laws, quietly check to see if one is in the works (or even being contemplated). If one is, quietly (again) check to see whether the sponsors or planners already intend such a repeal. Depending on local conditions, you may be able to give them some help in terms of literature, arguments, lobbying, and public support—or they may advise keeping completely out of it so they can "slip it through" without alarming their more hidebound colleagues. (In some cases legislators have voted for and governors have signed such legislation without realizing what they were doing.) If they do not plan on it, you should make every effort to persuade them to include it. Try to work quietly and behind the scenes for as long as it seems anything is to be gained by such caution; if this does not prove effective, "go public" and try to generate media and constituent pressure.

In cases where a state has already "reformed" its criminal code *without* decriminalizing private consensual adult homosexual acts, a frontal attack on the ban may be the only recourse. The first steps should be accomplished on an individual level, since you will get nowhere without first convincing at least one legislator to sponsor a repeal measure; but the later stages may have to be noisily public—because of backlash from antigay groups.

When a general criminal code reform is not in prospect, it may be possible to hitch sodomy repeal to another, less controversial issue, either as an integral part or as an inconspicuous "rider." One possibility is to make decriminalization part of a reform of laws governing rape and sexual assault—which, Lord knows, are usually much in need of reform! Legislators with a high enough consciousness about feminist issues to consider sponsoring a rape reform measure may also be hospitable to removing sanctions against so-called deviate *voluntary* sexual intercourse. Moreover, it is helpful in alleviating legislators' and others' (unwarranted) fears about gays "preying" on children or nongay adults to introduce decriminalization in the context of stiffening penalties for involuntary intercourse (among which it is a good idea to include rape of males).

CIVIL RIGHTS LEGISLATION

Civil rights are "entitlements": benefits, procedural guarantees, and opportunities that persons are entitled to simply by virtue of their citizenship. Ideally, all citizens have the same rights in our democratic republic; in practice, there are many official and unofficial gradations of status and treatment, so that some are "more equal" than others.

However, there is a strong trend in this country toward equalizing civil rights. Jews, blacks, Chicanos, Native Americans, Italian-Americans, and other ethnic minorities have asserted their claims and made various degrees of progress toward "first-class citizenship." And women, a "majority," are standing up for our rights against the institutionalized sexism that makes men the "masters."

The gay liberation movement, in calling for "gay rights," is firmly based in this tradition. The purpose of a gay rights law, like any other civil rights measure, is simply to eliminate *unfair* discrimination based on factors irrelevant to the entitlement being sought; and to provide legal recourse, usually through a human rights commission, to file complaints and redress grievances.

There are three levels on which the struggle for gay rights is being waged: federal, state, and local. So far, the only relatively complete successes (in the form of broadly ranging gay rights legislation) have been at the local level. About forty cities, towns, and counties around the country have passed local gay rights ordinances. They range from small college towns like Alfred, New York, and Chapel Hill, North Carolina, to major cities like Detroit, Washington, D.C., and Minneapolis.

At the state level no gay rights bills have been passed, though they are under consideration in a number of states (and will be introduced in many more) and the chances look good for passage of this type of legislation in several states within the next couple of years. In Pennsylvania, Governor Milton Shapp in 1975 issued an executive order barring discrimination against gays in all state government employment, and has held his ground despite repeated attempts by a homophobic legislature to overrule him.

There are two federal gay rights bills before Congress, though at this writing neither has been voted out of committee. Former Representative Bella Abzug (D–N.Y.) introduced a bill amending the Civil Rights Act of 1964 to prohibit discrimination in employment, housing, and public accommodations, and other areas on the basis of affectional or sexual preference. The current principal sponsor is Representative Edward Koch (D–N.Y.), with forty cosponsors. Passage of this bill would create nationwide civil rights protections for gays, just as a U. S. Supreme Court ruling against state "sodomy" laws would have done in terms of decriminalization; in so doing, it would save an enormous amount of time and effort in gay lobbying. On the other hand, passage of a federal bill would not make state and local gay rights laws completely superfluous, since the latter would bring with them additional resources for enforcement. (The Abzug bill would put the burden of enforcement on the Equal Employment Opportunity Commission, for employment discrimination, and the appropriate Cabinet departments—e.g., Housing and Urban Affairs—in the other areas.)

On the Senate side of Congress, it is expected that a bill prohibiting antigay discrimination in employment will soon be introduced. It provides for enforcement through the courts, with the Justice Department empowered to initiate suits. The Abzug-Koch bill has gained widespread attention in Congress—and in part thanks to opponents like Anita Bryant, who help publicize it—the media. Hearings on the bill are planned, which will further focus attention on the issues and permit airing of progay arguments and myth-shattering facts. Whether or not it passes anytime soon, the whole process is likely to be worthwhile in terms of educating politicians and the public.

One general point about gay rights legislation requires discussion, and that is the concept of "affirmative action." While lesbians and gay men deserve the same rights as other minority groups, it may not always be equally appropriate to use the same means of securing those rights. Affirmative action, which means making a special effort to extend opportunities (usually in employment) to members of discriminated-against minority groups, would in the case of gays actually involve an invasion of privacy, because we would all have to declare our gay identity at the time of hiring. Forcing someone to admit to being gay *in order to be hired* is just as bad as forcing people to live closeted lives when they'd rather be open. It is good to have visible, open gay people in positions of trust and responsibility as role models, but expecting everyone to come out of the closet as a precondition for fair treatment is a gross violation of the right to privacy and is, moreover, counterproductive.

As for general legislative strategies, the main thing is to carefully build support for the principle of gay rights—among legislators, the media, and the public—before getting down to the details of particular bills. Be prepared with the facts, support statements from influential organizations (e.g., church and scientific groups), and familiarity with the kinds of negative reactions one can expect *before* you go in to start lobbying legislators. Finding a sympathetic sponsor is often a good first step, but it may be easier to convince him or her to take on this controversial issue if you have previously canvassed the rest of the legislature to assess the depth of support (or virulence of the opposition). All members should be visited at least once, preferably by their own constituents. Do not automatically write anyone off. In Massachusetts, for instance, an otherwise extremely conservative legislator has strongly and publicly supported efforts to pass a gay rights bill there—on the grounds that he doesn't want to have to pay to support gays on welfare who are denied jobs because of prejudice!

Working with the media is extraordinarily important, at all levels. In promoting local gay rights legislation, meetings with the editors of the local papers should be a first priority. Inform them about the nature of the discrimination gays suffer from, the background of the gay rights movement, the support that has already been received, and the specifics of the legislation being proposed. Give them reasonable answers to all the objections, reasonable or otherwise, that you can think of or that they raise themselves. They will be the public's main source of information about the proposed legislation, and it is vital that they at least be given the chance to tell the truth. (And, unless they are so hopelessly sunk in homophobia that nothing but prolonged psychotherapy could possibly shake them out of it, don't give up on them after the first unfavorable editorial or slanted story.)

Public hearings of any kind on a proposed gay rights law can be a wonderful opportunity to educate the public. (The people holding the hearings scarcely ever change their minds because of anything that they hear—though it does sometimes happen.) Plan your presentation(s) carefully. Try to arrange for supportive testimony from friendly psychiatrists, politicians, religious leaders, and business people, as well as from other civil rights organizations and from gay people willing to tell how they personally have been discriminated against. Do everything you can to secure good media coverage.

Generally, a proposed bill should not be reported out of committee, even favorably, until a head count of the full body (legislature, council, commission, or whatever) has been made to determine what chance it has of passage. If it's bound to be miserably defeated, better it die in committee than let the negative vote go on the record. If the vote is going to be close, however, it may be worthwhile chancing it, in the hope that debate on the floor, last-minute letter-writing campaigns, and personal lobbying will pull it through. A *close* defeat does not affect a bill's future chances the way an overwhelming one does.

When dealing with elected bodies, remember that every member will be most swayed by his or her own constituents (since the main concern is to be reelected). In heavily populated areas, setting up tables in high traffic spots such as shopping centers, and major intersections can be a good way to generate letters, petition signatures, and even receive donations. Provide sample letters, but encourage people to vary them slightly; legislators tend to discount piles of letters that sound identical. If the climate seems favorable, polling people on the issue may be a good way to convince legislators that their constituents support gay rights (and thus that it is safe for them to do so). It is also important in the long run for lesbians and gay men to have a continuing political presence. The more a local gay community contributes to the election or defeat of local candidates, the more its needs will be taken seriously by those in office. This can be done through campaigns, fund raising, and voter registration.

Finally, though legislation is probably the most generally effective way to secure civil rights, other, more limited measures should not be neglected. Each organization that issues a statement of support, each union that unilaterally reforms itself, each agency that mandates nondiscrimination in its own area of concern, each professional association that supports its gay members, brings us that much closer to our goal of full citizenship, as well as providing weighty precedents for timorous legislators to cling to when the antigay zealots start howling.

It is also important to remember that changes in government can be made not only through passage of legislation but also through administrative decisions. Perhaps the mayor of your city can be persuaded to issue an executive order barring discrimination against gays in municipal employment or to appoint an open lesbian to the Human Rights Commission. Perhaps the Board of Education or the university in your town would be willing to establish a fair employment policy for gays in education. Any local agency that has control of its own employment policies is a likely place to lobby.

In the remainder of this section we will consider a series of particular areas in which gay people face unfair discrimination.

AREAS OF DISCRIMINATION

Employment

Gay people suffer from employment discrimination in several different ways, some of them obvious and some quite subtle. Most obvious is when an employer, whether private or governmental, simply refuses to accept gay employees: An open gay person cannot be hired and any closeted gays already working are fired if their sexual orientation becomes known (or, perhaps, even suspected). In many such cases there is not even a shabby rationale for such practices; they are based on rank prejudice. As revealed in various public opinion samplings, a surprisingly large percentage of the American people, perhaps a majority, is already willing to reject and condemn this sort of discrimination.[2]

Far more difficult to combat, however, is employment discrimination that is based on false assumptions about us. For instance, there is still considerable resistance to hiring acknowledged lesbians or gay men for any jobs, such as teaching or counseling, involving close contact with young people. The assumption is that homosexuality can be learned and there is great fear of positive gay role models. It is also thought that gays cannot be trusted with children and young people without "molesting" them sexually. This is *not* the view of those in a position to know the facts—for instance, the National Education Association, the American Federation of Teachers, and the United Federation of Teachers, who have all issued statements of support for gay rights. The truth is that child molestation is overwhelmingly a *heterosexual* phenomenon (usually adult males attracted) to young girls), and that it is almost nonexistent among lesbians.

There is also great resistance to hiring lesbians or gay men as police officers or fire fighters. The fear persists that gay and nongay police officers or fire fighters cannot work together without the former seducing or attacking the latter. This is the same rationale used to keep those services fairly well segregated by sex. Although some police departments are beginning to integrate, there is hardly a woman fire fighter in the country.

Employment discrimination against gays does not end with unfair hiring restrictions. There continue to be problems even after a gay person is hired. Simply avoiding being "found out" and fired as a result can require an elaborate pattern of deception and dissimulation. It is always assumed that one is either married or looking for someone to marry, and office gossip tends to center around "the dating game." Lesbians must fend off proposals, or just propositions, from members of the opposite sex, as well as well-intentioned efforts at match-making, without arousing suspicion. If a lesbian has a lover, she cannot talk about her in the way others talk about their mates, nor come to an office party with her, nor claim any joint benefits. And not only do we thus tend to become isolated from our working colleagues, in many corporations and institutions there are definite bars to advancement for *any* single persons. It is assumed that a single person is "less stable" than someone who is married; he or she is less burdened with dependents and thus more inclined to change jobs and even careers if dissatisfied. On the other hand, there is great fear that an unmarried woman will marry and become pregnant, and thus be a bad job security risk. You can't win!

Perhaps more than any other civil rights problem

we face, employment discrimination must be combated on two fronts: legal and attitudinal. Explicit legal guarantees are of use only to someone who is willing to identify herself as gay in order to file a complaint. There must be a considerable shift in attitudes before most gays will feel that they risk less by claiming their rights under law than by suffering unfair discrimination in silence.

Housing

Much of the discrimination in housing is directed toward single lesbians living alone and is largely shared with other singles; this can often be fought under existing laws prohibiting discrimination based on marital status. Lesbians living together can face more difficult problems, particularly if they are of an age when the "roommate" dodge is no longer plausible, and especially if they wish to rent or purchase a house together. The right to buy or rent may be refused not explicitly because of the fact or suspicions of homosexuality, but simply because an area is zoned for "family use" and two women (or two men) are not considered a family.

Most lesbians do not feel free to be affectionate with each other in their neighborhoods in a way that heterosexuals take for granted: We often avoid holding hands or kissing good night on the doorstep out of a realistic fear that the landlord might evict us and, if so, we'd be without recourse to law.

Municipal ordinances barring housing discrimination on the basis of sexual or affectional preference are of some help with these problems, as a general federal (or state) gay rights law would be. As a preliminary step, efforts are being made to persuade the Department of Housing and Urban Development to amend its own regulations so that all federal housing grants explicitly prohibit discrimination against gay people by the governmental or private grant recipients.

Child Custody

Many lesbians and gay men either first realize or first come to accept their own sexual orientation after they are already conventionally married, and often after they have had children. Such marriages often end in divorce, and the laws are usually interpreted so as to deny custody of the children—and, sometimes, even adequate visitation rights—to the gay parent. This pattern of discrimination affects lesbians most since in our sexist society, which assigns women the role of nurturing, custody is generally awarded to the mother. However, judges often decide that a mother's lesbianism makes her "unfit" to care for her own children, who are then either given to the father or else institutionalized. But homosexuality as such, besides being neither immoral nor sick, has nothing at all to do with a given person's ability to love and nurture children. (There may be gay parents who are in some way "unfit" to raise children, but it is not because they are gay.)

There have been some scattered victories for lesbian mothers in child custody cases, but there is as yet

---

2. A 1977 Gallup Poll indicated that 56% of those surveyed felt that gays should have equal rights in terms of job opportunities. A Harris poll conducted the same year found that 55% felt that gay people were the "most discriminated-against" group in our society.

no widespread trend toward reform in this area. Indeed, as gay women and men become more open about their life-styles, we can expect ex-spouses to insert the issue of their "fitness" into custody hearings more often, giving more judges an opportunity to decide according to their prejudices. What is needed is reform of the laws in order to leave judges less discretion in awarding custody; the law should spell out precisely what constitutes unfitness, and should explicitly state that homosexuality *as such* does not. Such legislation has already been passed in Washington, D.C. (See also "Lesbian Mothers in Transition," page 207.)

Marriage

Persons of the same sex are denied the right to marry each other in our culture. Lesbians and gay men who wish to marry should be able to do so. The same practical advantages that accrue from heterosexual marriages should be available to persons of the same sex by having their relationships sanctioned by law and religion. There is no good reason to deny this right, particularly if one conceives of marriage essentially in terms of mutual love and support between two individuals, since this is as present in long-lasting gay unions as in any successful heterosexual marriage.

The real source of the often virulent opposition to the possibility of gay marriages is simply prejudice against homosexuality itself. The feeling of many anti-gay persons is that permitting legal or religious marriage between persons of the same sex would "legitimize" what they view as an immoral relationship.

Taxes

Currently the federal income tax laws, as well as those of most of the states (and those municipalities that tax incomes), favor married couples over singles when only one partner has an income, but favor singles over couples when both do. This is obviously a relic of the "a woman's place is in the home" stereotype. It is unfair to both groups, and the "social goal" of discouraging working mothers is no longer an acceptable justification. If two adults share a single income, they should be able to divide it between them for tax purposes, as if each individually had an income half the total. Similarly if both have an income but one is larger, they should be able to pool them and assign equal shares to each. Deductions for children or other dependents, if any, should also be able to be shared. But there is no reason to distinguish between heterosexual and homosexual, married and unmarried, couples in determining who is qualified for this option; all that should count is the fact that the income is shared to maintain a single household.

Gay organizations are no longer discriminated against by the Internal Revenue Service. Its policy had been to deny tax exemptions to nonprofitable charitable or educational groups if they take the position that homosexuality is a normal, healthy, acceptable alternative life-style. Thus, the only nonprofit organization aimed at "helping" gay people that could get a tax exemption was one that was *anti*gay in ideology. Since the policy was not based in any statute but was merely a matter of interpretation on the part of IRS administrators, this form of discrimination was remedied by administrative action on the part of the IRS. It is now possible for gay groups to qualify for tax-exempt status if they meet the standard criteria.

Credit and Insurance

Because of the prejudicial assumption that gays are somehow "less stable" than nongays, open lesbians or gay men (or those who are closeted but suspected) often find it more difficult to secure credit for major purchases or expenditures (e.g., an automobile or house or a business), regardless of their past credit record and current financial situation. There is clearly a need here for legal guarantees of nondiscrimination.

Insurance presents similar problems, as well as additional ones peculiar to the business. Gays are often considered to be higher risks than nongays, so premiums are higher for all insurance, when it is obtainable at all. Moreover, the insurance industry's rules on naming beneficiaries for *life* insurance policies have frequently worked to the detriment of gays. The insurer requires that a beneficiary have an "insurable interest"—that is, that she or he stands to lose more by the insured person's death than is to be gained from payment on the policy. Relatives and legal spouses are generally assumed without question to have such an interest, but until recently a gay person's lover was not generally accepted as a beneficiary. Some of the major companies have now made it their explicit policy to recognize "established" relationships outside of marriage (both heterosexual and homosexual), but the waiting period demanded (usually at least one year) is still an onerous requirement not imposed on conventionally married persons, who can insure each other from the moment they are pronounced "man and wife."

Similarly, to return to the question of credit, a heterosexual married couple may cosign loans, but a gay couple often may not, even if both partners are employed and have good individual credit records. Both of these difficulties could be removed were gay marriages recognized in law—and so would the problem of establishing inheritance rights in the absence of a will. But single gays would still have to be protected by explicit inclusion in civil rights laws.

Military Service

Open lesbians and gay men are refused entry into this country's armed forces, and those discovered to be gay while in the service are invariably discharged, frequently with a "less-than-honorable" label that can be a barrier to employment or promotion for the rest of the person's life. In order to keep the services "free" of the homosexual "taint," outrageous invasions of privacy and unconstitutional methods of intimidation are routinely used by military investigators. As with other forms of employment discrimination, which this is, the notion that lesbians and gay men cannot effectively and honorably serve in the military is based on falsehoods and myths that have no basis in fact. (See also "Lesbians in the Military," page 211.)

Immigration and Naturalization

The United States immigration policy excludes homosexuals, although exceptions are often made for the wealthy and famous. The basis for the exclusionary policy is that gays are held to lack the "good moral character" required and because homosexuals are defined as "sexual deviants" and "psychopathic personalities," despite the American Psychiatric Association's removal of homosexuality from the mental disorder list in 1973. The INS, however, maintains that the Supreme Court ruled in the Boutilier case that the intent of Congress was to exclude homosexuals by using such "terms of art."

On the other hand, the naturalization policy has been relaxed somewhat; gays are not automatically ineligible for citizenship, but this privilege can be denied if a person has a history of arrests relating to homosexual acts in other countries, or if it can be shown that she was gay at the time she entered the country. Aliens for whom this can be proven may be deported.

Prisoners

Lesbians sent to prison, for whatever reason, generally suffer a great deal more than heterosexual women. There is pervasive official discrimination against gay prisoners, in both state and federal institutions, in job assignments, work release programs, educational opportunities, furlough and parole decisions, living conditions, and recreational facilities. Gay prisoners are not permitted to receive gay publications in the federal prison system, on the specious grounds that having such publications will make them more of a "target" for abuse than they are already. The Universal Fellowship of Metropolitan Community Churches, Dignity, Integrity, and other gay religious groups often find it difficult or impossible to be recognized by prison authorities and allowed to give counseling, hold services, or dispense literature. Here again, while there are many things that may be done now to ameliorate the lot of lesbians and gay men in prison, their condition cannot ultimately be redeemed until homosexuality is accepted by society as a whole. When that happens there will be far fewer gays in prison at all, and the gay offenders who are justly sentenced will not be punished ten times over for their crimes. (See also "Prison Ministry," page 171.)

Security Clearance

Another subcategory of employment discrimination involving government attitudes is the denial of security clearance. These must be approved by either the Defense or the State Department, and in the past they have routinely been denied to known gays (including those discovered to be gay only in the course of a security check). The rationale has been—again!—that gays are inherently "less stable" than heterosexually oriented

persons, and thus less trustworthy generally; regardless of an individual's prior record, there is the lurking fear that at any moment she or he may "go off the deep end." Government agencies have used the argument that gays, being engaged in usually illicit and in any case disreputable activities, are especially vulnerable to blackmail. The assumption that a lesbian would automatically prefer to betray her country than to come out of the closet shows more about the mind set of homophobes than about our trustworthiness.

In any event, an *open* gay person is no more vulnerable to blackmail than anyone else, so any gay who is denied a security clearance on that ground is in a very good position to win an appeal; if she or he is willing to take the government to court to protect this right, there can hardly be any "guilty secret" an enemy agent could exploit. Increasingly the courts have been ruling in favor of the gay plaintiffs in such cases.

Media

Lesbians and gay men very often "get it in the neck" from the media, both print and broadcast, and at present there isn't a great deal one can do about it except protest and educate influential media people. The Federal Communication Commission has explicitly ruled that the gay community is *not* one that licensees must take into account in their programming (which is supposed to meet the needs of those living within the broadcast area). Gays sometimes succeed in getting on the air to "balance" an antigay spokesperson, but under present policies there is no requirement that the progay position be presented.[3]

Bigotry in newspapers and magazines is legally sacrosanct under the First Amendment, and there is no central agency like the FCC or the networks where one can concentrate pressure. (See also "Lesbians and the Media," page 239).

Campus Gay Groups

Campus lesbian and gay organizations must often struggle with an antigay administration for the right to hold meetings on school property, to advertise in the school newspaper (or on the campus radio), and generally to be treated like any other legitimate student group. The legal situation at present is unclear, with several important cases decided for the gay groups and at least one against; there is no national precedent binding on all the states. Since campus groups are an important source of knowledge and energy for the gay liberation movement, as they were for the peace and the black civil rights movements, it is important for all gay people to

---

3. Both FCC policies are being challenged. The National Gay Task Force, joined by 143 lesbian and gay organizations, has filed a petition with the FCC asking that gay leaders be added to the checklist of community groups which broadcasters are required to "ascertain." A "Petition to Deny" based on the Fairness Doctrine has also been brought against a San Francisco TV station. For details, contact the Media Access Project, 1609 Connecticut Ave., N.W., Washington, D.C. 20009.

support these struggles, whether they are personally concerned in them or not.

Mental Institutions

Lesbians who are under age have sometimes been committed to mental institutions by their parents. This may be a less frequent occurrence since the removal of homosexuality from the mental disorder list, but it can still happen, and does—as indicated by personal testimony on page 205. The hospital, however, if challenged, might claim that the patient was hospitalized not because of gayness, but because of "adolescent problems," though lesbianism may be the real reason.

Lesbians who are institutionalized are usually subjected to heavy pressure to "go straight," and often pretend they've converted in order to get out. So far there have been several cases challenging parents' absolute power to have their children committed (for whatever reason). In *Bartley* vs. *Kremens*, a federal court ruled that parents do not have such power, and that the children are entitled to a full-fledged committal hearing. Generally, the inclination of the courts is to rule that you cannot be committed unless you're suicidal or homicidal. If your parents try to have you committed to a mental institution, contact your local chapter of the American Civil Liberties Union. Whether or not you can establish that the attempt to commit you is based on your lesbianism (which both your parents and the hospital may deny), the ACLU may be willing to sue the hospital, and you have a fair chance of winning your case.

Civil Rights Commission

The U. S. Civil Rights Commission has thus far refused to recognize discrimination against gay people as an appropriate subject for its investigations and recommendations (it has no other powers), except in the area of "Administration of Justice." The same is true of many of the various agencies, commissions, boards, and so on established around the country at the state and local levels to oversee the process of extending full civil rights to a previously discriminated-against minority. What this means is that, for the public at large, gay civil rights is not yet perceived even as a *problem*. We are now roughly where blacks were when the NAACP was founded; before we can hope to achieve full citizenship, we must convince the heterosexual majority that we don't yet have it, and *then* we will have to persuade them that we *should* have it. In this process, we may find that open opposition is far preferable to being ignored, which is why temporary setbacks should never deflect us from our ultimate goal.

RESOURCES

"Connecticut's Lobbying Effort," by Christine Pattee, in *Gay Community News*, March 12, 1977. A blow-by-blow account of the gay lobbying campaign for Connecticut's gay rights bill, by the coordinator of

the gay lobby. Inquire: Gay Community News, 22 Bromfield, Boston, Mass. 02108.

The Majority Wins, by Linda Joy, available for $3.00 from the National Women's Political Caucus, 1411 K St., NW, Washington, D.C. 20005. Lobbying strategies.

Sexualawreporter. A journal reporting legal developments in sex-related law. 3701 Wilshire Blvd., Suite 700, Los Angeles, Calif. 90010. Bimonthly, $15/year; libraries $25, prisoners $5, students $10. Sample issue $3.

"Gay Civil Rights Support Statement and Resolutions Packet." National Gay Task Force, 80 Fifth Ave., New York, N.Y. 10011. $2. A collection of statements from groups such as the American Bar Association, National Council of Churches, the YWCA, the American Psychiatric Association, etc., supporting gay civil rights legislation and the repeal of consensual sex laws. A helpful lobbying tool.

"Corporate Business Support Statements Packet." National Gay Task Force, 80 Fifth Ave., New York, N.Y. 10011. $1 prepaid. Letters declaring nondiscrimination employment policies from IBM, Bank of America, AT&T, CBS, Eastern Airlines, McDonald's, etc.

"A Legislative Guide to Gay Rights," an 86-page pamphlet addressed to the Oregon State legislature. Portland Town Council, 320 SW Stark, Rm. 303, Portland, Oregon 97204. $4.50.

"Twenty Questions About Homosexuality." Gay Activists Alliance of New York, 1972. Order from GAA, Box 2, Village Station, New York, N.Y. 10014. 75¢; 10 or more copies 25¢ each plus 50¢ postage and handling per order.

"Press Release on New Guidelines for Federal Employment," issued July 3, 1975, by the United States Civil Service Commission. National Gay Task Force, 80 Fifth Ave., New York, N.Y. 10011. 25¢.

The Rights of Gay People, by E. Carrington Boggan et al (an American Civil Liberties Union Handbook). New York: Avon, 1975.

"Gay Rights Protections in U.S. and Canada." List of legislative changes, updated monthly. National Gay Task Force, 80 Fifth Ave., New York, N.Y. 10011. Free for stamped, self-addressed envelope.

"Being a lesbian and working with girl children . . . I felt vulnerable."

After appearing on the *David Susskind Show* as one member of a lesbian couple in 1973, I lost my job at the Girls Club of New York. When I learned I was going to be doing the taping, I told the director of the club, and she panicked and called the president of the board, who said, "We'll have to ask for her resignation." Then I had the choice to say, "No, I will not do the taping," and they could sit back and say, "Whew—it's not that we care you're a lesbian; it's just that in your sensitive job ..." that kind of bullshit. I said, "No way. I'll just go ahead and do the taping and if they ask for my resignation, then I will resign." I had been very active in lesbian political activity, and doing a television show was nothing that I thought would frighten me or be threatening to others. But by the time the show was taped, I knew from the flack coming down from the Board of Directors at my job with the Girls Club that this was not an acceptable thing to do.

If I had stayed in the closet, they would have kept me on. I had been a recreational group leader. I started out working with adolescents, twelve to fourteen. I also ran an evening program of weekend dances for older teen-agers, fifteen through eighteen. Later I worked as the group leader for eight-to-eleven-year-olds, and I saw the community needed some kind of tutorial program for girls. They had all kinds of things for boys, and the girls needed a lot of attention, academically. I started a tutorial program with about five kids and ended up with about twenty. My work performance was excellent. I was getting raises and working more hours, and being given more responsibility. Their request for my resignation was only due to my being out as a lesbian.

By the time the show was aired on television, a month after the taping, I was no longer working at the Girls Club, and women at Lesbian Feminist Liberation were saying to me, "We've got to do something other than writing letters. What are *you* going to do?" and I could not do anything. I was frozen. It was like playing with Tinker Toys and having fun, and finding out that you have built a structure that is going to explode and annihilate everything. That's fear, panicking kind of fear. At the time I could not protest this loss of a job.

What I would like to have done was explain to the seventy-odd kids that I came in contact with on my job every day, "This is what is going to happen; I am going to be involved in a mass protest, it has everything to do with sexuality, sexual identification, and I want you to understand what that means to me. I am still the person who has been with you every day for the last two years." But I could not do it.

If I had not been working with children, I would probably not have gotten that kind of flack, and I would not have had to deal with my own fears. Being a lesbian and working with girl children, not even mixed boys and girls, I felt vulnerable, because I thought the parents might be afraid of the spectre of child molester. If there had been a big protest and all those parents had withdrawn their children from the Girls Club program, then that would have been the end of the club. In fact, the Girls Club of New York is supported by bankers' wives, big business, the whole economic structure. The wife of a president of a bank could have been sitting on the board where lesbians were running rampant through the Girls Clubs, right? Who knows?

Ironically, the one reaction from a parent I ever heard about after I left was one mother who came in and told the director that she had seen me on television and that I had done a great job. She wondered how come I

wasn't there anymore. So the reaction of the Board of Directors was based on groundless fears, but it was my imagination at work, too.

I felt totally supported by the gay community at large, by all the letter writing instigated by Lesbian Feminist Liberation and the Gay Activists Alliance. What I know now, with a great deal of hindsight, is that I wish there had been a counselor then for me, to help me deal with the fears I had internalized, because at the time I was stepping back and withdrawing, saying, "No, I can't handle this." I knew that years from then I would regret the inaction. It's too bad that we all couldn't have been a little further along politically, or I had been somewhere else in my head, so I would say, "This is panic and fear I'm dealing with, not reality. If I protest this loss of job, if we all have a picket line, they're not going to call out the national guard." The fear was a reminder of fifties' mentality, when people got thrown in prisons for being lesbians, that kind of harassment. I was paralyzed. We should have had a court action or mass demonstration and sit-in. I'm sure that once an action is decided upon, then you can delve into the political structure of an organization, find the loopholes, where some kind of pressures might have been effective.

—Dinah

"As a nonimmigrant alien, I am at the mercy of the immigration authorities."

I never had the time nor the expertise to look up the statutes governing the "admissibility" of aliens into the United States. But after my "ordeal" not so long ago, I at least learned that lesbians are "excludable" under the United States immigration laws.

I was to board a regular scheduled flight bound for the States at the end of my visit to Country X when the United States immigration officer at the boarding gate routinely asked for my passport. When he saw that I had an F-1 (Foreign Student) visa, he asked to see my Form I-20 (Certificate of Eligibility). It turned out that the only "proof" I could have that I was a legitimate full-time student in the United States was the I-20 from my school, or the Form I-94 (Record of Arrivals and Departures). My I-94 was surrendered to the airline personnel before I departed for Country X. Without either an I-20 or I-94 in my possession, the suspicious officer asked for my student identification card, which I gladly produced. He then asked for further identification, and in the process of taking my driver's license out of my wallet, I sensed that he had noticed my Gay Activists Alliance membership card next to my driver's license. What followed was a move of questionable legality by a law enforcement agent: He simply snatched my wallet and looked through my collection of ID cards. I came from a country where the law enforcement agents themselves are the law, and at that time I had not heard of the right against "illegal search and seizure" (but even now I doubt whether aliens—as opposed to United States citizens—are protected by the constitutional rights). I therefore did not dare to protest against his "seizure" of my wallet.

After a thorough inspection of my IDs, he said: "There's no way we can readmit you into the States without the I-20 or the I-94." The plane took off without me. But I decided that with my student ID and valid visa, I could at least try to plead my case to the supervising officer at the airport U. S. Immigration Office. I was interviewed by another officer who proceeded to issue me a new I-94 when the first officer (the one at the boarding gate) suddenly reappeared and demanded to have my wallet and "the card." So, it was *indeed* my lesbianism (GAA membership) that was in issue! He asked, gesturing with my GAA card, "Do you believe in this?" I said, "What is 'this'? I believe in civil rights. . . ." He cut me off with a wry grin: "I am not talking about civil rights; I am talking about this." He was raising his voice: "Do you believe in this?!" "Yes," I replied. It wasn't even a matter of courage for me at that point; it was a matter of principle and dignity. I had never intended to be a "test case" or a "martyr," but any lesbian with any sense of pride and decency simply could not afford to betray our cause under those circumstances.

After more questioning—and again, I was not informed of my rights under "custody" and "interrogation"—he finally said, "Now, do you want a hearing?" He concluded that under the immigration laws, "this" would make me "unfit" for entry into the States. And until I requested such a hearing, I would not be able to reenter the States. I later phoned some friends in the United States who then contacted some lawyers from the American Civil Liberties Union. I gave it another try at the airport two days later, only to find that my case was indeed on record there. Moreover, the officer this time gave me the nebulous explanation that "a person who is 'this way' is not admissible [to the States]; he [sic] is excludable." So much for his understanding of the law.

After being "stranded" in Country X for two weeks, I went to Country Y, stayed there for a week or so, reentered the United States through another port of entry and took a train to my final destination in the United States. I was able to reenter the States without further incidents after I detoured to Country Y. I also had the new I-20 that my school sent me then. My experience with the immigration authorities in Country X may be just a typical case of police harassment and intimidation, but I am not taking any chances now, as I do not know whether, and where, they have me on file.

The unexpected "side trip" to Country Y completely wiped me out financially. But I learned a valuable lesson that as a nonimmigrant alien *and* a lesbian in the United States, I am in "double jeopardy." The "exclusion" clauses in the present U. S. immigration laws discriminate against lesbians in much the same manner the laws in many states discriminate against lesbians in employment, housing, and public accommodation. A person's sexual preference should have abso-

lutely no bearing on her job performance or her eligibility to be naturalized as a U. S. citizen. Denial of a job or citizenship on account of sexual orientation to an otherwise well-qualified person is a form of blatant discrimination that, unfortunately, not enough of us (yet) dare to openly criticize.

I intend to seek U. S. citizenship. And until these discriminatory laws are struck from the books, I am a "hopeless" case unless I lock myself in the closet. As a nonimmigrant alien, I am at the mercy of the immigration authorities; I can theoretically be deported or be denied reentry anytime they discover my sexual orientation. It is ironic that the United States Government talks about "human rights" abroad while much of that is still to be desired at home!

—Isabelle

"We got an eviction notice to get out in five days, just before Christmas."

My eviction happened in 1966 and it involved an apartment building on Second Avenue in Manhattan. I was taking the place in my own name because I was afraid to say then that it was with another woman. The owner of the building came to visit me in my office, where I had a respectable job, and he proceeded to tell me he was happy to have me move in because he was getting rid of two gay men. He didn't say it was because they were gay. He said it was because they were "dirty and noisy." I rationalized to myself, "Well, if they're dirty and noisy, nobody would want them," and I wasn't dirty and noisy, so it wasn't a matter of being gay.

I moved in and Celia moved in with me and was very openly loving. This was long before the movement, but she was very proud of her love for me and did not hide it. We held hands in the street and she was openly affectionate, and even wore a ring which she showed everybody. At that time I was very unliberated and I found it very difficult. The situation was clear to anybody that saw us together.

The owner of the building and the superintendent could always see us going by, and before I knew what was happening we were being accused of writing pornography on the walls of the hall—dirty, right? Also that we were making noise. We didn't even know anybody. We had two friends that occasionally came to visit us, but we were alone most of the time. It was ludicrous and ridiculous that we were made to take on the stereotypes of these gay men as noisy and dirty. They evicted us on this basis because I think they were afraid then that we were a menace.

We got an eviction notice to get out in five days, just before Christmas. It was extremely cold, and we packed in a hurry. We didn't know whether we had any recourse because those were totally subjective accusations. When you're told you're evicted, if you feel alone and have no recourse, you're going to get out. Otherwise they are going to break in and take your things.

It was very depressing because Celia had decorated the place for Christmas. She was sentimental and wanted things just right; the holidays were special to her. She cried at night, and it was very difficult. It was snowing the night we left. We had a U-Haul without heat. It was painful physically and painful emotionally. It was just horrible. We moved to this little place in Queens, a one-room place, and it was a depressing Christmas. And it was even worse because it was Celia's last Christmas; she was killed in an automobile accident that April.

—Barbara Love

"Parents can have their minor children sent to a hospital simply by seeing a psychiatrist . . ."

I was recently discharged from a state hospital. I was admitted two years ago by my parents because I was a lesbian. I was hospitalized in ten private places before that and I've had over forty shock treatments. I had Thorazine; every medication that you can imagine is used in a psychiatric institution—I've had it. I've been experimented on with drugs. I've been beaten. I was put in a padded cell; I've been locked up on security—you name it—all because I was a lesbian.

I came out to my parents when I was fourteen, and everything exploded. My mother got very upset and started screaming and yelling about what kind of a pervert I was. Then there was silence in the house. I got very depressed and tried to kill myself, and they put me in a private hospital in Jersey City. When I got out I was fine, but they put me back in maybe three months later. Afterward I went to live with my father; I was not allowed out of the house. If I did go out, I was questioned as to whom I was with; I didn't get phone call messages; I was a prisoner. Every time I rebelled my father put me in the hospital, making up some kind of story about being suicidal. When I was hospitalized a couple of years ago I had shock treatment. They gave me so many treatments I was a vegetable. During my latest stay there they gave me some more. They said it was for depression, and they said I was violent, but I wasn't—I was withdrawn because I lost all my friends when I came out.

We had group therapy three times a week, and one person running the group said to me, "How do you fuck?" and other personal questions, and when the other attendants in the ward found out I was a lesbian, they tied my sheets in knots and wrecked my room. If I said something to the nurses or caught somebody at it, they locked me up in a room, but no one ever did anything to the attendants who had done these things to me. At this particular hospital I was put on a trial drug which had only been out two weeks. I had a very bad reaction—my eyes rolled up in the back of my head and my tongue protruded and I couldn't get it back in. I almost suffocated. It was three hours before they gave me a shot to counteract it and then they locked me up—they call it a

"quiet room," but it's just a mattress on the floor and bars on the windows.

Parents can have their minor children sent to a hospital simply by seeing a psychiatrist who thinks you're crazy just because your parents brought you. They don't ask you anything. They ask your parent or guardian, and if the doctor thinks that you should stay, and 99 percent of the time they do, that's it.

Since I was a lesbian, my door was locked every night and no one else's was. I was always observed. I wasn't allowed to form close friendships because every time I did get close to somebody there'd always be an extra pill in my medication cup. The nurses called me "dyke" and "faggot," and if I said anything they beat me up. I have a cigarette burn on my middle finger and a scar on my upper arm that shows what kind of beatings I got. I was kicked down the stairs one day by one of the attendants.

Once one of them slapped me across the face and broke my glasses and I hit her over the head with a chair because I had just had enough. They're very cruel to somebody who's different. I was there almost two years, and it was almost four months before they even let me go on a day visit home. I used to masturbate occasionally, and they observed me, through an observation window in my door, and I never knew about it until I left. They used to put down on the chart what time, how many times, and report it to the doctor.

The men do pretty well. But the treatment toward women is the worst. There are open showers and we all took a shower together. When we had to go to seclusion they called four or five men from the men's area, stripped us, and hauled us into the back rooms and locked us up. The men take advantage of you when there's no female nurse in sight. There's supposed to be a female nurse around when they do that, but there never is. Mental patients have a bill of rights that we're supposed to have privacy and dignity, and it's never followed. We get to write letters and we get to make phone calls, but I've written to Lesbian Liberation in Cambridge and to some of my friends who visited looking "dykey" and they don't get the mail. I've had relatives send me money, and I never got it. They don't rip it open—they just return it. The pay phones were probably tapped, because one woman called her friend with an escape plan, and the nurses knew about it the next day. It's Gestapo tactics; the people who work there have no feelings. They think lesbians are sick, disgusting people who molest little children, and who should be locked up or killed. One woman staff person told me she believed all homosexuals should be locked up in concentration camps.

The New Jersey law says that if you're in a state hospital you have to go to court within thirty days to find out if you're insane enough to stay. I was there a year before I had a court hearing. Each time I was recommitted the doctors and lawyers made a big fuss over my lesbianism and included one or two fights that I had been in with the attendants and the nurses, and they said I was crazy. Finally my lawyer, a public defender, advised my mother to take me home, and the judge agreed. Now I'm not a minor. My mother would have to go to court and prove that I'm incapable of handling myself if she wanted to recommit me now. I don't think she could do that because I hold a job.

I will be nineteen soon. I've come out. I go to Lesbian Feminist Liberation, but I really have to watch my step because the police could arrest me for anything —if I were caught smoking pot, they could take me in and lock me back up. An institution is harder to get out of than jail, because in jail you have a sentence, and in a hospital you never know when you're going to get out. It's very easy to get into a hospital, but very difficult to get out.

Definitely there are some changes necessary in the system I'm talking about. Minors should be allowed to tell their side of the story to the doctors, because I tried, and the doctor wouldn't even listen. I gather this can be the case with adults too. I think if the sodomy laws in New Jersey would be repealed it would help. Even though the American Psychiatric Association removed homosexuality from the list of mental illnesses, I know that in the hospitals many people were there just because they were gay. They don't put down that you're mentally ill, but that you're "sexually deviant," and they usually slap the word "schizophrenia" or "paranoid" or both terms on you. They don't let anybody out who has that diagnosis, because a certifiable schizophrenic is very dangerous. Even the patients on the grounds believe that. They use labels very loosely, if they don't know what's the matter with you. If you complain to the doctors that the nurses are bothering you, the doctor will write down that you're paranoid. They say it's a figment of your imagination.

—Karen

Lesbian Mothers in Transition

MARY L. STEVENS, J.D.

Some lesbians stay married to their children's father. Some, living apart from men, decide they want children and have them. This is written especially for the lesbian mother who was a mother before she knew she was a lesbian. To her we say: "Congratulations! After how many years you have recognized where your heart's desires really lie." When a woman's sexual orientation is at last clear to her, her personal and emotional life becomes deeper, more satisfying, and more exciting. It is, at last, a source of strength. But the time when a mother "comes out" is often a time of hardship and

danger as well as opportunity and joy. The future looks both rosy and scary.

Hold on tight! For you are about to enter a maze of decisions central to your life and your children's, to embark on a roller coaster of emotions, and to be politicized in every area of your life.

The safest way to deal with all that is and with all that will soon be happening is to keep yourself very clear about all of the separate processes you are going through and deal with them one at a time. You may find that the constellation of new stresses on your mothering role will distort your relationship with your kids; don't forget that it's the stresses, not the kids, that cause this. Find the best solution to each problem for you. You'll still have anger energy, of course. What should you do with it? *Use it—politically!*—in the streets or in the legislature, depending on your style.

LESBIAN MOTHER CASES

There are fewer than fifty reported lesbian mother cases; lesbians are winning more of these but not all of them. The earliest clear-cut victory also teaches an interesting lesson in life. When Nadler went to trial in 1967, the mother lost on the ground that she was "unfit": The judge said he would be unable to find that *any* lesbian mother was a fit mother. But the appellate court held that homosexuality was *not* by itself proof of unfitness and ordered the trial judge to "exercise his discretion" in determining who should have custody. So the trial judge heard evidence from a psychologist that homosexuality would not have an adverse impact on the children and that the mother was a "reasonable, sensible, sensitive, aware person," but that she would be impaired in teaching her children a "traditional concept of morality." Then, in the exercise of his discretion, the trial judge found her unfit and she lost custody.

In thinking about change, probably the best solution available is legislation. One effective approach is a law to exclude any evidence or consideration of sexual orientation. A Washington, D.C., bill was originally worded this way but an amendment accepted during floor debate substituted language with the same effect as the *Nadler* holding.

Sandy Schuster and Maddy Isaacson have been through five years of almost continual litigation to keep their children. Their struggle was widely reported and focused movement attention on the problem; a film was made: "Sandy and Madeline's Family."[1] Both fathers have challenged the mothers' right to custody. On the first round, the fathers lost, but the judge forbade the mothers to live together, a not uncommon stipulation. The mothers appealed this decision and finally won the

[1] "Sandy and Madeleine's Family," by Sherrie Farrell, John Gordon Hill and Peter M. Bruce, 1973. 16 mm film, color, sound, 29 mins. Multi Media Resource Center, 540 Powell, San Francisco, Calif. 94108. Rental $50 (for gay groups, $40), sale $330.

right to be both lesbians and mothers (and live together), but this victory has again been challenged.

The victories so far have been hard-won, even against fathers who were clearly less suitable parents. And those victories have been costly. In June 1976, in Maine's first lesbian mother custody case, Carol Whitehead won custody of her two children. In any other context, we would say that the father lost custody: He once kidnaped the children, he had episodes of violent behavior, he was two thousand dollars delinquent in child support payments, and he did not even produce evidence of his fitness as a parent or his plans for the children.

The court battle cost Carol dearly. She reported that her antique business failed, and she was unable to get a job or to pay her court costs, until appeals through the gay press netted donations for her litigation debts.

Mary Jo Risher's case in Texas[2] is one of the few with an opportunity to set a precedent. To understand why, you need to know a little about how courts work. Custody cases seldom go before a jury. In fact, they are usually not held in civil court at all, but in family or juvenile (domestic relations) court. Male priorities being what they are, domestic relations judges do not enjoy the status of civil court judges, nor are the "due process" protections as thorough when child custody, rather than contract rights, are at stake. Appeals are seldom successful because the standards that judges have to use are very broad, the appellate courts give them "broad discretion" in using those standards, and many court records are sealed rather than published so that it is difficult for judges or attorneys to know what the current "law" really is. Texas, however, does use a jury. Risher's appeal will test the right to sexual orientation based on freedom of association and privacy and the constitutionality of Texas law requiring that parents provide a "religious home."

There are now several good law review articles that discuss all the cases, and you can read them if you're feeling hopeful or depressed and looking for a reason to feel that way. The cases, as you can see, go both ways. They are not yet following a pattern that is consistent enough to give you much help in deciding what to do.

DEALING WITH THE LAW IN YOUR OWN CASE

As a lesbian mother you will also encounter all of the problems that face every woman in transition. You should arm yourself as well as possible for this: Read *Women in Transition*[3] carefully, and *Momma—The*

Sourcebook for Single Mothers.[4] There are handbooks on doing your own divorce; some are written for individual states. Look at these even if you have an attorney so that you will know what is going on. Knowledge is power.

You will have to pay your lawyer; it is no longer routine to have the father pay in most states. Negotiate with your attorney about this on your first visit. S/he should help you decide whether you may qualify for free legal services in your state. You might get some help from a legal defense fund, but don't count on getting enough. Resources are very scarce.

You will need the advice of a good attorney who knows how to handle this type of case and has the interest to do a good job for you. Lesbian mother cases are still too unpredictable and difficult to proceed without an attorney. You must first choose and then evaluate your attorney. *Women in Transition* and *Mom's Apple Pie* (January 1977)[5] tell you how.

PUT EVERYTHING IN WRITING. Keep all notes and letters from your husband in one place that is secure. Buy a date book, label it "Harry the Husband," *and use it* to keep track of every support payment, every visit, even every talk with your husband. Keep track of your own "maternal activities" too: PTA meetings, teacher conferences, medical care, psychological care and testing (if any), even church. These things will be useful many times. In a custody battle you may need to appear invincibly Victorian; then these materials will be as good as money in the bank.

Here are a few handles for you to grab onto as you thread your way through the maze of the Law. I hope they will be helpful, but they are no substitute for the other books. Winning your case as a lesbian mother is going to be a major motion picture! Don't proceed without preparing yourself thoroughly or without legal counsel. (Even if you file "pro se" you will still need some legal assistance.)

Most lesbian mother cases are settled out of court. You are more likely to keep your kids if you can avoid a showdown in court. It is only because of the legal reporting system that we know more about court cases than settled cases. You may have the impression that a court victory will vindicate you or the movement. Don't believe it! The best thing you can do for yourself and for all of us is to *win*. The second best thing you can do, *after you win,* is put some of that money and energy you saved back into the movement to support your sisters who could not keep their cases out of court. Literally, take the money you set aside but didn't have to spend and *send it,* right way, to a local defense fund, to the tax-exempt Lesbian Mothers National Defense Fund, or to another group involved in this struggle.

---

[2]Mary Jo Risher lost custody of her youngest son, Richard, in a Texas courtroom trial in 1975. She and her lover, Ann Foreman, are in the process of appealing this decision. Their story is recorded in *By Her Own Admission: A Lesbian Mother's Fight to Keep Her Son,* by Gifford Guy Gibson with the collaboration of Mary Jo Risher, Doubleday, 1977.

[3]*Women in Transition.* Women in Transition, Inc., New York: Scribner and Sons, 1976.

---

[4]*Momma—The Sourcebook for Single Mothers,* Karol Hope and Nancy Young, New York: New American Library, 1976.

[5]Two other helpful resources are: "The Lawyer Evaluation Tool," available free from The Lesbian Mothers National Defense Fund (see resource list); and "Custody Rights of Lesbian Mothers: Legal Theory and Litigation," *Buffalo Law Review,* 1976.

WHAT YOU THOUGHT MARRIAGE WAS ALL ABOUT VERSUS WHAT IT IS

When you married and had a child you probably thought that child was the joint responsibility of both of you, no matter what happened, until s/he reached majority. Maybe you relied on the difficulty of divorce for some security. It was only fair that you would help your husband out "in the beginning." Now that you're splitting, you think you can settle your own differences and mutually tell "the law" to stay out of it. And I'll bet you think that the courts won't interfere again after the divorce is over.

Unfortunately, this is *not* how it is. The state has an interest in your marriage overriding your own. One mother lost custody to the husband's *parents* over the objections of the kids, the mother, *and* the husband. The state law can change at any time but you will have to abide by the law when your marriage is ending, even if you can prove you counted on the protection it gave when you married and you wouldn't have married otherwise. The children do not have a vested right in each parent's income to the extent of half their support. If the father is a surgeon and the mother with custody a nurse, they will probably live on the mother's income alone after a few years, all of them enjoying a drop from upper-class status to lower-class while the father improves his own standard of living. You may have put him through seven years of medical school and college, but it makes headlines when he has to put you through law school for three years. If your husband was poor you may encounter trouble from the state. One such mother lost her children to foster care because she was "unfit." Marriage is still a fiefdom: Your husband was a vassal of the state with dominion over how and where you and the kids lived in return for which he kept you all off the public dole and conned you into raising "legitimate" citizens. He's not really expected to pay for something he no longer controls.

States vary widely and domestic relations is overwhelmingly a state law matter. Even constitutional challenges have little hope of success because in real life everything depends on what happens at trial. You may live in a "fault" or a no-fault state; that will determine the right to divorce. For allocating property, the state may follow community property or common law rules. But there are some bits of "received wisdom" that are generally applicable.

The legal process of splitting up involves separation, divorce, custody and visitation, and child support. If there is a lot of property, it will be divided at the time of the divorce. If not, you split it between yourselves and tell the judge what you did. Some "child support" may be labeled "alimony" to save taxes for the husband. Real alimony is rarely awarded and almost never paid. Child support is almost never equal to the actual cost of maintaining the child at its former standard of living; it is also seldom paid in full or on time or for the full term. If the two parents are both "fit" to care for the child, custody is determined by the "best interests of the

child" test. The judges have to use these tests. The words mean almost what you think they mean but a lot depends on the judge. If a parent is "unfit," the court can place the children elsewhere, even in a foster home. This has happened to lesbian mothers. At a divorce hearing, the only final determination that can be made is that the marriage is over. Everything else is subject to change: alimony, child support, custody, and visitation can all be reopened for "changed circumstances." Discovery for the first time that the other parent is gay is a "changed circumstance," and so is remarriage by either parent.

Child-naping is becoming more common. It is used to avoid court decisions on custody and unfortunately it is often successful. Most courts place a high value on continuing custody in the parent who has it, no matter how it was obtained, because change is so disruptive to children. Courts say that returning the child to the "right" parents would punish the child rather than the kidnaping parent. But there may be a double standard if a lesbian mother does the kidnaping. For the same reason it is important for you to get custody *and keep it.* Don't let anyone take the kids while you "get your head together" unless (a) you *really* need to and (b) you both put it in writing that it's temporary.

Separation is your best opportunity to gain the upper hand. As soon as you know you're likely to split up, prepare your own separation agreement (with legal help). Do your own thinking about what you want and what you can dicker on. This is the time when you decide whether to keep the kids or not; this is one of the most important decisions you will ever make. If you don't want custody, decide how much visitation you want (don't be vague on this). When you know what your bottom line is, add some to leave room for bargaining, but be firm where it matters to you. Don't get involved in unnecessary fights with your husband. It will do no good to "talk it out" now; you're leaving, remember?

After separation there will be a hearing on the divorce. If you've worked it out with your husband and if the judge is not alarmed by anything, then s/he will probably grant the divorce on the terms you agreed upon.

But you still have to deal carefully with your husband from then on. All the terms (especially custody, visitation, and money) can be reviewed and modified if there are changed circumstances. If he's not living up to his end of the bargain, figure out the best way to get him to do it. If you just blow up at him, you may be paying heavily for your victory.

What can you expect when he "finds out the awful truth"? He may be furious or he may play it cool. But don't be misled by too-easy acceptance; he may be too insecure to lash out at you now, and that might change should he remarry. It seems that a husband is seldom mature enough to see your sexual orientation as the logical explanation for that lack of "marital bliss." To him it may be a personal affront, an irreparable and unforgivable injury to his "masculinity." You want to avoid his coming to view it that way. The best way to do that is with a "low profile." Focus on your "bottom line"; forget the rest.

If all of your attempts have failed to prevent a challenge to your custody or visitation, settle in for a big battle. Gather all the support you can, read everything you can, *reevaluate your strategy in light of the challenge,* and make your plans. Carefully select or evaluate your attorney. You'll have to decide whether to stipulate that you're gay or force the father to prove it. There are advantages and disadvantages to each position. You'll be relying heavily on expert witnesses for psychological evaluations of you and your kids. Find out everything you can about their views and their reliability on the witness stand before they're hired.

You now have a political case. You can't avoid that even if you want to. You have to decide *how* to handle the political side of the case; do you want publicity and public pressure or not? Before, during, or after the trial court level? Do you want a defense fund? How will it be organized? Do you want organizational support? In some cases judges will restrict publicity that mentions the names of the parties; they have more leeway in this than in other sorts of cases because of the harm it might do to the children. If your name is Jane Doe, you might still be able to have a defense fund under another name (the Suzy Jones Defense Fund). This political work should not be your responsibility; you have enough to do. But any defense fund worth its salt listens to what you have to say.

The judge *may* be influenced by your life-style. Be prepared to relate its values to his/her values. If you're involved with a woman while you're dealing with the divorce or a custody challenge, and if you have a choice of living with her or near her, opt for the second. It can make a big difference.

The courts are not your only problem in this transitional period. You'll find you have to deal with the same problems all single mothers face and then some. Here, especially, you *need* the other books mentioned earlier.

A lot of problems center on money. You'll have to do some very shrewd financial management to minimize the disruption of your life-style. You should take the opportunity to decide whether further education or skill training would be advantageous for you. You are likely to become acquainted with the ins and outs of welfare for the first time. Call your local welfare rights organization for help. Being a lesbian does not disqualify you but it would be unwise to bring it up. You should learn a few basics about insurance. If your kids depend on anyone's earned income, buy term insurance on that person if you can.

Job discrimination is the biggest headache. In some localities you have some civil rights protection as a lesbian but it doesn't amount to much in most cities. Nationwide there is protection for most women on the job, but if the objection is that you're a lesbian, you'll have no success using those laws. Even the best remedies in the best circumstances leave a lot to be desired. Contact your local or state Human Rights Commission and the Equal Employment Opportunity Commission if you experience discrimination on either basis. The local NOW chapter can show you the ropes. A few corporations have publicly declared that they don't discriminate against gays.

The next problem will be re-creating your network of support. Lesbian mothers spend a lot of time running between a community that rejects them and a community that rejects their children. There are some lesbian mothers groups now but not enough. Consider starting your own. If you don't mind living schizophrenically you can build a pretty good network by making the most of both worlds. On the mother side, many institutions you didn't need in your cozy straightness may be very helpful to you now: the library, the YWCA, neighbors, youth groups for the kids, school events, and (some!) churches. On the gay side, investigate everything first; find out what supports you and stay with it. You might try gay groups, separatist and mixed feminist groups, the bar scene, dances, gay or all-women's spiritual groups. You'll find as many gays who appreciate your kids and you as a mother as you will who reject motherhood. The difference is that straights just assume kids are here to stay; gays are more apt to have definite opinions and are much less aware of the problems of raising children.

You have some important decisions to make about your life-style. The central decision is whether you want custody, and if not, how you want to arrange visitation. You and your kids can live alone, with another mother, in a group situation, or with your lover. You are in a transitional phase of your life. You could take what looks best for the moment knowing it will change, but you'll have to consider the impact of change on the kids, too. Kids do adjust but they don't adjust without effort on their part and on yours. The question is how much of an improvement a change would be and whether you all have enough "bounce" for it. You'll probably miss married life in some ways, and that might make a nuclear lesbian family awfully attractive to you. Before you do it, consider seriously the extent to which you positively like "marriage" and the extent to which you can be happy alone. If you can't make yourself happy on your own, you owe it to yourself and those around you to learn how. Secondly, if the divorce teaches you anything, it should teach you the value of planning. You and your lover—while you're still happy and loving—should sit down and decide (1) how to arrange things if the time ever comes that you have to split; (2) exactly what your material commitments are, assuming you stay together; (3) how to arrange things when one of you dies. I know you think you'll never part and you'll "take things as they come" and you're both immortal, but experience proves otherwise.

Political action is important. It strengthens you to channel your anger this way and if you've had any breaks at all, you owe it to your less fortunate sisters to help them. Raise money for the LMNDF or local funds, or get to work in feminist and gay political action groups.

Deciding what to tell the children is a very personal matter but it may help you to think about it this way. First of all, be thankful that talking about sex and lesbians has nothing to do with how babies are made! It is as though you have to decide two questions: "How do I tell the kids we're Jewish" and "How do I tell the kids what I want them to know about lovemaking?" In other words, an eight- or nine-year-old may not need to know the difference between copulation and cunnilingus and she already knows that her Mom loves women. What she needs to know is how to handle kids who don't like Jews (or gay people) and what to do if she hears the word "kike" (or "dyke").

About psychology. This will be a very stressful time for you; you are adjusting to a new identity and you may have paid a price you didn't know about for submerging your sexual orientation. The stresses you must learn to handle skillfully. Not everyone knows how to do this: Basically (1) take good care of yourself physically; (2) take life "one day at a time," one problem at a time; (3) trust yourself and trust the future. The adjustment you'll be making eagerly, no doubt. It's the price you paid for acting straight that you'll need a lot of insight to deal with. That may lead you to consider some form of therapy or lesbian mothers group. While you're at it, take a good look at your kids. They'll have a lot to handle, too, and it'll take something out of them.

You have to expect that the enormous stresses you'll be under will cause problems. But if you sort them out, and tackle them one at a time, you'll find you can cope very well. And you'll become a much stronger and happier person in the process. Congratulations again! Not only have you found "Paradise Island," you'll find you're quite a Wonder Woman, too!

RESOURCES

A comprehensive resource list for lesbian mothers has been compiled by Mary K. Blackmon as a part of a master's project and as a supplement to Iris Films' documentary on the issue of custody for lesbian mothers. The film, entitled "In the Best Interests of the Children," is available from Iris Films, 2130½ Elsinore St., Los Angeles, Calif. 90026. Rental $60; 60 min., color, sound.

The "Lesbian Mothers Resource List" is available for $1.00 from Mary K. Blackmon, 2327 Glyndon Avenue, Venice, Calif. 90291. It includes national listings of groups, legal counseling, sources of emotional support, classes, hotlines, research for testimony in court cases, expert witnesses, videotapes, documentation of cases all over the country, and a bibliography.

Chicago Lesbian Mothers Group, 3032 N. Sawyer, Chicago, Illinois 60618. 312 528-3303; 312 772-2655.

Custody Action for Lesbian Mothers (CALM) 1427 Walnut St., Philadelphia, Pa. 19190. 215 563-3055, day; 215 667-7508.

National Gay Task Force, 80 Fifth Avenue, New York, New York 10011. 212 741-1010, weekdays 10 A.M.-6 P.M.

Lesbian Mothers National Defense Fund, 2446 Lorentz Place North, Seatle, Wash. 98109. 216 282-5798.

Los Angeles Lesbian Mothers Group, c/o Women's Center, 237 Hill St., Santa Monica, Calif. 213 980-7905.

"Motherhood, Lesbianism, and Child Custody," by Francie Wyland, Falling Wall Press and Wages Due Lesbians, 1977. $1.20 each, 32 pages; group rates available. For less than 10 copies, order from (Canada) Wages Due Lesbians, Box 38, Station E, Toronto, Canada; or from (USA) Women in Distribution, Box 8858, Washington, D.C. 20003. For bulk orders write to Falling Wall Press, 79 Richmond Rd., Montpelier, Bristol BS65EP, England.

Lesbians in the Military

SASHA GREGORY-LEWIS

Private First Class Barbara Randolf: stationed in an honor platoon at the Army's Security Agency Training School in Fort Devens, Massachusetts. Selected WAC of the month and soldier of the month.

Airman First Class Carmen Baños: assigned to the Air Force intelligence service as a radio monitoring specialist in Spanish and Russian. Top secret security clearance.

Sergeant Miriam Ben Shalom: first female drill sergeant in the 84th Division of the U. S. Army Reserve.

Barbara, Carmen, and Miriam were just three of tens of thousands of American women joining the armed forces each year to take advantage of opportunities that might otherwise be closed to them. The armed forces offer a regular income (starting at $347 a month), room, board, clothing, medical care, specialized training, a chance to travel, thirty days' paid vacation each year, two-for-one matching benefits to help finance college educations, and other veterans benefits that follow an honorable discharge.

Some women join because of these benefits. Others join because of patriotism—the chance to serve their country, outmoded as this notion might seem.

Military recruiters are notorious high-pressure salespeople for their services, and between tangible economic benefits and patriotism, they have a lot to hawk.

What the recruiters never say, however, is that the armed forces don't want lesbians—no matter how well qualified, no matter how physically fit they are, regardless of their test scores, regardless of their patriotism, and regardless of the country's need for highly qualified dedicated people to serve.

As Barbara, Carmen, Miriam, and dozens of other servicewomen have learned, Uncle Sam needs you—unless you're a lesbian, in which case your friendly uncle will turn unlimited resources loose to hunt you out, spy on you, humiliate and harass you, and unceremoniously kick you out (often without any money to get back home, and sometimes without unemployment insurance benefits).

Lesbian life in the American armed forces is an underground life. Lesbian members of the military services don't often talk about their experiences because they fear harassment and discharge. The military itself, meanwhile, tries to deny that lesbians serve in the armed forces with honor and distinction. This is an obvious evasion on their part.

Even a study of military records discloses little about the true number of lesbians serving in the armed forces. About the only revealing statistic the military makes available is the number of gay people it admits to kicking out—an average of a few hundred each year. This number, however, is meaningless because most lesbians who are ousted from the services capitulate to "deals" so that the real reason for their ouster need never be revealed.

Periodically, the gay underground learns of purges at various military bases where lesbians are being searched out and eliminated. Once in a rare while news of these purges, usually released by the military for its own public relations purposes, reaches the media. The best publicized lesbian purge in recent years was at Key West Naval Air Station (Boca Chica, Florida), where at least one dozen women were investigated in both the Navy and the Air Force. The Marine Corps, during the same year, also purged suspected lesbians at a Virginia Marine base. News of the Marine purge, however, barely reached the local press, where it was promptly ignored.

The ever-vigilant armed forces, fearing they might miss someone if the only purged women they could prove had engaged in lesbian sex acts, also seek out and discharge women with so-called homosexual tendencies (a phrase even the military admits it can't define) and people who "habitually associate with 'known homosexuals.' "

From the *Air Force Manual:*

It is the duty of every member of the Air Force to report to his commander any facts concerning overt acts of homosexuality or association or tendency by any member which comes to his attention. . . .

Navy Instruction 1900.9A:

Commanding officers receiving information that a person in the naval service has been involved in a homosexual act or possesses homosexual tendencies shall in-

quire thoroughly into the matter to determine all the facts and circumstances of the case. The development of information should be directed toward the eventual alternative course of action which includes: (1) dismissal of the matter if it is clearly the product of erroneous or false report (2) referral of charges to courtmartial in appropriate cases; and (3) processing for an administrative separation. In order that the proper course of action may be selected, it is essential that great care be exercised in the development of evidence and that all facts and statements be documented and prepared in the proper manner. In documenting a homosexual case, care must be exercised that all persons involved are investigated and reported. Initial information, if deemed appropriate, should be referred to the nearest Naval Investigative Service Office, which will render professional investigative assistance and advice. . . .

When news of lesbian purges does leak out of the military machine, the number of women who are discharged always seems to total about 10 percent of those in the unit.

This would suggest that at least 10 percent of the women in the armed forces today are lesbians. Actually, the percentage is probably much higher. A recent survey undertaken by the lesbian publication *Lesbian Connection* (East Lansing, Michigan) found that of some one thousand women responding, sixty-three had been in the military service, or about 6 percent. This seems to be quite high when it is compared to the percentage of all American women who serve in the armed forces. The *Lesbian Connection* number, indeed, suggests that the population of lesbians in the armed forces is much higher than 10 percent.

Whatever the number of lesbians in the military services, their lives are dominated by fear of exposure—regardless of their work records, and despite commendations, military honors, and promotions.

To date, no court and no agency of government has done anything to secure basic civil liberties protections for lesbians who wish to serve their country in the armed forces.

Members of other minority groups don't think the government has a right to exclude them from military service and, needless to say, neither do lesbians. Lesbians do join the armed forces, and thousands have served honorably in both war and peace.

Most fulfill their terms of service without discovery, but dozens are hounded out each year. Only a handful, like Barbara, Carmen, and Miriam, decide to fight for their right to serve.

STAYING IN SECRETLY

Fortunately for lesbians who, despite the obvious disadvantages, are intent on getting into the armed forces and staying in, the government is not yet omniscient. There are a few simple guidelines which, if followed, will ensure that this aspect of your private life will never come to the attention of the United States government.

The following guidelines are summarized from the *Gay Military Counselor's Manual*, available from the Gay Center for Social Services (see resource list at the end of this article).

The military usually relies on informants and occasional patrols of gay bars to weed out lesbians. Often authorities will only learn of your affectional preference because you told someone about it who either was pressured into giving your name or wants to get even with you for something. The essential self-defense rule, therefore, becomes: Don't tell anyone! The fewer people you tell, the greater your chances are of not being discovered. As the *Counselor's Manual* advises, what a person does say will hang them, what a person doesn't say won't hurt them.

Here are guidelines that will help you avoid being discovered:

1. Don't confide in anyone in your unit (or to military chaplains, doctors, or psychiatrists).

2. Don't have sex with anyone in your unit.

3. Don't give your real name to your friends unless you can really trust them or, if they are lesbians they have more to lose than you have.

4. Don't use military ID in gay bars.

5. Don't receive gay mail—lesbian publications, gay lib literature, or love letters—at your military address. Get an off-base post office box. And don't keep any of this material in a place that is subject to search by military authorities, like your barracks or your car.

6. Don't expose or inform on other lesbians.

7. Don't park cars with military ID stickers near gay bars or community centers.

8. Don't go to gay bars that are frequently patrolled by military police.

9. Don't get picked up in a gay bar for being drunk!

Point number six: "Don't expose or inform on other lesbians" has more than altruism in its favor. Once authorities learn about the existence of one lesbian in a unit, they won't stop until they have ferreted out every other person they suspect might be a lesbian, including the informant!

IF YOU ARE SUSPECTED

If you are suspected, you'll probably know about it long before anyone tells you. Rumors about the investigation will circulate in your unit (as they did in Barbara's and Carmen's units) months before you are actually questioned or confronted. The military likes to build its case *before* it talks to the suspects.

At this point you will have two choices: You may decide to be outfront about your private life because you want to fight for your and other lesbians' rights, or you may decide to try to stay in the service and survive the purge.

In either case you should get help from a qualified military rights counselor (see resource list) immediately —*before* you are questioned or interrogated.

COMING OUT FOR LESBIAN RIGHTS

If you decide, after advice from a military rights counselor, that fighting for the rights of all lesbians is more important than your military career, you should be prepared for a battle that will last from two to three years and may not be successful.

To date, the military has discharged all of the open lesbians who have decided to fight for their right to stay in. The courts have sustained the military's right to do this, with the highest court ruling coming in the case of a male homosexual Air Force sergeant, Leonard Matlovich.

The judge in Matlovich's case, U. S. District Court Judge Gerhard A. Gessell, ruled in Washington, D.C., on July 16, 1976, that the military was completely within its rights to discharge Matlovich despite the fact that he had served almost thirteen years with distinction and had been awarded a Purple Heart.

In a ruling delivered orally (in *Matlovich* v. *Secretary of the Air Force*, Civ. No. 7501750) Judge Gessell condemned the military police, but said that "there is no constitutional right to engage in homosexual activity," and that legal precedents show that the armed forces can "establish standards of acceptable behavior when conduct impinges directly or indirectly on discipline and the fullest advancement of appropriate military objectives."

While Judge Gessell admitted he thought the Air Force decision was a bad one, he ruled that the discharge was not "so irrational that it may be branded arbitrary" or in violation of Matlovich's constitutional right to due process of law.[1]

Other court cases, including those of Barbara Randolf, Deborah Watson (who came out publicly as Randolf's lover), and Mary Boner, who was also stationed at Fort Devens, are still in the works, but prospects for winning any of them are poor.

One of the major benefits of fighting, however, is not so much that you might someday win in court, but that your case will draw public attention to how unfair

---

[1] As this book was being completed, some gay media were investigating leads that President Carter, under his amnesty program, might make provisions for gay people who had been discharged from the armed forces because of their sexual orientation to upgrade their discharges. Interested women should check with a good military counselor on the ways currently available to upgrade military discharges.

and inhumane the military policy on gay people is. This kind of attention may cause enough public pressure that the military will be forced to stop its purges.

The need for public attention, though, has special drawbacks you should think about carefully before deciding to fight openly. As Barbara Randolf explained to a reporter for Boston's *Gay Community News,* "The whole publicity trip was just amazing. I had never known anything like it. I'm much more nervous since then, and have trouble sitting still."

Aside from the emotional cost of fighting, there is also a dollars and cents cost. Few attorneys can or will take on military test cases for free, and legal costs can run into thousands of dollars. This money can be hard to raise, as Sergeant Miriam Ben Shalom is finding as she travels from city to city trying to raise money for her defense.

Women are also at a disadvantage when raising money because the press, in general, pays less attention to lesbians, favoring male homosexuals. Leonard Matlovich, for example, had his picture on the cover of *Time* magazine, while all of the women who have decided to fight the military have been virtually ignored by the mainstream media. This lack of media attention can cripple a fund-raising effort, and the lesbian who decides to fight should take these financial problems into account before making a commitment to a long and costly defense.

TRYING TO STAY IN

The chances of your being able to stay in the service if you decide not to make a public test case out of your lesbianism are much better, especially if you follow certain critical guidelines, the first of these being to never admit that you are a lesbian or that you have "homosexual tendencies" (which you shouldn't admit anyway since no one knows what it means).

Navy Petty Officer Patricia Veldon was caught up in the same purge as Airman Carmen Baños. Veldon, an air traffic controller and good conduct award winner, admitted nothing and was charged with "homosexual tendencies."

Represented by lawyer Carol Scott, Veldon was recommended for discharge by the air station's command, but this decision was overturned on appeal to the Bureau of Naval Personnel. As lawyer Scott explained to *The Advocate,* discharge from the Navy is not actually mandatory, and what cinched the appeal was the fact that the Navy could not "substantiate the nebulous charge of homosexual tendencies."

Six other women were discharged during the same purge that Veldon and Baños were caught up in, but they made no effort to fight. Had they decided to fight, the chances are that they may have stayed in as well.

THE DISCHARGE PROCESS: SURVIVAL TACTICS

The first phase of the discharge process is the investigation, which follows a complaint that someone in your unit or on your base is a lesbian. Neither you nor the person who was the subject of the complaint will be told, at this time, that there is an investigation going on. Generally, however, investigations become common knowledge because of rumors that someone from the service is going around to friends and acquaintances (both in and out of the service) asking a lot of questions.

When you first hear these rumors, you should get help from a qualified military rights counselor immediately. You and your counselor can then create the best strategy for your particular situation. (The information that follows should give you a general idea of what will happen, but don't let it substitute for good advice from a military counselor!)

During the investigation process, military investigators will interrogate other people and, trying to build an airtight case against you, may follow you or other people, search through your mail, or search your room. Some of these activities may be illegal. Check with your counselor.

After the military thinks it has built its case against all of the lesbians in the unit, it will begin to interrogate its suspects. The purpose of these interrogations is to get the victims to confess. Such confessions save the military the cost of fighting their case, public embarrassment, and also look good on the interrogator's records.

Interrogation techniques are often vicious and unscrupulous. You should be prepared for the worst and should know your rights.

The investigator will probably tell you that the military already has a strong case against you, that they know all about your lesbianism, and that they have witnesses ready to testify. These statements may even be true (although they are usually outright lies), but the information isn't enough for them to build their case on. Then, the interrogator will ask you to sign a statement admitting to the charges and perhaps naming others. Women who have made the mistake of signing such statements say that after you sign, the interrogator will probe you about all of the intimate details of your sex life, asking you to name all of your sexual contacts from the first time you knew you were a lesbian.

Such a probe is not only humiliating, it can be dangerous for the people you name as well. The military, we have learned at *The Advocate,* keeps files on all the people you name, even if these people aren't in the military!

If you don't sign, expect to be threatened. The most popular threat seems to be the threat of a court-martial. This threat is almost always a bluff—if they had enough evidence against you to call for a court-martial, they would do it, not threaten you with it. The investigator may also threaten to tell your friends about your lesbianism or may imply that your friends and relatives will find out about it. Telling friends about your affairs is an illegal invasion of your privacy and you can file charges against the investigator who threatens to do this to you.

Perhaps the most popular of the interrogator's bag

of tricks is to offer you a deal. If you disclose the names of other lesbians, the "deal" goes, you will get a general (instead of dishonorable) discharge. This offer is a lie. The interrogator has no legal or military authority to make deals.

When you sign your "confession" (which you should never sign except on the specific advice of your military counselor), you will also be asked to sign a waiver of your rights for a hearing. If you are thinking it might be easier just to sign and get it over with, read the waiver carefully. Every word is true!

Excerpt from waiver of privileges (Navy):

. . . I understand that an undesirable discharge is under other than honorable conditions and may deprive me of virtually all veterans' benefits based upon my current period of active service, and that I may expect to encounter substantial prejudice in civilian life in situations wherein the type of service rendered in any branch of the Armed Forces or the character of the discharge received therefrom may have a bearing.

The investigators may also forget to tell you about your rights, as they are legally required to do. Remember, you do have rights. These rights are: You are entitled to a lawyer, not only at your hearing, but during your interrogation. You are entitled to be informed of the charges against you. You have the right to remain silent. You have the right of confidentiality of your military records. You have a right to have access to and copy your military records and may take another person of your choice with you when you look at your records.

What is the best strategy during an interrogation? Stick to your rights: SAY NOTHING, SIGN NOTHING, TERMINATE THE INVESTIGATION, and SEEK LEGAL COUNSEL.

It's the best advice available.

WHAT'S IN THE FUTURE[2]

Black people weren't always welcome in the military. Neither were women. Gradually, as the American people were aroused about the unfairness of these policies, and as the military discovered the need for more and more qualified people, these policies were eliminated.

Other sections of the government have gradually eliminated their bans on gay people during the last few years. Gay people in civilian jobs can now get security clearance. Gay people can work in most federal civil service jobs. It is only a matter of time before the military eases its policy as well.

RESOURCES

There are three national groups that can provide help to lesbians in the military. It's a good idea to contact all three to find out which one is able to give you the best help:

Central Committee for Conscientious Objectors (CCCO), 2016 Walnut St., Philadelphia, Pa. 19103. 215 568-7971.
National Gay Task Force, 80 Fifth Ave., New York, N.Y. 10011. 212 741-1010.
National Organization for Women, Action Center, 425 13th St., N.W., #101, Washington, D.C. 20004. 202 347-2279.

If you are stationed on the West Coast you should contact the Gay Center for Social Services, 2250 B St., San Diego, Calif. 92102. 714 232-7528.

A relatively new organization, which is active in lobbying for gay rights in the military is the American Armed Forces Association, Box 1863, Pensacola, Fla. 32589.

"Once they were branded 'queers' they were immediately corralled into separate barracks."

I am a lesbian who just finished serving in the United States military for a full term of four years. While I was in active duty I was extremely fearful of being "discovered" as a lesbian. I have seen firsthand the punishment of lesbians in the military, and, not knowing how to go about eradicating it, I want to expose this treatment.

When I was tested for entry, I discovered the first prejudice against homosexuals. The questionnaire asked if I had ever been addicted to or taken marijuana or hard drugs, if I was a frequent user of alcohol, belonged to any anti-American organizations, or was attracted to members of my own sex. The way this questionnaire was laid out made it natural to assume that any of these "offenses" would mean not being selected for the military. I was wrong. I later found out that drug users, alcoholics, kleptomaniacs, and others were allowed entry. These people are sent to a "redirecting" school after they have committed an offense once they are in

---

[2] As this book was being compiled, the United States Navy was due to decide if it would appeal a federal district court decision in San Francisco which ordered that Navy personnel policies should be "free of any policy of mandatory exclusion" of gay people.

The February 1977 ruling by Judge William Schwarzer was made in the case of Mary Saal, a woman who has fought for her right to serve for the last four years.

Saal's four-year battle to stay in the Navy began in March 1973, when the Navy investigated her private life and found that she had had sexual relations with other women. Saal acknowledged her homosexuality in a signed statement and the Navy began discharge proceedings.

Eventually, the Navy, apparently to avoid the expense of fighting the matter in court, gave Saal an honorable discharge at the end of her enlistment contract. Saal, however, wanted to reenlist, but her application was denied because of her sexual orientation. Judge Schwarzer ruled that the Navy's refusal to reenlist the air traffic controller violated her due process rights and would unfairly impose a "stigma" on Saal's future employment opportunities.

the military. However, lesbians, once discovered, were immediately ostracized by the military organization and by their peers. And they were discharged.

While I was attending a school for hospital training, a so-called ring of lesbians was kicked out of the school. These girls had never forced their attentions on anyone, never disrupted classes. They had committed no crime. Once they were branded "queers" they were immediately corralled into separate barracks of substandard quality. This was December in Illinois, and there was no heat or hot water, and often no light. These women were forced to stay in these conditions for several months. They were withdrawn from classes and forced to perform menial tasks around the compound. The others ridiculed or ignored them. Any woman seen in their company was immediately up for suspicion and watched by the faculty. I was one of the "watched." The girls were lonely and bitter. This is how they spent Christmas of 1972.

Not only were they kicked out of school and then out of the military, but also on their discharge papers they were coded as homosexuals and this is forever on their government files. This means that in civilian life any government employer or large corporation may send for their dossier and see that they were discharged for lesbianism. Many employers will take one look and never call the woman in for an interview. On that little coded space often falls the hopes of a good job.

Because I saw this and knew the women before their punishment and after their confinement, I chose to keep my love for women a secret for four years. Instead of cultivating friendships with women, I shunned all women and turned to more accepted activities with men.

Now I want to know why the military got away with this treatment and how to stop them in the future from injuring other women.

–Chana Lopez,
from *Lesbian Connection*

Legal Planning for Loving Partnerships

THE LESBIAN LAW SECTION COLLECTIVE

Note: The Lesbian Law Section was a mini-conference held the first day of the Eighth National Conference on Women and the Law. The following article is a product of the Collective formed at one of its strategy workshops. Members of the Collective who were able to contribute to this project are: Katharine English; Sandra Blair, Esq.; Nancy Gertner, Esq.; and Prof. Rhonda Rivera, Esq. (editor). The National Coordinator of the Section was Mary L. Stevens. Some of the Collective are non-gay feminist law women.–Ed.

The "lesbian relationship"–two women living together in a committed relationship–has no social model, no supporting legal or economic structures. Often there is no marriage ceremony to symbolize community support and acceptance. There are no legal procedures such as joint tax returns to aid everyday financial management problems; there is no "divorce" to guide the couple who fall "out of love" in dividing joint property. None of the structures are there to buttress the lesbian relationship that marriage with all its ramifications, good and bad, provides for the heterosexual couple.

The "lesbian relationship" needs protection and support. First it needs protection from external sources. Unfortunately, the main external source from which lesbians need to be protected is their own families, parents, siblings, etc. Parents step in and interfere at various times, and since the lesbian partner usually has no formal, legal relationship to her lover-partner, she is often shunted aside. For example, when one lesbian dies the family often steps in and takes custody of the deceased lesbian's natural child. Her lover is, in all likelihood, the psychological parent of the child, but the lover has no legal rights. When one of the lesbian partners becomes ill and hospitalized, her partner often finds herself kept out of the hospital room while Mom and Dad are in–not only in, but making decisions. When one lesbian partner dies, her grieving lover sometimes finds their property accumulated together being claimed by her deceased lover's parents. And so it goes–families have formal legal rights that cut off the ethical and moral but unrecognized rights of the lesbian partner.

Another source of external interference and discrimination is government. For example, if one lesbian partner dies without a will, state law will dictate how her property is distributed. The living partner does not have the automatic claim on part of the assets that a heterosexual spouse has. Also, the government will tax lesbian partners not as a family unit but at the higher single-person rates.

A second level of protection and support is needed for the ongoing relationship. How should lesbian partners manage their financial affairs? Should they have joint bank accounts? Should they buy a house together? If yes, how should they title it? Can they get a second-car discount on auto insurance? Trivial questions? Maybe yes, but custom and tradition, financial and legal institutions, automatically respond in these situations for the married couple. The routineness of such matters for the heterosexual couple supports the relationship.

The fact that each issue presents obstacles for the lesbian couple is a source of daily irritation for even the most loving partners.

Lastly, the lesbian relationship needs protection and support when it is going to end. Some lesbians need to "uncouple" and they need a reasonable and fair method to disentangle their affairs. Divorce, while certainly lacking in much, does provide a formal, structured method of "uncoupling." Lesbians need a structure of uncoupling that is already in place when the partners break up. Lesbians are in the enviable position of custom-designing a method that really meets their felt needs. This is a freedom that is not so available for nongay couples.

For lesbians, seeking to live with and love one another, the paths are open. We are not bound by the customs and traditions of heterosexuals. Some will undoubtedly make great use of the current system, some will successfully adapt it to serve the real needs of loving lesbian partners, while others may strike out in new directions.

From our freedom and our identity is born the power to change.

WHAT ARE THE ALTERNATIVES AVAILABLE?

There are two situations to consider—a planned lesbian relationship and a crisis lesbian relationship. But good planning for the future economic and legal relationship and its potential pitfalls is not common. In the first blush of love, disability, death, or dissolution seem far away. Few wish to focus on the everyday problems of who pays the vet bill and who is responsible for the new lawn mower. Most people plan (and plot) only after catastrophe has already struck. Let's see how lesbians can use the current system to meet their needs, first when they have foresight, and secondly, when problems have already arisen.

Creating Legal and Economic Structures

1. A contract for the loving partnership. The best time to plan for the unexpected (death, dissolution, disability) is when no one has an interest in the outcome. When both are loving and want to be fair.

We all operate within our relationships on a contract. It is rarely written, but definitely implicit, with unspoken (or well-hashed-out) terms being things like: You will share responsibility for the children; we will share our income; you will not sleep with anyone else unless you tell me beforehand; I need time alone and space to myself so I don't feel smothered; since you don't have a car, we will share mine; I will learn to play bridge if you'll quit smoking; and so on.

To make a contract legally binding lesbian partners must make two contracts. One should deal only with financial and property arrangements and be very businesslike to ensure its enforceability. This problem comes up because courts avoid enforcing contracts where part of the value given is as hard to measure as "affection." The safest way is to make it look like a business partnership. The second contract can deal with housekeeping arrangements, fidelity, child care, etc. It is a personal document.

Lesbian partners should give great thought to how they want to enforce the contract and settle disputes that arise under it. Many lawyers who aid lesbians suggest providing for arbitration rather than using the courts. Each party can agree to abide by the decision of an arbiter (or arbitration panel). The agreement to abide by arbitration is binding, so that a dissatisfied partner is not free to try for a better deal by filing a lawsuit.

Lesbians could use existing arbitration groups such as the American Arbitration Association (unless they seem too male) or they can provide that each lesbian partner pick one arbiter each and those two in turn pick a third person. A new alternative is to involve the lesbian community as a whole in working out separate arbitration institutions.

Contracts can always be modified or revoked. It is wise to have contracts renegotiated and renewed in whole or in part on a regular basis. This avoids applying the 1959 expectations of youth to the 1979 relationship between two older women.

2. The first question two lesbians should deal with is sharing. In the first blush of love, sharing everything seems the ideal! Later it may not seem so great. Ask yourselves: Why do we want to share everything? Are we seeking some proof of each other's love? Are we looking for a formal symbol of commitment? Think it through. Most feminist lawyers today counsel both gay and nongay women against financial comingling.

What if sharing is important to you? The legally appropriate method is to use the "joint tenancy" form of ownership. For example, one can have joint savings and checking accounts and own a home as joint tenants with the right of survivorship. Joint tenancy provides relatively strong protection against potential governmental intrusion and interfering families, although joint tenancies can sometimes be attacked by families who claim that one lesbian partner used "undue" influence on the other, or committed fraud. But jointly owned property makes breaking up a mess and, in the case of joint bank accounts, provides no protection against the partner who cleans out the account and skips.

3. A third method of structuring the legal and economic aspects of a lesbian relationship provides for the other partner at death (protection against families and government), provides a rational method for potential dissolution (protection against each other), and gives a working structure for daily living (support for the lesbian relationship).

Step 1. *Pre-coming together inventory.* Make a list of all the possessions each partner brings into the relationship. Each partner should sign the other's list acknowledging that the property does not belong to her.

Have the signatures witnessed and notarized. Store the document in a safe place.

Step 2. *Establish a joint "household" checking account.* Agree on how much per month each partner will contribute and exactly for what bills it will be used.

Maintain separate individual checking and savings accounts for personal funds.

Step 3. *Post-coming together inventory.* Keep a running inventory of items purchased jointly. Indicate the cost of the item and each partner's contribution. Each partner should initial each item on the list as it is added. (This list would be the basis for a division if dissolution should occur.)

Step 4. *Each partner should make a will.* Remember to mention your family in the will (e.g., "I leave nothing to my dear loving mother because she is well provided for by my father's insurance. I leave $1.00 to my sister Agnes"). That way the family can't claim you forgot them! Follow strict rules in signing the will. Choose stable witnesses with a permanent address. Name a neutral person you can trust as the executrix (your lawyer?). Remember wills can be revoked (torn up) and changed (by codicil). Again do it very formally so the family can't claim undue influence, coercion, or fraud. Drawing a new will with identical terms annually gives further protection.

Step 5. *Get life insurance.* Take out term insurance in a small amount ($5,000) with the lesbian partner as beneficiary. It can be used for burial expenses, meeting bills while finances are unsettled, and paying a lawyer to fight the interfering family or the intrusive government.

Step 6. *Power of attorney.* Each lesbian partner can give a power of attorney to the other partner so that should one of them be disabled or hospitalized the other can make decisions and manage affairs. Remember powers of attorney can be limited in scope and time, and may be revoked.

Crisis Action for the Lesbian Relationship

All of the above procedures are great with hindsight but are not helpful when one has ignored these issues and then is faced with a breakup in the relationship or the partner's death. What then?

Unfortunately at this point it is almost always necessary to obtain a lawyer. Find a good feminist attorney. They used to be as rare as hen's teeth, but not anymore! Check with local women's organizations, the National Lawyers Guild, the ACLU, Lesbians in Law, women studies at your closest university, the local gay organization, ask your sisters in the community—one will be available.

Where two persons have lived together, comingled their income and property, and have given no thought to future problems, splitting up can be a mess. If reasonableness could be used they could disentangle themselves by themselves. Unfortunately, the pain of a broken relationship often robs people of their instincts of fairness. So a third party or representatives are needed to arrive at a fair and mutually satisfactory arrangement. As

in divorce, no one will win, and no one will come out ahead.

The courts can apply certain legal theories with regard to property to divide it between opposing parties. For example, if the lesbian partners have purchased a home jointly, one can bring an action for "partition" against the other. Where one lesbian partner has contributed funds to the business of the other, it is possible to have the courts impose a "constructive trust."

These and other legal solutions are possible, but there are two main problems in utilizing them. First is the question of whether the partners want to go to court at all. In order to "explain" the situation, one's personal, private life becomes an open book. If the lesbian has been in the closet or is in a state where homosexual behavior is illegal, bringing a public action risks exposure, loss of job, family estrangement and harassment. Secondly, the court may refuse the case because of the sexual element involved claiming that it is against public policy to provide a remedy in this situation. Good lawyering *may* keep the sexual element out of the court proceedings but there is no guarantee.

This is not to say that lesbians shouldn't go to lawyers and consider lawsuits. But the ultimate decision as to whether to press for trial or settle for less than one thinks is fair may be colored by external factors.

It is highly likely that two feminist lawyers negotiating for their clients can reach some mutually agreeable settlement solution and avoid trial.

CREATING A NEW SYSTEM

The above outlined approaches all utilize, to a greater or lesser degree, the current system by adapting it to suit lesbian needs. There is a strong moral and political argument on the side of ignoring that system altogether and trying to create a system utilizing the lesbian community as a source and foundation.

Domestic relations law today is without a doubt basically a product of a white, male, heterosexual, capitalistic ethic. Most lesbians find that ethic repugnant in many ways. A separate and more functional system certainly would be appealing.

Some of us believe that we mustn't throw out the tool just because it has been misused against us. The concept of presenting explanations, evidence, and proof to a group of persons who are our peers as workers and community dwellers, and of asking those persons to objectively determine a solution that seems fair, is a good concept. It is better than battle. It is better than years of unresolved bitterness. Used in its best sense, it can create a feeling of caring, love, interest, and compassion. The court system in this country has not done that for lesbians, but as members of a lesbian community, we have the responsibility to do it for ourselves: to create or rediscover our own theory of justice, and to conceive a system that reflects it.

To create our own laws and our own "courts" is a

monumental vision, as full of powerful excitement and hidden disasters as any vision. All lesbians do not share the same politics, life-styles, or life goals simply because we are lesbians. We are diverse, and that diversity must be recognized and accounted for. The issues are terribly important. They require thought and reflection, experimentation and sharing.

1. *Deciding to evolve an alternative legal structure.* The first step in any solution is to come to agreement among ourselves in our community that we *do* want to create new ways to protect ourselves in relationships.

2. *Loving partners write their own partnership agreements.* The second step in a solution might be to encourage the *writing* of contracts between lesbian couples. The important aspect of this solution step is writing out the contract. It should and must include all property aspects of our relationships. A separate contract should include all intimate expectations and agreements.

3. *The Lesbian Fairbody.* If and when expectations are not fulfilled or the relationship dissolves, someone in the community who serves as our "court" will need a written statement of expectations to read and react to.

Women in our community whom we like and trust, who serve as an assembly to determine justice for us, are the Lesbian Fairbody. They could be called a lesbian court, a community assembly, facilitators, an arbitration board—whatever name seems right to the community.

Who are members of the Lesbian Fairbody? In the event a conflict arises that is not resolvable by the lovers, each contract can determine for itself the way the members of the Fairbody are chosen. The community could elect or self-select or by some method determine a standing Fairbody to which everyone agrees. Or each lover might have the option of picking three persons, and between the two lovers all but two would be eliminated. Or out-of-community lesbians, perhaps unknown to "in-community" lesbians, may have agreed to be "on call" for weekly meetings of the Fairbody, before which all women in need appear. It may be that certain women are named within the contract as Fairbody women, and that they can be changed when the contract is renewed, or we may choose to ourselves become part of the Fairbody making any decision a collective consensus.

The formulation of the Fairbody is a personal and community issue of great importance. Many factors must be considered. Does the community have a lot of sexual openness: Could Diana's Fairbody woman be sleeping with Diana's lover next week? Is the community particularly grapevine inclined; that is, how can privacy be ensured? How can the Fairbody be provided for closet couples? Should the Fairbody be paid?

To begin, we need models. All of us who are in relationships need to sit down and work out contracts that we can share with each other in the community to get ideas on how it's done, what to include, how we feel comfortable selecting our own Fairbody.

We need a herstory of the self-help law movement. A central contact in our own communities who can share with other contacts in other communities for ideas, models of contracts, models of Fairbodies, models of practice.

In this way we legitimate ourselves in a way the law never has. In this way we elevate our own capabilities to determine justice for ourselves above those of a male, patriarchal court system.

9.
The Spectrum of Lesbian Experience

and working-class sisters. As we look more and more into ourselves and our history, many of us have become persuaded that the "isms" of racism, classism, and age-ism are traceable to the ultimate, underlying "ism" of them all—sexism, created by the patriarchy, of which we are all the victims. This basic oppression is our common bond and the source of our common revolutionary strength.

The following statements will, hopefully, add to our enlightenment on these issues and encourage commitment on all parts to remedy the inequities, transcend the barriers, and seek our common cause.

In the first section on "Race," statements appear from representatives of the black, Hispanic, Asian-American, and American Indian (Native American) communities. These are followed by a series of personal testimonies on the subjects of class, age, and religion.

These women offer important insights and a challenge we must meet if we are ever to put into practice the lesbian-feminist philosophy that unites us. When we fully understand where each of us is coming from, and we *care enough,* we will be in a better position to accomplish the revolutionary work that addresses the survival and quality of life for us all.—Ed.

Introduction

Lesbians are members of every race, class, religion, and age group. The differences in our background affect our experiences as lesbians in important areas: our attitude toward homosexuality, our families' reactions to our coming out, the level of repression we feel in acting on our love for women, our degree of inclination toward role-playing, and so on.

These subcultural identities also have much to do with our attitudes toward the white middle-class-dominated lesbian-feminist movement. Racial minorities and working-class whites, in particular, have put relatively little of their energy into lesbian feminism because (1) they are too busy just trying to survive economically and (2) they encounter racist and classist attitudes in the movement community. The sisterhood they hope to find is often more available to the "privileged" among us—to whites and the more prosperous.

Like everyone else, we lesbians do not escape our conditioning. We are steeped in cultural biases. Nonetheless, by virtue of being lesbians we have already rejected one basic "commandment" of male culture ("Thou shalt love men") and we are often inclined to question others. Moreover, *we care about women in a way that no one else does.* Slowly, and painfully, we have begun to explore and overcome the barriers that divide us—often after being challenged by Third World

I've Been Standing on This Street Corner a Hell of a Long Time!*

AUDRE LORDE

All too often for so many years, silence has been a burden laid upon us by our mothers: creating a lack with which we all struggled, and of which some of us sometimes died, screaming: Why? I do not wish to share in laying that same burden upon my younger black sisters who search for some word intimating, Yes, indeed, we did exist, and Yes, we did suffer before them, and Yes,

*Excerpted from *I've Been Standing on This Street Corner a Hell of a Long Time!* Copyright 1977 by Audre Lorde.

some of us did indeed survive. The hows of our survival are needed now, for them to either copy or avoid. I hear young black women who love themselves and other women seeking to underline their own strength with some word that we have always been before, and all too often they find only white women, some well intentioned, saying, "Look at us and wait, maybe someday someone will write pieces of your history, too."

You see, I remember how being young and black and gay and lonely felt. A lot of it was fine and knowing I had the truth and the light and the key, but a lot of it was purely hell and lonely. There were no mothers, no sisters, no role models, as we call them these days. In other words, we had to do it alone, cold turkey, like our sisters and amazons, the riders on the loneliest outposts of the kingdom of Dahomey. We, young and black and fine and gay, sweated out our first heartbreaks alone, with no school or office chums to share that confidence over lunch hour that help young women a little over the rough places. Just as there were no rings to make tangible the reason for our happy secret smiles, there were no names or reasons given or shared for the tears that messed up the lab reports or the library bills.

We were good listeners, and never asked for double dates, but didn't we know the rules? Why did we always seem to think friendships between women were important enough to care about? Always we moved in a necessary remoteness that made "What did you do this weekend?" seem like an impertinent question. We discovered and explored our woman-focus alone, sometimes in secret, sometimes in defiance, sometimes in little pockets that almost touched ("Why are those little black girls always either whispering together or fighting?") but always alone, against a greater aloneness. We did it cold turkey, and although it resulted in some pretty imaginative, creative, tough, and powerful women when we survived, too many of us did not survive at all.

During the fifties in the Village, I didn't know the three or four other black women who were visibly gay at all well. We acknowledged each other's presence by avoiding each other's eyes, and since all too often we found ourselves sleeping with the same white women, we recognized ourselves as exotic sister outsiders who might gain little from banding together. It was as if we thought our strength might lie in our fewness, our rarity. That is the way it was downtown, and uptown, meaning the land of black people, seemed very far away, and hostile territory. Or so it seemed.

There were not enough of us. But we surely tried. We were brave and true, but I remember thinking I was the only black lesbian living in the village until I met Felicia. Felicia, with the face of a spoiled nun, skinny and sharp brown, sat on my sofa on Seventh Street, with her enormous fantastic eyelashes that curled back up on themselves twice. She was bringing me a pair of Siamese cats that had terrorized her junkie friends who were straight and lived on a houseboat with the two cats until they brought their new baby home from the hospital and both cats went bananas back and forth all over the

boat, jumping over everything including the box that the baby screamed in, because Siamese cats are very jealous. So instead of drowning the cats they gave them to Felicia whom I happened to meet for the first time having a beer at the Bagatelle that night, and when Marion who introduced us said I liked cats, Flee insisted on bringing them over to my house right there and then. So she sat on my sofa seven stories up on Seventh Street with her box of cats and her curly eyelashes and I thought to myself, "If she must wear false eyelashes you'd think she'd make them less obviously false."

In those days we didn't think "lesbian," we thought "gay girl," and soon Felicia didn't count because we decided that we were really sisters, which was much more than friends or buddies, particularly when we discovered while reminiscing about the bad old days that we had gone to the same Catholic school for six months in the first grade.

Felicia and I came to love each other very much, even though our physical relationship was confined to cuddling. We were both part of the "freaky" bunch of lesbians who weren't into role-playing, and who the butch and femmes, black and white, disparaged with the term AC/DC. Flee loved to snuggle in bed, but then she would always hurt my feelings by saying I had shaggy breasts. Besides, Flee and I were always finding ourselves in bed together with other people, usually white women.

Then I thought we were the only *two* gay black women in the world, or at least in the Village, which at the time was a state of mind extending all the way from river to river below Fourteenth Street, even in pockets throughout the area still known at that time as the Lower East Side.

I had heard tales from Flee and others about the proper black ladies who came downtown on Friday night after the last show at Smalls Paradise to find a "gay girl" to go muff diving with, and bring her back up to Convent Avenue to sleep over while their husbands went hunting, fishing, golfing, or to an Alpha's weekend. But I only met one once, and her pressed hair and all too eagerly interested husband who had accompanied her this particular night to the Bagatelle, where I met her over a daiquiri and a pressed knee, turned me off completely. And this was pretty hard to do in those days because it always seemed forever between warm beds in the cold mornings seven flights up on Seventh Street.

Downtown in the gay bars I was a closet student and an invisible black, while uptown at Hunter College I was a closet dyke and a general intruder. Maybe four people altogether knew I wrote poetry, and I usually made it pretty easy for them to forget.

It was not that I didn't have friends, and good ones. There was a loose group of young lesbians, white except for Flee and me, who hung out together, apart from whatever piece of the straight world we each had a separate place in. We not only believed in the reality of sisterhood, that word that was to be so abused two decades later, but we also tried to put it into practice, with varying results. We all cared for and about each other, sometimes with more or less understanding, regardless of who was entangled with whom at any given time, and there was always a place to sleep and something to eat and a listening ear for anyone who wandered into the crew. There was always somebody calling on the telephone, to interrupt the fantasies of suicide.

However imperfectly, we all tried to build a community of sorts where we could, at the very least, survive within a world we correctly perceived to be hostile to us; and we talked endlessly about how best to create that mutual support that twenty years later was being discussed in the women's movement as a brand-new concept. Lesbians were probably the only black and white women in New York City in the fifties who were making any attempt to communicate with each other on a genuine feeling level, and we learned lessons from each other, the values of which are not lessened by what we did not learn.

But when Flee and I talked about racism we usually made sure our white friends weren't around, because who wanted to hurt anybody's feelings? And for the most part, our white friends, when they admitted to thinking about race, were very busy pretending that there was absolutely no difference at all.

But only on the full moon or every other Wednesday was I ever convinced that I really wanted it different. A bunch of us, maybe Noel and Joan and I, would all be standing around having a beer at the Bagatelle or deciding whether to inch onto the postage stamp dance floor for a slow intimate fish, garrison belt to pubis and rump to rump, and did we really want to get that excited after a long weekend with work tomorrow, when I'd say sorry but I was tired and would have to leave now, when in reality what I meant was I'd have an overdue paper for English the next day and needed to work on it all that night.

That didn't happen too often because I didn't go to the Bag very much. It was the most popular gay girls' bar in the Village, but I hated beer and was scared to dance, and besides the bouncer was always asking me for my ID to prove I was twenty-one, even though I was older than the other women with me. But of course you could never tell with collud people. And we would all rather die than have to discuss the fact that it was because I was black, since, of course, gay people weren't racists. After all, didn't they know what it was like to be oppressed?

Sometimes we'd pass on Eighth Street, the invisible but visible sisters, or in the Bag or at Laurel's, and our glances might cross, but we never looked into each other's eyes. We acknowledged our kinship by passing in silence, looking the other way. Now I write poems to some of the dark sisters whom I passed by in those days, yearning for and afraid of some connection with. But often when I send them the poems I write now, I get only silence. And I mourn the time we could have grown up together and shared the strength of each other that young black women needed so badly, and are so programmed to avoid.

Today, the younger sisters who are gay seem to be wiser with each other. They take their ease where they can find it together or separately, and compare notes all the time. They don't seem quite so fragmented from their dreams as we were, nor from their fantasies of power, possession, and the differences between all of these and love, or simple desire. The differences seem clearer now, and therefore less important.

We were always on the lookout, Flee and I, for that telltale flick of the eye, that certain otherwise prohibited openness of expression, that definiteness of voice which would tell us, I think she's gay. After all, doesn't it take one to know one.

I am the darkest member of my family and I've worn my hair naturally since I finished high school. When I moved to East Seventh Street, every morning that I had the fifteen cents I would stop into the Second Avenue griddle on the corner of St. Marks Place on my way to the subway and school and buy an English muffin and coffee. It was a tiny little counter place run by an old Jewish man named Sol with a tough right arm who'd been a seaman (among other things) and Jimmy, who was Puerto Rican and washed dishes and who used to remind Sol to save me the hard Englishes on Monday. For over eight years, we shot a lot of bull over that counter.

So on the last day before I moved away from the Lower East Side to Mount Vernon after I finished college, I went in for my last muffin and coffee and to say good-bye to Sol and Jimmy in some unemotional and acceptable-to-me way, and I told them both I'd miss them and the old neighborhood, and they said they were sorry and why did I have to go and I told them I'd gotten a fellowship for Negro students, and Sol said: "Oh? I didn't know you was collud."

I went around telling that story for a while, but a lot of my friends couldn't really see why I thought it was funny, in a gallows-humor way. But this is about how difficult it is at times for people to see who or what they are looking at, particularly when they don't want to. Or maybe it does take one to know one.

When I was twenty I went to Mexico, which was still a place of light, and color, and beauty, and for the first time in my life I walked down the streets of a city where most of the people were brown-skinned, everywhere I went. It was like coming into sunlight, and I began to talk to strangers and finish my sentences, even in a language that was new to me. I felt myself opening like a blossom or a clenched fist, even before I fell in love with a residentista newspaperwoman who drank too much. I watched McCarthy's censure and Oppenheimer's trial from across the border, and I read about the Supreme Court decision on desegregation in Spanish. I wept because I wasn't home for the start of it all, not even knowing what *it* was or might be. I think it was called hope.

Upon my return I found that Felicia had vanished into the bosom of Detroit. I came back to New York in the middle of winter, with days that were too short and not enough sun. I was twenty-two, and there was a certain kind of freedom I felt in the pain of thinking I would always be alone. There were no jobs and little money, and I felt myself growing hard and angry sometimes in that desperate winter, blowing through the midnight streets like an angry wind, last year's snow in my tears. Sometimes even now I weep for that black girl whose hands were warmed by nothing so much as her own hidden furies. But still, there was a certain freedom in knowing myself as alien, alone. That way, even when I functioned as a part of a group, I could always consciously disclaim any connections with any piece of the group identity that I happened not to like, or with which I had psychic or emotional or spiritual difficulty. Because obviously I wasn't really a part of the group anyway—or at least I felt that I always stood in a different relationship to the corporate entity of the group, as well as to each individual member within the group; different from the relationship other members had with the total as well as with each other. I was black. That fact was irrevocable: armor, mantle, and wall. Often, when I had the bad taste to bring that fact up in a conversation with other gay girls who were not black, I would get the feeling that I had in some way breached some sacred bond of gayness, a bond that I always knew was not sufficient for me.

This was not to deny the closeness of our group. It is only to say that I was acutely conscious—from Gay Head Beach at Riis Park in the summer, where I was the only one who could sun for hours and not worry about burning, to the Bag on Friday nights, where I would still have to produce my ID every time or be turned away—that my relationship as a black woman to the parts of our day-to-day life that we all shared was different from the others, and would be, gay or straight. The question of acceptance had a different weight for me.

In a paradoxical sense, once I accepted my position as one different from the larger society as well as from any single subsociety—or subculture—black or gay, I felt I didn't have to try as hard. To be accepted. To look fem. To be straight. To look straight. To be proper. To look nice. To be hired. To be loved. To be approved. What I didn't realize or couldn't admit then was how much harder I had to try merely to stay alive, or rather to stay human. Yet how much stronger a person I became in that trying.

But in this plastic, antihuman society in which we live, there's never been too many people buying fat black girls born almost blind and ambidextrous, gay or straight. Unattractive, too, or so the ads in *Ebony* and *Jet* seemed to tell me. Yet I read them anyway, in the bathroom, on the newsstand, at my sister's house, whenever I got a chance. It was a furtive reading, but it was an affirmation of some part of me, however frustrating.

So if nobody's going to dig you too tough anyway, it really doesn't matter so much what you dare to explore. I had already begun to learn that when I left my parents' house at seventeen. Particularly when your black sisters on the job think you're crazy and collect money between themselves to buy you a hot comb and straightening iron on their lunch hour and stick it anonymously into your locker in the staff room, so that later when you come down for a coffee break and open your locker the damn things fall out on the floor with a clatter and all 95 percent of your library co-workers who are very very white want to know from what it's all about. Again when your black brother calls you a ball-buster and tricks you up into his apartment and tries to do it to you against the kitchen cabinets just, as he says, to take you down a peg or two, when all the time you'd only gone up there to begin with fully intending to have a little in the first place (because my lover Marion had gone back home indefinitely and all the other girls I knew who were possibilities were too damn complicating and involved for one-night stands, and I was plain and simply just as horny as hell). I finally got out of being raped although not mauled by leaving behind a ring and a batch of lies and it was the first time in my life since I'd left my parents' house that I was in a physical situation that I couldn't handle physically—in other words, the bastard was stronger than I was. It was an instantaneous consciousness-raiser.

As I say, when the sisters think you're crazy and embarrassing; and the brothers want to break you open to see what makes you work inside; and the white girls look at you like some exotic morsel that has just crawled out of the walls onto their plate (and don't they love to rub their straight skirts up against the edge of your desk in the college literary magazine office after class); and the white boys all talk either money or revolution but can never quite get it up; then it doesn't really matter too much that you have had an Afro long before the word even existed.

"I cannot ignore my own oppression as a Puerto Rican."

In May 1971 I attended my first Gay Activists Alliance meeting. Although there were only a few women among the men, I experienced for the first time a sense of real pride and excitement about my lesbian identity. I was no longer alone. Here were people who had made the first step in coming out of the closet and identifying themselves to the world. They would be ashamed no longer. It was a momentous occasion in gay history and in my life.

Working with GAA and then with Lesbian-Feminist Liberation, the women's organization that split with GAA in order to concentrate on lesbian-feminist issues, my strength in my own lesbian identity grew. I will always be grateful to those organizations for what they gave me—helping me to break out of my role-identified relationships, giving me the chance to learn to articulate my feelings about my lesbianism effectively to such people as my family, City Council members, and other politicians, and helping to enlarge my scope of friends to include other women who were exploring their feelings in many of the same ways I was. I didn't have to remain in the closet most of the time any longer. The community provided a network of communications so that I became more aware of the activities and places that were available to lesbians. However, as time passed, I became increasingly aware of my differences with the women with whom I was working. The lesbian-feminist movement was white. I was alone in my struggle for a complete identity—that of a Puerto Rican lesbian.

Although I have gotten a lot out of the lesbian-feminist movement and wish that more of my Puerto Rican sisters would participate, I understand why they remain apart. Quite simply the lesbian-feminist movement will not help Puerto Rican women get better jobs, better education, and positions of power in the community. When quotas are set for minorities it is the Puerto Rican male and the white women who fill their respective quotas. The problems of the Puerto Rican community are manyfold and often seem to be contradictory to the goals of the lesbian-feminist community. We are fighting for survival—jobs, housing, education, and most importantly struggling for a sense of dignity in a country dominated by whites. Our problems are immediate, not long-range. We as women in that community in order to be effective must accept these priorities as our own. We must put aside our lesbian-feminist perspectives and work within the framework that exists.

In the Puerto Rican community, the patriarchal family unit is inviolate. Anyone who threatens the maintenance of the family unit is not respected, and even worse, is ostracized from the community. Most lesbians who have achieved higher eduation and power within the community and are dedicated to leading the community in obtaining its goals realize that they must remain in the closet in order to be effective. They cannot jeopardize their position of trust by alienating the very people with whom they want to effect change. As one lesbian said to me, "My community comes first, my private life second."

Therefore, in order to work in the Puerto Rican community, a lesbian must remain in the closet. However, even if she chooses to remove herself from the community for a while and concentrate on lesbian-feminists issues, as I have, there are still problems.

Everyone needs to feel a sense of closeness with others who understand their roots and why they react to certain situations in a certain way. A sense of identity with others of the same upbringing and ethnic uniqueness is essential to feeling a part of any group. From consciousness-raising groups, to meetings, to social functions, we all bring a perspective that is at least partially influenced by our background.

For example, in a discussion of roles, which was an important concern in most consciousness-raising groups, the argument that was presented by most of the women who identified with the "butch" role was that it gave

them more freedom. Granted that this society is certainly male-dominated, but very few cultures are oppressed as much by the male figure as in the Latin countries. The term *machismo* defines the male with no weakness, superior to the female in all respects, and entitled to a freedom to be as arbitrary in his actions toward her as he wants simply because he is male. Therefore, when I identified myself with the butch role it meant total strength with no room for tears or any other signs of weakness. I was also perceived by other women as a symbol of the macho role and forced to adopt a position of protector in many situations, such as being called to break up fights at dances or getting men out of our all-women's meetings. If there was a problem that needed someone strong, I was called upon to help. My identity was as much defined by how others saw me as how I saw myself. Therefore, it was always difficult for my white sisters to understand why I had more problems breaking out of the butch role than they did. The lesbian-feminist movement was helping destroy the stereotypical role of women in regard to men, therefore allowing butch-femme roles in the lesbian community to dissolve, but it was not concentrating on destroying the stereotypes that women placed on other women because of their ethnic backgrounds.

There are other major differences between me and my white sisters. I come from a community that is regulated by the family unit. While this is restrictive in the ways I have already noted, it is also a community that is close-knit, filled with warmth and a sense of caring. We look out for each other and will spend more time helping a friend or family member than we might spend on ourselves. Parties are lively with loud music and dancing and a general atmosphere of closeness. Entertaining is basically done in the home and if someone arrives unexpectedly to visit around dinnertime, there is always room for more people around the table. I guess because we are alienated from so many other people, we created a sense of belonging among ourselves.

In the lesbian-feminist community socializing is rarely done in private homes. Except for my closest of friends, I see people at meetings or community social functions. I don't get the sense of warmth and closeness that I feel in the Puerto Rican community. My Puerto Rican heritage and Spanish language are very important to me. Yet there is no place in the public life-style that predominated in the lesbian world to share with others my music, my language, and my food. I feel distant and set apart in a world that expresses itself completely differently from that to which I am accustomed. I even tried to join a black feminist organization, thinking that I might better be able to identify with their life-style and goals. However, when I went to their first meeting I was asked to leave and was told that this group was only open to black women. [The policy has since changed.]

Another difference I sense in the lesbian-feminist community is the lack of family ties of the kind that I have. Puerto Rican children are brought up to remain under the jurisdiction of their parents until they are married, and even then, parental influence is minimized only slightly. Phone calls must be made often and visits must be frequent. If there is great physical distance between parent and child, as in my case where my parents have recently moved back to Puerto Rico, I must answer every letter I receive immediately, and if there is any indication of trouble, I have to get on a plane and go to see them, regardless of the cost in money or loss of work time. When my white sisters advocate that we try to create our own family structure within the lesbian-feminist community and spend holidays together or ignore the parents that won't accept our lesbianism, they have difficulty understanding the internal struggle I have. My sense of obligation comes not only from my parents and other relatives telling me I must do certain things, but because *I* feel I must. I may be looked upon as unliberated by lesbian feminists, and would like not to feel as totally obligated to my family as I do, but I ultimately don't want to lose that sense of family identity as much as my white sisters do.

I am extremely grateful for what the lesbian-feminist movement has given me. I think all Puerto Rican lesbians could benefit in much the same way. But I am caught between two worlds, neither of which gives me a sense of totality and strength. My Puerto Rican lesbian sisters have chosen to work for the Puerto Rican community and not concentrate on their oppression as women and as lesbians. I cannot do that as completely as they have. I have to deal with it every day. Yet I cannot ignore my own oppression as a Puerto Rican. I feel caught between two irreconcilable worlds which *should* be able to exchange the benefits of the respective cultures but, because of their priorities, cannot do so at the present time. As a lesbian who has actively participated in both, I am pained by the contradiction I experience because my feelings are warm and loving for the good things I see in each one. I want to hold on to those good feelings and am always fighting to reconcile the two worlds. Yet as a single person, I do not have the strength to effect the changes I would like to see. It remains a frustrating situation and I unfortunately have yet to find the answer.

—Zulma Rivera
(written testimony)

"It is unthinkable to disobey one's parents if you are a properly brought-up Chinese."

The Chinese are very reticent about sex and male-female relationships. Needless to say, female-female relationships (i.e., lesbian relationships) simply do not exist; it would be too shocking to the Chinese conscience to even acknowledge their existence. At least this was true when I was growing up; Western influence in the sixties and seventies might have slightly changed that attitude.

I didn't even know the Chinese word for "homosexuality" until I was in my late teens. But I have always been aware of my "feelings" for other women since I was four or five years old. Well, I did not play with my sisters or my girl friends in the neighborhood that much because all they wanted to play was housekeeping and cooking. Instead, I grew up playing soccer, badminton, and Chinese chess with the boys. In particular, I adored two neighborhood girls who could play a good game of badminton and always beat the boys. By the time I was eleven, I could beat all the boys in badminton, too. I simply gravitated toward female figures since early childhood. I went to an all-girls' school as a third-grader, and have been in all-women schools ever since—including college and graduate school!

These women-oriented environments helped me build a very strong and *positive* sense of being female. I was lucky in this respect, because otherwise I would have grown up just like any other girl from a traditional Chinese family. I can see the reflection of what could easily have been "me" in 99 percent of my girl friends and schoolmates. They all grew up with the very stifling —to me, at least—notion of belonging to a man and *submitting* to him in the not-so-distant future. It is a Chinese virtue for a woman to be a submissive wife—gentle and obedient.

I knew what was expected of me as a Chinese woman. It is terribly improper for Chinese women to even speak up in the presence of men. But I must say my parents are, in certain ways, frightfully unconventional by Chinese standards. Perhaps because I am the eldest daughter, my father always enlisted my help in "manly" jobs like waxing the floor, moving furniture, fixing the stereo, etc. Moreover, they often stepped out of the way to encourage me to excel in my studies, in sports, and gave me (and my sisters) plenty of opportunities for extracurricular activities, such as joining the Girl Scouts, taking music lessons, and so on. Such parental attitudes for bringing up *girls* were quite unheard-of then in a Chinese community.

So, I grew up a free spirit, full of self-confidence and ambitions unseeming for a Chinese woman. Unlike the "average" Chinese young women, who is usually reluctant to achieve or express herself knowing that she will have a husband who will speak and provide for her anyway, I learned young that I am an individual who has to fend for myself. Therefore, the idea of my submitting to a man (i.e., my supposed husband) was sickening to me. Besides, I have always felt that I "love" women, which, by the way, made me even more aware of my "oddity" among other Chinese women, as if being such an "un-Chinese free spirit" were not enough.

It is therefore easy to imagine that lesbians in a Chinese community—a culture imbued with Confucian morality and decency—are extremely hard to come by (to put it rather crassly). Even as liberal as my parents are, when it came to my *lesbianism,* they were alternately shocked, offended, shamed, despaired, and out-raged. And I, in turn, was startled too, because I thought—innocently enough—my parents would support my un-Chinese, unconventional mode of life *all the way.*

My high school experience was an episode of my one-sided infatuations with various girls in the senior classes. This sort of thing, I learned, was quite common in all-girls' high schools. But deep inside, I knew that in my case it was a *serious* emotional and physical attrac-tion, and I was not just doing what was "in" under the circumstances. (Sure enough, many of my schoolmates whom I thought were also courting other girls are now "happily married" and raising their children.) I cannot speak for all Chinese lesbians, but I certainly did not feel any guilt about having love feelings for other women. I just felt strange that I did not have the kind of feelings for boys as my schoolmates had. So I kept my lesbian—I didn't know the word then, of course—feelings to my-self, and paid lip service whenever they talked about boys. I felt positive and good about loving other women even then. I felt as if I could be the exception: that I could be a woman-loving woman and be accepted by my Chinese environment.

A temporary setback came when I was sixteen. My lesbian feelings were getting too intense for me to com-fortably live with. At the same time, peer-group pressure was bearing especially hard on me. It was the time when everybody (so it seemed) in my class started actively dating boys. I had never felt so odd, isolated, and totally confused. Finally I succumbed to societal pressure—a move that I bitterly regret till this day. I started dieting in order to look more "feminine" and appealing (I was far too muscular and athletic then); I learned to walk and talk like a "lady"—that is, when I couldn't help *not* talking. The pressure on me to be "normal," or rather, to be like any other Chinese girl, was just overwhelming. My dieting resulted in a not-so-mild case of malnutrition; but at least I got what I thought I wanted—boy friends. It took another two years before I could force myself to feel marginally comfortable with going out on a date.

Just as I began to feel success in conforming to the expectations for me as a young Chinese woman, I met my first love. It totally took me by surprise, because I thought I had by then gotten my lesbian feelings well under control, and that I was on my way to become a bona fide heterosexual. I was a senior in high school at the time, and she was my classmate.

I was so thoroughly excited by how supremely good it felt to love a woman that I started indirectly publicizing our relationship in school. That was very naïve and foolish of me; my positive attitude toward lesbianism certainly proved to be one of a kind. When my parents found out about it, they took me out to lunch one day, and discussed it with me in a restaurant (as unbelievable as it may sound). Throughout the two-hour discussion, the word "lesbianism" never came up—

but we certainly knew what we were talking about. They wanted a confession from me that I "will never do it again." They never got a word of remorse from me, but instead I defended my love unequivocally. It is unthink-able to disobey one's parents if you are a properly brought-up Chinese. I am sure my parents were very hurt as well as indignant. But I had absolutely no shame or guilt. Mine was quite a "gutsy" coming out considering my cultural background and the circumstances.

My lover left me, rather reluctantly, probably be-cause of all the publicity. My family "ostracized" me for a few months. It was emotionally an extremely trying time for me, but I still would not "confess" that I had done anything wrong. Then came the good news that I got a scholarship to attend college. And the whole mat-ter was dropped instantaneously as far as my parents were concerned.

They somehow had this illusion that once I went to college, I would "turn a new leaf," that is, I would be able to leave the "bad influence" in my hometown that got me into "perversion." Of course, just the opposite happened once I left home. My long-suppressed lesbian feelings were set free. But most importantly, having gone through the painful experience of being misunderstood (even by one's own dear parents) and condemned—because of a love so powerful and beautiful—I was deter-mined to work for the liberation of all lesbians. If society is so stubborn and blind as to continue its bigoted oppression of lesbians, at least my (our) efforts can inform our sisters that it is *not* "sinful" or "perver-ted" to love other women.

I am sure that other Chinese lesbians may have quite a different story in terms of self-esteem and pride in their lesbianism. Several years ago, I came into con-tact with other Chinese lesbians in my hometown for the first time. I then realized that there was an "under-ground network" of lesbians that I was not aware of in my high school days. They were mostly high school students from middle-class families. They would meet at private parties since there were no "women's bars" as such. It was a very close-knit and secretive social circle. It took quite a bit of "leverage" for me to "crack in" at first. But I had a hard time blending into the group anyway because they were very much into role-playing. Since feminism apparently hadn't yet made any impact there, they were unaware that they did not have to pattern their relationships upon the sexist structure of a stereotyped heterosexual relationship. It was almost ironic to see how submissive women could be even to other women (i.e., to their male-identified lovers).

Perhaps submissiveness is a distinctive charac-teristic of Chinese women . . . but perhaps it is a universal phenomenon among women—we who have been subject to the indoctrination of male "supremacy" since birth. For this reason, I am committed to freeing my sisters from guilt and shame for loving other women. Lesbianism is the ultimate defiance vis-à-vis the subjugation of women by men—an oppression that recognizes no racial or cultural boundaries.

—Yee Lin
(written testimony)

"I could not be an open lesbian among my people on the reservation."

I come from the nations of people whose land this government was founded upon. I am a Native American lesbian. My identity is primarily as a Dakota (Sioux). My beginnings are in sacred mother earth, in my ancestors who fought to defend their land and their people from the European invaders, in my grandparents who raised me. My beginnings are also in my gay ancestors who lived peacefully and as equals among my people before the arrival of the European settlers. As a Native American lesbian, I have come a long way to proclaim who I am.

It is probably a little known fact to the gay community that prior to European arrival in this country, homosexual people were accepted by the Indian nations. They were often thought of as sacred, and some of the highly respected medicine people were gay. This traditional acceptance has been unfortunately almost wiped out among my people, through the influence of Christianity. In many instances this religion was forced upon my people, who were considered savage and heathen by the Christians.

The written accounts of Native American homosexuals by whites are usually distorted by the disdain and prejudice for homosexuals that the Europeans brought with them. The spoken history of gay Native Americans has a totally different impact from white recorded history when heard in one's own language, from one's own people.

As I was growing up on the reservation and becoming aware of my lesbianism, I could see that it was not going to be an easy task for me to live as a lesbian among my people. I was painfully conscious of the mild ridicule that the few gay Indians on the reservation received, but noted that they were nonetheless not abandoned by their people.

At the age of sixteen I reached what I felt was an impasse in my life. I had come to many revelations about myself and my place in this world.

I was at the same time a symbol and an actuality of resistance. I had no desire to be a member of American society or heterosexual existence. My experience spanned both the nineteenth and twentieth centuries. I met and lived with my great-grandparents and other relatives who had traveled freely on the prairies before

white people came. I can remember riding across the prairie with my grandparents in a wagon pulled by a team of horses. I would lie in the back, staring at the sky, listen to the wooden wheels turning, and smell the sacred sage which grew abundantly in the prairie. Memories like this, the voices of my grandparents, and the familiar sound of my language eventually brought me to a place of understanding.

During my sixteenth year I accepted my lesbianism, and much to my surprise it was during this year that I met my first woman lover on the reservation, a VISTA worker from Massachusetts. It was an interesting, somewhat difficult and contradictory experience to have a white woman lover on the reservation.

I could not be an open lesbian among my people on the reservation. Existence there is often so much a matter of life and death that other issues become less significant and less tolerable. Poverty-level income as the government defines it is far above what most of the Indian people on the reservation will ever have.

From South Dakota, I went to Santa Fe, New Mexico, to attend a school for American Indian artists, and I was finally able to be openly gay among my people. I was delighted to find other gay Indians—and my first Indian woman lover. My first experiences in being an open lesbian weren't all positive, but I left New Mexico feeling strong and reassured because I had established contacts with other gay Indians and because I found I could totally be myself with my people.

In San Francisco, where I currently live, my friend Randy and I decided to organize a group named Gay American Indians, to share our experiences and to develop a gay Indian community. Gay American Indians was a step forward in the organizing process for all Third World gay communities. It is important that Third World gay people organize because our needs and struggles are much different from those of the white gay community.

During the three years that I have lived in San Francisco and been in the lesbian community, I have begun to see and experience various forms of racism, which I thought I had left behind in South Dakota. I had the misconception that lesbians, because of their own oppression, would have a high consciousness about oppressed people. But I discovered that many of the lesbians I met did not know about Native American people except what they learned in the distorted history book accounts and through the Hollywood movie image. I discovered that many of the lesbians did not know whose land they are living on, or the real history of how they got to live on this land.

My identity is primarily as a Native American; my people's struggles come first for me. I do see myself as a member of the gay community, and feel that internal education of the gay community is necessary to make us stronger and truly able to respect one another, to break down the barriers that sometimes exist between us as lesbians, gay men, Third World, and non-Third World. I also feel that new leadership and new gay images are necessary for the gay community. I hope that new direction can come from Third World gay people. For far too long, life in this country has been defined by the white male power structure and by whites in general.

I hope that more Native American women who are gay will be able to come out and find the strength of spirit to stand proud as Native American lesbians.

—Barbara Cameron

"The lower-class lesbian doesn't have much 'respectability' to lose."

I grew up in a working-class home, and I think most of the lesbians that I knew twenty years ago when I was coming out were working-class women. It's been my experience all along that those who are most heavily into role-playing are generally from the working class. I did have some experience, though, with women who were not into such obvious roles—they were often upper-middle-class women who had maybe been kicked out of college for being lesbians.

There were three categories—butch, femme, and kiki. And nobody wanted to be a kiki—it was ridiculed. If you didn't know what role you wanted to play, you were considered confused. Kikis were the "queers" of the gay world.

I found it very easy to choose the butch role. I had already been a tomboy and had a desire to wear boys' clothes. A lot of us choose clothes because of different fantasies about one activity or another—and clothes symbolize those activities. Once I was free to choose my own clothes, I began to dress in a way that enabled me to act out all these fantasies. I had my hiking boots and my sailor suit and just about everything I had ever had a fantasy about.

The male role seemed more attractive because I thought it put me in control. I also think it was a little bit closer to what seemed natural for me. But there are lots of ways that I squelched what so-called femininity I had because it didn't fit in with a butch image. One thing the women's movement has done for me is to help me explore the tender parts of myself—get in touch with myself as a woman. In the past, for example, I would never cross my legs because it didn't fit in with my butch image—but I've found that it's nice to cross your legs.

When I first came to New York I was a female transvestite, therefore obviously lesbian. But after the unisex styles came in, for the first time I was finding that I had to come out to people because they couldn't tell from the way I was dressed that I was gay. So I fit in among movement lesbians, appearance-wise, more than I would have expected, and more than I did in my mind. Everyone was wearing mostly jeans and denim jackets and blue work shirts. And I had always worn boys'

shirts, jackets, shoes, and pants. So there wasn't any extreme difference except in the length of my hair, which was very short. My appearance did make a difference to some people, and I think the way they saw me had a lot to do with what was in their heads. I remember one woman saying that when she first came to Lesbian Liberation Committee and saw me she was terrified of me—I fit some image in her mind of what a tough dyke was. There were a lot of negative attitudes expressed about role-playing, and I knew I was guilty of this, and was really afraid of being rejected because of it. I did move away from the role image, because as it happened, I was open to change at the time; it was kind of a miraculous period in my life. Otherwise, I think I might have had too much invested in my butch identity to respond to feminist thought and handle the attitudes that I was coming into contact with.

I think my working-class background might have had something to do with my coming out earlier than middle-class lesbians. Most women I knew in the fifties were lower-class. I think that's probably because middle-class lesbians have more of a stake in the system, in being respected by the general society. The lower-class lesbian doesn't have much "respectability" to lose. The middle-class women tend to be more closeted and more repressed about acting on their sexuality.

I think there is a difference in the reactions of the working-class families to our coming out. In general, communication is more open and direct in working-class homes—they tend to have fights about things. So it's common, when a lesbian comes out, for her to get kicked out of the house, to be beaten, to experience heavy reactions. Middle-class people, when they come out to their families, often experience a pretense that the subject was never mentioned. I think there is some contrast there.

There are some specific signs of classism that we need to deal with in our own movement. One that I'm most conscious of and have put the most energy into doing something about is the fixed-price policies of all kinds of movement activities—dances, benefits, programs, etc.—that exclude poor women, or that add an extra burden to their ability to attend the same event that others can easily afford. At the time I started coming to the Sunday programs at the Firehouse, I was on welfare and was recovering from an illness, and I desperately wanted to be at the Firehouse but very often I didn't have the fifty cents. Even though the sign said "Donation," I didn't know that it meant I could come without paying. Most poor people have this feeling of being looked down on if they don't pay the full amount, and they would be the last people to come and ask for the break. More than likely, the middle-class woman who's short of money would feel entitled to ask to be let in for less. The poor woman would feel more embarrassed and less deserving. And I think that comes out of a lifetime experience of not having much money and feeling that you're looked down upon.

There's the class that you come from—what your childhood experience is—but there's also the class that

Women at Salsa Soul Sisters Meeting, New York City

you identify with, and these may not be the same. Often people in the movement with working-class backgrounds are assimilated, but they're usually identifying with middle-class values. They've left their class, or are hoping to. I've come from a long working-class background, but got into a long eight- or nine-year period of upward mobility and began to identify with the goals and values of the middle class as I saw an opportunity to move there.

There is definitely a class division among women in the lesbian community in New York. It's very easy to see: All you have to do is name the places where women go—you can almost identify what class goes there. It's shifting and changing, but clearly at the Women's Coffeehouse, for example, it's predominantly working-class women—and a fair number of middle-class women who identify with them. The uptown bars, on the other hand, are mostly middle- and upper-middle-class.

I think if we're ever going to have a strong lesbian movement, we've got to find some way to get women of different classes mixing together.

—Doris Lunden

"The biggest problem for a young person coming out is worrying about being put away by your parents."

When I was thirteen I knew I didn't have any feelings for guys. I had sexual feelings for women, and I got along better with them. I knew nothing about the gay movement then. I kept these feelings to myself until I was sixteen.

Then I saw the TV program "Outreach." I saw in *TV Guide* that it was about lesbians and gay men and I tuned in. Lesbian Feminist Liberation was mentioned and I went down to a meeting. I was scared to death. I called on the phone first. Erica answered and invited me to an orientation meeting. She was really very nice and made it a lot easier for me. If it wasn't for her I don't think I would have come. It took her a long time to talk me into coming, and when I got there I didn't know how to react, whether to tell people I was sixteen. If there was an age requirement I was afraid I wouldn't be accepted. I didn't say anything, but eventually someone asked me my age and I didn't want to lie. I told her and found out you only had to be thirteen!

I thought the women in LFL were great. They were nice to me and things were very comfortable. I had gone to libraries and read that lesbians were abnormal. It really blew my mind. I thought, I have to go to one of these meetings; I don't believe this is true. I knew how I felt and I realized all the books were wrong.

When I first read the books I didn't know if I wanted to change myself, if I wanted to be gay or not. But after I met other lesbians I realized that's how I wanted to live and I didn't want to change for anything.

It can be hard, though. All the hassles, the guilt

trips, straights lay on you. I told my parents a couple of weeks ago, and they are reacting pretty badly. My mother cries. My father has a bad Irish temper. They're threatening to put me away in a hospital. It's bullshit. I told them, "Hospitals are not going to accept me. What are you going to do? Tell them, 'Here's my daughter, she's gay'?" But the biggest problem for a young person coming out is worrying about being put away by your parents. When you're not eighteen you don't know what can happen to you. In another six months, at eighteen, I'll be able to do what I want.

I was scared to tell them. I didn't know how they would react. One night my mother said, "I don't want you hanging around with them people." I said, "Ma, I'm one of 'them people.'" She started crying, "Why are you doing this to me? And ruining my life?" She doesn't understand how I feel. My parents don't want anyone to know. I'm a disgrace to the family.

I quit high school. There was an incident with a teacher. I asked her if she was gay, and she took it wrong, or got scared. She got me in a lot of trouble with the principal. I went to the assistant principal and told her that I was gay. She is a nun and she took it very well. It was a very good school, but with the hassles at home and school I just couldn't continue. My marks were going down. I used to have an 85-90 average and it was going down to 65-70. I'm looking for a full-time job now so I can get out of the house.

Coming out takes a lot of energy and nerve. I had an idea because of what I read, of what society thinks of lesbians in general, but I figured I'm not going to live my life closeted. I would have never come out without the movement. I don't think I would have gone to the bars. The first time I went into a bar, I was nervous; I thought people might stare at me. Eventually I met more and more people. It was like making friends at any new place, just like making friends at school.

I'm not very religious. I was afraid of the nuns' reaction at school and I was surprised when the assistant principal tried to help. She said she would talk to my parents if I wanted. She said, "It's not all that bad." I was very surprised and I started to laugh. She said, "No, really, I'm being very honest with you." That helped a lot.

If things are not going to get better at home I will regret telling my parents, because I don't want our family to be broken up. But it was making me a very nervous person hiding everything. I couldn't be myself. I feel a lot better since I let it out.

There's a counselor at school, Sally. I go when I need to talk and she always has a willing ear. It's good to have someone to tell what's happening. She was going to talk to my mother to ease the tension, but my mother refused to talk to her. My mother said, "I'm not going to see that counselor; you're the one that needs counseling." Sally works with a counselor named Richie whose sister is gay. I spoke to Richie a couple of times, and he said, "I know what you're going through." He told me about his parents not accepting his sister. He told me it takes a long time for parents to understand. I still see Sally even though I'm not in school. I'm glad I went to see her instead of seeing a psychiatrist like the school and my parents suggested. I didn't want to have my parents spend the money when I knew I wasn't going to change. It would just be a waste of time and energy. Sally doesn't try to make me change.

My mother keeps bringing it up. She thinks it's her fault. I told her it's not her fault; it's the way I want to be. I don't want to live any other way. It hasn't been easy for me. I tried to commit suicide about a year and a half ago, because things were building up inside of me. Sometimes I try to solve my problems by drinking. I don't know why I do that to myself. It's a waste.

My parents are completely against gay people. My father can't even talk about it without getting into a rage. If I start talking with my mother, and my father is in the room, he's ready to choke me. My mother says, "You're going out with a bunch of queers, I can't believe you're a queer." It really gets to me. I wish I could change the way people felt. That's why I'm thinking about marching in the Christopher Street Parade. I don't know if it would change people, but I think it would help. I think it's important to get more lesbians to march. If my parents had been supportive, or if they had just left me alone, I would have stayed in school.

I've made friends with women in their twenties, thirties, forties. I get along with a lot of people. The only problem that I've had with the community is their reaction to my seeing someone who's a lot older than me. I'm seventeen and she's almost twenty-nine. People think, "What can you possibly get out of a relationship if you're so young and she's so much older than you and knows so much more?" One woman, after I had just told her I was in love with someone who is twenty-eight, said to me, "What can she possibly see in you? That must be hell for you, Donna, and it must be hell for her, too." She said it in a really insulting way.

But I feel that as long as you're comfortable with each other and you're happy I don't think that age matters. The person I'm involved with and I have our hassles and feel that our age difference is significant at times, but we're willing to work on that.

Basically, I haven't encountered any tendency for women to take me or my ideas less seriously because of my age. My friends accept me for what I am. They don't treat me like I'm twelve, they treat me like I'm eighteen.

—Donna

Winifred M. Johnson, photo courtesy of The Lesbian Tide

"We need some kind of retirement place for older gay women."

I was forty-three years old when I came out. I was fortunate in that I came out when the gay liberation movement was around. I didn't come out before that because the movement wasn't around for support, but I regret not coming out earlier. There were two sides of that coin—one side is that I feel I've missed a whole lot of things in my life. My affinity to women was always there in the background but I was denying it, elaborately disguising it to myself and to others. But the other side of the coin is that at forty-three years of age I was reborn, and that was very exciting. I had a whole new life at that age, like starting over again.

When I first came out, for the first few months I was high as a kite. I was getting only two hours' sleep. I did everything, went everywhere, running around, having a great time. All of a sudden it occurred to me that I was always with younger women, often young enough to be my children. I would go down to the Firehouse with young women, dance with them, talk with them, very unselfconscious about the whole thing, because I felt much younger: I felt like I was in my teens. But I also had a problem relating to many of my age peers, because many had been old-time dykes who had come out a long time ago. They had a whole different mentality from someone coming out at the height of the feminist and gay liberation movements, and they were not as politically aware as some of the younger women I was meeting. A lot of these older women had "made it in a man's world." They did not have too much feminist consciousness.

There are two kinds of older lesbians—those who have come out just recently with the help and security of knowing there's a movement behind them, and those who went through all the hardship of premovement years before. I would not have called myself a radical, but I was much more radical than they were. I needed to find women my own age who had some political awareness.

Then, with two other women I helped start a cultural discussion group for older women—Gay Women's Alternative—to attract women of various backgrounds and diverse interests, and that's what it's been doing, attracting all kinds of women, politically aware or not—it doesn't really matter. It's not a moralistic group. Younger women also come and are welcome. We try to cater to everyone's needs, but I think the women who are politically unaware have a problem, because it's very hard for them to tune into the politics of women today.

The younger women at the Firehouse were more politically aware, but in many ways they were also politically naïve and unrealistic, and there has to be some kind of synthesis of those two things; I think you have to have realistic goals and understand that we're living in a world where there are men. It's a different kind of revolution that I see.

I see a revolution happening by us just being who we are, by our coming out. I think coming out is revolutionary not only for the person who is doing it but to all the people she touches; family and friends. You can watch the gradual process of change in attitudes. To me, that's a revolution. Ripples will become waves.

One woman was saying the other day, "The tide is really rising, when we see so many activities going on and so many things happening." In spite of what we hear from different sources that the women's movement is dying or dead, I don't believe it. It might be less visible than it was a couple of years ago, but there are more real things happening in the ways of women's communities, publications, etc. I'm absolutely awed when I go into Womanbooks and see all those books that women continue to write—every time I go in there there's a new book or two on some aspect of women's new consciousness. This, to me, is a revolution.

I think that gay women age more gracefully than straight women do. There's a certain amount of what society calls immaturity among gay women, but I'm saying it not in a pejorative way. I think it's a good thing, for a lot of gay women. We can be refreshingly childlike, not to be confused with childishness. I think we go through menopause without the same kinds of problems straight women do. Many problems are cultural rather than physiological. The lesbian's sexuality is more encouraged than discouraged as she gets older. Gay women, I think, are more sexually active, which acts hormonally to ease menopause. Lesbian women are more outside the culture which says that at menopause such-and-such is going to happen, and we're less influenced by a lot of the "old wives' tales." We have more independence from cultural expectations of what's going to happen.

But it isn't necessarily easier to grow old as a lesbian. Some things are harder. A gay woman alone has more of a problem because in many ways she has either severed relationships with her family and the straight world, all the things that spell security, or perhaps she lives with those things and is frustrated because she hasn't come out to her family and friends. There's a great inner turmoil in hiding things. I think there is still no real community yet for older gay women. Some

women are working toward it. That's why I believe in communities, feminist retreats like Women's Ways, etc. I know some women who are in their late sixties, approaching seventy, who are alone and frightened, because there's no place for them. We need some kind of retirement place for older gay women. One woman's idea is to establish land trusts. Every woman we could get hold of would give five dollars to buy pieces of land throughout the country, and use them until they're built up to the kinds of places older women could retire to. In the meantime we could use them as retreats, communities where women could live year-round, or come to visit. All women would own it—no one person would own it.

I haven't seen many lesbians over sixty. They're around but not visible. The few women that I know are in great shape, very active and healthy, more so than a lot of straight women. My observation is that they have much more vitality than straight women. But what takes away from vitality is the depression some women will sink into if they're alone and feel isolated. There's one older woman who comes up to Women's Ways and she enjoys herself but she doesn't have age peers there. Every once in a while she wakes up to the fact she is surrounded by younger women, and how does she fit in? She doesn't want to be treated like the grandmother; she wants to be one of the group. Even that kind of thing, though, is much easier in the lesbian world. Ageism is not as much of a problem. Lesbians are not as susceptible to the cultural myths that women are supposed to internalize. They are much more independent, much more supportive of who you are and where you are in the lesbian community.

There's nothing in the lesbian culture that says you're less attractive as you grow older, or encourages that way of thinking, but lesbians are coming from other places, too. There are influences in their lives from the straight world, too. I don't like to look in the mirror and see I'm getting older, mostly because I don't want to lose my physical vitality. Even though older gay women have more vitality than a lot of straight women do, you can't argue with the aging process of slowing down. I'm very often terror-stricken by it. The most fearsome thing to me is the idea of being dependent on anybody. I don't ever want to feel physically dependent on anybody. I think I would feel that if I were a straight woman too. Maybe that fear is even greater for lesbians than straight women, since we tend to value our independence so much.

I've been referred to as an older woman only recently. There is less ageism in the lesbian community, but I'm being called an older woman when I never thought of myself that way. Part of it has to do with what society calls immaturity. I've always pictured myself as a kid, never really grown up, never having reached adulthood. A lot of gay women feel that. All of a sudden when you're being called an older woman, you look at yourself and say, "I really am getting there."

Otherwise, I don't feel it. It's all relative to everyone else.

There is a bit of a youth culture among lesbians. Wherever you go you see younger women. It's impossible to avoid envy. You say to yourself, "Why didn't I come out at that age? They have their whole lives to live as lesbians!"

—Batya

"If there is a group of people who can claim more oppression than Jews, it is homosexuals."

Some twenty years before I came out, I got deeply involved in the Zionist movement. I studied for a year in Israel and then returned to join a kibbutz. Although I enjoyed many aspects of kibbutz life, I was unhappy. I did not understand why. Now, in retrospect, I know. Israel, and particularly the kibbutz, is fanatically family-oriented, and the pressure to marry is very strong. I knew marriage was not for me and that a single woman is never fully integrated into a kibbutz. I left, came back to the United States, climbed the bureaucratic ladder and achieved a measure of success and satisfaction. I worked for several national Jewish organizations over the years on behalf of the Jewish people, doing something I felt was important and fulfilled many of my needs as well.

But when I came out, I simply could not continue my pattern of deceiving and playing games. I did not feel my Jewish associates were ready for my coming out to them. I had three choices: I could stay in the closet on the job; I could come out publicly; or I could drop out of the environment that forced such a decision. To stay in the closet, when every fiber of my being was reaching for openness and expression of the joy I was feeling, was psychically impossible. To come out publicly would force many people to deal with something I felt instinctively they were not ready for (perhaps I, myself, was not ready, either). So I had to drop out. I could no longer channel my energies into and produce the kind of work I had produced in the past in an atmosphere that I felt could not appreciate who I really am and that was, therefore, oppressive to me.

The catalyst that changed my life was a TV talk show featuring four gay couples—four women and four men. I watched and listened intently. These were beautiful, intelligent people who loved being just who they were and who articulately affirmed their life-styles. For the first time in my life I saw positive role models for the me I had spent a lifetime elaborately disguising to myself and to others.

The next day I set out to make contact with the gay community. I found a cultural discussion group and paced up and down at length before gathering the courage to venture inside. I was scared. Both men and women, recognizing a new face and the usual terror of the first step, came up to me and tried to ease my anxiety. They talked to me. They offered me coffee. They showed me around. I was eventually seated next to another woman. It was then that I froze up completely. I wouldn't speak to her or even look at her. Later I found out that this was also her first step into the gay world and she was just as scared as I was.

After the formal program, the group broke up into what could just as well have been an Oneg Shabbat. People drinking coffee, talking with each other about everything and anything. What also surprised me was the preponderance of Jews.

As for me, I was clinging to the woodwork, not speaking to anyone and answering in monosyllables when spoken to. I stuck it out for a half hour and then fled.

On the way home, my anxiety gave way to a warm glow. I had taken the first step into realizing myself.

Since that time, I have become involved in women's and gay activities. I cofounded a social cultural group for women over thirty. I was somewhat involved in the Gay Synagogue—Beth Simchat Torah in New York—and enjoyed the close connection to Judaism this congregation provides. It is hard to find another congregation of people with more intense and knowledgeable Jewish expression and devotion to Judaism and to each other; a number of Jewish scholars belong to BST and the scholarly level of the *divrei* (discussion of) *Torah* is unique among synagogues. The spirit of the *Ongei* Shabbat can only be compared with that of young Zionist movement kids. Such singing, such dancing! Such love!

But I have not been attending the Gay Synagogue very often because it is composed of and run predominantly by men, and for now, I want to spend my energies with other women. For the past two years, I have conducted gay women's seders on Pesach where we are rediscovering Jewish women heroes throughout the ages. Jewish history has been a record of men written by men, and it is only the occasional outstanding woman who is recorded for posterity.

I enjoy being with other Jewish lesbians. Some of us who know Hebrew speak with each other in that language and it helps us to feel our Jewish roots profoundly. Of course, there are many Jewish lesbians who feel that Judaism is so patriarchal at its very core and that the roles for men and women are so precisely defined that there is not much to salvage. They feel that recent attempts to "include" women by creating new rituals and by certain concessions allowed us by the male-run institutions such as women in the *minyan* (quorum of worshipers) and the glorification of woman's role as queen of the household do not really give us the psychic equality that we lesbians—perhaps the most independent of all women—need and want. We are rejecting in the man-created myths that which diminishes us as equal participants in our heritage as Jews. In digging deep into the sources of these myths, we are finding that our ancestors, in order to firmly establish their patriarchy, rejected and suppressed much that came before them; following their precedent after some two thousand years, we are revoking existing myths for our own edification as women. We pin our hopes on the evolutionary nature of Judaism and in this age of future shock, feel it must evolve more rapidly than it has to embrace a wider range of human experience. I believe that the various Jewish countercultures will save Judaism from its present slide into obsolescence.

It is noteworthy that I have no trouble affirming my Jewish identity in mixed groups of lesbians, even though there might be much disagreement as to the salvageability of the Judaic and the Christian traditions. I'm not sure I could express my lesbian identity in the mainstream Jewish community. I don't believe there would be the same appreciation of who I am.

While the entire heterosexual world finds it difficult to relate to homosexuality in general, some segments of the Church have been making efforts to come to terms with their hitherto pejorative attitudes about homosexuality, as more and more practicing Christians who are homosexuals are coming out of the closet. As a Jew, I find it painful that the Jewish community, often at the forefront of progressive causes, has not as yet risen to this particular challenge, even as Jews count significantly in the emerging homosexual community. (It is estimated that homosexuals number 10 percent of the population. My own experience would indicate more.)

If there is a group of people who can claim more oppression than Jews, it is homosexuals. Although there are few Jews alive today who do not know about the yellow Star of David patch that Jews were forced to wear under Nazi-dominated Europe, there are probably few Jews who ever heard of the pink triangle patch that the Nazis forced homosexuals to wear, identifying them and leading them to the same crematoria as Jews. We were consumed together in the fires of the Holocaust and were united in our ashes. We Jews will never forgive or forget ordinary Germans who looked the other way as the smoke rose from the crematoria incinerating Jews. But I can't help wondering how many Jews, had we not been targets in that period of monumental evil, would have stuck our necks out to save homosexuals, or even uttered mild words of protest.

Many Jews have been in the closet, concealing their Jewishness (often behind changed names and noses) for business, social, and personal reasons; many lesbians and male homosexuals have been hiding their true identity in the closet for similar reasons. Just as the establishment of the State of Israel in 1948 and Jewish self-love through Zionism brought many Jews out of the closet, the women's movement of the 1960s and the gay liberation movement of the 1970s brought many lesbians and male homosexuals out of hiding.

The Zionist movement, the women's movement, and the gay liberation movement have been the most important factors in affirming myself and my identity as a Jew, as a woman, and as a lesbian. Zionism brought me out as a Jew. The women's movement brought me out as a feminist. The gay liberation movement brought me out as a lesbian. All are self-affirming. All are life-affirming. All have made the difference between the denial of who I am and the affirmation of who I am.

—Batya Bauman*

"In high school the nuns would caution you against 'particular friendships.' "

I grew up in an Italian household. Because my mother was afraid I'd get pregnant in public high school, the perfect solution was to send me to parochial high school, to keep me a virgin.

I was very impressed with the nuns. I liked the idea of a lot of women living together. By this time I knew I was different. I felt more comfortable around women. I had not had a lesbian experience, but I had an active imagination. At sixteen I tried to gain entry into a convent. My mother shouted to me that I couldn't possibly enter because I was illegitimate. That was how I found out I was illegitimate. In those days, most orders would not accept an illegitimate woman.

My religious training presented a problem with my first lesbian relationship, which lasted two years. I felt I was a bad person, that there was no redemption possible for me. This devastated me. I didn't want to be bad, but I felt this was an unnatural, overwhelming sin, probably the worst sin ever. Up until the time I was twenty-nine I believed there was only a handful of whatever we were in this world. I also felt responsible for my lover. She had actually made the overtures to me, yet I felt responsible for whatever sin she was living in now. It was a double guilt.

The Catholic Church didn't talk about it, but in high school the nuns would caution you against "particular friendships." Even unnamed it can oppress you. There was no hope for me; I was irrevocably destined for eternal damnation. The hopelessness of what Christianity was saying to me led me to religions and philosophies of the East. The East didn't see creation and destruction as two separate things, but part of a chain. Spirits didn't go to hell and stay there.

Then I looked at the Church again. I entered the convent to examine my life and determine what direction I wanted to take. At twenty-six years of age I had been chair of a history department. I had just gotten tenure. I had a lover who is a marvelous woman. I tried to explain to her that I wasn't entering the convent for the Church; it was my need to pull away and see where I was. This woman would come and sit outside the convent to try to get me to come out. It was terribly sad; she just didn't understand. There was no way I could communicate it.

I began to see Christianity as a radical ethic of love

---

*Excerpted from *Lilith*, the independent Jewish women's magazine, winter 1976/1977, New York. © Copyright Lilith Publications, Inc., 1976.

and that was exactly what I was looking for. It led naturally to my commitment to civil rights, as a response to working in ghetto areas as an educator. That was the first time I could accommodate where I came from and who I was. I felt I had a contemporary definition of what redemption means. One could redeem oneself in commitment to work that would free all people.

The other day on a talk show someone asked me a question, "We hear a lot of funny stories about homosexuality in the convent." I said, "If the question is, Was there homosexuality in the convent? my answer is yes. If the question is, Was it funny? my answer is no."

Sexuality was considered an oppressive aspect of one's life in the convent. Homosexual relationships there were denied. I had a woman come into my room one night who said, "Sister, I tie my hands to the top of my bed at night for fear I'll commit a sin of impurity." She was afraid she'd masturbate at night. It was *the* sin. When I was teaching in midtown, you would see nuns disappear at lunchtime and go down to St. Francis Church, where they could have confession twenty-four hours a day. You would know that these nuns probably masturbated the night before and couldn't wait to go down and get themselves absolved.

After the convent experience, I met Betty, my present lover. She was not intimidated at all by her background and the Church in terms of being able to say, "I am a lesbian," and that gave me a certain amount of strength. I remember that both of us had made a commitment to speak at a Gay Academic Union conference a few years ago. We were sitting on a stage and I said something about being a lesbian and stopped. There were about 110 men and 13 women in the audience, and I said, "I want you people to know that is the first time I have ever heard myself say, 'I am a lesbian.'" I had a loving partner who helped me articulate and accept what took years to say, and having said it, I dove in in terms of celebrating it.

—Ginny Apuzzo

Members of lesbian feminist panel on Channel 13 program,
New York City, 1976

10. Lesbians and the Media

The Lesbian Image in the Media

GINNY VIDA

The media *is* the message; it is our main tool for creating a cultural image, changing public attitudes, and reaching closeted lesbians. Every successful political movement has learned to use it effectively. Think about it: *Most people have learned practically everything they know about lesbians from the media.* The sooner we learn to use the mass communications system effectively, the sooner we will break down stereotypes in the public mind and reach out to our own people. We have already begun this effort—and I can think of no more important work for us to do.

Like all great instruments of power in this country, the media is controlled by men. Men are the news editors, the network executives; men are the producers and the writers. (At last count the Screenwriters' Guild had less than ten percent women in its ranks.) Since the media's tendency is to ignore women, its message about lesbians has mainly been that we don't exist. And too often, the few images projected of us are mostly the creation of a male sexploitation club peddling Cheap Lesbian Thrills to the public to titillate viewers and boost network ratings. We've strangled old ladies with piano wire; we've raped a young girl with a broom handle. Physically we're frightening, emotionally we're a wreck, and personally we're the last people you'd want to meet.

Before 1969, for all the media told us, there were no lesbians or gay men; we were absent from TV dramas and situation comedies, radio and TV talk shows, magazine articles, and news stories in both the broadcast and print media. There had been a few books such as *The Well of Loneliness,* which was hard to come by in many areas, and some pitiful portrayals in a few films like *The Killing of Sister George, The Children's Hour,* and *The Fox.* (People who saw those films will probably recall the sadist who made her lover eat cigars, the guilt-ridden soul who hanged herself, and the dispensable third party in a bisexual triangle who met her death beneath a falling tree.) These were not glorious moments, to be sure.

After the Stonewall Riots in 1969, gays (mostly gay men) began to surface in news stories and occasional articles. But it was not until 1972 that the first gay character appeared in a television drama, and the first lesbian surfaced on NBC's *The Bold Ones,* in an episode entitled, "A Very Strange Triangle." In this "debut," the lesbian, a pathetic victim of her rejecting mother (the obvious cause of her lesbianism), is spurned by her bisexual woman lover. This was not exactly the "breakthrough" we'd been hoping for.

In 1973 the picture began to improve when CBS gave us an attractive, successful lesbian psychiatrist on *Medical Center,* played by Lois Nettleton. The characterization was flawed, however, by the psychiatrist's attempt at the end of the program to persuade a young girl that her lesbian feelings needn't be taken seriously.

Nineteen seventy-four was the Year of the Gruesome Lesbian. NBC's made-for-TV movie, *Born Innocent,* showed two lesbians raping fourteen-year-old Linda Blair with a broom handle in a juvenile detention home, and a few weeks later, a *Policewoman* episode, "Flowers of Evil," had three lesbians murdering and robbing all the patients in a rest home which they owned. An actress who played one of the lesbian roles said she had been instructed to flatten her breasts, shorten her hair, lower her voice, and wear masculine clothing.

This episode resulted in nationwide protests by lesbian and gay groups at TV stations and network offices on both coasts, including a demonstration and sit-in by Lesbian Feminist Liberation at the executive offices of NBC in New York. The sit-in delegation, which included a lesbian mother and her three children, held out for twenty-four hours in the broadcast standards office. Shortly afterward, NBC promised not to rerun the program, and the network president agreed to a series of meetings with representatives of the National Gay Task Force and other groups concerned with improving our image.

The 1975-76 season brought three programs dealing with lesbianism. A segment of *Bronk* featured a story about a heterosexual policewoman falsely accused of being a lesbian and molesting a female suspect. (She is finally cleared of the "terrible" charges.) Next, a lesbian murdered her lover on an episode of *Cannon*. The third program was a TV movie, *Death Scream*, based on a true incident, the fatal stabbing of a young lesbian (Kitty Genovese) in view of fifteen neighbors who ignored her cries for help. Initially the police suspect that someone in the lesbian community might have committed the crime, but the villain turns out to be a man. In one scene, an ex-lover of the victim tells the police, "A woman would never do that [murder] to another woman."

The 1976-77 season represented a dramatic breakthrough in visibility for gay men—and to a far lesser extent, for lesbians. All in all, there were lesbian images in eight programs (compared to about twice that number for gay men). Two programs that aired early in the season brought glimmers of hope. First, we were presented with a successful and courageous lesbian executive in another episode of *Policewoman*. The season's best offering, however, was *The War Widow*, a drama that aired on public broadcasting stations around the country, accompanied by a good deal of publicity. Set during World War I, the story featured a wife who has a beautiful love affair with another woman while her husband is away fighting in France. She eventually leaves her husband and daughter to join her female lover. Most remarkable about this story was its feminist insight into the benefits of love between women; the lesbian relationship is seen as a liberation from the protagonist's heterosexual role which has, until now, stifled her personal growth.

NBC's made-for-TV movie *In the Glitter Palace* got mixed reviews from the lesbian community, but whatever its limitations, it certainly represented a breakthrough for commercial TV in its presentation of a loving relationship between two women. At the end, when one of them is cleared of a false murder charge, they go off lovingly, hand in hand, into the sunset. There were many objections, however, to the sordid bar scene, the theme of blackmail, another lesbian murderer (this time a judge), a violent scene in which lesbians beat up the defense attorney, and the fact that a male hero was called in to rescue a woman.

On the negative side, the season brought a lesbian mother on *Executive Suite* who got run over by a truck (with her lesbian mother custody case pending), and a lesbian on *Seventh Avenue* who threw herself from a bridge after her brother-in-law refused to sleep with her so that she could prove she was a "real woman." We were also subjected to ABC's first lesbian portrayal on *The Streets of San Francisco*, where a lesbian murders her lover's best friend because she thinks they're having an affair.

The soap opera *Mary Hartman, Mary Hartman* dealt positively with bisexuality in the character of Tippytoes, but no lesbian couple appeared as the counterpart of Howard and Ed, the gay couple of the 1976 season. Things went from passable to worse, however, when Wanda began having an affair with her maid,

Lila, who threatens her with blackmail and tries to poison Wanda's husband.

Late in the season, a CBS daytime serial, *The Young and the Restless*, broke new ground by dealing with the lesbian theme, but conjured up several damaging stereotypes in the process. The story centered on Kay, a woman in her fifties, who is emotionally and sexually attracted to Joanne, twenty-six. But Joanne is "saved" from seduction in the nick of time by homophobic pressure from Kay's son and Joanne's ex-husband.

With the exception of *Mary Hartman*, lesbian characters have appeared only in TV dramas. We've been totally nonexistent in situation comedies, while gay male characters have appeared in *Phyllis, Alice, The Practice, Barney Miller*, the *Nancy Walker Show, Bob Newhart*, and *CPO Sharkey*, to name a few sit-coms. It almost seems as though the very existence of gay men is seen as cause for instant hilarity. Game shows, too, thrive on endless jokes and innuendoes around the words "fruit," "queen," and "fairy." But the words "butch" and "dyke" do not have comparable comic value. In the straight-male fantasy, the equation seems to be: gay male = cheap laughs; lesbian = cheap thrills.

Why is this so?[1] First of all, the heterosexual model (nuclear family) on which our society is based requires relating sexually to the *opposite* sex in order to qualify as a "real woman" or a "real man." Therefore, gay men are seen as not real men but as women; and lesbians are seen as not real women but as men. (The failure to actually accomplish this gender switch, however, is reflected in the old phrase the "third sex.")

The stereotypic assumption that gay men are taking on a female role and being sexually passive represents *downward mobility;* and as a powerful class condescending, they are perceived as funny, just as minstrels used to be considered funny when white men dressed as blacks. (The reverse, however, isn't funny. In a recent TV movie, *Minstrel Man*, a black minstrel is lynched after he puts on white makeup and makes jokes about rednecks.) It is also "funny" to be lower class—and part of Archie Bunker's humor derives from this phenomenon.

Laughter is always a release of tension and always has to do with a serious issue, deep down. If you don't laugh, you cry. It's the men, not the women, who find gay "jokes" funny; laughing *at* the reduction of men to a sexual object level allows a release of male sexual tension created by an inability to deal with their own homosexual feelings of love.

Lesbians, on the other hand, in being identified (in the public mind) with the male role, are seen as upwardly mobile, and therefore as threatening, usurping male privileges and stealing male property (other women). It is also threatening that we are (correctly) perceived as not desiring to relate to men (therefore constituting a threat to patriarchal society), whereas a

[1] I am much indebted to Bonnie Gray for many of the insights in the next few paragraphs.

gay man is understood to be "one of the girls," and therefore, harmless.

There are differences, too, in the sexual titillation potential of the lesbian and gay male images. Lesbianism is titillating to men (as cheap thrills) and to many women (in a nonexploitive way), although oddly, gay male sex is not that titillating to women. Probably it is to straight men—but butch gays are avoided as too threatening, too close to the sexuality of the male viewer; so instead, we have *Starsky and Hutch* male-bonding relationships that stop just short of being sexual, but that are the primary relationship in several programs.

Though we've seen definite progress, obviously we're still waiting for important breakthroughs. We need *frequent* stories about loving relationships between women. We need scenes of *affection.* We need stories that break the myth that we are purely sexual. We need sympathetic portrayals of lesbians on daytime serials, lesbians on situation comedies (in which it's *not* our affectional preference that's made fun of), and stories about *our* lives (not just other people's reactions to us). We are still waiting for the first lesbian kiss and a series featuring a lesbian couple. Daydreams, you may say? Granted, it won't be easy. But these images are all somewhere down the pike, I believe, if we are clever and persistent in our media efforts.

The point has been made by some, of course, that television doesn't portray people's real lives anyway—so why should we want any part of this wasteland? The value, however, is for millions of isolated lesbian viewers who think "I'm the only one" to have *someone* to identify with who's not murdering or raping people—even if the characters are stick figures.

TALK SHOWS

Fortunately, we've had some exposure on TV and radio talk shows, and here we've had more control of our image because we've had a chance to present *ourselves* (not withstanding frequent homophobia from hostile, condescending, or ignorant interviewers). Perhaps our earliest breakthrough on the TV network level was an all-lesbian panel on the *David Susskind* show in 1971. Late-night programs such as the *Tomorrow* show have also featured lesbian guests. But both lesbians and gay men have had less frequent access to network shows aimed at a family audience, such as *Today* and *Good Morning America.*

We've had a fair amount of exposure on local programs, but in some very conservative areas there is still a good deal of resistance on the part of broadcasters to deal with the gay issue at all, let alone invite us as program guests.

As lesbian feminists, we have additional problems that go beyond the concerns of gay men. First of all, we are continually shortchanged in representation by comparison with them. I am often called upon by talk show producers to find gay panelists, and in nearly all cases the request is for men. Not long ago I had a call from a producer who was organizing a program on "Coming Out to Parents." He had already found *three* gay men for the panel and was calling to ask us to find some gay people to be in the audience. It had never occurred to him that a panel of gays should include even *one* lesbian, let alone equal numbers of women and men, which is what we always push for. We finally persuaded him to add a lesbian and a parent to the panel.

I think we must be particularly forceful on this point when we're dealing with people who book these programs to insist on equal representation wherever possible, and to obtain total commitment for equality from gay men in joint media efforts with them, because the media will shortchange us at every opportunity. If anything, lesbians need *more* exposure to compensate for being ignored in the past.

An additional problem is *what we say* when we get a chance to say something. Persuading the public that "we're just like everyone else" or that we don't molest children or that we need gay rights laws to protect our jobs and homes are all important efforts. But how often do we talk about lesbian feminism? How often have we communicated the *advantages* of the lesbian life-style to the public and the connection between feminist principles and devoting one's life and energy to other women? In an important sense, we're *not* just like everyone else, and the public—and especially the women in the audience—should hear this. They need to hear not only from those of us who feel we were "born that way," but from previously heterosexual women who have gotten in touch with their feelings of love for women and have made a *choice* for a *better life-style,* one that satisfies their own personal needs for nurturance and is compatible with their feminist politics. This is a message that, I feel, we have not made effective use of the media to communicate.

OTHER MEDIA IMAGES

Coverage of lesbian news has been scanty. Among those who have received some measure of national media attention are Elaine Noble, Massachusetts State Representative; Ellen Barrett, the first open lesbian to be ordained an Episcopal priest; Mary Jo Risher, a lesbian mother who lost custody of her son in a Texas courtroom trial (her book has been published by Doubleday); and several lesbians who have been hounded out of the military, including Carmen Baños, Pat Veldon, Debbie Watson, Barbara Randolph, and Miriam Ben-Shalom. Of course, the lion's share of media attention has gone to gay men with distinguished military careers such as Leonard Matlovich. (Women, of course, have never had the opportunity to achieve comparable military distinction.)

From time to time the advice columnists deal with lesbianism. The best known of these are the twin sisters Abigail Van Buren and Ann Landers, whose positions on homosexuality are like night and day. "Dear Abby" counsels lesbians to accept their life-style, while Ann Landers advises going for a psychiatric cure. Not too long ago she urged a woman who had had some lesbian experiences to burn her diary. (We immediately wrote Ann that we had just set fire to a stack of old Ann Landers columns. She never printed our reply.) As for magazines, with the exception of an occasional piece here and there, the lesbian theme has been quite invisible. The only publication to print anything substantial has been *Ms.* magazine, where articles have appeared by Del Martin and Phyllis Lyon, Charlotte Bunch, Jill Johnston, Joan Larkin, and a few others.

EFFORTS TO IMPROVE THE IMAGE

Concerted efforts by the National Gay Task Force and local groups to promote a positive image of lesbians and gay men in the media are beginning to pay off to some degree. At the National Gay Task Force, we've concentrated our energies on positive TV portrayals and adequate and fair coverage of gay news, with emphasis on lesbian visibility in both areas.

Since the executive offices of the TV networks and NGTF's headquarters are located in New York, we've taken every opportunity to meet with network executives in the programming and broadcast standards departments. These meetings have increased the network's sensitivity to the lesbian and gay community and their recognition of us as a legitimate minority which is entitled to the same consideration regularly accorded other groups.

In 1973 we helped establish the Gay Media Task Force in Los Angeles, an advisory board of lesbian and gay male consultants working with writers, producers, and the networks in the preparation of programs involving gay themes and characters. We've worked closely with GMTF to coordinate East and West Coast gay media strategies. Their efforts have been extremely valuable. The second *Policewoman* program which aired in 1976 started out to be very antilesbian in the script stage. But with guidance from GMTF and the cooperation of NBC, the final result was a program that was uniformly well received by our community.

When meetings haven't produced the desired results, we've resorted to nationwide protests via our Gay Media Alert Network (a list of lesbian and gay groups across the country located strategically in the various broadcast markets) to generate national protests when we know in advance that a program is objectionable. Through "GMAN," we supply tips on how to persuade station managers to cancel an offensive program. We also notify groups of forthcoming lesbian and gay portrayals —negative or not—to get them to monitor the programs and respond to the networks and their local affiliates with compliments or complaints.

In 1973 the National Gay Task Force and local groups persuaded a large number of network affiliates, including Boston and Philadelphia, to cancel an offensive episode of *Marcus Welby*. We also convinced several sponsors to drop the show, and ABC was forced to lower its advertising rates to fill the space. In 1974 we helped persuade eight NBC affiliates and four sponsors to drop the rerun of *Born Innocent*.

Other pressure points have been the regulatory agencies and organizations that control or influence the broadcast media. NGTF has made presentations before the National Association of Broadcasters, the Federal Communications Commission, and the House of Representatives Subcommittee on Communications. In 1976 our presentation to the FCC at its *en banc* meeting in Washington, D.C., received coverage by both the Associated Press and United Press International, which was carried by news media across the country.

In the area of news coverage, our best results came from a mailing—a letter sent to over 150 people at the TV networks, wire services, and news weeklies, along with a Summary of National Gay News, pointing to important gay news events that had gone unreported in the national media. This mailing produced an appearance by gay representatives on the *Today* show, meetings with the editors of *Newsweek* and *U.S. News & World Report* (each followed by gay stories in the magazines), and national wrap-ups of gay news by both wire services, AP and UPI.

We are continuing to meet with executives, producers, and assignment editors at the TV network news departments and have sent out frequent press releases drawing their attention to important gay events.

LOCAL EFFORTS

Local groups often report to us on some of their most successful media activities. Gay Media Action in Boston was able to launch a gay public-service advertising campaign and to persuade one of the local TV stations to hire a gay consultant. Some groups have been able to persuade local radio stations to initiate gay programming or do a lesbian documentary on the local news. Some have succeeded in getting local newspapers to do a feature story on lesbian mothers or gays in the arts. Some have invited the local media to cover conferences they've sponsored. Several groups have responded to NGTF media alerts and persuaded local TV stations to cancel a program or run a disclaimer with it.

The variety of things that individuals and local groups can do is enormous. But some of the most important are:

1. Complain when negative images are projected. If it's a network TV program, call your local affiliate, then follow up with a letter of complaint to the station manager and send copies to the appropriate network:
CBS-TV, 51 W. 52 St., New York, N.Y. 10019.
NBC, 30 Rockefeller Plaza, New York, N.Y. 10020.
ABC-TV, 1330 Ave. of the Americas, New York, N.Y. 10019.

Public Broadcasting System, 475 L'Enfant Plaza West, S.W., Washington, D.C. 20024.

Be sure you record the name of the program, date, channel, and network, who said what and what was said that offended you. Phone calls to the local station should be made during business hours so that you can reach the station's executives. People to contact are the program director for entertainment shows and the news director for news shows. Or you might direct your complaint to the Station General Manager, who is responsible for the station's FCC license.

Send copies of your complaint to the Federal Communications Commission (the agency created by Congress to regulate the broadcasting industry) and to the National Association of Broadcasters, a self-regulating agency whose code most radio and TV stations subscribe to. The NAB has ruled that offensive and inaccurate statements about segments of society (including gays, although we're not specifically mentioned) are in violation of the code. Addresses are:

Federal Communications Commission, Washington, D.C. 20554.

Director, NAB Code Authority, 485 Madison Ave., New York, N.Y. 10022.

When you write a letter of complaint, it's important to do it in a closely reasoned, calm manner explaining *exactly why* something was offensive. Don't call the people you're writing to "finks" or "bigots" and don't use offensive language. Remember that we need to *educate* people. It is useful, when complaining, to make parallels with other minorities, explaining that we are not asking for special favors, but just the same sensitivity accorded other groups, and that this means (1) no abusive terms like "dyke" or "queer," (2) no victories for bigotry, (3) no presentation on talk shows of the bigot's point of view without our having the right to reply, (4) and no shows about homosexuality without gay people to speak for themselves.

Explain why we're insisting on a ban on negative images of gays in entertainment programming until positive images are *frequently* appearing. It isn't enough for the networks to tell us that they show the "good and bad of everybody" when so many viewers still believe the worst about us.

To complain about offensive items in newspapers and magazines, clip the article and record the newspaper's name, date, page number, and city. Register your complaint by sending a letter to the publisher or managing editor. Don't forget to send a "Letter to the Editor" which can be printed. You may also wish to respond immediately by phoning in your complaint.

In lodging complaints, it's important to recognize that there are basic differences in the broadcast and print media. The broadcast media is licensed and regulated with rules administered by the Federal Communications Commission, while the print media is free from such restraints. The rationale for regulating one type of media and not the other is that there are a limited number of airwaves available, but, theoretically, an unlimited number of publishers, newspapers, etc. Television, especially, is loaded with rules because it has a monopoly on the airwaves. (There are many more radio channels available than TV channels.)

And so, in complaining about offensive images of lesbians on TV or radio, it's helpful to know what some of these rules are. Under the FCC's Fairness Doctrine, for example, a station is obliged to present both sides of a "controversial issue of public importance." In practice this means that if your local station invites Anita Bryant to discuss the gay rights bill, it is obliged, if it has not already done so, to interview proponents of the measure as well.

It's also good to keep in mind that the media is not only the shaper of society's attitudes but a product of them as well. You can't really expect it to do a whole lot more than the society is ready for—or be any better informed than the general public. So if you are just plunging into media work, dissolve any fantasy you may have of the "good press."

2. Compliment the media when they do something right: If you see something positive, follow the procedures outlined in (1) above to let the media know they're on the right track.

3. Make up a list of lesbian leaders in your area and send it to the station managers of your local TV and radio stations, asking that they invite representatives of the lesbian community to ascertainment meetings. If you don't hear from the stations, call up and check on the status of your request. (Send for "How to Participate in Community Ascertainment," available from NGTF.) This will give you an opportunity to make contact with broadcast executives in your area and to air your concerns with them. (Don't forget to mention media visibility as one of the "needs of your community.")

4. Arrange for meetings with editors of local newspapers, TV news assignment editors, etc., to stimulate stories and familiarize the local media with your group. This might be a joint project with gay men; if so, be sure you have an equal number of women and men in your delegation.

You can often use complaints on news and talk shows to make initial contacts. Ask for a meeting to discuss the offense, saying, "Our purpose is not to dwell on this but to help you understand what's happening in the lesbian community and establish a connection." Be sure you walk away from the meeting with the name of one person who can be your news and complaint contact whom you can talk to, and who will see you as a resource.

Remember, in order to get coverage of lesbian news, you have to be promoting the *kind* of event that the media recognizes as news in your area. Obviously, lesbian groups have to be doing something that has news value. In your meetings with news people, give examples of *real* news: legislative efforts, child custody cases, assaults by bigots, statements of support from unexpected sources—but not a panel of "coming out."

By the same token, we can't complain about the media's failure to cover kinds of events not generally recognized as news, no matter how we may feel about them personally.

5. Make a list of all the TV and radio talk shows in your area, find out who books the programs, and try to get lesbians invited as guests. For help, send for NGTF's guidelines on "How to Book a TV or Radio Show."

If you get invited, try to anticipate offensive questions that may come from poorly informed interviewers. Think through the parallels with other minorities mentioned in (1) above and discuss these in advance with the show's producer. If the host is a bigot who asks you to defend yourself, answer the question, but point out in a rational manner that the interviewer would not have asked the B'nai B'rith, "Are you people really misers?" As an aid in keeping your sanity in such a situation, try to remember where we are in the context of history.

6. Appoint someone in your group to be responsible for publicizing your group's activities. Send out press releases in advance if you have an important event you want the media to cover, for example, a demonstration or conference; or if you wish to react to a homophobic attack or national or local gay news event. For help, send for "Making News" (how to write a press release), by Sasha Gregory-Lewis, and "How to Make the Media Work for You," available from the Women's Action Alliance (see resource list below).

7. If there is an effort to pass gay rights legislation in your area, be sure that lesbians play a major role in it and receive prominent media attention along with the men. Legislation is something that the media often *does* take seriously, so don't miss this opportunity to cash in on media attention. Offer your spokeswomen to news shows, talk shows, and newspapers in your area.

8. If there is currently no lesbian or gay minority programming in your area on radio or television, try to stimulate some. When you make your pitch to the station, connect lesbians with the rationale for minority programming, which is specifically for those groups in the culture whose concerns are unique and so little understood that special programming is needed. In our case, lesbian programming is needed because heterosexuals don't have the background necessary to do justice to the subject.

9. Advertise the activities of your group in the local movement media and nonmovement media. Don't overlook community "bulletin boards" or public announcements on radio or TV stations.

RESOURCES

"How to Make the Media Work for You." Available from the Women's Action Alliance, 370 Lexington Ave., New York, N.Y. 10017. $3.50. Includes information on most of the above-mentioned media efforts. An excellent manual.

"How to Book a TV or Radio Program and Why, How to Complain to the Media," by Loretta Lotman. Available from NGTF, 80 Fifth Ave., New York, N.Y. 10011. 50¢

"Making News—Getting Your News in Print," by Sasha Gregory-Lewis. Available at no charge from *The Advocate,* 1800 N. Highland Ave., Los Angeles, Calif. 90028. Information on how to write a press release.

"Gays and the Press." Available from NGTF, 50¢. How to get coverage in your local newspaper.

Access Magazine, publication of the National Citizens Committee for Broadcasting, 1028 Connecticut Ave., N.W., Washington, D.C. 20036. Subscription $12/year (2nd-class mail); $15 (1st-class mail).

"National Gay News Summary" and covering letter to TV networks. Covers period from January 1975 through June 1976. Serves as a sample for local groups to follow. Covering letter contains good arguments to use with straight media for covering lesbian/gay news.

NGTF Statement Presented to the FCC, Nov. 15, 1976. Available from NGTF, 50¢. Contains specific recommendations on what the FCC should do to protect access of the lesbian/gay community to the broadcast media.

"How to Participate in Ascertainment." Available from NGTF. 50¢. Information for lesbian/gay groups on how to participate in the ascertainment process, a procedure that all broadcasters must follow in order to qualify for license renewal. This is a must!

Media News Keys. A guide to national and local radio and TV talk shows, news shows, names of producers, etc. $50/year. Media News Keys, 150 Fifth Ave., New York, N.Y. 10011.

"Guidelines for Portrayals of Lesbians/Gay Men in Broadcasting." Available from NGTF. 50¢.

Guidelines for the Portrayals of Lesbians in the Media." Available from Lesbian Feminist Liberation, 243 W. 20th St., New York, N.Y. 10011.

Media Report to Women 1977 Index/Directory, edited by Martha Leslie Allen. Available from Women's Institute for Freedom of the Press, 3306 Ross Pl., N.W., Washington, D.C. 20008. 202 966-7783. $8. Includes a five-year index of *Media Report to Women,* a monthly publication ($10/year by personal check or money orders; otherwise $15/year) and a comprehensive Directory of Women's Media groups, periodicals, presses, etc.

A Survey of Lesbian Publications

JACKIE ST. JOAN, ESQ.

LESBIANS NOT ONLY HAVE SOMETHING TO SAY—BUT WE HAVE SOMETHING TO SAY IT WITH!

This is not a rave review. Nor is it a pessimistic survey of lesbian publications. It is an attempt to describe with some perspective the unique explosion of woman-identified print media which has developed over the past six years. This article includes analysis by format, content, readership, and political perspective, as well as some observations of recent themes in lesbian publications and a critique of lesbian publications, both as journalism and as political propaganda.

From a historical perspective this subject is a first in written history—the expression by lesbians of their own minds' contents in media owned and controlled by lesbians. What printed words may have existed before this time have been eliminated or suppressed by male publishers long ago. To start with, I want to reveal my own biases as a reviewer, so as not to produce simply another personal comment to toss into the hopper. My biases are these: I look for quality of production reflective of a seriousness of purpose; I look for a political content reflective of a commitment to overcoming male domination; I look for news reflective of an appreciation of the overall news blackout about lesbians in the male press. Also I am always searching for stimulation to keep the oxygen going to my brain tissues.

What is meant by a lesbian publication? Simply put, it includes those publications that are owned and managed by lesbians, that are intended for a lesbian readership, and that are committed to serving, speaking, and fighting for the lesbian community. Naturally, lesbians, being the varied, untamable creatures that we are, read more than those publications identifiable as "lesbian publications." Such feminist publications as *Big Mama Rag, Off Our Backs, Quest,* and assorted NOW newsletters may in fact be a primary source of information about women for many lesbians. However, this article will focus on those publications that are lesbian by definition, and some of the gay publications, which contain material relevant to lesbians.

According to *format,* lesbian publications can be roughly categorized as (1) a newsletter, (2) a magazine or journal, or (3) a newspaper. According to *content,* however, the distinctions begin to fade. Newsletters produced by mimeograph or offset press are usually defined as internal organs of communication among organi-

zational members. Among lesbians, as often as not, there is no formal organization, but a loose network of individuals. In fact, the term newsletter is more revealing of the finances of a group (or an initial production decision of a preceding group) more than it is of the substance of the publication itself. There may be little relation between format and content—a newsletter may contain as much theoretical material as announcements of local events. By content, the line between what is a magazine or journal and what is a newspaper practically disappears altogether.

Most publications begin with a focus on local readership, but it is often difficult to maintain that focus for several reasons. To support a publication's growth financially, it often must be geared to purchasers beyond its local area. In addition, the geography of the lesbian ego and of lesbian-feminist communities extends beyond the political geography of the local area. A lesbian living in upstate New York is concerned about issues and identifies with lesbians living in Vancouver or Arizona, as readily as she does with the lesbian who lives down the road. The *political perspectives* of lesbian publications range the spectrum from reform (gay rights) to radical (lesbian-feminist opposition to patriarchy and capitalism) to dyke separatism (active political withdrawal). Contrary to the periodic Death Certificates devised and irregularly issued by the male media,[1] the feminist movement is alive, and the lesbian-feminist movement, in particular, continues to grow. It is worthwhile to mention those lesbian publications that have met various voluntary and involuntary deaths along the way, however, not with a sense of failure, but with appreciation and respect to the foremothers who produced them. *The Ladder,* first published by Daughters of Bilitis in 1956 in San Francisco, was the first lesbian publication to put ink to paper, followed some fourteen years later by *Ain't I a Woman?* (Iowa City) and *The Furies* (Washington, D.C.). Both *The Furies* and *AIAW* expressed the rage of dyke separatism and revealed the depths of the class schism within the feminist movement. *Amazon Quarterly,* principal literary and theoretical journal among lesbians for several years, ceased publication about three years ago. Along with these should be added a number of local publications that have stopped publishing or have evolved into something else—*Lavender Woman* (Chicago), *Lazette* (New Jersey), *The Pedestal* (Vancouver), *Cowrie* (New York), and *Desperate Living* (Baltimore).[2]

In the tradition of Wicca, the eldest enters the circle first. Thus the distinction of being the oldest, living lesbian publication goes to *The Lesbian Tide* (current circulation: 6,700). Publishing bimonthly since 1971, *The Tide* also ranks highest in the criteria of journalistic excellence—integrity, fairness, and technical excellence. A magazine-on-newsprint published in Los Angeles, *The Tide* offers consistently good news writing,

---

[1] See cover story, "Requiem for the Women's Movement," *Harper's,* November 1976.

[2] *Desperate Living* published its last issue in 1977.

interspersed with analysis and opinion material, as well as in-depth features. Instead of serving up yesterday's leftovers to its readers, *The Tide* takes responsibility for local investigative news coverage and origination of news elsewhere—an outstanding quality which many publications lack. Politically insistent but flexible, the Tide Collective encourages controversy as a source of political growth. It is the only lesbian newspaper of its kind—would that it were a daily on my doorstep![3]

The newest born babe of lesbian publications comes from the South—*Sinister Wisdom,* published in Charlotte, North Carolina. A neat, impressive triannual magazine with definite literary leanings, it welcomes "ALL forms of material . . . related to the creation of a revolutionary lesbian imagination in politics/art." What it lacks in illustrations it compensates for in the depth of both its undertaking and its content. *Sinister Wisdom* is a journal that demands thinking, sophistication, and occasional long-suffering, of its readers. Vulnerable, intense, imaginative—the magazine is reminiscent of the best relationships I have known.

Withdrawing a deep breath and myself from what *Sinister Wisdom* arouses, I change gears to discuss the most exciting development in lesbian publications—*Lesbian Connection.* Having the largest circulation of any lesbian publication (at this writing, well over 7,000) and still growing, *LC* is a vital, informative monthly newsletter by, for, and about lesbians, produced by the ever-optimistic, ever-well-organized Ambitious Amazons of Lansing, Michigan. The concept is simple—a centralized round-robin printing of letters and news from lesbians all over the world. The publication is free, supported entirely by donations and the labors of the Ambitious Amazons themselves, who share *LC's* processes—financial, editorial, administrative—with readers, and promote a sense of well-being and unity among its individual subscribers. *LC* is a particularly well suited avenue of expression for lesbians who are just "coming out," as its format is informal, its style is unintimidating, its attitude is tolerant. It is a simple way of keeping current with developments among lesbians, as well as a means of receiving letters and diminishing isolation.

Linking lesbians to the north, *Long Time Coming* (Montreal) is the national Canadian lesbian publication, which, after publishing for several years, ceased publication temporarily due to a fire in their offices. Soon to be revived this year, *Long Time Coming* (circulation: 3,000) plans to publish every two months—with Canadian news from the prolific Canadian feminist press, features, letters, reviews, and its regular Lesbian Lifestyle section. Using a mimeo newsletter format, *LTC* encourages the development of a visible dyke culture in Canada.

Albatross, the radical lesbian-feminist satire quarterly, operates by a standard of its own, hardly capable of evaluation in an article like this one. Tacky Productions has created a medium offensive, beautifully designed magazine that may find you straining to laugh.

Created in reaction to lesbian suppression in its local area (East Orange, New Jersey), *Albatross* appears confused and halfhearted in carrying out its purposes, mixing serious comment with attempts at satire, which often barely reach the status of sarcasm. However, with a novel approach to politics (destroying patriarchial myths)—such as "Jesus Christ on a Bicycle Comix" or "Betty Frypan [Friedan] Funnies" mixed with personal ramblings and stoned raps—*Albatross* does encourage lesbians' continued hope for a high-quality satire magazine.

There are a number of lesbian publications that, upon careful reading, appear to be held together by the labors of one or two women, with contributions from other writers. This kind of structure often weighs against diversity and development, but sometimes can produce a particularly well fashioned publication. *Lesbian Voices* (San Jose, California) is one such publication. *Lesbian Voices* is a small quarterly journal of ideas, opinions, and poetry, with some very good writing and research between its attractive lavender pages. The journal is influenced by the anarchist politics of its editor (Rosalie Nichols), and by her genuine love for writing and quality.

Among struggling journalists, wasting copy space is probably one of the most serious offenses there is, and *Dyke* magazine (Preston Hollow, New York) thus may be the greatest sinner of them all. This visually enticing quarterly magazine abuses valuable news space by filling it with trite meanderings on such superficial subjects as dyke fashions and interior decorating. Lacking political analysis (even of dyke separatism) or the talents to express the written word, *Dyke,* fortunately still a baby in the lesbian publishing world, unfortunately displays the temperament of a spoiled brat.

A number of lesbian newsletters/journals specifically serve the local communities where they are published. *Focus* (Boston) and *ALFA* (Atlanta) are two of the best. *Focus,* a small mimeo journal, is published by the Boston Daughters of Bilitis. Its design is clean and simple; its contents are mostly fiction, reviews, and poetry with local DOB news; its political perspective is of the "gay is good" variety. *ALFA,* the monthly newsletter of the Atlanta Lesbian-Feminist Alliance, is a free-floating grass-roots information and political organ that packs a lot of spirit into its mimeo pages. It contains local comment on recent lesbian activities, as well as some reviews and interviews. Other lesbian newsletters are listed in the section following this article. The listing also includes lesbian publications outside of North America—from New Zealand, England, and Germany—which, unfortunately, I was unable to obtain for review.

Most gay publications are owned and controlled by men, and thus do not fit the criteria for lesbian publications. However, since some lesbians identify more readily with gay liberation than with dyke separatism or lesbian feminism, lesbians do pick up gay publications, hoping to find some mention of their existence under the covers. The following publications are recommended pickups.

---

[3]Note my biases at the beginning of this article.

Christopher Street, the new *New Yorker* of the gay world, complete with appropriate cartoons and middle-class marketing, contains some material that is significant to lesbians. Published in New York, the monthly magazine appeals to the literary lesbian in particular—with interviews, short stories, novel excerpts, and personality snaps on lesbian celebrities. Other than presenting the "gay is good" propaganda, its political inclinations are manifested more in the selection of persons interviewed and writers published than in editorial rousings. With a one-third representation of females listed on the masthead, *Christopher Street* offers lesbians more quality than quantity.

The Gay Community News (Boston), also known as *The Gay Weekly,* is a newspaper written mostly by men of the gay rights movement, and contains some coverage of lesbian news. *GCN* is particularly valuable to the lesbian press as a news source. About one third of *GCN* is ad copy, so, like most male publications, it is able to afford the amenities (necessities, really) of respectable journalism (typesetting, weekly publication, correspondents, origination of news). Unlike some gay male skin-sheets, *GCN*'s display advertising has a minimum of sexism, and its publishers maintain a consistent liberal political stance. *GCN* reflects community involvement, diversity, growth, and straight press credibility. It contains some interesting stories which are valuable to lesbians, particularly to those on the East Coast, and news of gay rights developments internationally.

Body Politic is my most exciting discovery in reviewing gay publications. Published ten times a year in Toronto, the newspaper is published by what is apparently a collective of feminist leftist faggots. The special double issue that I found contains a short story by Jane Rule, a speech by Delores Klaitsch about the state of the women's movement, and an interview with a Canadian lesbian activist, as well as several lesbian cultural reviews. *Body Politic*'s international approach is refreshing and balanced—for example, the speech by Klaitsch was a "token" American subject, offered in a series that included features about homosexuality in the German Democratic Republic, Cuba, Argentina, and Mexico. *Body Politic,* which is partially funded by a grant from the Ontario Arts Council and which recently passed its fifth birthday, also contains a literary supplement, "Our Image," which offers book, film, and music reviews, many of relevance to lesbians.

THE STATE OF THE LESBIAN PRESS

The lesbian press is new, bearing the marks of its birth— the subjectivism of the sixties counterculture, the arrogance of Marxist politics, the reactions of separatism, the vision of a woman-identified world. It also bears the trappings of childhood—limited control of material resources, uncertainty of goals, unfamiliarity with new skills, reaching for maturity in a movement that itself is new. An analysis of lesbian publications cannot ignore these facts, whether approaching the topic from the point of view of journalism or of propaganda.

Lesbians must operate with some criteria in judging a publication as a piece of journalism. Some criteria[4] would include: (1) *integrity*—being detached from "any particular feminist politics, yet responsible and accountable to feminists"[5] as a whole; (2) *fairness*—giving many sides of a story, printing the source of opinion statements, and generally making distinctions between facts and opinions; (3) *technical excellence*—legibility, readability, originality, and a general concern about quality of production.

By propaganda I do not mean the popularized notion of social thought control (and its negative connotations), but more precisely a set of methods and symbols used by a political group to cause participation in its actions by a mass of individuals psychologically unified through media.[6] (Some lesbian examples of propaganda would be: Sisterhood is powerful; Gay is good; The personal is political; A woman without a man is like a fish without a bicycle.) Propaganda fortifies an ideology within a political group and eventually spreads that ideology beyond the group's borders. To be effective it requires a level of organization that lesbian feminists have not yet attained. However, some tentative propaganda objectives of current lesbian media would be the following: (1) *psychological*—to rid lesbians of guilt and to instill pride in being a lesbian and in being a woman; (2) *political*—to transmit certain feminist beliefs and ideas, thus developing a feminist theoretical base as well as group identity; (3) *cultural*—to communicate a growing lesbian culture expressive of those ideas (humor, music, art, fantasy); and (4) *social*—to provide an outlet to the individual's need for expression of opinion, design, and organizational functioning.

Through its strength as spirited new journalism, the lesbian press has succeeded in some of these propaganda objectives. However, the attainment has been a by-product of journalism, more coincidental than deliberate. To advance to the level of genuine propaganda, the lesbian press would require more political intent and organization than currently exists. If and how this would happen remains to be seen, although politically conscious lesbian journalists cannot retreat from its consideration.

As spirited as the lesbian journalism has been, its weaknesses are also glaring. Possibly the two most dangerous weaknesses are these: (1) There is *too little news,* and (2) there is not enough emphasis on *quality writing*

---

[4]Adapted from Roland E. Wolseley, "Pro and Con on the Black Press," *The Black Press, U.S.A.* (Ames, Iowa: Iowa State University Press, 1971).

[5]"The Ethics of Feminist Journalism," *Quest: A Feminist Quarterly* (Communication and Control issue), Vol. III, No. 2 (Fall 1976), p. 35.

[6]Adapted from a definition by Jacques Ellul, *Propaganda, the Formation of Men's Attitudes,* trans. from the French by K. Kellen and J. Lerner (New York: Alfred A. Knopf, 1965).

and production skills. Lesbian publications rely largely on one another and on feminist, gay, and other "alternative" media for news. Thus, most contain reprints of news and features with little attention given to investigative journalism. In fact, investigative journalism and original features are luxuries to the struggling lesbian publication, striving to keep its head above water and unable to pay its workers.[7] One result is that lesbian publications (as well as feminist publications, generally) focus on *personalities and ideas as news.* This reflects both our need for symbols and our need for developing political theory. However, from a practical standpoint, the imbalance also results from a lesbian news blackout. Good news is hard to find; writing reviews is easier than investigating a story. Thus personalities fill our pages and their ideas become our headlines.

The danger here is that journalists may see themselves simply as passive observers and not as women generating their own stories and their own power. We desperately need information. As I. F. Stone has stated, "The fault I find with most American newspapers is not the absence of dissent. It is the absence of news. . . ."[8]

Lesbian publications also suffer from a lack of journalistic expertise and quality writing. The feminist movement has affirmed the subjective approach to writing and the validity of personal experience as a source of consciousness. Thus, much writing, while having an authentic letter-writing quality, is often disorganized and evasive. As Jeanne Cordova, a founder of *The Lesbian Tide,* has stated: "Authenticity does not a writer make. . . . A dozen times I have read the same story written by three different women, and invariably one version is more imaginative, more capturing, and more accurate than the other two."[9]

Reviewing the past several years of lesbian publications, I am struck by certain recurring themes within: (1) an examination (often ad nauseam) of relationships—monogamy vs. nonmonogamy; long- vs. short-term, recovering from the lost lover—all reflective of the personal pain in lesbians' lives and of the desire to confirm some kind of public existence; and (2) the defensiveness of political dialogue—reflective of our political immaturity and personal insecurity about political ideas.

To make an analogy to the black press: A black historian has written: "The early protest papers [in the 1840s] were influential and important not for their total content but for their value as outlets for opinion. As sermonizers, as exhorters, they were effective, but their readers still had to become informed of facts and strategies after the sermons were over. For those simpler times the protest papers performed a function, but it was not and still is not, the sole fuction of a press that wants protection of its freedom."[10] What this suggests is that the next stage of development of communications among lesbians should be an acknowledgment of a passing political phase of lesbian journalism as an emotional outlet, and a recognition of the need for expansion and specialization.

Maintaining an ongoing publication means renewing the interest of the reader and continuously challenging her intelligence and spirit. In a world in which people assume a certain level of media sophistication, a lesbian publication must compete to some extent for the attention of its readers. Lacking the privileges and resources that commercial publications have, lesbian publications, and their readers as well, often have to settle for less. "The danger in the compromise [of quality for survival] is that it can result in a contentedness with slovenly reporting, careless writing, confusing makeup, and a generally mediocre publication."[11] A frenzy of production ("Get it to the printer, whatever it is!") disperses energy as much as a frenzy on group process, and both deny the purpose of lesbians linking ourselves for survival and for taking power. The continued development of the lesbian press is essential. It is important not only that lesbians have something to say, but that we have something to say it with![12]

Members of The Lesbian Tide Collective: Sharon McDonald, Shirl Buss, and Jeanne Cordova

[7]A feminist news service is currently being organized in the United States—FNS, P.O. Box 18417, Denver, Colo. 80218. The Feminist News Service in Canada has been functioning for several years. With the development of these organizations, local publications should be somewhat freed-up to pursue local investigations and to contribute them to the news services.

[8]I. F. Stone, *The Haunted Fifties* (New York: Random House, 1969), p. xxi.

[9]"Advocacy Journalism," *Quest: A Feminist Quarterly* (Communications and Control issue), Vol. III, No. 2 (Fall 1976), p. 40.

[10]Wolseley, *The Black Press,* p. 300.

[11]Ibid.

[12]Adapted from Maurice Sendack, *Higgelty Piggelty Pop or There Must Be More to Life.* Note: Jennie, the dog, ate all the leaves off her friend the talking plant, so that soon the plant not only had nothing left to say, but nothing left to say it with. Beware!

11. Lesbian Culture

Kay Gardner

Women's Music

JOAN NIXON and GINNY BERSON

Note: The richly creative and unique talents of lesbian feminists have become much more visible over the past few years, with the emergence of a women's cultural community that is producing and enjoying its own literature, art and music. Of these forms, women's music has so far attracted the widest audiences (gathered in one place, at least) with the additional draw of providing a much-needed social outlet.

The qualities of women's music are gentleness, passion, sensitivity, and strength—in sharp contrast to the blasting hard rock fed to us by the male culture. The themes of our music are self-love, love of other women, love of animals and living things, the damage done to women by the patriarchy and the need to separate from men, the healing powers of sisterhood, ourselves as a spiritual source, the rising tide of feminist power, and the creation of a new social order based on feminist principles of nurturance.

Inspired by the folk-art tradition as well as a political awareness, our troubadours travel from coffeehouse to coffeehouse, city to city, and festival to festival. Everywhere they go, women gather in great numbers to hear them, and are enthralled and transported. For that period of time they are immersed in sisterhood

and protected from the outside culture which drains their energies.

In the following statements, Joan Nixon, a former writer for *Lavender Woman,* traces the growth in popularity of women's music and music festivals, and Ginny Berson describes the philosophy and services of Olivia Records, a national women's recording company whose pioneering efforts have served as a model for this type of enterprise.

This article is entitled "Women's Music" instead of "Lesbian Music" because not all entertainers in this community identify (openly, at least) as lesbians (despite their strong presence in this context). All photographs reproduced here, however, are of acknowledged lesbians.—Ed.

My first experience with the power and joy of women's music began in October 1972, in Chicago, with the first Family of Woman concert. Family of Woman was a four-woman band, Linda Shear, Joan Capra, Ella Szekely, and Sherry Jenkins, and their concert blew my mind. They had hundreds of women stomping, clapping, and dancing. The Family gave a concert about once a month thereafter, and women came from miles around to hear them. In April 1973 FOW and other Chicago dykes went to California for the West Coast Lesbian Conference, where M'Lou Brubaker from Chicago organized a music and politics workshop. Linda Shear, M'Lou Brubaker, and I stayed in California for Kate Millett's Feminist Music Festival at Sacramento in early May 1973. Kate even had a women's film crew to document the event. We met many women musicians and wanted to start a women musicians' newsletter to help everyone get in contact with each other. Our newsletter idea never got off the ground. Later *Paid My Dues* from Milwaukee and Indy Allen's *Musica* newsletter fulfilled some of that need.

In June 1974 Kristin Lems and others organized the first National Women's Music Festival in Champaign-Urbana, Illinois, an event that was repeated again in June 1975 and June 1976. NWMF One brought women musicians together who had never heard each other play before and inspired much musical sharing and celebration. Margie Adam, Cris Williamson, Meg Christian, Vicki Randle, and Woody Simmons gave an unforgettable concert on Saturday night, paving the way for later collaborations and joint concerts. Casse Culver and her womanager, Spotts, put together a concert tour from contacts made at Champaign and shared the information and contacts with the Clinch Mountain Back-Steppers and the Berkeley Women's Music Collective and others so that a whole network of women concert producers has been established around the country. Kay Gardner developed her ideas about circular modes in women's music.

After Champaign, women's music seemed to take off. In August 1974, an Amazon Music Festival was held in Santa Cruz, California, and Margie Adam, Cris Williamson, and Vicki Randle performed together in Los Angeles. That fall a large Womansphere festival was held in Maryland. More women's bands were forming and more women were getting their music out on high-quality women-produced records. Cris Williamson, Jackie Robbins, and June Millington, and later Holly Near and Meg Christian, made extremely successful concert tours in 1976.

Maxine Feldman was probably the first musician in the country to perform publicly as a lesbian—she wrote her song "Angry Atthis" in 1969, about wanting to hold her lover's hand in public. In 1972 the Chicago Women's Liberation Rock Band and the New Haven Women's Liberation Rock Band came out with their fine album celebrating feminist music and politics, *Mountain Moving Day*. Jody Aliesan produced her record "You'll Be Hearing More from Me," in Seattle. "Lavender Jane Loves Women," by Alix Dobkin and Kay Gardner, was the first lesbian album to enjoy national distribution. Willie Tyson produced and distributed her first album, *Full Count*. Olivia Records, which started in Washington, D.C., and later moved its base to Los Angeles, produced albums by Meg Christian and Cris Williamson. Ginni Clemmens's album *I'm Looking for Some Long Time Friends* came out of Chicago. Casse Culver's *Three Gypsies* and Margie Adam's *Songwriter* albums appeared in late 1976. Be Be K'Roche and the Berkeley Women's Music Collective have albums now, both distributed by Olivia.

Few performers have been willing to make their lesbian politics and life-style the focal point of their musical performance partly because their job opportunities as musicians thus become limited. Maxine Feldman was alone as a lesbian performer in 1969. Linda Shear and Ella Szeckely performed as lesbians in April 1972 in Chicago. The Family of Woman band stated in their contracts that they had to be billed as lesbian-feminist musicians. Alix Dobkin's latest album, *Living with Lesbians* celebrates women loving women. Linda Shear currently wants to play concerts for lesbians only.

As the women's movement gains momentum, women's music will be an increasingly important vehicle to bring women together. Women are beginning to remember and reclaim our ancient rites and traditions. Perhaps the Amazons and witches are among us again. A time for celebration is at hand. Linda Shear's wonderful song "Family of Woman" proclaims this hope:

We are bringing in the dawn. Family of woman we have begun; family of woman we will become; family of woman, we are tearing down the walls; family of woman, we are more than slaves and dolls. Women sing of mountain moving days—the day is now! Armies of lovers cannot fail. [1]

—Joan Nixon

---

[1] "Mountain moving days" is quoted from the Chicago Women's Liberation Rock Band; "Armies of lovers cannot fail" derives from a phrase by Oscar Wilde quoted by Rita Mae Brown.

OLIVIA RECORDS

There are no lesbians in the world. Nor are there many (if any) strong women, or women who care about anything other than the men in their lives. If you don't believe this, just listen to popular music. The women sing about the men they're in love with, who are usually the men who just left them or the men they're trying to get. There are no songs about women caring about other women or even women caring about themselves.

Olivia Records, a national women's recording company, was formed in 1973 with the specific intent of providing women with a chance to create and disseminate their own musical definitions. It was started by a group of lesbian feminists new to both business and recording who set for Olivia Records the following goals: (1) to make high-quality women's music (music that speaks honestly and realistically about women's lives) available to the public, (2) to provide talented women-oriented musicians with access to the recording industry and control over their music, (3) to provide music-industry-related jobs for large numbers of women, with reasonable salaries and in unoppressive situations, and (4) to provide training for women in all aspects of the recording industry.

In four years of existence we have produced one single, six albums, and two songbooks. We have set up our own distribution network, which covers the United States, Canada, and parts of Europe, and in addition to distributing our own products, we distribute three other albums, all of which are woman-produced. We have grown from an initial volunteer labor force to a full-time staff of thirteen. At first our records were carried by a hundred or so feminist stores throughout the country; now many major record chains and stores stock and display them. Because of the growing demand for woman-identified music, some stores have set up "women's music" sections. We have gone from almost no radio play to spots on the play lists of major FM stations all over the United States. We have sold over eighty thousand records. In short, with the help of many women, we have learned the business and found that there is a tremendous need for and response to the music we are providing.

What does it matter that we are all lesbians? Olivia is a political organization as well as a recording company. We are not interested in becoming a female version of the male record industry. We operate collectively, in a nonhierarchical fashion. The basis of our ability to operate collectively is that we trust each other politically. We trust, after many years of working together, that when decisions are made they are made with the best interests of Olivia Records in mind, given the goals we have set for ourselves. And the basis of our political trust comes from the fact that we are all lesbian feminists, who see our present and future intimately connected with the future of all women. We love women; we put all our energy into women; we get all our energy from women; we define ourselves in terms of women; we recognize that we are oppressed because we are women and that we will end our oppression with the help of other women, especially women who are willing to make a full-time, lifelong commitment to women's struggles. We have weathered a thousand crises together because we have never had to question our basic assumptions or our basic woman-identification.

Not only is Olivia a recording company and a political organization, it is also a money-generating institution. We know that what we create, we control. By creating our own structures, we are providing jobs for women who would otherwise be working for men, very possibly in jobs that drain their energy, don't pay them enough, don't treat them like human beings, and are not concerned with making basic societal changes. Most women have to work at such jobs (unless they are very rich, or very lucky, or can't find any jobs at all). The more women who can be freed from situations that are oppressive, the more women will be able to devote their lives to building a better world.

We also know that huge amounts of money are needed to build a movement—for travel, for communication, for salaries, for food and rent, for health. We must have money in order to pay people who are doing important political work so that they can do it full-time. We must have money so that groups of women who are involved in non-money-making but crucial political activities have the money they need to do their work.

We must also be able to publish our own books and newspapers; produce our own music and films; provide our own health care; supply food, housing, clothing; take care of our children. And we must be sure that the products and services we provide are relevant to all women—regardless of class, race, or age.

Finally, we must be sure that whenever we can, we support our institutions, even though they might not yet be as wide-reaching as male institutions; for how else will our own structures grow if they don't have the support of the women who will ultimately benefit from them?

The records that we have and will continue to produce reflect the full range of women's experiences—our joys, our anger, our pain, our friendships, our loves, our growth, our strength. Our first album, *Meg Christian: I Know You Know,* includes songs about women supporting and caring for each other ("Joanna," "Valentine Song"), a song about the pain caused by a society that degrades women and lesbians ("Scars"), and the hilarious "Ode to a Gym Teacher." The response we have gotten from women around the world tells us that in this album women are finding carefully arranged and exquisitely performed music centered around Meg's voice and classical guitar; and comfort, personal validation, and political support; strength, help to change, laughs from deep inside, pride, and the power and happiness that come from being a woman who is learning to take control of her life.

Cris Williamson is one of the finest singer-songwriters we have ever met. Her album *The Changer and the Changed* includes "Waterfall," a song about life's cycles; "Dream Child," a celebration of sensuality and the experience of feeling good in one's body; and "Sweet Wom-an," a song about the beautiful strength of women. Cris sees herself as a healer, and her album is a source of comfort and inspiration to women.

Our third album, *Be Be K'Roche,* a four-woman band, was a complete departure for us from our other albums. We were excited to move into a whole new area of women's experiences and music. The album is a sensual, rhythmic blend of Latin, rhythm and blues, jazz, and rock music and features songs such as "Strong and Free," "Gotta Make Something of My Life," and "Kahlúa Mama." It's hard not to dance to this album. But it's not just a dance album. Each song is carefully crafted and is rich with the addition of back-up vocals, percussion, synthesizer, clavinet, and flute to the basic band tracks of drums, bass, guitar, and piano.

Where Would I Be Without You: The Poetry of Pat Parker and Judy Grahn is our first spoken-word record; it is an intense, extraordinarily moving statement by two women who express their poetry in the forceful words and concrete images that come from the real places where all women live. Included are Pat Parker's "Womanslaughter" and "For Straight Folks Who Don't Mind Gays but Wish They Weren't So Blatant" and Judy Grahn's "A History of Lesbianism" and poems from the "She Who" collection.

Album number five is Teresa Trull's *The Ways a Woman Can Be.* Teresa had performed as a soloist for many years, but when she made her album she worked with a band and combined their musical vision with her own southern soul roots. Teresa's voice is remarkably expressive and gutsy. She sings of her love for women ("I Hope She'll See," "I'd Like to Make Love with You") and our struggles for survival ("Don't Say Sister," "Women-Loving Wimmin"). This album comes from a woman who knows that living her politics is a most joyful, exhilarating means of self-expression.

Linda (Tui) Tillery, who produced the Be Be K'Roche and Teresa Trull albums, is the featured musician on Olivia's sixth album. Tui's album is an exciting blend of jazz and rhythm and blues and speaks particularly to the experiences of Third World women. All Tui's talents shine through—as a singer, drummer, producer, arranger, songwriter, and interpreter.

Olivia has also produced songbooks of Meg's and Cris's albums. Our next project will be Meg Christian's second album.

Additionally, Olivia distributes the records on the Urana label, produced by Wise Women enterprises, including Kay Gardner's *Mooncircles,* an album of classical flute, guitar, cello, small percussion, and piano. Kay also accompanies herself on autoharp or guitar for her songs of growth, change, and spirituality such as "Wise Woman" and "Beautiful Friend." *Mooncircles* is part of Kay's search for women's musical forms and instrumental combinations.

Casse Culver's *Three Gypsies,* also on the Urana label, is a combination of country, folk, and pop music that takes the listener on a journey into the open spaces and sharing of life embraced in songs like "Good Old Dora" and "Desert Eyes." The album features a wide range of instrumentation, and there is an intimate, down-home feeling present, especially on the country side.

Olivia also distributes the *Berkeley Women's Music Collective,* an album of strong woman-identified music, featuring "The Bloods," "Gay and Proud," and "Fury." The group approached the whole album collectively; each of the four members wrote songs, and they trade off instruments. Their fine instrumentals and interesting harmonies create incredible, whimsical energy, and the joy of women working together comes through in every line.

Olivia Records is growing and expanding all the time. Eventually we hope to have control over all aspects of record production, including having our own studio, record pressing equipment, and jacket printing and fabricating facilities. We believe that women have much to say and that we are providing an opportunity for women to learn, teach, work, and make music that will enrich our culture and strengthen us all.

–Ginny Berson

RESOURCES

Women's Recording Companies

Olivia Records, P.O. Box 70237, Los Angeles, Calif. 90070. 213 389-4243.

Wise Women Enterprises, Inc./Urana Records, P.O. Box 297, West Station, New York, N.Y. 10014; 212 989-2998. Also: P.O. Box 33, Stonington, Maine 04681; 207 367-2783.

Pleiades Records, P.O. Box D, Dixon, Calif. 95620.

Project #1, Preston Hollow, New York 12469.

Submaureen Records, P.O. Box 147, Hyannis Port, Mass. 02467.

Full Count-Lima Bean Records, 217 12th St., S.E., Washington, D.C., 20003.

Atthis Productions, Sunset, Maine 04683.

Recording Artists

Margie Adam, "Margie Adam, Songwriter." Produced and distributed by Pleiades Records, P.O. Box D, Dixon, Calif. 95620.

"Berkeley Women's Music Collective," distributed by Olivia Records, P.O. Box 70237, Los Angeles, Calif. 90070.

Meg Christian, "I Know You Know," produced by Olivia Records.

Casse Culver, "Three Gypsies," produced by Wise Women Enterprises, Inc./Urana Records, available from Olivia Records.

Alix Dobkin, "Lavender Jane Loves Women" and "Living With Lesbians," available from Project #1, Preston Hollow, New York 12469.

Maxine Feldman, record in production, Atthis Productions, Sunset, Maine 04683.

Kay Gardner, "Mooncircles," produced by Wise Women Enterprises, available from Olivia Records.

Jade and Sarsaparilla, "Jade and Sarsaparilla," available from Submaureen Records, P.O. Box 147, Hyannis Port, Mass. 02467.

"Be Be K'Roche," Latin/jazz, available from Olivia Records.

Holly Near, "You Can Know All I Am," available from Redwood Records, 565 Doolin Canyon, Ukiah, Calif. 95482.

Teresa Trull, "The Ways a Woman Can Be," available from Olivia Records.

Willie Tyson, "Debutante," available from Wise Women Enterprises, P.O. Box 297 West Station, New York, N.Y. 10014, and from Willie Tyson, Full Count-Lima Bean Records, 217 12th St., S.E., Washington, D.C. 20003.

Chris Williamson, "The Changer and the Changed," available from Olivia Records.

Maxine Feldman

Production team for Casse Culver's album, Three Gypsies *(Wise Women Enterprises)*

Casse Culver

Lesbian Literature: An Introduction*

BERTHA HARRIS

Between the time of Sappho and the birth of Natalie Clifford Barney (between ca. 613 B.C. and A.D. 1876) lies a lesbian "silence" of twenty-four centuries. The *practice* of lesbianism, in its sexual and romantic meanings, never stopped: Every human phenomena, once expressed, will continue. somehow, to assert itself—if only in secrecy and disguise. For that terribly long time, however, *literary* expression of lesbianism was thwarted. There was no room, apparently, for *both* the assertion of the new patriarchal culture and the declaration of lesbian existence. If those 2,400 years tell lesbians nothing else about themselves, they may show that patriarchy regards lesbianism—and particularly "talking about" lesbianism—as anathema: as dangerous to the health. As Jeannette H. Foster stated in her pioneering work *Sex Variant Women in Literature* (1956), "No class of printed matter except outright pornography has suffered more critical neglect, exclusion from libraries, or omission from collected works than variant belles-lettres. Even items by recognized masters, such as Henry James' *The Bostonians* and Maupassant's *Paul's Mistress,* have been omitted from inclusive editions. . . . When owned by libraries such titles are often catalogued obscurely. . . ." But the problem is complicated by more than the simple fact of suppression—although that alone has been damaging enough. To make a body of work that can be immediately perceived as a "literature" (such as "French" literature, "Russian" literature, "Jewish" literature) there must first exist cultural *identity*: A group or a nation must know that it exists *as a group* and that it shares sets of characteristics that make it distinct from other groups: a sense of its own history, religion, myth, food, language, etc. From such group identity comes the literature of the group, which, like the cultural identity, flows from other sets of shared values and meanings: symbols, metaphors, narrative traditions, etc.—through which the language will evoke an explicit sense of "realness" for the group. Cultural (and therefore "literary") silence is first brought about through suppression of the group's sense of "realness"—especially through invalidation of experience. That which is unreal is unworthy of expression. Jeannette Foster's work, therefore, is more than an act of literary discovery: It is, in effect, an act of archaeology—a tremendous "dig" beneath the heterosexual literary mainstream to find surviving instances of lesbian erotic cir-

cumstance. But sexual experience alone does not a culture make—nor, again, does it incite what we have learned to discern as a literature.

The first modern attempt to make a lesbian "sensibility" based on considerably more than sexual activity happened in France around the turn of the century. Both the lives and the literary output of Natalie Clifford Barney and Renée Vivien (born Pauline Mary Tarn) were eloquent in their refusal of what they thought of as the "everyday"—bourgeois morality; and forthright in their declaration of lesbianism as a valid—indeed, superior—life-style. Their work is informed by a radicalism that would not find political expression until the late 1960s. In her novel *Une Femme m'apparut* (A Woman Appeared to Me), Renée Vivien has one of her characters ask: "In fact, San Giovanni, has a woman ever loved a man?" San Giovanni replies, "I can hardly conceive of such a deviation of the senses. Sadism and the rape of children seem more normal to me." Renée's friend and lover, Natalie Barney, while no less extreme in her assessment of heterosexuality and no less persuaded that lesbianism was the only natural, healthy—and thrilling—choice for a woman, was free of the fatal stress and conflicts that drove Vivien to an early grave (at thirty-two). And she was much more akin to contemporary lesbian feminists in style and outlook. Before her death at the age of ninety-six, in 1972, Barney had, with a cool reasonableness enraging to many of her lovers (including Vivien), dismissed sex roles, monogamy, possessiveness, sexual jealousy—in fact, all the contentions of heterosexual romance—as inappropriate to independent womanhood. Barney's work consists mainly of memoirs, brief fictional prose, some verse, most of it highly aphoristic; and, like Vivien's, it was composed in French. It is Natalie Barney's extraordinary person, rather than her work, that is mainly recalled—particularly as the model for some of the more fabulous figures in lesbian fiction. When the stalwart, but hapless, Stephen Gordon of *The Well of Loneliness* needs a "bad" character recommendation in order to drive her beloved Mary into the arms of a man and "normalcy," she turns to Valerie Seymour—and Valerie is unquestionably based on Natalie Barney, who found marriage, especially lesbian marriage, not only irrational but ludicrous. No amount of courage, insolence, or missionary effort, however, could save Barney and Vivien from the relative obscurity into which their work lapsed—probably because their celebration of lesbianism was also a celebration of female independence from men—a stance so abhorrent and threatening that, even in their own time, their writings were thoroughly suppressed outside the small homosexual society they mainly lived in. While the literary merit of Barney and Vivien's work is arguable, it does represent an end, historically, to lesbian silence—and, even more importantly, it established the precarious base for present lesbian literary expression. From this period, only the fiction of Radclyffe Hall, because it believes in God and male supremacy, because it argues for "tolerance," and Djuna Barnes's *Nightwood,* simply because it is a work of genius (*and* because it was introduced to the

*Copyright © 1977 by Bertha Harris.

Adrienne Rich, poet

truly bleak ages when hardly any woman was taught to read and write, lesbians have never stopped recording the stories of their lives—and somehow a handful have always been able to publish those stories. It is not the work per se we have lacked, but memory of the work that has gone before us: our literary past, and access to our literary present—which, by and large, is still being ignored or trivialized by the establishment press. The most serious effects of this deliberately induced amnesia have been prevention of that measure of truth that only fiction and poetry can express and prevention of that sense of community all writers need in order to learn and grow. During the Freudian fifties, the only publication that even attempted to meet those needs was *The Ladder*—first a mimeographed newsletter, then a magazine, created by the San Francisco chapter of Daughters of Bilitis. *The Ladder* published continuously for sixteen years; and *only* in its pages were lesbian fiction and verse noted, reviewed, discussed. One of the editors, Barbara Grier (alias Gene Damon), is the sole archivist of lesbian literature the world, as far as I know, has ever known. It has been only through her intrepid effort and attention that work from this period is remembered. Work from that time (pre-late sixties; before the feminist influence) falls very generally into two categories: fiction and poetry of genuine literary merit with a lesbian theme: work by Jane Rule, Maureen Duffy, May Sarton, Vita Sackville-West, Margaret Anderson, Dorothy Baker, et al.; and novels of the paperback pulp variety (by Ann Aldrich, Ann Bannon, Clair Morgan, Valerie Taylor, et al.), which, while meeting a commercial rather than literary market, nevertheless provided a romantic slice-of-life library for many lesbians of that generation.

The two novels that introduced the present stage of lesbian literature—and represent the first profound change in lesbian consciousness brought about by feminism—are Isabel Miller's *Patience and Sarah* (originally entitled *A Place for Us*) and Monique Wittig's *Les Guérillères*. Both works indicate, for the first time in lesbian imaginative literature, a sense of *shared* female experience and *shared* reevaluation of female and lesbian, identity and possibility. Both works achieve what Barney and Vivien, in isolation and without feminist community, could only attempt: a calm assumption of an independent female principle as a *reality*—a reality the authors were assured would be accepted and understood without question. While the two novels are utterly different in content, form, and style (Miller's is a naturalistic narrative; Wittig's, a mythic fantasy), both share the following premises in lesbian writing for the first time under patriarchal rule. Lesbianism is *natural* in human experience; women are capable of bonding together to make work as well as love; men are not as important as they think they are; lesbian experience is not analogous to male-female experience. At about the same time, Judy Grahn—in "Edward the Dyke," "A Woman Is Talking to Death," and "The Common Woman," poems—articulated the experience of the working-class lesbian, and that, too, was for the first time. Grahn's founding of the Women's Press Collective

general public by T. S. Eliot), have entered the literary mainstream. Gertrude Stein, another American lesbian in Paris whose time overlapped Barney's and Vivien's, has only of late begun to receive the critical attention she is due (mainly as a result of feminist demand). While her work is female-centered and, frequently, lavishly erotic, Stein lacked the "gay consciousness" of Barney and Vivien. Her own survival strategy consisted of an outright refusal to be a woman at all. Through her character Adele, in her lesbian novel *Q.E.D.,* Stein washes her hands of the problems of womanhood in general (and paraphrases the Jewish patriarch's prayer): "I always did thank God I wasn't born a woman." (An excellent analysis of this novel, as well as the biographical circumstances surrounding its composition, can be found in Jane Rule's *Lesbian Images*.) Again, until relatively recently, Stein has been popularly dismissed as "teacher" to those other American expatriates, Hemingway and Sherwood Anderson.

In her introduction to the new edition of *A Woman Appeared to Me* (Naiad Press), Gayle Rubin succinctly summarizes the critical problem of both lesbians and lesbians who want to make a lesbian literature: "It is notoriously difficult to maintain the memory of the past. But groups which are socially marginal are particularly relegated to the fringes of historical discussion. Lesbians, suffering from the dual disqualification of being gay and female, have been repeatedly dispossessed of their history." Emphasis should be placed on the word "repeatedly." Until the present, since the lesbian-feminist movement established the need for political as well as cultural identity, each impulse to make a lesbian sensibility has withered on the vine. Each new effort has been a process of reinventing the wheel. The sense of historical continuity, of "heritage," crucial to cultural formation, has been absent. Except for those in Oakland was a further challenge to the notion that writing and publishing are the perogatives of the elite. By the mid-seventies the press gave us the poetry of Pat Parker, a black lesbian feminist, and *Yesterday's Lessons,* a white working-class lesbian novel. These examples, however, are only a clue to the great changes in both quality and quantity lesbian writing has undergone under the feminist influences. In a relatively short space of time, we have gone from a starvation diet to a feast. One of the most significant effects of the lesbian-feminist movement on the writing and production of lesbian literature has been the building of independent women's presses, of which the Oakland group is only one example—and each with its own distinct areas of emphasis and priorities. Early in the women's movement, lesbian writers understood that the result of lifting the internal (self-made) censor would be the exercise of another kind of censoring by the establishment presses. Accustomed to the literary stereotypes of the lesbian as embittered, manlike, self-destructive monsters, the "straight" world is only gradually catching on to literature in which lesbians are three-dimensioned human beings—fortunately, however, the "new" lesbian writers did not care to wait for establishment acceptance and proceeded to do it themselves. Isabel Miller had to publish *Patience and Sarah* herself and "distribute" it from her shopping bag before McGraw-Hill—realizing that the general public not only would enjoy a good read about good lesbians but also would pay good money to do so—finally bought the novel. In 1973 Daughters, Inc., publishers of fiction by women, printed Rita Mae Brown's *Rubyfruit Jungle,* and, within the feminist community, turned it into a best-seller. Bantam Books brought out the mass-paper edition of Brown's work this year, and Daughters, with the money from the sale, will double its production of lesbian novels. The general character of the new lesbian writing is perhaps best summarized in some lines Renée Vivien wrote about a lover—lines expressive not only of the passion but of the kinship the lesbian imagination has already sought and is at last finding: "With her I dare not pretend or lie, because at that moment she lays her ear over my heart."*

SOME SOURCES FOR LESBIAN FICTION AND POETRY

Damon, Gene, et al. *The Lesbian in Literature: A Bibliography.* The Ladder, P.O. Box 5025, Washington Station, Reno, Nev. 89503.

Klaich, Dolores. *Woman + Woman.* New York: Morrow, 1974.

Rule, Jane. *Lesbian Images.* Garden City, N.Y.: Doubleday & Co., 1975.

The New Woman's Survival Sourcebook. New York: Alfred A. Knopf, 1975.

Women's Presses and Distributors

Several of the women's publishers and distributors listed here have catalogs available on request.

Publishing Houses

Persephone Press, P.O. Box 7222, Watertown, Ma. 02172.

Diana Press, 12 W. 25th St., Baltimore, Md. 21218.

Womanpress, Box 59330, Chicago, Ill. 60645.

Naiad Press, Box 5025, Washington Station, Reno, Nev. 89513. 816 633-4136.

Daughters, Inc., 22 Charles St., New York, N.Y. 10014.

Out-and-Out Books, 476 Second St., Brooklyn, N.Y. 11215. 212 499-9227.

Women's Press Collective, 5251 Broadway, Oakland, Calif. 94618.

Amazon Press, 395 60th St., Oakland, Calif. 94618.

Ladysmith Publishers, P.O. Box 8879, Minneapolis, Minn. 55408.

Distributors

Women in Distribution, P.O. Box 8858, Washington, D.C. 20003 (write for catalog).

Old Lady Blue Jeans, A Lesbian Distribution Process, P.O. Box 515, Northampton, Mass. 01060.

Amazon Reality, P.O. Box 95, Eugene, Ore. 97401.

Book Clubs

Women's Small Press Book Club, Box 9279, Long Beach, Calif. 90810.

Barbara Deming, author of We Cannot Live Without Our Lives

---

*Quoted by Gayle Rubin in the Introduction to *A Woman Appeared to Me* by Renée Vivien, Naiad Press, 1976.

Kate Millett, artist and author, with a sculpture from her environmental project "Naked Ladies," exhibited at the Woman's Building in Los Angeles

Lesbian Artists

Note: In the following statements, two lesbian visual artists–Harmony Hammond and Betsy Damon–speak to the lesbian community about their visions and experiences in a world of art dominated by men and heterosexuals.–Ed.

"Where I put my creative energy is a political decision."

What can I tell you except the truth? We do not have a history. We are not even visible to each other. Many well-known women artists of the twentieth century have been lesbians, but if they are famous as artists, it is never mentioned that they are lesbians, or how that might have affected the way they live, their work, or work processes. The best we have is Romaine Brooks, but she was rich and ensconced in villas, surrounded by monocled countesses. As wonderful as this sounds, it is unrealistic on my $360 a month. Rosa Bonheur lived with her Natalie for forty years and dressed in pants, but she didn't think that other women should.

In my search for contemporary lesbian artists, I spend much energy wondering and fantasizing about women who rejected passive female roles and committed themselves to art. After all, they did have young women as assistants and companions. But there is a space between us–time..., a silence, as large as the desert, because history has ignored lesbian visual artists. The patriarchy has taken them.

The silences, the words omitted from the biographies of lesbian artists, have denied us role models and the possibility of developing work that acknowledges lesbian experience as a creative source for art making and a context in which to explore it. I refuse to let them dispose of me in this way–to obliterate my existence as a lesbian and as an artist. I refuse to be quiet; I want lesbian artists to be visible.

Art not only reflects but creates and transforms cultural reality. Cultural reality is a whole made up of individual realities. I first came out as a lesbian through my work. I knew and identified myself as a lesbian before ever sleeping with a woman. My work is the place where I confronted myself, gave form to my thoughts, fears, fantasies, and ideas. I had been drawing on a tradition of women's creativity in my work, so it was only natural to acknowledge my feelings and desires for women. My work is a lover, a connection between creativity and sexuality. Since I came out as a lesbian through my work, I came out as a lesbian artist– meaning the two are connected and affect each other. This was relatively easy, perhaps as a matter of evolu-

tion. As lesbians we have the possibility of the utmost creative freedom to make the strongest, most sensitive statements. Passion gives substance.

I believe that there is something as yet indefinable in my work, and other work that we might call "lesbian sensibility," but for the most part it is hidden. As our work becomes more visible, public recurring themes and approaches will emerge and we can examine and develop them. How can lesbian sensibility exist in the context of patriarchal art? In some works lesbian imagery is overt– at least to other lesbians. In others, it is hidden or perhaps less important. That is okay; it's there and will come out. We do not need to define or limit it.

I feel that we are at a very important time, with new creative energy coming from political consciousness in our work. To be a lesbian artist is not a limitation or a box any more than being a feminist is, unless you make it so. It is a statement of commitment, energy, interest, and priority. As a feminist, and as a lesbian, I can express myself in any media, and I can use any technique or approach to art making. But, whatever I do, be it overt lesbian imagery or a more covert statement, it will come from a consciousness of myself as a lesbian and an artist. It is a question of where you get your support and whom you give your energy to and not just a matter of whom you sleep with, nor your life-style. Where I put my creative energy is a political decision. It is important that we identify ourselves as lesbians as well as artists. No one is going to give us space or visibility. We must take it. Since we have no history, we can begin to paint, draw, weave, and write our own. In sisterhood . . .

–Harmony Hammond

"If you're a lesbian, you've related to your own power; you own your own Muse."

I first began exploring the woman in me through my work. It led me deep into myself, to that place where, in spite of a husband and two children whom I loved, I saw very clearly that I, the woman, was the center, that my roots, spirit, and energy were lesbian, and that the total expression of this meant living with women.

This released a rush of energy so great that for several years I lived in terror of being swallowed by it. I was paralyzed by fear until I understood that my greatest fear was a fear of myself. Slowly and painfully my work has taken on new forms. I am my own gardener–I prune, grow, plant, water, and weed myself, and I am nurtured by women.

I am "out" the way most lesbians are, selectively. I am totally out to other lesbians and to my straight-women friends, but I don't identify myself as a lesbian on my press releases. If a group of women comes into the gallery from out of town, I don't insist that I'm a lesbian. For most people who walk into my gallery and like my work, that information seems to get in the way of their seeing or feeling my art.

My work is the most important thing to me, and I want people to get the substance of it. I don't want all their red flags about sexuality to get in the way of their beginning to understand my work first of all. Afterward, if they can absorb the additional information that I am a lesbian, great.

When I was in Minnesota as a guest artist, it seemed to me that everybody knew I was a lesbian; I used to insist on being out to everybody. I would go around giving lectures on lesbianism, but it was too big a burden. It was too hard, and it got in the way of their hearing what I had to say about my art.

Now I am the center for my art, and I believe that when people look at it, it becomes very clear that I have nothing to do with men. Everyone who wants to is able to make all the right associations. It tells them everything about being a lesbian, about being a strong woman, and where my energy comes from, without hitting them over the head.

I founded a feminist studio at Cornell University while I was still married, and a year before I came out. The thesis behind it was that women couldn't discover their creativity while they had to work with men, or in a male-defined space. For a year we had our own space and I taught at Cornell.

I was one of the most energetic and best young artists in the community, and I think the Cornell Art Department was very threatened, and they were threatened by the studio. The studio women did incredible artwork, much more exciting than anything Cornell had ever put out before. A lot of the Cornell teachers really liked my work. They even liked me; they were just scared to have any relationship with me or to allow me to have any relationship to the student body. I didn't hesitate about being out; I was out from the first minute that I thought about it up there, so I'm certain that had a lot to do with it. Consequently, I had no professional feedback or associations.

I think the men there are endemically afraid of strong women. If you're a strong creative woman, you "castrate" men. It's different from being a good historian, because gut-level creativity isn't tied up in history. Almost all those men have wives and girl friends they exploit terribly.

Very covert lesbians sometimes feel threatened by the overt female sensuality of my work. And men have felt threatened by its *bigness* and aggression.

My dealing artistically with female sexuality and my own sexuality led me to be a lesbian. I set out to explore myself, and the conclusion I came to was that the only way I could be totally myself was to be a lesbian. The sexual exploration came naturally, before I even recognized it, in my work, in the kind of flowers I did. Everything was a "cunt" image. That's no longer true in my work; I didn't stay in that place. But there continues to be a highly sensual quality in my work that is missing in straight women's work. It just isn't there. If you're a lesbian, you've related to your own power; you own your own Muse. That's what my art is all about, and that particular power has a strong fantastic ecstatic sensual nature to it.

—Betsy Damon

RESOURCE LIST FOR LESBIAN ARTISTS

1. The lesbian issue of *Heresies* (a feminist art journal), September 1977. All material is by and about lesbians.

2. The Feminist Studio Workshop, Woman's Building, 1727 N. Spring St., Los Angeles, Calif. 90012. This is an art program for women which includes many lesbians both as teachers and as students and deals with lesbianism. Lesbian Art Workshop: Arlene Raven. Lesbian Experience: Sheila Bob. Lesbian Literature: Alice Bloch.

3. The Feminist Studio, 136 E. State St., Ithaca, N.Y. 14850. Quite active.

4. Video tapes and films and lesbian artists (only "out" lesbians are listed):
Kate and Lyn on Louise Fishman. Video tape. Data Bank School of the Art Institute, Columbus at Jackson, Chicago, Ill. 60603.
Harmony Hammond. Video by Hermine Freed. A.I.R. Gallery, 97 Wooster St., New York, N.Y. 10012.
Harmony Hammond Making Rug Pieces. Film by Dale Anderson. 28 Cornelia St., New York, N.Y. 10014.
Betsy Damon. Video by Lynne Berman, Art Department, Buffalo State College, Buffalo, N.Y. (There are numerous video tapes on Betsy Damon at the Cornell University Library, Ithaca, N.Y.)
Donna Hennes. Video by Gloria Allen, 351 Jay St., Brooklyn, N.Y. 11201.
Electric Affinities. Video about George Sand (a poetic opera), by Ann Wilson, 60 Pearl St., New York, N.Y. 10004.

5. Articles and books:
The Lavender Herring, by Sarah Whitworth, Diana Press, 1977. A collection of articles that Whitworth wrote for *The Ladder* about lesbian artists and images of women in art.
Between Me and Life: a Biography of Romaine Brooks, by Meryle Secrest, Doubleday, 1974.
Lesbian Lives, by Barbara Grier and Coletta Reid, Diana Press, 1976.

6. Some women artists in history who definitely were lesbian, or who we have good reason to believe were lesbians: Rosa Bonheur, Romaine Brooks, Emily Carr, Mary Cassatt, Harriet Hosmer, Suzanne Valedon, Marie Laurencin.

7. Lesbian art historians:
Arlene Raven, Women's Building, 1727 N. Spring St., Los Angeles, Calif. 90012.

Ruth Iskin, same address.

Alexandre Comini, Professor of Art History, 7 Methodist University, Meadows Schools of the Arts, Dallas, Tex. 75275.

Sandy Langer, 3261 Rivera Dr., Coral Gables, Fla. 33434.

8. Lesbian artists who give lectures and/or workshops as "out" lesbians:

Betsy Damon, 24 Bond St., New York, N.Y. 10012. Lecturer and workshop facilitator, painter, sculptor, performer of rituals.

Louise Fishman, 151 W.18 St., New York, N.Y. Painter.

Su Friedrich, 159 Second Ave., New York, N.Y. 10003. Photographer.

Harmony Hammond, 129 W. 22 St., New York, N.Y. Painter. She is compiling a slide registry of lesbian artists and will lecture on the material; she is on the panel for the College Art Association of Lesbian Artists discussing the issue of lesbian art and is working on a major exhibition of lesbian art.

Deborah Jones, Perry City Rd., Trumansburg, N.Y. 14886. Sculptor, lecturer.

Ann Wilson, 60 Pearl St., New York, N.Y. Performer and painter, multimedia theater pieces. Gives workshops on theater.

9. The Young Lesbian Artist Groups.

We began meeting while working on a magazine (*Heresies*) that is devoting an entire issue to a consideration of lesbian art and the lesbian artist. We aren't the only women working on that issue but we feel a special connection exists for us as young artists. Our experience is different from that of women who have been "out" as artists for a long time before coming out as lesbians.

We formed an ongoing support group. We don't mean to concentrate on being "young"; we don't want to define "younger" and "older."

We cannot consider ourselves exactly a resource for two reasons: (1) We aren't open to new members as of this writing, and (2) we don't have any group goals or politics; we are a group of individuals who meet together despite the fact that our media, our involvement, our feelings, hopes, politics, sometimes differ.

We do see ourselves individually as contacts for other individuals or groups of lesbian artists, particularly those of you who feel that your lesbianism and your being an artist are somehow entwined. We are involved with various forms: Several of us are painters, some of us writers, one a photographer, one a performer. We are interested in an ever-widening network of lesbian artists.

Amy Sillman, Su Friedrich, Radishes, 159 Second Ave., New York, N.Y. 10003. 212 473-6459.

Kathy Webster, 462 Greenwich St., New York, N.Y. 10013. Painter/collage boxes.

Rose Richtenholtz, 462 Greenwich St., New York, N.Y. 10013.

Christine Wade, 492 Greenwich St., New York, N.Y. 10013.

Alix Dobkin

Cynthia Gair and Helaine Harris, of Women in Distribution, a national distributor of books by women

12.
Some Help
From Our Friends

The Politics of Supporting Lesbianism

GLORIA STEINEM

Why is lesbianism a central issue for all feminists? To put the question a different way, since the-personal-is-political, why do I, as a "straight" feminist, feel so strongly that I have a personal interest in supporting lesbianism as a valid life-style?

Those are the questions I've been asked to answer here. I want very much to say to heterosexual feminists that we have clear and self-interested reasons for supporting and defending lesbianism. I want to say to lesbians that there are so-called straight feminists who understand this common cause and can be trusted. (For that matter, I hope that men reading this will feel supported in their questioning of what sexuality and individual human rights are or could be, and the profound political reasons why they, too, are discouraged from discovering their own humanity.) Yet ever since I agreed to contribute to this anthology, I've been wondering just how and where to start. After nine years of working and lecturing and trying to build feminist coalitions, plus reading and witnessing the struggles of countless other feminists, the answers to these questions have progressed from seeming very complex and controversial to being so obvious that they sound condescending when explained. To go back again over this

well-traveled road is like trying to recapture the freshness of discovering that control of our reproductive lives is basic to women's freedom.

As it turns out, I needn't have puzzled over the problem. I should have understood that any truth will be proven by everyday life; not just once, but over and over again. All you have to do is wait, pencil in hand.

This time, the catalyst for life's lesson was the Pope's recent edict that women could never be priests in the Catholic Church. (If you'll remember, the Pope argued that we lacked a certain crucial resemblance to Jesus Christ.) A radio talk show host, the sort who solicits live on-the-air interviews plus phone calls from listeners, called for a comment on the papal edict. Realizing that I had got trapped into addressing a large radio audience through my telephone, I tried to be as well reasoned as I could about why this edict had mostly to do with enshrining the patriarchal power structure, and little to do with religion.

I hung up the phone—and immediately began to get calls from listeners. It seems that the radio host had ended our polite, scholarly conversation, and then announced to his listening millions: "All right. Now let's hear from some *other* lesbians."

Did our exchange have anything to do with lesbianism? Or with my personal life at all? Of course not. But I had rejected the idea of patriarchy and the power of men to define and restrict women—*therefore I must be a lesbian.* What else could a non-male-defined woman possibly be?

This was only one experience, and a rather mild one compared to those that many women reading this have certainly had. But it echoes back through the years since I became a feminist, and such incidents first began.

There was my longtime journalist colleague, for instance, who forgot everything he had known about me from the past when my first obviously feminist article was published in 1969. "I never realized Gloria was a lesbian," he announced conspiratorially to a mutual woman friend. "Did she ever . . . ah . . . approach you?"

When I began traveling around the country to lecture as a team with a black feminist—first Dorothy Pitman Hughes, then Florynce Kennedy and Margaret Sloan—the hostile questions from audiences increased. After all, what could a black woman possibly have in common with a white woman—except sex? The comments grew more hostile when I was colecturing with Margaret Sloan, who was a lesbian and had the courage to publicly say so. How could a heterosexual woman possibly be friends with a lesbian?

Most people did accept our shared reasons for speaking together in each case: to show that feminism included *all* women, and that the twin caste systems of sex and race were interdependent and could only be fought together. But there was often one hostile man in the audience (in our case, always white, and always focusing on me as the one who was inexplicably "slumming"). He asked a question that either assumed or sought to confirm my lesbianism. (The best answer I ever found to a man's head-on query, "Are you a lesbian?" was "Are you my alternative?" Not only did it frustrate the curiosity of the questioner, but it tended to make him sit down.)

The most elaborate examples of this "any-rebellious-woman-is-a-lesbian" problem were the two full-length novels that are still circulating somewhere in the world. (Based both on their literary merit and on their exploitation-for-profit of peoples' lives, I feel no obligation to give their titles publicity.) Each had a major character whose appearance and work pattern are exactly like mine; each had a plot assumption that this woman writer-editor was also a lesbian. I remember waking up to NBC's *Today* show one morning three or four years ago, and being confronted with the following commercial. An actress, with hair and glasses like mine, inches suggestively toward a table with feminist symbol on it. As she slowly puts her glasses down next to the symbolic necklace, a male voice-over confides intimately something about how this sensational new novel reveals the true story of the famous feminist who manipulates men, but prefers women.

I'm not suggesting that these events are equal to the punishments suffered by women who are lesbians. As Charlotte Bunch has pointed out, women can only begin to guess at those penalties by living as a lesbian for a while. "Announce to everyone—family, roommate, on the job, everywhere you go," Bunch suggests to heterosexual feminists, "that you are a lesbian. Imagine your life, economically and emotionally, with women instead of men. For a whole week, experience life as if you were lesbian, and you will learn quickly what heterosexual privileges and assumptions are . . . and that self-loving and independent women are a challenge to the idea that men are superior, an idea that social institutions strengthen and enshrine."[1]

Furthermore, to say that lesbian and heterosexual feminists could or should share exactly the same experience and viewpoint would be to limit the full human range of insights, and therefore the complete human knowledge, that feminism hopes to set free. As Bunch wisely pointed out, "True unity is grounded not on a false notion of sameness, but on understanding and utilizing diversity to gain the greatest possible scope and power."[2]

The lesson of my experience—and that of other women who have acted on their belief in feminism, whether they also have a husband and children or not—is simply that sooner or later, all nonconforming women are likely to be labeled lesbians. True, we start out with the smaller punishments of being called "pushy" or "aggressive," "man-hating" or "unfeminine." But it's only a small step from those adjectives, whether bestowed by men or by other women, to the full-fledged epithet of "lesbian."

Prefeminism, I would have been hurt by that word. I might have denied it explicitly, or modified my offending "unfeminine" behavior in order to deny it by word or by deed. And that's exactly what the accusers have in mind: to scare female human beings out of exercising all our human rights and talents, and thus to keep us from upsetting the male-superiority applecart.

It's for this reason that lesbians have often been the pioneers at the forefront of change that has benefited women as a group, even when the lesbians involved were not acting for feminist reasons. Just by working and surviving as women without the protection of some status vis-à-vis a man, lesbians may force institutions into some acceptance of women on their own. And this pioneering act helps break a barrier for all autonomous women.

But that accidental impact cannot be either directed or maximized without the consciousness that feminism brings. Certainly, we're all aware of old-style, nonfeminist lesbians, for instance, who can be just as conservative and antichange, just as hooked on role-playing as many of the heterosexual couples around them. But they are far from alone in their fearful allegiance to the very system that oppresses them. Like every Jew who has ever been proud to be judged "not like those other Jews," or every woman who has ever been complimented by phrases like "You think like a man," they have come to believe that deserting their "inferior" group and integrating with the dominant one is their only hope for survival.

Self-hatred is the blight of every discriminated-against group; lesbians no less than any other.

But the positive, conscious, affirmative act of choosing to identify with your own "inferior" group, of refusing to be defined by the rules of the "superior" one—that is revolutionary. And male supremacists know a revolutionary act, in sexuality or any other area, when they see one.

In a practical, day-to-day sense, therefore, all feminists have a self-interest in taking the sting out of the word "lesbian," and making it as honorable a life-style as any other. Until we do, we ourselves will continue to be limited by fear of losing jobs and career possibilities (not to mention housing, child custody suits, credit, and access to public accommodations) because of this accusation; or at a minimum, of losing society's esteem and our friends' or family's approval. As long as we shrink back in fear from the word "lesbian," we are giving it the power to keep all women in line.

Acting together with other women and becoming self-identified, *female*-identified, is a very long and inevitable part of gaining the power to reach a humanistic society in which we can integrate female and male, black and white as individual, equally powerful human beings. It's true that we also protect our own much-needed pioneers when we protect lesbian-feminist sisters. By "pioneers," I don't mean that lesbians are somehow the only true feminists. Though the lesbian need to compensate for past suffering makes that assertion some-

---

[1]Charlotte Bunch, "Learning from Lesbian Separatism," *Ms.*, November 1976.

[2]Ibid.

times understandable, the truth is that positing lesbianism as a requisite of feminism depends on the acceptance of heterosexual sex as always an act of conquering by the man. It depends, in other words, on accepting a male definition. Yet we are all most likely to get radicalized on our own concerns. And the truth is that heterosexual feminists *ourselves* will remain male-identified and "man junkies" to some degree until we dare to kick the habit of identifying with, and being given our self-image by, the patriarchy. That practice of female identification and autonomy, whether sexual or not, is exactly what much of society condemns as lesbian.

So much for the personal end of the argument. It's the most relevant to the practical world and the time frame we live in. For many of us, it is reason enough. But it's also possible to start at the causal, long-term end of our reasons for coalition; to do a more radical analysis, in the true sense of "going to the root."

We must begin by asking the very basic why. Why do women end up on the underside of this sexual caste system in the first place? Why should there be a caste system based on sex at all, when the sex difference is infinitely smaller than the human similarities shared by both sexes?

There need be no rational reason, of course, as there is no intrinsically rational reason for the differentiations based on race. One group can simply establish a historical upperhand, and then entrench and internalize it with culturally produced arguments and mythologies that appear to endow that inferiority with a "natural" base.

Like other radical feminists, however, I find logic in the argument that the sexual caste system evolved first among the various oppressive systems, and was the model on which other caste systems—based on the equally visible marks of race difference—were patterned. (And both became the models, of course, for later systems based on socially produced institutionalized differences of class.) That means tracing all this historical sickness of birth-determined power structures to the unjust dominance based on endemic difference between sex groups, their reproductive functions.

Of course, there is the controversial theory of some gynocratic prehistory in which women's superiority was based on this same child-bearing capacity. According to that theory, the power shift to a male-centered society began with the discovery of men's role in conception. Prior to that time, women had been assumed to bear fruit mysteriously, like the seasonal bloomings of plants and trees. And that mysterious gift caused us to be worshiped as superior, and even as the women goddesses whom we see in ancient religions. Certainly, this discovery of paternity helps to explain men's gradual and growing attempts to restrict women's freedom. They were attempts to determine paternity and men's "ownership" of children. As patriarchal systems solidified, the need to determine the patriarchal line of descent, to pass down power, name, and property, restricted and oppressed women more and more. We were controlled by family, tribe, or nation-state as, literally, the most basic means of production.

But whether or not there ever was a gynocratic, prehistorical time when the current sexual caste system was nonexistent or even reversed, it is still clear that women's reproductive function has always been the source of her oppression. The double standard of behavior and the restriction of her sexuality, the idea that a woman must be possessed by and faithful to one man in order to earn society's respect, the lesser value of women who produce the progeny of lower-caste or lower-class men, the restriction of women to child care or other unpaid, undervalued supportive roles—all these generalities of the female caste can be traced directly to our role of reproduction. It is the power of some patriarchal structure to decide the reproductive life of its females. Women deciding for ourselves is often equated with disorder, anarchy, and danger.

Is it any accident that the societies most oppressive to women as a group are also most repressive of *all* sexuality that cannot end in reproduction? I don't think so. Contraceptive knowledge has existed since the understanding of conception, yet its political control has been a mark of patriarchies in every era. The calculated release or suppression of contraception has depended on whether the national interest was seen as an expanding, stable, or lowered population. But the point is always the same: It is not to be controlled effectively by women, or by any force except some structure of the patriarchy.

The allowing or restricting of homosexual and lesbian sexuality, or any heterosexual forms that do not result in conception, has also been controlled by the same societies—and for exactly the same reasons: the need to manipulate sexuality so it produces (or curtails) the production of population. After all, witches were rebellious women who also taught contraception and performed abortion in a time when the Church and State wanted a growing population. The word "faggot," as Kenneth Pitchford has pointed out, became synonymous with male homosexuals because these men were thrown on the funeral pyre first, as human kindling, in order to make the fire "foul enough" to burn a witch. There is common cause there—not only with all women, lesbian or not, but also with homosexual men. It is the same centralized, self-justifying drive of patriarchal nationalism that restricts all of us. At that political level, whatever our differences, we have a reason to act together and to give each other mutual support.

What we are doing, together, is struggling to expand the area of individual human rights to include reproductive freedom. That's especially important to women, since we must assert power over our own bodies, the basic means of production, before we will have any control of our lives. But it's also important to men whose sexuality is being politically governed. After all, human beings are the only animals capable of experiencing orgasm at times when we cannot conceive. That means sexuality is also a form of expression, of reaching out and communicating with each other, and not only a way of reproducing.

It's this human birthright that patriarchy has taken away from us as individuals. It has restricted us all for its own political, self-perpetuating reasons.

There will continue to be those who say to feminists, "Don't mention lesbianism. Never support the cause of male homosexuals. You will only damage your cause." But we must look at our longer term goals and our real self-interest. We must understand that what we are attempting is a revolution, not a public-relations movement. As long as we fear the word "lesbian," we are curtailing our own strength and abandoning our sisters. As long as human sexuality is politically controlled, we will all be losing a basic human freedom.

By working together, we have our full selves and the future to gain.

A Mother's Support

BETTY O'LEARY

When I was first asked to write this article, I hesitated, wondering if some other parent couldn't do a better job. It would be less than honest to say that hearing the news that my darling daughter is a lesbian made me jump for joy. I was heartsick. But when the initial shock was over, one thing I was sure of—my love for her never wavered one bit.

The news came four years ago, Christmas of 1972, when Jean came home from New York for the holidays. She had left Cleveland after college to settle in New York and pursue graduate work at Yeshiva University ... and also, unknown to me at the time, to become part of one of the largest gay communities in the country.

There was nothing that had given us any real indication that this might even be a remote possibility. The only inkling we had that anything was different was a note some months earlier from our son at the University of Maine, who had stopped in New York to visit Jean on his way back to school. After his visit he had written, just on a postcard: "My, Jean's life-style has changed so much since she was back home—W-O-W!" I knew that he didn't mean just any little thing; it sounded like "Wow!" So I began to question him. Had she been married and we didn't know it? Had she become a communist? (I knew it must be something pretty outrageous.)

My son never did say what it was. He wanted to leave it up to Jean to tell us. But then—I don't know

whether he thought it would be easier for Jean, or what—but that Christmas, as he was going out the door to pick Jean up at the airport, he turned and said, "Hey, Mom, guess what. Jean is gay!" His comment really didn't register on me. Did he mean she was happy? But then he said, "She's a lesbian, Mom." And I was just thunderstruck. I can remember not saying anything at all. I don't even think I cried, because I was that stunned.

The trip back from the airport was only a fifteen-minute drive, but it seemed forever before they returned. Finally, when they walked in, my husband Jim put his arms around Jean and said, "Well, we still love you—we love you a lot." But we didn't talk about it right away.

When we finally did sit down and talk, the first thing I thought of was, Why hadn't she told me before? I felt that perhaps I had let her down. Shouldn't a child have been able to approach her mother with this problem? I especially felt that way because we had been very close and confided in each other.

I was thinking, too, "She must be terribly unhappy." "How long has she known this—we never dreamed ..." "Is a sexual preference something that might be remedied with psychiatric help?" I worried about how her friends would react—whether they might reject her, and she'd be alone. Jean tried to assure us that she was happy in her new life, but that was beyond our comprehension at the time.

In those first days I cried a great deal when I thought about it. I plagued myself with an endless series of questions: Were we to blame in some way? Growing up, she had been a tomboy who loved sports ... but that was kind of cute and the fellows liked her. There was nothing unusual about her appearance; she was and is obviously female—not the buttons-and-bows type, but that was not out of the ordinary. Would it have been different if we had directed her toward things like sewing and the things that little girls do? She was so definitely *not* a sewer; where do you start with someone like that?

One of the biggest questions that occurred to us was, Is this hereditary? I'm sure that my husband must have been experiencing the same soul-searching questions. On the night of the "big news" he said he was thinking over *my* relatives, wondering from whom Jean had inherited this condition.

Another conflict for us was religion. We're Roman Catholic, and our Church teaches that sex is for procreation. In recent years the position of the Church on homosexuality has been challenged, but the official teaching is that it's wrong. My faith has been a great comfort to me during my life and I was concerned that Jean wouldn't have this to turn to. I must say, in honesty, that these religious conflicts, for me, have never been reconciled.

I also felt concern about her bold public stance. Why did she have to be a public figure? Wouldn't she be happier keeping her sex life quiet? Why this crusade, this

Barbara Love and her mother in gay march

devotion to helping gays acquire equal rights? It seemed like such an uphill struggle. How could she begin to make a dent in public attitudes?

I worried, and still worry, about the lack of permanency in her relationships. First she'd be with one woman, then another, and in the meantime I would have heard four or five other names. I wondered if she was going to be a playgirl all her life. I felt that in the long run, the best thing would be for Jean to find some nice woman that she could be happy with and settle down with her—rather than try to convert the whole world to feeling that gay is good.

But if it was true—and it was—that Jean was gay, I was glad we knew. One of the reasons that prompted her telling us when she did was that she was getting to be a public movement activist and wanted us to hear the news from her, not from the newspaper or neighbors. I'm glad she told us when she did and didn't let it go any further, because I would have just hated to hear it from someone else. Our being "tuned in" did not in any way alter the love that we have always had, and always will have, for her.

Then there was the question of what to say to people—if anything. I felt as though I were holding a hot potato in my hands. Would I tell people about it? Rather heavy conversation over the bridge table. How about the relatives? "Maybe later on," I told myself. And even after I'd known for a while, I thought it wouldn't be necessary to say anything, because after all, maybe she would forget this as she grows older and settles down. At the same time, though, I was also thinking about Jean's happiness. She said she was happy, and I knew that Jean had always been a fighter for what she wanted. Of course, she has not changed, and this has been a fact that I've had to accept.

Gradually, my attitudes did change. I read *Sappho Was a Right-On Woman* and just about everything I could find on the subject. My whole frame of reference for homosexuals had been nonexistent, other than some vague notion that these people were "weird." Someone had once told me that Liberace was a homosexual, and I remembered a male nurse whom I had met in the hospital who wore lipstick and carried a shoulder bag; but certainly I knew little about gay men and absolutely nothing about lesbians.

Through reading and exposure to new information and meeting Jean's loves and friends, I began to have a new feeling about her life-style. Jean did indeed seem happy, and we welcomed whomever she brought home. I can't think of one who visited us who was ever anything but a joy to have here, and I mean that sincerely.

Eventually, the publicity Jean was getting finally solved my problem of what to tell the neighbors. First there was an article in the *National Observer*; then she appeared on the *Today* show and the ABC network news. After that there was an article in the Cleveland *Plain Dealer,* and more recently she and Bruce Voeller

appeared on a very popular TV talk show in Cleveland, *The Morning Exchange.*

When the first article appeared on the front page of the *National Observer,* one neighbor brought it over. At that time I was still waiting for people like her to introduce the subject, because it wasn't easy for me to bring it up without getting a little bit teary-eyed.

When the article came out with Jean's picture in the Cleveland *Plain Dealer,* telling all about the work she was doing with the National Gay Task Force, a lot of neighbors reacted. People didn't really know what to say. One friend telephoned me and said, "Are you saving newspaper clippings these days? Do you want my copy?" That was just a way of getting on the subject and talking about it. Then there were others who said, "Well, I often wonder about my children; they were tomboys, too." Some of them thought I had just heard about it for the first time because I hadn't discussed it before.

My reaction to the neighbors finding out was one of sheer relief. I was really glad about it because as these articles were publicized, I could only wonder who had heard and what their reactions were. When Jean appeared on *The Morning Exchange* with Bruce Voeller, everybody saw that (I told some friends in advance so they could watch it!) and thought the two of them made an excellent appearance. All of my friends know about it now, and the media exposure has been a great relief to me because now I can and do talk about it openly.

By and large, most people have been understanding, with some memorable exceptions. My daughter Diane had a sad experience at work after the article appeared in the Cleveland *Plain Dealer.* I had called her there to tell her about it, so during her break she began to read the article. Before she had a chance to finish it, she had been called away from the lounge. When she returned, the paper was still there with the article visible. One of the young nurses said, "Say, Di, here's a chick who's got her picture in the paper and she's got the same name as you have. And she's a fag—isn't that funny?" The nurse was carrying on, thinking it was so hilarious. Diane turned around—she could feel herself getting very, very angry and also feeling like crying—and said, *"That's my sister!"* She walked out leaving the other woman stunned.

As for other members of the family, Jean's brothers and sisters are fully accepting of her lesbianism. After Jean's coming out her two brothers both made trips to see her in New York within the next couple of years and went to some of the gay meetings and met a lot of her friends. Ken even went to one of the bars with her and was very open-minded about it. I do think the young people today are a lot more liberal and able to adapt to various concepts of living. When some of the young people that I know heard about it, they just said, "Oh, really?" And with a few more questions, that was it. It doesn't seem to strike them one way or the other. I must say, it was a much harder adjustment for me, and even more difficult for my husband, Jim. He's tried to say as many nice things as he could. Jim's love for Jean is very great. But I know he'd be surprised but happy if she announced her engagment to a man.

When I first heard the news about Jean, my attitudes about lesbianism were terribly harsh and negative. Now they have become more tolerant. My own Jeanie is gay. I know now that there are many wonderful gay people. Like all human beings, they are another segment of our human race. Our world is divided into innumerable segments: male and female, people of different religions and ethnic backgrounds, with the good and bad in all of us no matter in what niche people find themselves. I'm not emotionally equipped to be gay, but many people have this preference. One thing we all have in common is the right to love . . . and this no one should be denied. I hope someday there will be no discrimination whatsoever due to one's choice of whom to love. I hope that all parents can learn to give their gay children the love and support that they need and deserve.

Parents of Gays

Note: One of the most important developments of the movement has been the founding of Parents of Gays groups in various parts of the country. Often our parents have great difficulty, even more than we do, in dealing with our coming out because their generation's attitudes toward homosexuality are even more conservative than those of our generation.

Parents of Gays helps mothers and fathers of lesbians and gay men get over their own feelings of "Where did I go wrong?" and encourages them to give loving support to their own children and the larger gay community.

In the following testimony, edited from taped interviews, three parents recount the various stages they went through in accepting their daughters' life-style. The first statement is from Charlotte Spitzer, a licensed marriage, family, and child counselor who founded Parents of Gays in Los Angeles and represented that organization nationally at the White House meeting in March 1977. Now in private practice, she is writing a book for parents of gays, lecturing and making media appearances, and is actively searching for funding to develop a center to work with families with a gay child.

The second and third testimonies were contributed by Esther and Ken Morgan, who are working within the Quaker congregation to help members become more accepting of the gay life-style. Esther is a prospective graduate student in social work; Ken is a practicing social worker. —Ed.

"I see parents as an important bridge between heterosexual and homosexual communities."

When my daughter was twenty-one she came to me and told me she was a lesbian. I was shocked. I thought we had a close relationship and I knew her well, yet I had no idea this was going on. She told me that she had known for a while but had wanted to be sure. She had been dating in high school and had been involved emotionally with a young man and this is why it had been a surprise. My first reaction was "Where did I go wrong?" and I have since found out that most parents do assume guilt: that we did something wrong that "caused" our children to be homosexual. I have since found out that nobody makes anybody anything, that there is nothing wrong, but at the time I felt ashamed and guilty.

I made it my business to investigate what homosexuality was all about, because I had internalized a lot of myths and misinformation that I had grown up with.

Though I thought of myself as a very sophisticated, well-educated person, and had friends who were gay, it was only *intellectually* that I accepted it, not emotionally. I started to read, attend lectures, talk to people. As I got more information I realized it was not sick, there is nothing unnatural; gay people are just different. I felt much better and realized that if I were going through this, and I was relatively sophisticated, what must be happening for other parents who were not in the same position? Maybe it would be a good idea for someone to be here for them so they could talk about it, so I offered my services to the Gay Community Services Center hotline for parents who were having a hard time accepting their children.

In the meantime I met lots of gay people who were going through their own kinds of pain because they were afraid to tell their parents. In some cases they had told them and had been rejected. I met kids who had come thousands of miles from home to avoid having to confront this in their own communities. They shouldn't have to change their whole lives just because they're gay. I would like to work with the heterosexual community, of which I am a part, to see that things get better, so everybody can live without harassment.

It took me about six months to go through the whole process. I've checked it out with other parents, and it's universal. First the guilt, then the shame: "How am I going to tell anybody? What if anybody finds out?" There were a couple of components in that, too. I didn't want anybody to feel sorry about us, or be cruel to my daughter, like pull their kids away if she were with their children.

Then there's a period of denial, when a parent says to herself, "Maybe my child is going through a phase, it'll go away," or "Maybe my kid got in with the wrong people and is being influenced." That is part of the denial process and it can go in any direction. Often after that there's anger: "Why me?" or "My kid is doing this to get even with me." It didn't happen specifically to me, but I have seen it happen to others. After the anger, there's usually reconciliation, when parents get to the point where they can ask themselves, "What do I really want for my child?" where they're ready to put it into perspective. Once that happens, the healing starts. I find that when people can talk out their feelings they go through the process faster. It's bottled-up feelings that stick people in an attitude that doesn't change.

It took me some time until I could feel good about myself. The interesting thing was when I felt good about it, people were so matter-of-fact that it surprised me. I haven't had one bad response from anybody I know. Some people have avoided it, and I feel if they can't handle it that's their problem. But wherever there's been anyone genuinely interested in my daughter, I'm very matter-of-fact about it. They say things like, "Is she going with anybody, is she going to get married?" and I say, "No, Robin is a lesbian. She's very happy. She has a wonderful relationship and she's as married as she's going to be." They say, "Oh, that's good, as long as she's happy." And that seems to be the predominant theme. That's what I came to: What do I really want for my child—I want her to be happy. It may not be my way of being happy, but how can I tell another person what his or her happiness is going to be.

Robin has two brothers. The younger was fourteen at the time and she decided she wasn't going to tell him because he might be having his own sexual identity crisis. She told her older brother and he became even closer to her. He was marvelous; he would do things he had never done before. He would say, "Do you need money, help? What can I do for you?" It was beautiful to see how he came through for her. I knew all along that my younger son was ready, but I respected her wanting to wait. We had a gay friend who came out to us one night, and Paul, my younger son, sat in and said later, "Dick is a neat guy—What a nice guy." I thought this was a good time. He knew Dick, felt positive about him, and knew he was gay. And I said, "You know, Paul, Robin is gay, too." He said, "Really, Mom, hey that's neat." That was his reaction, and it has been that way ever since. I have a feeling that a lot of young people, especially if they're not raised with prejudices, accept most things better than my generation would.

I had made the decision that I wouldn't tell my mother, who grew up in a very different time. I didn't think she would have the understanding or even that she knew what a homosexual was. But then I was asked to appear on television, and I had to face the fact that she might get wind of it, and I wanted to tell her in a positive way, rather than have some gossipy person tell her in a negative way. I went into town to tell her and said, "I have something I want to discuss with you, Mother. Do you know what a homosexual is, do you know what *gay* is, do you know what a lesbian is?" She

said, "Oh yes, Paul said something about it the other day." I thought, "Oh, my God. She's lived eighty-four years and somebody just said something to her the other day." At that moment my son came to the door and we talked with him and never got back to the subject. While I was riding home, it struck me that I hadn't discussed it with her, and I knew I wasn't going to get into town to see her again before the show. Friday morning I called and she said, "I saw you on television yesterday. Did you *have* to be on television? Does the whole world have to know?" I said, "Yes, I had to be on television. This is something I feel is very important to discuss." I have a relationship with my mother where we're in different worlds but she respects me for the things I care about. She knows I have lots of deep-seated convictions. I talked to her about how I needed to do this.

I reminded her that every time my daughter went to visit my mother, the standard question was "Are you going with anybody? When are you getting married? When you get married, I will make you a big wedding." This was my mother's dream. Finally one day, my daughter said, "Grandma, if I were to tell you that I might never get married, but that I could be happy, could you be happy for me?" My mother thought about it and said, "I never looked at it that way, but yes, darling, if you were happy, I could be happy for you." I thought my daughter handled it beautifully. It was one of those spontaneous things that was just right.

I reminded my mother about this conversation and said, "Mom, she's happy. She's in a relationship with another beautiful woman and they're really happy and they love each other." She said, "Well, I'm not happy." I said, "I don't expect you to be happy right now, but I hope you will accept her, and not reject her." She said, "I'll never stop loving her. She's my grandchild." And that's the way it's been. The next time my mother saw her she embraced her, and whenever she sees her she's warm and friendly. She doesn't altogether understand and probably never will, but she could never reject her. It's nice to see that an eighty-four-year-old woman can make that kind of an adjustment.

I'd like to encourage other parents of lesbians to find a support group if they can, and if there isn't one in their community to start one, because it can be very gratifying and important for them. I think people who have been through the same thing can help. I know what happens in our group. Parents come in in very bad shape and in a short time they're helping other parents. We get lots of education, too. We meet other gay people, we meet other parents, we meet people who can give us information and shatter some of the myths we've lived with most of our lives. I say, "Get thee to a group." For me that's the best way. And don't stop talking to your gay children, because they need validation from their parents more than anything in the world. That world is a rejecting one still, and if they don't get it from their parents, it really is painful, and they can end up rejecting themselves in the process. They need some good vibes from somebody, and who better to give it to them than the parents who love them and care about them? It's brought her even closer to me and Robin's father. I've gone up there and stayed with them and it's perfectly comfortable.

Her father, from whom I am divorced, took it very well. He was a little uncomfortable at first. Robin said, "Mom, I think my father is kind of uncomfortable now," and I said, "That's understandable; give him time," and that's all it took. He and his wife go up and stay with them, and they come down and stay in his house with him. It's beautiful.

Our experience with gays used to be only with stereotypes, because they were so obvious. But we didn't know that the person next door, the unmarried school-teacher who was living with her best friend, could have been gay, because they didn't fit the stereotype. I am sure we all know people—the maiden aunt, the bachelor uncle. Who knows how many people in our lives had to be gay, many of them married, who never dealt with their own gayness, because they would have been perse-cuted and they couldn't live with that. There are many gays I've met who've said they came out after twenty or thirty years of marriage, because the climate has changed and they decided they can't live with a lie anymore. Could you imagine having to submerge that for all those years? Dreadful. I had a woman call me after reading an article in the paper and she said, "I am fifty years old; I have never had an experience with a gay person, even talking to a gay person. I have literally lived alone all my life and I am dying of loneliness." I just wanted to weep for that woman. She said, "What shall I do?" I said, "Go and meet some people. Even if you just make friends, there are loads of people who will befriend you." And I told her about the Gay Community Services Center and she had never known it existed.

People who are gay who are forty years old and older have really had a tough time. It's hard to imagine what it's like to live in a small, conservative rural town. The absolute terror. I met a man from Kentucky who knew he had homosexual feelings and never acted on them. He said he had never shared his feelings with another person. "What do I do? I can't go back to Kentucky and be a homosexual. I'd be ridden out of town." I said, "Do you have to stay in Kentucky?" He said, "That's my home." "Can you be happy there?" "No, I don't think so." I said, "Then get out." And he did. He's living his life now as a gay man, and happy for the first time in his life.

I did a workshop with lesbian women for a NOW conference on changing life-styles, and my counseling consisted of telling them that before they tell their parents they ought to decide *why* they want to tell them. If they're in a good relationship, this is something that might be standing in the way, and by all means tell them. Give them time to absorb it—expect shock reac-tions. Don't hit and run. Stay and give them lots of time to work with it, keep talking to them, don't break off the communication; if they react shocked and rejecting

at first, it doesn't mean that they are going to stay that way. The parent and the child almost reverse roles in this situation; the child becomes the patient, understanding listener to the adult.

I caution people not to act out of anger in telling their parents. I advise them to wait until they're feeling good about themselves, and to continue the relationship until the parents come around, because I'm convinced that most parents will come around.

If it's possible for them to get their parents to attend a parents' group, this is a marvelous way of getting them through that process quicker with people with whom they can be comfortable, more comfortable than talking to their children. Give them literature that may help correct some of the misinformation they have gotten during their lifetimes. The stereotype of homo-sexual misery, living furtive lives, was probably true a long time ago, and no longer is necessarily true. It doesn't mean that everything is easy, but it certainly is easier, and I think it is important to let parents know they can be instrumental in making the world a better place for their children. They can play a vital role if they come out of the closet too and talk to their nongay friends and relatives in the community.

Most important, though, is that we bring parents and children together so they can continue in a healthy, loving relationship. I would like to see young people treated with dignity and respect for who they are, whether homosexual or heterosexual. I think we're also going to have to get sex education into the school system early so that it isn't a taboo subject and can be discussed openly, so we don't raise a generation who grow up with negative attitudes toward people just be-cause they aren't exactly the same as they are.

I see parents as an important bridge between heterosexual and homosexual communities. We will have the heterosexual ear much more easily than the homo-sexual community can get it. We are not just talking about our kids, but *their* kids, too, because in every audience we address, there are parents that are going to learn their children are homosexual, and we want to help them understand it so their kids don't have to go through fear of telling their parents; so their parents can give the support and loving care they so deperately need when they're discovering their own sexuality.

—Charlotte Spitzer

"She . . . trusted our relationship enough to know I would not reject her."

I am also a member of Parents of Gays in Southern California. I have a lesbian daughter who is twenty years old. Two years ago, she called me up on the phone and said, "I've got something to tell you. I'm happy, I'm in love." "Terrific," I replied. She said, "Her name is

Jaime." And I said, "Oh." I don't know what I said after that because I could hardly respond at that point. I remember hanging up the phone thinking, "What am I going to do with this information?"

Fortunately, some experiences had prepared me to deal with Karen's lesbianism and to accept it. Jean had been a good friend of mine of fifteen or twenty years. Her marriage broke up and she fell in love with a woman, and had a similar conversation with me, saying, "I'm in love with Ruth," and I said, "Give me a few months to think about it. Right now I don't think anything adverse. Maybe I will, maybe I won't." As it turned out I didn't, but it helped me realize I wouldn't reject somebody I cared for who was gay. This happened four or five years before Karen came out as a lesbian.

Some initial gut feelings I had to Karen's lesbianism were "No, I don't want it in my life; it's too hard. I don't know how to relate to it, I wouldn't know how to tell other people about it. What did I do wrong? How did I help this happen? It will be a hard life for her." It took me a few days to go through that section of it and realize that that reaction was ridiculous. She was the same person that loved people and animals and never hurt anybody, and I had a lot of respect for her in terms of making choices for herself. After I got over the initial shock, I was amazed Karen had told me. She has since told me she felt close enough to me and trusted our relationship enough to know I would not reject her, that I would accept her.

Telling friends and relatives was another stage of my developing and coming out. When I told Ken, he didn't say anything, so I knew he was uncomfortable. It took me several months to tell one of my dearest friends, who said, "How neat!" I thought, "She didn't fall apart; maybe I can trust one more person." So I began to feel that I could very carefully tell people. I got some backlash. I was in a consciousness-raising group and it began to bottle up. We had shared so much—I decided I would share this. A couple of them really were uncomfortable and showed it. I knew this would happen but I felt better having told them. I realized this was some of the backlash Karen would feel when she told other people she was a lesbian, and that was the day I said to myself, "I've got to find another parent, another mother of a lesbian I can relate to." I remembered meeting a woman at a Quaker conference the summer before whose daughter was a lesbian who was dealing with it okay, and I wrote her a letter. She wrote me saying, "You're doing great. You don't have to worry about it so much." That was a big help. The process for me was telling a good friend, then writing this letter, telling the rap group I was into, plus reading some books. I had asked Karen to help me find some books to read. One of them was *Lesbian/Woman*, by Del Martin and Phyllis Lyon. Another book was *Rubyfruit Jungle*, by Rita Mae Brown. That's a really good one. She gave me *Woman + Woman*, by Dolores Klaich, for my birthday and on the inside cover she said, "To Mom for your birthday. I really appreciate having you for a friend." That felt good. I began to look around for a parents' group. Ken said he would go with me if I found one, and I found an announcement of the Parents of Gays group in *Sister* and our contact with them started.

Karen's older brother was nineteen when she came out, and he's a quiet sort of person, but he accepted Karen where she was. It's fine with him. He was more concerned about how his life was going than with her life. Her younger brother was thirteen at the time and just takes the world as it rolls along. "So she loves a woman—big deal." That's the way he acted.

My sister and her husband kept saying, "Karen's going to be the next grandchild to get married," and I said, "No, she's not." He said, "How do you know she's not?" So I threw it at him: "Because she's a lesbian." Dead silence. My sister said nothing; she was uncomfortable. My brother-in-law, who had initiated the conversation, said, "How do you know?" and I said, "She told me and I believe her." He asked, "Has she ever had a male lover?" It was as if somehow you're not tried and true unless you've tried men first. You can't just start out with women, because otherwise he believes you've obviously missed a great experience if you haven't had men first, or else you haven't met the right man.

My other sister, when I told her, said, "I just don't understand young people. They're always trying to make life so difficult for themselves." I said, "I don't think she is trying to make life more difficult. Could it be that that's just the way she is?" Then she did come around, "Yeah, probably that's so, and if that's what she wants, that's okay."

It was a real shock to me to find out and realize how intolerant and how rejecting some parents are. I couldn't imagine turning my back on my daughter. I found out some of her friends' parents could not deal with it, were really very rejecting, saying, "Don't come home, I don't want to see you," or "If you come home don't bring a lover or don't talk about it." I met one of Karen's friends and she looked at me, her eyes big, and said, "You *really* are that accepting? You don't mind that Karen is a lesbian?" and I said, "No, I don't mind at all," and she said, "You are really amazing." I just started laughing. I don't consider myself amazing. I do wish to be of help to some of these parents who feel so much as if their child is doing something to *them*, to realize it's not that way at all, just a natural part of that person growing up and finding herself as a sexual and emotional person.

We were invited through Parents of Gays to be a resource to a lesbian rap group at the Gay Community Center in Los Angeles. We didn't have any idea what to expect. It was a shock to me how many people walked out of the room and didn't stay with us.

I was impressed at the difficulty some of these women were having with their parents. There were probably twenty women in the group and there were at least four who said nothing. There was one woman there who kept saying over and over, "We don't *have* to tell our parents." I was trying to give them a lot of support, saying, "You feel a rift. There's some tension and you'd like to get beyond that, and if you need some support here I am, you can ask me anything. I'll be glad to encourage you."

One woman who didn't say anything at all came up to me after the meeting was over, grabbed my hand, and said, "I really appreciate your coming. My parents are in Ohio and there's no way I can tell them, but I'm so glad you came and I appreciate hearing from you." I thought maybe it's good for her to listen to parents that are dealing with it and maybe someday she'll be able to deal with it herself, with her parents. I felt pretty good about the rap group.

One thing I would say to lesbians who are wondering about talking to their parents is maybe you ought to consider that your parents already know. I think we often leave a long dribble of symbols behind us when we want to tell somebody something and can't get our guts together. If it's possible for you, try to sit down and talk to your parents about it, and if you can help them understand that you are happy and secure in your decision, that this is what makes you feel good, they'll probably come around.

—Esther Morgan

"We wouldn't think of telling Karen that she couldn't bring home a lover and sleep together."

I found out about Karen's lesbianism from Esther. I was quite upset and taken aback and felt as though Karen was upset with me, or if not me, certainly men, and I really felt in some way I had done something that helped her decide that she didn't want anything to do with men. It was a big relief to talk to her and find out that she had had affairs with men, and that she really was not angry at men, even though she had had both good and bad experiences. It took me a year or more to get better acquainted with Karen and to share a bit of her life so I could understand her better. After that, I was able to get to know some of her friends and go with them to a gay bar and other places and enjoy them as people. I had always been fond of Karen's lover; she and her parents are friends of the family.

I told our Quaker group that I had a gay daughter and that I was very interested in trying to help the organization to be more open and accepting of gay life-styles. The dramatic thing about this was that two other people in the group, a man and a woman, acknowledged their own gayness.

I've also been telling some of my associates that Karen is gay, and I was really amazed. I told one that Karen was an active lesbian and his reaction surprised me. He didn't ask any of the usual questions. What he wanted to know was, did we accept her bringing home a lover and allow them to sleep together in our house? He was quite pleased that I said that was never an issue. We wouldn't think of telling Karen that she couldn't bring home a lover and sleep together. It turned out he had personal friends who had gone through this experience and had difficulty in dealing with their parents.

I've previously had both good and bad experiences with gay people. I'm a professional social worker, and I'd worked in a hospital setting for many years, and in the course of those years I had met many disturbed gay people, so my early attitudes about gays were pretty mixed up around sick people.

More recently, though, and before Karen came out, I had gotten to know a number of gay people as friends and being able to visit with them certainly improved my relationship with Karen, too. She said she's felt good about the support and the interest. I feel much closer to Karen than before.

—Ken Morgan

PARENTS OF GAYS CONTACT LIST

Arizona
Faith and Ed Parker, 4217 E. Hazelwood, Phoenix, 85018.

California
Long Beach
Parents and Friends of Gays of Long Beach, 700 E. Roosevelt Rd., 90807. 213 427-4347.
Los Angeles
Parents and Friends of Gays, P.O. Box 24528, 90024. Adele Starr, 213 472-4804.
San Diego
Al Johnson, Gay Center for Social Services, 2250 B St., 92102. 714 232-7528.
San Francisco
Parents of Gay People, c/o Operation Concern, Pacific Medical Center, P.O. Box 7999, 94120. 415 563-0202.
San Mateo
Leslie Bunch, 426 E. 16th St. 94402. 415 349-0542.

Colorado
Betty Fairchild, 700 Emerson St., Denver, 80218. 303 831-8576.
MCC of the Rockies, 303 831-4787.

Florida
Jacksonville
Parents of Gays, c/o MCC, P.O. Box 291, 32201. 904 354-1318.
Pensacola
Parents of Gays, P.O. Box 4479, 32507. 904 453-1923.

Georgia
Jake Shipp, 816 Piedmont Ave., N.E., Atlanta, 30308. 404 876-5177.

Sister Constance Peck speaking in favor of New York City gay rights bill, 1974

Eleanor Holmes Norton, former New York City Human Rights
Commissioner, testifying for gay rights legislation

Iowa

Bill and Louise Miller, 3428 Brandywine Rd., Mason City, 50401. 515 423-5911.

Kentucky

Barbara Maynor, 418 Marret Ave., Louisville, 40208. 502 636-0649.

Maine (Summer only)

Evelyn and Floyd Bull, RFD #2, CP80, Kennebunkport, 04046. 207 967-4837.

Maryland

Parents of Gays—Baltimore, 301 235-HELP, 366-1415.
June Durham, 5434 Relcrest Rd., Apt. A. Baltimore, 21206. 301 483-4042.

Massachusetts

David Griffith, Coord., Parents of Gays, 80 Boylston St., Suite 855, Boston, 02116. 617 542-5188.

Michigan

Parents of Gays, MCC—Detroit, c/o Trinity Methodist Church, 13100 Woodward Ave., Highland Park, 48203. 313 534-9314.

Minnesota

Families of Gays, c/o Neighborhood Counseling Center, 1801 Nicollet Ave. South, Minneapolis 55403. 612 874-5369.

Missouri

Kansas City

Phyllis Shafer, 1838 E. 49th St., Kansas City, 64130. 816 921-7779.

St. Louis

Arthur and Marian Wirth, 7443 Cromwell Drive, St. Louis, 63105. 314 863-2748.

New Jersey

Evelyn and Floyd Bull, Princeton Arms North, Apt. 150, Cranbury, 08512. 609 448-4537.

New York

Parents of Gays and Lesbians, Metropolitan Duane Methodist Church, 201 W. 13th St. at 7th Ave., New York, 10011.
Jules and Jeanne Manford, 212 353-4044.

Ohio

Liselotte Sherwood, 1177 Northwest Blvd., Columbus 43212.

Oregon

Portland

POG/Portland, The Portland Town Council, 320 S.W. Stark St., Rm. 303, 97204. 503 227-2765.

Pennsylvania

Philadelphia

POG—Philadelphia, Gay Community Center, 326 Kater St., 19147.

Pittsburgh

Parents of Gays, c/o Persad Center, Inc., Shadyside Center Bldg., 5100 Centre Ave., 15232. 412 681-5330.

Vermont

Ruth and Hank Abrams, Highgate Apts., Barre, 05641.

Washington, D.C.

Parents of Gays of D.C., c/o Ilse Mollet, 263 Congressional Lane, #407, Rockville, Md. 20852. 310 468-0091.

Canada

D. F. Cassidy (all efforts in French/English), POG—Montreal, 5311 Sherbrooke W., #916, Montreal, P.Q., Canada H4A 1U3, 514 288-1101.

Ready or Not, Here We Come!

FLO KENNEDY, ESQ.

In *Our Right to Love* a whole 'nother set of the niggerized have issued a "Declaration of Human Rights." Gay people have hereby withdrawn consent to oppression. Eat your heart out, Anita Bryant, Jocks, PTA Clubs, Aileen Ryan, John Birch Society, Matthew Troy, Pope Paul, et al.

It would, however, be inaccurate, ungracious, and unpolitical to deny the boosts such detractors have given to the gay movement. The alliance of the alienated has been largely strengthened by this proud addition to the liberation struggle.

Hassling homosexuals, chasing whores, conning consumers, and districting neglected elderly by villainizing unemployed black teen-agers are but a few of the niggerizing techniques of a society where institutionalized oppression is a major gross national product.

The National Gay Task Force in this book provides a pinpoint of light in a tunnel of corporate manufacturing crises, government subsidized cancer-causing products, tax-financed Pentagonnorhea, and bank-directed raids on workers' pension funds. Ecclesiastical values, trumpeted by media, enforced by criminal laws, misdirect a mass of brutal hysteria against sexuality while imperalism, Pentagonnorhea, waste-ism, and racism approach cancerous levels.

We are surrounded by a volcanic range of bullshit mountains, and everybody gets a plastic teaspoon. *Our Right to Love* is calculated to dispel a noticeable layer of the pall of guilt that functions as a smoke screen to fog our perceptions as to where the shit is coming from.

The "good people" keep telling us to be industrious and to clean up our act, but every time we bend over to hoe a row or pick up the soap, we seem, without our consent (or Vaseline) to get it from the pigocracy. Enough, already!

An "Innerview" with Lily Tomlin*

Note: The following "innerview" with Lily Tomlin is excerpted from her album Modern Scream *and is reprinted here with her permission.—Ed.*

Interviewer: I want to talk to you about your frank film about heterosexuality. Did it seem strange to you, seeing yourself making love to a man on the big screen?

Lily: Oh, well, I did a lot of research, you know, and by the time we began shooting I was used to it. I've seen these women all my life, so I know how they walk, and I know how they talk. Of course I did interview some psychiatrists, but they don't have the answers.

Interviewer: No, I don't suppose anyone does, really.

Lily: Of course I got a lot of flack from straight liberation groups—some thought I went too far, some not far enough. . . .

Interviewer: Well, you have your radical element in every group.

Lily: And my family said, "How could you do such a thing?" People just don't understand—you don't have to be one to play one.

Interviewer: I guess people are pretty amazed that a woman who looks like you do can play a heterosexual so realistically, and still be perfectly normal.

*Copyright © 1975 Omnipotent, Inc.

The Hite Report

SHERE HITE

Note: Following is the conclusion of Shere Hite's chapter entitled "Lesbianism" in The Hite Report, *Macmillan, 1976.*

It is important for women to recognize their own potential for having sexual feelings for other women. If we want to grow strong, we must learn to love, respect, honor, and be attentive to and interested in other women. This includes seeing each other as physically attractive with the possibility of sexual intimacy. As long as we can relate sexually only to men *because they are "men"* (and as long as men can relate only to women because they are "women"), we are dividing the world into the very two classes we are trying to transcend.

Any woman who feels actual horror or revulsion at the thought of kissing or embracing or having physical relations with another woman should reexamine her feelings and attitudes not only about other women, but also about *herself.* A positive attitude toward our bodies and toward touching ourselves and toward our physical contact that might naturally develop with another woman is essential to self-love and accepting our own bodies as good and beautiful. As Jill Johnston has written: ". . . until women see in each other the possibility of a primal commitment which includes sexual love they will be denying themselves the love and value they readily accord to men, thus affirming their own second-class status."

Revolution: Tomorrow Is NOW!

WILMA SCOTT HEIDE

(From a speech delivered by Wilma Scott Heide at the Sixth Natonal Conference of the National Organization for Women, 1973, during her term of office as president of NOW.)

As a further matter of integrity, feminism includes the freedom and power to love ourselves *and* each other as women, as men and as women and men loving each other as persons and embracing such children as we choose to have or have had in that love. No particular sexuality preference, if any, is either a requirement of or a barrier to feminism in NOW. That orientation, in my view, is the sine qua non for getting on with the business of educating and being educated by our children vis-à-vis the full potential of human sexuality. We do not equate normal with natural and in neither do we see bases for praise or censure. Our sexuality is; that is its own validity, and though often vital is not the totality of our identity. I would propose that philosophy as a societal imperative to help hang up our sex hang-ups. Though we've resolved this in NOW, we have *yet* to exhibit the courage of our convictions. This Conference must move beyond resolution to action programs for NOW and society.

What we are about is love in its deepest, most abiding sense. If we did not care, we would not be here; indeed, if we did not care, NOW would not be.

Equal Protection for All

BELLA ABZUG

It is time to recognize that lesbians and homosexuals are individuals like anyone else, who happen to have made certain personal choices about their private lives. These choices are their own business; they have no greater effect on their work than their color, size, shape or ethnicity, and they should not be subjected to discrimination of any kind because of their sexual preferences. They are fully entitled to the same Constitutional protections as all other Americans.

The Lesbian Label

LOIS GOULD

Lesbian is no longer just a sexual term. Many feminists—myself included—now consider it a highly charged political word, used to describe any woman who chooses to live independently from men.

It is, as the feminist theorist Charlotte Bunch has said, a logical extension—in the sense that if a woman's life is not bound up with or defined by men, then in men's eyes she might as well be a lesbian.

For some non-lesbian women, the act of declaring oneself one is a political statement—like the King of Denmark wearing a yellow armband to mark himself a Jew because the Nazis had ordered all Danish Jews to be marked.

We need new words that support women and all forms of women's sexuality. Until we have them, the word *lesbian* must be accorded at least as much respect as the words wife, mother, daughter, fiancee, mistress, sister—and friend.

Edward I. Koch, mayor of New York City, former congressional sponser of federal gay rights bill

NBC News Producer Sharon Sopher filming a documentary in a lesbian bar

Appendix

Bibliog-raphy

compiled by KAROL D. LIGHTNER

The following bibliography lists nearly two hundred titles of pamphlets, nonfiction, fiction, poetry, periodicals, bibliographies, and biographies. Premovement literature should be read critically, with the understanding that a liberated view of lesbianism was unavailable to most authors at the time of writing.

For those readers who have not read widely on the subject of lesbianism, we suggest the following books as a good introduction (see complete entries on the following pages):

Nonfiction:
Sappho Was a Right-On Woman, Love and Abbott
Lesbian/Woman, Martin and Lyon
Woman + Woman, Klaich
Loving Someone Gay, Clark
Out of the Closets, Jay and Young
After You're Out, Jay and Young
Gay American History, Katz
Society and the Healthy Homosexual, Weinberg

Fiction:
Rubyfruit Jungle, Brown
Patience and Sarah, Miller

BIBLIOGRAPHIES AND GUIDES

Bibliography of Lesbian Related Materials. 1974. Lesbian Resource Center, 2104 Stevens Ave. South, Minneapolis, Minn. 53404. Free.

Bullough, Vern L., et al. *An Annotated Bibliography of Homosexuality.* 2 vols. 1976. Garland Publishing, 545 Madison Ave., New York, N.Y. 10022. $75.

Damon, Gene; Watson, Jan; and Jordan, Robin. *The Lesbian in Literature: A Bibliography.* 96 pp. 1975. The Ladder, Box 5025, Washington Station, Reno, Nev. 89503. $10.

Dignity. *A Catholic Bibliography on Homosexuality.* 1975. Dignity-National, 775 Boylston, Rm. 514, Boston, Mass. 02116. Free.

Gay and Lesbian-Feminist Organizations List. Complete United States, updated monthly. National Gay Task Force, 80 Fifth Ave., New York, N.Y. 10011.

Gay Bookstores and Mail Order Services, U.S. and Canada. National Gay Student Center, 2113 S St., N.W., Washington, D.C. 20008. 25¢ prepaid.

Gay Professional Organizations and National Caucuses (U.S.). National Gay Task Force, 80 Fifth Ave., New York, N.Y. 10011. 25¢.

Gittings, Barbara, ed. *A Gay Bibliography* From the Task Force on Gay Liberation (Social Responsibilities Round Table) American Library Association. Pamphlet. 25¢. Box 2383, Philadelphia, Pa. 19103.

Green, Frances, comp. *Gayellow Pages,* National Edition. For United States and Canada only. Organizations, bars, restaurants, businesses, etc. *Gayellow Pages,* Box 292, Village Station, New York, N.Y. 10014. Single issue $5, 4 issues $10.

———, comp. *Gayellow Pages,* New York Edition. A guide to gay organizations, bars, businesses, restaurants, etc., for gay women and men. *Gayellow pages,* Box 292, Village Station, San Francisco, N.Y. 10014. Paper, $1.25.

Horn, Sandy, comp. *Gaia's Guide.* Yearly updated lesbian travel guide, international and United States (includes bars, organizations, switchboards, bookshops, restaurants, etc.) Gaia's Guide, 115 New Montgomery St., San Francisco, Calif. 94105. $6.

Kuda, Marie J., ed. *Women Loving Women: A Select and Annotated Bibliography of Women-loving Women in Literature.* 1974. Womanpress, Box 59330, Chicago, Illinois 60645. 32 pp., $1.50.

Nicolson, Nigel. *Portrait of a Marriage: Biography of Vita Sackville-West and Harold Nicolson.* 1973. Bantam Books, 1974.

Student Gay Groups, U.S. and Canada. 3rd ed, 1975. National Gay Student Center, 2115 S St., N.W., Washington, D.C. 20008. 50¢ prepaid.

NONFICTION

Abbott, Sidney, and Love, Barbara. *Sappho Was a Right-On Woman: A Liberated View of Lesbianism.* Stein & Day, 1972. Cloth and paper eds.

Bailey, Derrick S. *Homosexuality and the Western Christian Tradition.* Longmans Green, 1955 (out of print). Reprint 1975 by Archon-Shoe String Press.

Birkby, Phyllis; Harris, Bertha; Johnston, Jill; Newton, Esther; and O'Wyatt, Jane. *Amazon Expedition: A Lesbian Feminist Anthology.* Times Changes Press, 1973.

Boggan, E. Carrington, et al. *The Rights of Gay People.* The American Civil Liberties Union Handbook, Avon, 1975.

Brittain, Vera. *Radclyffe Hall: A Case of Obscenity.* A. S. Barnes & Co., 1968. Trial of author of *Well of Loneliness.*

Brown, Rita Mae. *Plain Brown Rapper.* Diana Press, 1977. Essays, speeches.

Burns, Edward, ed. *Staying on Alone: The Letters of Alice B. Toklas. 1973.* Vintage, 1975.

Clark, Don. *Loving Someone Gay: A Gay Therapist's Guidance for Gays and People Who Care About Them.* Celestial Arts, 1977.

Covina, Gina, and Galana, Laurel, eds. *The Lesbian Reader: An Amazon Quarterly Anthology.* Amazon Press, 1975.

Crew, Louie, ed. *The Gay Academic,* Etc. Publications, January 1977.

Damon, Gene. *The Lesbian in Literature.* Ladder, 1975.

———, *Lesbiana.* Naiad Press, 1976. Book reviews from *The Ladder,* 1966-72.

———, and Reid, Colletta, eds. *The Lavender Herring.* Diane Press, 1976. Essays from *The Ladder.*

Deming, Barbara. *We Cannot Live Without Our Lives.* Grossman Publishers, 1974. Essays, poems, letters.

Falk, Ruth. *Women Loving: A Journey Toward Becoming an Independent Woman.* Random House, 1975.

Foster, Jeannette H. *Sex Variant Women In Literature: A Historical and Quantitative Survey.* Afterword by Gene Damon. Diana Press, 1975.

Galana, Laurel and Covina, Gina. *The New Lesbians.* Moon Books, dist. by Random House, 1977.

Gearhart, Sally, and Johnson, William. *Loving Women/Loving Men: Gay Liberation and the Church.* Glide, 1974.

Gibson, Gifford Guy, with the cooperation of Mary Jo Risher. *By Her Own Admission: A Lesbian Mother's Fight to Keep Her Son.* Doubleday, 1977.

Hodges, Beth, ed. *Margins,* No. 23 (August 1975). Special issue on lesbian-feminist writing. $1.

Hope, Karol, and Young, Nancy. *Momma— The Sourcebook for Single Mothers.* New American Library (Plume), 1976.

Jay, Karla, and Young, Alan. *After You're Out*. Links Books, 1975.

———, eds. *Out of the Closets: Voices of Gay Liberation*. Pyramid, reprint, 1974.

Johnston, Jill. *Gullibles Travels*. Links Books, 1974.

———. *Lesbian Nation: The Feminist Solution*. Simon & Schuster (Touchstone), 1973.

Katz, Jonathan. *Coming Out: A Documentary Play About Gay Life and Liberation in the USA*. Arno Press Series on Homosexuality, 1975.

———. *Gay American History*. Crowell, 1976.

Klaich, Dolores. *Woman + Woman: Attitudes Toward Lesbianism*. Morrow, 1974.

Lehman, Lee, ed. *Gays on Campus*. National Gay Student Center, 1975.

Lesbianism and Feminism in Germany, 1895-1910. Arno Press Series on Homosexuality, 1975. An original Arno Press anthology.

McNeil, John J. *The Church and the Homosexual*. Sheed Andrews and McMeel (formerly Sheed & Ward), September 1976.

Martin, Del, and Lyon, Phyllis. *Lesbian/Woman*. Bantam Books, 1972.

Millett, Kate. *Sita*. Farrar, Straus, and Giroux, 1977.

Morgan, Robin. *Going Too Far*. Random House, 1977. The personal chronicle of a feminist.

Morgan, Robin, ed. *Sisterhood Is Powerful: An Anthology of Writings from the Women's Movement*. Vintage, 1970.

Myron, Nancy, and Bunch, Charlotte. *Lesbianism and the Women's Movement*. Diana Press, 1975.

Newton, Esther, and Walton, Shirley. *Womenfriends: A Journal Dialogue Between a Lesbian and a Heterosexual Woman*. Friends Press, Inc., 1976.

Nomadic Sisters. *Loving Women*. Illus. by Victoria Hammand. Nomadic Sisters, 1975.

Rich, Adrienne. *Of Woman Born: Motherhood as Experience and Institution*. Norton, 1977.

Rule, Jane. *Lesbian Images: Critical Studies of Lesbian Literature and Lives*. Doubleday, 1975.

Sarton, May. *A World of Light: Portraits and Celebrations*. Norton, 1977.

———. *Journal of a Solitude*. Norton, 1973.

Simpson, Ruth. *From the Closets to the Courts: The Lesbian Transition*. Viking, 1975.

Sisley, Ph.D., Emily and Harris, Bertha. *The Joy Of Lesbian Sex*. Crown, 1977.

Teal, Don. *The Gay Militants*. Stein & Day, 1971.

Tobin, Kay, and Wicker, Randy. *The Gay Crusaders*. 1972. Arno Press Series on Homosexuality, 1975.

Weinberg, George. *Society and the Healthy Homosexual*. Doubleday/Anchor, 1972.

Weltge, Ralph W., ed. *The Same Sex: An Appraisal of Homosexuality*. United Church Press, 1969.

What Lesbians Do. Godiva, 1975. Essays, poems, drawings.

Wolff, Charlotte. *Love Between Women*. Harper Colophon Books, 1971.

Womanshare Collective, *Country Lesbians*. Womanshare Books, P.O. Box 1735, Grants Pass, Ore. 97526.

Women in Transition, Inc. *Women in Transition, a Feminist Handbook on Separation and Divorce*. Scribner's, 1976.

Women Loving, Women Writing. Womanpress, 1976. Women's Press Collective. *Lesbians Speak Out*. Women's Press Collective, 1974. Anthology of essays, poems, photos, drawings.

Wysor, Bettie. *The Lesbian Myth: Insights and Conversations*. Random House, 1974.

BIOGRAPHY

Acosta, Mercedes de. *Here Lies the Heart*. 1960. Arno Press. Series on Homosexuality, 1975. Biography of woman who knew Garbo and Dietrich.

Aldridge, Sarah. *Cytherea's Breath*. Naiad Press, 1977.

Grier, Barbara, and Reid, Coletta, eds. *Lesbian Lives*. Diana Press, 1976. Short biographies that originally appeared in *The Ladder*.

Mellow, James R. *Charmed Circle: Gertrude Stein and Company*. Avon Books, 1974.

Millett, Kate. *Flying*. Ballantine, 1974.

Nicolson, Nigel. *Portrait of a Marriage: Biography of Vita Sackville-West and Harold Nicolson*. 1973. Bantam Books, 1974.

Secrest, Meryle. *Between Me And Life: a Biography of Romaine Brooks*. Doubleday & Co., 1974.

Simon, Linda. *The Biography of Alice B. Toklas*. Doubleday & Co., 1977.

Spencer, Virginia. *The Lonely Hunter: Biography of Carson McCullers*. Doubleday/Anchor, 1975.

Stein, Gertrude. *The Autobiography of Alice B. Toklas*. Vintage Books, 1933.

(Vincenzo) Una, Lady Troubridge. *The Life of Radclyffe Hall*. 1963. Arno Press Series on Homosexuality, 1975.

Wickes, George. *The Amazon of Letters: The Life and Loves of Natalie Clifford Barney*. G. P. Putnam's Sons, 1976.

FICTION

Aldridge, Sarah. *The Latecomer*. Naiad Press, 1974.

———. *Tottie*. Naiad Press, 1974.

Arnold, June. *The Cook and the Carpenter*. Daughters, Inc., 1973.

———. *Sister Gin*. Daughters, Inc., 1975.

Bannon, Ann. *I Am a Woman*. 1959. Arno Press Series on Homosexuality, 1975. One of the best of lesbian pulp writers.

———. *Journey to a Woman*. 1960. Arno Press Series on Homosexuality, 1975.

———. *Odd Girl Out*. 1957. Arno Press Series on Homosexuality, 1975.

———. *Women in the Shadows* 1959. Arno Press Series on Homosexuality, 1975.

Note: The four Bannon titles are a serial and should be read as follows: (1) *Odd Girl Out*, (2) *I Am a Woman*, (3) *Women in the Shadows*, (4) *Journey to a Woman*.

Barnes, Djuna. *Nightwood*. Introduction by T. S. Eliot. New Directions, 1961.

Beal, M.F. *Angel Dance*. Daughters, Inc., 1977.

Brown, Rita Mae. *In Her Day*. Daughters, Inc., 1976.

———. *Rubyfruit Jungle*. Daughters, Inc., 1973.

Bryant, Dorothy. *The Kin of Ata Are Waiting for You*. Moonbooks/Random House, 1976. Fantasy/Science fiction.

Colette. *The Pure and the Impure*. Farrar & Rinehart, 1932.

Dykewoman, Elana. *They Will Know Me By My Teeth*. Women In Distribution, P.O. Box 8858, Washington, D.C. 20003, 1977.

Frederics, Diana. *Diana: A Strange Autobiography*. 1939. Arno Press Series on Homosexuality, 1975.

Gregory, Roberta. *Dynamite Damsels*. Women In Distribution, P.O. Box 8858, Washington, D.C. 20003, 1977.

Grier, Barbara, and Reed, Colletta. *The Lesbians Home Journal*. Diana Press, 1976. Short stories from *The Ladder*.

Gay, Rosa. *Ruby*. Viking Press, 1976. Novel of two black women's relationship.

Hall, Radclyffe. *The Well of Loneliness*. 1928. Pocket Books, 1974. The lesbian classic for many years. Grossly outdated, but historically interesting.

Harris, Bertha. *Catching Saradove*. Harcourt Brace Jovanovich, 1969.

———. *Confessions of Cherubino*. Harcourt Brace Jovanovich, 1972.

———. *Lover*. Daughters, Inc., 1976.

Hauser, Marianne. *The Talking Room*. Fiction Collective, 1976. As seen through the eyes of the thirteen-year-old daughter of a lesbian mother.

Isabell, Sharon. *Yesterday's Lesson*. 2nd ed., Women's Press Collective, 1974.

Jones, Sonya. *The Legacy*. Vanity Press, 1976.

Jordan, Robin. *Speak Out, My Heart*. Naiad Press, 1976.

Jullian, Phillipe, and Phillips, John. *The Other Woman: A Life of Violet Trefusis.* Houghton Mifflin Co., 1976. Includes previously unpublished correspondence with Vita Sackville-West.

Lehmann, Rosamond. *Dusty Answer.* 1927. Harcourt Brace Jovanovich.

Marie, Linda. *I Must Not Rock.* Daughters, Inc., 1977.

Miller, Isabel. *Patience and Sarah.* McGraw-Hill, 1972. Originally published by the author as *A Place for Us.*

Morgan, Claire. *The Price of Salt.* 1952. Arno Press Series on Homosexuality, 1975.

Nachman, Elana. *Riverfinger Woman.* Daughters, Inc., 1974.

Pass, Gail. *Zoe's Book.* Avon Books, 1976.

Renault, Mary. *The Middle Mist.* Popular Library, 1945. Renewed 1972.

Rule, Jane. *Against the Season.* Manor Books, Inc., 1971.

———: *The Desert of the Heart.* 1964. Arno Press Series on Homosexuality, 1975.

———: *Themes for Diverse Instruments.* Talon Books, 1976. 13 short stories.

———: *This Is Not for You.* 1970. Popular Library, 1972. Currently out of print.

———: *The Young in One Another's Arms.* Doubleday, 1977.

Sarton, May. *Mrs. Stevens Hears the Mermaids Singing.* 1965, Norton, 1974.

———: *The Small Room.* Norton, 1961.

Shockley, Ann. *Loving Her.* Bobbs-Merrill, 1974.

Vivien, Renée. *A Woman Appeared to Me.* Translated from the French by Jeanette Foster. Naiad Press, 1976.

Wilhelm, Gale. *Torchlight to Valhalla.* 1938. Arno Press Series on Homosexuality, 1975.

———: *We Too Are Drifting.* 1935. Arno Press Series on Homosexuality, 1975.

Wittig, Monique. *The Lesbian Body.* Avon Books, 1973.

———: *Les Guérillères.* Translated by David LeVay. Avon Books, 1969.

———: *The Opoponax.* Translated by Helen Weaver. 1964. Daughters, Inc., 1976.

Woolf, Virginia. *Orlando.* Harvest Books, 1928.

POETRY

Aldridge, Sarah. *Cytherea's Breath.* Naiad Press, 1976.

Barnard, Mary, trans. *Sappho.* University of California, 1958. Considered best translation of Sappho's poetry.

Bernikow, Louise, ed. *The World Split Open.* Vintage Books, Random House, 1975.

Brown, Rita Mae. *The Hand That Cradles the Rock.* Diana Press, 1971.

———: *Songs to a Handsome Woman.* Diana Press, 1973.

Bulkin, Elly, and Larkin, Joan. *Amazon Poetry.* Out-and-Out Books, 1975. Anthology of lesbian poetry.

Cavin, Susan. *Me and Them Sirens Running All Night Long.* The Print Center.

Griffin, Susan. *Dear Sky* (poetry 1971, 1973). Shameless Hussy Press.

———: *Let Them Be Said* (poetry 1973). Shameless Hussy Press.

Foster, Jeanette, and Taylor, Valerie. *Two Women: The Poetry of Jeanette Foster and Valerie Taylor.* Womanpress, 1976.

Gidlow, Elsa. *Sapphic Songs: Seventeen to Seventy.* Diana Press, 1976.

Grahn, Judy. *Edward the Dyke and Other Poems.* Women's Press Collective, 1971.

———: *A Woman Is Talking to Death.* Women's Press Collective, 1971.

Greenspan, Judy. *To Lesbians Everywhere.* Violet Press, 1976.

Lorde, Audre. *From a Land Where Other People Live.* Broadside Press, 1973.

Louys, Pierre. *The Songs of Bilitis,* Capricorn Books, 1966.

McArthur, Pam. *Mountain Lore.* Privately printed.

Morgan, Robin. *Lady of the Beasts.* Random House, 1976.

Parker, Pat. *Pit Stop.* Women's Press Collective, 1973.

Passeri, Margaret. *Going Down in Silver.* The Gilded Sparrow, Iowa City Women's Press, 1976.

Rich, Adrienne. *Twenty-one Love Poems.* Effie's Press, 1976.

Sherman, Susan. *With Anger/With Love.* 1963-1972. Mulch Press.

———: *Women Poems Love Poems.* Out-and-Out Books, 1977.

Stevens, Wendy. *I Am Not a Careful Poet.* Privately printed, 1975.

Taylor, Valerie. *Love Image.* Naiad Press, 1977.

Vivien, Renée. *The Muse of the Violets.* Naiad Press, 1976.

We Are All Lesbians. Violet Press, 1973, Poetry anthology.

Wiackley, Mildred, ed. *From Deborah and Sappho to the Present: An Anthology of Women Poets.* New Orlando Publications, 1976.

Winant, Fran. *Dyke Jacket.* Violet Press, 1976.

PERIODICALS AND JOURNALS

The Advocate. 2121 S. El Camino Real, San Mateo, Calif. 94403. National gay newsmagazine. Biweekly. All United States subscriptions $10/year.

Albatross: The Radical Lesbian Feminist Satire Magazine. Tacky Productions, Box 112, 111 S. Harrison St., East Orange, N.J. Quarterly. $7/year.

Amazon: A Midwest Journal for Women. Amazon Collective, 2211 E. Kenwood, Milwaukee, Wis. 53211. Bimonthly. $3/year, 65¢ sample.

Apple: A Journal of Women's Sexuality and Erotica. Sister, 100 N.E. 56th St., Seattle, Washington, 98105. $7/4 issues. Sample copy $2.

Armed Forces Informer. American Armed Forces Assn., Box 1863, Pensacola, Fla. 32589. Monthly. Free to service members.

Association of Gay Psychologists Newsletter. Box 29527, Atlanta, Ga. 30357. 3 issues, $5.

Atalanta: Atlanta Lesbian Feminist Alliance Newsletter. Box 5502, Atlanta, Ga. 30307. Monthly. Donation $1.50, single issue.

The Barb. Box 7922-Y, Atlanta, Ga. 30309. Gay newspaper. Monthly. 12 issues, $5.

Best Friends. Nancy Gage Staley, 800 Carlisle, N.E., Albuquerque, N.M. 87106. Feminist poetry publication.

Big Mama Rag. 1724 Gaylord, Denver, Col. 80206. $6/year. Feminist newspaper.

The Body Politic: Gay Liberation Journal. Box 7289, Station A, Toronto, Ont., Canada. Bimonthly. Single issue $1.

The Bright Medusa. Nancy Stuckwell, ed., Box 9321, Berkeley, Calif. 94709. Lesbian-feminist arts journal.

Christopher Street. 60 W. 13th St., New York, N.Y. 10011. Monthly. Single issue $1.25; $5/year. Magazine for gay women and men.

Chrysalis. Woman's Building, 1724 N. Spring St., Dept. A, Los Angeles, Calif. 90012. $10/year. Feminist magazine for women's culture.

Conditions. P.O. Box 56, Van Brunt Station, Brooklyn, N.Y. 11215. $6.50/year (3 issues). A magazine of writing by women with an emphasis on writing by lesbians.

Country Women. Box 51, Albion, Calif. 95410. $4/year (5 issues).

Diana. 6368 Heitzler, Cincinnati, Ohio 45224.

Dignity. Room 413, 755 Boylston St., Boston, Mass. 02116. Monthly. $15/year. National publication of the gay Catholic community.

Dyke. Tomato Publications, 70 Barrow St., Dept. G, New York, N.Y. 10014. Quarterly, $8/year.

Ecstasy. New Time Press, Box 32236, San Jose, Calif. 95132. $10/year. Feminist erotic journal.

Emergence. Darlene Miller, 7027 Rt. 534, Windsor, Ohio 44099. Bimonthly. Newsletter for women artists.

Focus. Boston Daughters of Bilitis, 419

Boylston, Rm. 323, Boston, Mass. 02116. Monthly. Single issue 60¢; $6/year. Journal for gay women.

Gay Academic Union Journal: Gai Saber. Gay Academic Union, Inc., Box 480, Lenox Hill Station, New York, N.Y. 10021. Quarterly. $18/year; $12.50 student rate.

Gay Community News (GCN). 22 Bromfield St., Boston, Mass. 02108. $15/year. Weekly from Boston, for Northeast.

Gay Lutheran. Lutherans Concerned for Gay People, Box 1911 4A, Los Angeles, Calif. 90019.

Gay News (England). United States and Canada: unsealed seamail $14/12 issues, $23/24; sealed seamail $20/12, $38/24; unsealed airmail $20/12, $38/24; sealed airmail $30/12, $58/24. Sample (United States and Canada), $1 unsealed seamail, $1.50 sealed seamail, $1.50 unsealed airmail, $2.50 sealed airmail.

Hera. 2041 Walnut, Philadelphia, Pa. 19103. $6 for 12 issues. Philadelphia feminist publication.

Heresies. P.O. Box 766, Canal St. Station, New York, N.Y. 10013. $2.50. Feminist publication on art, women's culture and politics.

Homosexual Community Counseling Journal. Homosexual Community Counseling Center, 30 E. 60th St., New York, N.Y. 10022. $10/year.

Integrity. Gay Episcopal Forum, 701 Orange St., #6, Fort Valley, Ga. 31030. $10/year (10 issues).

Interchange. National Gay Student Center, 2115 S St., N.W., Washington, D.C. 20008. $3/year (every 2 months).

In Unity. Universal Fellowship of Metropolitan Community Churches, Box 5770, Los Angeles, Calif. 90055. $10/year.

It's Time. National Gay Task Force, 80 Fifth Ave., New York, N.Y. 10011. Bimonthly. Free with $15 membership. Sample 25¢. Newsletter of NGTF.

Journal of Homosexuality. 130 W. 72nd St., New York, N.Y. 10023. Quarterly. $15/year. Scholarly and psychological research in mental health field.

The Ladder, vols. 1-16. Arno Press Series on Homosexuality, 1975. Includes an index to *The Ladder* by Gene Damon, 1956-72.

Leaping Lesbian. Hibben and Silver-rod, 1003 Packard, #5, Ann Arbor, Mich. 48104. Free.

Lesbian Connection. Ambitious Amazons, Box 811, East Lansing, Mich. 48823. 8 times yearly. Suggested donation, $1 per copy. National lesbian journal.

The Lesbian Feminist. Lesbian Feminist Liberation, 243 W. 20th St., New York, N.Y. 10011. Free

Lesbian Front. Box 8342, Jackson, Miss. 39204. Monthly. $4/year. Newsletter in Mississippi and Southeast.

Lesbian Herstory Archives Newsletter. Box 1258, New York, N.Y. 10001. Free.

The Lesbian News. Box 2023, Culver City, Calif. 90230.

The Lesbian Tide. 8855 Cattaraugus, Los Angeles, Calif. 90034. $6/year (6 issues). Lesbian-feminist national news.

Lesbian Voices. R. Nichols, P.O. Box 3122, San Jose, Calif. 95116. Quarterly. $5/year.

The Longest Revolution. P.O. Box 350, San Diego, Calif. 92101. $3/year. Feminist publication.

Maine Freewoman's Herald. 193 Middle St., Portland, Maine 04111. $4/year.

Majority Report. 74 Grove St., New York, N.Y. 10014. Biweekly. $5/year. Feminist newspaper.

Mamma Ry. S. Craig, 938 W. Oakdale, Chicago, Ill. 60657. By/for/about lesbians and feminists—a celebration of women's artistic and intellectual talents.

Mom's Apple Pie. Lesbian Mothers National Defense Fund, 2446 Lorentz Pl. North, Seattle, Wash. 98109. Bimonthly. $2/year.

New Women's Times. 1357 Monroe Ave., Rochester, N.Y. 14618. $5/year.

Off Our Backs. 1724 20th St., N.W., Washington, D.C. 20009. $6/year. Feminist newspaper.

The Other Woman. Canadian feminist. Box 928 Station Q, Toronto, Ontario, Canada. United States, $4/year; Canada, $3.

Paid My Dues. Women's Soul Publishing Co., Box 11646, Milwaukee, Wis. 53211. $4/year (irreg.). Journal of women and music.

Plexus. 2600 Dwight Way, Rm. 209, Berkeley, Calif. 94704. $5/year. Bay Area women's newspaper.

Pointblank Times. P.O. Box 14643, Houston, Tex. 77021. $5/year. Lesbian-feminist publication.

Prisoner Yellow Pages. Prisoner Ministry of Metropolitan Community Church, Box 5570, Los Angeles, Calif. 90055. Free to prisoners; nonprisoners, $2.

Quest: A Feminist Quarterly. Box 8843, Washington, D.C. 20003. $9.

Second Wave. Box 344, Cambridge, Mass. 02139. Quarterly. $3.50/year. Feminist magazine.

Sexualawreporter. Reporting on legal developments in sex-related law. 3701 Wilshire Blvd., Suite 700, Los Angeles, Calif. 90010. Bimonthly, subscription $15.

Sister. The Women's Center, P.O. Box 597, Venice, Calif. 90291. $5/year. Feminist newspaper.

Sister Courage. P.O. Box 296, Allston, Mass. 02134. Monthly. Single issue 35¢; $4/year. Feminist publication.

So's Your Old Lady. Lesbian Resource Center, 2104 Stevens Ave. South, Minneapolis, Minn. 55404. Bimonthly. Single issue $1; $6/year. Lesbian-feminist journal.

Wicce. Box 15833, Philadelphia, Pa. 19103. 65¢ (irreg.). Lesbian-feminist publication.

Woman Rising. P.O. Box 2792, Tempe, Ariz. 85282. $2.50 (12 issues).

Womanspirit. Box 263, Wolf Creek, Ore. 97497. Quarterly, $6/year.

Women: A Journal of Liberation. 3028 Greenmount Ave., Baltimore, Md. 21218. $1.25 per issue (United States).

PAMPHLETS

Bender, David, and McCuen, Gary. "Determining Family and Sexual Roles." Greenhaven Press, Box 831, Aoken, Minn. 55303. $1.35.

"Corporate Business Support Statements Packet." National Gay Task Force, 80 Fifth Ave., New York, N.Y. 10011. $1 prepaid. Letters declaring nondiscrimination employment policies from IBM, Bank of America, AT&T, CBS, Eastern Airlines, McDonald's, etc.

Crew, Louie, and Norton, Rictor, eds. "The Homosexual Imagination." National Council of Teachers of English, 1111 Kenyon, Urbana, Ill. 61801. $2. Special issue of *College English,* November 1974.

Fairchild, Betty. "Parents of Gays." Revised 1975. Lambda Rising, 1724 20th St., N.W., Washington, D.C. 20009. $1 plus 35¢ for postage.

Gay Academic Union. "The Universities and the Gay Experience." Proceedings of the first GAU Conference, November 1973. Gay Academic Union Publication Committee, Box 1479, Hunter College, New York, N.Y. 10021. $2.

"Gay Civil Rights Support Statement and Resolutions Packet." National Gay Task Force, 80 Fifth Ave., New York, N.Y. 10011. $2.

Gay Military Counselor's Manual." Gay Center for Social Services of San Diego, 2250 B St., San Diego, Calif. 92102. $9.

"Gay Parent Support Packet." National Gay Task Force, 80 Fifth Ave., New York, N.Y. 10011. $1 prepaid. Statements on gay parents' custody and visitation rights.

Gidlow, Elsa. "Ask No Man Pardon. The Philosophical Significance of Being Lesbian." Pamphlet, photos by Ruth Mountaingrove. Druid Heights Books, 685 Camino del Canyon, Mill Valley, Calif. 94941. $1.

Grammick, Jeannie, et al. "Catholic Homosexuals: A Primer for Discussion." Dignity, 1975. Dignity National, 755 Boylston, Boston, Mass. 02116. $1.50 prepaid.

Hodges, Beth, ed. "Sinister Wisdom Special Focus: Lesbian Feminist Writing and Publishing." Vol. I, No. 2, November 1976. Sinister Wisdom, 3116 Country Club Dr., Charlotte, N.C. 28205. $2 prepaid.

Martin, Del, and Lyon, Phyllis. "Lesbian Love and Liberation." Multi-Media Resource Center, 1973. 540 Powell St., San Francisco, Calif. 94108. $1.95.

Motive, Inc. "Motive: Lesbian Feminist Issue." Illus. 1972. National Gay Student Center, 2115 S. St., N.W., Washington, D.C. 20008. $1 prepaid.

National Council of Churches. "A Resolution on Civil Rights Without Discrimination as to Affectional or Sexual Preference." National Council of Churches, Rm. 711, 475 Riverside Dr., New York, N.Y. 10027. Free with stamped reply envelope.

"Policy Statement on Homosexuality." April 13, 1975. American Civil Liberties Union, 22 E. 40th St., New York, N.Y. 10016. Free with stamped reply envelope.

Portland Town Council. "A Legislative Guide to Gay Rights." $4.50. 86-page large pamphlet addressed to legislature of state of Oregon. 320 S.W. Stark, Rm. 303, Portland, Ore. 97204.

"Resolutions on Homosexuality." December 15, 1973. American Psychiatric Association, APA Division of Public Affairs, 1700 18th St., N.W., Washington, D.C. 20009. Free.

Sex Information and Education Council of the United States." SIECUS Study Guide No. 2. rev. ed. Behavioral Publications. 72 Fifth Ave., New York, N.Y. 10011. $1.00 prepaid.

Shapiro, Lynne D. "Write On, Woman. A Writer's Guide to U.S. Women's/Feminist/Lesbian Alternate Press Periodicals." 1977 ed. Lynne Shapiro, 92 Horatio St., #4S, New York, N.Y. 10014. $3.50.

"Twenty Questions About Homosexuality." 1972. Gay Activists Alliance, Box 2, Village Station, New York, N.Y. 10014. 50¢.

United States Civil Service Commission. "Press Release on New Guidelines for Federal Employment." July 3, 1975. Copies from National Gay Task Force, 80 Fifth Ave., New York, N.Y. 10011. 25¢.

"Workforce: Gay Workers out of the Closet." Gay Issue of *Workforce*, September-October 1974. Vocations for Social Change, 5951 Canning, Oakland, Calif. 94609. 85¢.

Youth Liberation Press. *Growing Up Gay.* Youth Liberation, 2007 Washtenaw Ave., Ann Arbor, Mich. 48104. 75¢

Lesbian National Resource List

This section contains a national listing of movement organizations, religious groups, services, coffeehouses, feminist retreats, publications, radio programs, women's centers, and other helpful contacts.

Most entries were compiled from a survey mailed to all seventeen hundred groups on the National Gay Task Force national list. Priority was given to lesbian organizations and to gay and feminist groups indicating a significant lesbian presence.

We are grateful to *Gaia's Guide* and the *Gayellow Pages* for allowing us to reprint entries from their publications that were not part of the NGTF list.

We have tried to make this listing as comprehensive as possible, but in some areas, resources are still very few. In general, bars are listed only in those areas where movement groups and services are unavailable. For a more complete listing of bars and a regularly updated national groups listing, we suggest you consult the following:

Gaia's Guide, 115 New Montgomery St., San Francisco, Calif. 94105. $6.00.

Gayellow Pages, Renaissance House, Box 292, Village Station, New York, N.Y. 10014. $5.00.

If all else fails, contact NGTF: National Gay Task Force, 80 Fifth Ave., New York, N.Y. 10011. 212 741-1010.

ALABAMA
Auburn
Bars
. Pete's, 816 Opalika Ave.
Birmingham
Bars
. Gismo's, 909 S. 22nd St.
Dothan
Bars
. Upstairs Lounge, Dothan Hotel, 314 N. Foster.
Huntsville
Publications
. Gayseed, 2310 Country Club Ave., N.W., 35805. Quarterly. 50¢.
Mobile
Bars
. Princess House Lounge, 254 Government St. 205 432-2238.
Services
. Society Lounge, 51 S. Conception.
Montgomery
Bars
. Rainbow, 305 Randolph St.
Tuscaloosa
Bars
. Chukker, 2121 6th St. 205 758-9445. Friendly, provides gathering place for gays. Stafford Hotel Bar downstairs, 3209 9th St.

ARIZONA
Coolidge
Religious Groups
. Gay Episcopalian Caucus, Box 1631, 85228.
Florence
Organizations
. Caucus on Concerns in Human Sexuality, Box 906, 85232.
Phoenix
Bookstores
. Womansplace Bookstore, 2401 N. 32nd St., 85008. 602 956-0456. Mon.-Sat. 10 A.M.-6 P.M.
Media
. NOW on the Air, 93.3 FM, 1510 AM. 5 P.M. each Thursday.
Organizations
. Gay People's Alliance, Box 21461, 83036, 602 252-2135. Counseling, raps, etc.
. Lesbian Task Force of N.O.W., P.O. Box 16023, 85011. 602 966-0039 and 255-0154.
Publications
. Who Do You Know? Semco Publishers, P.O. Box 1816, 85001.
. Woman Rising, P.O. Box 27292, 85282; 602 255-0154. Regular activities, 11 A.M. on Sat. on or following the 15th of every month at 2401 N. 32nd St., Phoenix 85008. A publication with feminist oriented articles by, for, and about women and women's events locally. Single issue, 30¢; subscription $2.50—9 issues. Circulation: 1,000 (Est. 50% lesbians.)
Religious Groups
. Metropolitan Community Church, 426 E.

Maricopa Freeway. 602 271-0125. Mailing address: Box 21064, 85036. Phone counseling, Fri.-Sun. 8 P.M.-midnight. Legal referrals, parents' group, prisoner services, social. Publishes *The Carpenter*.

Services

- Caterpillar Wings, 602 967-1994. "Lesbian poets and songwriters. Let's get together and share."
- Phoenixbird, 602 268-8856. Softball (*Woman Rising* has details).
- Women's Clinic, 2021 N. Central. 602 275-1743.

Scottsdale
Services

- Counseling for Women, 4216 N. Brown Ave., 85251. 602 994-5742, Mon.-Fri. 9 A.M.-4 P.M. A private agency with wide range of services for individuals, couples, and families. The need for continual evaluation of sex role attitudes and its impact on counseling relationship. Major focus on women, needs, issues, and concerns.

Tempe
Bookstores

- Womansplace, 9 E. 5th St., 85281. 602 966-0203, Mon.-Sat. 10 A.M.-6 P.M.; Sun. noon-5 P.M. Extensive mail-order service available for 13¢ stamp.

Organizations

- Free Spirit, P.O. Box 117, 85281. 602 966-5090. Helpline 271-0125, Sat. and Sun. 8 P.M.-midnight.
- Gay Liberation Arizona Desert (GLAD), Box 117, 85281. 602 252-0713. Gay rap and counseling.

Services

- Founders (The Committee to Form a Gay Caucus Organization at ASU), Box 117, 85281. Professional and peer counseling, legal and medical referrals, accommodation-finding.
- The Women's Center, P.O. Box 27292, 85282. 602 959-8675, 967-8175, or 994-5742. Group in existence for four years, now in the process of finding a new space. Provides crisis information, referral phone service, child care, library, coffeehouse and restaurant, etc.
- Women's Colorado Land Collective, 110 West Geneva Dr., 85282. 602 966-0039. "Planning for a Southwest Women's Land Trust—one primary location will probably be in western Colorado—exploring and expanding the collective concept."

Tucson
Bookstores

- Antigone Books, 415 N. 4th Ave., 85705. 602 792-3715, Tues.-Sat. 10 A.M.-5 P.M. Feminist bookstore with extensive selection of lesbian literature and paraphernalia.

Religious Groups

- Metropolitan Community Church, 4831 E. 22nd St. (study group). Mailing address: Box 50412, 85703. 602 622-0330.

Services

- Gay Law Collective, Box 3065, 85702. Tuscon Center for Women, 646 S. 6th Ave., 85701. 602 792-1929. Crisis center for women, prisoner services, legal and medical referrals, coffeehouse, crash pad for needy

travelers. Fantastic staff, helpful, really nice women.

Vail
Services

- Nourishing Space, Cave Canyon Ranch, Box D-11, 85641. 602 791-7686, 24 hours daily. Camping on the land except Dec. and Jan. Learning and teaching of self-sufficiency skills. A place for women to find their center.

ARKANSAS
Eureka Springs
Services

- New Orleans Hotel, 63 Spring St., 72632. 501 253-8955. Feminist-owned Victorian hotel, restored to period. Beer, wine, food. Highly recommended.

Fayetteville
Bars

- 42nd Street, 649 West Dickson St. Very gay with a huge dance floor. Entire building is owned by gay people, tons of potential. Gay men and women.

Religious Groups

- Metropolitan Community Church Study Group. 501 521-5367.

Services

- The Women's Center, 207 Razorback, 72701. Has a lesbian cooperative.
- Women's Land Trust, Box 521, 72701. Razordykes, University of Arkansas Associated Lesbians, Women's Center, 207 Razorback, 72701. 501 443-4998. Weekly meetings Wed. 8:30 P.M. Supportive base for political activity to promote more positive image of lesbianism, outreach for isolated lesbians; providing speakers, films, music, discussions (panel) for the university, etc.

Fort Smith
Bars

- Peacock Lounge, 220 Central. 501 623-0227.

Little Rock
Bars

- Drummers Club, in the Manning Motor Hotel. 501 372-5141. Recommended as being very gay and a good place to ask for more information on the local scene.

Services

- Switchboard, 415 W. 20th St., 72206. Mailing address: P.O. Box 483, 72203. 501 376-9141. 5 P.M.-midnight daily. Information of all sorts, primarily telephone hotline but also organizational help and counseling.

CALIFORNIA
Albany
Services

- Bacchanal, 1369 Solano Ave., 94706. 415 527-1314, 5 P.M.-1 A.M. except Wed.; Wed. midnight-1 A.M. A women's tavern, coffeehouse, and entertainment center. Poetry on Wed. evening; musicians, Sunday; older lesbian night, Thurs. Discussions, workshops, films, dramatics on other days; also small art gallery. Mellow, hassle-free environment where women can rap, dance, play pool or table tennis, and feel support of the women's community.

Albion
Publications

- Country Women Magazine, P.O. Box 54, 95410. Articles on women's experiences focused on specific topics; work, personal power, practical how-to information about country skills. Published 5 times a year. $1.25/issue; $5/year. Staff is predominately lesbian; writers are not necessarily.
- Times Change Press, Box 187, 95410. Purpose is to publish and sell books and posters with primary focus on women's and gay liberation.

Anaheim
Services

- Gay Community Center of Orange County. 415 534-3280. Mon. 7:30 P.M.

Atascadero
Services

- Atascadero Gay Encounter, Drawer A., 93422. Counseling, social activities, library.

Berkeley
Bookstores

- Granma Books, 3264 Adeline St., 94703. 415 658-8407. Women's gay, socialist, nonsexist, and Third World books and periodicals.

Media

- Fruit Punch, KPFA, 94.1 FM, 2207 Shattuck Ave., 94704; 415 848-6767. Wed. 10-11 P.M.
- Radio Free Lesbian, KPFA, 94.1 FM, 2207 Shattuck Ave., 94704. 415 848-6767. Sat. 5-6 P.M.

Organizations

- Slightly Older Lesbians, 2329 San Pablo Ave., 94701. Thurs. 7:30-9:30 P.M. A way for slightly older lesbians to meet and share feelings and build a support system in the gay community.

Publications

- Dykes and Gorgons, Box 840, 94704.
- Plexus, 2600 Dwight Way, Rm. 209, 94704. Tremendous source of information for all lesbians in the Bay area. $5/year.

Services

- Alice B's Bookservice, P.O. Box 4190, 94704. 415 845-1308. A book service specializing in lesbian and feminist literature, with emphasis on the out-of-print book. Mail order catalogue listing titles, prices, annotations, etc., available prepaid $1.00. Browsers welcome. Call 415 845-1308 for appointment.
- Berkeley Women's Center, 2112 Channing Way, 94704. 415 548-4343. Mon., Tues., Thurs., Fri. 11 A.M.-5 P.M.; Sat. 11 A.M.-2 P.M.
- Berkeley Women's Health Collective, 2908 Ellsworth, 94706. 415 843-6194.
- Cheese and Coffee Center, 2110 Center St., 94704. 415 848-9664.
- Gay People's Union, Rm. 320, Eshleman Hall, U.C. 94720. 415 848-7142.
- Kafeneo, 1543 Shattuck Ave., 94704. 415 848-9664. A restaurant.
- Pacific Center Community Services, P.O. Box 908, 94701. 415 841-6224. Mon.-Fri. 10 A.M.-10 P.M. Sat. noon-4 P.M. Counseling services and social events, gay switch-

board and crisis line, rap groups, speakers' bureau, and peer counseling.

The Pacific Center for Human Growth, 2329 San Pablo Ave. Mailing address: Box 908, 94701. 415 841-6224.

- San Francisco-East Bay Women's Yellow Pages, Berkeley Women's Center, 2112 Channing Way, 94704.
- Student Health Service, U.C. Berkeley, 94720. 415 642-5012. Counseling for lesbians and gay males, free of charge.

Claremont
Organizations
- Gay Student Union of the Claremont Colleges, Counseling Center, 735 Dartmouth Ave., 91711. 714 626-8511, ext. 3038.

Concord
Services
- Everywoman's Clinic, 2600 Park Ave., 94520. 415 825-7900 or 825-7903. Gynecological services.

Corte Madera
Bars
- Electric Banana, 5625 Paradise Dr. 415 924-1546. A bar with disco.

Costa Mesa
Bars
- Newport Station, 1945 Placentia Ave. 714 631-0031. Disco dancing and restaurant. Gay women and men.

Cotati
Organizations
- Gay Students' Union, Sonoma State College. 707 795-9950.

Culver City
Publications
- The Lesbian News, P.O. Box 2023, 90230. Monthly newsletter to provide an outlet for lesbian news and viewpoints. Mail rate $2/year.

Davis
Organizations
- Gay Students at U.C. Davis, Student Activities Office, Memorial Union, 95616. 916 952-3495.

Emeryville
Services
- Janice Macomber, P.O. Box 8292, 94662. 415 652-6789. Piano tuning.

Eureka
Bars
- Fogg's, "E" Street and Second.

Felton
Publications
- Rubyfruit Readher, Box 949, 95018. Published monthly. Donation asked for single issue; $3 for six-issue subscription. News, analysis, reviews, stories, poems. A forum for lesbian communication.

Fontana
Bars
- Acacia, Citrus and Arrow. Sunday brunch, good dinners. Open until 4 A.M.
New Alibi, Foothill Boulevard at Fontana.

Fresno
Organizations
- Gay People's Union, Student Affairs, California State University, 93704. 209 237-6536.
- Lesbian and Sexuality Task Force, 420 North Van Ness, 93721. 209 233-2384.

Fullerton
Bookstores
- The Horny Toad, 716 W. Commonwealth, 92632. Lesbian titles plus sexuality and health.
Organizations
- Gay Students Educational Union, Student Activities, CSU, 92634. 714 497-1687.

Garden Grove
Services
- Gay Community Center of Orange County, 12732 Garden Grove Blvd., Suites G & H, 92643. 714 534-3261, 6-11 P.M. daily. Provides services to the gay community, especially counseling, referrals, rapes. Hotline (information and crisis). (Est. 25% lesbians.)

Gardena
Bars
- The Club, 16805 S. Western.
- Mama Jeans, 15215 S. Crenshaw

Grover City
Services
- Emma's Place, P.O. Box 717, 93433. 805 489-9633. A women's retreat.

Hayward
Bookstores
- The Oracle, 22640 Main St., 94541. 415 886-1268, Mon.-Fri. 10 A.M.-6 P.M. Sat. 10 A.M.-4 P.M. Center for feminist literature and information operated collectively by women. Coffee and easy chairs. Children welcome.
Organizations
- Advocates for Women, 1303 A St., 94542. Gay People's Union of Alameda County, Box 3935, 94540.
- Lesbians and Kids. 415 652-6780.
Services
- South County Women's Center, 25036 Carlos Bee Blvd., 94542. 415 537-2112, Mon.-Fri. 10 A.M.-5 P.M. Information and referral, counseling, lesbian rap group Thurs. 8 P.M. Publishes *Women to Women* monthly; free.

Hollywood
Services
- Homosexual Information Center, 6715 Hollywood Blvd., #210, 90028. 213 HO4-8431, 2-6 P.M. daily, 8-10 P.M. Tues. and Fri. Publishes bibliographies and reading lists. Offers social service referrals and resource assistance to researchers and students.
- Lesbian Resource Program, Gay Community Services Center, 1213 N. Highland Ave., 90007. 213 464-7400, ext. 32 or 33. Staffed Mon.-Fri. 10 A.M.-6 P.M.; Sat. 12-5 P.M.; Tues., Thurs. 8-10 P.M. Office hours, Mon.-Fri. 10 A.M.-6 P.M., Women's Clinic. Women's Raps Tues.-Thurs. 8-10 P.M. All women's dance, first Sat. of each month, 8 P.M. Provides referrals to women's resources, information to and about lesbians; emergency services, housing employment, counseling, alcoholism and drug abuse aid.

Laguna Beach
Bars
- Little Shrimp, 1305 South Coast Highway. 714 494-4111.
Religious Groups
- Metropolitan Community Church, 964 Noria St., 92651. 714 752-1220 and 497-2142.

Long Beach
Bookstores
- Sojourner, 538 Redondo Beach, 90814. 213 433-5384.
Organizations
- The Gay Outdoor Club, P.O. Box 14403, 90803. Backpacking and hiking, open to lesbians and gay men. Club was organized and is directed by lesbians. Monthly flyer of activities is available. $2 membership fee. (Est. 65% lesbians.)
Gay Service League, Box 5014, 90805. 213 591-7611. Service Club with biweekly parties and other social functions.
- Parents and Friends of Gays of Long Beach, 700 E. Roosevelt Rd. 90807. 213 427-4347.
Services
- Gay Hotline. 213 591-7611.

Los Angeles
Bookstores
- Sisterhood Bookstore, 1351 Westwood Blvd., 90024. 213 477-7300. Staffed Mon.-Sat. 10 A.M.-6 P.M.; Thurs. 10 A.M.-9P.M.; Sun. noon-5 P.M. Feminist bookstore, community bulletin boards, tickets sold for local activities, referrals. (Est. 66.6% lesbians.)
Media
- IMRU, Gay Radio Collective, KPFK, 90.7 FM, University City, 91608. Messages, 213 877-2711. Second and third Tues. of the month, 10:30 P.M.
- Lesbian Sisters, KPFK, 90.7 FM, University City, 91608. First Tues. of the month, 10:30 P.M.
Organizations
- Lesbian Activist Women, 1213 N. Highland Ave., 90038.
- One, Inc., 2256 Vencie Blvd., 90006. 213 735-5252. Largest library on female and male homosexuality in the world; research, counseling.
- Southern Californians for Whitman-Radclyffe, 9171 Wilshire Blvd., Suite 310-88, 90210.
- USC Gay Student Union, Stu 313B, USC, 90007. 213 746-6920, Mon.-Fri. 11 A.M.-5 P.M. Provides social and educational activities for gay people at USC. Speakers and information for the entire USC community. (Est. 10% lesbians.)
Publications
- Chrysalis, Women's Building, 1727 N. Spring St., 90012. Articles, etc.
- Lesbian Tide, 8855 Cattaraugus, 90039. 213 839-7254 (tape on always). Regular activities, Thurs. 7:30 P.M. A national lesbian-feminist journal published every other month. News analysis, features, reviews, graphics, poetry, etc. 75¢/issue; $6/year.
- SexuaLaw Reporter, 1800 N. Highland Ave., 90028. 213 464-6666. Mon.-Fri. 9 A.M.-5 P.M. Articles on sexual law. Bimonthly. $3/issue; $15/year. ($25 libraries).

Religious Groups

- Congregation Beth Chayim Chadashim, 1945 Westwood Blvd., 90025. 213 559-0320 (tape machine). Reform Jewish Sabbath services Fri. 8:30 P.M. Religious and social activities for the gay Jewish community. (Est. 30% lesbians.)
- Dignity, P.O. Box 6161, 90055. 213 664-2872.
- Integrity/Los Angeles, 4767 Hillsdale Dr., 90032. 213 225-7471. Gay Episcopalians and friends of gay Episcopalians.
- Lutherans Concerned for Gay People, Box 19114A, 90019. 213 663-7816.
- Metropolitan Community Church, 1050 S. Hill St., 90015. 213 748-0121, 9 A.M.-5 P.M. Hotline 24 hours. Religious outreach to the gay community. Activities, Sun. 11 A.M. and 7:30 P.M.; Tues. 7:30 P.M. (in Spanish); Wed. 7:30 P.M. Alternative coffeehouse, Fri. 7:30 P.M. (Est. 40% lesbians.)

Restaurants

- Identified Woman Cafe, 1727 N. Spring St., Women's Building. 213 254-7540. A feminist restaurant in the Women's Building.

Services

- Alcholism Center for Women, 1147 S. Alvarado St., 90006. 213 381-7805. AA meetings, self-development, counseling, social services, and job counseling.
  Amazon Airways Collective, KPEK-FM, "Woman to Woman," 213 390-7356. "Need women to produce new shows—no previous experience in radio is necessary."
- Annu Unlimited, 12817 Indianapolis St., 90066. 213 397-1268. Feminist note cards, one design or assortment. Cards for and about women. Photo notes, etc.
  Christopher Street West Association, Box 3949, 90028.
- Dianic Mechanics, 5721 Venice Blvd., 90019. 213 931-0460, 10 A.M.-5 P.M. daily. Open to the public by appointment only. Basic preventive maintenance for cars. Teaches women the how and why of a tune-up.
- Feminist Horizons, 10586½ W. Pico Blvd., Mon.-Sat. 10 A.M.-5 P.M. Largest feminist gift store in the world, caters to a large gay women's community.
- Gay Alliance for Professionals (GAP), 4779 Cromwell Ave., 90027. 213 660-6249, noon-9 P.M. Student and gay academic counseling and professional services by anthropologists and university professors of gay subculture.
- Gay Community Services Center, 1213 N. Highland Ave., 90038. 213 464-7485. Switchboard. Highly organized center.
- Gay Liberation Front, East L.A. College, 5357 E. Brooklyn Ave., 90022.
- Gay Persons Alliance, 3701 Wilshire Blvd., 7th fl., 90010. 213 386-7855.
- Gay Rights Chapter, American Civil Liberties Union. 633 S. Shatto Pl., 90005. 213 H-O-M-O-S-E-X, 24 hours daily. Works for parity in the society for gay women and men.
- Gay Sisterhood, UCLA, Women's Resource Center, 90 Powell Library, 405 Hilgard Ave., 90024. 213 825-3945.
- Gay Students of People's College of Law, 2228 W. 7th St., 90057. 213 661-5135.

Only law school to openly recruit gays.
- Gay Students of People's College of Law Black Caucus, Gloria Brown and Ron Grayson, 2228 W. 7th St., 90057.
- Gay Students' Union, UCLA, Kerkhoff Hall No. 411, 308 Westwood Plaza, 90024. 213 825-8053, 24 hours daily. Counseling, etc.
- Homophile Effort for Legal Protection (HELP), Box 3416, 90028. 213 463-3146. 24-hour emergency service for women and men.
- Insight Dynamics Corporation, 8235 Santa Monica Blvd., 90046. 213 654-3491. A private club that sponsors activities and parties for gay women as well as providing one-to-one introductions.
- IRIS Films, 2130½ Elsinore St., 90026. Mailing address: Box 26463. 213 483-5793. Produces and distributes films by and about women. Sharing of skills and resources through workshops, working toward a responsible media.
- Lavender and Red Union, 6844 Sunset Blvd., 90028. 213 465-9285.
- Lavender People, Hunter, 507½ Glenrock, 90024.
- Lesbian Resource Center, 1213 N. Highland Ave., 90038. 213 464-7485. Located at Gay Community Services Center.
- Los Angeles Guidance and Counseling Service, 924 Westwood Blvd., #535, 90024. 213 477-6017. Mon.-Fri. 9 A.M.-8 P.M. (Est. 30% lesbians.)
- Olivia Records, Box 70237, 90070. 213 389-4243, Mon.-Fri. 9:30 A.M.-5:30 P.M. Makes women's music available to the public, provides women-oriented musicians with access to the recording industry and control over their music, provides training and jobs for women in the recording industry.
- Parents of Gays, Los Angeles, Gay Community Services Center, 1213 N. Highland Ave., 90038. 213 464-7485. Helps parents and their daughters and sons to a better understanding of each other. Helping to pass the National Gay Civil Rights Bill, consenting adults in private, repeal "lewd and lascivious" statutes, and change attitudes in the community and throughout the nation.
- Prisoner, Parole and Probation Program, Gay Community Services Center, 1213 N. Highland Ave., 90038. 213 464-7485.
- The Ski Closet, Box 3213, 90028. 213 980-0448. Bimonthly trips to Mammoth Mt., parties, etc. Women and men.
  The Women's Building, 1727 N. Spring St., 90012. Houses studio workshops, art gallery, a restaurant, a performance space, a bookstore, feminist study programs, dances, etc.
- Zero to Success, Box 17719, 90017. 213 469-5128. Organization for needs of handicapped and disabled. Jobs, loans, blood bank, etc.

Manhattan Beach
Services

- Califia, Inc., 3415 N. Highland Ave., 90266. 213 545-8717. Open on Tues.-Sat. 11 A.M.-6 P.M., Sun. 11 A.M.-4 P.M. Closed Mon. Books, periodicals, arts and crafts, by women for women.

Menlo Park
Services

- Everywoman's Coffeehouse, 1921 Menalto Ave., 94025. 415 328-3295.

Modesto
Bars

- Mustang Club, 413 N. 7th St.

Monterey
Bars

- Righteous Ram, 430 Washington.

Religious Groups

- Metropolitan Community Church, 1154 2nd St., 93940. 209 375-2338.

Newport Beach
Services

- U.C. Irvine Gay Students Center, ASUCI, Irvine, Calif. 92717, Trailer No. 304, U.C.I. 714 833-7229, Mon.-Fri. 9 A.M.-5 P.M.

North Hollywood
Religious Groups

- Metropolitan Community Church in the Valley, 11717 Victory Blvd., 91606. 213 762-1133.

Services

- Dummy Up, 1217½ Ventura Blvd., Studio City, 91604. Open noon-2 A.M. every day. Pool table, dancing, softball team.

Restaurant and Bar

- Hialeah House, 8540 Lankershim Blvd., Sun Valley. 213 767-9334, Wed.-Sun. 5 P.M.-2 A.M. Sandwiches, dancing, wine and beer.

Oakland
Bookstores

- A Woman's Place, 5251 Broadway at College, 94618. 415 654-9920, Mon.-Thurs. 10 A.M.-6 P.M.; Fri.-Sat. 10 A.M.-10 P.M.; Sun. 1-5 P.M.

Organizations

- June 28 Union, Box 8704, 94608.

Religious Groups

- East Bay Metropolitan Community Church, 2624 West St., 94612. 415 763-1592.

Services

- Bishop's Coffeehouse/Womanspace, 1437 Harrison, 94612. 415 444-9805, 451-0395, 465-3986.
- Information Center Incorporate, I.C.I., 5251 Broadway, 94618. 415 547-9920. Lesbian books, magazines, and newspapers.
- The Women's Press Collective, 5251 Broadway, 94618. Collects, prints, and distributes material women have written, are writing, and will continue to write. Emphasis on sharing work skills.
- Womonworks, Box 23984, 94623. Feminist and lesbian symbols, $2.25 per package. 12 packages or more 40% discount. 25¢ postage or 15¢ per package when ordering a dozen or more.

Oceanside
Religious Groups

- Pamomar Metropolitan Community Church, Box 228, Escondido, 92025. 714 746-5660. Meetings at 113 North Tremont.

Orange
Services

- LIFE (Lesbians in the Feminist Effort), P.O. Box 5374, 92667. 714 633-1192. Meet in homes of members Wed. 7-8 P.M. (business),

*Charlotte Spitzer, Parents of Gays,
Los Angeles*

8-10 P.M. (rap group). Provides a place for women to explore their lesbian-feminist identity; provides services and helps build community.

Palm Springs
Bars
• Desert Knight Motel, 435 Avenida Olancha. Doll House, 68-961 B St.

Pasadena
Bars
• Daily Double, 3739 E. Colorado Blvd. 213 449-8271.
Bookstores
• Page One, 26 N. Lake Ave., 91101. 213 792-9011, Mon.-Sat. 11 A.M.-5:30 P.M. A retail feminist bookstore with a good selection of books of interest to gay women. Nonsexist children's books are also featured.
Services
• Gay Discussion Group, California Institute of Technology, Winnett Center, 218-51, 91109.

Pomona
Bars
• Alibi East, 225 S. San Antonio. Disco.
Religious Groups
• Metropolitan Community Church, Box 1082, 91786. 714 982-7642.

Redding
Religious Groups
• Metropolitan Community Church, Box 1228, 96001. 916 246-9982.
Services
• Gay Line, 916 246-9686.

Redlands
Services
• Lesbian Rap Group, YWCA, 16 E. Olive Ave., 92373.

Riverside
Bars
• Circus Room, 3800 7th St.
Services
• Metropolitan Community Church, Box 2451, 92506. 714 682-7445. Services held

at 5539 Mission Blvd., Rubidoux, Calif. Rap groups, counseling, social activities.

Rohnert Park
Organizations
• Gay Students Union, Student Resources, California State College, Sonoma, 94928. 707 795-2391.

Rubidoux
Bars
• Red Shade, 5539 Mission Blvd.

Russian River
Bars
• Noah's Ark, 9117 River Rd., Forestville, 95436.

Sacramento
Organizations
• California Committee for Sexual Law Reform, 4949 13th Ave., 95820.
• Gay Students Union, Sacramento City College Student Activities, 3835 Freeport Blvd., 95822. 916 422-9313.
• Lesbian Feminist Alliance, ASSC, California State University, 95810.
Religious Groups
• Dignity/Sacramento, Inc., Box 9643, 95823. 916 422-6305. 5-9 P.M.
• Metropolitan Community Church of Sacramento, 2741 34th St., 95817. Mailing address: P.O. Box 5282. 916 451-5552, Tues.-Sun. 11 A.M.-4 P.M. Christian outreach to the homophile community. Activities: Sun. 11 A.M. and 7:15 P.M.; Tues. 7 P.M. (rap group); Wed. 7:30 P.M.; Fri. 7 P.M. (Gay AA).
Services
• Gay AA, Metropolitan Community Church, 2741 34th St., 95817. 916 451-5552.
• Gay Crisis Line and Referral Service, Box 215, Broderick, Calif. 916 391-1544, 24 hours daily. Therapy to current local community social activities.
• Sacramento Gay People's Union, Programs Advising, California State University, 6000 J St., 95819. 916 454-6595.
• Sacramento Women's Center and Bookstore, Inc., 1230 H St., 95814. 916 442-4657 (24-hour crisis line). Hours: Mon.-Fri. 9 A.M.-5 P.M.; Sat. 11 A.M.-3 P.M. Center has three components: rape crisis which helps rape victims emotionally, medically; Mother's Emergency Stress Service which has a 24-hour crisis line for mothers and discussion groups, and Women's Informational Services which has a referral service, counseling and legal clinics, discussion groups and various projects. 916 446-7663.

San Bernadino
Bars
• Grand Central, 345 West 7th St., 94201. Skylark, 8917 Inland Dr., 92408.

San Diego
Bookstores
• Book Mark, 4077 Adams Ave., 92116. 714 280-3091, Mon.-Sat. 10 A.M.-6 P.M. General bookstore with gay literature, information center.
Organizations
• Gay Nurses Alliance, P.O. Box 17593, 92117. National organization. Advocates for gay patients and gay nurses. Speakers' bur-

eau, workshops and conferences, legislative activity, referral services for counseling. Publishes *Signal* 3 times a year. Subscription: contribution of at least $5.
• Parents of Gays, Gay Center for Social Services, 2250 B St., 92102. 714 232-7528.
Publications
• Pacific Coast Times, P.O. Box 7173, 92107. 714 222-9687. $8 for 12 issues.
Religious Groups
• Dignity of San Diego, 2422 Congress St. Mailing address: P. O. Box 19071, 92119. 714 448-8384 (answering service). Meetings Sat. 7:30 P.M.; every other Wed. 7:30 P.M. An organization of gay Catholic men and women providing religious and social activities. (Est. 14% lesbians.)
• Gay Center for Social Services, 2550 B St., 92120. 714 232-7528. Office 10 A.M.-10 P.M. Publication. *This Way Out.* Counseling, lending library, speakers' panel, gay awareness rap groups, prisoner assistance, drop-in center.
• Integrity, Rev. H. C. Lazenby, 4645 W. Talmadge Dr., 92116.
• Metropolitan Community Church, Box 33291, 92103. Church Center at 1335 Fern St. 714 239-0714. Women's activities, two women deacons.
Services
• Echo House, 108 Ivy, 92101. Temporary housing and food, also employment.
• Gay Center for Social Services, 2550 B St. 92120. 714 232-7528, 24 hours.
• Las Hermanas, 4003 Wabash Ave. 714 280-7510. Activities and events.
• Pathways, 4312 Cass, Pacific Beach, 92109. 24-hour counseling service for gay women and men.

San Fernando Valley
Religious Groups
• Dignity/San Fernando Valley, Box 911, Van Nuys, 91408. 213 894-7982.

San Francisco
Bookstores
• Old Wives' Tales, "Women's Visions and Books," 532 Valencia, 94110 (between 16th and 17th). 415 552-1015. Store open Tues.-Sat. noon-7 P.M.; Thurs. noon-9 P.M. New and used books, lending library, pamphlets, records, ideas of women available to women. Bulletin boards, comfortable space, and tea and coffee. Often some event on Thurs. night.
Organizations
• Artemis Society, 1199 Valencia, 94110. 415 647-4144.
• Black Gay Caucus, 32 Page, 94117.
• Daughters of Bilitis, 1209 Sutter St., 94109. Quarterly organization meetings, bimonthly events, newsletter. An organization to continue the interrelations with lesbians in San Francisco and across the nation, offers support and events of interest to lesbians in Bay Area. Approximately 300 members. Gay Latino Alliance, 32 Page, 94117.
• Lesbians in the Law ("LIL"), Women's Association Golden Gate University Law School, 536 Mission St., 94105.
Publications
• Paragraph, Box 14051, 94114. Provides an outlet for quality gay fiction by women and

men, and brings that work to the lesbian and gay male communities.

Religious Groups

- Church of the Androgyne/United States Mission, 182 F Clinton Park, 94103. Mailing address: P.O. Box 6437, 94101. 413 626-4317, Mon.-Fri. 1-9 P.M. (Est. 30% lesbians.)
- Committee of Concern, Friends Meetinghouse, 2160 Lake St., 94121. 914 431-3344. Quaker lesbians and gay men.
- Council on Religion and the Homosexual, 83 6th St., 94103. 415 781-1570. Metropolitan Community Church, 1076 Guerrero, 94110.

Services

- Full Moon, Inc. (coffeehouse for women), 4416 18th St., 94114. 415 864-9274, Tues.-Sun. 4-11 P.M. Open Tues. 4-11 P.M.; Wed. 4-11 P.M., Fri. 4 P.M.-midnight; Sat. noon-midnight; Sun. 2-10 P.M. Bookstore with large selection of lesbian literature and poetry, buttons, posters, record albums. Lesbian raps (Tues.), poetry (Wed.), music, workshops, speakers, etc., are among the current activities. A worker-owned consensus collective. (Est. 90% lesbians.)
- Gay Information Line, 415 647-0433.
- Gay Referral Line, P.O. Box 6046, 94101. 415 994-1522, 8 A.M.-midnight. A phone-in referral service only. Six years in existence. Lesbian Counseling Service, 200 Golden Gate Ave. (at Leavenworth), 94102. 415 885-6027.
- Lesbians Organizing, 32 Page St., 94117.
- Lesbian Mothers and Friends, 63 Brady St., 94103.
- Operation Concern, Parents of Gays, San Francisco, P.O. Box 7999, 94120. 415 563-0202. Helps parents and their gay sons and daughters to a better understanding of each other. Pass National Gay Civil Rights Bill, consenting adults in private, repeal lewd and lascivious statutes, and change attitudes in the community and throughout the nation. Printed material available for 24¢ stamped legal-sized envelope.
- San Francisco-East Bay Women's Yellow Pages, Berkeley Women's Center, 2112 Channing Way, 94704. Donation, 50¢. San Francisco Gay Community Group, 415 652-6789. Nonsexist program coordinators and social group facilitation can help get new groups started.
- San Francisco Women Against Rape, Box 40709, 94140.
- San Francisco Women's Center, 63 Brady St., 94103. 415 431-1180.
- Women's Litigation Unit, 1095 Market St., Rm. 417, 94103. 415 626-3819, Mon.-Fri. 9:30 A.M.-5 P.M. A law office specializing in sex discrimination and problems of poor women who live in San Francisco.
- Women's Switchboard, 63 Brady St., 94103. 415 431-1414, Mon.-Fri. Referral service for groups and activities in the area.

San Jose

Bookstores

- Ms. Atlas Press and Bookstore, 53 W. San Fernando St., 95113. 408 289-1088. Promotes self-esteem, ambition, and individual achievement among lesbians. Commercial printing of all types suitable to small press.

Bookstore carries gay, feminist, and liberation literature; also functions as an information center and meeting place.

Publications

- Lesbian Voices; Feminist Lesbian Quarterly, P.O. Box 3122, 95116. 408 289-1088. A quarterly of articles, fiction, poetry, photos, drawings. Ideas and attitudes covering a range of viewpoints. Dignified format. $1.50/issue; $5/year.
- Women Inc., P.O. Box 32236, 95132. 408 923-1298. A new cooperative feminist press. Feminist oriented books, lesbian titles. Write for list of books and information.

Religious Groups

- Integrity/San Francisco, P.O. Box 6444, 95150. 408 268-3378, staffed days and evenings. Regular activities: second Wednesdays, home eucharist; fourth Sundays, general meetings, at Grace Cathedral House, 1051 Taylor St. Purpose is to challenge anti-gay attitudes and actions in Episcopal Church in Bay Area, minister to gay persons, and promote acceptance in church community. Local chapter of national caucus of gay Episcopalians. Publishes *SFI Newsletter,* a monthly. $10/year with membership. (Est. 25% lesbians.)

Services

- Lesbian Feminist Alliance, 170 S. 10th St., Women's Center, 95112. Mailing address: c/o Student Services and Activities, Box 19, San Jose State University, 95117. 408 294-7265, Mon.-Fri. 9 A.M.-5 P.M. Activities on Sun. nights, 6-8 P.M.; other nights' scheduling happen through Sun. planning. Speakers' bureau, referral in counseling, etc., lesbian rap group. Provides a place where any lesbian can come in and fulfill herself.

San Luis Obispo

Religious Groups

- Metropolitan Community Church, 793 Higuera, #10, 93401. Mailing address: P.O. Box 1706, 93406. 805 544-8210, 24 hours daily. Meetings Sun. 2 P.M. and 7:30 P.M., Wed. 7:30 P.M. Pot luck one Sat. each month; rap group Thurs. 7:30 P.M. Open to public Wed.-Fri. noon-5 P.M. Gay church. Raps, women's awareness groups, etc. Monthly newsletter. *Outreach.* (Est. 45-50% lesbians.)

San Mateo

Publications

- The Advocate, One Peninsula Place Bldg., 1730, Suite 225, 94402. 415 573-7100. Mon.-Fri. 8:30 A.M.-5:30 P.M. News and features magazine on all aspects of lesbians' and gay men's lives.

San Pablo

Services

- San Pablo Women's Center, 1515 Market Ave., 94806. 415 233-1084.

San Rafael

Bookstores

- Everywomen's, 1560 4th St., 94901. 415 456-3496.

Organizations

- The Other Side, P.O. Box 132, 94902. All-lesbian social organization.

Santa Barbara

Bars

- The Odyssey, 221 State St.

Organizations

- Gay People's Union, P.O. Box 15048, 93107.

Services

- Libertarians for Gay Rights, 3755 San Remo Dr., #186, 93105.
- Western Addiction Services Program (WASP), 137 E. Anapamu, 93101. 805 962-7235 (24-hour hotline). Open to public 10 A.M.-6 P.M. Mon.-Fri. A gay non-profit organization providing information and referral services, alcohol and drug abuse counseling, legal assistance, referrals, CR groups, etc. (Est. 33% lesbians.)

Santa Cruz

Bars

- Mona's Gorilla Lounge, 1535 Commercial Way.

Bookstores

- Mother Right Bookstore, 538 Seabright, 95062.

Services

- Lesbian Umbrella, Snails Ankles' Press, 248 Seaside St., 95060.
- Snails Ankles' Press, 248 Seaside St., 95060. Two Sisters, 815 41st Ave., 95062. Restaurant.

Santa Monica

Services

- Westside Women's Clinic, 1711 Ocean Park Blvd., 90405. 213 450-2191, Mon.-Sat. 9 A.M.-9 P.M. Gynecological services, counseling, referral. (Est. 50% lesbian.)
- Woman Space, 237 Hill St., 90405.

Santa Rosa

Bars

- Star and Crescent, 447 Sebastopol Rd. (at Dutton Ave.).

Bookstores

- Rising Woman's Books, 151 Montgomery Dr., 95404.

Publications

- The Wishing Well, P.O. Box 1711, 95403. A rapidly expanding mini-magazine dedicated to helping gay women find others with similar interests, needs, and objectives.

Services

- Pat 'n' Laddie's Ventures, Inc., P.O. Box

1711, 95402. Tours for gay women exclusively who are seeking adventure and new relationships. Run by certified Tour Directors. '77-78 season group tours include Caribbean Cruise, Europe, Hawaii, etc. Publish *The Wishing Well,* a quarterly; single issue, $2.00; subscription rate, $10 ($3.50-$13.50 other countries).

South San Francisco
Organizations
- Gay American Indians, P.O. Box 2194, 94080. 415 621-4716 (no staffing). Do not have permanent office. Social, political, education programs which vary. Bringing together Indian gay women and men with common identity to reeducate Indian community in Bay Area as well as gays. In existence since July 1975. (Est. 15% lesbians.)

Stanford
Organizations
- Gay People's Union, Stanford University, Box 8265, 94305. 415 497-1488.

Stockton
Bars
- Gay 90's, 925 El Dorado.
Organizations
- San Joaquin County Gays, Anderson Y Center, University of the Pacific, 95211. 209 466-1496. Rap groups, occasional social activities.
Religious Groups
- Metropolitan Community Church, 2606 Wilson Way, 95205. 209 463-0478.

Studio City
Organizations
- Southern California Women for the Whitman-Radclyffe Foundation, 13033 Ventura Blvd., 91604. 213 766-6811 (answering machine). Steering committee meets every other week with topic. Raps once a month. The group sponsors educational, social, and community outreach activities. Free newsletter every other month.

Van Nuys
Religious Groups
- Dignity/San Fernando Valley, P.O. Box 911, 91408. 213 894-7982, 5-10 P.M. Purpose is to work within the Catholic Church to accept gays as full and equal members, work for justice and acceptance through educational and legal reform, help reinforce individual gays to reinforce their self-acceptance. Publishes bimonthly, *The Owl,* free to members. (Small number of lesbians.)
Services
- Women's Basic Automotive Class, P.O. Box 906, 91408. 213 980-0884, 3-6 P.M. daily. Classes and workshops explaining parts of car, function, malfunction, basic maintenance, tire changes, etc. A general introduction class to help women become knowledgeable enough to take care of their cars. By appointment only. Contact for dates, hours, location.

Venice
Services
- The Feminist Wicca/Sisterhood of the Wicca, 442 Lincoln Blvd., 90291. 213 399-3919, Mon.-Sat. noon-6:30 P.M. (regular store hours). A matriarchal spiritual center, home of Susan B. Anthony Coven #1. Activities include sabbat and solstice celebrations. Self-healing tools, supplies of the craft, and reference books, available through mail order.

Ventura
Organizations
- Ventura County Gay Alliance, 362 N. Ventura Ave., 93003. 805-648-7060, Fri., Sat., Sun. Regular activities on the first and third Tuesdays of each month at 8 P.M. at Ventura County Main Library, Topping Room, Main St. Social and educational services. Monthly VCGA newsletter. (Est. 30% lesbians.)
Religious Groups
- Metropolitan Community Church, 362 N. Ventura Ave., 93001. 805 648-7060.

Colorado
Aspen
Organizations
- Aspen Gay Coalition, Box 3143, 81661.

Boulder
Bookstores
- Little Professor Book Center, 1344 Pearl, 80302. 303 443-3390.
Organizations
- Boulder Gay Coalition, Box 1402, University Memorial Center, 183E, 80302. 303 492-8567. Mon.-Fri. 10 A.M.-2 P.M.
- Lesbian Caucus, UMC 181, University of Colorado, 80309. 303 492-7735. Hours and days vary for staffing. Meetings every other Thurs. at 7 P.M. Monthly dances. Complete library for women, offers CR groups, cosponsors a work exchange with Women's Liberation Coalition and the Women's Line. Also offers coming-out meetings and speakers' bureau.
Religious Groups
- Dignity Denver/Boulder, Box 2943, Denver, 80201. 303 377-8691.
Services
- Boulder County Women's Research Centers, 2750 Spruce St., 1408 Pine St., 80302. 303 447-9675.
- Women's Crisis Line, 303 492-8910.

Colorado Springs
Bars
- Sappho's, 2028 Sheldon Ave.
Services
- Colorado Springs Gay Relief Fund, Hide and Seek, 512 W. Colorado Ave., 80904. Lambda Services Bureau, Box 911, 80901. 303 475-8409. Help and information.
- Women's Health Service Clinic, 1703 N. Weber, 80907. 303 471-9492 or 471-8196, generally Mon.-Thurs. 9 A.M.-5 P.M. A nonprofit corporation organized by feminists to provide high-quality medical care at reasonable prices for all women. Gynecological care, sexuality counseling, sexual preferences, self-health, etc. (Est. 90% lesbians.)

Denver
Media
- Woman Everywhere, KFML, 13.90 AM. Lesbian material is included. Radio program.
Organizations
- Gay Students Association, Metropolitan State College, 250 W. 14th Ave., 80204. Office: 710 W. Colfax Ave., Rm. 140. 303 892-6111.
- Gay Youth, 815 E. 18th, #9, 80203.
- Lesbian-Feminist Workers, Woman to Woman Bookstore, 2023 E. Colfax, 80206.
- NOW Lesbian Task Force, 1400 Lafayette, 80218. 303 831-7707.
- Parents of Gays, Betty Fairchild, 700 Emerson St., 80218. 303 831-8576. Also contact MCC of the Rockies, 303 831-4787.
Religious Groups
- Dignity/Denver, P.O. Box 2943, 80201. 303 831-7684, daily 6-10 P.M. Sun. 5 P.M. (Liturgy) at the cathedral. Provides social, educational, and spiritual concern for and service to gays and homophiles. Publishes *Dignity-Counterpoint,* monthly news of chapter, articles relative to gay Catholics. (Est. 6% lesbians.)
- MCC of the Rockies, 14th and Lafayette (First Unitarian Church Building). Mailing address: P.O. Box 9536, 80209. 303 831-4787, Mon.-Fri. 9:30 A.M.-4:30 P.M. Provides Christian ministry to gay persons. Free monthly newsletter. (Est. 40% lesbians.)
Services
- Feminist Switchboard, 303 320-5972.
Gay Coalition of Denver, Box 18501, 80218. 303 831-8838. Classes, counseling, referrals, etc.
- Gay Community Services Center of Colorado, P.O. Box 2024, 80201. 303 831-6268. Gay Legal Workers, 412 Majestic Blvd., 80202.
- Woman to Woman Feminist Bookcenter, 2023 E. Colfax 80206. 303 320-5972, Tues.-Sat. 10 A.M.-8 P.M. First Sun. of month 7 P.M. (community coffee); second Sun. 5 P.M. (business coordinating meeting), first and third Sun. 5 P.M. (bookstore meetings), fourth Sun. 5 P.M. (political, personal meetings), Tues.-Sat. 8-10 P.M. (unscheduled meetings). A collective feminist project established to provide women's center, including bookstore, library, switchboard, political action groups, etc. (Est. 80% lesbians.)
- Women's Video Workshops at Denver Community Video Center, 1459 Ogden St., 80218.

Durango
Services
- Women's Colorado Land Collective, P.O. Box 1429, 81301. 303 259-1367. Planning for a women's land trust, exploring and expanding the collective concept.

Fort Collins
Organizations
- Fort Collins Gay Alliance, Student Center, Box 210, Colorado State University, 80521. Sisters of Sappho, Fort Collins Gay Alliance, Student Center, Box 210, Colorado State University, 80521.
Services
- Fort Collins Women's Center, 629 Howe St., 80521. 303 484-1902.

Milliken
Services
- Broad Street Journal, Box 377, 80543. 303 587-4224. Phone counseling, printing, etc.

CONNECTICUT
Bridgeport
Bars
- Black Rock Inn, Black Rock Turnpike, 2931 Fairfield Ave. (western part of Bridgeport). Restaurant.

Organizations
- Gay Academic Union, University of Bridgeport Chapter, Prof. Rene Boux, Bernhard Humanities Center, University of Bridgeport, 06602. 303 576-4425.

Danbury
Bars
- The Answer Cafe, Route 7, New Milford. Restaurant.

Darien
Services
- The League, Box 2143GA, 06820. 203 359-3141. Discreet introduction between sisters.

Hartford
Bars
- The Lib, 132 New Park Ave. Owners are lesbians.

Media
- None of the Above, WWUH, 91.3 FM. 203 728-0653.

Religious Groups
- Church of the Eternal Flame Universal, 39 Dorothy St., Apt. 1A, 06106. 203 527-2626. Female pastor, ministry to gay women in prison.
- Integrity/Hartford, Christ Church Cathedral, 45 Church St. 06103. 203 522-2646. Meetings: Church of the Good Shepherd, 155 Wyllys St.
- Metropolitan Community Church, 11 Amity St. Mailing address: Box 514, 06101. Gay switchboard and information: 203 522-8651; gay counseling: 203 522-5575.

Services
- Church of the Eternal Flame Universal, 5 Dorothy St., 06106. 203 232-3761. Lesbian groups, activities, library, switchboard, etc.

Manchester
Bars
- Peppino's Place, 623 Main St. 203 649-5544.

Middleton
Organizations
- Wesleyan Gay Alliance, Box 233, Wesleyan Station, 06457. Meet 9 P.M. on first and third Thursdays while school is in session (University of Wesleyan). Contact for information. Provides information and entertainment for students and residents, gay and bisexual. Provides resources to educate community about gays. (Est. 15% lesbians.)

New Haven
Bars
- Partners, 365 Crown St. 203 624-5510. In addition to bar, it services as center for activities, referrals geared to gays.

Media
- Come Out Tonight, Box WYBC, 94.3 FM, Yale Station, 16520.

Organizations
- Gay Alliance at Yale, 2031 Yale Station, 06250. 203 436-8945. Tues.-Fri. 9P.M.-

midnight. Women's caucus on Thurs. 7 P.M. Yalesbians, Room B018, Bingham Hall, Old Campus Yale University, 330 College St., 06510. Mailing address: Gay Alliance at Yale/Yalesbians, 2031 Yale Station, 06250. 203 436-8945. Meetings on Wed. 8 P.M. at Gay Alliance Office, 330 College St. Support group for lesbians at Yale. Political group to raise consciousness of students and administration to gay rights. Coproduce only gay radio show in area with gay men at Yale, Come Out Tonight, WYBC, 94.3 FM, Sun. 7:30-8:30 P.M.

Religious Groups
- Dignity/New Haven, Box 3712, Amity Station, 06525.

Services
- Lesbian Rap Group, The Women's Center, 215 Park St., 06511.
  New Haven Women's Liberation Center, 148 Orange St., 06510. Mailing address: 3438 Yale Station, 06520. 203 436-0272, Mon.-Fri. 10 A.M.-5 P.M. Counseling, rap groups, classes in self-defense. Speakers' bureau, rape crisis center. Women's coffeehouse with feminist entertainment and refreshments. Open to all women of the community.

New London
Bars
- The Corral, 727 Bank St. 203 624-5510. Gay women and men. Hotel.

Storrs
Organizations
- UCONN Gay Alliance, U-8 University of Connecticut, 06268. 203 429-1448.

Waterbury
Bars
- The Road House, 1388 Thomaston Ave.

Westport
Bars
- The Brook, 919 E. State St. 203 226-6204.

DELAWARE
Bethany Beach
Bars
- Nomad Village, Inc., Rte. 14, Box 158, Tower Shores. 302 539-7581. Mon.-Sat. 9 P.M.-1 A.M.

Dewey Beach
Bars
- The Boat House. 302 227-7337. Restaurant.

Greenville
Services
- Delaware Separatist Dyke Group, Box 3526, 19807. 302 478-1246. A contact group composed of lesbians only. Peer counseling, emergency housing, open meetings for women, Tues. 7:30 P.M. at 30 Homewood Rd., Lynnfield.

Rehoboth Beach
Resorts
- Sandcastle Ltd., 1st and Brooklyn Ave., 19971. 302 227-6217. Lesbians and gay men.

Wilmington
Bars
- The Ark Club, Inc., 5101 Governor Printz Blvd., 19809. 302 762-5429, 8 P.M.-4 A.M.

A wholly owned gay club by members to offer social and legal benefit for its members. Disco, BYOB bar, after hours. Publishes *Captains Lounge,* a report of monthly board meetings, current events, new business. (Est. 40% lesbians.)

DISTRICT OF COLUMBIA
Bookstores
- First Things First, Feminist Bookstore, 2427 18th St., N.W., 20009. 202 234-2722. Tues.-Fri. noon-7 P.M.; Sat. 11 A.M.-6 P.M. Books by, for, and about women, nonsexist children's books, posters, pins, buttons. Walk-in business and also mail-order service. Publishes *A Catalogue of Our Books,* which includes sections of books of particular interest to lesbians.
- Lambda Rising, 1724 20th St., N.W. 20009. 202 462-6969. Open 7 days. Lesbian and gay lib bookstore. Periodicals, nonfiction, poetry, buttons, T-shirts, etc. New annotated bibliography—cost $1. Mail-order service available.
- Lammas Women's Shop, 321 7th St., S.E., 20003. 202 546-7292. Tues.-Fri. 11 A.M.-6 P.M.; Sat. 10 A.M.-6 P.M. Lesbian-owned business. Finest arts, crafts, books, records. Publicizes women's events and sponsors several sports teams each year.

Organizations
- Gay Activists Alliance, D.C., Box 2554, 20013, 202 331-1418, 6-11 P.M.
  Gay Youth, 1724 20th St., N.W. 20009. 202 387-3777, evenings.
- Northeast District Women's Collective/ Universal Fellowship of Metropolitan Community Church, P.O. Box 514, Hartford, Conn. 06101. Att'n Nancy Katherine Award. Or: 945 G St., N.W., 20001. Att'n: Jennie Bull. 202 232-6333, leave message. Actively working for increased female leadership in MCC, inclusive language, feminist theology. Concerned with nonsexist publications.
- NOW Sexuality Task Force, Greater Washington Area. Mailing address: c/o Edda Sonnenberg, 4504 East-West Highway, Riverdale, Md. 20840. 301 927-3275, irregular staffing. Meetings each month at the Towne House, 506 8th St., S.E. (upstairs). Supports and stimulates lesbian-feminist consciousness within the community; explores sexuality and provides conducive setting for social exchange among feminists in supportive environment.
- Parents of Gays of D.C., Ilse Mollet, 263 Congressional Lane, #407, Rockville, Md. 20852. 301 468-0091.
- The Task Force on the Status of Lesbian and Gay Psychologists, BSERP, American Psychological Association, 1200 17th St., N.W., 20036. 202 833-7600. A fact-finding and advisory committee of the APA Board of Social and Ethical Responsibility for Psychology. Purposes include documenting present number and status of gay psychologists, attitudes of psychologists toward their gay colleagues; providing information and support for gay psychologists; making recommendations to APA about how to "take the lead in removing stigma of mental

illness long associated with homosexual orientation"; and developing resource materials for educating. Care and custody of minors, etc. Over half of members of the Task Force are psychologists who are openly gay. They are doing a comprehensive study of experiences of lesbian and gay male psychologists within their profession.

Publications

- Blade Communications, Inc., 2430 Pennsylvania Ave., N.W., 20037. 202 785-3009, Mon.-Fri. 1-5 P.M. Meetings every other Tues. (Board of Directors); biannually (general membership); first Mon. of every month (writers and editors). A monthly gay newspaper, informative and interesting, with news, features, information, events, etc. Single issue free; subscription rate, $5/year (3rd class); $6 (1st class). (Est. 40% lesbians.) Off Our Backs, 1724 20th St., N.W., 20009. 202 234-8072, Mon.-Fri. 10 A.M.-5 P.M. A newspaper that expresses the ideas, interests of all aspects of feminism: news, analysis, commentary, culture. Published 10-12 per year. Single issue, 60¢; subscription, $6. (Est. 90% lesbians.)
- Quest: A Feminist Quarterly, 1901 Que Street, N.W., 20009. Mailing address: P.O. Box 8843, 20003. 202 667-7779, usually staffed 10:30 A.M.-5:30 P.M. daily. The publication concerns long-term feminist political analysis and provides a forum for development of feminist theory and practice. (Also publish books.) Quarterly. $2.75/issue; $9/year. (Est. 83% lesbians.)

Religious Groups

- Jewish Gays of Baltimore-Washington Area, Box 34038, 20034. 202 547-4562 and 544-1615. Helps with emergency housing, counseling, social events, etc.
- Unitarian Gay Community, All Souls Unitarian Church, 16th and Harvard, N.W., 20009. 202 722-0439.

Services

- Alcoholics Anonymous Gay Group, 202 332-3775 and 544-4598.
- Bread and Roses, 1724 20th St., N.W., 20009. 202 387-6264. A record shop. Emergency Mental Health Services, 202 629-5222.
- Feminist Counseling Collective, 202 439-6848.
- The Gay Connection, Box 622, Riverdale, Md. 20840. 202 277-9183, 24-hour service. Gay Switchboard of Washington, D.C., 1724 20th St., N.W. 20009. 202 387-3777, Mon.-Fri. 7:30-11 P.M.; Sat.-Sun. 2-11 P.M.
- Gay Women's Open House, 703 671-3762, Wed. 9-11:30 P.M. Lesbian and bisexual women get together and talk.
- Moonforce Media, Inc., P.O. Box 2934, Main City Station, 20013. 202 544-7243 or 546-7292. Main project is coordinating National Women's Film Circuit, a nationwide series of showings of films by and about women. Arranges showings in different cities around country. Film packages distributed are composed of feminist and lesbian films. Involved in film production. Will screen films for possible inclusion in future film packages.
- Parents of Gays, 203 965-4673, 6-11 P.M. Washington Area Women's Center, 17th and

M Streets, N.W., Sumner School Basement, 20036. 202 347-5078, Mon.-Fri. 10 A.M.-2 P.M. A referral service, information clearing house, and contact place. Provides alternative feminist environment for projects such as rap groups, art display, study groups, self-defense, workshops, etc. Monthly publication: In Our Own Write. $2.50/year.

- Wednesday Nite Women's Clinic, Washington Free Clinic, 1556 Wisconsin Ave., N.W., 20007. 202 965-5476, Wed. 6-11 P.M. Operating as a collective, providing self-help classes, gynecology exams, treatment of gynecological problems in a nonhierarchical, nonmystifying manner. Particular concern that the atmosphere be comfortable for lesbians.
- Writing-On, Douglas, 3616 Connecticut Ave., N.W., No. 300, 20008. Washington area lesbian-feminist writers' collective.
- Woman Sound, 1735 New Hampshire Ave., N.W., #104, 20009. 202 322-4220. A P.A. and recording company owned and run by women.

FLORIDA

Boca Raton

Organizations

- Gay Academic Union of Florida Atlantic University, Student Activities Office, 305 395-5100.
- Southern Gay Liberator, Box 2118, 33434. 305 391-8693. Publishes Florida Gay Liberation News.

Clearwater

Organizations

- Florida Coalition of Gay Organizations, Joe Finger, Chairperson, Legislative/Political Committee, P.O. Box 2423, 33517. 813 839-7871. Kip Hamm, Media Committee Chairperson. A new statewide organization, five committees. No office or phone (as yet) other than the individual residences of five board members throughout the state. Membership costs $5 per year. Actively supports lesbian rights and has one (out of five) lesbian board member.

Daytona Beach

Bars

- Damien's Yum Yum Tree, 703 N. Ridgewood Ave. 904 255-9177.
- Zodiac, 1564 S. Ridgewood. 904 767-4264.

Fort Lauderdale

Bars

- Annie's Odds 'n' Ends, 3148 E. 12th Ave.

Religious Groups

- Metropolitan Community Church, 1127 S.W. 2nd Court, 33312. 305 462-2004.
- Universal New Age Church, 1426 Lauderdale Villa Dr., 33311. 305 763-5775, 10 A.M.-5 P.M.; emergency 24 hours.

Gainesville

Bars

- Melody Club, 4130 N.W. 6th St. Dancing.

Services

- Gainesville Women's Health Center, 805 S.W. 4th Ave., 32601. 904 377-5055 or 377-5551, Mon.-Sat. 9 A.M.-10 P.M. 24-hour hotline. Open to the public 9 A.M.-11 P.M. Mon., Tues., Thurs.; 9 A.M.-6 P.M. Wed., Fri., Sat. Lesbian-feminist self-help workshop. Gynecology clinics which include

services for lesbians but are not exclusively for lesbians.

Hallandale

Bars

- Lou's Back Room, 800 N. Federal Highway (U.S. Highway No. 1). Sandwiches, snacks, dancing.

Hollywood

Organizations

- Stonewall Committee, Box 2084, 33040. Political activities, referral service, library, etc.

Jacksonville

Organizations

- Gay Alliance for Political Action, Box 52043, 32201. 904 354-4640. Medical and legal referrals, some emergency housing, etc.
- Lesbian Task Force of Jacksonville Women's Movement, P.O. Box 10551, 32207. Monthly Task Force meeting held the last Mon. of each month at Regency Square Library, 7-9 P.M., Conference Room. A political organization concerned with community education, consciousness-raising groups, developing services, etc. This Task Force arose from local women's movement which was largely lesbian. 904 724-3340.
- Parents of Gays, MCC, P.O. Box 291, 32201. 904 354-1318.

Religious Groups

- MCC of Jacksonville, 729 N. Laura St. Mailing address: P.O. Box 291, 32201. 904 354-1318, Mon., Wed., Fri. 11 A.M.-5 P.M. Meetings held at 729 N. Laura St. (MCC Social Hall). Provides spiritual, social, and social action improvements toward all, especially the gay community. (Est. 10% lesbians.)

Miami

Publications

- Lesbiana Speaks, Dade County NOW Lesbian Task Force, Box 330265, 33133. Free bimonthly.

Organizations

- Alliance for Individual Rights, Inc., Box 330414, 33133.
- Dade County Lesbian Task Force, 1431 N.W. 43rd St., 33142. 305 633-7108.

Religious Groups

- Metropolitan Community Church, N.W. 22nd Ave. (at 25th St.). Mailing address: P.O. Box 370963, 33137. 305 758-7190. Includes a separate women's group called Affinity.

Services

- Blue Boy Forum, WKID-TV, Channel 51. Mondays at 11 P.M. First regularly scheduled, commercially sponsored TV show in United States prepared by and for members of the gay community. Will be directed and involve participation by lesbian community as well as with their gay brothers.
- Center for Dialog, 2175 N.W. 26th St., 33142. 305 638-4085, Mon.-Fri. 9 A.M.-4 P.M.
- Gay Community Services of South Florida, Box 721, Coconut Grove Station, 33133. 305 445-3511. 7-12 P.M.

Orlando

Organizations

- Florida Coalition of Gay Organizations, P.O. Box 26274, 32816. Communication with other gay organizations, and get all potential gay voters in the state to the polls.

Florida Technological University Gay Student Association, Florida Technological University, 32816. Mailing address: P.O. Box 26, 274, 32816). 305 275-9101, 8 A.M.-5 P.M. A gay civil rights consciousness-raising and recreational group. (Est. 40% lesbians.)
- Lambda Society, Box 4479, 32507. 904 456-9034 after 5 P.M. Referrals, counseling, parents' groups, etc.

Publications
- Gayzette, Parliament House Resort Hotel, 410 N. Orange Blossom Trail, Suite 147, 32805.

Services
- Parliament House, 410 Orange Blossom Trail, 32805. 305 425-7571. Disco, three bars, motor inn accommodation. (Est. 50% lesbians.)

Pensacola
Bars
- Aquarius Lounge, 6120 Lillian Highway. 904 455-9006.

Services
- Parents of Gays, P.O. Box 4479, 32507; 904 453-1923. (No office.) Helps parents and their gay sons and daughters to a better understanding of each other; pass National Gay Civil Rights bill, consenting adults in private, and change attitudes in the community and throughout the nation. Printed material available for 24¢ stamped legal-sized envelope.

St. Petersburg
Bars
- Kitty's Bar, 1020 S. 4th St.

Organizations
- Lesbian Task Force of Pinellas County—NOW, 210 5th Ave. South, 33701.

Religious Groups
- King of Peace Metropolitan Community Church, 6702 54th Ave. North. 813 581-5587. Mailing address: 1050 Parkview Lane, Largo, Fla. 33504.

Services
- Female Awareness Counseling Enterprises, Twin Towers, 12945 Seminole Blvd., Bldg. 2, Largo, Fla. 33462. 813 586-1110. Workshops, speakers' nights.

Sarasota
Media
- Gayspace, WQSR, Box 7700, 33578. 813 974-2637. Last Sun. of every month, 6 P.M.

Organizations
- Sarasota Daughters of Bilitis (DOB), P.O. Box 15621, 33579. 813 924-8968. Meetings on second Sat. and fourth Wed. of every month at MCC facilities. A group by and for gay women offering moral support and social gatherings.

Tallahassee
Bookstores
- Herstore, 112 E. Call St., 32301. 904 224-2728. Mon.-Sat. 11 A.M.-6 P.M. Tues. night collective meetings at 6 P.M. Open to all interested women. A nonprofit, collectively managed feminist bookstore selling books, periodicals, posters, crafts, etc. Also an information center and meeting place for women in the community.

Services
- FSU Women's Center, 110-112 N. Woodward Ave. Mailing address: FSU, Box 6826, 32306. 904 644-4007. Open noon-5 P.M. Lesbian rap group, rape crisis center, etc.

Tampa
Bars
- Cucujo's, 1725 W. Kennedy Blvd. 813 251-9453.

Bookstores
- Feminist Connection, 1202 W. Platt St. 33606. Mailing address: 1200 W. Platt, 33612. 813 258-6421, Mon.-Sat. 10 A.M.-6 P.M. Coffeehouse and teahouse offering wide variety of literature, posters, buttons, herbal aids, stationery, T-shirts, etc. Also carries woman-made crafts and will sell on consignment.
- Our Place, 12315 N. Nebraska Ave., 33612.

Organizations
- Tampa Daughters of Bilitis, Feminist Women's Health Center, 1200 W. Platt St., 33606.
- University of South Florida Gay Coalition, 4202 Fowler Ave., 33620. Mailing address: Ctr. 2466, 33620. 813 974-2749, Mon.-Thurs. 6-10 P.M. Coalition meetings at USF University Center, Rm. 158 (subject to quarterly change), Sun. 8 P.M. Information Center—CBA 335 Mon.-Thurs. 6-10 P.M. Registered student organization. Provides a support system for gays, educates the community, and works for political and legal changes in the system. (Est. 30% lesbians.)

Religious Groups
- Metropolitan Community Church, 2904 Concordia Ave., 33609. 813 839-5939.

Services
- Feminist Women's Health Center, 1200 W. Platt St., 33606. 813 251-4089.
- The Women's Center, 1208 West Platt St. 33606. 813 251-4089. Coffeehouse, bookstore, clinic.

West Palm Beach
Bars
- Le Cabaret, 6910 S. Dixie Highway. 305 588-3751. Disco, show bar. Recommended.

GEORGIA
Athens
Organizations
- Committee on Gay Education, Box 2467, University Station, 30602. 404 599-4015, evenings. Publishes Gay Sun.

Atlanta
Bookstores
- The Hobbit Habbit, 298 E. Washington, 30601. 404 549-4299.

Media
- Gay Atlanta, Box 5332, 30307. 404 523-3471. WRFG, 89.3 FM. Fri. 9-10 P.M.
- Gay Digest, Box 5332, 30307. 404 523-3471. WRFG, 89.3 FM. Tues. 2-2:30 P.M.

Organizations
- Atlanta Lesbian Feminist Alliance. 1326 McLendon St., N.E., 30307. Mailing address: Box 5502, 30307. 404 523-7786, irregular hours. General meetings first Sun. of month, 6 P.M. An umbrella organization serving the social, political, cultural, and educational needs of lesbians. Yearly dues

$6. Monthly ALFA newsletter (can be subscribed to separately), $3/year for individuals; $5/year for institutions.
- The Atlanta Socialist Feminist Women's Union, ALFA, 1326 McLendon Ave., N.E. Mailing address: Box 5502, 30307. Meetings, second and fourth Tuesdays of each month at Alfa House.
- Gay Center, 20 4th St., N.E., 30308. 404 872-3495. New expression of political interest in Atlanta gay community.
- Gay Pride Alliance, 20 4th St., N.E., 30308. Libertarians for Gay Rights, 2936 Skyland Dr., 30341.
- Parents of Gays, Jake Shipp, 816 Piedmont Ave., N.E., 30318. 404 876-5177.

Religious Groups
- Dignity Atlanta (Catholic), Box 77013, 30357. 404 355-1416.
- Metropolitan Community Church, 800 N. Highland Ave., N.E., 30306. 404 872-2246, Mon.-Fri. 9 A.M.-4 P.M.; Sun. 1-8 P.M. Responds to the spiritual and social needs of gay people, counseling, job and housing referrals, educational programs, etc. (Est. 35% lesbians.)

Services
- Alternative Therapy Center, 20 4th St., N.W., 30308. 404 873-2000.
- Atthis, P.O. Box 5533, 30307. 404 688-7978 or 523-8977, 6-10 P.M. daily. Workshops and consultations in lesbian sexuality. Five workshops primarily with all lesbians. Also available to do workshops in other cities. Contact for arrangements.
- Gay Help Line, Box 7974, 30309. 404 892-5855. Publishes Gay Help Liner.

Augusta
Bars
- The Peacock, 1321 New Savannah Rd. Ray's Riverview, 29 Water St.

Columbus
Bars
- C. and G.'s, First Ave. and 14th St.

Macon
Bars
- Anne's Tic Toc, 408 Broadway. We Three Lounge, 434 Cotton Ave. 912 746-9193.

Savannah
Bars
- The Basement, Bull and Charlton Sts., 912 234-9148, Mon.-Sat. 8 P.M.-3 A.M. A bar-lounge. (Est. 50% lesbians.)
- Woodies, 229 W. River St.

HAWAII
Honolulu
Bars
- Hula's, 2103 Kuhio Ave. 808 923-0669. Your best bet: outdoor area. The Tomato, 240 McCully (at Ala Wai, half block south of Kalakaus). 808 955-5688.

Publications
- The Paper, 1186 Fort St. Mall, Rm. 212, 96813. Free monthly. Affiliated with Metropolitan Community Church. (Est. 30% lesbians.)

Religious Groups
- Dignity of Hawaii, P.O. Box 15825, 96815. 808 573-9478.

• Metropolitan Community Church, 1186 Fort St. Mall, 96813 (office). 808 537-9478. Service: Sun. 10 A.M., 240 McCully; and 7:30 P.M. at 2500 Pail Highway.
Services
• Love and Peace Together/Sexual Identity Center, 2457 Kanealii Ave. Mailing address: Box 3224, 96801. 808 524-4699, 8 A.M.-5 P.M.; other times, 538-7940.

Wahiawa
Organizations
• Gay Liberation Hawaii, 95-065 Waikalani Dr., F205, 96786. 808 623-4334.

IDAHO
Boise
Bars
• Shuckey's, 233 S. 10th St. 208 342-9558.

Moscow
Bookstores
• Bookpeople, 512 S. Main St. 208 882-7957.
Organizations
Northwest Gay People's Alliance, P.O. Box 8758, 83843. Executive meetings every other Tues. Membership and open meetings monthly; meeting place varies. Provides resources, speaker's bureau, and education for general public. Political group aimed at organizing locally and fighting discrimination in housing codes, etc. Bimonthly publication, *Update for Action*. (Est. 40% lesbians.) 208 882-0836.
Services
• Women's Center, University of Idaho, Administration Center Building, #109, 83843.

Pocatello
Bars
• Atom Club, 230 W. Lewis. 208 232-9821.

ILLINOIS
Calumet City
Bars
• Our Place, 706 State Line. 312 862-9706.
The Patch, Wentworth at 155th St. 312 891-9854.

Champaign
Organizations
• Gay Women's Group, Box 1096, Station A, 61820.
• Lavender Prairie Collective, P.O. Box 2096, Station A, 61820. 217 384-8040, 7 P.M.-1 A.M. (gay switchboard, men and women staff with information for lesbians). Activities at coffeehouses about once a month. Provides an alternative to bars where women can meet and talk—also place for lesbian entertainment—and just be together (bars are mixed). Publishes about once a month, *Lesbian News*. 25¢ issue.
Religious Groups
• Metropolitan Community Church, Box 5015, Station A, 61820.
Services
• Gay Switchboard (Urbana), 217 384-8040, 7 P.M.-1 A.M.

Chicago
Organizations
• Blazing Star, Chicago Women's Liberation Union, 3411 W. Diversey Ave., 60647. 312 772-2655. Hours vary, call first. Group of lesbian and bisexual women. Members of CWLU who do outreach and organizing in the lesbian community. Offers classes, rap groups, and educational forums. Publishes, *Blazing Star*, approximately every two or three months. $3/10 issues.
• Chicago Women's Liberation Union, 3411 W. Diversey Ave., 60647. 312 772-2655. Hours and regular activities vary, call for information. A socialist-feminist women's organization working on health care, legal problems, sports for women, job discrimination, and other areas. Publications include *CWLU News* newsletter, dues $12/year; *Blazing Star*, published every two or three months, $3/10 issues (single issue free). Membership includes lesbians (10% to 15%) and bisexual women.
• Gay Task Force of the Alliance to End Repression, Clark House, 22 E. Van Buren St., 60604. 312 427-4064.
• Gay Youth, Gay Horizons, Beekman House, 2745 N. Clark St., 2nd floor. Mailing address: Box 1319, 60690. Meetings, Sat. 3 P.M.
• University Feminist Organization, University of Chicago, 1212 E. 59th St. 60637. 312 684-3189, hours irregular. Tues. night meetings, Wed. night rap group. Thurs. noon discussions at the Blue Gargoyle, 5655 S. University Ave. Promotes the welfare of university women, sponsors women's center, lectures, readings, library, coffeehouse. Publishes *Primavera* (women's literary magazine) once a year. $3.50/issue; $9.50/3 issues. (Est. 5% lesbians.)
• University of Chicago Gay Liberation, Rm. 301, Ida Noyes Hall, 1212 E. 59th St., 60637. 312 753-3274.
University of Chicago Gay Peoples Center, Rm. 301, Ida Noyes Hall, 1212 E. 59th St., 60637. 312 753-3274, Sun.-Thurs. 8-10 P.M. Discussion group, Thurs. 7 P.M. Provides information and referral services, sponsors social activity to Hyde Park-Kenwood community, and represents interests of gay students in university-wide affairs.
• Gay Life (newspaper), 205 W. Wacker Dr., Suite 1416, 60606. 312 236-7575, Mon.-Fri. 9 A.M.-6 P.M. Regular activities in office. Disseminates information, advertises gay organizations and businesses, features a lesbian life section. Published twice monthly. $10/year.
• Mamma Ry, S. Craig, 938 W. Oakdale, 60657. Private phone; can be contacted by letter only. A quarterly publication to celebrate the literary, visual, and intellectual talents of women. Poetry, drawings, essays, photographs. $1.50/issue; $5/year.
• Womanpress, P.O. Box 59330, 60645. 312 334-8561 daily. Publishes several newsletters, monographs, and books. Provides communication and exchange of resources to lesbians and other women interested in lesbian writing, music, and graphic arts.
Religious Groups
• Lutherans Concerned for Gay People, Ron Anderson, 656 Buckingham Place, 60657. United Clergy (Gay Rap), Mary Houlihan, 1221 W. Sherwin, 60626. 312 262-9609.
Services
• Alexandria Library for Lesbian Women,

3523 N. Halstead, 60657.
• Blue Gargoyle, 5655 S. University Ave., 60637. Coffeehouse.
• Chicago Counseling and Psychotherapy Center, 5711 S. Woodlawn Ave., 60637. 312 684-1800. Staffed throughout week by appointment. Center open for flexible hours, by appointment and when groups begin at above address and at 6354 N. Broadway. Provides low-cost psychotherapy to clients, clarifying their sexual orientation, etc. Individual psychotherapy, gay couple counseling, personal issues for lesbian women, over-thirties group for gay and bisexual women. Costs for groups and services given on request. (Est. 20% lesbians.)
• Chicago Women's Health Center, 745 W. Armitage, 60614. 312 787-2031, staffed Tues. 2-10 P.M.; Wed. A.M.; some Sats. Meetings: Well-woman gynecological, self-help clinic, Tues. 6:30-10 P.M.; collective meetings first and third Thurs. each month; Saturdays, health classes. Open Tues. 6:30-9 P.M.; Sat. 10 A.M.-noon; Wed. 11 A.M.-1 P.M. and 6:30-9 P.M. Services for self-help clinic, health referrals, women's health courses, slide show presentations. Provides health education and gynecological care.
• Counseling Resource Center for Lesbians, 3523 N. Halstead, 60651. 312 935-4250.
• Emma Goldman's Women's Clinic, 1317 W. Loyola, 60626. 312 262-8870.
• Gay People's Legal Committee, 413 W. Fullerton, 60614. 312 248-1508.
• Gay Speakers Bureau, Box 2377, 60690. 312 348-8243, 5-11 P.M. Lesbians and gay men speak at universities, etc.
Illinois Gays for Legislative Action, Larry
• Gullan, 1921 N. Bissell St., 60614. 312 871-3198.
• Institute for Human Relations, Gay People's Counseling and Education Center of Chicago, 561 W. Diversey Parkway, 60614. 312 248-8588.
• Lavender Elephants, Lambda Associates, 2745 N. Clark St., Suite 210, 60614. 312 281-0686. A weight watchers' group.
• Lesbian Feminist Center, 3523 N. Halstead, 60657. 312 935-4250.
• Midnight at Harlow's, WVVX, 103.1 FM. Chicago's first gay radio program, Mon.-Fri., 10 P.M.-midnight.
• Midwest Women's Legal Group, Ms. Renee Hanover, 54 W. Randolph St., 60601. 312 641-1905.
• Mother-Right Feminist Rock Band, Nancy Katz, Lesbian Feminist Center, 3523 N. Halstead, 60657. 312 935-4207.
• North Loop Cab Service, Box 1003, 60690. 312 337-2262. Radio-dispatched cabs for gays on the North Side. Regular cab fares. Rogers Park Gay Center, 7109 N. Glenwood. 312 262-0537.
• WICCA, Women in Crisis Can Act, 1139 W. Webster, 60614. 312 528-3303.
• Women's Graphics Collective, 3100 N. Southport, 60657. 312 477-6070, irregular hours. Meet sporadically, but someone usually in studio every afternoon. Make hand silk-screened posters, done from a feminist perspective. Strongly woman-identified, and have about five posters that are specifically lesbian. Free catalog of their posters. Twelve

members in group. (Est. 50% lesbians, fluctuates.)

De Kalb
Organizations
- Gay Liberation Front, Northern Illinois University, Box 74, 60115. Student activities. 815 753-0518.

East St. Louis
Bars
- Helen Schrader's, 205 N. 5th St. (off Missouri Ave.).

Evanston
Organizations
- Women at Northwestern University, 619 Emerson, 60201. 312 492-3146, Mon.-Fri. 10 A.M.-5 P.M. Meetings Wed. 8 P.M.-midnight; Fri. at lesbian coffeehouse (lesbian hotline 312 492-3146, Fri. 8 P.M.-midnight). Group of undergrads and grads of N.W.U. committed to feminist goals and improving women's conditions. Publishes *Mountain Moving*. $1/issue; $3/year (3 issues).

Services
- Evanston Women's Liberation Center, 2214 Ridge, 60201. 312 475-4480, Mon.-Fri. 10 A.M.-3 P.M. irregularly. Meetings on first Thurs. 8 P.M. and any time services are offered. Weekly rap group for lesbians. Purpose is to combat sexism, support women in need of legal help, etc. Provides open forums, education, telephone referrals. Publishes *Rapport*. Monthly. $5/year.
- Women's Collection, Special Collections Department, Northwestern University Library, 60201. 312 492-3635, staffed Mon.-Fri. 8:30 A.M.-5 P.M.; Sat. 8:30 A.M.-noon. A library, open to the public, extensive lesbian periodical titles, posters, records. Are documenting contemporary women's liberation movement (soliciting since 1970), have retrieved many sixties' documents. Publishes irregularly *Women's Collection Newsletter*. Free.

La Grange
Religious Groups
- Holy Covenant Community Church, 900 S. La Grange Rd. (at 51st St.). Mailing address: Box 9134, 60690. 312 274-5582, 7-10 P.M. 312 274-5586, weekdays.

Macomb
Organizations
- Friends, Western Illinois University. Mailing address: Box 296, 61455. Gay students and community organization.

Normal
Organizations
- Gay People's Alliance of Illinois State University, 225 N. University St., #1C, 61761. 309 438-3411, afternoons Mon.-Fri. Meetings Thurs. 8 P.M. on ISU campus. A social environment for gays, film festivals, social functions, local crisis center, and workshops. Provides education through guest speakers and raps. (Est. 50% lesbians.)

Peoria
Bars
- Club Peorian, South West Adams at Oak. 309 674-5623. Disco bar. Recommended.

Quincy
Religious Groups
- Metropolitan Community Church/Illiamo, 16 Skyview Ct., Keokuk, 1A, 52632. 319 524-7700.

Rockford
Bars
- The Office, 513 E. State St.

Streamwood
Organizations
- Fox Valley Gay Association, Box 186, 60130. 312 697-0623.

Urbana
Organizations
- Gay Illini, 284 Illini Union, 61801. 217 333-1187, variable hours. Meetings Sun. 7:30 P.M., Rm. 270. Gay switchboard, 217 384-8040, 7 P.M.-1 A.M. daily. Provide support for gay people, to educate and raise consciousness of the Champaign, Urbana, populace. Publishes *Gay Illini*. Free. (Est. 20% lesbians.)

Services
- Gay Switchboard, 217 384-8040, 7 P.M.-1 A.M. daily.

INDIANA
Bloomington
Bookstores
- A Room of One's Own, 101½ W. Kirkwood, 47401. Rms. 9 and 10.

Organizations
- Lesbian Liberation Organization, 212 W. Kirkwood Ave., 47401. 812 332-3535.

Services
- Gay Rap Line, 812 332-3535.
- New Horizons Gay Community Services, 212 W. Kirkwood Ave., 47401. 812 332-3535, Thurs.-Sun. 7 P.M.-1 A.M. Women's Crises Service, 812 332-0181. Mon.-Fri. 2 P.M.-7 A.M.; Sat. and Sun. 8 P.M.-7 A.M. Gay-oriented, trained paraprofessionals.
- Xanthippe Women's Collective, 101½ W. Kirkwood Ave., 47401. Regular activities Mon.-Sat. 11 A.M.-8 P.M. The purpose of the collective is to further women's interests in the community. Presently operating a feminist bookstore and plans to sponsor women's concerts, dances, movies, and lectures.

Fort Wayne
Organizations
- University Gay Activists, IPFW Student Union, 2101 Coliseum Blvd., 46805.

Religious Groups
- Metropolitan Community Church, P.O. Box 5443, 46805. 219 744-3898.

Indianapolis
Organizations
- Gay People's Union of Central Indiana, 146 E. 19th St., #12, 46202.

Services
- Everywoman's Center, 1018 S. Laurel St., 46203. 317 632-4637, Mon., Wed., Fri. 10 A.M.-3 P.M.; Sat. noon-6 P.M. Membership meetings usually third Sun. of every month. Other events and activities may be scheduled anytime. 24-hour answering service for referrals and information. Counseling, refer-

rals for legal, medical, emergency shelter, services to women in crisis, social center, etc. Open to all women. Collective structure, membership self-defining. Monthly calendar of events distributed. (Est. 80% lesbians.)

Notre Dame
Organizations
- Gay Community of Notre Dame, P.O. Box 206, 46556. Meetings Thurs. 8 P.M. Lesbians in minority but welcomed.

South Bend
Bars
- Downtowner, 411 E. Jefferson.
- Seahorse, 1902 Western.

Religious Groups
- Michiana Christ Community Church, 1527 Kemble St., 46613. 219 287-2552.

Terre Haute
Bars
- Meg's Place, 1801 Wabash.

Religious Groups
- United Ministries Center at Indiana University, 321 N. 7th St., 47807. Mailing address: P.O. Box 727, 47807. 812 238-1454/5, 9 A.M.-5 P.M. daily. Activities office open daily 9 A.M.-4 P.M., some Sundays, some evenings, by announcement in Indiana State University newspaper *Statesman*. Arm of four major Protestant denominations—United Methodist, United Presbyterian, United Church of Christ, Disciples of Christ (Christian)—on campus. Actively serving the gay population. Counseling and church services.

West Lafayette
Organizations
- Purdue Gay Alliance, Box 510, Purdue Memorial Union, 47906. Meetings every other Thurs. during school year at 7:30 P.M. in Stewart Center, Purdue University campus. A social, political and educational organization (gay and straight). Dances, sports activities, speakers' bureau, CR groups etc. Publish free *Rap Sheet*, supposedly once a month. (Est. 33% lesbians.)

IOWA
Ames
Organizations
- Open Line, 2502 Knapp St., 50010.

Cedar Rapids
Organizations
- Pride of Lambda, Box 265, 52406. 319 362-2629.

Des Moines
Bookstores
- A Mind of Your Own, 1926 Francis, 50314.

Religious Groups
- Metropolitan Community Church, Box 4546, 50306. 515 244-4342.

Services
- Gay Community Services Center, 3905 Crocker, 50312.

Grinnell
Organizations
- Grinnell College Gay Community, Student Affairs Office, 50112.

Iowa City
Organizations
- Iowa City Lesbian Alliance, 3 E. Market St., 52240. 319 353-6265.
- Lesbian Alliance, Women's Resource and Action Center, 130 N. Madison, 52240. Wide range of activities, facilities, social, sports. etc. Publishes *Better Homes and Dykes*. Free.

Services
- Emma Goldman Clinic for Women, 715 N. Dodge, 52240. 319 337-3042, Mon.-Fri. 9 A.M.-5 P.M.; Sat. 10 A.M.-2 P.M. Provides services such as feminist patient advocates for lesbians (both in clinic and other doctors' offices and hospitals). Informal discussions on lesbian sexuality, lesbian health concerns book in process, and a contact for new women in town. Also self-help, gynecology, etc. (Est. 33% lesbians.)
- Grace and Rubie's, 209 N. Linn, 52240. 319 351-9550, Mon.-Fri. 11 A.M.-midnight. Natural food. Private membership.

Mason City
Organizations
- Parent of Gays, Bill and Lois Miller, 3428 Brandywine Rd., 50401. 515 423-5911.

KANSAS
Emporia
Organizations
- Gay People of Emporia, Student Organizations Office, Memorial Union, Kansas State College, 66801. 316 342-0641.

Kansas City
Bars
- Pete's Pub, 2550 W. 47th St., 66103.

Lawrence
Services
- Dyke Patrol, Kansas Union 104 B, 66044. Mon.-Fri. 9:30 A.M.-4:30 P.M. A subgroup of the Women's Coalition, this is a resource group for lesbians entering the community or needing counseling.
- Gay Services of Kansas, Box O, Kansas Union, University of Kansas, 66045. Rm. 104B. 913 842-7505. 9 A.M.-5 P.M. Womanspace, 643 Rhode Island St., 66044. Care space, therapy services, monthly dances, Yoga, bike repair, classes.
- Women's Coalition, Kansas Union 104 B, 66044. 913 864-4934, Mon.-Fri. 9:30 A.M.-4:30 P.M. No regular activities at this time. Classes in self-health, self-defense, Yoga CR, etc. A resource center for referrals for information and counseling, small library, periodicals. Sponsors classes and workshops and films. Main meeting place for lesbians and social center. Publishes *Women's Resource Guide 1976-77*. Free. (Est. 90% lesbians.)

Manhattan
Services
- Children of Sappho, Gay Counseling Service, UFM, 615 Fairchild Terrace, 66502.
- Gay Counseling Service, UFM, 615 Fairchild Terrace, 66502. 913 539-2311, Fri., Sat. 7 P.M.-3 A.M.; Sun. 7 P.M.-midnight.

Topeka
Bars
- Guys and Dolls, 415 Kansas Ave., 66601.

913 235-5241. Food and dancing.
- The Midnight Sun Club, 2633 N. Kansas, 66617. 913 354-9745.

Wichita
Organizations
- Lesbian Rap Group, Free University, Wichita State University, 67208. Activities every Wed. 7:30 P.M. at 251 Campus Activities Center, WSU. Provides a forum for lesbians to express a point of view, get support, counseling.
- Wichita Gay Community Association (WGCA), P.O. Box 13013, 67213. 316 942-6619. Newsletter. $3/year.

Religious Groups
- MCC of Wichita, 147 N. Emporia, 67202. 316 681-1573, staffed 24 hours. Mailing address: P.O. Box 2639, 67201. Office only open during evenings. Church group instruction given. (Est. 33% lesbians.)

KENTUCKY
Lexington
Religious Groups
- Metropolitan Community Church, 507 N. Broadway, 40507. 606 233-1082.

Services
- Lexington Gay Services Organization, Box 1677, 40501. 606 269-5192. Peer counseling, referrals.

Louisville
Organizations
- Gay Liberation/Daughters of Bilitis, 416

Belgravia Ct., 40208. 502 635-5841.
- Parents of Gays, Barbara Maynor, 418 Marret Ave., 40208, 502 636-0649.

Services
- Mother's Brew, 204 W. Market St., 502 582-9758. A coffeehouse for women.

LOUISIANA
Alexandria
Publications
- Louisiana Gay Blade, P.O. Box 1583, 71301.

Baton Rouge
Bars
- Mirror Room, 311 N. Boulevard.
- Thirsty Tiger, 3205 Plank Rd.

New Orleans
Organizations
- Daughters of Bilitis (DOB), P.O. Box 52113. 504 945-2217, 737-7671, 891-4339, 866-3124, 866-7765.
- NOW, P.O. Box 13604, 70183. 504 865-9550.
- Tulane University Gay Students Union, Associated Student Body, University Center, 70118. 504 865-6208 and 865-4735.

Religious Groups
- Dignity, P.O. Box 15586, 70175. 504 861-1663.
- MCC of New Orleans, 1934 Burgundy St., 70116. 504 945-5476, Tues.-Fri. Services Sun. 11 A.M., 7:30 P.M.; Wed. 7:30 P.M. Religious services and educational classes; VD clinic, counseling, social functions.

Services
- New Orleans Gay Service Center, Box 51315, 70151; 504 947-GAYS. Center: 2006 Burgundy St.

Shreveport
Bars
- Florentine Room, 728 Austin Place. K-9 Club, 1724 Barksdale Blvd. (Bossier City).

MAINE
Bath
Services
- Women's Counseling Service, 72 Front St., Rm. 23, 04530. 207 443-9531, Mon. 7-10 P.M.; Wed. 11 A.M.-2 P.M.; Thurs. 4 P.M.-7 P.M.; Sat. 10 A.M.-1 P.M. Counseling for all women in informal atmosphere, little or no cost. Referral center, library. Counselors 25% lesbians, all nonhomophobic.

Belfast
Organizations
- Maine Lesbian-Feminists, P.O. Box 125, 04915. Statewide meetings every two months at a different location around the state. Purposes are to give support to selves and each other, sponsor lesbian-feminist political activities, initiate projects; create strong lesbian presence within Maine's gay community, issues brought to media attention, etc. Publish *MLF Newsletter*. Monthly. $5/year (for those who can afford price). (Approximately 250 lesbians in group.)

Lewiston
Organizations
- Gay Rights Organization, Box 1163, 04240.

Ogunquit

Bars

- Annabelle's, U.S. Highway 1. Disco, brunch, dinner, etc.

Orono

Organizations

- Lesbian Caucus, Fernald Hall, University of Maine, 04473.
- Wilde-Stein Club, Union, University of Maine, 04473. 207 581-2571.

Services

- Orono Women's Center, Fernald Hall, University of Maine, 04473.

Pleasant Point

Organizations

- Maine Gay Indians, Deanna Francis, Passamaquoddy Library, 04667.

Portland

Organizations

- Gay People's Alliance, 92 Bedford St., 04103. 207 773-2981.
- Maine Freewoman's Herald, 193 Middle St., 04111. Feminist and lesbian; Maine-oriented. Publishes bimonthly. 40¢ issue.
- Maine Gay Task Force, 193 Middle St., 04111.

Services

- Evelyn and Floyd Bull, Parents Group, Maine Gay Task Force, Box 4542, 04112. Southern Maine Lesbian Caucus, Johnson/ Breeding, 205 Spring St., Apt. 5, 04102.
- University of Maine Gay Students Group at Portland-Gorham, Maine Gay Task Force, Box 4542, DS, 04112.

Presque Isle

Services

- Lesbian Community Center, 3028 Greenmount Ave., 04769. 207 235-8593.
- Persephone Press, P.O. Box 7222, 04769. A lesbian publishing house run by four lesbians.

Sunset

Services

- Atthis Productions, 04683. Promotes women's culture, especially music.

MARYLAND

Baltimore

Bookstores

- The 31st St. Bookstore, 425 E. 31st St., 21218. 301 243-3131; Mon.-Sat. 10 A.M.-6 P.M. Lesbian-feminist bookstore.
  A Women's Bookstore, Diana Press, 12 W. 25th St., 21218. Mon.-Fri. 9:30 A.M.-4:30 P.M.

Organizations

- Baltimore Gay Alliance, Box 13438, 21203. Parents of Gays, 301 235-HELP, 366-1415. Ultimate Woman, Women's Growth Center, 1110 St. Paul St., 21202. 301 539-3588, varied hours. Rap session, Thurs. 7:30-10 P.M.; political committee meetings on Sun.; newsletter and social committees on Tues. 7:30 P.M. (all meetings open). Trying to raise consciousness of all women (esp. lesbians) to be fully aware of the need to fight oppression. Also provide warm, loving atmosphere to share feelings, ideas, etc. Publishes *The Sapphic Connection,* a free monthly. (Est. 95% lesbians.)

Publications

A Cold Day in August, 101 E. 25th St., B-2, 21218. 301 366-6475. 40¢/issue; $4/year.

Women: A Journal of Liberation, 3028 Greenmount Ave., 21218; 301 235-5245. $1.25 an issue; free to women prisoners. Thematic approach to lesbian-feminism; has fund-raising events several times a year.

Religious Groups

- Dignity, 761 W. Hamburg St., 21230. 301 235-0333.
- Jewish Gays, 301 685-0736.
  Metropolitan Community Church of Baltimore, 4201 York Rd. Mailing address: Box 1145, 21203. 301 435-3443.

Services

- Baltimore Women's Liberation Center, 101 E. 25th St., 21218. 301 366-6475, Wed. 10 A.M.-2 P.M. Business meeting third Sun. of month, 6 P.M. Open house, craft and plant sale once a month. Publishes *Cold Day in August* (newsletter). Monthly. 40¢/issue; $4/year. Lesbian speakers' bureau, lesbian rap session, art gallery, consciousness-raising. (Est. 90% lesbians.)
- Gay Switchboard, 301 235-4357.
- Lesbian Community Center, 3028 Greenmount Ave., 21218. 301 235-8593. Child sharing project; social events, sports, etc. Lesbian switchboard, same number, Mon.-Fri. 7-10 P.M.
- Lesbian Speaker's Bureau, Women's Center, 101 E. 25th St., Suite B-2, 21218. 301 366-6475, Wed., Thurs. noon-4 P.M.
- Sappho's, 100 S. Albemarle St., 21202. 301 752-1263, 8 P.M.-2 A.M. Live music, a variety of entertainment. Free use building to women's organizations for fund raising, benefits. Honor women's holidays, not traditional Christian or Jewish ones. Nonexploitive of women's and lesbian groups.
- The Women's Growth Center, 1110 St. Paul St., 21202. 301 539-3588, Mon.-Sat., hours irregular. Counseling and educational workshops scheduled according to availability of participants and staff. Individual, family, and group therapy on a scaled-fee basis. CR groups weekly. Education and growth workshops on quarterly basis with provision for women who cannot pay. (Est. 50% lesbian.)

College Park

Organizations

- Gay Students Alliance, Student Union Building, University of Maryland, 20742. 301 454-4855.

Columbia

Organizations

- Coalition of Gay Sisters (COGS), P.O. Box 222, 21045. 301 997-1593, staffed 7-10 P.M. Meetings Wed. evenings, 7:30 P.M. at The Other Barn, Oakland Mill Village Center. To provide a sense of community among gay women and support cultural and legislative change. Open to any woman regardless of background, ideological affiliation or personal self-definition. Rap groups, social activities, forums and workshops, hotline, information and referrals, etc.

Publications

- Lesbian Front, No. 203, 2619 Nicholson, 20782.

Largo

Religious Groups

- Gay People's Group of Prince George's Community College, Student Activities Office, 301 Largo Rd., 20870.

North Beach

Bars

- Golden Key Tavern, 5th and Chesapeake.

Simpsonville

Organizations

- Peet, Box 27, 21150.

Washington County

Services

- Elk Ridge Campground, Box 2846, RR1, Harpers Ferry, W. Va., 25452. Chestnut Grove Road (close to Washington, D.C.). 301 432-5024.

MASSACHUSETTS

Allston

Publications

- Sister Courage, Inc., P.O. Box 296, 02134. Monthly. 35¢/issue; $4/year. Feminist newsjournal open collective; resource to women's community.

Amherst

Media

- Gaybreak, WMUA, 91.1 FM, Marston Hall, University of Massachusetts, 01002. 413 545-2876. Radio programs on first and third Wed., 10:20 P.M.

Organizations

- Lesbian Union, C.C. 901, University of Massachusetts 01003. 413 545-3438, Mon.-Fri. 9 A.M.-5 P.M.; some evenings. Social events, counseling, political focus, speakers' bureau.

Services

- Amherst Gay Hotline, 413 545-1045.
  Everywoman's Center, 506 Goodell Hall, University of Massachusetts, 01003. 413 545-0883, Mon.-Wed., Fri. 10 A.M.-4 P.M.; Wed. 6-8 P.M.; Thurs. 1-4 P.M. Courses for women, some with lesbian focus, offered spring, fall, and summer. Counseling, support groups, workshops. Publishes bimonthly newsletter. Free to community; mailed, $3/year. (Est. 20% lesbians.)
- Lambda Travel, 233 N. Pleasant St., 01002. 413 549-1256. Travel agency.

Andover

Religious Groups

- Dignity/Merrimack Valley, Christian Formation Center, 475 River Rd., 01810. Mailing address: P.O. Box 348, Lowell, Mass. 01853. 617 851-6711, Mon.-Fri. 9 A.M.-3 P.M. Meetings for gay Catholic community second and fourth Sat. of month, 7:30 P.M. Newsletter published monthly; one issue free; $3/year. (Est. 40% lesbians.)

Bellingham

Services

- Bay and Valley Counseling Associates, 12 Dal Mor Road, 02169. Mailing address: P.O. Box 69, N. Quincy, Mass. 02171. Psychological counseling for gay persons.

Boston

Media

- Closet Space, WCAS, 740 AM, 02139. 617 492-6450. Radio program, 10:30-11 P.M. Gay News, WCAS, 740 AM. Radio program, Mon. 10 A.M.
- Gay Way, WBUR, 90.9 FM, 630 Commonwealth Ave., 02215. 617 353-2790. Radio program, Tues. 8-9:30 P.M.

Organizations

- Boston University Gays, 31 Program Resources Office, Student Union, 775 Commonwealth Ave., 02215. 617 353-2000.

- Cambridge Gays, GCN Box 6500, 22 Bromfield St., 02108.
- Daughters of Bilitis (DOB), 419 Boylston St., Rm. 323, 02116. 617 262-1592. Lesbian social group and referral service; lesbian rap, Tues. 7:30 P.M. and socials listed in *Focus*. Publishes *Focus: A Journal for Gay Women*. Monthly. 60¢/issue; $6/year.
- Gay Academic Union of New England, Box 212, 02101. 617 266-2069.
- Gay Legislation, Box 8841, JFK Station, 02114. 617 661-9362.
- Gay Nurses' Alliance, P.O. Box 530, Back Bay Annex, 02117. 617 266-5473. National organization. Advocates for gay patients and gay nurses. Speakers' bureau, workshops and conferences, legislative activity, referral services for counseling. Publishes *Signal* 3 times a year. Subscription: contribution of at least $5. (Est. 75% lesbians.)
- Gay People's Group at the University of Massachusetts, Center for Alternatives, Rm. 620, University of Massachusetts at Columbia Point, 02125. 617 287-1900, ext. 2396.
- Gay Professional Women's Association, P.O. Box 308, Boston University Station, 02115. Meets monthly in members' homes. Founded to help women meet others who share both a gay life-style and professional experiences.
- Lesbian Liberation, Women's Center. 617 354-8807.
- Lesbian Mothers, Women's Educational Center, 46 Pleasant St., Cambridge, 02139. 617 354-8807.
- Northeastern Gay Students Organization, Student Activities Office, 155 Ell Center, 360 Huntington Ave., 02115. 617 253-5440.
- NOW, 45 Newbury St., 02116. 617 267-6160.
- Parents of Gay, David Griffiths, 80 Boylston St., Suite 855, 02116. 617 542-5188.
- Radcliffe Gay Students Association, 198 Memorial Hall, Harvard University, Cambridge, 02138. 617 495-1927, 24 hours during school year.

Publications
- *Focus*, Daughters of Bilitis, 419 Boylston St., Rm. 323, 02116. Monthly. 60¢/issue.
- *Gay Community News*, GCN Inc., 22 Bromfield St., 02108. 617 426-4469. 25¢/issue; $2/year.

Religious Groups
- Metropolitan Community Church, 131 Cambridge St., 02114. 617 523-7664.

Services
- Amethyst Women, Gay Community News, Box 800, 22 Bromfield St., 02108. Do not have an office, just a mailing address. A collective of lesbians that sponsors social gatherings for lesbians, recovering alcoholics, and their women friends. A space to relax or socialize in alcohol-free environments and be with women committed to sobriety. (Name derived from the lavender stone used in ancient times to ward off drunkenness.)
- Beacon Tours, 160 Commonwealth Ave., 02116. 617 247-1832, Mon.-Fri. 9:30 A.M.-5 P.M.; Sat. 11 A.M.-2 P.M. Gay travel agency, lesbian-owned and managed. (Est.

40% lesbians.)
- Boston Gay Hotline, 617 426-9371, Mon.-Sat.
- Focus, Women's Counseling, 186 Hampshire St., Cambridge, 02138. 617 876-4488.
- Gay Alert, 617 523-0368 and 267-0764 (emergencies).
- Gayline Greetings, P.O. Box 1715, 02105. Mail-order greeting cards designed by gay artists. (Est. 66% lesbians.)
- Gay Health Collective of Boston, Fenway Community Health Center, 16 Haviland St., 02115. 617 267-7573. Office Mon.-Fri. 9 A.M.-5 P.M.; open Mon. and Wed. 6:30-8:30 P.M. by appointment. Lesbian health night second Mon. of each month. Provides total primary health care. (Est. 10% lesbians.)
- Gay Media Action, GCN Box 5000, 22 Bromfield St., 02108. 617 354-2079.
- Gay Speakers' Bureau, P.O. Box 2232, 02107. 617 354-0133, 11 A.M.-11 P.M. intermittently. Provides gay speakers for groups; general meetings two or three times a year. (Est. 50% lesbians.)
- Homophile Community Health Service, 80 Boylston St., Suite 855, 02116. 617 542-5188 or 542-6075, Mon.-Fri. 1-9 P.M. Licensed by Commonwealth of Massachusetts as a mental health clinic. Offers individual, group, and couple counseling by appointment. Three divisions: Boston Gay Hotline for crisis counseling and referrals; Division of Education coordinates library; and the Speakers Bureau does outreach to the community. Family services and alcoholism program. (Est. 40% lesbians.)
- Lesbian Therapy Research Project, Boston Psychological Center for Women, 617 266-0136.
- Meetinghouse Coffeehouse, 70 Charles St., 02114. 617 742-0405. Staffed by gays.
- Project Lambda, 70 Charles St., 02114. 617 227-8587, Mon.-Fri. 10 A.M.-6 P.M. Advocates for gay youth twelve to seventeen years old with regard to public and private agencies. Rap groups and activities. (Est. 50% lesbians.)
- WGBH Educational Foundation, Distribution Office, 125 Western Ave., 02134. 617 492-2777.

Cambridge
Bookstores
- New Words; A Women's Bookstore, 186 Hampshire St., 02139. 617 876-5310, staffed Tues., Wed., 10 A.M.-6 P.M.; Thurs. 10 A.M.-9 P.M.; Fri.-Sat. 10 A.M.-6 P.M.; Sun. 12-6 P.M.; closed Mon. (open same hours to public). Significant number of lesbian books, feminist press publications, all kinds of books by and about women, records, posters, etc.

Organizations
- Boston Dykes and Tykes, 46 Pleasant St., Cambridge, 02139. 617 354-8807. Brings together and supports lesbians involved with and/or interested in children. Lesbian mothers rap, Thurs. 8 P.M.

Publications
- The Second Wave, Inc., 20 Sacramento St. Mailing address: Box 344, Cambridge A, 02139. 614 491-1071, Tues. evenings. Radical-feminist publication. Publishes three or four times yearly; $1/issue; subscriptions

$4/individual; $4.50/institution. Staff 90% lesbians.
Restaurants
- Bread and Roses, 134 Hampshire St., 02139. 617 354-8371. Tues.-Sat. 5:30-9:30 P.M.; Sunday brunch, noon-2 P.M.; Sunday dinners, 6:30-10 P.M. by reservation, followed by concerts, movies, art shows of interest to women's community.
Services
- Janus Counseling Association, 21 Bay St., 02139. 617 661-2537. Mon.-Fri. by appointment. Empathetic and professional low-cost individual, group, and couple counseling to lesbians and women in transition. Massage and body work by appointment; lesbian-feminist workshop, Fri. 7:30-9:30 P.M.; lesbian mothers rap group, Thurs. 8-9 P.M. Counselors are lesbian.
- Women's Community Health, 137 Hampshire St., 02139. 617 547-2302, Mon.-Fri. 9 A.M.-5 P.M. Self-help educational groups concerned with lesbian health issues, etc. Participates in organizing functions to provide better health care to women. Publishes free annual report. (Est. 25% lesbians.)
- Women's Educational Center, Inc., 46 Pleasant St., Cambridge, 02139. 617 354-8807. Lesbian research project, lesbian liberation, etc.

Charlemont
Organizations
- Pioneer Valley Gay Union, Windy Hill Grace Church, 01370. Thurs. 7:30 P.M. Raps, political, social.

Fitchburg
Organizations
- Homophile Union of Montachusett, Box 262, 01420.

Haverhill
Services
- Gaypeople Drop-In Center, Campus Center, 100 Elliott St., 01830. Gayline: 617 327-0929.

Lowell
Religious Groups
- Dignity/Merrimack Valley, Box 348, 02853.

New Bedford
Services
- New Bedford Women's Health Center, 15 Chestnut St., 02740. 617 999-1070.

Northampton
Organizations
- Lesbian Gardens, 200 Main St., 01060. Irregular hours; events most week nights and occasional weekends. Any lesbian can schedule an event or meeting. Drop-in center, lesbian library, and bookstore. Publishes *Dyke Doings* once a month; free.
- Valley Women's Union, 200 Main St., 01060. 415 586-2011.
Publications
- Megaera Press, W.I.T., Inc., P.O. Box 745, 01060.
Services
- Greasy Gorgon Garage, W.I.T., Inc., Box 745, 01060.
- Nutcracker Suite (women's karate school), P. Turney, 23 Smith St., 01060.
- The Women's Film Coop, W.I.T., Inc., P.O.

Box 745, 01060. Lesbian distributors of lesbian and women's films.

North Quincy
Services
•Bay and Valley Counseling Associates, 29 Cottage Ave., 02169. Mailing address: P.O. Box 69, 02171. 617 883-8220, staffed as arranged. Psychological counseling for gay persons, individual, couples, group, family. Purpose is to help persons achieve their own designated maximum potential and relieve pain and suffering.

Provincetown
Organizations
•Gay Activists Alliance, General Delivery. 617 487-3393, 487-3234, 487-3344.
Services
•Everywoman's Resource Center, 14 Center, 02657. Mailing address: P.O. Box 949, 02657. Meetings Sun. 2 P.M. Ann Weld Harrington, Group leader, always open for information. Information given to women coming into Provincetown looking for jobs, housing, counseling. etc. (Est. 90% lesbians.) Gay Community Services, Box 815, 02657. Lower Cape Women's Center, Box 675, 02657. 617 487-3075.
•Provincetown Drop-In Center, Inc., 6 Gosnold St., 02657. Mailing address: P.O. Box 579. 617 487-0387, 24 hours daily. Center building open 10 A.M.-11 P.M. daily.
•Womancrafts, 373 Commercial St. Mailing address: Box 190, 02657. 617 487-9854. Women's Health Clinic, 14 Center St., 02657.

Randolph
Services
•Randolph Country Club, 44 Mazeo Drive, Rte. 139, 02368. 617 963-9809. Private club, swimming, disco.

Somerville
Bookstores
•New Words, 419 Washington St., 02143. 617 876-5310.

Springfield
Organizations
•Springfield Gay Alliance, P.O. Box 752. 413 583-3904.
Religious Groups
•Dignity, P.O. Box 488, Forest Park Station, 01108.

Westfield
Services
•Sexual Identity Awareness Organization, Sue Elmasion, Scanlon Hall, Westfield State College, 01085.

Worcester
Organizations
•Clark Gay Center, Wright Hall, Rm. 148, Downing St., 01610. Mailing address: Clark University, Box A-70, 01610. 617 793-7287, irregular hours. Political, social, educational organization. Gay rap, Tues. 8 P.M. Peer counseling, Sun.-Wed. 7-10 P.M. Socials, speakers' bureau. (Est. 40% lesbians.)
Religious Groups
•Metropolitan Community Church, 2 Wellington St., 01601. Gay Helpline, 75o-0730.
Services
•Gay Women's Rap Group, at "Another

Way," 64 Chandler St., 01609. 617 756-0730.

MICHIGAN
Allendale
Organizations
•Gay Alliance, Grand Valley State College, 49401.

Ann Arbor
Bookstores
•A Woman's Bookstore, 225 E. Liberty St., 48108. 313 995-3400. Mon.-Thurs. noon-8 P.M.; Fri. noon-5 P.M.; Sat. 11 A.M.-5 P.M. Women's bookstore and resource center. In process of forming Women's Social and Political Union. (Est. 75% lesbians.) Also: Feminist Library, 1003 Packard, #5, 48108.
Organizations
•Amazon Union, Gay Women's Advocates Office, 326 Michigan Union, 48104.
•Gay Advocates Office, 3405 Michigan Union, 48104. 313 763-4186.
•Gay Community Center, Guild House, 802 Monroe, 48104.
•Gay Liberation Front, 325 Michigan Union, 48104. 313 763-4186.
•Gay Women's Advocates Office, 326 Michigan Union, 48104. 313 763-4186.
Publications
•Her-Self, 225 E. Liberty, Suite 200, 48108. Community Women's newspaper.
Services
•Ann Arbor Lesbian Band, Susan, 533 N. Main, 48104.
•Gay Hotline, 616 761-2044.
•Library Project of A Woman's Bookstore, 1003 Packard, #5, 48104. 313 663-3027.

Birmingham
Services
•Identity Center, Inc., 37060 Garfield, Mt. Clemens. Mailing address: P.O. Box 464, 48012. 313 469-3311, by appointment. Individual, joint, and group psychotherapy.

Detroit
Media
•Lesbian Radio Collective, WDET-FM, 101.9 FM, 5035 Woodward Ave., 48202. 313 577-4146. Thurs. 11:30 P.M. (taping of shows on Tues.).
Organizations
•Parents of Gays, MCC-Detroit, Trinity Methodist Church, 13100 Woodward Ave., Highland Park, 48203. 313 534-9314. Sappho Sisters Rising, Box 573, 48232. 313 063-7193.
Publications
•Metro Gay News, P.O. Box 445, 48232. 313 956-7423. A paper for gay women and men that covers local, national, and international news.
Religious Groups
•Dignity, 2846 17th St., 48216. 313 894-1064.
•Metropolitan Community Church, 13100 Woodward Ave., 48203. 313 868-2122 and 869-8159. Publishes The Way.
Services
•Feminist Women's Health Center, 2445 West 8 Mile Rd., 48203. 313 892-7790, Mon.-Thurs. 9 A.M.-7 P.M.; Fri. 9 A.M.-5 P.M.; Sat. 9 A.M.-3 P.M. Preventive health care, gynecological services, prenatal and

abortion clinics, self-help, phone counseling and referrals. (Est. 50% lesbians.)
•Gay Switchboard, 313 577-3450, Mon.-Thurs. 6-10 P.M.; Fri., Sat. 6-11 P.M.

East Lansing
Bookstores
•Womanself Bookstore, University Mall, 220 M.A.C., 48823. 517 337-2404. Mon.-Sat. 10 A.M.-5:30 P.M. Feminist bookstore offering wide selection of lesbian titles, feminist books, feminist posters and stationery, lesbian and feminist jewelry, leather items, and records.
Organizations
•Gay Liberation Movement, 309 Student Services Building, Michigan State University, 48823. 517 353-9797, Mon.-Fri. noon-5 P.M.
Services
•Ambitious Amazons, P.O. Box 811, 48823. 517 371-5257, 24-hour service. A forum for and about lesbians nationwide. Publishes Lesbian Connection, eight times a year (news, articles, reviews, directories, etc.). Free.

Flint
Religious Groups
•Dignity, P.O. Box 281, 48501.

Grand Rapids
Organizations
•Western Michigan Gay Alliance, 250 Charles St., 49503. 616 456-7129.

Highland Park
Bookstores
•Her Shelf Wimmins Books and Crafts, 2 Highland, 48203. 313 869-4045. Wed.-Fri. 2-7 P.M.; Sun. noon-5 P.M. Collective meetings Tues. 7:30 P.M. Workshops and events monthly. Alternative children's books. Outlet for local craftswomen. (Est. 75% lesbians.)

Kalamazoo
Organizations
•Lambda of Kalamazoo, Inc., P.O. Box 2213, 49003. 616 344-7629. Staffed seven days, 9 A.M.-11 P.M. Meetings Thurs. 7:30 P.M. at People's Church, No. 10th St. Weekly meetings held to promote understanding of the dignity of individuals regardless of sexual orientation. Offer local information, legal referrals, speakers' bureau, raps, social events, political activities. Publishes Lambda Monthly at no charge locally. (Est. 25% lesbians.)

Lansing
Services
•Let's Be an Apple Pie, 427 Spring St., 48912. 517 484-3475. A lesbian center. Social, educational, political activities.

Mt. Clemens
Services
•Identity Center, Inc., 37060 Garfield (at Metro Parkway), 48043. Mailing address: P.O. Box 464, Birmingham, Mich. 48012. 313 469-3311. Psychotherapy for the gay community.

Mount Pleasant
Organizations
•Central Michigan Gay Liberation, Inc., Box 34 Warriner Hall, Central Michigan University, 48859. 517 774-3822 or 774-3823, Mon.-Fri. 8 A.M.-5 P.M. Regular activities

on Thurs. 8-10 P.M. in the University Center. A nonprofit organization open to all members of community and students at CMU. Provides peer counseling, speakers' bureau, research materials, library, etc. (Est. 75% lesbians.)

Okemos (Ann Arbor area)
Religious Groups
- Lutherans Concerned for Gay People—Michigan, 1577 Cranwood, 48864. 517 349-1843, anytime. Meets monthly at Lord of Light Lutheran Church, Hill at Forest, Ann Arbor. National newsletter *The Gay Lutheran* published ten times a year. 85¢/issue; $12/year with low income rates. (Est. 80% lesbians.)

Saginaw
Bars
- Dutch's Bar, 1742 E. Genesee Ave. 517 752-9179. Gay women and men.

Saugatuck
Hotel/Motel
- Saugatuck Lodges, 3169 Blue Star Highway, 49453. 616 857-4269, 24 hours daily. Indoor and outdoor sport and fun recreation. (They estimate 40% lesbians, but their flyer is very male-oriented!)

MINNESOTA
Duluth
Organizations
- Duluth Gay Group, Rt. 6, Box 382, 55804.
Services
- Arrowhead Gay Resource Center, Box 538, Civic Center Station, 55802.
- Women's Growth Center, 2 E. 5th St., 55805. Not yet staffed. Workshops, lesbian CR, etc. (Est. 40% lesbians.)

Manketo
Organizations
- Manketo Gay Consciousness, Box 58, Centennial Student Union, Manketo State College, 56001. 507 387-4408.

Minneapolis
Bookstores
- Amazon Bookstore, Inc., 2607 Hennepin Ave. South, 55408. 612 374-5507, Mon.-Fri. noon-8 P.M.; Sat. 10 A.M.-6 P.M. (Est. 50% lesbians.)
Organizations
- Families of Gays, Neighborhood Counseling Center, 1801 Nicollet Ave. South, 55403. 612 874-5369.
- Lesbian Feminist Organizing Committee, LRC, 2104 Stevens Ave. South, 55407. 612 871-2601, Mon.-Fri. 11 A.M.-4 P.M. General membership meeting second Sun. of month 7-9:30 P.M. Autonomous political organization to identify issues and create strategies, especially relating to lesbian visibility and power. Standing committees: FBI-grand jury resistance, class consciousness, self-defense, and ad-hoc committees.
- Lesbian Resources Center, 2104 Stevens Ave. South, 55404. 612 871-2601. Publishes *So's Your Old Lady, Le'sbeinformed.* Metro Gay Students Union, Metropolitan State Junior College, 50 Willow St., 55403. Minnesota Committee for Gay Rights, Box 4226, St. Anthony Falls Station, 55414. 612 871-3111 (messages).

- Minnesota Women's Alliance, Box 14362, 55414. Professional gay women's group.
Religious Groups
- Dignity/Twin Cities, P.O. Box 3565, 55403. Meets second and fourth Fri. of month 7:30 at Newman Center, University of Minnesota, 1701 University Ave., S.E. Provides support and alternative social settings for gay Catholics, education, and works for reform. Publishes *Minnesota Gay Christian.* Monthly. $3/year. (Est. 10% lesbians.)
- Gay Quakers, 3208 Portland Ave., South, 55407.
- Gay United Methodists, 923 Fuller St., S.E., 54414.
- Metropolitan Community Church of the Twin Cities, 44th and York Ave. South, 55410. 612 920-3787. Emergency number 612 432-8499. Wed. evenings and Sundays 2 P.M. Other events throughout the week. (Est. 30% lesbians.)
Services
- Christopher St., 1111 W. 22nd St., 55405. 612 374-9550, Mon.-Fri. 10 A.M.-6 P.M. Provides counseling and treatment for drug-dependent gay people, also counseling on sexual abuse for both gay and straight communities. Mon.-Fri. 6-10 P.M. (Est. 50-80% lesbians.)
- Gay Community Services, 1725 Nicollet, 55403. Mailing address: P.O. Box 3589, Upper Nicollet Station, 55403. 612 871-3111, noon-10 P.M. Counseling and advocacy for gay and lesbian community. Workshops, educational services.
- Gay House, Inc., 4419A Nicollet, 55409. 612 824-4449, Mon.-Fri. 2-10 P.M.
- Lavender AA for Gays, Pharm House, 1911 Pleasant Ave. South, 55403.
- Maiden Rock: Women's Learning Institute, Inc., Box 8587, 55408. 612 824-5706, Mon., Tues., Thurs., Fri. 2-5 P.M. Collective working to establish a feminist learning institute. Various programs offered each month.
- Sagaris, 2619 Garfield Ave. South, 55408. 612 825-7338.
- Women's Coffeehouse, 2104 Stevens Ave. S., 55404.

Northfield
Organizations
- Carleton College Gay Friends, Carleton College, 55057.

Ortonville
Organizations
- Shalom, Box 523, 56278.

Rochester
Organizations
- Lambda Friends, P.O. Box 454, 55901.

St. Paul
Bars
- Townhouse, 1415 University Ave. 612 646-9267. Recommended.

MISSISSIPPI
Biloxi
Bars
- Casa Blanca, 220 Pat Harrison Ave. Recommended.

Jackson
Organizations
- Jackson Women's Coalition, P.O. Box 3234,

39207. Regular meetings, discussions, study groups.
- Mississippi Gay Alliance, P.O. Box 8342, 39204. 601 353-6447 and 372-3449 (switchboard).
- Mississippi Lesbians, 1003 Walnut. Mailing address: Box 8342, 39204. 601 355-6935.
Publications
- Lesbian Front, P.O. Box 8342, 39204. $5/year.
Services
- Mississippi Prisoners' Defense Committee, Ms. L. C. Dorsey, 223 N. Farish St., 39201. 601 948-5400.

Mississippi State
Services
- Gay Counseling and Educational Projects, Mississippi Gay Alliance, Box 4470, Mississippi State University, 39762.

MISSOURI
Columbia
Organizations
- Gay Liberation/Columbia, Box 1672, 65201. Gay Liberation Executive Board, Ecumenical Center, 813 Maryland Ave.
- Gay Liberation Front, University of Missouri, Lawrence Eggleston, 1723 Worley Rd., Apt. 6A, 65201.
- Missouri Alliance for Gay Rights, Box 1672, 65201.
Publications
- Women's Defender, 110 W. Ash, #48, 65201. 314 442-2329.

Joplin
Organizations
- Committee for Gay Justice, Pride Community Center, 207 W. 4th St., 64800. Free monthly publication.
Religious Groups
- MCC of Joplin, 207 W. 4th St., Suite 321, 64801. 314 781-9494, 7-11 P.M. Worship Sun. 8 P.M. Counseling, holy unions, religious services. (Est. 10% lesbians.)
Services
- Pride Community Center, 207 W. 4th St., 64800. 314 781-9494.

Kansas City
Bookstores
- New Earth Bookstore, 24 E. 39th St., 64111. 816 931-5494, Mon.-Sat. 9 A.M.-6 P.M.; Thurs. 9 A.M.-9 P.M. Feminist-owned and -operated bookstore which serves as a referral network for getting women in touch with services. (Est. 75% lesbians.)
Organizations
- Joint Committee for Gay Rights, Box 19522, 64141.
- Lesbian Alliance, KC Women's Liberation Union, 3621 Charlotte, 64109. 816 276-1470.
- Parents of Gays, Phyllis Shafer, 1838 E. 49th St., 64130. 816 921-7779.
Religious Groups
- Metropolitan Community Church, 4000 Harrison. Mailing address: Box 5206, 64112. 816 921-5754.

Maplewood
Services
- Tigmait Press, 7213 Lanham, 63143. 314 644-3059. Mon.-Fri. 10 A.M.-5 P.M. Lesbian print shop. Typesetting, layout, design,

printing, and binding. Charge on sliding scale.

St. Joseph
Bars
- First Word, 2102 St. Joseph Ave.

St. Louis
Bookstores
- Left Bank Bookstore, 6254 Delmar, 63130. 314 862-9327.
- Woman's Eye, 905 Yale Ave., 63117.

Organizations
- Gay People's Alliance, Box 1068, Washington University, 63130.
- Parents of Gays, Arthur and Marian Wirth, 7443 Cromwell Dr., 63105. 314 863-2748.

Publications
- Moonstorm, P.O. Box 4201, Tower Grove Station, 63163. Meetings Mon. 8 P.M. Issues focus on political analysis and changing attitudes on sexism, racism, classism. Publicizes women's news, activities. Twice a year. 75¢/issue; subscription $4.50/6 issues.

Religious Groups
- Dignity/St. Louis, Box 10075, 64111.
- MCC of Greater St. Louis, 5108 Waterman Ave., 63108. Mailing address: P.O. Box 3147, 63130. 314 361-7284, Mon.-Fri. 11 A.M.-4 P.M., 7-10 P.M.; Sat. 9 A.M.-5 P.M. Worship Sun. 2 P.M. and Wed. 8 P.M. A.I. and Alanon Thurs. 7:30 P.M. Coffeehouse Fri. 8 P.M. Ecumenical Christian church. Free monthly newsletter. (Est. 50% lesbians.)

Services
- Independent Contractors Association, 4539 Gibson St., 63110. 314 865-2832, various hours or tape message. Office open 9 A.M.-4:30 P.M. or by appointment. New roofs, repairs, painting, chimney rebuilding. Sliding scale payments, time payments, skill and tool sharing. Provide free labor to limited number of poor people. A collective. (Est. 50% lesbians.)
- Metropolitan Life Services Center, 4748-A McPherson Ave., 63108. 314 367-0447. Referrals, space to rap, health clinic, gay older people. Publishes *Prime Time.*
- Metropolitan Life Services Center Gay Hotline. 314 367-0084.
- St. Louis Women's Counseling Center, 6808 Washington Ave., 63130. 314 725-9158, 24-hour answering service. Counseling, medical and legal referrals, workshops, etc.
- Women's Car Repair Collective, 3610 Botanical Ave., 63110. 314 644-0922.

Springfield
Organizations
- L.I.F.E., P.O. Box 161, 65801.

MONTANA
Billings
Organizations
- Billings Coalition for Women's Rights, Rm. 300, 804 N. 29th, 59101. 406 248-8892.

Great Falls
Bars
- Forum Club, 204 First Ave. 406 761-9580. Recommended.

Missoula
Organizations
- Lambda, 770 Eddy, #4, 59801. Now just gay men, but they are trying to start a group for women.
- Women's Resource Center, University of Montana at Missoula, 59801. Gay women's rap group.

NEBRASKA
Lincoln
Organizations
- University of Nebraska Gay Action Group and Lincoln Gay Action Group, 333 N. 14th St., 65808. 402 475-5710, 8 P.M.-2 A.M. (Gay Rap Line); other times, 402 432-6561. Publishes *Gay Nebraskan.*

Publications
- Growing Season, 520 N. 28th, 68503. Regular gay movement column and feminist concerns.

Services
- Gay Rap Line, 402 475-5710, evenings. Women's Resource Center, Rm. 126, Nebraska Union, 1400 R St., 68588. 402 472-2597.

Omaha
Bars
- Bottleneck, 402 472-2597 for details. Dance bar. Only open Sun. evenings.
- The Cave Under the Hill, 506 S. 16th St. (at Howard). 402 346-9983.

Omaha
Religious Groups
- First Metropolitan Community Church of

Nebraska, 803 N. 20th St., 68102. 402 345-2563.

NEVADA
Reno
Organizations
- The Ladder (Reno Daughters of Bilitis), P.O. Box 5025, Washington Station, 89503. 816 633-4136.

Publications
- Naiad Press, Inc., P.O. Box 5025, Washington Station, 89503. 816 633-4136. A lesbian-feminist publishing company specializing in lesbian fiction, nonfiction, and poetry. Only lesbian material considered and published. Seven titles in print.

NEW HAMPSHIRE
Concord
Organizations
- New Hampshire Lambda, P.O. Box 1043, 03301. 603 228-8542. Political support for lesbian life-style. Membership lesbians only. Meets third Sun. of the month 6:30 P.M. Call for place.

Lebanon
Services
- New Victoria Printers, 7 Banks St., 03766. A women's collective.

Littleton
Bookstores
- Tigris-Euphrates, Women's Concern Center, 20 Main St., 03561. Mailing address: Box 6, Plainfield, Vt. 05667. 603 444-3349. Tues.-Sat. 11 A.M.-6 P.M. Books, records, magazines available in store and traveling van. Finances women's activities with profits and maintains a directory of women with skills to offer. (Est. 99% lesbians.)

Manchester
Bars
- 484 Club, 484 Chestnut. Dancing, show bar.

Northwood
Organizations
- Occupant, Box 137, 03216. Contact group to women who want to meet others, rap, etc. A chapter of Daughters of Bilitis.

Portsmouth
Organizations
- Seacoast Area Gay Alliance, Box 1424, 03801. 603 436-7196.

NEW JERSEY
Atlantic City
Bars
- Chez Paree, 235 N. New York Ave. Ocean House, 127 S. Ocean Ave. 609 345-8203.
- Other Door, 12 S. Mt. Vernon Ave.

Belvidere
Services
- Lambda Book Club, P.O. Box 248, 07823. Features quality gay literature. Lifetime membership $10.

Convent Station
Organizations
- Gay Activist Alliance in Morris County, P.O. Box 137, 07961. 201 884-0653, 347-6234 eves. Meetings 8:30 P.M. Mon., Morristown Unitarian Fellowship, Normandy Hts. Sapphic Sisters, P.O. Box 137, 07961. 201

627-4340, Mon.-Fri. 4-11 P.M. Meetings third Wed. of the month 8:30 P.M. at Valley Stream Gardens, Apt. D-7, Savage Rd., Denville. Provides a supportive forum to develop new consciousness of self in relation to other women, and focal point for social, educational, and political activities. (Est. 50% lesbians.)

Cranbury
Organizations
• Parents of Gays, Evelyn and Floyd Bull, Princeton Arms North, Apt. 150, 08512. 609 448-4537.

Dover
Bars
• Mine Hill Tavern, Randolph Ave.

East Orange
Bars
• Penelope's, 611 Central Ave. 201 673-7710. Highly recommended.
Publications
• Albatross, 111 S. Harrison St., Box 112, 07017. 201 OR4-4111. Radical lesbian-feminist satire magazine. News, poetry, fiction, humor-comix, etc. Quarterly. $1.50/ issue; subscription $7/6 issues.

Elizabeth
Bars
• The Barrel House, 40 W. Grand.

Garwood
Organizations
• United Sisters, P.O. Box 41, 07027. 201 233-3848, Mon.-Fri. 10 A.M.-3 P.M. (try other times). Meeting second Fri. of month; third Fri. when month has five Fridays. Meeting place varies; call or write for information. Social-service group for women by lesbians. Educational, civil rights; emphasis on helping lesbians. Referrals to professionals of all types, hotline, peer counseling, speakers' bureau, etc. Publishes *The Puce Mongoose* eleven times a year. Local news, political articles, etc. $5/year. (Mainly lesbians.)

Glassboro
Organizations
• Together, Inc., 7 State St., 08028. 609 881-4040.

Hackensack
Organizations
• Gay Activists Alliance of New Jersey, 178 Kansas St. Mailing address: Box 1734, South Hackensack, 07606. 201 343-6402.
• Gay Teachers Caucus of National Education Association, 32 Bridge St., 07601. 201 489-2458.

Irvington
Religious Groups
• Dignity/Metro New Jersey, P.O. Box 337, 07111. 201 575-0338, 6:30-10:30 P.M. daily. Provides gay Catholics with religious and social experience, counseling, and educates the Church on gay needs as Christians. Home liturgies. Free monthly publication, *Icthus.*

Jersey City
Organizations
• Gay Rights of People Everywhere (GROPE),

Jersey City State College, SGAC, 2039 Kennedy Blvd., 07305. 201 432-8815.
Religious Groups
• United Inter Faith Church, 132 Bergen, 07305. 201 659-3840.

Mahwah
Organizations
• Alternative Sexual Lifestyles Association, Ramapo College. 201 825-2800, ext. 463, Mon.-Wed. 12:30-2:30 P.M.; Thurs. 6-8 P.M.; Room 1204 Student Life Building. Counseling, dances, speakers.

Montclair
Services
• Drop-in Center, Montclair State College, Upper Montclair, 07043. 201 893-5271.

Morristown/Convent Station
Organizations
• Gay Activists Alliance in Morris County, P.O. Box 137, Convent Station, 07961. 201 884-0653 or 347-6234, evenings. Meets Mon. 8:30 P.M., Morristown Unitarian Fellowship, Normandy Heights Rd. Publishes *Challenge*, free with membership. (Est. 40% lesbians.)

Newark
Organizations
• Rutgers Activists for Gay Education (RAGE), Box 8, 350 High St., 07102.
Religious Groups
• Dignity/Metropolitan N.J., Box 337, Irvington, 07111.

New Brunswick
Organizations
• Rutgers University Coalition of Lesbian-Feminists, Women's Center, Tillet Hall, Livingston College, 08903. 201 932-4678.
• Rutgers University Homophile League, RPO 2901, Rutgers University, 08903. 201 932-7886. Rutgers Student Center, Rm. 304.
Publications
• The Jersey Lesbian, J. Lee Lehman, Botany Department, Rutgers University, 08903.
Services
• Women's Crisis Center, 201 828-7273.

Orange
Organizations
• Organization for Gay Awareness, Box 41, 07050.

Paterson
Bars
• The Coach, 541 Union Ave.
• Joan's Key Club, Union Ave.
• Pad I, 389 Madison Ave.

Plainfield
Bars
• Colonial House, Park Ave. and 7th St., 07060. 201 756-4434. Dinner and dancing.

Princeton
Organizations
• Gay Alliance of Princeton, 306 Green Annex, Princeton University, 08540. 609 452-5338.
• Gay People, Princeton, Box 2303, 08540.
Services
• Gay Switchboard, 602 921-2565.

• Princeton Women's Center, 201 Green Annex, Princeton University, 08540.

Princeton Junction
Services
• New Jersey Gay Switchboard and Information Center, Box 323, 08550. 609 921-2565.

South River
Services
• The Sea Shell Lounge, 21 Ferry St., 08882. 201 254-9812. Tues.-Sun. 8:30 P.M.-2 A.M. Closed Mon. A bar, with women's nights on Thurs. and Sun.

Trenton
Bars
• Forty West, 40 West State St.
 Zodiac, South Clinton Ave.
Organizations
• Gay Student Organization Mercer C.C.C., Box B, 08690.

Union
Bars
• Nite Light, 509 22nd St. 201 863-9515.

Wayne
Organizations
• Gay Activists Alliance, William Paterson College, Student Center, 300 Pompton Rd., 07470. 201 881-2151.

NEW MEXICO
Albuquerque
Bookstores
• A Woman's Gallery, 302 Rio Grande Blvd., N.W., 87104. 505 243-0291. 10:30 A.M.-5:30 P.M. daily (store open). Art gallery and bookstore carrying feminist and lesbian titles. (Est. 66.6% lesbians.)
Organizations
• Juniper, Student Union Building, University of New Mexico, 87131. 505 777-2564.
• New Mexico Gay People's Union, 3214 Silver, S.E., 87106.
Religious Groups
• Metropolitan Community Church, P.O. Box 26554, 87155. 505 299-0512. Worship: 113 Alvarado, N.E. Parsonage: 9905 Bellamah, N.E., 87112.
Services
• The Women's Center, 1824 Las Lomas, N.E., 87106. 505 277-3716.

San Juan Pueblo
Organizations
• Circle of Loving Companions, P.O. Box 8, 87566. 505 852-4404. A self-sustaining, labor-intensive collective to further gay consciousness' growth, development, and nationwide contributions.

NEW YORK
Albany
Organizations
• Capital District Gay Political Caucus, Box 131, 12201.
• Gay Alliance, SUNY Albany, Box 1000 DD, SUNY Station, 12203.
• Lesbians for Liberation in the Capital District, Gay Community Counsel, Box 131, 12201. 518 462-6138.

Religious Groups
- Dignity, 95 Chestnut St., 12210. 518 462-6138.

Services
- Capital District Gay Community Center, 332 Hudson Ave., 12210. Mailing address: Box 131, 12201. 518 462-6138, 7-11 P.M. daily. Counseling, rap sessions, movies, speakers, assertive workshops, social events, meeting space for political or religious groups, backpacking, life drawing, etc. (Est. 10% lesbians). Publishes *Gay Report.* Monthly. Single issue free; subscription rate $2.
- Gay Community House, 332 Hudson Ave., 12210. 518 462-6138. Mon.-Sat. 7-11 P.M.; Sun. 3-11 P.M.

Annandale-On-Hudson
Organizations
- Gay Liberation Front, Bard College, Box 87, 12504.

Athol
Services
- A Woman's Place, Athol, 12810. 518 623-9541. Feminist retreat open all year.

Aurora
Organizations
- Gay Students Organization, Wells College, 13025.

Bayshore
Bars
- Pat and Scottie's Lounge, 24 Ackerson, Long Island, 11706.

Binghamton
Organizations
- Binghamton Gay Liberation, Box 2000, Harpur College, State University of New York, 13901. 607 798-4470.

Buffalo
Bookstores
- Emma, Buffalo Women's Bookstore, 2223 Fillmore, 14214. 716 836-8970. Tues.-Sat. noon-7 P.M. Carries literature about lesbian and feminist movement, nonsexist, nonracist children's books. Also resource center for community, coalition work, cosponsor feminist and progressive events. (Est. 50% lesbians.)

Media
- Sappho, WBFO-FM, 88.7 FM, 3435 Main St., 14214. 716 831-5394. Mon. 9:30-10 P.M.

Organizations
- Gay Liberation Front/SUNYAB. College F (Tolstoy) House, Winspear Ave., 14212. 716 831-5386.
- Sisters of Sappho, c/o Buffalo Women's Center, 499 Franklin St., 14202. 716 881-5335 (switchboard). Publishes *Lavender Grapevine.*
- Student Alliance for Gay Equality (SAGE), 1300 Elmwood Ave., 14222.

Services
- Gay Community Services Center, 1350 Main St., 14209. 718 881-5335, Mon.-Fri. 2-10 P.M.; Sat. 1 P.M.-3 A.M.; Sun. 1-6 P.M.

Congers
Bars
- Porthole, 75 Rt. 9 West.

Craryville
Services
- Women's Ways, Box 375A, Rte. 11, 12521. 518 325-6612. A women's retreat, open all year. 2½ hours north of New York City.

Elmira
Bars
- Mary's Grill, 112 Lake St., 14901.

Farmingdale
Services
- Gay Evolution Center, 3 Dolphin Dr., 11735; 699 Oriole Ave., West Hempstead, N.Y. 11552. 516 752-0225. Mon.-Fri. 10 A.M.-10 P.M. Offers psychotherapy for gays and bisexuals. Lesbian therapists available.

Fredonia
Organizations
- Fredonia Women's Collective, c/o SA; Campus Center, State U. at Fredonia 14063. 617 673-2381,2. Mon.-Fri. 9 A.M.-5 P.M.
- Homophile Education of Fredonia, State University College, Student Center, SGA office, 14063. 617 673-3424.

Gardiner
Services
- Women's Communique, Scarlet Pimpernel, P.O. Box 248, 12525. 914 255-5525, 9-5 P.M., or 914 255-5984 anytime; opens at 4 P.M. Professional and referral services provided. Regular activities held at Oh Susannah, Inc., Cafe, 171 Main Street, New Paltz, N.Y. 12561.

Genesco
Organizations
- Gay Freedom Coalition, Box 38, College Union, State University College, 14454. 716 245-5891.

Greenlawn
Organizations
- New York National Assciation of Social Workers, Lesbian Committee, Lucy Lenner, 10 Northgate Dr., Long Island, 11740. 516 261-1931.

Hempstead
Organizations
- Hofstra United Gays, Box 67, Student Center, Hofstra University, Long Island, 11550.

Services
- Women's Liberation Center of Nassau County, 14 W. Columbia St., Long Island, 11550. 516 292-8106, Mon. Thurs., Fri. 11 A.M.-2 P.M.

Ithaca
Organizations
- Cornell Gay Liberation, Gay People's Center, 306 State St., 14850.

Services
- Ithaca Gay People's Center, 306 E. State St., 14850. 607 277-0306. Counseling and social events. Publishes *Lavender Opinion.*

Jamestown
Services
- Lambda, 14 E. 12th St., 14701. Mailing address: Box 273, 14701. 716 487-1878. Discussions, dances, etc.

Lake Ronkonkoma
Bars
- Chardy's, 2850 Ponds Rd., Long Island, 516 588-6868.

Lindenhurst
Bars
- Dockside, 771 South, Long Island. 516 226-9838.

Liverpool (Syracuse area)
Bookstores
- Sister Bear Bookstore, 401 1st St., 13088. 315 457-7777, Thurs., Fri. 3:30-9 P.M.; Sat. noon-5 P.M. Wide selection of lesbian literature, also posters, jewelry, records, and resource information. *Spokesbear* published monthly. Single issue free; subscription for stamps.

Livingston Manor
Organizations
- Sullivan County Gay Liberation, Tim, Box 191, 12758.

New York City
Bookstores
- Djuna Books, 154 W. 10th St., 10014. 212 242-4868. Winter hours: Tues.-Thurs. 8 A.M.-11 P.M. Fri., Sat. noon-9 P.M.; Sun. noon-7 P.M. Books, posters, records, nonsexist children's books. Good selection of lesbian books. Open to all women. Monthly readings and women's art exhibition.
- Feminist Book Exchange, 37 St. Marks Place, 10033. 212 777-7240. Out of print, feminist, mail order.
- Oscar Wilde Memorial Bookshop, 15 Christopher St., 10014. 212 255-8097. Mon.-Sat. 11 A.M.-6 P.M.; Sun. noon-5 P.M. Literature on gay themes and/or by gay authors. Periodicals, etc., for lesbians and gay males. Catalog $1. Also permanent mailing list.
- Womanbooks Bookstore, 201 W. 92nd St., 10025. 212 873-4121. Open to public, Tues.-Sat. 10 A.M.-8 P.M.; Sun. noon-6 P.M. Closed Mon. Featuring women's presses, periodicals, books, records by and about women. Nonsexist children's books, children's play area, bulletin board, lounge area. Coffee, tea available. Sponsors events, discussions, readings, etc.
- Gay and Women's Alliance for Responsible Media, Box 48, GPO, 11202. 212 624-8067.

Media
- Gay Media Alert Network, National Gay Task Force, 80 Fifth Ave., 10011. 212 741-1014.
- Gay Media Coalition, Women's Center, 243 W. 20th St., 10011. 212 691-5460.

Organizations
- All the Queens Women, 36-23 164th St., Flushing, N.Y. 11358. 212 359-9204, Mon.-Thurs. 10 A.M.-5 P.M.; Fri.-Sat. 10 A.M.-4 P.M.; Sun. noon-4 P.M. A resource center, help line, Rap groups (lesbians, older women, sexuality, mothers, divorce), employment counseling, brunches, bimonthly lesbian dance. Publishes *Womanspace.* Monthly. 25¢/issue; $2/year. (Est. 50% lesbians.)
- Dykes and Tykes, Box 621, Old Chelsea Station, 10011. 212 929-0096 or 677-7626. Rap groups, events for women and children,

benefits, dances, concerts. Support organization for lesbians relating to children. Summer training program in paralegal custody counseling will lead to custody counseling clinic in the fall. Benefits for East Coast Lesbian Mothers Defense Fund. Publishes *Dykes & Tykes Newsletter.* Bimonthly. Single issue free; $3/year.

- Gay Academic Union, Box 480, Lenox Hill Station, 10021.
- Gay City Workers, 916 Union St., 11215. 212 857-6549.
- Gay Community at Queens College, Queens, Student Activities, 11367.
- Gay Human Rights League of Queens County, Box 1224, Flushing, Queens, 11352. 463-2938.
- Gay Liberation Front, Long Island University, Student Activities, 365 Flatbush Ave. Extension, 12201.
- Gay Parents, Church of the Beloved Disciple, 348 W. 14th St., 10014. 212 242-6616.
Gay People at City College, City College, Finley Student Center, Rm. 408, 10031. Mon.-Fri. 10 A.M.-11 P.M. Provides community and social atmosphere conducive to gay life-styles, rap sessions, culture festivals, counseling, referral services. (Est. 33% lesbians.)
- Gay People at Columbia, 304 Earl Hall, Broadway and 116th St., 10027. 212 280-3574.
- Gay People's Union at NYU, Loeb Student Center, 566 La Guardia Place, Rm. 810, 10003.
- Gay Socialist Coordinating Committee, Box 1039, Cathedral Station, 10025.
- Gay Social Services Alliance, 345 W. 21st St., Apt. 1A, 10011. 212 243-8683 (ask for Ron Ginsberg or leave message).
- Gay Students League of New York Community College, Student Activities, 300 Jay St., 11201. 212 824-6334.
- Gay Women's Alternative, Unitarian-Universalist Church, 4 West 76th St. (Central Park West), 10023. 212 532-8669. Holds Thurs. night talks, 8 P.M., followed by wine and cheese social. Dances on holidays. Speakers etc. mid-Sept. through mid-June.
- Hiking Dykes, 212 569-1888 or 699-2553.
Lesbian Activists at Barnard College, McIntosh Center, Rm. 106, 10027.
- Lesbian Feminist Liberation, Inc., 243 W. 20th St. 10011. 212 691-5460, Mon.-Fri. 2-6 P.M. Meetings Mon. 7:30 P.M. (general business); Sun. afternoon (various programs and discussions). Political and social group to serve the lesbian community. Dances and concerts. Publishes every two months, *Lesbian Feminist,* which addresses issues of interest to the lesbian community. Donation—no set price.
- Lesbians Rising Collective, Hunter College Women's Center, 47 E. 65th St., 10021. 212 360-5162. Meetings Mon. 1-3 P.M. Gay peer counseling at Hunter, 360-2118.
Lesbians United, Richmond College, Student Government, 130 Stuyvesant Place, Rm. 542, Staten Island, 10301.
- National Gay Task Force, 80 Fifth Ave.,

10011. 212 741-1010, Mon.-Fri. 10 A.M.-6 P.M. Membership, $15. A clearinghouse for the national gay movement, and a political force promoting gay civil rights legislation and a positive image of lesbians and gay men in the media. Lesbian visibility is a special concern.
- Parents of Gays, Metropolitan Duane Community Church, 201 W. 13th St. (at 7th Ave.), 10011; Attn. S. Montgomery. 212 674-5543. Helps parents and their gay daughters and sons to a better understanding of each other. Helping to pass the National Gay Civil Rights bill, consenting adults in private, repeal lewd and lascivious statutes, and change attitudes in the community and throughout the nation. Printed material available for 24¢ stamped legal-sized envelope.
- Pratt Gay Union, Student Affairs, Pratt Institute, 11205. 212 636-3505.
Rainbow Empire Alliance, Thomas P. Kane, 189 Second Ave., 10003. Deaf gay community.
- Third World Gay Women, Washington Square Church, 133 W. 4th St., 10012.
Women's Liberation Center, 243 West 20th St. (8th Ave.), 10011. 212 255-9802, Mon.-Fri. 2-6 P.M. Activities for lesbians and feminists. Lesbian Feminist Liberation, AA, Al-Anon, Switchboard, Lesbian Overeaters (Thurs. 8:30 P.M.), and Gay Older Women's Liberation (Mon. 8:30 P.M.), Lesbian Feminist Liberation (Mon. 7:30 P.M.).

Publications
- Dyke Quarterly, Tomato Publications, 70 Barrow St., 10014. Publication has essays, interviews, photos, drawings, reviews of lesbian culture and politics. Single issue price, $2.25 at stores ($2.75 by mail); subscription rate, $8/year; Canada, $10/year; overseas, $16/year.

Religious Groups
- Church of the Beloved Disciple, Eucharistic Catholic, 348 W. 14th St., 10014. 212 242-6616, 10 A.M.-5 P.M. daily. Morning liturgy 11 A.M.; parish eucharist 2 P.M.; evening liturgy, 7 P.M. Parish hall open to the community during the week. Monthly publication. (Est. 20% lesbians.)

Services
- ACLU Sexual Privacy Project, 22 E. 40th St., 10016. 212 725-1222.
- City College Women's Center, 133rd St. and Convent Ave., 10031, Rm. 152, Finley Hall. 212 690-8153, Mon.-Fri. 9 A.M.-2 P.M. Programs, usually Thurs. noon-2 P.M.; place varies. Provide information on women's activities; counseling; political caucus; women's prison collective; library. (Est. 35% lesbians.)
- Come! Unity Press, 13 E. 17th St. 212 675-3043. Gay anarchist collective teaching printing to movement groups and individuals. Provides access to photo-offset equipment for noncommercial use.
- Earth and Fire Productions, 16 Jane St., Apt. 2D, 10014. 212 691-7380. Irregularly staffed; answering service. Produces fundraising events for women only. Cosponsors events with lesbian or gay groups. Does pub-

licity and technical arrangements.

- Eve's Garden, Ltd., Suite 1406, 119 West 57th St., 10019. 212 245-1432. Open to public: Mon.-Fri. noon to 6:30 P.M.; Sat. noon to 5 P.M. A body awareness and sensuality boutique created by women for women. A place where women can obtain books on female sexuality, and pleasurable things in a supportive, feminist environment. A mail order catalog is available on request.
- Gay Older Women's Liberation (GAY OWL), Women's Center, 243 W. 20th St., 10011.
- The Homosexual Community Counseling Center, 30 E. 60th St., 10022. 212 688-0628. Appointments made by calling at any time. Moderate fees charged. Trained and experienced specialists (certified psychiatrists, psychologists, psychoanalysts, clergy, sex educators, etc.) committed to optimal development of each client in terms of his or her own values through a broad spectrum of counseling and psychotherapy. Also sponsors conferences throughout America, a speakers' bureau, and publishes a professional quarterly, *Homosexual Counseling Journal.*
- Identity House, 544 Sixth Ave., 10011. 212 243-8181, Sat.-Tues. 6-10 P.M. Sat., women only. Free peer counseling for lesbians. CR groups, raps, Sat. 2:30-5 P.M. $1.50 donation.
- Institute for Human Identity, 490 West End Ave., 10024. 212 798-9432. Counseling for gays and bisexuals. Individual and group therapy. Staffed by peers and professionals. Fee based on ability to pay.
- Lambda Legal Defense and Education Fund, Inc., Box 5448, Grand Central Station, 10017. 212 758-1905.
- Lesbian Al-Anon, 243 W. 20th St., 10011. 212 473-6200. Meets Fri. 6:30 P.M. For lovers and families of alcoholics.
- Lesbian Alcoholics Anonymous, Women's Center, 243 W. 20th St., 10011. 212 473-6200. Meets Wed. 6:30 P.M.
- Lesbian Discussion and Social Group, Metropolitan Community Church, 201 W. 13th St. Mailing address: Box 1757, 10011. 212 691-7428.
- Lesbian Herstory Archives, P.O. Box 1258, 10001. 212 874-7232 or TR3-9443 (all by appointment). Both a library and a "family album." Place for lesbians to do reading and research. Over 2,000 books, most lesbian newsletters, journals, tapes, records, photos, original poetry, research papers. Publishes *Lesbian Herstory Archives Newsletter* three times a year. Donation payment. Run by a five-woman collective.
- Lesbians and Gay Men's Counseling at NYU, 566 La Guardia Place, Rm. 608, 10003. 212 598-3806. Walk-in and phone counseling.
- Lesbians of New York University, Loeb Center, 566 La Guardia Place, Rm. 408, 10012. Coffeehouse on Thurs. 8 P.M.
- Lesbian Switchboard, Women's Center, 243 W. 20th St., 10011. 212 741-2610, Mon.-Fri. 6-9 P.M. Serves as referral, help, and rap line. Publishes *Referral Portfolio*, a listing of

organizations, social places, etc. for lesbian community (updated every two months). 20¢ contribution.

- Onawa; A Growth Center for Women, 76 Clinton Ave., Staten Island, 10301. 212 351-5300. Presents a variety of one-time and ongoing workshops on the interrelationship between our emotions and relationships. A referral for individual, couple, or family therapy or an ongoing therapy group. Out and Out Books, 476 Second St., Brooklyn, 11215. 212 499-9227, hours staffed flexible, 7 days. A women's independent press, publishing and distributing books by women. The emphasis is on lesbian literature. Wide selection of fine books, can be ordered by mail; add postage/handling of 35¢ for each order of up to 2 books, 15¢ for each additional book.
- St. Marks Clinic, 44 St. Marks Place, 10003. 212 533-9500. Tues. 5-10 P.M., women's night. General medical clinic serving women. Emphasis is on whole body care; preventive care and screening as well as diagnosis and treatment are done. Would like to function as a family doctor for the lesbian community. The clinic has been operating for three years and has a staff of eight to ten women.
- The Virginia Woolf House (for Women in Conflict or Crisis). Temporary address: 2 Stony Hill, W. Nyack, 10994 or Kupferman, 305 E. 11st St. Meetings at Women's Coffee House and members' homes. Planning a house or loft by September 1977. Lesbians only; other women will be referred to other appropriate agencies or groups.
- West Side Discussion Group, 37 Ninth Ave. Mailing address: Box 611, Old Chelsea Station, 10011. 212 675-0143. Counseling, free therapy groups.
- Wise Women Enterprises, Inc., P.O. Box 297, West Station, 10014. 212 989-2998, 9 A.M.-5 P.M. daily. Also has mailing address: P.O. Box 33, Stonington, Maine 04681. 207 367-2783. Seven women now working together to make women's creative ventures available through recordings, audio/visual media, publications, live theatrical events, and musical happenings. Recordings include *Mooncircles*, Kay Gardner (ST-NWE-80); *3 Gypsies*, Casse Culver (ST-WWE-81); and *Debutante*, Willie Tyson (ST-WWE-82).
- Women's Action Alliance, 370 Lexington Ave., 10017. 212 532-8330, Mon.-Fri. 9 A.M.-5 P.M. A nonprofit educational organization. Helped to coordinate the National Women's Agenda. Nonmembership resource center for women of all ethnic and economic groups. Model projects, referral system, publications for feminist projects. Library houses many publications about, by, and for lesbians.
- Women's Center Karate Club, 243 W. 20 St., 10011. 212 633-7108. Karate instruction. Women's Coffee House, 54 Seventh Ave. South, 10014. 212 691-8715. Entertainment, sandwiches, good place to meet and talk.
- Women's Health Alliance, Peggy Farber, 68 Perry St., 10014. 212 989-2751.
- Women's Health Forum, 175 Fifth Ave.,

10010. 212 674-3660, Mon.-Fri. 10:30 A.M.-6 P.M.
- Women's Institute for Psychotherapy, 105 W. 13th St., Apt. 12F, 10011. 212 741-1278, Mon.-Fri. 9 A.M.-5 P.M. (basically). Support group for feminist therapists to meet, rap, or hold workshops. Open by appointment. (Est. 50% lesbians.)
- Women's Martial Arts Center, 155 Chambers St., 10007. 212 349-2449. Staffed usually weekdays plus Sun.-Thurs. till 9 P.M. Sun., Mon., Wed. 7:30 P.M. (karate); Wed. 6:30-7:30 P.M. (Tai Chi Chuan); Tues. 6 P.M. (practice), Sun. 7:30 P.M. (boxing); Mon. and Thurs. 6 P.M., Tues. noon, Sat. 1:30 P.M., Sun. 7:30 P.M. (street technique/self-defense). Schedule may vary with the season. Free counseling for rape and wife abuse victims, speakers' bureau on women's physical strength, violence against women, child abuse, etc. Fees for classes are $25 and $35 per month.
- Women's Psychology Collective, 35 W. 20th St., 10011. 212 929-3353, 24-hour answering service. Lesbian-feminist therapists: as speakers, on panels, conferences; for therapy.

Oneonta
Organizations
- Gay Rights Organization of Oneonta, Box 541, 13820.
- People's Association for Gay Expression, Box 541, 13820. 607 432-2111, "85-Hotline," 24 hours daily, referral only. Weekly meeting Tues. 8-11 P.M. at Unitarian Universalist Church, 12 Ford Ave., 13820. Free bimonthly publication, *Gayzette*; political news, poems, articles. (Est. 40% lesbians.)

Potsdam
Organizations
- Potsdam-Canton Gay Community, College Union, State University College, 13676.

Poughkeepsie
Organizations
- Lesbian Feminist Liberation, 20 Carol St., 12601. Meet at Christ Episcopal Church. Stonewall Society, 914 471-8885.
Vassar Gay People's Alliance, Box 1921, 12601.

Riverdale
Services
- Women on the Move, P.O. Box 182, 10471; 212 548-4717-staffed 7 days, 24 hours. Activities vary, some almost monthly. A travel and social club for gay women.

Rochester
Bookstores
- Irondequoit Book Rack, Inc., Greece Town Mall, 14626. 716 225-0890. Mon.-Sat. 10 A.M.-9 P.M. Offers resource materials.
Media
- Lesbian Nation, WCMF, 96.5 FM. Radio show. Every other Mon. midnight.
Organizations
- Lesbian Resource Center, 713 Monroe Ave., 14607. 716 244-9030, Mon.-Fri. 7:30-9:30 P.M. Meetings first and third Wed. of each month, 7:30-9:30 P.M. at the center. Pro-

vides peer counseling, referrals, social events, speakers' bureau, political activities, etc.

Publications

- The New Woman Times, 1357 Monroe Ave., 14618. 716 271-5523.

Religious Groups

- Dignity/Integrity Rochester, 17 South Fitzhugh St., 14614. Mailing address: P.O. Box 8295, 14617. 716 232-6521 or 458-8628 weekday evenings. General business meetings every other Fri. 7:30 P.M. Roman Catholic mass followed by coffee hour every Sun. 5 P.M. Ministry to gay Christians in social, religious areas, counseling, etc. Monthly publication $5/year; single issue free on request. (Est. 15% lesbians.)

Services

- Lifeline, 716 275-5151. Crisis Center, 24-hour service.
- Women's Video Collective, 716 586-5072.

Saratoga Springs
Organizations

- Skidmore Sapphic Society, Casey Crabill, Skidmore College, 12866. 518 584-5000.

Stony Brook
Services

- Lesbian Outreach, Stony Brook Union, SUNY, 11794. 516 246-3540.

Suffolk County
Services

- Gayphone, 516 751-6380, Tues.-Sat. 8 P.M.-midnight.

Syosset
Services

- Feminist Hotline, Claudia Rubin, 10 Woodbury Way, 11791. 516 364-1364.

Syracuse
Organizations

- Gay Political Caucus, Box 399 Colvin Station, 13205. 315 476-5157.
- Lesbian Feminists of Syracuse, Franklin St., Syracuse University Women's Center, Ostrom Ave., 13210. 315 472-3917. Sponsor annual New York State Lesbian Feminist Conference.
- Syracuse University Gay Students Association, 103 College Place, Suite 6, 13210. 315 423-2081.

Services

- Gayphone, 315 423-3599.

Utica
Bars

- The Hub, 224 Bleecker St.
- Midnite Mary's, Columbia at Broadway.

Organizations

- Hamilton-Kirkland Gay Alliance, Hamilton College, Clinton, 13323. Peer counseling and social activities.

West Hempstead (Nassau County)
Bars

- T.C. and Company, 121 Woodfield Rd. 516 486-9516. 7 P.M.-4 A.M. Pool table, dancing, bowling parties, fund raisers held to serve Long Island community.

White Plains
Organizations

- Task Force on Sexuality and Lesbianism, Southern Westchester NOW. Meetings second Mon. of each month at Westchester People's

Action Coalition, 100 Mamaroneck Ave., 10601. 914 949-0088; NOW phone no. 914 682-8445. Open meetings, political action work.

Services

- Lesbian Feminist Coalition, WESPAC, 100 Mamaroneck Ave., 10601. 914 949-0088 (leave message). Bimonthly meetings, day and time vary; call to check–Patty, 914 834-4227. Counseling, referrals, social gatherings, dances, parties, discussion groups, films, raps, etc. Free publication, monthly, Green Thursdays. (Est. 95% lesbians.)

Woodstock
Services

- Woodstock Women's Center, 59 Tinker St., 12498.

NORTH CAROLINA
Chapel Hill
Organizations

- Carolina Gay Association, Box 39, Carolina Union, 27514. 919 942-2039.

Publications

- Feminary, P.O. Box 954, 27514. A biweekly publication. Provides forum for local women to express opinions, calendar of events, national news, reviews. Collective meets in members' homes. $5/year.

Charlotte
Organizations

- Carolina Gay Alliance for Freedom, P.O. Box 10205, 28202.
  Drastic Dykes, P.O. Box 3302, 28203.

Publications

- Sinister Wisdom, 3116 Country Club Dr., 28205. 704 377-0333, staffed all the time. A lesbian literary journal which includes poetry, fiction, essays, graphics, reviews, etc. Published three times a year. $2/issue; $4.50/year.

Durham
Organizations

- Duke Gay Alliance, 6298 College Station, 27708.
- Triangle Area Lesbian Feminists, P.O. Box 2272, 27702.

Services

- Crosspoint Counseling Service, 2715 Chapel Hill Rd., 27707. 919 493-1159. Open to servicing anyone who can benefit from their skills, particularly dedicated to the concept of nonsexist counseling. A strong commitment to offering counseling to lesbians and gay men which is free of heterosexist theory or homophobic bias.

Fayetteville
Bars

- Twilight Zone, 459 W. Russell St.

Greensboro
Organizations

- Gay People's Alternative, P.O. Box 6806, 27405.

Greenville
Organizations

- Eastern Gay Alliance, Box 1126, 27834. 919 752-4043.

Raleigh
Bars

- Mouse Trap, 1622 Glenwood Ave. 919 755-9123.

Religious Groups

- Metropolitan Community Church, 900 W. Morgan St., Apt. BA, 27603. 919 832-1582.

Wilmington
Bars

- The Other End, 1622 Glenwood Ave.

NORTH DAKOTA
Fargo
Bars

- Take Five, 515 Second Ave. North. 701 232-4967.

Leonard
Organizations

- Aware, Lynn Runck, Box 177, 58052.

OHIO
Akron
Organizations

- Sisters and Brothers, Newman Center, 143 S. Union St., 44304. 216 253-2790

Religious Groups

- Dignity/Akron, 143 S. Union St., 44304. Metropolitan Community Church, Box 563, 44309. 216 253-8388.

Bowling Green
Organizations

- Bowling Green Gay Union, Box 9, University Hall, B.G.U., 43403. 419 352-2831, staffed 24 hours (private home). Business meetings Wed., 7 P.M., Rm. 205, Mosley Hall, B.G.S.U. A social, political, and educational organization. Free quarterly newsletter. (Est. 65% lesbians.)

Canton
Bars

- Hal's Corner, 1432 Tuscaraways (Rte. 30). 216 454-0868.
- The Horseshoe, 1701 Harrison S.W. 216 452-7396.

Cincinnati
Organizations

- Labyris, Box 6302, 54206. Lesbian group and bookstore.
- Lesbian Activists Bureau, Inc., 6368 Heitzler, 45224. 513 541-7393 Mon.-Tues. 8 A.M.-6 P.M., Wed. 8 A.M.-12 noon. Weekly coffees Thurs. 7:30 P.M.
- University of Cincinnati Gay Society, Student Affairs Office, 420 Tangeman University Center, 45221. 513 475-6876.

Publications

- Dinah, 6368 Heitzler, 45224. 513 541-7393 and 541-5132. Newsletter.

Religious Groups

- Dignity/Cincinnati, Box 983, 45201. 513 621-4811.
- Metropolitan Community Church, St. John's Church, 320 Resor Rd. Mailing address: Box 39235, 45239. 513 591-0303.

Services

- Cincinnati Free Clinic, 2444 Vine St., 45219. 513 621-5700. Gay Saturday, 1-5 P.M.
- Gay Line Cincinnati, 65 E. Hollister, 45219. 513 241-0001.
- Lesbian Activist Bureau, Inc., 6368 Heitzler, 45224. 513 541-7393, Mon.-Tues. 8 A.M.-6 P.M. Wed. 8 A.M.-noon. Weekly coffees, Thurs. 7:30-9:30 P.M. Nonprofit. Provides a director to work on organizing in Ohio and

Midwest, working with groups on civil, social, economic issues of lesbians; organize and develop funding, etc. Publishes *Dinah*. $5/year donation.

- Lesbian Line, 513 621-2273.
- Women Helping Women, 513 861-8616.

Cleveland
Bookstores
- Coventry Books, 1832 Coventry Rd., 44118. 216 932-8111. General, with feminist and gay titles.
Media
- Radio Free Lambda, WRUW, 91.9 FM, 11220 Bellflower Rd., 44106. 216 368-2208. Mon. 10 P.M.
Organizations
- Cleveland Area Lesbian-Feminist Alliance, Box 18458, Cleveland Heights, 44118. 216 932-2669, Sun.-Thurs. 7-10 P.M. Publish *Calfa Notes*.
- Cleveland Gay Political Union, GEAR, Box 6177, 44101. 216 696-5330.
Publications
- High Gear, Box 6177, 04101. 216 696-5330. Paper. Gay news, etc. Monthly. 50¢/issue; $5/year.
- What She Wants, WomenSpace, 3201 Euclid Ave., 44115. 216 391-6651, Mon.-Thurs. 5-9 P.M. Monthly publication concerning local Cleveland women's news and cultural events, poetry, and graphics. 50¢/issue; $6/year.
Religious Groups
- Community of Celebration, Box 18226, 44118. Interfaith, interracial.
- Fellowship Metropolitan Church, Box 99234, 44199. 216 696-3649.
Services
- Gay Education and Awareness Resources Foundation (GEAR), Box 6177, 44101. 216 696-5330.
- Gay Switchboard, Box 6177, 44101. 216 696-5330, Sun.-Thurs. 8 P.M.-3 A.M.; Fri., Sat. 6 P.M.-4 A.M.
- Hope for the Gay Alcoholic, 216 687-0416.

Cleveland Heights
Services
- Oven Productions, P.O. Box 18175, 44118. Production of feminist and/or lesbian events every two to four weeks to make women's culture accessible to Cleveland Heights women's community. Events publicized in *What She Wants* (Cleveland).

Columbus
Bookstores
- Fan the Flames Feminist Book Collective, c/o The Women's Action Collective, 127 E. Woodruff Ave., 43201. 614 291-7756, Mon.-Fri. 1-7 P.M.; Sat. 1-5 P.M. Non-profit feminist bookstore providing books, periodicals, and pamphlets from women's and other presses. Good selection of posters and women's records.
Organizations
- Central Ohio Lesbians, P.O. Box 8393, 43201. 614 291-9114 (home phone). Meetings Mon. 7:30-10 P.M. at 82 E. 16th Ave. Working to achieve full civil rights for lesbians through political awareness and activism. Also social, educational, and service

needs. Monthly newsletter. $1/6 months. (Forty lesbians in group.)
- Columbus Gay Activists Alliance, 232 Ohio Union, 1739 N. High St., 43210. 614 422-9212, 10 A.M.-5 P.M.
- Lesbian Task Force of NOW. Inquire locally. OSU-Women's Liberation, Ohio Union, 1739 N. Hight St., 43210.
Religious Groups
- Dignity/Columbus, Box 4826, 43202.
Services
- The Gay Clinic, Open Door Clinic, 237 E. 17th Ave., 43201. 614 294-6337 (or phone for appointment on Mon.-Fri. noon-9 P.M.). Open door clinic Mon. and Thurs. 7-9 P.M. One-hour appointments (walk-in or appointment). Peer counseling, referrals, mental health, speakers' bureau. (Est. 25% lesbians.) Lesbian Peer Support, c/o The Women's Action Collective, 127 E. Woodruff Ave., 43201. Mailing address: Box 3321, University Station 43210. 614-291-7756, Mon.-Fri. 9 A.M.-7 P.M.; Sat. 1-5 P.M. Peer counseling, all lesbian, a member group of Women's Action Collective, a radical feminist organization of working groups. Specializes in short term problem-solving for lesbians, relatives and friends of lesbians, couples, and women struggling with sexual identity. Members of LPS trained in counseling skills under professional supervision. Donations are voluntary. Also referral and consultation, speakers' bureau. Publishes an irregular quarterly, *Purple Cow*. 25¢/single issue; $1/year.
- Women's Action Collective, 127 E. Woodruff Ave. 43201. 614 291-7756. A nonprofit association of feminist groups providing services for women. Encourages self-help approach; serves as focal point for work, programs and social gatherings. Houses Women Against Rape, Single Mothers Support Group, Women's Cooperative Garage, Lesbian Peer Support and others.

Dayton
Bars
- The World, 2312 N. Main St. 513 276-9673. Recommended.
Organizations
- Dayton Lesbian Feminist League, 1938 Rugby Rd., 45406. 513 275-3606. Peer counseling, CR groups. Meetings second and fourth Tues. of month, 8 P.M.
Publications
- Dayton Gayzette, 665 Salem Ave., 45406. Monthly. $10/year.
Religious Groups
- Lutherans Concerned for Gay People/Columbus-Dayton, Box 134, 45401.
Services
- Dayton Gay Center, Inc., 665 Salem Ave., 45406. 513 278-3963, Mon.-Fri. 10 A.M.-4 P.M.; Fri.-Sun. 8-11 P.M. Counseling, referrals, parents' groups.

Kent
Organizations
- Kent Gay Liberation Front, Rm. 308, Student Center, Kent State University, 44242. 216 672-2068 or 672-2581; staffed irregularly. Women's rap groups Fri. 8-10 P.M. (when school is in session). Working for gay-

lesbian rights, speaking engagements (about 100 a year); social, peer counseling. (Est. 30% lesbians.)

Lorian
Bars
- Buck's Tavern, 1052 Broadway (Rte. 57).

Mansfield
Bars
- Hugel's, E. 5th and Main Sts. Food and dancing. Recommended.
Retreat, 1030 W. 4th St. 419 529-2428.

Pique
Bars
- The Water Main, 202 N. Main St. 513 773-9277 and 773-9095.

Rockbridge
Organizations
- Society for Individual Rights of Ohio, Inc., Rte. 1, Box 298, 43149. 614 385-6823.
Services
- Summit Lodge Resort, 26500 Wild Cat Rd., 43149. 614 385-6823. Camping, swimming pool, restaurant, bar, bath club for lesbians.

Springfield
Bookstores
- Book and Cranny, 27 W. Sasilly, 45504.
Bars
- Why-Not Cafe, 1400 W. Main St. 513 324-9353. Open 8 P.M.-1 A.M.

Steubenville
Bars
- David's Lounge, 160 N. 4th St. 614 283-9274. Private club.

Toledo
Bars
- Sahara Club, 3402 Dorr St. 419 535-9021.
Organizations
- Personal Rights Organization, Box 4642, Old West Station, 43620. 419 243-9351. Publishes *Pro-gram*. 25¢/issue; $3/year.
Religious Groups
- Metropolitan Community Church of Toledo, 513 Magnolia, 43604. Mailing address: P.O. Box 1052, 43697. 419 241-9092, Mon.-Fri. 9-? Sat., Sun. 5-10 P.M. Rap Mon. 7 P.M. God Talk Thurs., 7 P.M. Services Sun. 6:45 P.M. A Christian church with a special outreach and ministry to the gay community. Free bimonthly publication, *Casing the Closet*. (Est. 50% lesbians.)

Warren
Bars
- The Outpost, Rte. 5, one mile from turnpike, Exit 14.

Yellowsprings
Organizations
- Antioch Gay Center, Antioch College, 45387. 513 767-7331, ext. 217.
- Antioch Radicalesbians, Women's Center, Antioch College Union, 45387.

Youngstown
Bars
- Troubador, 2010 Market St. 216 788-0872.
Organizations
- Gay Rights Organization, Youngstown State University, 44503.

Religious Groups
- Dignity/Youngstown, P.O. Box 4204, Austintown, Ohio 44515. 216 482-2481.

OKLAHOMA
Oklahoma City
Bars
- Funny Girl, 2422 N.W. 23rd St. Private club.
- Our Place, 1302 N. Pennsylvania Ave. 405 524-9396.

Organizations
- Libertarians for Gay Rights, 1206 N.W. 40th St., 73118.

Religious Groups
- Christ the King Metropolitan Community Church, 401 S.E. 22nd St., 73129.

Tulsa
Organizations
- Tulsa Gay Community Caucus, P.O. Box 2792, 74101.

Religious Groups
- Metropolitan Community Church, P.O. Box 4187, 74104. 918 939-0417.

OREGON
Eugene
Bookstores
- Book and Tea Shop, 1646 E. 19th Ave., 97403. 503 344-3422. Mon.-Sat. 10 A.M.-6 P.M.; Sun. afternoons. Women's books, non-sexist children's section, lesbian and gay periodicals.
- Mother Kali's Books, 541 Blair, 97402. 503 343-4864. Mon.-Sat. 10 A.M.-9 P.M. Collectively owned and operated by the workers. Women's bookstore, complete lesbian section, feminism books, Indian struggles, black women, women in prison, etc. Meetings are held at bookstore, upstairs. Women's groups and educational meetings every two weeks on any and all topics. Dyke hangout.

Organizations
- Gayouth, 503 343-8130 or 746-6755. For those under twenty-three.
- Gay People's Alliance, Rm. 318, EMU, University of Oregon, 97403. 503 686-3360, 10 A.M.-4 P.M., five days a week. Meetings Tues. evening, 1236 Kincaid St. Education and outreach, panels, peer counseling, referrals, political activities. (Est. 25% lesbians.)

Publications
- Women's Press, 371 N. Lawrence (upstairs). Mailing address: P.O. Box 562, 97401. Publishes a women's newspaper every six to eight weeks. Local, national, international news, features, and reviews of interest to women. 25¢/issue; $4/year. (Est. 50% lesbians.)

Religious Groups
- Metropolitan Community Church of the Willamette Valley, Box 3076, 97403. 503 746-7427.

Services
- Amazon Kung Fu, 503 345-2084.
- Communitype, 454 Willamette, 97401. 503 687-2556. Printing, etc.
- Gay People Alliance, University of Oregon, EMU Suite 1, 97403. 503 686-3327. Social meetings, rap groups, etc., at 1236 Kincaid St., Tues. 8 P.M. Counseling, legal and medical referrals.

- Jackrabbit Press, 454 Willamette St., 97401. Commercial print shop run by women.
- Lesbian Rap Group, Women's Center, 2nd and Washington, 97401.
- Mountain Movers, 454 Willamette St., 97401. Sells lesbian materials.
- One Step Beyond, 323 E. 12th, 97401.
- Oregon Women's Land Trust, 1821 Jefferson St., 97402. 503 342-4671. Permanent living and camping.
- Switchboard, 503 686-8435.

Grants Pass
Services
- Womanshare Feminist Retreat, 1531 Gray's Creek Rd., 97526. Mailing address: P.O. Box 1735, 97526. 503 862-2807, 24 hours daily. Five-day sessions scheduled on holidays and throughout summer. A place in the country where women can feel their own environment and work on creating a new culture. Book, *Country Lesbians,* the story of the collective, $5.50.

Portland
Bookstores
- A Woman's Place Bookstore, 1300 S.W. Washington St., 97205. 503 226-0848. Mon.-Sat. 10 A.M.-6 P.M.; Sun. 1-4 P.M. Meetings on alternate Mondays, 7 P.M. at bookstore. Bookstore selling feminist books, posters, records. Also meeting place, lounge, and library. Publish *A Woman's Place,* a monthly. Local Portland women's events and book reviews. 25¢/issue; $2/year.

Media
- Optimistic Voices, c/o Radio KINK, 1501 S.W. Jefferson St., 97201. 503 223-0245.

Organizations
- Gay Liberation Front, Portland State College, Steve Fulmer, #403, 1232 S.W. Jefferson St., 97201.
- Gay Student Affairs Board, Room 438, Smith Center, Portland State University, 97201. 503 229-4458, Mon.-Fri. 8 A.M.-5 P.M.
- Gay Teens, Moon Brothers Collective, 729 S.E. 33rd Ave., 97214. 503 238-0148. Lambda House, 1867 S.W. 14th Ave., 97201.
- Parents of Gays/Portland, The Portland Town Council, 320 S.W. Stark St., Rm. 303, 97204. 503 227-2765.
- Portland Gay Liberation Front Communications Committee, 4226 N. Montana Ave., 97217. 503 287-7894.
- The Portland Town Council, 320 S.W. Stark St., Rm. 303, 97204. 503 227-2765, Mon.-Fri. 1-5 P.M. Political action, community organization. Also some counseling, referral, media work, public speaking. Regular monthly business meetings at Old Church, 1422 S.W. 11th, first Tues. of each month 7 P.M. Free monthly publication. (Est. 50% lesbians.)
- Salem Group, Portland Town Council, 320 S.W. Stark St., 97204.

Publications
- Northwest Gay Review, 118 W. Burnside St., 97209. 503 227-0432. 50¢/issue; $5/year.

Religious Groups
- Metropolitan Community Church, Box 8348, 97207.

Services
- Mountain Moving Cafe, 532 S.E. 39th, 97214. 503 236-7541. Wed.-Sun. 9 A.M.-1 A.M. A restaurant-community center. One all-women's night a week, music, bands, dancing. Different activities every night, lots of women's music, lots of gay people come in. (Est. 50% lesbians.)
- Women's Place Resource Center, 1915 N.E. Everett, 97232. 503 234-7044, Mon.-Fri. 11 A.M.-6 P.M. Center collective meetings Tues. 7:30-10 P.M. Phone counseling, umbrella for rap groups, lesbian mothers, women in prison project, housing, etc. Monthly newsletter. $1/year. (Est. 50% lesbians.)

Roseburg
Services
- Oregon Women's Land, P.O. Box 1692, 97470. 503 673-7649, sporadically. Land trust meeting about every three months. Time and place in newsletter, free (donations requested). 147 acres of open women's land, to serve travelers, women in need. No money needed. (Est. 95% lesbians.)

Wolf Creek
Publications
- Woman Spirit, Box 263, 97497.

PENNSYLVANIA
Bethlehem
Organizations
- Lehigh Valley Homophile Organization (LEHI-HO), Box 1003, Moravian Station, 18018. Meeting fourth Sun. of month, Unitarian Church, 701 Lechauweki Ave. (Fountain Hill). Educational organization with library, speakers, filmstrips, etc.

Bridgeport
Bars
- The Lark, 302 De Kalb, Rt. 202.

Bryn Mawr
Organizations
- Bryn Mawr/Haverford Gay People's Alliance, Rm. 24, College Inn, 19191.

Duncansville
Bars
- Danny's Hideaway, Rt. 220, R.D. 1.

Erie
Bars
- Washington Grill, W. 10th and Washington.

Harrisburg
Publications
- The Gay Circle, Gay Community Services, Box 297, Federal Square Station, 17108. Free.

Religious Groups
- Dignity/Central Pennsylvania, P.O. Box 297, Federal Square Station, 17108.
Integrity/Greater Harrisburg, P.O. Box 3809, 17108.
- Metropolitan Community Church/Harrisburg, 1001 W. Spring St., #1-2, Middletown, Pa. 17057.

Services
- Gay Community Services, P.O. Box 297, Federal Square Station, 17108. 717 232-2027. Counseling and meetings.
- Gay Switchboard of Harrisburg, P.O. Box

872, 17108. 717 234-0328, Mon.-Fri. 6-10 P.M. Meetings first Sun. and third Thurs. each month. Provides peer counseling, information, legal and medical referrals to gay women and men. Speaking engagements and training sessions. (Est. 33% lesbians.)

Indiana
Organizations
- Homophiles of Indiana University of Pennsylvania, Box 1588, Indiana University, 15701.
Services
- The Open Door, 948 Wayne Ave., 15701. Counseling.

Lancaster
Publications
- Gay Era, 3002 Marietta Ave., 17601. 717 898-2876. Monthly. 50¢/issue; $6/year.
Services
- Gays United Lancaster, 3002 Marietta Ave., 17601. 717 898-2876. Peer counseling. Tues., Thurs. 8-10 P.M. Sun. 6-10 P.M.
- JRM Cooper Feminist Notecards, 3002 Marietta Ave., 17601. 717 898-2876. Feminist-designed notecards based on illustrations in nineteenth-century children's books.
- Women Oriented Women, Lancaster Women's Center, 230 W. Chestnut St., 17600. 717 299-5381. Meetings second and fourth Sun. of month, 2-4 P.M.

Lebanon
Organizations
- Gay League of Lebanon, Box 431, 17042.

New Hope
Bars
- January's, at the Inn at Hope Ridge Farms, Aquetone Road. Disco.
- Old Cartwheel Inn, Rte. 202 West.
- Prelude, Rte. 202 West.
- The Rendezvous, Highway 202 North.

Philadelphia
Bookstores
- Alexandria Books, Inc., 328 S. 17th St., 19103. 215 732-2420, Mon.-Sat. 10 A.M.-7 P.M. Meetings Mon.-Sat. 10 A.M.-7 P.M. Feminist bookstore collective, weekly workshops, readings, concerts, politics of motherhood, etc. At present the only public women's space in Philadelphia. (Est. 90% lesbians.)
- Penelope and Sisters, 603 S. 4th St., 19147. 215 PE5-1389. Books, also crafts collective. Together Books, 233 S. 13th St., 19107. 215 732-3334. Mon.-Sat. 11:30 A.M.-7 P.M.
Organizations
- Amazons, Inc., 2114 Locust St., 19103. Mailing address: P.O. Box 18521, 19129. Purpose is to provide a variety of services for the lesbian community. Immediate plans (new organization) are for a coffeehouse, library, hotline, space for workshops and meetings, and a film series.
- Dyketactics!, P.O. Box 18521, 19129. A radical lesbian-feminist (and activist) group of women loving women. Sisters are encouraged to send their support and ideas. Group in constant state of growth and evolution.
- Gay Community Center of Pennsylvania, 346 Kater St., 19147. 215 922-1623. Staffed Mon., Wed., Fri. 12:15-6 P.M.;

Mon.-Fri. 7:30-10 P.M. Free school courses, Fri., Sat. 9 P.M.-1 A.M. (coffeehouse). A nonprofit corporation. Promotes positive self-acceptance by gay people, appreciation of gay culture, literature, life-styles. Also to educate general public. (Est. 25% lesbians.)
- Gays at Drexel, Educational Activities Center, 33rd and Chestnut, Drexel University, 19104.
- Gays at Penn, Christian Association, 3601 Locust Walk, 19104. 215 243-3888.
- Gays in the Northeast, Eromin Center, 1735 Naudain St., 19146. 215 638-0739. All sorts of social events for gays of northeast Philadelphia and Bucks County—bike rides, picnics, etc.
- Gay Students at Temple, Rm. 205, Student Activities Center, 13th and Montgomery Sts., 19122. 215 787-7902.
- Gay Women's Alternative. No set location at this; phone the Gay Switchboard, 215 928-1919, for information about CWA. A social and cultural organization for gay women over thirty.
- Parents of Gays/Philadelphia, Gay Community Center, 326 Kater St., 19147.
- Philadelphia Wages Due Lesbians, 602 S. 48th, 19143. 215 SH8-7303. Part of International Wages for Housework campaign to win wages for housework for the government of all lesbians. Also focus on child custody for lesbian mothers.
Publications
- Hera, 112 S. 16th St., 19103.
- WICCE, Box 15833, 19103. Newspaper of lesbian-feminist news, fiction, poetry, etc. 35¢/issue; $3.50/year (6 issues).
Religious Groups
- Gay Pagans and Atheists, Box 25083, 19147. An alternative to the usual—nonsexist.
- United Church of Christ Gay Caucus, P.O. Box 24005, 19139.
Services
- Amazon Country/Sunshine Gaydream, WXDN-FM, 3905 Spruce, 19104. 215 387-5401. Weekly show Sun. 1-3 P.M.
- Eromin Center, Inc., 1735 Naudain St., 19146. 215 732-3212, Mon.-Thurs. 10 A.M.-10 P.M.; Fri. 10 A.M.-6 P.M. Professional counseling center for sexual minorities, individual couples, groups, and families. Fees on a sliding scale. (Est. 50% lesbian clientele, 50% women staff.)
- Feminist Therapy Collective, 2132 Lombard St., 19146. 215 KL6-1234.
- Gay Media Project of Philadelphia, Box 2186, 19103. 215 387-0716 or 724-1247. Meetings at the Christian Association, 3601 Locust Walk.
- Gay Nurses Alliance, Box 5687, 19129. 215 849-1171.
- Gay Peer Counseling at University of Pennsylvania, 3601 Locust Walk, C8, 19104. 215 243-8888, Tues. 2-4 P.M., 7:30-11 P.M. (lesbian staffing also); Thurs.-Fri. 2-4 P.M. Thurs.-Sat. 7-11 P.M. Meetings Tues. 6-7 P.M. Telephone and drop-in peer counseling by trained University of Pennsylvania graduate and undergraduate students for university and nonuniversity people. (Est. 33% lesbians.)
- Gay Raiders, Box 15786, 19103. 215

248-2228. Problems concerning media, etc.
- Gay Speakers Bureau, 8111 Fayette St., 19150. 215 CH8-2228.
- Gay Switchboard of Philadelphia, 326 Kater St., 19147. Mailing address: P.O. Box 15748, 19103. 215 928-1919, Mon.-Fri. 6-11 P.M., Sat., Sun. 7-10 P.M. Counseling via phone, medical and legal referrals.
- Gay Women's Coffeehour, Deana Lang, 702 Wynnewood Rd., 19151.
- Lesbian Hotline, Box 5474, 19143. 215 SA9-2001, Mon.-Thurs. 6-11 P.M.
- Out Front Productions, Box 2186, 19103. 215 GL5-0659 or EV7-0716. First gay co-produced public affairs TV show.
- Women in Transition, Inc., 3700 Chestnut St., 19104. 215 382-7016.
- Women's Cultural Trust, 3601 Locust Walk, 19174. 215 243-5110, staffed Mon.-Fri. 11 A.M.-6 P.M. Dedicated to furthering women in the arts. Operate a crafts gallery and bookstore. (Est. 50% lesbians.)
- Women's Switchboard, Pennwalt Building, 3 Parkway, 19103. 215 563-8599.

Pittsburgh
Organizations
- Lesbian Feminists, Persad Center, Inc., 5100 Center Ave., 15232.
- Parents of Gays, Persad Center, Inc., 5100 Center Ave., 15232. 412 681-5330.
- Pittsburgh Gay Parents, 1412 Alton Ave., 15216.
- Pittsburgh Gay Political Caucus, Box 10236, 15232. 412 661-8570 or 681-6330.
Publications
- Pittsburgh Gay News, 233 S. 13th St., Philadelphia, Pa. 19107. Mailing address: Box 10236, 15232. 412 363-0594. Monthly. 35¢/issue; $5/year.
- Gay Alternatives, Box 10236, 15232. 412 363-0594. Meetings Sat. 8 P.M. Coffeehouse on Sat. 9 P.M.-midnight at First Unitarian, Ellsworth and Morewood Aves., Shadyside.
- Gay Students at Pitt, Box 819, Schenley, University of Pittsburgh, 15260. 412 624-5944, 7-11 P.M. Meetings Wed. 8 P.M. and 520 Pitt, Student Union.
- Persad Center, Inc., 5100 Center Ave., 15232. 412 681-5330, Mon.-Thurs. 12:30-9:30 P.M.; Fri. 12:30-4:30 P.M. Mental health center for sexual minorities of all kinds. Counseling, consultation, research services; library; Pittsburgh gay parents.
- Pittsburgh Gay Clinic, S. Highland and Alder Sts., 98195. (Shadyside) in East End Christian Church. 412 661-5424.

Reading
Bookstores
- Alternative Booksellers (corporate name: Feminist Enterprises, Inc.), 10 N. 4th St., 19601. 215 373-0442. Store hours, Mon.-Wed. 10 A.M.-5 P.M.; Thurs., Fri. 10 A.M.-9 P.M.; Sat. 10 A.M.-5 P.M. A bookstore with shelf for lesbians and supportive lesbian community that makes suggestions for titles, etc.
Organizations
- Gay Coordinating Society, 616 Locust St., 19604. Mailing address: P.O. Box 3131, 19604. 215 373-3643. Meetings at 6 P.M. third Sun. of the month. Provides social and

political events and handles cases of discrimination. (Est. 50% lesbians.)
Services
- Gay Coordinating Society, Box 3131, 19603. 215 372-5123. Counseling, emergency housing, social activities.

Shaverstown
Organization
- Northeast Pennsylvania Gay Alliance (NEPGA), Box 1710, 18708.

Shippensburg
Organizations
- Shippensburg Students for Gay Rights, CUB, Shippensburg State College, 17257.

State College
Bars
- My-Oh-My Bar, 128 E. College St. 814 238-2345.
Organizations
- Homophiles of Penn State, P.O. Box 218, 16801. 814 863-0588, Mon.-Fri. 1-3 P.M. and 7-9 P.M. General meetings once a month; coffeehouses once a month. Free publication, *Zap*, monthly, with an exchange subscription. A social, political, and supportive group in existence almost seven years. (Est. 30% lesbians.)
- Hops Lesbian Collective, 212 HUB, 16802. Mailing address: P.O. Box 218, 16801. 814 863-0588. Weekly meetings Wed. 8:30 P.M., Women's Resource Center, 108 W. Beaver St. Serves needs of local lesbians for discussions, political action, social activities, personal counseling, readings, etc. Monthly publication, *Zap,* free

Swarthmore
Organizations
- Swarthmore Gay Liberation, Swarthmore College, 19081. 215 544-7900, ext. 296, or LO6-9467.

West Chester
Organizations
- Gays of West Chester, Box 2303, West Chester State College, 19380.

York
Bars
- Town Tavern, 41 N. Georgia St.

PUERTO RICO
San Juan
Bars
- The Abbey, 251 Calle Cruz (near Calle Fortaleza).
- Boccachio (Hato Rey) Ave., M. Rivera (near Domenech).
- Small World, 250 Calle San José (near Fortaleza).
  Top of the Aquarium, 255 Calle San Justo (upstairs).
Organizations
- Comunidad de Orguillo Gay, Box 5523, Puerta De Tierra, 00906. Casa Orguillo, Calle Saldana, #3, Rio Pedras. 809 722-4669.
Religious Groups
- Dignity/Puerto Rico, Box 22000, UPR Station 00931.

RHODE ISLAND
Central Falls
Bars
- Marti's Lounge, 176 Railroad St. 401 728-5460. Almost a gay community center.

Newport
Bars
- David's, 28 Prospect Hill (off Thames). 401 847-9698.
Services
- Franklin Spa, Spring St. at Franklin, 02840. 401 847-3540.

Northsmithfield
Bars
- Town and Country, Rte. 44, Farnum Pike. Lesbians like it because it's not in downtown Providence.

Providence
Bars
- Club Cabana, 681 Valley St. 401 621-8366. Open 7 P.M.-2 A.M. Bar with all-women's bands, dancing weekends. (Est. 90% lesbians.)
Bookstores
- Dorrwar Bookstore, 224 Thayer St. 02906. 401 521-3230. Mon.-Sat. 9 A.M.-6 P.M. Retail books, strong emphasis on sexual politics, gay concerns, women's concerns, socialism, etc.
Organizations
- Brown Gay Students Organization, Box 49, Student Activities Office, Brown University, 02912. Meetings Tues. 8 P.M., third floor.
Religious Groups
- Metropolitan Community Church Women's Rap Group, 63 Chapin Ave. Mailing address: Box 1942, 02901. 401 274-1693. Meets Wed. 7 P.M.
Services
- Gay Help Line, 401 831-9491.
  Gay Women of Providence, 401 831-5184.

Woonsocket
Bars
- High Street Cafe, 281 High St. Dancing, live bands. (Est. 50% lesbians.)

SOUTH CAROLINA
Charleston
Bars
- Bacchus, 135 Calhoun St.

Columbia
Bars
- Fortress Club, 5729 Shakespeare Rd. 803 754-9848.
- H & M Club, 2300 Notch Rd., Disco.
Religious Groups
- Metropolitan Community Church, Box 11181, 29211. 803 798-3916.

SOUTH DAKOTA
Rapid City
Organizations
- Black Hills Gay Coalition, Box 8034, 57701.

TENNESSEE
Chattanooga
Bars
- Powder Puff Lounge, 28 E. Main St.

Knoxville
Bars
- Carousel, 1501 White Ave.
Services
- Gay Switchboard, 615 726-4299. (Est. 50% lesbians.)

Memphis
Bookstores
- Community Bookshop, 1907 Madison. 901 726-4531. Mon.-Sat. 11 A.M.-6 P.M.
Media
- WEVL, 90.3 FM, Box 2118, 38101. Radio program, Tues. 7:30-8:30 P.M.
Services
- Gay Switchboard, Box 3620, 38103. 901 726-4299.
- The Last Laugh, 1335 Madison. Gay women, feminists, college students.

Nashville
Bars
- Other Side, 615 242-9547. Super bar, highly recommended.
Organizations
- NOW Lesbian Task Force, 615 276-8876.

TEXAS
Amarillo
Bars
- Pal's Lounge, 717 W. 16th.

Austin
Bookstores
- Common Woman Bookstore, 2004½ Guadaloupe St. 78705. 512 472-2785. Tues., Wed., Fri., Sat. 11 A.M.-6 P.M.; Thurs. 11 A.M.-9 P.M. Weekly collective business meetings. "Bookstore is lesbian-related—materials unavailable anywhere else in Austin area." Women's writings, art, music, information on community resources, etc.
Organizations
- Austin Lesbian Organization, P.O. Box 3301, 78764. 512 472-3053 (Woman/Space). Business meeting second Sun. each month at 7 P.M.; program meeting third Sun. each month, 7:30 P.M. at Woman/

Space, 2330 Guadaloupe St. Sponsors a variety of educational activities, deals with political issues of importance to lesbians. Aims to develop and strengthen lesbian community.

- Gay People of Austin, 2330 Guadaloupe St., 78705. 512 477-6699.
- Gay Political Committee, Box 1255, 78767. Gay/Texas, Office of Student Activities, University of Texas, 78712.
- The South Central Region of the U.S. Gay Academic Union, 900 West Ave., 78701.

Publications

- Goodbye to All That Collective, P.O. Box 3301, 78764. 512 441-1130. Monthly publication on news, articles, poetry of interest to lesbians. 50¢/issue; $4/year.
- Red River Women's Press, 2204 San Gabriel, 78705. 512 478-8939, Mon.-Fri. 9 A.M.-5 P.M.Printing and publishing at reasonable rates. Also training women in nontraditional skills in printing. (Est. 50% lesbians.)

Services

- Gay Community Services, 2330 Guadaloupe St. (in University Y), 78705. 512 477-6699, 4-7 P.M.
- Woman/Space, 2330 Guadaloupe St. (in University Y) 78705. 512 472-3053, Tues.-Fri. 7-10 P.M. Walk-in peer counseling to women from feminist perspective (Tues., Thurs., Fri. 7-10 P.M.). Medical, legal, psychological information. Child care referrals. Community information. Sponsor coffeehouse and women's groups Fridays. (Est. 75% lesbians.)

Corpus Christi
Bars
- Chez Paris, 2207 Ayers. 512 884-0063.

Dallas
Media
- Just Before Dawn, Helen Margaret, 4703 Live Oak, 75204. Radio program, KCHU, 90.9 FM, Wed. 7 P.M.

Organizations
- Dallas DOB, 3220 Lemmon Ave., 75204.
- Task Force on Lesbianism, Dallas County NOW, Box 12431, 75225.

Religious Groups
- Metropolitan Community Church, 3834 Ross Ave., 75204. 214 826-0291.

Services
- Community Service Center, 3834 Ross Ave., 75204. 214 826-2192. Many activities.
- Gayline of Dallas, Ms. Rob Shivers, Box 5944, 75222. 214 241-4118, 6 P.M.-6 A.M. Counseling and referrals.

El Paso
Bars
- Apartment Bar, 804 Myrtle St. 915 544-7175.

Fort Worth
Organizations
- Daughters of Bilitis, Box 1564, 76010.

Religious Groups
- Agape Metropolitan Community Church, 151 Vanek, 76107. 817 335-7355. Legal, medical referrals, emergency housing, etc.
- Dignity/Dallas-Fort Worth, Box 813, Arlington, Tex. 76010. 817 640-0482.

Galveston
Bars
- Kon Tiki Wahine, 2214 Mechanic.
- Mary's, 2502 Ave. Q½.

Grand Prairie
Religious Groups
- Metropolitan Community Church, Box 718, 75050. 214 436-6805.

Houston
Bookstores
- Albraxas, 1200 W. Alabama, 77006. 713 528-9129.

Organizations
- Gay Activists Alliance of Houston, Box 441, U.C. On-campus activities, Rm. N-11-G, University of Houston, 77004, 713 749-3489, Mon.-Fri. 8 A.M.-10 P.M. Regular meetings Tues. 7:30 P.M., Spindletop Room, University Center. Political, social, educational; responds to discrimination and harassment of gays. Monthly newsletter, *The Lambda Letter.* Free (if mailed, just postage). (Est. 50% lesbians.)
- Gay Political Caucus, Box 16041, 77022.
- Houston NOW Sexuality Lesbian Task Force, Women's Center, 3602 Milam, 77002. 713 524-5743, Mon.-Thurs. 7-10 P.M. Referrals, speakers, etc.
- Texas Gay Task Force, Integrity, Box 16041, 77022.

Publications
- Montrose Star, 900 Lovett, 77006. 713 527-8961, 9 A.M.-8 P.M. six days a week. "Leading gay newspaper in Texas, includes lesbian news and advertising." Circulation ca. 7,000. Sub. $9.75/16 months.
- Pointblank Times, P.O. Box 14643, 77021. A monthly lesbian-feminist publication with news, features, photos, etc., trying to facilitate communication in the community. Also produces occasional get-togethers, concerts, picnics, women's Olympics, etc. 50¢/issue; $5/year.

Services
- Parents of Gays, Houston, The Depository, 2606 Peekham, 77006. 713 527-0260. Helps parents and their gay daughters and sons to a better understanding of each other. Helps pass National Gay Civil Rights bill, consenting adults in private, repeal lewd and lascivious statutes, and change attitudes in the community and throughout the nation. Printed material available for 24¢ stamped legal-sized envelope.

Lubbock
Bars
- David's Warehouse, 2402 Marshall St.

Services
- Lubbock Gay Awareness, Box 4002, 79409.

McAllen
Services
- New Age Community, Melnyk, 306 S. 11th St., 78501. Gay organic farming, community into survival/spiritual growth, healing, activism. Publishes newsletter.

San Antonio
Bars
- The 200 Club, 3240 N.W. Loop.

Services
- Gay Switchboard of San Antonio, 1136 W.

Woodlawn, 78201. 512 733-7300, 7-11 P.M. daily.

Universal City
Organizations
- Texas Gay Task Force, Box 2036, 78148.

UTAH
Salt Lake City
Religious Groups
- Metropolitan Community Church, Box 11607, 870 W. 4th South, 84111. 801 531-9434, 24 hours daily.

Services
- Gay Community Center, Box 6077, 84106. Nature Note Cards, N.E. Lake, 1899 Sycamore Lane, 84117. 801 278-8335. Pen and ink drawings on brightly colored paper with envelopes, twelve assortments. $3 plus 50¢ postage.
- The Open Book, 1025 Second Ave., 84103. 801 364-6152, Mon.-Fri. 10 A.M.-6 P.M.; Sat. 10 A.M.-4 P.M. A bookstore specializing in human liberation, female and male, gay and straight, anyone who's open to growing. Central meeting place. Art shows by local women artists, openings (nine artists) first Sun. of every month, 2-5 P.M. Free newsletter published about three times a year.
- Women Aware, Box 25532, 84119, 801 261-0777. Activities on the second Sun. of each month, 2 P.M. at the UWCA Cottage, 322 E. 300 South. To unite Salt Lake's lesbian community and to meet its varied needs through social activities, educational experiences, workshops, CR groups, political action, etc. Sponsors performers, musicians. Attempting to establish a legal defense fund for lesbians.

VERMONT
Bellow Falls
Bars
- Andrew's Inn, 802 463-3966. Ski resort with two bars and dance bar. (Est. 30% lesbians.)

Burlington
Bookstores
- Book Stacks, Inc., 118 Pine, 05401. 802 862-8513. Open to public 10 A.M.-8 P.M. most nights. Run as collective. Feminist and lesbian titles, intensive political theory section, etc.

Organizations
- Gay in Vermont, Box 3216, North Burlington Station, 05401.

Services
- Counseling for Gay Women and Men, Vermont Women's Health Center, 158 Bank St., 05401. 802 863-1386.
- Gay Student Union, Billings Student Center, University of Vermont, 05401. 802 656-4173, Mon.-Fri. 7-9 P.M. Regular activities vary, but one monthly meeting held first Mon. of each month at 8 P.M. Always has staffed desk in student center. Service organization with some political and social activities for gays. Primarily for campus community with speakers' bureau, hotline,

monthly coffeehouse and meetings, gay awareness weekend in spring. (Est. 40% lesbians.)

Middlebury
Organizations
• Gay People at Middlebury, Middlebury College, 05753.

Windham
Resorts
• Gay Ski House, c/o Oscar Wilde Memorial Bookshop, 15 Christopher St., New York, N.Y. 10014. 212 794-2770.

VIRGINIA
Arlington
Services
• Gay Women's Open House, 5411 South 8th Pl., 22204. No mailing address. 703 671-3762. Wed. 8-11:30 P.M. Meetings in private home at above address. A protected social setting where lesbians and bisexual women and women who think they're gay can meet and talk. Legal, psychological, and roommate referrals.

Charlottesville
Organizations
• Gay Student Union, Peabody Hall, University of Virginia, 22901.

Norfolk
Organizations
• Virginia Lesbian/Feminist Group, Box 11103, 23517.

Richmond
Organizations
• Gay Liberation Front, Kenny Pederson, 505 Brookside Ave., 23327. 703 266-2691.

Services
• Gay Rap, 10 W. Cary St., 23220.

Roanoke
Bars
• Tradewinds, 717 Franklin Road (at Elm Ave.).
Services
• Roanoke Valley Trouble Center, Inc., 3515 Williamson Rd., 24012. 703 563-0311, 24-hour crisis intervention and referrals.

Williamsburg
Organizations
• Gay Liberation Group, College of William and Mary, Campus Center, 23185.

WASHINGTON
Bellingham
Organizations
• Gay People's Alliance, Viking Union, Rm. 212, Western Washington State University, 98225. 206 676-3460, 9 A.M.-4 P.M.

Olympia
Services
• Evergreen State College Gay Resource Center, CAB 305, Evergreen State College, 98505. 206 866-6544.

Pullman
Organizations
• Gay People's Alliance and Gay Awareness, Rm. 304, CUB, Washington State University, 99163. Meetings Wed. 8 P.M.

Seattle
Bookstores
• It's About Time, 5502 University Way, N.E., 98103. 206 525-0999. Mon.-Fri. 1-7 P.M.; Sat. 5-11 P.M. A feminist bookstore.
Media
• Lesbian Feminist Media Collective, KRAB, 1406 Harvard Ave., 98122. 206 322-8059.
Organizations
• Gay Feminists Coalition, Metropolitan Community Church, Box 12020. 98112.
• Gay Students Association, Box 96, HUB (FK-10), University of Washington, Student Union, SB29, 98119. 206 543-6106.
• Responsible Gay Mothers, Lesbian Resource Center, 4224 University Way, N.E., 98105.
• The Woman's Woman, 910½ E. Pike St. 98122.
Publications
• Out and About—Seattle Lesbian Feminist Newsletter, 110 Boyleston Ave. East, 98102. A monthly newsletter including calendar of events, announcement, and articles of interest to the Seattle lesbian community. Published by a collective of six women. 15¢/issue; $3/year.
• Seattle Gay News, 110 Boyleston Ave. East, 98102. Monthly. $10/year. Free to prisoners.
Services
• Chemical Dependency Program of Stonewall, Inc., 300 Vine St., 98121. 206 623-5661, Mon.-Fri. 8:30 A.M.-5:30 P.M. One-to-one and group counseling, outpatient treatment and education for alcohol and drug abusers, outreach to gay and non-gay organizations. (Est. 50% lesbian clientele and 75% lesbian staff.)
• Gay Community Center, 110 Boylston Ave. East, 98102. 206 322-2000, Mon.-Fri. 10:30 A.M.-10 P.M.; Sat., Sun. 1-5 P.M. Meetings Mon.-Fri. 10:30 A.M.-10 P.M. Switchboard, emergency housing, jobline, drop-in services, archives. Publishes monthly *Seattle Gay News.* 10¢/issue; $2/year.
• Gay Community Social Services, Box 2228, 98122.
• Lesbian Feminist Media Collective, KRAB, 1406 Harvard, 98102. 206 322-8059, afternoons. Radio programming (KRAB radio, Sun. 7-8 P.M.), local, national, and international news from a feminist perspective.
• Lesbian Mother's National Defense Fund, 110 Boylston Ave East. 98102. Mailing address: 2446 Lorentz Pl. North, 98109. 206 EA2-2000, messages taken Mon.-Fri. 9 A.M.-8 P.M. Meetings on Tues. 7 P.M. Provides legal, financial, and emotional support to lesbian mothers for custody of their children. Publishes bimonthly, *Mom's Apple Pie,* 25¢/issue; $2/year.
• Lesbian Resource Center, 4224 University Way, N.E. 98105. 206 632-4747, ext. 7, Mon.-Fri. 9 A.M.-5 P.M.; Sat. noon-4 P.M. A nonmembership organization (open to public, hours above, plus Thurs. till 7 P.M.). Drop-in center, library, peer counseling, speakers' bureau (by prearrangement), social events, job referrals, medical care, housing,

etc., for Seattle area women. Provides resources and supportive atmosphere for lesbian women and those exploring that option.
• Seattle Counseling Service for Sexual Minorities, 1720 16th Ave., 98122. 206 329-8737, Mon.-Fri. 10 A.M.-10 P.M. Discussion on sexuality Mon. 8-10 P.M. Women encouraged to call or drop in to rap, join groups. (Est. 75% lesbians.)
• Sister (Seattle Institute for Sex Therapy, 100 N.E. 56th, 98105. 206 522-8588, Mon.-Fri. 10 A.M.-5 P.M.; Mon. to 8 P.M. Services in lesbian sexuality, therapy groups, workshops, individual counseling, couples' counseling, women's sexuality, etc. Events scheduled on weekends and evenings as well as regular office hours. Publishes *Apple,* a quarterly journal of women's sexuality and erotica. $2/issue; $7/year. Approximately 200 people (est. 50% lesbians) served in the last year.
• Women's Coffee Coven, P.O. Box 5104, 98105. 206 324-2818, staffed 7-9 P.M. A nonprofit corporation producing women's music concerts for women alone. Events occur on Fri. nights, usually once or twice a month. No permanent location, consequently must rent halls. Membership; $5 for 6 months, $10 for year. Reduced cost to low-income women applying in writing. Child care and refreshments provided at events.

Spokane
Bars
• Sonja's Magic Inn, 425 W. First Ave.

Tacoma
Services
• Tacoma Counseling Service, 712 S. 14th, 98405. 206 272-3847.

WEST VIRGINIA
Charleston
Bars
• Tradewinds Restaurant and Lounge, 500 Carolina St. 304 342-9429. Restaurant.

Huntington
Bars
• Chateau Club, 1121 7th Ave. 304 696-9623. Private club. Women and men.

WISCONSIN
Appleton
Bars
• Doris' Super Bar, 343 W. College Ave. 414 733-9757. Dancing, sandwiches, women and men.

Fox Valley
Organizations
• Fox Valley Gay Alliance, Box 332, Menaslia, Wis. 54952. 414 233-2948.

Green Bay
Bars
• Gail's Bar, 1101 Main St. 414 432-9924.

Madison
Organizations
• Gay Activists Alliance, Renaissance of Madison, Box 687, 53701. 601 257-7575.

- Gay Law Students Association, 608 257-4611.

Publications

- We Got It! Lesbian Communication Collective, Lesbian Switchboard, University YMCA, 306 N. Brooks St., 53715. Monthly. 25¢.

Services

- Gay Switchboard and Information Service, 1001 University Ave. Mailing address: Box 687, 53701. 608 257-7575.
- Lesbian Switchboard, 306 N. Brooks, 53715. 608 257-7378, Mon.-Thurs. 7-10 P.M. Peer counseling, information, social events, educational services(panels) for any interested group, dances, coffeehouses (irregular), library, etc.
- Madison Committee for Gay Rights, Box 324, 53701. 608 256-2479 or 244-6739.

Milwaukee

Bookstores

- Sistermoon, Feminist Bookstore and Art Gallery, 1625 E. Irving, 53202. 414 276-0909, Tues.-Sun., noon-6 P.M. Provides space for reading, talking, art exhibits, women's music, poetry reading. Large selection of lesbian literature. (Est. 95% lesbians.)

Organizations

- Gay People's Union, Farwell Center, 1568 N. Farwell. Mailing address: Box 92203, 53202. 414 271-5273.
- Grapevine, Women's Center, 2211 E. Kenwood Blvd., 53211.
- University Wisconsin-Milwaukee Gay Student Association, Box 10, Student Union, 53211.

Publications

- Amazon: A Midwest Journal for Women, 2211 E. Kenwood, 53217. 414 964-6117, Mon.-Fri. 9 A.M.-1 P.M.; Tues. 7-10 P.M. Meetings on Tues. 8 P.M. at above address. A forum for feminist ideas, views, news, reviews, poetry, events, fiction. Documents Amazon Midwest women's culture. Submissions welcome. (Est. 75% lesbians.)
- GPU News, Farwell Center, 1568 N. Farwell, 53202. 414 271-0378, 24 hours daily. A monthly publication providing news of the gay world, national and local, poetry, fiction, reviews, classified, directory. To help more closet doors swing open. 60¢/issue; $6/year; $11/two years. (Est. 20% lesbians.)

Services

- Dyke Productions, 2927 N. Frederick, 53211. 414 964-4616. Produces lesbian performers openly political in their content. Maxine Feldman, Linda Shear, etc. Would include poets, singers, comics, plays.
- Gay Alcoholics Anonymous, Newman Center, 2528 E. Unwood, 53211. 414 271-5273. Meetings Sun. 6 P.M.
- Gay People's Union, Inc., 1568 N. Farwell Ave., 53202. 414 271-5273, 7-10:30 P.M. Counseling, rap sessions, classes, venereal disease examinations, library. Woman counselors available Wed. and Fri. evenings. Publishes *G.P.U. News* monthly. 75¢/issue, $7/year. (Est. 20% lesbians.)
- Salvatorian Gay Ministry Task Force, 3517 W. Burleigh, 53210: 414 873-1521, 9 A.M.-5 P.M. A basic resource for priests and ministers wishing to understand and develop progressive attitudes and deal with gay persons in a Christian and human manner. Publishes *A Model for Ministry to the Gay Community,* single issue, $6/year.

Racine

Bars

- Gus' Bar, 2201 Meade St. 414 634-9403. Jodee's Bar, 2139 Racine.

WYOMING

Cheyenne

Bars

- The Green Dor, 301 E. 16th St.
- The Shamrock (about five miles south of Cheyenne). Dancing.

CANADA
ALBERTA

Calgary

Bars

- Cecil Hotel Bar, 4th and 5th Sts., S.E.
- Club Carousel, 1632 Centre St. West.

Edmonton

Publications

- Club 70 Newsletter, Box 1716, Main Post Office, T5J 2P1. Free quarterly.

Services

- Gay Alliance Toward Equality, Box 1852/8225 109th St. 403 433-8160. References and counseling, etc.

BRITISH COLUMBIA

Vancouver

Bookstores

- Vancouver Women's Bookstore, 804 Richards St. 604 684-0523, Mon.-Sat. noon-5 P.M. Books on feminist theory, bibliographies, non-sexist children's books, feminist music, newspapers, journals, etc. Phone referral information. Much of above material is by and for lesbian feminists. Publishes *Woman's Bookstore Catalogue,* free, approximately every two years.

Organizations

- Gay Alliance Toward Equality, Box 1463, Station A. 604 255-7820.
- Gay People of UBC, Box 9, Student Union Building, University of British Columbia, V6T 1W5.
- Lesbian Caucus of the BC Federation of Women, Box 4294.
- Rights of Lesbians Subcommittee of the British Columbia Federation of Women, Vancouver Status of Women, 2029 West 4th. 604 736-3746.

Services

- Gay People of Simon Fraser, Student Society, Simon Fraser University, Burnaby. 604 876-4704.
- Lesbian Drop-in at Vancouver Status for Women, 2029 West. 4th. 804 736-3746. Society for Education, Action, Research and Counseling (SEARCH), Box 48903, Bentall Centre, V7X, 1A8.

Victoria

Bookstores

- Everywomen's Books, 2033 Oak Bay Ave.

Services

- Victoria Women's Centre, 552 Pandora St. 604 385-3843.

MANITOBA

Winnipeg

Organizations

- Gays for Equality, Box 27, University Centre, University of Manitoba. 204 747-8216. Counseling, referrals at 269 474-8216.

Services

- Happenings, 242 Manitoba Ave. 204 528-2049. A social club.
- A Woman's Place, 143 Walnut St., R3G 1P2. 204 786-4581.

NEWFOUNDLAND

Corner Brook

Organizations

- Community Homophile Association Newfoundland (CHAN), Box 905.

St. John's

Organizations

- Canadian Homophile Association of Newfoundland (CHAN), Box 613, Station C; ALC 5K8.

NOVA SCOTIA

Halifax

Organizations

- Gay Alliance for Equality, Box 161, Armdale Station, B3L 4G9. 902 429-6969. Counseling.

Services

- Halifax Women's Centre, 5673 Brenton Place, Box 5052, Armdale Station. 902 423-0643.

ONTARIO

Guelph

Services

- Guelph Gay Equality, Rm. 221, University of Guelph, N1E 4U5. 519 824-4120, ext. 8575, or 836-4550. Dances, counseling, etc.

Hamilton

Organizations

- McMaster Homophile Association, Rm. 607, Chester New Hall, McMaster University. Mailing address: Box 44, Station B, L8L 717. 416 527-0336.

Kingston

Organizations

- Queens Homophile Association, 51 Queen's Crescent, K7L 2S7. 613 547-2836, Mon.-Fri. 9 A.M.-4 P.M. Thurs. 7-9 P.M. General organizational meetings every second Sun. at 2 P.M., drop-ins every Fri. 8 P.M.-midnight. Open to public and members as noted above and also by appointment. Purposes are to eliminate homophobia and sexism (work in high schools, on radio and TV); provide social outlets for gay people at Queen's University and in Kingston; and counseling services through phone lines, peer counseling, referral services to and from local psychiatrists, etc. Publishes free

monthly, *QHA News,* with news and political comment. (Est. 40% lesbians.)
Services
- Kingston Women's Center, 200 Montreal St. 613 542-5226.

Kitchener
Bars
- Dark Lady, 15 Scott St.

London
Organizations
- Homophile Association of London, Ontario, 649 Colboume St., N6A; 37 3Za. 519 433-3762.

Mississauqa
Organizations
- Gay Equality Mississauqa, Box 193, Station A, L5A 2Z7.

Ottawa
Bars
- Coral Reef, 30 Nicholas St. 613 234-5118.
Bookstores
- Sister Book Shop, 35 Clarence.
Organizations
- Gay People of Carleton, CUSA, Carleton University, Colonel By Drive, K1S 5B6.
- Gays of Ottawa, Box 2919, Station D. 613 238-1717. Center: 378 Elvin St. Publishes *Go-Info.*
- Lesbians of Ottawa NOW, Ottawa Women's Centre, 821 Somerset St.
Religious Groups
- Metropolitan Community Church, 91½ 4th Ave. 613 233-6463.
Services
- Just Women Folk, Gail Joy, 33 Irving Ave. Quiet woods, 100 acres for women.
- Ottawa Women's Centre, 821 Somerset St. 613 233-2560 and 235-4035.

Thunder Bay
Bars
- Backstreet Athletic Club, 539 Simpson St. 802 622-9555.
Services
- Northern Women's Centre, 132 N. Archibald St. Mailing address: Box 314, Station F. 807 622-3989.

Toronto
Bookstores
- Toronto Women's Bookshop, 85 Harbord St.
Publications
- The Body Politic, P.O. Box 7289, Station A. $2.50/6 issues.
- The Other Woman, Box 928, Station Q. $3/year; $4 (United States).
Organizations
- Community Homophile Association of Canada, 199 Church St. 416 862-1544. Center: 201 Church St. 416 862-1169.
- Gay Academic Union, Box 396, Station K, M4P 2EO.
- Gay Alliance at York, CYSF, CS105, York University, 4700 Keele St., Downsview, M3J 1P3. 216 Vamier College Residence. 416 667-3509 and 667-3632.
- Gay Alliance Toward Equality, 193 Carleton St., M5A 2K7.
- Toronto Wages Due Lesbians, Box 38, Station E. 416 466-7457 or 465-6822. Irregular

activities; part of International Wages for Housework campaign to win wages for housework from the government for all lesbians. Autonomous group within WFH. Also focus on custody for lesbian mothers, etc. Publishes sporadically a free (donation) campaign bulletin, *Wages for Housework.* Ten members in group, all lesbians.
- Women's Place and Lesbian Collective, 137 George St. 416 929-3185 and 363-8021.
Religious Groups
- Hamishpacha, Gay Jewish Group, 1179A Bloor St. West. 249 960-0053 and 653-0498.
Services
- Radio Women, 416 961-0722. Weekly program for two hours.
- Toronto Area Gays, Box 6706, Station A. 413 964-6600. Counseling.
- Women's Yellow Pages, P.O. Box 153, Station Q; 416 964-0354.

Waterloo
Organizations
- Waterloo Universities Gay Liberation Movement, Federation of Students, University of Waterloo, N2L 3G1. 579 885-1211, ext. 2372.
Services
- The Women's Place, 42-B King South. 519 886-1820.

Windsor
Organizations
- Windsor Gay Unity, Box 7002, Sandwich Station, Stan, N9C 3Y6. 519 252-0979.
Services
- Women's Place, 327 Ouellette Ave., #202, N9A 4J1. 519 252-0244.

QUEBEC
Montreal
Bars
- Babyface, 1235 Dorchester. 510 861-0896. Lesbians who are older.
- Hollywood, 1252 Stanley.
- Jillys, 1425 A. Bishop.
Bookstores
- Androgyny/Alternatives Bookstore, 1217 Crescent St. H3G 2B1. 514 866-2131, Mon.-Wed. 11 A.M.-6 P.M.; Thurs.-Fri. 11 A.M.-9 P.M.; Sat. 11 A.M.-5 P.M. A non-profit volunteer collective. Books on feminism, lesbian, radical sociology, libertarian, etc. Advertising and communications space for lesbian community provided—also a meeting place where many women have found support for coming out. (Est. 50% lesbians.)
- Librairie des Femmes, 375 Rachel St. East. 510 843-6273.
Publications
- Long Time Coming, Box 128 Station G. Lesbian bimonthly.
Organizations
- Central Homophile Urbain de Montréal, 6581 St. Laurent. 510 279-5381.
- Gay Coalition Against Repression/Comité Homosexual Anti-Répression, CP26, Succursale C, H2L 4J7. 510 866-2131.
- Gay Teenage Group, 4515 Ste.-Catherine West. 510 934-0721.
- Montreal Lesbian Women/Lesbiennes de Montréal, 3585 St.-Urbain. 514 842-4781,

Women's Information Center, Mon.-Fri. 9 A.M.-5 P.M., messages taken. Thurs. lesbian drop-in; Sunday discussion, 1 P.M.; dances and coffeehouses. Phone for information. Provides lesbians with both social activities and an opportunity to grow politically. Also provides peer counseling and referrals to lesbian social workers and other therapists. Free newsletter.
- Parents of Gays—Montreal, D. F. Cassidy, 5311 Sherbrooke West, #916, H4A 1U3. 514 288-1101.
Services
- Gay Information. 510 288-1101, 7-10 P.M. Eric Hill, 695 Moffat Ave., Verdun, H4J 1Y7.
- Gayline, Family Services Association, 3515 Ste.-Catherine St. West, Westmount. 510 931-5330 7-11 P.M.
- Groupe Homosexual d'Action Politique, C.P. 235, Station N.
- Montreal Women's Yellow Pages, Woman's Referral Centre, 3595 St.-Urbain. Annual resource directory, $2 plus 25¢ postage.
- Powerhouse Gallery, 3738 St. Dominique. A women's art gallery.
- Women's Referral Centre, 3595 St.-Urbain. 510 842-4781.

Quebec
Bars
- Le Balloon Rouge, 811 rue St. Jean.
- Le Perigord, 30 rue St. Stanislaus.
Organizations
- Centre Humanitaire d'Aide et de Liberation, BP 596, Haule Ville, G1R 4R8; 283 rue des Franciscains. 418 525-4997.
Services
- Service d'Entraide Homophile de Quebec, BP 596, Haute Ville; G1R 4R8. 418 524-8344. Counseling, referrals, etc.

SASKATCHEWAN
Regina
Bars
- Artopus, 2242 Smith St. 306 651-0975 and 525-3941.
- Hotel Saskatchewan Bar, Victoria and Scott Sts.

Saskatoon
Bars
- Apollo Room, Ritz Hotel, 21st St. between First and Second Aves.
- The Cove, King George Hotel, Second Ave. and 23rd St.
Organizations
- Gay Academic Union, Prof. Peter Millard, Box 1662, S7K 3R8.
Services
- Gay Community Centre of Saskatoon, #2, 310 20th St. East (second floor). Mailing address: P.O. Box 1662, S7K 3R8. 306 652-0972, Mon.-Fri. 11 A.M.-4 P.M. 7:30-10 P.M. Social activities, counseling, educational and political programs. (Est. 25% lesbians.)

Photo Credits

Liza Cowan, 263
Denise Crippen, courtesy *The Lesbian Tide,* 112
Diana Davies, 5, 10, 252, 256, 258, 259, 282, 288
Robin Evans, 220
Donna Gray, 1, 20, 39, 75, 94, 219, 231, 284, 293
Linda Guthrie, 42
Cary Herz, 37, 42, 44, 70, 114, 182, 270
JEB (Joan E. Biren), 1, 2, 47, 178, 237, 256, 263, 283,
     305, 308
Bettye Lane, 6, 9, 78, 93, 120, 122, 123, 130, 133, 140,
     150, 168, 179, 194, 238, 255, 264, 265,
     277, 278, 281, 283
Bruce Larson, 158
Cynthia MacAdams, 260
Robert McKeever, 46
Marcelina L. Martin, 136
Chie Nishio, 315
From *Loving Women,* copyright © 1976 by Nomadic
     Sisters, 96, 98, 102
Anita Schloss, 15, 47
Richard Stanley, 292
Nicole Symons, 13
Kay Tobin, 48, 128, 176, 179, 251
E K Waller, courtesy *The Lesbian Tide,* 249
Williams, courtesy *The Lesbian Tide,* 233
F. Carol Wood, 108
Irene Young, 5, 250

3026-1
5-17

3285-1
3-77